THE CONTINE SE

Reality and Aspiration in the American Revolutionary Era.

~2nd Edition~

by Wm. Thomas Sherman

Gun Jones Publishing, Seattle, Washington, 2012

1604 N.W. 70th St.
Seattle, WA 98117
206-784-1132
Also, I can be reached by any of these email addresses.
wts@gunjones.com
williamthomasherman@gmail.com
gunjones1@yahoo.com

website: http://www.gunjones.com

Last updated: 26 Dec. 2018

Introduction

It is an odd but, for some, all too noticeable fact that many recent popular studies of the American Revolution, including as well studies of the early Republic, tend to overlook or give short shrift to the spirit and personality of those tumultuous and colorful times. Offered typically instead are sociological, psychological, and military analyses; gossip or anecdotal trivia; or would-be revisionist scolding and the putting of the moral characters of historical figures on trial; or else patriotic platitudes accompanied by a rehash of cardboard, stereotypical portraits; which latter those acquainted with the given subject or topic are already more than familiar with. *One* reason for this too routine and lopsided state of things has been the traditional separation of ordinary history versus *literature.* And yet it is frequently in the literature, rather than history as such, that more genuine and uninhibited emotions of a bygone era are properly and vividly conveyed and brought to recognizable life. Private papers, correspondence, orderly books, diaries, and memoirs have to some extent served to mitigate and significantly bridge the gap. Yet such sources, though utilized and highly regarded as they sometimes and rightly are, can only fill out portions of the overall picture. So that restricting oneself to and overly relying on them and standard histories almost invariably results in a one or two-dimensional perspective that seldom provides students, and readers with a deeper and more complete sense of how life was actually felt, seen, imagined, and *hoped for* way back when.

However, by adding to and melding with the more conventional records of the past the work of essayists, newspaper writers, poets, story tellers, and playwrights contemporaneous with the time frame one is addressing, we gain a fuller and enhanced outlook of what thinking and feeling people individually and at large *valued* and what they perhaps saw as being of greatest importance for them *and* posterity. In so doing, we expand our perspective and understanding of personalities beyond the mere imparting of contemporary opinions, incidental details, chronological information, and the immediate or seeming causes of successive events.

It was for the purpose then of helping to better join, complement, contrast, and synthesize the history of the American Revolution and early America, roughly from 1750 to 1830, with contemporary and post-contemporary literature that this anthology of short pieces and excerpts from larger works took form. I say *took form* because the project originally began as a desultory series of short articles and impromptu pieces written for amusement and leisurely edification. Yet with time, these accumulated to a point where they began to shape into a more or less, if far from perfect, unified whole. And despite the seemingly odd or semi-random assortment of topics and titles, the separate articles often echo and chime with each other with respect to recurring notions, insights, and themes. The collection as whole is titled "The Continental Army series;" with a mind to make reference to the ideals, steadfastness, and courage of the more high-minded Revolutionary soldiers; mindful of the intimidating challenges they faced; while, at the same time, alluding to the sometimes haphazard or ad hoc formulation of that army -- which army, in truth, founded the United States -- and that from often very humble and all too human beginnings, and over trying and despairing times, ultimately became an indomitable and victorious, if also patched and threadbare, force to reckoned with.

Because these monographs, articles, and literary selections were initially chosen and composed as exigency prompted and present interest moved me, rather than according to a pre-set plan, the sequence of subjects, as intimated, is somewhat, though not entirely, hodgepodge and random. Nor is the focus exclusively American; so that every now and then are included British, Irish, Scotch, French and other European viewpoints. The very first article, "Lee's Legion Remembered," became a sort of prototype for all that followed, and this will help explain also the occasionally repeated mention or reference to Lee's Legion. For were I to credit a single individual for providing the impetus and inspiration for this series, that honor would, without hesitation, go to Alexander Garden "of the Legion;" whose Revolutionary War anecdotes, more than any other collection of writings, furnished the heart and conception of Revolutionary American *character* that originally formed the idea and basis of this work.

William Thomas Sherman
Seattle, Washington

Table of Contents

LEE'S LEGION REMEMBERED:
Profiles of the 2d Partisan Corps as taken from Alexander Garden's *Anecdotes* (1822 & 1828 eds.)

Lee's Legion, or more formally the 2d Partisan Corps, and led by Lieut. Col. Henry Lee (1756-1818), is and was one of the most well known units of the Continental army's history; so much so that it even received mention several times in the histories of the war contained in the *Annual Registers* of that time. Yet most of what we know about the Legion and its members usually originates with Lee's own *Memoirs* (in its various editions.) And though we are extremely fortunate to be able to avail ourselves of that indispensable work, we cannot help coming away from it feeling that with regard to the Legion itself, there is still much that is left vague and incomplete; and as much and more we would like to know about both the corps and its individual members in order to attain a more fully rounded out picture.

General Washington's initial reason for forming Legions or Partisan Corps,[1] that is, special elite units which incorporated both cavalry and infantry formations, was for the purpose of carrying out reconnaissance and raids against the enemy.[2] At the same time, they were seen as encouraging initiative and acts of boldness which in turn bolstered the army morale; while fostering an offensive spirit in a conflict where pitched major engagements were normally avoided and where, due to both logistical constraints and lack of training, it was ordinarily ill advised for large bodes of American forces to be on the attack.

Henry Lee's preliminary unit of light dragoons, and precursor to the Legion, was formed at Williamsburg, Virginia on June 8, 1776 as the 5th Troop of the Virginia state light cavalry battalion commanded by Col. Theodorick Bland (and who also happened to be a kinsman.) Lee himself was commissioned the troop's Captain on June 18th. After spending time in Virginia enlisting, equipping, and training, in December of that same year, Bland's five cavalry troops were sent north to reinforce Washington's army. They arrived in mid-January, and later, on March 31st 1777, the regiment was by order of Congress officially incorporated into the Continental Army as the 1st Continental Light Dragoons.[3]

Almost from the beginning, Lee's 5th troop found itself operating freely of Bland's parent regiment, and was attached to different generals, such as Lincoln and Stirling; usually situated in New Jersey and eastern Pennsylvania, to assist in scouting, espionage, foraging (rustling cattle and sheep for example), suppressing loyalists, skirmishing, and surprising small British detachments. In the course of the operations of 1777, Lee's men alone took prisoner some 125 British and Hessian soldiers. Though present at the battle of Brandywine, they were, as best we can tell, not actually engaged there; while at Germantown they served as Gen. Washington's bodyguard. So impressed was Washington himself by their energy, zeal, and diverse accomplishments in small operations, by October he viewed and treated them as an independent unit that took their orders exclusively from him.

The troop went on to garner further notoriety when on 20 January 1778 they thwarted a surprise attack by numerically superior British forces at the Spread Eagle Tavern,

---

[1] Lee's Legion, technically speaking and for most of the time it was engaged, was a Partisan Corps rather than a Legion as originally intended; a Legion having 60 men per troop (of either cavalry or infantry); while a Partisan Corps had only 50. It was thus easier for Partisan Corps to supply itself, travel greater distances, and operate more freely than a formal Legion. Revolutionary War legion formations, whether American, British, or French, first entered the war by way of John Graves Simcoe's elite Queen's Rangers, and who, it could be said, were the inspiration and preliminary exemplars of all the (Rev War) legions that came after them.

[2] Ancient Roman legions, while principally comprised of infantry, did have a cavalry contingent; this in addition to being highly professional, organized, and versatile corps compared to ordinary Roman Auxiliaries.

[3] For this and subsequent information on the Legion's organizational history see Fred Anderson Berg's *Continental Army Units*, pp. 60-61, and Robert K. Wright's *The Continental Army*, pp. 161-162, 348-349.

in Philadelphia.[4] Although both Alexander Garden and Lee biographer Cecil B. Hartley speak of this attempted ambush as taking place at that tavern, some recent historians, based on Washington and Lee's correspondence, are inclined to believe it occurred *instead* at Scott's Farm located sixteen miles west of Philadelphia. The question has perhaps yet to be completely resolved, but one explanation, and that is consistent with accounts of the action, is that the fight itself, involving a very small number of Lee's men, transpired at the tavern while the *main body* of the 5th troop was stationed at Scott's farm two miles distant.

On 7 April 1778, Lee's contingent was formally separated from the 1st Light Dragoons. Lee was promoted to Major-commandant and authorized by Congress, at General Washington's request, to augment his unit from one to two troops with a mind to forming what was subsequently denoted "Maj. Henry Lee's independent light dragoon corps."[5] The

---

[4] Cecil B. Hartley: "As Captain Lee was particularly active, a plan was formed, late in January [1778], to surprise and capture him in his quarters. An extensive circuit was made by a large body of cavalry, who seized four of his patrols without communicating an alarm. About break of day the British horse appeared; upon which Captain Lee placed his troopers that were in the house, at the doors and windows, who behaved so gallantly as to repulse the assailants without losing a horse or man. Only Lieutenant [William] Lindsay and one private were wounded. The whole number in the house did not exceed ten. [Hartley's note –'Major [John] Jameson was accidentally present, and engaged in this skirmish.'] That of the assailants was said to amount to two hundred. They lost a sergeant and three men, with several horses, killed; and an officer and three men wounded.

"The following is Captain Lee's report of this affair to General Washington: 'I am to inform your Excellency of an action, which happened this morning, between a party of the enemy's dragoons and my troop of horse. They were near two hundred in number, and by a very circuitous route endeavored to surprise me in quarters. About daybreak they appeared. We were immediately alarmed, and manned the doors and windows. The contest was very warm ; the British dragoons trusting to their vast superiority in number, attempted to force their way into the house. In this they were baffled by the bravery of. my men. After having left two killed and four wounded, they desisted and sheered off. We are trying to intercept them. Colonel Stevens has pushed a party of infantry to reach their rear. So well directed was the opposition, that we drove them from the stables and saved every horse. We have got the arms, some cloaks, &c. of their wounded. The only damage I at present know of, is a slight wound received by Lieutenant Lindsay. I am apprehensive about the patrols. The enterprise was certainly daring, though the issue of it very ignominious. I had not a soldier for each window.'-- January 20th.

"Again: 'We have at length ascertained the real loss of this day. Four privates, belonging to the patrol at the square, were taken. I am told they made a brave resistance. The quartermaster-sergeant, who imprudently ran from our quarters prior to the commencement of the skirmish, was also taken. The loss sustained stands thus: one sergeant and four privates taken; one lieutenant and two privates wounded. By what I can learn from the people of Derby, the enemy's loss is as follows: three privates dead; one commissioned officer, one sergeant, and three privates wounded.'

"The following letter of General Washington to Captain Lee attests his sense of the merit of his young protégé: ' My Dear Lee, Although I have given you my thanks in the general orders of this day, for the late instance of your gallant behavior, I cannot resist the inclination I feel to repeat them again in this manner. I needed no fresh proofs of your merit, to bear you in remembrance. I waited only for the proper time and season to show it ; those, I hope, are not far off. I shall also think of and will reward the merit of Lindsay, when an opening presents, as far as I can consistently; and I shall not forget the corporal, whom you have recommended to my notice. Offer my sincere thanks to the whole of your gallant party, and assure them, that no one felt pleasure more sensibly, or rejoiced more sincerely for your and their escape, than your affectionate, &c." -- Hartley, *Life of Maj. Gen. Henry Lee*, pp. 32-34. And see Capt. Henry Lee, Jr. to Gen. Washington, in two dispatches of 20 Jan. 1778 (292, 293). *The Papers of George Washington* Digital Edition, ed. Theodore J. Crackel. Charlottesville: University of Virginia Press, Rotunda, 2008, and taken originally from *Revolutionary War Series* (16 June 1775–14 January 1779), Volume 13 (26 December 1777–28 February 1778); and also John Laurens to Henry Laurens, 23 Jan. 1778, *The Army Correspondence of Col. John Laurens in the Years 1777-78, with a Memoir by William Gilmore Simms* (1867), pp. 110-112, and Marshall, *Life of Washington*, Vol. III, p. 377.

[5] Washington's letter to the President of Congress soliciting Lee's promotion to Major: "Captain Lee of the light dragoons, and the officers under his command, having uniformly distinguished themselves by a conduct of exemplary zeal, prudence, and bravery, I took occasion, on a late signal instance of it, to express the high sense I entertained of their merit, and to assure him, that it should not fail of being properly noticed. I was induced to give this assurance from a conviction, that it is the wish of Congress to give every encouragement to merit, and that they would cheerfully embrace so favorable an opportunity of manifesting this disposition. I had it in contemplation at the time, in case no other method more eligible could be adopted, to make him an offer of a place in my family. I have consulted the committee of Congress upon the subject, and we were mutually of opinion, that giving Captain Lee the command of two troops of horse on the proposed establishment, with the rank of major, to act as an independent partisan corps, would be a mode of rewarding him very advantageous to the service. Captain Lee's genius particularly adapts him to a command of this nature; and it will be the most agreeable to him of any station in which he could be placed.

"I beg leave to recommend this measure to Congress, and shall be obliged by their decision as speedily as may be convenient. The campaign is fast approaching, and there will probably be very little time to raise and prepare the

first troop was command by Capt. William Lindsay; the second by Capt. Henry Peyton; with a focal recruiting post being set up in Charles County, Maryland. On 28 May, their number was further increased to three troops, the third of these placed under Capt. Robert Forsyth, and a quartermaster added; though one troop acted as a *dismounted* formation. The later inclusion of foot soldiers with the cavalry, and advocated by Lee himself, was seen as measure necessary to insure the flexibility and survivability of the unit. Much of 1778 and early 1779 was spent recruiting, training, and arming the corps. However, they continued scouting, foraging, putting fear into tories, and were occasionally skirmishing, including one retaliatory foray on Sept. 30th, 1778 -- two days after the infamous Baylor massacre at Tappan, N.J. -- when, accompanying some infantry from the 9th Pennsylvania Regt. under Col. Richard Butler, they put to flight a contingent of German riflemen, led by a hessian Capt. Von Donop, and in which they slew 10 and took another 20 prisoners.[6]

At Lee's and subsequently Washington's request, Congress, on 13 July 1779, assigned Captain Allan McLane's Delaware infantry company as a fourth troop or foot company. McClane joined up with them by mid June; so that by the end of August "Lee's cavalry" mustered a total of about 200.[7]

Both Lee and McLane played vital roles in the preparation of Gen. Anthony Wayne's victorious assault on Stony Point, 15-16 July 1779; with their unit itself acting as a reserve. For their part in this enterprise neither Lee or McLane received much credit. Notwithstanding, they not long after did secure fame and laurels, including an acknowledgment of thanks and a gold medal for Lee from Congress (28 Sept. 1779), for the their hatching and spearheading a daring and mostly successful night raid on the British outpost of Paulus (also "Powles") Hook, New Jersey on 19 August 1779.[8]

In addition to routine duties of gathering supplies; which on a few occasions incurred the rancor of friendly civilians and the intervention of Washington to help settle disputes relating to impressments, in September the Legion was sent by the to the coastal area of Monmouth County, N.J. to secretly keep watch for the anticipated return of D'Estaing's fleet; while under the guise of feeding and refurbishing the unit. D'Estaing, however, ended up in Georgia; so that it is possible that Washington, by placing Lee's cavalry to keep eyes out for the French fleet, was attempting to mislead British intelligence.

In mid-January 1780, two attacks were carried out against Sandy Hook, New Jersey. In the first of these on Jan. 12th, Captain Michael Rudolph with a party of the Lee's men landed at "The Hook," and seized seven loyalist and some $45,000 in counterfeit Continental currency. The second raid occurred on the 15th; when Captain Henry Peyton and 40 others burned two ice bound schooners and a sloop while capturing some prisoners. Lee reported Peyton's excursion to Washington as follows:

---

corps for it. It is a part of the plan to give Mr. Lindsay the command of the second troop, and to make Mr. Peyton captain-lieutenant of the first." Dated 3 April 1778, Valley Forge.

[6] See Brig. Gen. Charles Scott to Gen. Washington, 30 Sept. and 2 Oct. 1778. *The Papers of George Washington* Digital Edition, ed. Theodore J. Crackel. Charlottesville: University of Virginia Press, Rotunda, 2008, and taken originally from *Revolutionary War Series* (16 June 1775–14 January 1779), Volume 17 (15 September–31 October 1778).

[7] In his *Light-Horse Harry; A Biography of Washington's great Cavalryman, General Henry Lee* (pp. 59, 65, 68, 71), Noel B. Gerson asserts that 40 Oneida braves, and who it is otherwise known and established served as partisan auxiliaries for McClane when the latter acted on diverse missions in and between Valley Forge and Philadelphia in 1777, became the Legion's 3rd troop up until and including Paulus Hook. I, however, have as yet no corroboration of this from elsewhere.

[8] Although Capt. Allan McLane (1746-1829) played decisive roles in both Stony Point, N.Y., and Paulus Hook (with the former being the inspiration for the latter undertaking), he was unjustly neglected when the honors for both these victories were handed out, and this no doubt contributed to his falling out with Lee (whom he did not subsequently get along well with), and his leaving the corps ultimately to be re-assigned to a separate duty in Jan. 1781. His men notwithstanding remained with the Legion and served in the south. For an account of McLane's war services and related amazing adventures, see Garden, vol. 2, pp. 76-83, and *American Heritage Magazine*, Oct. 1956, vol. 7, Issue 6; available at: http://www.americanheritage.com/content/allan-mclane-unknown-hero-revolution

"The noise of the [Peyton's] men marching occasioned by the snow, alarmed the garrison: of course the attempt on the light house [at Sandy Hook] was omitted agreeable to orders. The shipping were assaulted, and three burnt, vizt. one tender one schooner and one sloop. The prisoners taken amounted to twelve; these with the British officer captured some time since will be sent to Philada [sic]. The counterfeit money [captured by the Legion on the 12th] I have sent to the loan office to be burnt. Unfortunately the owner of it, was mortally wounded and left behind, so that no discovery can be made."[9]

On 14 February 1780, Lee was, as was also at that time Col. Charles Armand, granted Congressional authorization[10] to form a Legionary Corps; with, as additionally proposed by Maj. Gen. Von Steuben, an increase of 70 men. Many of the best soldiers from other units either volunteered or were specially invited to join its ranks; with resultant Legion members hailing from Virginia, Maryland, Delaware, New Jersey, New York, Pennsylvania, and Connecticut. So that by April, the newly created Legion numbered 300 with three troops of cavalry and three of infantry.

In March 30th, they were directed to be prepared to march south in support of then besieged Charleston. By mid-May, they were duly supplied and accoutered for that purpose and just en route, when on the 20th of the same month Washington rescinded the command and summoned them back to the main army.

The unit subsequently distinguished itself, fighting alongside Col. Matthias Ogden's 1st New Jersey Regiment, at the battle of Springfield, N.J. June 23, 1780; and which was the first engagement in which Lee's corps found itself acting under the leadership of Maj. Gen. Nathanael Greene.

Just three days before that clash, Lee wrote a letter (dated "Advance post."), worth quoting at length here, to President (i.e., Governor) Joseph Reed of Pennsylvania; which provides a rare and unusually close-up look at Colonel Lee's ideas concerning field tactics:

"Since my junction, which was the second day after we passed Philade[lphia], every measure with us seemed to be in consequence of something from them. The arrival of S[i]r Henry from Charlestown has urged us to motion. The main body of the army under his Excellency decamped last night, pointing its march toward the N. River. A secondary body remains in this country. Gen. Greene commands. My corps continue here, & with a detachment of Infantry form the advance. On my reaching the army, I was immediately ordered to the front, & honored with the command on the lines. In consequence of which line of life, I know the springs of action in both armys [sic]. Be assured that the enemy conduct themselves with much wisdom. Not only their movements are material & military, but their positions are circumspect, & their discipline rigid. A very different chief Mr. Clinton from Sr Will. Howe. They have made two fruitless excursions on my post; we have made prisoners one L[ieu]t. & his party -- every day we kill, & are killed.

---

[9] See Washington to Lee, Jan. 21, 1780; with the quoted text inserted with Washington's letter; and also, *The Virginia Gazette*, Feb. 12, 1780, and *This Old Monmouth of Ours* by William S. Hornor, Moreau Bros. Freehold, N.J., 1932, pp. 68-69.

[10] "Resolved, That recruiting money be furnished to major Lee, to enable him to inlist [sic] seventy privates, to serve as dismounted dragoons in addition to those now in the corps; the whole to be formed into three troops." Resolves of the Continental Congress. Pulaski's Legion had already been authorized on 28 March 1778 as a way to compensate Pulaski who had earlier been promised a Continental cavalry brigade, but which Congress decided it could not for financial and other reasons form. For this reason Pulaski's Legion held a special status all its own; separate from the other American Legions. Armand's, by the way, became the 1st American Legion while Lee's became this 2nd; with the title of Legion later being *formally* changed for both to "Partisan Corps" in Jan. 1781 to reflect a slight decrease in the size and composition of the units. The term "Legion," however, continued to be used as an informal designation.

"I have proposed this day to make an attempt on Mr. Kinsihausen [Knyphausen] with three hund[re]d men. My object is to bring off a picquet, & oblige Mr. Kinsihausen either to extend his picquets or to contract his lines. His caution has worked so far on him, as to induce him to proximate his picquets to his camp, least the former might be taken off. I am now speaking of his right flank -- his left is secured by the Elizabeth town creek; it is on his left I mean to strike seriously, & to storm his right. The alarm on his right I expect will shew him the impropriety of having his piquets so near his lines, as it is certain that in such a position his army is liable to surprize. He will therefore extend his picquets on his right; if he does, the prosecution of my plan orders them to be cut off at some opportune moment. This being done, he will necessarily contract his lines, or reinforce his army.

"Either of these objects will be very important to us; the first liberates E. town, the second prevents any important movement in another quarter.

"How this reasoning will relish I don't know; I fear the general will not consent because it might produce the loss of 20 or 30 lives in the operation of the plan.

"But done with these matters; I cannot but express my happiness in the movement taking place toward the N. river.

"The enemy are about one third superior to us in number; wisdom on our side will effectually prevent any injury to us; the succour we expect from our Countrymen will give us in time the ability of offence. In the interim, while the main body prepares a position capable of relieving W. point if besieged, or of striking on the enemy's right should they advance on Gen'l Greene, we shall be safe. The moment we lay und[e]r cover of the mountains in one body, the enemy will possibly hurt us by their maneuvers. This let[te]r is all in hurry..."[11]

Another occurrence deserving mention involving the unit, though of a quite different character than Springfield, was a largely auspicious cattle raid in the summer of 1780, under Gen. Anthony Wayne; that took place just below Fort Lee, New Jersey. This event was afterward celebrated in a poem-parody by Maj. John André entitled "The Cow Chace."[12]

In enumerating these various actions and escapades involving Lee's 5th troop and the Legion prior to 1781, it needs be emphasized that what we have related thus far are merely *highlights*, and that something like a full listing of *known* engagements (i.e., not to mention those for which there is no apparent record) is far too lengthy to include in a general introduction of this kind.

Despite the numerous tactical triumphs, questions continued to be raised in Congress regarding the utility of Legionary and Partisan corps to the army. The establishing of Legions as effectually *federal* military entities doubtless prompted reservations with some Congressmen with state's rights leanings. Washington in response to the nay-sayers, in a letter of 11 October 1780 addressed to the President, stated: "In general I dislike independent corps, I think a partisan corps with an army useful in many respects. Its name and destination stimulate to enterprise; and the two officers I have mentioned have the best claims to public attention. Colonel [Charles] Armand is an officer of great merit, which, added to his being a foreigner, to his rank in life, and to the sacrifices of property he has made, renders it a point of delicacy as well as justice to continue to him the means of serving honorably. Major Lee has rendered such distinguished services, possesses so many talents for commanding a corps of this nature, and deserves so much credit for the perfection in which he has kept his corps, as well as for the handsome exploits he has performed, that it would be a loss to the service, and a discouragement to merit, to reduce him, and I do not see how he can be introduced into one of the regiments in a manner satisfactory to himself, and which will enable him to be equally useful, without giving too much disgust to the whole line of cavalry."

---

[11] *The Virginia Magazine of History and Biography*, vol 6, Oct. 1898, pp. 153–58.

[12] See Benson J. Lossing's *Field Book of the Revolution*, vol. 2, pp. 622n, 684-686.

Ensuing upon this, Congress, on 21 Oct., reiterated the earlier resolve of April and officially confirmed its authorization of both Lee's and Armand's legions.[13]

While then the Legion was a Congressionally sponsored, as opposed to a state based regiment, the state of Maryland, for one, made provision for the Legion and some other independent Continental units, resolving on 11 April 1780: "That the officers and soldiers raised in this state, and now in colonels Hazen's [2nd Canadian Regt.], Spencer's, Gist's and major Lee's corps, be entitled to receive the same privileges, bounties, and cloathing, that the officers in the line have or are entitled to receive under the resolution of the 4th of December, 1778, and the act of assembly, entitled, An act relating to the officers and soldiers of this state, in the American army, and other purposes therein mentioned, passed at a session of assembly, begun and held at the city of Annapolis, on Thursday the 22d day of July, in the year 1779."

By 1 November 1780[14] Lee's force was detached from the Main Army and once more sent to reinforce the Southern Army badly mauled at the battle of Camden, 16 August 1780. On 1 January 1781, the Legion was re-designated the 2d Partisan Corps (in place of "Legion"), and when it joined General Greene by early January numbered some 100 cavalry and 180 foot which were organized into three troops of horse under Captains Joseph Eggleston, Ferdinand O'Neal, and James Armstrong, and 3 companies of infantry led by Captains Patrick Carnes, Michael Rudulph and George Handy. As the exploits and movements of the Legion in the South are extensively recorded elsewhere, an overview and recapitulation of such is unnecessary here.[15]

Among it marks of distinction, the "Legion" was one of the best disciplined, clothed and equipped units in the Continental Army; this due in no small part to Lee's dogged and persistent determination to make it so. His *mounted* legionnaires wore green jackets and on several occasions they were mistaken for men of both Simcoe's Queen's Rangers[16] and Tarleton's British; while Lee himself, in his *Memoirs*, speaks of his cavalry wearing "green coatees and leather breeches." Yet this is about as much incontrovertible information as we have to go on with respect to apparel and applies only to the cavalry.[17]

---

[13] "Resolved, That there be 2 partizan corps, consisting of 3 troops of mounted and 3 of dismounted dragoons, of 50 each, one of which corps to be commanded by col. Armand, and the other by major Lee, and officered by appointment of the commander in chief, with the approbation of Congress: and that the commander in chief be authorized to direct a mode for completing, recruiting and supplying the said corps." Resolves of the Continental Congress, 21 Oct. 1780.

[14] Lee himself was promoted by Congress to Lieutenant Colonel on 6 November 1780.

[15] For more on the Legion while in the south, see my *Calendar and Record of the Revolutionary War in the South: 1780-1781*, at: https://archive.org/details/CalendarAndRecordOfTheRevolutionaryWarInTheSouth1780-1781

[16] Lee, *Memoirs*, pp. 301n-302n.

[17] Nevertheless, there is a most intriguing cavalry figure -- dark green coated with white collar and facings; wearing a smaller version of the British Legion style helmet, and with tan vest and breeches -- in Alonzo Chappel's (1828-1887) painting "Washington's Farewell to His Officers, 1783" (c. 1857) that may very well be the uniform in question. While it is true Chappel did do a painting (now lost but that survives as an engraving) specifically of the Legion cavalry at Guilford Court House, it is uncertain whether it was done before or after "Washington's Farewell." In the "Legion at Guilford," the troopers wear a metal helmet very similar to the one worn by Thomas Young Seymour of the Connecticut Light Dragoons in the portrait by John Trumbull (1756-1843), but with shell covered in black rather than brass or gold; surmounted by a metal crest on which hanging horse hair is attached; with, as well, as metal visor broader than Seymour's. The green jackets are cut at the waists, and have relatively high collars and long cuffs, and which latter, as depicted in some colorings of the engraving, are buff-yellow. It is not impossible that both the dragoons shown in "Washington's Farewell" and or "Guilford" are accurate representations of how the unit appeared at different times. It was trying to keep any regiment in the Continental army properly outfitted in the field. And with Lee's Legion being one of the optimally clothed compared to other American units, they doubtless still had to make shift attiring themselves as best they could and as changing circumstances allowed; so that the result was still, at least in many instances in the course of several campaigns, something of an amalgam. The Legion infantry itself has been spoken of as being at one time in purple trousers and purple jackets when in the north (Don Troiani's *Soldier's of the American Revolution*, by Troiani and Kochan, pp. 156-160), and then there are records of scarlet and blue cloth being issued to them while in the south (*Uniforms of the Continental Army* by Philip Katcher, pp. 39-40) -- as well as the painting of Laurence Manning of the infantry; where he wears a conventional blue army coat with red collars and facing, and silver epaulette.

Otherwise supply records intimate that at least some of the unit, presumably the infantry, were attired in blue coats with red trim and white linen. For headgear, leather caps were most frequently used by Continental cavalrymen; and yet some are known to have worn visored black or brown leather helmets; with felt hats making an occasional appearance.[18]

While in the south, the Legion occasionally took in recruits from local Carolinians; some of whom became notable in its service. In May of 1781, about 25 North Carolina Continentals under Maj. Pinkertham Eaton were included in the ranks of the Legion Infantry; evidently to offer them temporary training; as well as to strengthen the Legion's numbers.

By early February 1782, Lee, in part because he felt he was not receiving sufficient support and cooperation from fellow southern army officers to continue leading effectively, removed himself (Eggleston accompanying him) from command and returned north. Greene then in June divided the Legion by combining its cavalry with detachments from the 3rd and 4th Continental Light Dragoons, under Col. George Baylor;[19] while assigning the infantry of the Legion to Lieut. Col. John Laurens' Light Infantry battalion: all as part of a plan to form a brigade under Brig. Gen. Mordecai Gist. The reaction on the part of remaining Legion officers was one of dismay and indignation, and all resigned in protest; this unanimity being a testimony to the Legion's continued pride and esprit d' corps, even with Lee absent. Greene, however, was able to somewhat appease and console them, and those who would not stay were granted furlough to return north.[20] The unit, which continued to exist on paper and payroll returns, finally and formally disbanded at Winchester, Virginia on 15 November 1783.

Part I.

But for Alexander Garden (1757-1829), son of noted Scotch-American physician, botanist -- *and Loyalist* -- of the same name,[21] our knowledge and idea of the officers and men under Lee's command would be considerably more shadowy and sketchy than it is. Born in Charleston, S.C., Garden for most of the war was in Scotland pursuing studies at the University of Glasgow. Yet in July 1780 he returned to British held Charleston, and sometime, but apparently not earlier than after the battle of Eutaw Springs in 8 September 1781, he somehow managed to join up with and enlist in Greene's army. Being first made a Cornet in Lee's Legion, he rose to Lieutenant by February 1782; and (presumably due to his cultured and well educated background) was subsequently recommended by John Laurens as aide-de-camp to General Greene, in which function he then served. After the war, his father's

---

Also the Legion, like other British and American legions, was inspired and styled itself in precedent on Simcoe's Queen's Rangers, who were very careful and strict about their uniforms, yet loved a little flourish and extra adornment for color; for example, in the crescent moon worn on their headgear, and, on one occasion, when they put on white and black feathers in mourning for André (Simcoe, p. 152; Simcoe also, incidentally, commends Lee's Legion for its discipline, p. 136.) Since lack of regular equipment prevented strict uniformity of the Legion's clothing, a concomitant harmony of élan, cut, and swagger (such as, say, Garden implies) not only permitted but encouraged divers clothing and gear to be used in a creative and colorful manner; providing at least they had good to better aesthetic taste; which it is probably safe to conclude the majority of legion officers and men had. That Lee prided himself on the unit's look and appearance, including their gentlemanly deportment (as, for instance, in the quasi-for its time knightly treatment of Brown and the King's Rangers at and after the fall of Augusta) added to Garden's dashing picture of the legion, would seem to strongly support such a surmise.

[18] See Lee, *Memoirs of the War in the Southern Department of the United States* (1869 ed.) p. 302n., Phillip Katcher's *Uniforms of the Continental Army*, pp. 36, 39-40.

[19] With respect to the 3d and 4th Continental Light Dragoons see Berg, p. 30-31. While for a no little helpful account and explanation of what happened to the Legion after Lee left in February, see William Johnson's *Life and Correspondence of Nathanael Greene*, vol. 2, ch. 17, pp. 325-331.

[20] Lee, *Memoirs*, pp. 550-553.

[21] Alexander Garden senior (1728–1793), a member of the Royal Society, was a colleague and or correspondent of fellow Americans Cadwallader Colden and John Bartram, and European scientists such as Linnaeus of Uppsala and John Frederick Gronovius of Leiden. The *gardenia* is named after him.

estate, that would otherwise have been confiscated, was awarded to him by the state of South Carolina. He later published two separate volumes of Revolutionary War Anecdotes, viz.:

* *Anecdotes of the Revolutionary War in America: With Sketches of Character of Persons the Most Distinguished, in the Southern States, for Civil and Military Services* A.E. Miller, Charleston, 1822.

* *Anecdotes of the American Revolution: Illustrative of the Talents and Virtues of the Heroes of the Revolution, Who Acted the Most Conspicuous Parts Therein.*
-- Second Series. A.E. Miller, Charleston, 1828.

These "anecdotes," although largely second or third hand in origin, were often enough taken from original participants themselves whom he knew personally; not least of which, for our purposes, his old comrades and fellow officers in Lee's Legion.

.

Although sometimes unabashedly patriotic even to the point at times of being suspect in their accuracy, and despite how other portions of his text merely re-relate David Ramsay, William Moultrie, or other early Revolutionary War historian (including Garden's former commander, Henry Lee), Garden's accounts often contain much rare, candid, and unusual information not found elsewhere and to that extent are much more original and reliable than perhaps initially and on their face we might otherwise take them to be.

What follows here then are Garden's reminiscences of some of the officers, non-commissioned officers and enlisted men of Lee's corps. These profiles and vignettes make up only a portion, though a substantial portion, of the *Anecdotes* as a whole; and for that reason might be easily overlooked or bypassed by those not specifically researching Lee's Legion. What we get is a very lively more detailed picture of the men; certainly as good or better as any we find elsewhere in the literature of that very early time of chronicling the Revolution; and which succeeds well both at imparting the spirit of loyalty and comradery that characterized the corps; providing records of their individual bravery and virtues; as well as filling in important, and occasionally amusing, dramatic, or touching, details we simply have no other means of knowing about. At the same time, this gathering of information affords the opportunity to fill some of the gaps in the record further by way of footnote and annotation; which we have striven to do here. While numerous facts are still unknown and primary materials often scarce if not altogether non-existent, hopefully we, with Garden's most unique and gifted assistance, will have at least managed to get significantly closer to our object of better comprehending and appreciating quite what the Legion was, and who the men were that filled its ranks and or led therein.

>>>>>>>>>>>>>>>>>>>>***<<<<<<<<<<<<<<<<<<<<

Excerpts from *Anecdotes of the Revolutionary War in America: With Sketches of Character of Persons the Most Distinguished, in the Southern States, for Civil and Military Services* A.E. Miller, Charleston, 1822. By Alexander Garden, of Lee's Partisan Legion; Aid-De-Camp to Major General Greene; And Honorary Member of the Historical Society of New-York. [Beginning at p. 123.]

Character and Conduct of Officers of the Legion

~*~

I feel too proud of the partial friendship experienced from my brother Officers of the Legion, not to be ambitious, in some degree, to acquit myself of my debt of gratitude, by recording the successes resulting from their exemplary good conduct, and the achievements that gave many of them, peculiar claims to celebrity. Where merited praise is not bestowed, I can truly aver, that it will not proceed from intentional neglect. The title of most of them to distinction, has been repeatedly acknowledged by their general, and confirmed by the flattering concurrence of their confederates in arms. I can only speak particularly of those with whom I was most familiar, and best acquainted. Major John Rudolph [Rudulph], the Captains [Henry] Archer and Hurd, the facetious Captain Carns [Patrick Carnes], bold in action, in quarters the delight of his associates; George Carrington, [William] Winston, [Jonathan] Snowden, [James] Lovell, [Robert] Power, [William Butler] Harrison, Lumford [Swanson Lunsford], and [John] Jordan, performed every duty with alacrity, and with the highest advantage to the service.

Captain Joseph Eggleston[22]

Cavalry.

This meritorious Officer was endowed with superior powers of mind, but decidedly better qualified to gain celebrity in the cabinet, than in the field. He had the most perfect knowledge of duty, and was ever prompt in its performance; but the spirit of enterprise particularly requisite in a Partisan, was foreign to his nature. There occurred, however, one recontre [sic] with the enemy, in which he acquired distinction, both for [p. 123] talent and intrepidity. On the retreat of the British army from Ninety-Six, Lee, knowing that the rich settlement South of Fridig's [also "Friday's"] ferry, could alone afford the forage which they would require, determined to avail himself of the probable chance of striking a blow, which should paralyze every future movement, Eggleston was detached for the purpose, to the expected scene of action, and choosing an advantageous position, anxiously awaited their approach. A party of sixty British dragoons, and some foraging wagons speedily appeared, evidently intending to reach the very farm he occupied. The legionary cavalry rushed forward with irresistible impetuosity, the enemy were at once put to rout, the wagons taken, and forty-five dragoons brought off prisoners, without the loss of a single man.[23]

It is painful to state, though the imputations of blame rest not on him, that the opportunity of totally destroying the British cavalry at Eutaw was lost, by his having, from his ardour to perform his duty, obeyed an unauthorized order to engage. Foiled, and compelled to retire, when summoned to advance by Lee, he was too far distant to support Armstrong, who was ready to engage, but unequal with a single troop to meet the superior force of [John] Coffin.[24] On the day following the battle, however, he rendered very essential service, charging the retiring enemy, and taking from them several wagons containing stores and baggage. On this occasion, his horse was killed under him – he himself escaping without injury, though five balls pierced his clothes and equipments.

At the conclusion of the war, turning his attention to literary pursuits, he was returned a Member of Congress, in which respectable body he obtained applause and distinction. [p. 124]

Of warm and impatient temper, while yet in the flower of his age, tormented by the irritation of a disordered leg, and insisting on amputation, mortification ensued, which caused his immediate and untimely dissolution.

---

[22] Eggleston (1754-1811), a William and Mary graduate and originally part of Lee's first troop of Virginia State Cavalry, served with distinction in the Legion throughout the war and was afterward, among other several public offices he held, a U.S. Representative from the state of Virginia from 1798 to 1801. His gravesite is located in the Old Grubhill Church Cemetery, near Amelia Court House in Amelia County, Virginia.

[23] 3 July 1781, Lee, *Memoirs,* p. 381.

[24] Regarding both Eutaw Springs, 8 September 1781, and the lost opportunity to defeat Coffin and turn the British left flank, see Lee, *Memoirs*, pp. 463-475, Gibbes' *Documentary History* Vol. 3 p. 151, and *Papers of Nathaniel Greene*, Vol. IX (Dennis Conrad, editor) pp. 335n-336n.

~*~

Captain James Armstrong[25]

Cavalry.

There was no Officer in the service of the United States, whose feats of daring, had made a more salutary impression on the minds of the enemy, than those of Armstrong of the Legion. The British did justice to his merits; they admired his valor; they gratefully acknowledged his humanity; and when he, by an accident, became their prisoner, behaved towards him with marked and flattering attention. Had they displayed the same generous conduct towards others, which they exercised towards him, the asperities of the war would have been softened, and nothing heard of those acts of intemperate violence, which debased their characters as men.

The details of his achievements are to be met with in every history of the war; it would be superfluous again to repeat them. But, one instance of his attention to a brave and unfortunate Soldier, has not, in my judgment been sufficiently dwelt upon. Lieutenant Colonel Lee was certainly a man of strong prejudices; but, where admiration was excited towards a gallant enemy, his generosity was unbounded. Fascinated by the consummate skill and bravery of Colonel Browne [loyalist, Thomas Brown], in the defense of his post at Augusta, his resolution was immediately fixed, to save him from the fury of an exasperated population, and the better to effect it, [p. 125] put him under the safeguard of Armstrong, to conduct him to Savannah. The precaution was the more necessary, as the inveteracy of party, in the neighbourhood of Augusta, had given birth to a war of extermination, and he saw that without such interposition a gallant Soldier, who had committed himself to his enemy, on their plighted faith, would otherwise have been sacrificed. Colonel [James] Grierson of the British militia, had already fallen by an unknown hand; and to have risked a repetition of the crime, would have subjected the victorious commanders to merited censure and reproach.[26]

I have often heard the gallant Armstrong declare, that he never had, in his own opinion, encountered equal peril with that which he experienced on this trying occasion. At every turn preparation was made for death – in every individual who approached, was seen the eager wish to destroy. Resentment was excited to the highest pitch, and called aloud to be appeased by blood. Yet, by dint of good management, by the gentleness of persuasion – by forcibly portraying the duty of humanity to a captured and unresisting foe, and occasionally

---

[25] Armstrong (1753-1800), according to one credible genealogist's report was born in Londonderry, Ireland. Some time shortly after the Revolutionary War broke out, we find him serving as an officer in the Pennsylvania line; where he was made lieutenant in the 3d Pennsylvania Regiment in April 1777. On 16 July 1778, at Peekskill, N.Y., he was "notwithstanding his good character as an officer and soldier," court-martialed and reprimanded by General Washington, (see *Archives of Pennsylvania*, 2d series, Vol. 11, p. 294.) Then in September 1778, his, with other officers of the 3d Regiment, was one of forty-one signatures affixed to a petition submitted to Washington protesting recently adopted promotion procedures. By January 1779, we find him a Lieutenant in Lee's corps; and some time, not clear, in 1780 was made a Captain heading one of Lee's troops of cavalry; (Heitman gives 1 January 1779 as the date of his being granted a captaincy, but this is apparently in error); and was commended for his part in the raid on Paulus Hook, 19 August 1779. Armstrong was later taken captive near Dorchester, S.C. in December 1781 (see Lee, *Memoirs*, p. 538), and was held a prisoner to the war's termination. An account of Armstrong's own last Revolutionary War and capture encounter just outside Dorchester, S.C. is found in "The Narrative of Col. Stephen Jarvis." *The Journal of American History*, vol.1, Issues 3-4, 1907. Following the conflict, he settled in Richmond County, Georgia; and in 1786 commanded a company of Dragoons guarding the border with Florida. One unofficial source (and which we have yet to confirm) states Armstrong received an electoral vote for President in 1789. He died at the Georgia plantation of fellow officer Ferdinand O'Neal, in McIntosh County, on 28 June 1800 (*Georgia Gazette*, 31 June 1800, p. 3.) For further on both Armstrong and O'Neal, see *Pennsylvania Magazine of History and Biography*, Vol. XXIX, by the Historical Society of Pennsylvania, Philadelphia, 1905, pp. 483-484; and Caldwell Woodruff's, "Capt. Ferdinand O'Neal of Lee's Legion," *The William and Mary Quarterly*, 2nd Ser., Vol. 23, No. 3 (July, 1943), pp. 328-330, and the well done, though more informal, "A Biography of Ferdinand O'Neal," by Dorothy Tribble; that can be found at The O'Neal Genealogy Association website at http://www.onealwebsite.com

[26] 6 June 1781, Lee, *Memoirs*, pp. 367-370.

well applied threats, he saved the contemplated victim, and delivered him in safety to his friends in Savannah.

A remarkable scene is said, by Dr. [David] Ramsay, to have occurred on this occasion, which well deserves to be recorded, as exemplifying the firmness of a female, labouring under the deepest affliction of grief. Passing through the settlement where the most wanton waste had recently been made by the British, both of lives and property, a Mrs. M'Koy [McKay, mother of Rannall McKay, the young man spoken of], having obtained permission to speak with Colonel Browne [loyalist, Thomas Brown], addressed him in words to the following effect: -- "Colonel Browne, in the late day of your prosperity, I visited your camp, and on my knees supplicated for the life of my son -- but you were deaf to my entreaties! You [p. 126] hanged him, though a beardless youth, before my face. These eyes have seen him scalped by the savages under your immediate command, and for no better reason than that his name was M'Koy. As you are prisoner to the leaders of my country, for the present I lay aside all thoughts of revenge: but, when you resume your sword, I will go five hundred miles to demand satisfaction at the point of it, for the murder or my son."[27]

While Armstrong remained a prisoner, he was treated, as I have stated, with distinguished politeness. To Colonel Thompson, afterwards Count Rumford,[28] I have heard him express great obligation; and still more to Commodore Sweeny, whose attentions were such as none but a generous enemy could have known to bestow. I have only to add, that ever high in he esteem and affection of his associates, admired and respected in every society, he lived beloved, and died lamented.

~*~

Captain [Ferdinand] O'Neal[29]

Cavalry.

O'Neal was one of the Officers of the Legion, who rose to rank and consideration by the force of extraordinary merit. He entered the army a private trooper in Bland's regiment, and was one of a gallant band, who, when Captain Henry Lee was surprised at the Spread-Eagle Tavern, near Philadelphia, resolutely defended the position against the whole of the British cavalry, and ultimately compelled them to retire. Lee, on this occasion, addressing his companions, and strenuously urging them rather to die than surrender, added -- "Henceforth, I consider the fortune of every individual present, as inseparably [p. 128] connected with my own! If we fall, we will fall like brothers! If successful in repelling the enemy, (and it needs but a trifling exertion of your energies to effect it) my fortune and my

---

[27] For Brown's own version and explanation of what took place with respect to the murder of Grierson and the hanging of McKay, see White's *Historical Collections of Georgia*, pp. 614-620.

[28] Benjamin Thompson (1753-1814) was a Massachusetts loyalist, and later Count Rumford world renown scientist, inventor, and honored member of the Royal Society. On 24 February 1782 he was commissioned a lieutenant colonel in the "King's American Dragoons" (formed in New York); and is said to have served in South Carolina with that unit later the same year.

[29] O'Neal, a Virginian reportedly of French origin or ancestry, was initially a Cornet in Lee's Light Dragoons in April 1777. By 5 September 1779 he was Lieutenant in the Legion; and in October 1780 Captain in which rank he served to the conflict's completion. Immediately after the war, along with Legion comrades James Armstrong and Michael Rudulph, he settled Georgia; O'Neal in particular in Camden County, Georgia, representing that county in the legislature in 1786. In Mar. 1787, he married Mary Ann "Polly" Woodruff; with whom he had at least three children. He later moved to Liberty County where he was elected representative there in 1790; and following that had a plantation in McIntosh County (which had been formed from Liberty County.) At the time of Quasi-War with France, he was made a candidate for Colonel in the then being raised provisional army, and in which James Armstrong was a Major. In 1801, MacIntosh County sent him to the state assembly a Senator; which office he held till sometime in 1803. The date of O'Neal's death is unknown, but it has been suggested that it would have been sometime before 1820. For more, see Woodruff's "Capt. Ferdinand O'Neal of Lee's Legion," *The William and Mary Quarterly*, 2nd Ser., Vol. 23, No. 3 (July, 1943), pp. 328-330; and "A Biography of Ferdinand O'Neal," by Dorothy Tribble at http://www.onealwebsite.com

interest shall be uniformly employed to increase your comforts, and secure your promotion." Nor did he ever swerve from his promise. Appointed, shortly after, with the rank of Major, to the command of a corps of horse, O'Neal and [William] Winston, another of his faithful adherents, received commissions, and to the last hour of the way, by uniform steadiness of conduct, and exemplary intrepidity, gained increase of reputation. It was said, on this occasion, that Tarleton, making his first essay as a military man, but for the accidental snapping of O'Neal's carbine, would have fallen a victim to a bold effort, which he made to enter by a window at which he was posted, the muzzle of the piece being, at the time, within a foot of his head. Tarleton behaved with great calmness; for looking up, he said with a smile, "You have missed it, my lad, for this time;" and wheeling his horse, joined his companions, who, deceived by false alarm, were retiring with precipitation.

Captain Michael Rudolph [Rudulph][30]

Infantry.

There was not, in the Southern Army, an Officer of the same grade, whose activity and daring spirit produced such essential advantages to the service as Michael Rudolph; yet, in the pages of history he is scarcely named. I never knew a man, so strictly inforcing [sic] the observance of discipline, who, at the same time, maintained so perfect an ascendancy over the [p. 129] affections of his men. He was their idol; and such was their confidence in his talents and intrepidity, that no enterprise, however, hazardous, could be proposed, where he was to be the leader, but every individual in the regiment became anxious to obtain a preference of service.

His stature was diminitive [sic]; but from the energy of his mind, and personal activity, his powers were gigantic.

Fully to detail his services, is beyond my ability, but that he merited the grateful applause of his country, must be allowed, when it is recollected, that he led the forlorn hope, when the post at New York, was surprised and carried by Lee; and that the same perilous command was assigned him at the storming of the Stockade Fort at Ninety-Six; that he bore a pre-eminently distinguished part in conducting the sieges of the several Forts reduced in the interior country, and particularly directed against Fort Cornwallis at Augusta; that at Guilford [Court House] his conduct was highly applauded, and that he was conspicuous from his exemplary ardour, leading the charge with the bayonet, which broke the British line at Eutaw; that shortly previous to the evacuation of Charleston, he, with sixteen men, took and burnt the Galley protecting the left of the British line at the Quarter House, bringing off

[30] Michael Rudulph (often and usually given, incorrectly, as "Rudolph" though ostensibly the pronunciation is very similar if not identical) and cousin of Major John Rudulph (also of the Legion), hailed, like John, from Cecil County, Maryland; being born in Elkton. He was Sergeant Major of Lee's Light Dragoons in April 1778; and by July 1779 was made Lieutenant. He was conspicuous for his gallantry in leading the forlorn hope in the capture of Paulus Hook in August 1779, and in consequence was in Sept. brevetted Captain by resolve of Congress. By 1 November 1779, he was a full Captain in the Legion; serving, as much as anyone else in the heat of the fighting, in the unit to the war's end. He at first settled in Georgia along with Ferdinand O'Neal and James Armstrong; in Rudulph's case in Sunbury; raising rice and cattle, and then appointed collector for the port there for 1787-89. In June 1790, he became Capatin again in the United States army and was stationed at Augusta; and was among Washington's greeters when the President visited in 1791. Transferred to join Josiah Harmar's ill equipped western army, he returned to Elkton on 1 June 1791; arriving at Pittsburgh (then Fort Fayette) to assume dragoon command by March, and where he was well known for both his sternness and affection as a commanding officer. In Feb. of 1793 while on Furlough in Maryland, he was made Adjutant General and Inspector of the United States Army.
Sometime in 1795, Rudulph sailed from Baltimore in a merchant ship carrying tobacco, and was subsequently (and seemingly) lost at sea; though in the mid 19th century there was a legend or rumor afloat that he actually ended up and France and somehow, through disguising his true identity, became Napoleon's Marshal Ney. For more, see "Michael Rudulph, 'Lion of the Legion,'" by Marilou Alston Rudulph, *Georgia Historical Quarterly*, 45 (September 1961), pp. 201-222, and "The Legend of Michael Rudulph," by Marilou Alston Rudulph, *Georgia Historical Quarterly*, 45 (December 1961), pp. 309-328.

twenty-six prisoners;[31] and that, finally, he dismounted and made a prisoner of one of the boldest black dragoons employed by the enemy.

Such were the Revolutionary services of the Captain, under whose auspices I entered the army, and whose virtues were no less estimable than his public utility.

At a later period in the war, with the Western Indians, he served with distinguished reputation; but [p. 130] anxious to provide for an increasing family, he left the service to engage in trade, and sailing on a voyage of speculation to the West Indies, was heard of no more.

~ * ~

Captain [George] Handy[32]

Infantry.

Animated by principles as pure and patriotic, Captain Handy gained distinction by his zealous performance of every duty, and the invincible coolness with which he encountered danger. His activity contributed very essentially, to the reduction of several Forts held by the enemy in the interior country, particularly that at Augusta, where his vigorous charge on the British, who had, by a bold sally, actually possessed themselves of the trenches of the besiegers, caused their expulsion, and precipitate retreat into their posts, from where they never ventured again.[33] On the retreat of [Francis] Lord Rawdon from Ninety-Six, while Lee was endeavoring to gain his front, Handy, deviating a few paces from his command, was seized and carried to a distance by a party of *banditti*, who robbed him of his watch, money, and every article of his clothing, leaving him in a state of perfect nudity, to find his way back to his party. The appellation which I have used is not too harsh; the ceremony of a parole was, indeed, insisted on and given; but on application, at an after period, to the British commander for the exchange of Handy, he candidly acknowledged, that he was not known as a prisoner, and that his captors must have been a set of lawless marauders, of whom the British had no knowledge. Captain Handy, again restored to the service, by patent endurance of all the miseries and privations of the last campaign, had great influence [p. 131] in tranquilizing the minds of men, driven almost to desperation by famine and disease. The departure of the enemy, at length, closed the scene of the calamity.

Handy led the van of the troops taking possession of Charleston, and having the command of the main guard, by his arrangement of patrols, and the correct conduct of his men, preserved a tranquility that could scarcely have been expected, from Soldiers so long deprived of every comfort, who had now a town, rich in spoil, and many of their most

---

[31] David Ramsay: "Though the battle of Eutaw may be considered as closing the national war in South-Carolina, yet after that period several small enterprizes, greatly to the credit of individuals, were successfully executed. The American army felt the elevation of conquerors, while the British, from the recollection of their former prowess, and the exactness of their discipline, though reduced in their limits, could not bear to be insulted. From among a variety of projects which were undertaken by detached parties of Americans, in the year 1782, the following is selected as meriting particular notice. On the nineteenth of March captain Rudolph, of Lee's legion, and lieutenant Smith, of the Virginia line, with twelve men, captured and burned the British galley Alligator, lying in Ashley river, which mounted twelve guns, besides a variety of swivels, and was manned with forty-three seamen. The Americans had the address to pass themselves for negroes who were coming to market with poultry. They were therefore permitted to come so near the galley that they boarded her with ease, while their adversaries suspected no danger. Three or four of the British were killed, and twenty-eight were brought off prisoners." *The History of the Revolution of South Carolina*, (1785) vol. 2, ch. 12, pp. 257-258.

[32] Handy was an Ensign in the 5th Maryland regiment in April. 1777, and on 10 May 1777 was promoted to Lieutenant. Though on 26 August 1778 he resigned his commission; by July 1779, we find him a Lieutenant of the infantry in Lee's Legion; ably led a detachment at Paulus Hook, August 1779. Later, on 20 November 1780, Handy was promoted to Captain. Receiving particular praise by Lee himself for his role in the Second siege of Augusta, April 1781, he remained with the corps till the war's close; and returned to Maryland sometime after.

[33] 24 May 1781, Lee, *Memoirs*, p. 362.

implacable enemies, altogether within their power. To his credit I can assert that no irregularity was committed – not a murmur heard.

~*~

Lieutenant Peter Johnston[34]

Infantry.

Imbibing, at a very early period of the Revolutionary war, an enthusiastic attachment to the cause of Liberty, and sensible, that the opinions of his father, whose political creed sanctioned the pretensions of Britain, would militate against his ardent ambition to serve, Peter Johnston, at the age of sixteen, eloped from his College, and avoiding successfully the pursuit of his tutors, joined the Legion as a volunteer. His eagerness to acquire military knowledge, and unceasing efforts to obtain distinction, very speedily attracted attention, and obtained for him, the commission to which he aspired, while the whole tenor of his conduct evinced, that it could not have been more judiciously bestowed. He was brave, enterprising, and where duty called, exemplary in its performance. I will give no further proof of it, than his intrepid conduct at the siege of the post at Wright's Bluff [Fort Watson or Scott's Lake], where [p. 132.] the removal of the abbatis, under the immediate fire of the British riflemen, connected with the appalling erection of the Mayham [Maham] Tower, struck the enemy with so great a panic, as to cause an instantaneous surrender.[35]

To the end of the war, he still acquired an increase of reputation, and so completely gained the favour of the parent he had offended, as to be received, on his return to the domestic circle of his family, not only with affection, but pride. Pursuing the study of the Law, he rapidly obtained professional reputation; and now promoted to a seat on the bench of Judges, is equally admired for the wisdom and justice of his decrees.

~*~

John Middleton[36]

Cornet in the Legion

Of Middleton, I would speak with justice, equal to his merit. It would, indeed, be a sacred duty were I competent to perform it. He was ever "the man nearest my heart." Brought up together from infancy, and united in our progress through life, by ties of the most disinterested friendship, he was to me as a brother; and I can with truth assert, that he never obtained an honor, nor progressed a step in public favor, which did not occasion, in my bosom, a sensation of delight, as perfect as if the merit had been my own. Every attention that could induce a man of less exalted feeling, of patriotism less pure, to remain in England at the commencement of hostilities, were held out to him. Wealth, connexion [sic], preferment courted his acceptance. A living in the established Church, of considerable amount, was his by inheritance; [p. 133.] but superior to every selfish consideration, and regarding the violated rights of his country, as injuries to his own honor, he nobly resolved,

---

[34] Johnston (1763-1841), from Osborne's Landing, Virginia, was originally intended by his family for the church; but, at the age of 16, without informing his father, ran off and enlisted in the Legion. Evidently, and as later proven, he was an able and intelligent lad for he quickly arose in the ranks. At Fort Watson, in mid April 1781, he led the assault on the works there, and was later commended before the unit for his bravery. Following war's end, Johnston settled down to study law; subsequently becoming the eminent Judge and jurist Garden speaks of him as. Further of note, he was the father of Joseph Eggleston Johnston, famed Confederate Civil War general.

[35] 23 April 1781. Lee, *Memoirs*, pp. 331-332.

[36] According to Heitman, Middleton (from South Carolina) was a Lieutenant in the Legion from 1780-1782. He died in Charleston, 14 November 1784.

by the devotion of his life to her service, to become her defender, and ward off the exterminating blow, which the resentments of a merciless administration had denounced against her. Quitting Europe, and arriving safely on the American shores, he joined the Southern Army, and offering himself as a volunteer for promotion, speedily exhibited so many instances of gallantry, and so great an ardour for enterprise, as to be rewarded with a Cornetcy in the Legion. No youthful candidate for fame could ever, with greater success, have acquired the admiration of his superiors, the love of the troops serving under him, the perfect esteem and friendship of his brother Officers. His career was short. He but lived to witness the expulsion of the enemy from our Capital, when seized by a mortal disease, he fell its victim. The regrets of every class of the community, affording the highest proof of his estimable character, his talents, and his virtues.

~*~

Clement Carrington,[37]

of the Legion Infantry.

Perhaps a more striking instance of the irregular action of fear upon the human mind, was never exhibited than at the battle of Eutaw [Springs.] Early in the action, Mr. Clement Carrington, then a volunteer in the Legion, received a wound which incapacitated him from advancing with his corps, successfully charging the British with the bayonet. He was leaning on his spontoon, anxiously regarding the intrepid exertions of [p. 134] his companions, when a militiaman, flying from the field, appeared immediately in his front, rushing directly on him with the blind impetuosity of terror. Carrington, finding that he must be overturned, unless he could arrest his flight, crossed his spontoon over his breast, the more effectually to check his progress, and upbraiding his cowardice in an authoritative tone, commanded him to halt. The terrors of the fugitive were too highly excited to suffer control, he snatched the weapon opposed to him from the hands of Carrington, and passing the blade of it through his body, with redoubled speed ran on. To the satisfaction of his friends, the gallant volunteer recovered – was speedily commissioned in the Legion, and at the conclusion of the war, applying to the study of the law, has since become a distinguished practitioner at the bar of Virginia.

~*~

Dr. Matthew Irvine.[38]

It would be difficult to speak with encomiums equal to his merit, of this excellent Officer. This is no flattery; a cursory review of his services, will afford ample proof, that he stands in need of no such aid. He commenced his career, in the cause of liberty, at the very dawning of hostilities, being one of that distinguished band, who, pausing through the wilderness, and surmounting difficulties, such as had never before been encountered by man, appeared suddenly before the lines of Quebec.

In the Middle States, he served with great distinction, being present at every action of consequence in the field, and participating in many Partisan enterprises, highly creditable to American arms. But, [p. 135] it was in the Southern war that he acquired the highest distinction, not only performing the duties of his profession with consummate skill,

---

[37] Carrington was from Virginia, and, says Heitman, was Cornet in Lee's Light Dragoons in 1780, serving to the close of the war.

[38] From Pennsylvania, Irvine was originally a Surgeon's Mate in Thompson's Rifle Battalion from July to December 1775; then from 20 July 1778 to the close of the war he acted as Surgeon in the Legion. He died 31 August 1827. For more on Irvine, see Joseph Johnson's *Traditions and Reminiscences chiefly of the American Revolution in the South*, pp. pp. 403-405, and also *The Pennsylvania Magazine of History and Biography*, vol. 5, no. 4 (1881), pp. 418-424.

and exemplary tenderness and humanity, but frequently serving as an able negotiator with the enemy, and constantly employed as the confidential agent betwixt the General and the Officers, on whose judgment he chiefly relied, in all consultations where important measures were contemplated, and secrecy regarded as essential to success. His great fault, if fault it can be called, was the too great exposure of his person. Possessing an intrepidity that could not be controlled, he was frequently to be found in the hottest of the fight; and it is well known, that he was wounded at Quinby [Bridge, South Carolina],[39] at the head of Armstrong's troops, when his proper station was in the rear of the army. His military services ended, the celebrity he had acquired, as a skilful Surgeon and Physician attended him in private life; and it is no exaggeration to say, that he continues the practice of his profession, with infinite advantage to the public, and constant increase of his own reputation.

~*~

Dr. [Alexander] Skinner.[40]

I had, during the last campaign in the South, continued opportunity of witnessing the eccentricities of this extraordinary character; but while I admired his facetious and entertaining conversation, his exquisite humour, and occasional exhibition of sportive or pointed irony, I could not but consider him as a very dangerous companion. Colonel Lee has stated, that he had a dire objection to the field of battle, yet in private society always ready for a quarrel; it might be truly asserted, [p. 136] that it required infinite circumspection not to come to pints with him, since he really appeared to consider tilting as a pleasing pastime, and he was (as an Irish soldier once said of him) "an honest fellow, just as ready to fight as eat." In his regiment, and among his intimates, he was regarded s a privileged man, and allowed to throw the shafts of his wit impunity. This was a fortunate circumstance, as he would at any time rather have risked the loss of his friend, than the opportunity of applying satirical observation in point. When first he appeared in the lower country, he wore a long beard and huge fur cap, the latter through necessity, the first from some superstitious notion, the meaning of which it was impossible to penetrate. An officer, who really esteemed him, asking him "why he suffered his beard to grow to such an unusual length," he tartly replied, "It is a secret, Sir, betwixt my God and myself, that human impertinence shall never penetrate." On a night alarm, at Ninety-Six, as Colonel Lee was hastening forward to ascertain the cause, he met Skinner in full retreat, and stopping him, said, "what is the matter Doctor, whither so fast – not frightened I hope?" "No, Colonel, no," replied Skinner, "not absolutely frightened, but, I candidly confess, most damnably alarmed." His strong resemblance to the character of Falstaff, which Colonel Lee has also noticed, was very remarkable. "He was witty himself, and the cause of wit in others." Like the fat knight, too, in calculation of chances, not over scrupulous in distinctions between *meum* and *tuum*;[41] and, I should decidedly say, in his narrations of broils and battles, too much under the influence of Shrewsbury clock. I have seldom met with a man more fond of good and dainty cheer, or a more devoted idolater of good wine; but when they were not to be met with, the plainest food, and most simple liquor, were enjoyed with the highest relish. [p. 137]

A lady of the lower country, addressing herself to a young officer who had been much accustomed to enjoy every species of luxury, asked, "how he had supported the privations experienced during the last campaign in the interior?" he replied "that hunger

---

[39] 17 July 1781, Lee, *Memoirs*, p. 390.

[40] Skinner was initially Surgeon in the 1st Virginia Regiment, 26 October 1776; but by 1780, was a Surgeon in the Legion where he remained till the war's close. For a sketch of him by Lee himself see *Memoirs*, p. 382n. It seems more than reasonable to assume Skinner was in some measure the model and inspiration of the "Captain Porgy" character in William Gilmore Simms' historical novel *The Partisan* (1835), and also *Eutaw* (1856); a character, incidentally, roundly deplored and lamented by reviewer Edgar Allen Poe and pointed out as one of *The Partisan*'s signal weaknesses; (keeping in mind, of course, that Poe's criticism is directed at the author's fictional personage being ill fitted to the work; rather than a real life person.) See *Southern Literary Messenger*, January 1836.

[41] Latin -- *mine* and *yours*.

made a simple rasher on the coals, as delicious as the most sumptuous fare, and that where wine could not be obtained he relished whiskey." "I am grieved, my young friend," said Skinner, with great gravity, "mortified, beyond expression, to hear such a declaration from your lips, since it has long been my opinion, that the man who would drink so mean a liquor as whiskey would steal."

In person, Skinner was not unlike the representation generally given of Sancho; in his government, exhibiting extravagant pretensions to state and self consequence. Nor was he insensible to the influences of the tender passion. He not only could love, but he believed himself possessed of every requisite to inspire passion, particularly priding himself upon a roguish leer with the eye, that he deemed irresistible. When disencumbered of his beard, he was presented at Sandy Hill (the point of attraction to all the military) to Mrs. Charles Elliott, the amiable and benevolent hostess of the mansion. The facetious Captain Carns [Carnes], who was his friend on the occasion, indulging his natural propensity to quiz, pointed her out to Skinner, as an object highly worth the attention of a man of enterprise. The bait was attractive, and he bit at it with the eagerness of a hungry gudgeon. On his first appearance of his cap, Mrs. Elliott had perceived it, and retiring, for an instant, returned with an elegant military hat, which she placed on his head, and gracefully bowing, run off. Skinner was mute with astonishment – he looked at the hat, and at the lady [p. 138] and then at the hat again, and turning to his friend, seemed, in the language of Falstaff, to say –

"Her eye did seem to scorch me like a burning glass."

The expression of his countenance was, to Carns, a sufficient indication of the agitation of his bosom. The hint was not lost. "Well," he feelingly exclaimed, "if ever a broad and palpable invitation was given, this certainly, may be considered as such! Why, Skinner, what charm, what philter do you use to produce such havoc?" "Fie, fie," said the enraptured Doctor, adjusting his dress, and rising upon tip-toe, "Tempt me not, my friend, and make myself ridiculous. Mine is not a figure to attract the attention of a fair lady – it cannot, cannot happen!" "I will not," rejoined Carns, "compliment you, Skinner, on your personal attractions. You are a man of sense, a man of discernment, too wise to be flattered; but I certainly have seen men less elegantly formed than you are; and altogether with that *je ne sais quoi*, so fascinating, that you pre-eminently possess; besides, you have a fine, open, healthy, countenance, a prepossessing smile, and a prodigiously brilliant and piercing eye." "Ah, ha," cried Skinner, "have you discovered *that*? You are man of penetration! A man of taste! Yes, Carns, I *have* an eye, and if it has its usual trick, its tender expression, (you understand what I would say) I may, perhaps be happy." Carns, for a time, gave indulgence to the effusions of his vanity, but would not suffer him to make himself completely ridiculous. Love was very speedily forgotten; and a kind of invitation to feel himself at home, in the most hospitable mansion in the State, made Skinner the proudest and happiest of men.

Falstaff maintained, that it was proper for every man "to labour in his vocation." Skinner asserted, "that every man had his sphere of action, beyond the limits of which he ought never to emerge." "Mine," [p. 139] said he, 'amidst the tumults of war, the conflicts of battle, is *in the rear*. – *There*, I am always to be found. I am firm at my post. What did Matthew Irvine get by quitting his?* -- a wound – a villainous wound! Shall I follow his example, step out of my sphere, and set myself up as a mark to be shot at? O no! I am a stickler for the strict performance of duty, but feel no ambition to shine beyond it.

Being asked, which of the Ladies of South Carolina possessed, in his estimation, the greatest attraction? He readily replied, "The widow Izard beyond all comparison. I never pass her magnificent sideboard, but the late seems ready to tumble into my pocket."

Arriving near re bank of the river, on the night of the contemplated attack upon John's Island, he was asked, whether he intended to pass the ford? "By no means," replied

Skinner. "I am not fond of romantic enterprise, and will not seek for the perilous achievements where the elements more than the enemy are to be dreaded. The river too is deep, and my spirits are not buoyant; I should sink to a certainty and meet a watery grave. Death by water drinking! I shudder at the thought of it! I will remain and take care of the baggage; and as many of you as can boast a change, may be sure to meet, at your return, the comforts of clean linen, and the most cordial welcome I can give you."

[Footnote in original text] *After the gallant charge by Captain Armstrong at Quinby Bridge, both himself and his Lieutenant George Carrington,[42] having passed the gap made in it by the enemy, Dr. Matthew Irvine put himself at the head of the dragoons who had failed in the attempt to cross, and made an entire company of the 19th Regiment prisoners, but in the conflict was wounded. [p. 140]

~*~

Lieutenant [Laurence] Manning,[43]

And Occurrences leading to the Defeat of Colonel [John] *Pyle.* [44]

That important consequences have resulted from accidental occurrences, and that achievements have been attributed to foresight and judgment, which originated in some fortuitous incident, cannot be doubted. The following Anecdote may possibly be disbelieved by some, yet I must record it as doing honour to a fellow-soldier, to whom I was bound by strictest ties of friendship. No man who knew Manning would question his veracity, and from his lips I received it. Nor is it credible, that *he* would wander into the regions of romance to exalt his reputation, when by the uniformity of his conduct, he was daily adding, to the laurels universally acknowledged to be his due. I have besides, in my possession, a letter from my highly valued friend, Judge Johnston of Abingdon, Virginia, at the period of its occurrence, an Officer in the Legion, corroborating the principal fact, though slightly differing in the detail. With regard to the worth and abilities of Manning, his coolness and intrepidity, our sentiments are the same. His delineation of his talents and character I regard as perfect. "I never," says the Judge, "knew any man who was more remarkable for that quality, which is called presence of mind. The more sudden the emergency, the greater the danger in which he was unexpectedly placed, the more perfect was his self-possession, as related to the faculties both of body and mind. In corporal vigour and activity, he was exceeded by few; and there was an ardour about him, which characterized every thing that he said or did. If he had enjoyed the advantages of literary culture, he would have been [p. 141] as much the object of our admiration every where else, as he was in scenes of danger and military adventure."

Most of the settlers in North Carolina, in the neighbourhood of Cross Creek, now Fayetteville, were emigrants from Scotland, who had brought with them strong prejudices in favour of monarchy. Few among them had imbibed the spirit of Liberty, fostered with enthusiasm by almost the entire population in their adopted country; but, to the credit of such as professed attachment, it must be remembered, that having once declared in favour of the cause of America, none more courageously, zealously, and faithfully supported it. No other

---

[42] Lee remarks that during the Race to the Dan that "Lieutenant Carrington, who commanded the dragoons near the enemy's van, reported from time to time, in conformity to custom, by which it appeared that Cornwallis was moving as usual..." *Memoirs*, pp. 239-240.

[43] Manning (1756-1804), originally from Pennsylvania (and whose first name is also seen spelled as "Lawrence"), began his army career in the 2d Canadian (also "Hazen's") Regiment, and was a Sergeant with that unit by early December 1776.was; and on 1 March 1777 was made Sergeant Major. He was wounded and captured at Staten Island, 22 August 1777; but by 19 September 1778 was back with his the regiment as an Ensign; and later, in July 1779, made Lieutenant. March 1780 found him being moved to the Legion Infantry whom he served with till war's finish. Interestingly, Manning's son, Richard Irvine Manning; his grandson, John Laurence Manning; and great-grandson Richard Irvine Manning III, all became South Carolina Governors.

[44] 25 February, 1781, Lee, *Memoirs*, pp. 254-260.

foreign nation contributed so many distinguished Officers in the line of our armies as Scotland. The intrepid [Hugh] *Mercer* sealed his devotion to our cause with his blood, and died in battle. *Lord Sterling* [William Alexander], Generals *M'Dougald* [Alexander McDougall], *Sinclair* [Arthur St. Clair], *Stephens* [apparently Adam Stephen or possibly Edward Stevens], *M'Intosh* [Lachlan McIntosh], and [William Richardson] *Davie*, were among the most gallant and strenuous champions of Independence. Knowing these facts, it cannot be imagined, that I could ever cherish or utter a sentiment injurious to a country, whose sons are brave, and daughters virtuous; where beauty is adorned with its most fascinating perfections, and manhood exhibits a vigour and activity that cannot be surpassed; where industry has produced an almost incredible influx of wealth, and the energies of mind an increase of literary acquirement, that places human knowledge on an eminence that it had never before attained; -- a country where, as a student in a College of celebrity, I, for four successive years, listened with delight to the eloquence of the amiable and enlightened Miller, teaching, how far more congenial to the best feelings of the heart, and productive of [p. 142] happiness to man, in the purity of genuine Republicanism, than any system of government that the world has ever known. Where I studied the theory of morals, and witnessed the perfection of their practice, under the immediate protection and tuition of the first of Philosophers, and most virtuous of men, the immortal Dr. Thomas Reid. Where Jardine, the teacher of Eloquence, honored me with his friendship; and the liberal kindness of other Professors, of the inhabitants of the city, generally gave birth to sentiments of gratitude and affection, that can never be effaced. Truly, then, I can assert, that prejudices are unknown in the following narrative:

The intrigues and efforts of Lord Cornwallis, to excite insurrection, backed by a very formidable force, had produced among the Highland emigrants a spirit of revolt, which it required all the energies of General Greene to counteract, before it could be matured. – The zeal and activity of Lieutenant Colonel Lee, whose usefulness exceeded calculation, united to his acuteness and happy talent of obtaining intelligence of every movement, and of the most secret intentions of the enemy, pointed him out as the fittest man for this important service. He was accordingly selected, with orders to impede the intercourse of Lord Cornwallis with the disaffected; to repress every symptom of revolt, and promptly to cut off every party that should take up arms for Britain. Constantly on the alert, and equally solicitous to give security to his own command, while he harassed the enemy. A secure position was, on one occasion, taken near a forked road, one division of which led directly to Lord Cornwallis' camp, about six miles distant. The ground was chosen in the dusk of evening; and to prevent surprise, patrols of cavalry were kept out on each fork during the night. An order for a movement before day had been communicated to every individual, and was executed with so [p. 143] little noise and confusion, that Lieutenant Manning, waking at early dawn, found himself, excepting one Soldier, left alone. Stephen Greene, attendant of Captain Carns, lay near him, resting on the portmanteau of his superior, and buried in profound sleep. Being awakened, he was ordered to mount and follow, while Manning, hastening towards the fork, hoped to fall upon the track, and speedily rejoin his regiment. Much rain had fallen during the night, so that, finding both roads equally cut up, Manning chose at hard, and took the wrong one. He had not proceeded far, before he saw at the door of a log-house, a rifleman leaning on his gun, and apparently placed as a centinel [sic]. Galloping up to him, he inquired if a regiment of horse and a body of infantry had passed that way? "Oh ho," Cried the man, (whistling loudly, which brought out a dozen others completely armed, and carrying each a red rag in his hat,) "you, I suppose, are one of Greene's men." The badge which they bore, marked their principles. Without the slightest indication of alarm, or even hesitation, Manning pointed to the portmanteau carried by Green [sic], and exclaimed – "Hush, my good fellow – no clamour [sic] for God's sake – I have *there* what will ruin Greene -- point out the road to Lord Cornwallis' army, for all depends upon early intelligence of its contents." "You are an honest fellow, (was the general cry) and have left the rebels just in time, for the whole settlement are in arms to join Colonel Pyle to-morrow, (naming the place of rendezvous) where Colonel Tarleton will meet and conduct us to camp." "Come," said the man, to whom he had first spoken, "take a drink – Here's confusion to Greene, and success to the King and his friends. This is the right road, and you will soon reach the army; or rather let me conduct you to it myself." "Not for the world, my dear fellow," replied Manning; "your direction is plain and I can [p. 144] follow it. I will never consent, that a faithful subject of his Majesty should be subjected to the danger of captivity or death on my account. If we should fall in with a party of rebels, and we cannot say that they are not in the neighborhood now, we should both lose our lives. I should be hanged for desertion, and you for aiding me to reach the British army." This speech produced the effect he desired. The libation concluded, Manning rode off amid the cheers of the company, and when out of sight, crossed to the other road, and urging his horse to full speed, in a short time overtook and communicated the interesting intelligence to his commander. Lee was then meditating an attack upon Tarleton, who had crossed the Haw River to support the Insurgents; but, perceiving the vast importance of crushing the revolt in the bud, he informed General Greene of his plan by a confidential messenger, and hastened to the point of rendezvous, where Pyle, with upwards of four hundred men, had already arrived. It is unnecessary to detail the sanguinary scene which followed. Pyle, completely deceived, and to the last believing the Legionary Dragoons the soldiers of Tarleton, was overpowered, and with a considerable portion of his force, became victims of credulity.

It has been remarked that "severity at first is often humanity in the end." Its policy, on this occasion, will scarcely be denied. As Lee permitted no pursuit, many escaped, and spreading universal alarm, so completely crushed the spirit of revolt, that opposition to government was put at once and effectually to rest. But had the Insurgents been cut off to a man, would not the act have been justified on the score of retaliation? The provocation would have sanctioned it. To Colonel [Abraham] Buford, but a little before, Tarleton had refused capitulation. Deaf to the voice of clemency, and intent on slaughter, a charge was made on an unprepared and unresisting foe. His heart was steeled [p. 145] against the claims of mercy, and Lee has forcibly said, "it needed but the Indian war-dance, and roasting fire, to have placed the tragedy which followed, first in the records of torture and death."

Many other proofs could be adduced of Manning's presence of mind, and cool intrepidity in action. It is grateful to me to mention one of these. At the battle of Eutaw, after the British line had been broken, and the *Old Buffs*,[45] a regiment that had boasted of the extraordinary feats that they were to perform, were running from the field, Manning, in the enthusiasm of that valour for which he was so eminently distinguished, sprang forward in pursuit, directing the platoon which he commanded to follow him. He did not cast an eye behind until he found himself near a large brick house, into which the [New] York Volunteers, commanded by [John Harris] Cruger, were retiring. The British were on all sides of him, and not an American Soldier nearer than one hundred and fifty or two hundred yards. He did not hesitate a moment, but springing at an Officer who was near him, seized him by the collar, and exclaiming in a harsh tone of voice – "damn you, sir, you are my prisoner," wrested his sword from his grasp, dragged him by force from the house, and keeping his body as a shield of defence from the heavy fire sustained from the windows, carried him off without receiving any injury. Manning has often related, that at the moment when he expected that his prisoner would have made an effort for liberty, he, with great *solemnity* commenced an enumeration of his titles -- "I am Sir, Henry Barry,[46] Deputy Adjutant General of the British Army, Captain in the 52d Regiment, Secretary to the Commandant of Charleston [Nisbit Balfour.]" "Enough, enough, sir,' said the victor, "you are just the man I

[45] The 3d Regiment of Foot. In fairness to the unit, a not insignificant number of its privates were relatively new recruits; and given *that* acquitted themselves at Eutaw Springs well enough and despite (and even conceding) what Garden speaks of otherwise. Referring to the British at Eutaw generally, Greene comments (in a missive to Pres. Thomas McKean, of 11 Sep. 1781) "...and I could hardly tell which to admire most the gallantry of their Officers or the bravery of the Troops. They kept up a heavy and well directed fire, and the Enemy returned it with equal spirit [as the North Carolina Continentals did], for they really fought worthy of a better cause, and great execution was done on both sides." See as well, Lee, *Memoirs*, p. 467n.

[46] (1750–1822) and see regarding this same occurrence at Eutaw Lee, *Memoirs*, p. 470.

was looking for; fear nothing for your life, you shall screen *me* from danger, and I will take special care of you." [p. 146]

He had retired in this manner some distance from the brick house, when he saw Capatin Robert Joiett [Jouett] of the Virginia line, engaged in single combat with a British Officer. They had selected each other for battle a little before, the American armed with a broad sword, the Briton with a musket and bayonet. As they came together, a thrust was made at Joiett, which he happily parried, and both dropping their artificial weapons, being too much in contact to use them with effect, resorted to those with which they had been furnished by nature. They were both men of great bulk and vigour, and while struggling, each anxious to bring his adversary to the ground, a grenadier who saw the contest ran to the assistance of his Officer, made a lunge with his bayonet, missed Joiett's body, but drove it beyond the curve of his coat. In attempting to withdraw the entangled weapon, he threw both the combatants to the ground; when getting it free, he raised it deliberately, determined not to fail again in his purpose, but to transfix Joiett. It was at this crisis that Manning approached – not near enough, however, to reach the grenadier with his arm. In order to gain time, and to arrest the stroke, he exclaimed in an angry and authoritative tone -- "You damn'd brute, will you murder the gentleman?" The Soldier, supposing himself addressed by one of his own Officers, suspended the contemplated blow, and looked around to see the person who had thus spoken to him. Before he could recover from the surprise with which he had been thrown, Manning, now sufficiently near, smote him with his sword across the eyes, and felled him to the ground; while Joiett disengaged himself from his opponent, and snatching up the musket, as he attempted to rise, laid him dead by a blow from the butt end of it. Manning was of inferior size, but strong and remarkably well formed. Joiett, literally speaking, [was] a giant. This, probably, [p. 147] led Barry, who could not have wished the particulars of his capture to be commented on, to reply, when asked by his brothers Officers, how he came to be taken, "I was overpowered by a huge Virginian."*

The reputation of a Soldier, so highly distinguished both for valour and discernment, whose firmness enabled him, in all emergencies, to maintain a composure that neither difficulty nor danger could disturb, has caused a the honour of giving birth to Manning to be claimed both by Ireland and America. If my recollection is accurate, he certainly declared himself a native of Carlisle in Pennsylvania. Yet, when I remember the general tenor of his conversation -- "the facility he possessed of involving in obscurity, the subject he meant to elucidate" -- the accent on his tongue – the peculiar turn of his expression -- his calling for example to his servant, walking with naked feet over ground covered by heavy frost -- "Shall I never teach you discretion, Drone! -- If you will go *bare foot*, why the Devil don't you *put* on your blue stockings." And on another occasion, returning to camp, and looking at a bottle of spirits, *half emptied*, which he had left full -- "Speak quickly, Drone, you big thief, and tell me what you have done with the remainder of my liquor?" My opinion is staggered, and I am inclined to acknowledge the superior claims of Ireland.

[Footnote in original text] * Henry Barry was an eccentric character. He aimed at singularity in words as well as actions. He would send "his *bettermost* kind of compliments" to a lady; and, in a simple flower, present "the sweetest of all possible flowers." But in nothing was his conduct regarded as so farcical, as in his claim to delicate and liberal feelings. On one occasion, it has been stated, that reading a Poem, of his own composition, on the blessings of Liberty, a gentleman present asked his frankly "How his actions could be so much at variance with this principles he professed?" "Because, Sir," he unblushingly replied, "I am a Soldier of fortune, seeking a strong and comfortable establishment. My feelings are as delicate as yours, or any other man's; but I never suffer myself to be humbugged by them." The day at Eutaw was certainly not his fighting day; but he is said to have distinguished himself in India. [p. 148]

Manning, at the conclusion of the war, married into a highly respectable family, and settled in South Carolina. His attachment to a military life continuing unabated, he became a candidate for the appointment of the adjutant General of the Militia of the State, obtained it, and performed the important duties attached to t, with the applause of the public, till his death. [p. 149]

~*~

Having briefly sketched the characters, and detailed the services of several of the *Officers* of the Legion, I am confident that I shall gratify my readers, by recording a few interesting Anecdotes relating to the *Soldiers* of that corps. In proportion as they were removed from that rank in society, in which an enlargement of ideas, and expansion of mind was to be looked for, must be *their* merit, who, under the exalted influences of military and patriotic enthusiasm, evinced a nobleness of soul, and chivalric intrepidity, increasing their own fame, and giving a higher stamp of celebrity to the American character. I fondly hope, that they will be received with cordiality by every patriotic bosom.

Sergeant Whaling.

When the importance of wresting the possession of the Stockade Fort at Ninety-Six from the enemy, was clearly ascertained, Lieutenant Colonel Lee, to whom the charge of directing all operations against it, was intrusted [sic] by General Greene, adopted (it must be acknowledged too hastily) the opinion, that it might be effected by fire.[47] Accordingly, Sergeant Whaling, a gallant, non-commissioned Officer, who had served with zeal and fidelity from the commencement of the war, and whose period of enlistment would have expired in a few days, with twelve privates, were sent forward in open day, and over level ground that afforded no cover to facilitate their approaches, to accomplish this hazardous enterprise. Whaling saw [p. 150] with certainty, the death on which he was about to rush, but by prospect of which he was unappalled. He dressed himself neatly -- took an affectionate but cheerful leave of his friends, and with his musket slung over his shoulder, and a bundle of blazing pine torches in his hand, sprung forward for the object of his attack. His alacrity inspired the little band with courage. They followed him closely up to the building around which the Stockade was erected, before the troops within fired a shot. Their aim was deliberate and deadly. But one individual escaped with life. Whaling fell deeply lamented by every Officer and Soldier of the Legion. Instead of the rash and unavailing exposure to which he was subjected, all admitted his just claim to promotion – grieved that his valuable life was not preserved for those services he had so often shown himself so capable of rendering.

Poor Whaling! – the Soldier's cherished hope was denied him,

"When all his toils were past,
Still to return, and die at home at last."

~*~

Sergeant Mitchell.

It was at Ninety-Six also, that another Soldier of distinguished merit lost his life, and unhappily under circumstances peculiarly distressing. Captain Michael Rudolph commanded the detachment of the infantry on duty on the night after the arrival of the Legion from Augusta, where the corps had been employed, during the early part of the siege of the post now threatened, in bringing Colonel Browne [loyalist, Thomas Brown], and his command, to terms of submission. Sergeant Mitchell went the rounds with Rudolph, after having two hours before planted [p. 151] the centinels at their posts. Unhappily, among them were several militiamen, who had never before seen service. One of these, without

[47] That is by setting the stockade fort on fire; the date for the attempt of which was 12 June 1781. See Lee, *Memoirs*, 373-374.

challenging, fired at the relief with which Rudolph and Mitchell were approaching his position, and shot Mitchell through the body. He fell to the ground—told his Captain that he was mortally wounded—warmly pressed his hand—asked if he had ever neglected or omitted any of the duties of a faithful Soldier and true Patriot—regretted that he had not closed his life on the field of battle, and conjuring him to bear evidence, that he died without fear, and without a groan, expired! He was a Virginian from the County of Augusta. I fondly hope that this tribute to his memory, may reach his friends. Whaling [incidentally] was a Pennsylvanian.

~*~

Bulkley and Newman.

Among the incidents in the Southern Army, that excited the highest interest, was the singular and romantic friendship which united two of the most distinguished Soldiers of the Legionary Cavalry. Bulkley and Newman were natives of Virginia, born in the same neighborhood, and from early infancy united by such a congeniality of sentiment, that it almost appeared as if one soul gave animation to both. Their attachment increased with their years—it strengthened with their strength. As school fellows they were inseparable; their task was the same, and he who was first perfect in acquiring it, was unhappy till he had impressed it, with equal force, on the mind of his friend. When an appeal to arms, at the dawn of our Revolution, had called forth the youthful heroes of America to fight the battles of their country, and defend her violated [p. 152] rights, *both*, on the same day, and animated with the same enthusiastic devotion to her cause, were enrolled in the ranks of her armies. The officers of the Legion, who yet survive, can testify, that through all the perils and difficulties of the Southern War, each seemed more anxious for the safety and alleviation of the sufferings of his friend, than his own. In action they invariably fought side by side; in the more tranquil scenes of encampment, they were constantly engaged in the same pursuits; their toils and pleasures were the same. When at Quinby [Bridge], the memorable charge was made on the 19th British Regiment, by the intrepid Armstrong, Bulkley and Newman were among the few Dragoons, who, having leapt the gap in the bridge, which the enemy were industriously attempting to widen, were able to support their commander. The display of gallantry exhibited could not have been surpassed. Armstrong, seconded by George Carrington, his Lieutenant, his gallant Sergeant Power, the brave Captain M'Cauly [James McCauley], of the militia [Marion's Brigade], and less than a dozen of his own troopers, actually cut his way through the entire regiment, when a heavy and fatally directed fire produced a most direful catastrophe. Power fell desperately wounded; and the youthful friends, Bulkley and Newman, closed their brilliant career in the path of glory forever. Mortally wounded at the same instant, they fell on the same spot, and with united hands, reciprocating kindness to the last, expired.

~*~

Corporal [James B.] Cooper.[48]

Making a tour to the North, in the year 1817, I was invited to visit the *Franklin*,[49] then lying at Chester, in company with the Commodores [Alexander] Murray and [Richard] Dale, and several other officers of distinction. On our passage to the ship, some mention being made of Carolina, a naval officer present, said, "I do not believe there exists at this day, an individual who has a more perfect knowledge of the Southern War of the Revolution

---

[48] For more on Cooper, who incidentally hailed from New Jersey, see Joseph Johnson's *Traditions and Reminiscences chiefly of the American Revolution in the South*, pp. 405-414, and also *Notes On Old Gloucester County, New Jersey* (1917) compiled and edited Frank H Stewart, pp. 132-138.

[49] The *Franklin,* a 74 gun ship and the first such built and used by the United States Navy, was launched in Philadelphia in August 1815 by naval architects Humphreys and Penrose. Eminent maritime historian Howard I. Chapelle remarks "(H)er appearance was much admired," *The History of the American Sailing Navy*, p 284.

than myself, particularly, all that relates to the battles fought in the Carolinas. I entered those States with the Legion commanded by *Harry Lee*, and witnessed the conclusion of our toils at the evacuation of Charleston." "Under such circumstances, Sir," I immediately replied, "it must be my good fortune to be in the company with an old companion, for I had the honor of holding a commission in the infantry of that regiment, and was, like yourself, attached to the command which took possession of Charleston, when given up by the British." "I am, Sir," rejoined the officer, "altogether at a loss even to guess at your name; nor do I recollect ever to have seen you before. Attached to the Legion, you must have known Armstrong, who commanded the Sorrel Troop, and probably have heard of *Corporal Cooper*, who belonged to it." "Good heavens, Cooper," I exclaimed, with delight, "is it you? I now am astonished at my own forgetfulness, for I as thoroughly recognize you as if we had parted but yesterday!" I mentioned my name in turn, and was happy to find I was not forgotten by him. I am confident that, on this occasion, the sensation of delight and good feeling to men who had served and suffered together, was strongly experienced by both. The surprise and satisfaction of the moment being at an end, Cooper, with a significant smile, said, "By the by, I believe you were one of the officers who sat on the court-martial when I was in jeopardy, and brought to trial at our encampment, near the Ashley River." "No, Cooper," I replied, "I was not; though I well remember, on another occasion, when we lay at M'Pherson's, that in consequence of your ---" [p. 154] "Hush, hush, my dear Sir," he exclaimed, "I find you have an excellent and accurate memory, the les we say on *that* subject the better." I had known Cooper well; and it is no exaggeration to assert a more gallant Soldier never wielded the saber. The character, indeed, of consummate intrepidity, distinguished very individual or Armstrong's troop. Disciplined by him, and animated by his example, they were invincible. But their were traits that characterized Cooper, that entitled him to still higher commendation. If activity and intelligence were requisite to obtain the desired information -- if gallantry to strike a Partisan blow, Cooper was always uppermost in the thoughts of Lee. He had a soul for enterprise, and by prompt discernment, and a happy facility of calculating from appearances of events to happen, of incalculable utility to the service. When Armstrong, by the falling of his horse, was made a prisoner, and a flag sent out from the British commander to say, that his servant and baggage would be expected, as he wished to show every civility to an enemy, whose bravery could only be exceeded by his generosity to all who fell into his power, Cooper was immediately directed by Lee, to act the part of a domestic, and sent forward for the purpose. I mentioned my recollection of the circumstance to Cooper, who replied, "and well I knew my Colonel's motives;" and so perfectly was I disposed to second his views, that while taking the refreshment which was ordered for me by General [Alexander] Leslie, in the front of his headquarters near the British lines, I was closely examining the course of a creek in his rear, by which I flattered myself, I should very speedily be able to conduct and introduce him at the Head-Quarters of our own army." He then went on to say -- "The arts used by a Captain Campbell, who tried every manner of cajoling, topic out of my conversation intelligence of our force and position, very highly [p. 155] amused me. I acted the simpleton's part so naturally, that I could clearly perceive, that he believed me completely entangled in his toils. When suddenly hanging my manner, I gave him such a burlesque and exaggerated an account of troops of dragoons and regiments of infantry, that had no existence but in my imagination, that perceiving my drift, he angrily exclaimed, "Damn you rascal, you are too cunning for me. Here, take a drink of grog and depart." I cannot conjecture why it was done; but finding that I was not to be deceived, I think they might have done me the credit to suppose, that I was not to be intimidated; but instead of conducting me to my Captain, I was led to and shut up in the Provost [jail], when looking through the bars, I perceived Armstrong passing merrily along with several Naval officers, who seemed to vie with each other in civility to him. My situation forbid ceremony, so I called out lustily – "Hollo, Captain Armstrong! Pray have the goodness to tell me, is it *you* or *I* that am prisoner?" My speech produced an explanation. I was immediately released; and profiting by every occasion to store my mind with useful intelligence, in a few days left he Garrison, a partial exchange having freed my Captain from captivity. My fortunes have since varied very much. I have gained nautical information – have commanded a ship of my own—have, as a Naval Officer, supported the flag of my country—and now the war being over, find a snug berth in the Navy Yard. My varied life would greatly amuse could I detail it, more especially, as its constant bustle but ill accords with *my religious principles*; for though you might not suspect it, whenever my thoughts take a serious turn, I am professedly a member of the Society of Friends, a genuine homespun Quaker." [p. 156]

Although the expedition conducted against Georgetown [South Carolina][50] by General [Francis] Marion and Lieutenant Colonel Lee, was not, from a combination of adverse circumstances, crowned with success. [sic] Although the flight of a guide who had engaged to conduct Captain Armstrong and the dragoons of the Legion to a point, which would have effectually prevented the British Soldiers, who had escaped the Legionary Infantry, from reaching a redoubt that afforded perfect security, had given ample grounds for the suspicion of treachery and disconcerted the plans that had promised the most perfect triumph; yet advantages arose from it of considerable consequence to the American cause. Colonel [George] Campbell, the Commandant, was taken, and about seventy men either killed or taken prisoners. It convinced the British, that however great the distance by which they were removed from the enemy, (the Continental Army being, at the period of attack, on the borders of North Carolina) that they were still vulnerable, and at every moment subject to attack. It checked their marauding, predatory expeditions, gave comparative security to the oppressed inhabitants in their vicinity, and to themselves, full assurance, that to be safe, they must continue inactive, and remain within the limits of their Garrison. It is pleasing to me, to record the singular gallantry of a most meritorious Soldier, who, on this occasion, gained high renown.

Sergeant [John] Ord.[51]

In every instance where this heroic Soldier was engaged in action, he not only increased his own reputation, but animated those around him by his lively courage. In camp, on a march, and in every situation, [p. 157] he performed all his duties with cheerfulness and vivacity, preserving always the most orderly conduct and keeping his arms, accoutrements, and clothing in the neatest possible conditions. He might, indeed, be considered a perfect Soldier.

At the surprise of Georgetown, being with a small party of the Legion Infantry, in possession of an inclosure [sic], surrounding a house from which they had expelled the enemy, the recovery of the position was sought by a British force, whose leader, approaching the gate of entrance, exclaimed – "Rush on, my brave fellows, they are only worthless militia, and have no bayonets." Ord immediately placed himself in front of the gate, and as they attempted to enter, laid six of his enemies, in succession, dead at his feet, crying out at every thrust – "No bayonets here – none at all to be sure!" following up his strokes with such rapidity, that the British party could make no impression, and were compelled to retire.

~*~

Perry Scott

There was no Soldier in the Legion Infantry, who appeared more completely to have gained the favour of Lieutenant Colonel Lee, than Perry Scott. His chief merit consisted in his consummate intrepidity, and readiness to engage in hardy enterprise. As often as a Partisan expedition was in contemplation, he was invariably selected as one of the daring spirits to insure success. I am tempted to call for the pity of his countrymen for his untimely end, from the recollection, that in all the battles of the South, from the junction of the Legion with the army of General Greene, till the final retreat of the enemy, he was [p. 158] noticed for distinguished valour and activity. He was present at the evacuation of Charleston, and

---

[50] 24-25 January 1781, Lee, *Memoirs* pp. 223-225.
[51] Ord was from New Jersey.

shortly after disbanded; but devoted to a military life, again enlisted with his former commander, Michael Rudolph, then at the head of a Legionary Corps, under the orders of General [Josiah] Harmar, and as Sergeant Major acquitted himself with reputation.

The Indian War terminated, Scott knowing, that many of the Officers of the Partisan Legion of Lee, and several of his old associates, had settled in Carolina and Georgia, resolved to visit them, and actually reached the Cheraws with that intention. Here, for the sake of repose, after a wearisome journey, he took up his quarters at a Public House, kept by an old Soldier, once attached to the volunteers of Ireland, the corps commanded by Lord Rawdon. An amicable intercourse, for a time, increased the attachment of these veterans to each other. Scott eulogized the bravery of the Irish, and is companion was lavish in his commendations of the Soldiers of the Legion, when unluckily drawing comparisons relative to the merits of their respective corps, a serious quarrel ensued, which they immediately determined to settle by the sword. The conflict was maintained with spirit and obstinacy, and its result long doubtful, but Scott gaining a superiority and actively maintaining it, was about to triumph, when the wide of his adversary interfering,, and putting a loaded pistol into her husband's hand, he discharged it at poor Scott, who fell dead at his feet. This conflict being considered as the settlement of a point of honour no effort had been made to prevent it, but the survivor was now arrested, and being shortly after tried for murder, was condemned and executed.

[Garden's anecdotes, respecting members if the Legion, end at this juncture of the main text but continue again at page 378; and at which point we resume.]

Lieut. Ballard Smith, of Virginia,
Attached to the Legion Infantry.

Shortly after the capture of the British Galley by Rudolph, where Captain Smith acted as second in command, a Partisan enterprise was undertaken by him, which, had it succeeded, must have filled the British garrison with confusion and dismay. A tavern, called at that time Dewees', was kept at a farm house about two miles from Charleston. To this the British [p. 379] officers frequently repaired for recreation. It was often the scene of entertainments, and on one occasion of a splendid ball. Lieutenant Smith being previously apprized [sic] of this, took with him twelve men, and Sergeant Du Coin, of the Legion, a soldier of tried courage, and passed the river with a boat rowed with muffled oars, from the American, to the opposite shore. The night was dark and gloomy. The Negro who served as a guide, bewildered by it, and probably apprehensive of consequences if discovered, missed the landing place, and ran the boat into the marsh that skirted the shore. Du Coin, to make discoveries, slipped silently overboard, but, from the softness of the mud, with infinite difficulty reached the shore, immediately below the house. Curiosity led him to see what was passing within; the noise of music and revelry facilitated his approach, he leapt the fence, and passing through the garden, gained access to a window, through which he perceived a large and elegant assemblage of company enjoying the delights of dancing. Alone and unarmed, and without chance of success, he returned to the water's edge, and after ascertaining the exact situation of the landing place, regained the boat. So much time had already been lost, the ebbing tide too being unfavourable to his purpose, lieutenant Smith thought it best to retire, hoping to return, on some future occasion, with better success. The following night being favourable to enterprise, the river was passed as before, and the boat, steered by Du Coin, made the landing. Lieutenant Smith immediately surrounding the house, entered it, in full expectation of making a handsome capture of officers, but his evil genius forbade it. Instead of twenty or thirty officers, many of them of high rank, a Hessian Major, and a Lieutenant of the volunteers of Ireland, who had sacrificed too freely to Bacchus, were the only persons found on the premises. These he parolled [sic] and returned without molestation.[52]

Part II.

Excerpts from *Anecdotes of the American Revolution: Illustrative of the Talents and Virtues of the Heroes of the Revolution, Who Acted the Most Conspicuous Parts Therein.*
-- Second Series. A.E. Miller, Charleston, 1828. [Beginning at p. 117.]

PETER JOHNSTON, AND SOLDIERS OF THE LEGION.

Some weeks, spent in the Summer of 1826, under the hospitable roof of my early companion in arms, and justly valued friend Judge; Peter Johnston, of Abingdon, Virginia, gave considerable increase to my collection of Revolutionary Anecdotes, particularly such as related to the conduct generally, and gallant achievements of the officers and soldiers of the Legion. I shall, without hesitation, record many of them, more especially such as give evidence of the foresight, unruffled temper in the hour of peril, and intrepid conduct in action of my friend the Judge; persuaded, that they will be perused, with as much satisfaction, by my readers, as attended, when related, with delight to myself. I shall begin with a narrative of the Murder of Gillies, particularly as it happened under the eye of my friend, in the first encounter which he ever had with the enemy.

[Cornet James] GILLIES.

On the retreat of the army of General Greene into Virginia, subsequent to Morgan s victory at the Cowpens, a rencounter took place with the enemy, which strongly evinces the sanguinary disposition of Tarl[e]ton s dragoons [the British Legion], and the great superiority both in strength and courage of the Legionary Cavalry. The officers of the Legion were about seating themselves at the hospitable board of a friendly farmer, when Colonel Otho Williams, who commanded the Light Corps, rode up, attended by a countryman, mounted on a miserable tackey, and exclaimed, "to horse, gentlemen, the enemy are at hand." This honest fellow, seeing them pass his field, quitted his plough, and hastened [p. 118] to give us information of their approach. Captain Armstrong, with a small party, were immediately ordered forward to reconnoiter [sic], arid the countryman directed to serve him as a guide, but he decidedly refused to do so, unless a better horse was allowed him than that which he rode. Lieut. Col. Lee, wishing no delay, said to his Bugler, Gillies, a gallant youth, yet in early life, "change horses with him, Gillies, you, I am confident, you do not fear to trust yourself on his tackey." The exchange was immediately made. Armstrong pushed forward, and Lee, with Lieut. [Stephan] Lewis, Peter Johnston, (then serving as a volunteer, arid a candidate for a commission) with eighteen dragoons, with all expedition followed him. After riding a mile or more, Lee became impressed with the conviction that the countryman was in error, and determined to return to the farm house where dinner had been left, untouched, on the table. For this purpose he; turned into the woods, through which the nearest course to the spot lay, and had gone but a short distance, however, from the road, when a report of pistols was heard, discharged by Armstrong s orders, to give notice that he had met the enemy. Lee immediately drew his men up in the wood by the roadside. When Gillies was perceived, urging his tackey to the utmost of his speed, striking him at every step with his cap, and smiling with the hope of enjoying the termination of the affair, not doubting but that relief was at hand. The moment that the British Dragoons arrived at a point opposite to the Legionary Detachment, the charge was ordered, but too late to save poor Gillies, who fell

[52] For more mention of some of the Legion, including a close call involving Garden himself when he was a member of the unit, see also pages 62-68, 366-372, 380, 389-393, 405, 420-423, 427-428 of the 1822 edition of *Anecdotes*. On page 421 in particular is found the "strict injunctions of Lee, never to enlist a British soldier, a foreigner, or a drunkard."

covered with wounds. Exasperated, almost to madness, to see an unarmed, beardless boy thus butchered while offering no resistance, the Legionary Cavalry rushed forward, and in a few minutes fourteen of the British lay dead on the field. Their captain, and eight men, of whom several were severely wounded, made prisoners. The remainder of the party fled and escaped. Great prowess was exhibited in this unequal conflict by individuals.

The British had thirty-seven dragoons engaged -- the Americans, [p. 119] but eighteen. Serjeant [Robert] Power killed two men with his own hand, the last of whom died a martyr to his unbending, political prejudices, for, when assured that good quarters would be granted him on the surrender of his sword, he disdainfully replied, "it is far more grateful to me to die than to preserve my life, by yielding my sword to a rebel." Peter Johnston, the volunteer, must have fallen in the conflict, had not Sergeant Broom at the instant that a deadly blow was aimed at his head by a back-handed stroke of his sabre, sliced off a considerable pan of the skull of the British dragoon who aimed it, and caused the uplifted weapon to fall without effect. The cry for revenge was universal, and Captain Miller, who commanded, would have been sacrificed, had it not been ascertained that the near approach of the main army of the enemy made it necessary immediately to retreat. The prisoners were, in consequence, sent to Colonel Williams, who sent them again forward to Head-Quarters. When the strong excitement of anger having subsided -- the Captain was spared.[53]

Interesting Sequel of the above Anecdote.

A strong and partial attachment to the country in which he had served, with distinguished reputation, and united with it an anxious desire to meet the early companions of his youth, several of whom still survived, induced the Judge to visit the South. He left Richmond with that intent, in the winter of 1826, and had proceeded on his journey, as far as Guildford Court-house in North-Carolina, when an accidental overturn of his gig put a check to his progress. He had broken a shaft, and was not without a sufficiency of bruises, to make a temporary suspension of his journey desirable. A happy chance pointed out a wagon-maker's work-shop, immediately at hand, and, at a little distance, the house of Mr. Tatam [Rev. Henry Tatum], a gentleman, of respectability, where he was assured he would meet with a kind and hospitable reception. It now occurred to Judge Johnston's [p. 120] recollection, that he could not be far removed from the spot in which he had first met the enemy, and witnessed the massacre of poor Gillies. To ascertain the fact, he related the adventure above stated to a company assembled around Mr. Tatam's fire-side, and speedily perceived by the expressive countenances of several of his auditors that the event was not unknown to them. When his narrative was concluded, a lady present feelingly exclaimed, "I have heard my father relate the circumstances of that appalling tragedy, and .the death of Gillies, an hundred and a hundred times over, and without the slightest difference from the statement you have just made. He is within a short distance -- I will summon him here. He will be delighted to converse with you, and I am sure you will be glad to see him, particularly when 1 tell you that he was the individual who had provided the dinner for yourself and brother officers, which the near and rapid approach of the enemy compelled you to leave untouched. In a little time, Mr. Bruce, the gentleman in question, arrived. I will not attempt to state what the feelings of two genuine patriots must have been, on meeting after a separation of forty-two years, near the very spot where the one first engaged the enemies of his country, and the other, at the conclusion of the action, with his own hands, committed the body of the murdered Bugler to the grave. I can only judge of their sensations by the pleasure I feel in giving it publicity. Mr. Bruce immediately offered to point out the spot where Gillies lay -- and received the kind offers of hospitality which had, at first distinguished his feelings

---

37 This clash with the British Legion, 12 February, 1781, took place at Bruce's Crossroads, near Reedy Fork, in north Guilford County, N.C. Gillies' (1767-1781) memory was commemorated in a number of local monuments, including one at Guilford Court House National Battlefield. For more, see Lee, *Memoirs*, pp. 239-243; Caruthers, *A Sketch of the Life and Character of the Rev. David Caldwell* (1842), pp. 227n-229n; "James Gillies, Lee's Bugler Boy," by Marie Lowrey Armstrong, Archivist, Oak Ridge Military Academy, Oak Ridge, N,C., Historic Preservation Commission newsletter, 31 March, 2006, Issue 2, Vol. I.

towards as the officers of the Legion, and a refusal of them was only accepted, on the Judge s pleading urgent business, which compelled him to go forward. When about to depart, he asked, as usual, "what was to pay for the shelter and entertainment afforded him." "Sir," said Mr. Tatam, "a word on the subject would cruelly wound my feelings, your account with me was settled in the year 1781. Your conduct was a receipt in full." [p. 121]

LIEUTENANT-COLONEL LEE.

The conduct of Lee upon this, as well as every other occasion, was highly honourable to him. Envy, hatred and malice have, on various occasions, assailed his character. Even personal courage has been denied him, but how is it possible to think ill of a man, of whom that intelligent Soldier, General Charles Lee said -- "this gallant youth came a Soldier from his mother s womb." Of whom General Greene said, in a letter, dated February 18, 1782, "Lieut. Col. Lee retires, for a time, for the recovery of his health. I am more indebted to this officer, than to any other, for the advantages gained over the enemy in the operations of the last campaign, and should be wanting in gratitude, not to acknowledge the importance of his services, a detail of which is his best panegyric." Who, in the memorable whiskey insurrection, was selected by General Washington to march into the interior of Pennsylvania, to put down, by his activity and decision, a revolt so disgraceful to America -- and of whom Lord Cornwallis was known to say -- "I am never at my ease when I know Lee to be in my neighbourhood, for he is prompt to discover the weak points in the position of my command, and certain to strike at them, when I am least prepared to repel his attacks." I doubt if the calumnies which were leveled at his character ever reached him. Had they been communicated, I have not a doubt but that in the language of the Great Fabius, when reproached for avoiding a general engagement with Hannibal, he would have said -- "I should be a coward, indeed, if I were to be terrified into a change of conduct by groundless clamours and reproaches. The man is unfit to be trusted, who can be influenced by the clamours or caprice of those he is appointed to command." [p. 122]

PETER JOHNSTON.

That implicit confidence should not be placed in the reports of deserters, has often been exemplified. Lieut. Col. Lee, in his Memoirs detailing the most interesting occurrences, which took place at the siege of Augusta, gives a striking example in point.* He states, that while rapid approaches were made by the besiegers against the British Post, commanded by Colonel Brown, an intelligent Sergeant of Artillery, who had pretended desertion expressly for the purpose of destroying the Maham Tower, likely from its commanding height to force a surrender, succeeded so far, by expressions of disgust, against the service he had quitted, and the commander under whom he had served, as to lull suspicion, and to be actually placed in the situation the best calculated to effect it -- *the Tower itself*. Lee, however, reflecting on the character of his adversary, of whom he had a very exalted opinion, and prepossessed in favour of his military talents, concluded that mischief was contemplated, and in that belief, removing the Sergeant from the Tower, committed him to the charge of the Quarter Guard. Subsequent information proved the prudence of his conduct. Colonel Brown, after the surrender of the Post, frankly declaring, that under the pretext of directing the fire of the besiegers against the Magazine of the Garrison, the Sergeant had engaged to use every art to gain admission into the Tower, and to destroy it. But, on the other hand, it has frequently happened that timely information received from deserters, of the intended movements of an enemy, has saved many a valuable life from destruction. I, with peculiar pleasure, mention one connected with the achievements of my friend, Peter Johnson, which happened at the same period, and at the same place, where, had not intelligence been [p. 123]

[Footnote in original text] * *Vide* Lee s Memoirs, p. 106.

communicated by a deserter of a contemplated attack on the trenches, Johnston and his entire command must have been cut off. The ditch of the besiegers was occupied by that officer, and twenty-four men. It was early in the night when a British soldier rushed into it, and said to Lieut. Johnston – "You know not, Sir, the danger which threatens you, a party of forty men, British soldiers and Indians, is now paraded, and ready to throw themselves on your command, and the labourers at the head of your entrenchment, and without immediate precaution, you will be cut to pieces." Information was instantaneously communicated to Captain Rudolph, who, with the Legion Infantry, was within a few hundred yards. Lieut. Johnston, at the same time, mounting his men on the reverse of the ditch, instructed them to remain, sitting on their hams, until an order to rise should be given; when they were suddenly to gain their feet, and, with deliberate aim, fire on the approaching foe. In the interim, he posted a sentinel a little in advance, in a situation in which he could perceive the first movements of the enemy leaving their works towards him. The sentinel soon brought intelligence that he had distinctly ascertained that the enemy were moving out of their fosse, which was not more than twenty yards from the head of the American entrenchment. Lieut. Johnston quickly heard, as a further evidence, the rattling of their cartouch[e] boxes, and allowing them time to approach still nearer, gave the word to rise and fire. The effect was decisive.

The British, instead of surprising, were themselves surprised. Contrary to expectation, they found their enemy prepared for their reception, and a very considerable portion of their force being cut off, the survivors fled with precipitation, and sought safety within their fortification. [p. 124]

*Interesting interview between Lieut. JOHNSTON and MANNER*ING, a Legionary Soldier.

In the Anecdotes of the Revolution, already published, the singular interview which took place between Cooper of the Legion and myself, is particularly detailed. I have lately heard from my friend, Peter Johnston, of one which occurred between himself arid a Legionary Soldier, which has equal title to be recorded. The Lieutenant, now Judge Johnston, was riding his circuit, and stopped at a stream to water his horses, where a wagoner had halted his team for a similar purpose. There was something in the man s countenance that reminded the Judge of a former acquaintance, and he said, "permit me, my friend, to ask if your name is not Mannering." "Yes, Sir, (replied the wagoner, it is.") "Did you ever serve," rejoined the Judge? "I did, Sir, in the Legion commanded by Henry Lee, I was attached to the infantry of that corps." "Do you remember your Lieutenant, friend?" (continued the Judge) "What! little Peter Johnston; O, full well do I remember him, the soldier s friend, as fine a white haired and spirited a youth as ever served." Then, "give me your hand, Mannering, and know that I am that very man." "You that man," replied the wagoner, "impossible, Peter Johnston was a very likely youth, with light hair and fair skin, and you old gentleman are infirm and weather-beaten, and over and above, grey as a badger." A short conversation, however, set matters to rights. I will not pretend to relate what the feelings of the parties were, words would be inadequate to do justice to them. Suffice it to say, that the Judge was delighted to learn that his former companion in arms had thriven in the world, and was, at the period of their meeting returning home, having advantageously sold, at Abingdon, the crop of the preceding season. [p. 125]

Interview between Lieutenant JOHNSTON and DENNIS HAMPTON.

I shall now record another interview between my friend and a soldier of the Legion, which is not without interest. Not long after Congress had passed the act of March 18th, 1818, granting pensions to the surviving soldiers of the Revolutionary army, who were reduced to indigence, the Superior Court of Law for Lee county, Virginia, was in session, when a man, who appeared to be about sixty-two or sixty-three years of age, presented himself before the Judge, claiming the benefit of the act. Judge Peter Johnston, who was on the Bench, was instantaneously struck with his countenance, and impressed with the belief, that he had served under his command in the Legion Infantry of Lee. To ascertain the fact, he therefore put the following interrogatories. "Did you at any time serve in the Continental army during the Revolutionary war?" "I was in that service from the commencement to the close of the war." "To what corps did you belong?" "To Lee s Legion." "Were you with your regiment when it left the Northern and joined the Southern army?" "I was." "Do you remember any thing remarkable that occurred on the march at Petersburg?" "Nothing but that Colonel Lee ordered a man to be hung there for an unpardonable offence." "Do you recollect any particular circumstance that caused a great confusion at Guildford Court- House?" "I only remember that a Tory was brought in a prisoner, about the time of our arrival there, who was picketted [sic] and severely burnt in the feet and between his toes to extort intelligence, and that no torture could induce him to speak." "What is your name?" "William Hampton." There was no man of that name attached to the Legion," said the Judge. "I have given my true name," said the soldier, "and did belong to the Legion." [p.126]

"Were you not wounded at Augusta, in Georgia, by a ball, which entered your foot at the instep, and passed out at the heel?" "I was, sir, but how came you to know that." "Let me first ask further, who commanded your platoon when you were wounded?" "Lieut. Peter Johnston." "Would you know your Lieutenant if you were now to see him" "Certainly, sir." "Do you recollect to whom you sold a stout flea-bitten horse, on the day after possession was obtained of the British post." He stared intently in the Judge's face for a few seconds, when recollection breaking suddenly on his mind, he exclaimed, rushing forward and extending his hand with an expression of great cordiality, "I sold him to you, sir." "Answer me truly then," said the Judge, "is not your name, William Dennis?" "William Dennis Hampton is my name." "You certainly were Dennis, when with the Legion." "True, sir, but ever since my return to the neighbourhood in which I lived before the war, I have taken the name of Hampton." "How is that to be explained," said the Judge. "Very easily," replied the soldier, "my mother's name was Dennis, my father's, Hampton; they were never married, and I was known by my mother s name till her death, when 1 took the name of Hampton, in addition to that which I had previously borne." These multiplied interrogatories were put in order to discover the cause of the change of name, which being explained to the entire satisfaction of the Judge, it gave him particular pleasure to sign the certificate, which secured a pension to a veteran, who had ever been distinguished as an intrepid soldier, and zealous friend to his country.

JOSHUA DAVISON [Davidson], OF LEE'S LEGION.[54]

Joshua Davison, a private dragoon in the Legion, who had, on all occasions, behaved with distinguished gallantry, received [p. 127] at the battle of Guildford, so severe a sabre wound, as to be rendered unfit for immediate service. That every facility might be afforded for his recovery, Colonel Lee gave him permission to quit the army, and retire to his father's house in Prince Edward s county, Virginia; and the more easily to accomplish his journey, allowed him to take his charger along with him. The injury received, was in his right shoulder, which totally incapacitated him from using his sword-arm. Before his recovery was perfected, the invasion of Virginia was effected by Lord Cornwallis, and Tarl[e]ton, with his usual activity, was scouring the country in every direction; his particular aim being to destroy the stores said to be deposited at Prince Edward's Court-House. Davison hearing that a large body of British cavalry was near the spot which he inhabited, resolved at once to take a look at the enemy he had so often encountered ; and his sword-arm being useless, loaded an old squirrel gun, and set out in search of them. It accidentally happened, that passing through a thick wood, he came upon a road, along which Tarlton had, but a moment before, led his command. Determined to take a nearer view, he at once fell into, and followed on their trail. He had, however, advanced but a small distance, when he perceived a British dragoon, who had been plundering in the rear, rapidly advancing, who drawing his sword, exclaimed," surrender immediately, you rebel rascal, or you die." "Not so fast, my good fellow," replied

[54] After the war, Davidson went back to Prince Edward County, Virginia, and was residing there in 1795. By 1823, he had moved to Franklin, Kentucky, and in 1833 was living in Nicholas County, Kentucky; from where he successfully applied for a pension, #S1182.

Davison, "I am not prepared to yield" when raising his squirrel gun, with his left hand, he fired it off, and laid his adversary dead at his feet; seized his horse and plunder, and carried them off in triumph. Some years after, a gentleman asking him if he had been satisfied by killing a single man?" By no means," he replied; "I re-loaded my piece, and went in pursuit, but my firing had excited such alarm, and Tarlton fled with such expedition, that I could never have overtaken him, or I would have had another shoot [shot?]." [p. 128]

ROBERT HARVEY, OF THE LEGION.[55]

Robert Harvey, formerly a private dragoon in Lee's Legion, lately died at Fincastle [Virginia.] While actively engaged at Pyle[']s defeat, his horse was shot, and fell so suddenly and heavily upon him, that he found it impossibly to extricate himself. A circumstance the more distressing, as a wounded Tory, who lay at a small distance, was using his utmost endeavour to take a decisive aim with his rifle, and dispatch him. His only chance for safety, rested on his remaining quiet under cover of his horse's body, till assistance could be afforded. At this moment, Captain Eggleston, with a few dragoons, passed by the wounded man, and perceiving one of them ready to thrust his sword through his body, forbade it, as an act of unnecessary cruelty. Harvey, observing that the Tory, unmindful of the favour shewn, (having a better aim at men elevated above him,) was about to fire, called aloud, "take care Captain Eggleston, or you are a dead man." The rifle was at the instant discharged, and the ball passed so near the Captain's ear, that it appeared to him that he had actually received a blow on the side of his head. Justly exasperated at the ingratitude of the wretch he had spared, Eggleston wheeled round, and by a thrust of his sword, dispatched him. Harvey was now relieved from the awkward position in which he lay, happy to escape not only the Tory, but the Catawba Indians [allies of the Americans], who were extremely active on this occasion, running over the ground for the sake of plunder, dispatching every wounded man, whether friend or foe. It gives me pleasure to state, that Harvey, at the conclusion of the war, by active industry, acquired a very handsome fortune; that he lived highly respected, and died regretted by all who knew him. [p. 129]

SERGEANT CUSACK, OF THE LEGION.

This important service was achieved before the Legion moved to the South; but as the credit of it is due to a soldier of the regiment, I do not think that the recording of it in this place, will be deemed improper. While the British held possession of New-York, a gang of desperate marauders from that post, infested every part of the Jerseys [i.e. New Jersey.] They were headed by FENTON, a robber of celebrity, whose activity destroyed every chance of travelling [sic] with security. To attempt his destruction, Sergeant Cusack, having six men under his orders, fitted up a wagon, in which such articles were exposed to view, as would,

---

[55] Harvey was originally from Head of Elk (present Elkton), Maryland, serving in the Maryland Line before joining the Legion. His brother, Matthew, enlisted in the Legion at about age 16 and served in Capt. Michael Rudolph's infantry troop; and at some point was taken prisoner and later exchanged about the time of Yorktown. Both he and Robert served at Guilford Court House. The following is an extract from Matthew's pension statement, #W19681, composed by his widow, and which mentions the incident involving Eggleston that Garden describes: "...And further that the said Mathew Harvey [after Yorktown] went to school in Bottetourt [County, Virginia] one year immediately after he came from Maryland was discharged from service – and then commenced merchandizing, by which he accumulated a vast deal of property – and was a very wealthy man at the time of his death – which was in the year 1823... That his present widow Magdalen [sic] Harvey has remained unmarried ever since the death of her husband as aforesaid to the present time – and is the widow of said Mathew Harvey dec'd. [deceased] Deponant [sic] also understood Harvey to say that Col. Watt[']s of said Co – and Jude [Judge] Peter Johns[t]on of Abington [Abingdon] Va. Was also in said Legion – and that she has heard Harvey say that he knew Francis Gray (in the Revo'y. [Revolutionary] war) Agents father; and moreover that she has heard said Harvey, and Henry Bowyer of Bottetourt – who was an officer in Lee[']s or [Lt. Col. William] Washington[']s horse – talk for hours at a time together about their Revo'y. Services – and that Henry Bowyer aforesaid distinctly recognized Mathew Harvey aforesaid as having been in the service as aforesaid in Lees Legion in the Revo'y. war. That it was Capt. Egleston [Eggleston] who shot the wounded Tory, and saved Harvey's life – Harvey being then on foot – met a Tory on horse back with a bag of provisions for Talton's [Tarleton's] Army – captured him and took his horse for himself &c."

probably, allure to plunder, his associates being snugly concealed in its body. The stratagem proved successful: Fenton, and four of his associates, who incautiously rushed forward from a place of concealment, were fired on and left lifeless on the spot, while a reward of five hundred dollars, offered by the Governor of Jersey, was paid to the contrivers of it.[56]

I have still another Anecdote to relate, but of so melancholy a cast, as to be considered by some of my friends unfit for publication. That great severity was exercised towards a prisoner is true; and that it would have been unpardonable had the slightest trait of humanity been exercised by the individual, when he first burst into the apartment of the man, whoso life he threatened to destroy, I am ready to grant. But the ferocity of his manner, gave just cause to apprehend that his object was to plunder, and his ultimate aim, death to the party assailed. It is difficult, at this late day, to form an idea of the savage mode in which the war was conducted, more especially between the native whigs and tories. I remember [p. 130] full well, to have heard a Lieutenant in the British 71st Regiment say, that a few days previous to the battle of Guildford [Guilford], when Lord Cornwallis in vain endeavoured to trace the movements of General Greene, and to penetrate into his intentions, a young lad was brought into camp, who, when questioned with regard to the position of the American army, steadily replied, "you will find it soon enough." TARL[E]TON, who stood by, being highly exasperated, drew his sabre, and making a chop at the youth's hand, deprived it of one of his fingers, saying, "Will you now tell me where is Greene." With steady and undaunted countenance, the reply was to the same purpose as before, "You will know time enough." Five times was the blow repeated, but with as little success. The youth had his secret, and he kept it. This cruelty was exercised by a Lieutenant Colonel of Dragoons, considered the pride of the army -- its greatest ornament. "I wish," said Lord Cornwallis, (writing to him) "you could divide yourself into three parts -- we can do nothing without you." Perhaps, the same spirit of decided attachment to the cause he supported, actuated him, and he was obstinately silent from the fear of answering questions, which might be put to him, improperly. At all events, the provocation was great, and examples of still greater barbarity were not wanting to palliate, if not to excuse the act. Immediately after the arrival of the Legion at Guildford Court-House, a countryman entered our quarters, (said my informant) having a prisoner in custody, and said to Colonel Lee, "While I was at table with my family, this fellow burst into the room, and putting the muzzle of his rifle to my breast, bid me deliver every thing that I had of value, or prepare to die. I knew that no sort of trust could be placed in this sort of gentry, and that the surrender of my property would be the signal for death. So I made a grab at his rifle, and turning it aside, it went off without doing me injury. A severe struggle followed, when getting entire possession of it, I struck him on the head with the butt, and drove the [p. 131] cock-pin pretty deep into his skull. The severity of the round made him my prisoner, and I brought him along for examination, for he seems a cunning chap, and I dare say, has plenty of intelligence, if he can be made to part with it." To all the questions put to him, not a word was returned in reply. The wounded man was obstinately silent. Dr. Irvine, Surgeon of the Legion, examining the head, found that the skull was fractured, and that the brain could be seen plainly through the hole made by the cock-pin. Thrusting his finger into it, and drawing it back again, a portion of the brain remained on the point of it. "His obstinacy must be overcome," was the universal cry. "Picket him," said Lee. The order was obeyed, but without effect. A red-hot shovel was applied to the bottom of his feet, and even introduced between his toes, but not a feature of his countenance was altered, nor did he utter a word of complaint. "The severity of his wound," said Dr. Irvine, "has produced insensibility -- all feeling is destroyed -- the man must die." "Place him," said Colonel Lee, to Cornet George Carrington, "under a corporal's guard, and be you answerable for him." The orders were obeyed. Night came on, and Carrington was quietly reposing, when a musket was discharged, and a loud shout proclaimed that the prisoner had escaped. The fact was so -- the wounded man, who had been playing a part, no sooner perceived that a chance of escape was afforded, (the sentinel placed over him, becoming careless, from a conviction

[56] For more on Fenton, the "Pine Robbers," and the incident described here, see Lossing's *Pictorial Field Book of the Revolution*, Vol. II, p. 162n.

that one so much injured, could not run) than he leaped up and ran off, and though fired on and closely pursued, could not be overtaken.

PETER JOHNSTON was originally intended for the Church, his father s great object was to make him an Episcopal Minister; but he, himself, giving a preference to a military profession, he clandestinely quitted the paternal mansion, and [p. 132] joined the Legion as a volunteer, and candidate for a commission. I have already said enough of him to prove, that he was a prudent, active and most intrepid soldier. His diligence in acquiring a knowledge of his profession was great his attachment to literature, very conspicuous. Whenever there was the least respite from duty, while his brother officers were seeking amusement, or indulging in dissipation, Johnston would always be found at his studies. The war concluded, he returned to his father s house, and was well received. His thoughts were immediately turned to law and politics. He acquired celebrity at the bar, and was elected to the honourable station of Speaker of the House of Representatives. He did not, however, throw aside his youthful propensities, and actually figured as a General Officer at the head of the Virginia Militia; but being now more inclined to civil life, he accepted the appointment of Judge in some of the upper districts of the State, and now honoured, esteemed and admired by all who know him, resides, in the enjoyment of great comfort, at Abingdon, in Washington county. The Judge was early married to a lady of a most estimable character, and particularly distinguished by her talents and accomplishments. He has been the father often children, nine sons and one daughter, all of whom now live, with the exception of the eldest son, who has been dead for several years, leaving a disconsolate widow, who needs only to be seen to be admired and loved. I have often heard her declared, the very counterpart of her mother-in-law. The sons are all active, industrious and amiable men, and the daughter, a young lady of high promise.

CAPTAIN J. [i.e. Joseph] EGGLESTON.

I must apologize to my readers, and, in a particular manner to his family, for the incorrectness of my statement relative to [p. 133] the impatience which he displayed at the period that he lost his leg by amputation.* To my friend, Judge Johnston, I feel particularly indebted for the information that has made me sensible of my error, and enabled me to correct it. He assures me that after the decree of the attendant surgeons on the necessity of taking off the leg, that Major Eggleston submitted to the operation with the most exemplary composure and becoming fortitude, and that not the slightest sign of impatience was shewn by him from its commencement till it was completely finished.

I have erred too in another respect. I have attributed to him the capture of an entire foraging party of the British, on the retreat of their army from Ninety- Six. Now I have no right to force upon him an honour that he never claimed. The act was Armstrong's, and Eggleston, with the frankness and generous feeling of a soldier, never failed to acknowledge it. Lee, knowing that the rich settlements south of Fridig's [also "Friday's"] Ferry could alone supply the enemy with the forage which they would require, detached Eggleston, having Armstrong under his command, to the probable scene of action. An advantageous position was immediately taken, and their approach expected with anxious solicitude. A party of dragoons very speedily appeared, but from the mistiness of the day, their numbers could not be ascertained, and Eggleston immediately countermanded the order to charge, which had been given to Armstrong, till it could be satisfactorily discovered. Armstrong, however, who was one of the best and most intrepid soldiers that ever existed, either did not, or pretended not to hear the order of his commander, and dashed forward with irresistible impetuosity. Disarmed the leader of the British party, and so completely put them to route, that forty-five prisoners, together with all the foraging wagons, were taken without the loss of a single man. Congratulated on the importance of so brilliant an achievement, Eggleston, with great modesty, acknowledged that the credit of it was altogether due to his gallant companion,

[Footnote from the original text] * *Vide* First Series [of Garden's Anecdotes, 1822], p. 125.

[p. 134] "for had my orders been obeyed," he said, "our triumph, in all probability, would not have been so perfect -- a greater number of the enemy might have eluded pursuit and escaped."

CAPTAIN [William] LINDSAY.[57]

With this officer I never had the honor to form an acquaintance; he had quitted the service before I joined the Legion; but I have heard his military character very highly spoken of, and there is one instance of his intrepidity and skilful management, in imposing upon his enemy, that entitles him to particular commendation. To him it was unquestionably owing that Colonel Lee, and the detachment of the Legion which he commanded, escaped captivity, when surprised at the Spread Eagle Tavern, near Philadelphia. Lindsay, while barricading the door of the Tavern, the more effectually to keep out the enemy, received a severe wound in the hand, which incapacitated him from the further use of his arms. Having nothing to do below, made his way to an upper apartment, and pretending to see the approach of friends from a neighbouring wood, set up a loud huzza, and beckoning with great eager ness, as if to accelerate their movements, so completely deceived the British, who imagined that a strong reinforcement was at hand, that they galloped off with precipitation, leaving Colonel Lee at liberty to quit the house, and retire at his leisure.

DR. MATTHEW IRVINE.

A short sketch of the services of this meritorious officer, is given in my First Series, page 134. I am not satisfied with it. 1 have mentioned that his great fault, if fault it can be called, [p. 135] was the two constant exposure of his person in action, being frequently found in the heat of battle, when his post should have been in the rear, attending to the wounded. A departure, however, from the strict line of duty was productive on some occasions of great advantage. At Eutaw, for instance, Irvine could not avoid the temptation of taking a near view of the battle, and seeing General Greene alone, (his aids-de-camp being detached to different pails of the line with orders) he rode up, and assured him that he was ready to execute any commands that he might honour him with. "Quick then," (said Greene) to Colonel O. Williams, "order him to bring forward his command with trailed arms, charge the enemy with the bayonet, and make the victory our own." The message was delivered with promptitude, and produced all the effect expected from it. Dr. Irvine married a lady at the conclusion of the war, distinguished for her patriotic attachment to her country, and settled, as a physician in Charleston. Let his medical friends speak more particularly of his professional celebrity. I shall be content to say, that for humanity to the poor, hospitality to strangers, warm and enthusiastic attachment to his friends, and perfect devotion to his family, no man has been more beloved and admired in society than Dr. Irvine.

[End of Alexander Garden's *Anecdotes* Excerpts.]

>>>>>>>>>>>>>>>>>>>***<<<<<<<<<<<<<<<<<<<<

[57] On 16 June 1776, Lindsay was made a Cornet in the Virginia (apparently State) cavalry, and was a 3d Lieutenant in the 1st Continental Dragoons by 15 March 1777; being wounded near Valley Forge on 21 January 1778. In April 1778, he was transferred to Lee's Legion where he became a Captain in April 1778; but resigned his commission on 1 October 1778. He died 1 September 1797.

Roster of Legion Officers and Soldiers not mentioned or else not discussed by Garden.[58]

Most of this information is taken from Heitman and whom we more or less reproduce. Unless noted otherwise, all listed here survived the war.

* Major Henry Peyton, Legion Cavalry, Virginia
Cornet in the Virginia cavalry, 18 June 1776; 2d Lt. in the 1st Continental Dragoons, 12th Feb., 1777, Captain-Lieutenant of Lee's Battalion of Light Dragoons, 7 Apr. 1778; Captain, 2 July 1778; Major, 17 February 1780. The *Heitman Register* states Peyton was killed at Charleston, 12 May 1780, but this is obviously an error. Lee speaks of Peyton's still being alive in a letter to Greene of 25 Jan. 1781 (*Nathanael Greene Papers*, vol. VII, Showman-Conrad editors, p. 197.). Quite what then became of Peyton is, to this writer at any rate, a mystery. Some genealogical sources make reference to a Henry Peyton dying at the age of 39 in July 1781 in Prince William County, VA.; having made and signed his will on 22 May 1781. Whether this is the same person in question isn't at present clear.

* Major John Rudulph, Legion Cavalry, Maryland
Cousin of Michael, and known as "Fighting Jack." Lieutenant of Lee's Battalion of Light Dragoons, 20 Apr. 1778; Capt, 1st Oct. 1778; Major, -- 1781; died 8 Dec. 1782.

* Captain Henry Archer, Legion Cavalry, Maryland
Cornet in the Legion, 1 January 1779; Captain, 1780; served till close of war.

* Captain Patrick Carnes, Legion infantry, Virginia
Surgeon's Mate, 1st Continental Dragoons, 31 March 1777; Lieutenant of Lee's Legion, 22 April 1778; Captain, -- 1780; served to close of war.
* Captain Hurd

* Captain Ballard Smith, Legion Infantry, Virginia
Ensign in the 1st Virginia, October 1776; 2d Lieutenant, 9 August 1777; 1st Lieutenant, 18 November, 1777; Captain-Lieutenant., 12 May, 1779,. At some point thereafter, assuming Heitman is correct with respect to the foregoing, he was transferred to the Legion and served to war's close. He died 20 March 1794.

* Lieutenant George Carrington, Legion Cavalry, Virginia
Lieutenant in the Legion 1779, at which rank he served till June 1783.

* Lieutenant George Guthrie (also Guthrey), Legion Cavalry, Pennsylvania
Cornet of cavalry, Pulaski's Legion – July 1778; Lieutenant, 4th Continental Light Dragoons – 1781.

* Lieutenant Heard, Legion Cavalry, see Lee, *Memoirs* p. 272.

* Lieutenant John Jordan

* Lieutenant Stephan [or Stephen] Lewis, Virginia
Sergeant in Lee's Legion; Aug 1778; Lieutenant and Regimental quartermaster, 20 August, 1779, served to close.

* Lieutenant William Lewis, Virginia
Lieutenant in Legion 1778; killed 14 Sept. 1779 at Genesee, N.Y.

---

[58] For a further Return and listing of the members of Lee's Legion than what is given in what follows, see: https://archive.org/details/AReturnOfLeesLegion1778-1780

* Lieutenant Swanson Lunsford, Legion Cavalry, Virginia
(1754-1799) From Petersburg, Virginia, died in Columbia, S.C. Cornet in the Legion – 1779; Lieutenant in 1781. For the dashing raid he participated in March 1781, see footnote marked in Garden's profile of Perry Scott above.

* Lieutenant Jonathan Snowden, Legion Cavalry, New Jersey,
Ensign 1st New Jersey, 26 April 1777; 2d Lieutenant, 14 April 1778; 1st Lieutenant, 26 October 1779; transferred to Lee's Battalion of Light Dragoons in 1780; wounded at Guilford Court House, 15 March 1781, Aide de camp to General Hand May, 1781, to close of war; Captain in the Levies in 1791; Military Storekeeper United States Army, 5 May, 1808. Died 25 December 1824.

* Lieutenant William Winston, Legion Cavalry, Virginia
Sergeant of Lee's of Light. Dragoons 7 Apr. 1778; Cornet 1 Aug. 1779; Lieutenant and Adjutant, 1781 and served to close of war. Died 1804.

* Ensign Cuthbert Harrison, Legion Cavalry, Virginia
Lieutenant Virginia Dragoons 15 June 1776; Captain 1st Continental Dragoons, 12 February, 1777, and served to ---

* Ensign James Lovell, Legion Cavalry, Massachusetts.
Ensign of Lee's Continental regiment, 25 May 1777; regimental Adjutant, 10 May 1778; transferred to Jackson's Regiment, 22 April 1779; transferred to Lee's Battalion of Light Dragoons in March, 1780, and was Adjutant of the same till war's end. Died 10 July 1850.

* Cornet William Butler Harrison, Legion Cavalry, Virginia
Cornet in the Legion – 1779. Died 28 Feb, 1835.

* Cornet William Middleton, Legion Cavalry, Virginia
Cornet in the Legion – 1779.

* Cornet Robert Power, Legion Cavalry, Pennsylvania
Cornet in the Legion – 1780; Lieutenant, 1781(?) Died 20 January 1811.

* Cornet Frank Thornton, Legion Cavalry, Virginia
Cornet in the Legion from 21 April 1778 to 1 January 1779.

* Cornet Albion Throckmorton, Legion Cavalry, Virginia
Born about 1740; Cornet in the 1st Continental. Dragoons--, 1779; retired 9 November 1782.

* Sergeant-Major John Champe, Legion Cavalry, Virginia
(1756?-1798?) In October 1780, Champe was sent on a secret mission (and which required his desertion from the Legion being feigned) designed to capture Benedict Arnold. Although the scheme failed, Champe managed to escape and make his way back to the Legion, then in South Carolina, in about May 1781. However, Greene shortly thereafter sent him north, "with a good horse and money," to Gen. Washington and who discharged Champe from further service "lest he might in the vicissitudes of war, fall into the enemy's hands; when if recognized he was sure to die on a gibbet." He died in Kentucky probably about 1798 or somewhat earlier. See Lee's *Memoirs*, pp. 394-411, and Boatner, pp. 193-194.

~~~***~~~
~~~

Note. The following and subsequent lists are not exhastive of all the rank and file that served in the Legion; and a list of troopers specifically from other states, particulalrly New Jersey given their reported numbers, is obviously wanting.

Return of the Legion, dated, 18 Feb. 1788, Richmond.

from William T. R. Saffell's *Records of the Revolutionary War, etc.* (1894 ed.), pp. 113-115.

Mark Kenton, *Sergeant.*
Thomas Hogan, "
William Strothers, "
John Alexander, "
Charles Moorehead, "
Julias Hite, *Corporal.*
Richard Marshall, "
John Hopper, "
James White, "
Richard Johnson, "
Joseph Braun, "
Richard Hall, "
Andrew Coon, *Trumpeter.*
William Haynes, *Private.*
James Bland, "
John Barber, "
Robert Furgeson, "
John Fennell, "
John Purcell, "
James Swart, "
Joseph Tankersley, "
Benjamin Tyler, "
John Walden, "
John Brannan, "
William Groves, "
Charles Owens, "
William Halbert, "
Joseph Owens, "
Samuel Thompson, "
Thomas Almond, "
John Green, "
William Rogers, "
Andrew Brann, "
George Foster, "
William Binns, "
William Huff, "
William Halley, "
Thomas Thornhlll, "
William Lewis, "
Randolph McDaniel, "
William Loden, "
William Bransford, "
William Bigbee, "
William Dennis, "
Daniel Gray, "
John Fleace, "
Brothers Thompson, "
John Brett, "
John Wiggonton, "
Silas Johnson, "
John Gardiner, "
Samuel Avery, "
William Garner, "
Berry Shields, "
David Partello, "
Robert Meydon, "
Robert Fishkin, "
Green Robinson, "
Andrew Tosh, "
Robert Welch, "
Daniel Campbell,"
Thomas Chapman, "
Richard Cooper, "
Thomas Fisher, "
Redman Cruze, "
Thomas Whitlock, "
James Selcock, "
James Hutchinson, "
Jacob Lynn, "
Wheedon Smith, "
David Hambrich, "
John Morris, "
Richard Riely [sic],"
Thomas Jones, "
William Hunt, "
Godfrey Smith, "
James Wood, "
Tandy Holman, "
Francis Ramsay, "
John Richmond, "
Benjamin Jackson, "
Isaac Fanchaw "
James Thompson, "
Charles Bryan, "
William Carpenter, "
Daniel Hailey, "
Darien Henderson, *Qr. Mr's Sergeant.*
John Champe, *Sergeant.*
Robert Paver, "
John Mitchell, "
Wm. B. Harrison, "
John Briggs, *Private.*
John Wheeler, "
James Wheeler, "
Benjamin Strother, "
William Buckley, "
George Newman, "

John Sorrell, "
Joseph Davidson, "
Peter Crawford, "
Henry Aires,
John Myers,
John Zachary,
Thomas Hattaway, "
Ranson Bridges, "
Elijah Walbrow, "
Isaac Mooney, "
John Johnson, "
Minor Smith, "
Conrad Patterson, "
Joseph Asberry, "

~~~***~~~

PENNSYLVANIANS IN MAJOR HENRY LEE'S PARTISAN CORPS.[59]

Surgeon.
Irvine, Matthew, resided in Charleston, South Carolina, in 1824.

Lieutenants.
Armstrong, James.
Manning, Lawrence, from Hazen's [Regt.].

Music-Master
Roth, Philip.

Trumpet Major.
Cryselius, Adolph

Cornet.
Power, Robert, died January 20, 1811.

Sergeant.
McCrum, Michael, resided in Huntingdon county, 1833.

Privates.
Brown, Archibald.
Brown, Benjamin.
Burd, Isaac, resided in Sussex county, New Jersey, 1829.
Chambers, James, resided n Monmouth county, New Jersey, 1829.
Clouzier, Matthias.
Cogler, Adam, January 10, 1778.
Collins, William, resided at Old's Forge.
Cutler, John.
Ford, Archibald.
Ford, Benjamin.
Golding, Benjamin.
Gray, Samuel.
Grinder, Jacob, of Philadelphia.
Hoagland, John.
McDonald, William, resided in Baltimore county, Maryland, 1828.
Mayes, John, resided in Gloucester county, New Jersey, 1834.
Meredith, John, resided in Franklin county, Ohio, 1834.
Morgan, John.
Page, John.
Rosamund, Robert.
Teace, Joshua.

---

[59] As found in *Pennsylvania in the War of the Revolution: Battalions and Line 1775-1783*, vol. II; edited by John B. Linn and Wm. H. Egle; Harrisburg, 1880, pp. 159-161
~~~

Thomas, John T., resided in Bracken county, Kentucky, 1834, aged seventy-four.
Welch, William.
White, George.
White, James.
White, John.

~~~***~~~

MARYLANDERS IN MAJOR HENRY LEE'S PARTISAN CORPS.[60]

David Henderson, Sgt. (pay beginning 1 Jan. 1779)
Jesse Crasby (or "Crosby"), Bugler, 1st Troop (7 Apr. 1778)
James Gillies, Bugler, KIA, (1 Aug. 1780)
William French, Bugler, 3rd Troop (7 Apr. 1778)
Abraham Sutton, Fife Major

Privates
James Arrants (8 Mar. 1780)
Richard Basset (7 Apr. 1778)
John Bennet (7 Apr. 1778)
George Boice, 2nd Troop (7 Apr. 1778)
Thomas Broom, 1st Troop (beginning 7 Apr. 1778)
William Chestnut (1 Jan. 1779)
Robert Crouch, 2nd Troop (7 Apr. 1778)
William Crookshank [sic], KIA (1 Aug. 1780)
John Cummins
William Dowdle, 2nd Troop (12 Mar. 1780)
Archibald Gordon
Joshua Harvey (1 Jan. 1779)
Joseph Hemphill (7 Apr. 1778)
George Hill, 2nd Troop (7 Apr. 1778)
John Howard (1 Apr. 1780)
Abiah Hukill (7 Apr. 1778)
John Johnson (10 July 1780)
John Kinard (7 Apr. 1778)
Thomas Manly, 2nd Troop (7 Apr. 1778)
John McColla (4th Regt. Light Dragoons, 10 Apr. 1777)
James McCracken (1 Apr. 1778)
Joseph Owens (7 Apr. 1778)
Thomas Owens
William Richardson
William Richardson, (miller)
Tobias Rudulph
Christopher Rutledge (7 Apr. 1778)
Jnonath [sic] Short
Samuel Tenkins (1 Jan. 1779)
John Jermain Thomas (7 Apr. 1778)
Samuel Thompson
John Towlin (16 Mar. 1780)
James Veazey (8 Mar. 1780)
James Wallace
John Ward
Daniel Williamson
John Wisham, 3rd Troop

---

[60] Extracted from *Archives of Maryland*, vol. 18, pp. 586-587.
~~~

>>>>>>>>>>>>>>>>>>>>***<<<<<<<<<<<<<<<<<<<<

Sources

Armstrong, Marie Lowrey. "James Gillies, Lee's Bugler Boy." Oak Ridge Military Academy, Oak Ridge, N,C., *Historic Preservation Commission* newsletter, 31 March, 2006, Issue 2, Vol. I.

Banks, Henry. *The Vindication of John Banks, of Virginia, Against Foul Calumnies Published By Judge* [William] *Johnson, of Charleston, South Carolina, and Doctor Charles Caldwell, of Lexington, Kentucky. Also Vindication of General Henry Lee, of Virginia, with Sketches and Anecdotes of Many Revolutionary Patriots and Heroes.* "Published By The Author," Frankfort, KY., 1826.

Berg, Fred Anderson. *Encyclopedia of Continental Army Units.* Stackpole Books, Harrisburg, Pennsylvania, 1972.

Boatner, Mark M. *The Encyclopedia of the American Revolution* (third edition). Stackpole Books, Mechanicsburg, PA., 1994.

Boyd, Thomas. *Light-horse Harry Lee.* Charles Scribner's Sons, New York, 1931.

Caruthers, Rev. E. W. *A Sketch of the Life and Character of the Rev. David Caldwell.* Swain and Sherwood, Greensborough, N.C., 1842.

Cecere, Michael. *Wedded to My Sword: The Revolutionary War Service of Light Horse Harry Lee.* Heritage Books, Westminister, Maryland, 2012.

Earle, Swepson and Skirven, Percy G., editors. *Maryland's Colonial Eastern Shore: Historical Sketches of Counties and of Some Notable Structures.* Baltimore, 1916.

Garden, Alexander. *Anecdotes of the Revolutionary War in America: With Sketches of Character of Persons the Most Distinguished, in the Southern States, for Civil and Military Services.* A.E. Miller, Charleston, 1822.

Garden, Alexander. *Anecdotes of the American Revolution: Illustrative of the Talents and Virtues of the Heroes of the Revolution, Who Acted the Most Conspicuous Parts Therein* -- Second Series. A.E. Miller, Charleston, 1828.

Gerson, Noel B. *Light-Horse Harry; A Biography of Washington's Great Cavalryman, General Henry Lee.* Doubleday & Co., Inc., Garden City, N.Y., 1966.

Gordon, William. *The history of the rise progress and establishment of the independence of the United States of America: including an account of the late war; and of the thirteen colonies from their origin to that period.* Vol. IV, Hodge, Allen and Campbell, New York, 1789.

Haller, Stephen E. *William Washington: Cavalryman of the Revolution.* Heritage Books, Bowie, Maryland, 2001.

Hartley, Cecil B. *The Life of Major General Henry Lee, Commander of Lee's Legion in the Revolutionary War and Subsequently Governor of Virginia; to which is added the Life of General Thomas Sumter.* G.G. Evans, Philadelphia, 1859.

Heitman, Francis B. *Historical Register of Officers of the Continental Army*. Washington, D.C. 1914.

Johnson, Joseph. *Traditions and Reminiscences chiefly of the American Revolution in the South*. Walker James: Charleston, S.C. 1854, pp. 403-414.

Johnson, William. *The Life and Correspondence of Nathanael Greene* (1822), 2 Vols. De Capo Press re-print, New York, 1973.

Katcher, Philip. *Uniforms of the Continental Army*. George Shumway, York, Penn., 1981.

Kennedy, John Pendleton. *Memoirs of the Life of William Wirt, Attorney-general of the United States,* ["A New and Revised Edition"], vol. I [pp. 26-27], Lea and Blanchard, Philadelphia, 1850.

Lee, Henry, the 4th (son of "Light Horse Harry.") *The Campaign of 1781 in the Carolinas; With Remarks, Historical and Critical, on Johnson's Life of Greene. To Which is Added an Appendix of Original Documents, Relating to the History of the Revolution.* E. Littell, Philadelphia, 1824. (Quadrangle Books -reprint, Chicago, 1962)

Lee, Henry. *Memoirs of the War in the Southern Department of the United States*. Arno Press reprint of the 1869 edition, New York, 1969.

Linn, John B., and Egle, Wm. H., eds. *Pennsylvania in the War of the Revolution: Battalions and Line 1775-1783*, vol. II, Harrisburg, 1880, pp. 159-161.

Lossing, Benson J. *Pictorial Field-Book of the Revolution* (1859), 2 vols., Caratzas Brothers Publishers re-print, New Rochelle, N.Y., 1976.

Marshall, John. *The Life of George Washington* (volumes III and IV.) The Citizen's Guild, Fredericksburg, VA., 1926.

Maryland Historical Society. *Archives of Maryland, vol. 18: Muster Rolls and Other Records of Service of Maryland Troops in the American Revolution, 1775-1783*. Maryland Historical Society, Baltimore, 1900.

McCrady, Edward. *The History of South Carolina in the Revolution*, 1775-1780. Russell and Russell, New York, 1901.

McCrady, Edward. *The History of South Carolina in the Revolution, 1780-1783*. Russell and Russell, New York, 1902.

Pennsylvania, Historical Society of. *Pennsylvania Magazine of History and Biography*, Vol. XXIX. Philadelphia, 1905.

Royster, Charles. *Light-Horse Harry Lee and the Legacy of the American Revolution*. Louisiana State Press, Baton Rouge, 1981.

Rudulph, Marilou Alston. "Michael Rudulph, 'Lion of the Legion.'" *Georgia Historical Quarterly*, 45 (September 1961), pp. 201-222. See also "The Legend of Michael Rudulph." *Georgia Historical Quarterly*, 45 (December 1961), pp. 309-328.

Saffell, William Thomas Roberts. *Records of the Revolutionary War: Containing the Military and Financial Correspondence of Distinguished Officers; Names of the Officers and Privates of Regiments, Companies, and Corps, with the Dates of Their Commissions and Enlistments.* Charles C. Saffell, Baltimore, 1894.

Showman, Richard K., and Conrad, Dennis M., editors-in-chief. *The Papers of Nathanael Greene,* vols. VII, 1994, vol. VIII, 1995, vol. IX, 1997. University of North Carolina Press, Chapel Hill, 1994-1997. Conrad is chief editor for volumes VIII and IX.

Stewart, Frank H. (ed.) *Notes On Old Gloucester County, New Jersey*, vol. 1, The New Jersey Society of Pennsylvania, 1917, pp. 132-138.

White, George. *Historical Collections of Georgia: Containing the Most Interesting Facts, Traditions, Biographical Sketches, Anecdotes, etc., relating to its History and Antiquities, from the First Settlement to the Present.* New York City Pudney & Russell, 1854.

Wilson, James Grant; Fiske, John; Klos, Stanley L., editors. *Appleton's Cyclopedia of American Biography*, in six volumes. D. Apple and Company, New York, 1899.

Woodruff, Caldwell. "Capt. Ferdinand O'Neal of Lee's Legion," *The William and Mary Quarterly*, 2nd Ser., Vol. 23, No. 3 (July, 1943), pp. 328-330.

Wright, Robert K., Jr., *The Continental Army.* Center of Military History United States Army, Washington, D.C., 1989.

Also:
"Pension Application of Matthew Harvey: W19681," Transcribed and annotated by C. Leon Harris.
Tribble, Dorothy. "A Biography of Ferdinand O'Neal," See O'Neal Genealogy Association WebSite at http://www.onealwebsite.com/

* Although Pulaski's (est. March 28, 1778) and Armand's (est. June 25, 1778) antedated Cathecart's or the British Legion (est. July 1778), all seemed to have been inspired and or took their cue from the Queen's Rangers first formed in August 1776 on Staten Island by Robert Rogers; and where horse units were combined with "rangers." Lauzun's Legion, for its part, made its appearance on March 5, 1780.

* Lee's Partisan Light Dragoons came into being April 7 1778. Then on July 13, 1779, Capt. Allen McLane's elite Delaware company was joined to it to form (at least on paper and in intention though never formally realized) a "legion." The unit was finally designated the 2nd Partisan Corps on Jan. 1, 1781; so that the origin then of the Legion cavalry was the 1st Continental Light Dragoons, while the Legion infantry was founded on McLane's company.

* Most of the Legion, circa 1780-82, were Virginians, and after that men from Maryland. But in addition to this, the unit had soldiers from Delaware, Pennsylvania, Connecticut, South Carolina, North Carolina, Massachusetts, and New Jersey.

* The Legion's farriers marked the shoes of the cavalry horses; so that the troopers, if need arise, might better track each other. See LMS p. 401.[61]

* Was the Legion ever taken completely by surprise? Almost! While advancing on their way into S.C. in early April 1781 (following Guilford and the sojourn at Ramsey's Mill), the Legion one very dark night believed itself under imminent attack by Cornwallis' forces; only to learn next morning that what had set off the muskets of the pickets in the bleary hours was actually a pack of wolves scavenging the pine barrens. See LMS pp. 326-330.

* What was often or occasionally on the menu for the Legion while in the south? Bacon, beef, corn-ash cake, corn mush, rice, sweet potatoes, and later alligators and frogs! The horses for their part loved cane-brake and "Indian peas" (by which I believe he means peanuts.) LMS p. 523.

* Was Napoleon's "Bravest of the Brave," Marshal Michel Ney, in reality Michael Rudulph (1758–1795) of the Legion infantry? Well, there is one "legend" that asserts as much. See *The Southern Literary Messenger*, Jan. 1847, Vol. XIII, no. 1, p. 17; found at: https://tinyurl.com/ydxghbnh While I don't know myself whether it was ever done, one apparently easy way to test this question would be to compare the handwriting of the two officers.

Benson J. Lossing, in his Pictorial Field Book of the Revolution, *vol. II, p. 162n, relates the following unusual story of the infamous "Pine Robbers," and respecting the demise of whom members of the Legion played a not inconspicuous part.*

"The Pine Robbers were a band of marauding Tories, who infested the large districts of pine woods in the lower part of Monmouth county [New Jersey], whence they made predatory excursions among the Whigs of the neighboring country. They burrowed caves in the sand-hills for places of shelter and retreat, on the borders of swamps, and, covering them with brush, effectually concealed them. From these dens they sallied forth at midnight to burn, plunder, and murder. Nor were the people safe in the daytime, for the scoundrels would often issue from their hiding-places, and fall upon the farmer in his field.

[61] "LMS" refers to the 1869 edition of Lee's *Memoirs*.

The people were obliged to carry muskets while at their work, and their families were kept in a state of continual terror.

Of these depredators, the most prominent were Fenton, Fagan, Williams, Debow, West, and Carter. Fenton was the arch-fiend of the pandemonium of the Pines. He was a blacksmith of Freehold, large and muscular. He early took to the business of the Tories, and began his career of villainy by robbery. He plundered a tailor's shop in Freehold township. Already a committee of vigilance was organized. They sent Fenton word that, if he did not return the plunder, he should be hunted and shot. Intimidated, he sent back the clothing, with the following savage note appended:

"I have returned your damned rags. In a short time I am coming to burn your barns and houses, and roast you all like a pack of kittens!"

Fenton soon proceeded to put his threat into execution. One summer night, at the head of a gang of desperadoes, he attacked the dwelling of an aged man near Imlaytown, named Farr. Himself, wife, and daughter composed the family. They barricaded the door, and kept the scoundrels at bay for a while. Fenton finally broke in a portion of the door, and, firing through the opening, broke the leg of the old man with a musket-ball. They forced an entrance at last, murdered the wife, and then dispatched the helpless old man. The daughter, badly wounded, escaped, and the miscreants, becoming alarmed, fled without taking any plunder with them. Fenton was afterward shot by a young soldier of Lee's legion, then lying at Monmouth court-house. The robber had plundered and beaten a young man while on his way from a mill. He gave information to Lee, who detailed a sergeant and two soldiers to capture or destroy the villain. The young man, and the sergeant disguised as a countryman, took a seat in a wagon, while the two soldiers, armed, were concealed under some straw in the bottom of the vehicle, and proceeded toward the mill, expecting to meet Fenton on the road. From a low groggery among the Pines the robber came out, with a pistol, and commanded them to halt. He then inquired if they had brandy, to which an affirmative was given, and a bottle handed to him. While drinking, one of the soldiers, at a signal from the sergeant, arose, and shot the villain through the head. His body was thrown into the wagon, and conveyed in triumph to Freehold.

Fagan and West were also shot by the exasperated people. The body of the latter was suspended in chains, with hoop-iron bands around it, upon a chestnut by the road-side, about a mile from Freehold, on the way to Colt's Neck, where it was left to be destroyed by carrion birds.

The sufferings of the people from these marauders made such a deep impression, that the lapse of years could not efface it from the hearts of those who felt their scourge, and even the third generation of the families of Tories were objects of hate to some of the surviving sufferers. An old lady, ninety years of age, with whom I conversed at Boundbrook, became greatly excited while talking of what her family endured from the Pine Robbers and other Tories, and spoke indignantly of one or two families in Monmouth county who were descendants of Loyalists. Philip Freneau, from whose poems I have frequently quoted, was a native of this county. He was graduated at Princeton College in 1771. His poems, written chiefly during the Revolution and immediately after, were vigorous, and sometimes beautiful. He was found dead in a bog, in which he was mired, near Freehold, on the 18th of December, 1832, and was buried in that village."

FRONTPIECE to *The Old Joe Miller: Being a Complete and Correct Copy from the Best Edition of his Celebrated Jests*, Wilson & Co., London, 1800. "Ride si sapis" ("Laugh if you know.")

~~~***~~~

A REVOLUTIONARY JOE MILLER

An assortment of choice Bon Mots, Jests, & Repartees from the pages of Almon, Garden, and Lyman Draper, et al.

1. In the beginning of the war, an American cruizer having captured a rich British ship, the master coming on beard the cruizer, and not having heard of any reprisals made by the Americans at sea, seemed in no little surprise, -- and asked the commander whether he really meant and had authority to make prize of him; upon being assured that it was truly so, he cast his eyes upon the Colours, and inquired further, what motto the flag had, and what was particularly intended by the STRIPES. Oh, Sir, replied the American commander, the meaning of our colours is to be found among the maxims of the wisest Prince that ever reigned -- STRIPES *for the back of fools.*

2. *Ethan Allen*: "Among the great numbers of people, who came to the castle[62] to see the prisoners, some gentlemen told me that they had come fifty miles on purpose to see me, and desired to ask me a number of questions, and to make free with me in conversation. I gave for answer that I chose freedom in every sense of the word. Then one of them asked me what my occupation in life had been? I answered him, that in my younger days I had studied *divinity*, but was a *conjuror* by profession. He replied, that I conjured *wrong* at the time I was taken; and I was obliged to own, that I mistook a figure at that time, but that I had *conjured* them out of Ticonderoga."

3. *The following is found in T.R. Saffell's* (American) Records of the Revolutionary War: "Pay Office, Main Army, Nov. 8, 1780. Sir. -- Inclosed I transmit you my last month's account, and a letter of stoppages in the Southern department, which I wish you to forward. Money! money! money! or rather the want of it, is the word. It will oblige me much to hear what prospects you have of obtaining any. I am, with much respect and friendship, yours, John Pierce. Col. Palfeet, P. M. Gen."

4. A British officer was sent from the garrison at Georgetown, to negotiate a business interesting to both armies; when this was concluded, and the officer about to return, the general said, "If it suits your convenience sir, to remain for a short period, I shall be glad of your company to dinner." The mild and dignified simplicity of Marion's manners, had already produced their effect; and, to prolong so interesting an interview, the invitation was accepted. The entertainment was served upon pieces of bark, and consisted entirely of roasted potatoes, of which the general eat heartily requesting his guest to profit by his example, repeating the old adage, that "hunger was an excellent sauce." "But surely general," said the officer, "this cannot be your ordinary fare." "Indeed it is sir," he replied, "and we are fortunate on this occasion, *entertaining company* to have more than our usual allowance."

5. A detachment of mounted militia, had been sent out by the General to watch the movements of the enemy, hastening, under the command of Lord Rawdon, to the relief of Ninety-Six, and came up with their rear guard at a place called the Juniper Springs, about fifteen miles distant from Granby. The British cavalry, who composed it, were of much superior force, and being in every respect better prepared for

[62] [*Edit. Note*. Pendennis Castle, just on the outskirts of Falmouth, England.]
~~~

action, quickly disconcerted the American detachment, and put them to flight. A poor German, named Loaster, belonging to the American party, mounted on a sorry poney, with a rope bridle, and corresponding equipments, with no other arms than a musket, which he had already fired off, was assailed by a British dragoon, who aimed several desperate blows at him with his sabre, which were warded off with extraordinary dexterity, Loaster calling out alter every parry, "Huzza for America." While in this perilous situation, a Mr. Fitzpatrick, determining, if possible, to save him, rode up, and with the butt end of his pistol, which had been previously discharged, struck the dragoon so violent a blow in the face as to fell him to the ground. Loaster, thus happily rescued, rode off and escaped, vowing most earnestly never again to go into action Without a cutting iron, his musket being nearly severed in two, in five different places.

6. The haughty Tarleton, vaunting his feats of gallantry to the great disparagement of the Officers of the Continental Cavalry, said to a lady at Wilmington, "I have a very earnest desire to see your far-famed hero, Colonel Washington," "Your wish, Colonel, might have been fully gratified," she promptly replied, "had you ventured to look behind you after the battle of the Cowpens." It was in this battle, that Washington had wounded Tarleton in the hand, which gave rise to a still *more pointed* retort. Conversing with *Mrs. Wiley Jones*, Colonel Tarleton observed -- "You appear to think very highly of Colonel Washington; and yet I have been told, that he is so ignorant a fellow, that he can hardly write his own name." "It may be the case," she readily replied, "but no man better than yourself, Colonel, can testify, that he knows how to make *his mark*."

7. About the period of the final departure of the British from New-York, an excellent repartee made by Major Upham, Aid-de-Camp to Lord Dorchester, to Miss Susan Livingston, has been much celebrated. "In mercy, Major," said Miss Livingston, "use your influence with the Commander in Chief, to accelerate the evacuation of the city; for among your encarcerated belles, your Mischianza Princesses, the *Scarlet* fever must continue to rage till your departure." "I should studiously second your wishes," replied the Major, "were I not apprehensive, that freed from the prevailing malady, a worse would follow, and that they would be immediately tormented with the *Blue Devils*."

8. At the battle of Eutaw, when General Marion's Brigade was displaying in face of the enemy. Captain Gee, who commanded the front platoon, was shot down, and supposed to be mortally wounded. The ball passed through the cock of a handsome hat, that he had recently procured, tearing the crown very much, and in its progress, the head also. He lay for a considerable time insensible; the greater part of the day had passed without a favourable symptom; when, suddenly reviving, his first inquiry was after his beaver, which being brought him, a friend, at the same time, lamenting the mangled state of the head, he exclaimed -- "O, never think of the head; time and the Doctor will put that to rights; but it grieves me to think, that the rascals have ruined my hat for ever!"

9. When on his last visit to America, while at Montgomery, in the State of Alabama, he [Lafayette] was visited by a veteran who had served under him in many battles, whom he immediately recognized, as an orderly and most gallant soldier. After much interesting and familiar conversation, the old man said, "there is one thing, General, which it puzzles me to account for when we served together, I believed myself to be the youngest man of the two. But my locks are now perfectly grey, and you do not appear to have a grey hair in your head." "My good friend," replied the General, "you are altogether in error, the advantage is totally on your side. The hair of your head is grey while I cannot beast a single hair on my head I wear a wig!"

10. It happened during the Revolutionary war, that a treaty was held with the Indians, at which La Fayette was present. The object was to unite the various tribes in amity with America. The majority of the Chiefs were friendly, but there was much opposition made to it, more especially by a young warrior, who declared that when an alliance was entered into with America, he should consider the sun of his country as set forever. In his travels through the Indian Country, when lately in America, it happened at a large assemblage of Chiefs, that La Fayette referred to the treaty in question, and turning to Red Jacket, said, "pray tell me if you can, what has be come of that daring youth, who so decidedly opposed all our propositions for peace and amity? Does he still live and what is his condition?" "I, myself, am the man," replied Red Jacket, "the decided enemy of the Americans, as long as the hope of opposing them with success remained, but now their true and faithful ally until death."

11. Samuel Clowney...was a most determined Whig, and had joined Colonel Thomas at the Cedar Spring, early in July. Obtaining with several others a brief leave of absence, to visit their friends, and procure a change of clothing, they set off for the settlement on the waters of Fair Forest, known as Ireland or the Irish Settlement, on account of the large number of settlers from the Emerald Isle. On their route, the party left, with a Mrs. Foster, some garments to be washed, and appointed a particular hour, and an out-of-the-way place, where they should meet her, and get them, on their return to camp.

In accordance with this arrangement, when the party reached Kelso's creek, about five miles from Cedar Spring, they diverged from the road through the woods to the appointed place, leaving Clowney, and a negro named Paul, to take charge of their horses until they should return with the washing. Presently five Tories, making their way to a Loyalist encampment in that quarter, came to the creek; when Clowney, conceiving himself equal to the occasion, and giving the negro subdued directions of the part he was to act, yelled out in a commanding tone: "Cock your guns, boys, and fire at the word;" and then advancing to the bank of the stream, as the Tories were passing through it, demanded who they were? They answered: "Friends to the King." To their utter astonishment, not dreaming of a Whig party in the country, they were peremptorily ordered by Clowney to come upon the bank, lay down their arms, and surrender, or "every bugger of them would be instantly cut to pieces." Being somewhat slow in showing signs of yielding, Clowney sternly repeated his demand, threatening them, with his well-poised rifle, of the fatal consequences of disobedience; when the terror-stricken Tories, believing that a large force was upon them, quietly surrendered without uttering a word.

Paul took charge of their guns, when Clowney, giving some directions to his imaginary soldiers to follow in the rear, ordered the prisoners "right about wheel," when he marched them across the creek, directly before him, till he at length reached the rest of his party at Mrs. Foster's washing camp. They were then conducted to Colonel Thomas' quarters. The prisoners were not a little chagrined, when they learned that their captors consisted of only two persons -- one of whom was an unarmed negro. After arriving safely at Cedar Spring, his Colonel, when told that Clowney and the negro alone had captured the whole party, seemed at first a little incredulous that they could accomplish such a feat.

"Why, Paddy," said the Colonel, "how did you take all these men?"

"May it plase yer honor," he replied, exultingly, "by me faith, I surrounded them!"

12. Francois-Jean de Beauvoir, The Marquis de Chastellux (1734-1788), who served on Major-General Rochambeau's staff at Yorktown, in his justly celebrated journal and memoir, furnishes the following singular description of American living at the time of the Revolution. In addition are appended here two accompanying footnotes: the first by Chastellux's translator (who happened to be an Englishman), and the second by an American annotating an 1828 edition of the work.

[p. 296] "The Virginians have the reputation, and with reason, of living nobly in their houses, and of being hospitable; they give strangers not only a willing, but a liberal reception. This arises, on one hand, from their having no large towns, where they may assemble, by which means they are little acquainted with society, except from the visits they make; and, on the other, their lands and their negroes furnishing them with every article of consumption, and the necessary service, this renowned hospitality costs them very little. Their houses are spacious, and ornamented, but their apartments are not commodious; they make no ceremony of putting three or four persons into the same room;*[1] nor do these make any objection to their being thus heaped together; for being in general ignorant of the comfort of reading and writing, they want nothing in their whole house but a bed, a dining-room, and a drawing-room for company...

[English Translator: 1]* Throughout America, in private houses, as well as in the inns, several people are crowded together in the same room; and in the latter it very commonly happens, that after you have been some time in bed, a stranger of any condition, (for there is little distinction,) comes into the room, pulls off his clothes, and places himself, without ceremony, between your sheets. Trans.

[American editor's footnote: 2] This was probably the case at the time the translator wrote; but at the present day there is no country in which travellers can be more retired, or better accommodated than in the United States.

~~~*~~~

1. Almon's Remembrancer *(1780) part 1 pp. 21-22, 2. Ethan Allen's* Narrative *(1779), 3. Saffell's* Records of the Revolutionary War *(1894) pp. 83-84, 4. Garden's* Anecdotes of the Revolutionary War *(1822) pp. 21-22, 5. Garden's* Anecdotes of the Revolutionary War *(1822) pp. 403-404, 6. Garden's* Anecdotes of the Revolutionary War *(1822) p. 237, 7. Garden's* Anecdotes of the Revolutionary War *(1822) p. 417, 8. Garden's* Anecdotes of the Revolutionary War *(1822) pp. 385-386, 9. Garden's* Anecdotes of the Revolutionary War *(1828) p. 185, 10. Garden's* Anecdotes of the Revolutionary War *(1828) pp. 185-186, 11. Draper's* King's Mountain and Its Heroes *pp. 126-128. 12.* Travels in North America in the Years 1781-1782, *Part II, ch. V.*
~~~

CONTEMPORARY REVIEWS OF TARLETON'S *CAMPAIGNS*

Despite his being traditionally vilified as a notorious and ruthless cavalry leader, Banastre Tarleton has in recent decades come to receive more impartial appraisal and, for that matter, greater sympathy. Indeed, in retrospect and on the whole, it does seem that Tarleton, rather than the cold hearted monster he has been depicted as being, was rather and simply a young, ambitious, and energetic officer attempting merely to do what he saw as his assigned task and duty. That things at times, such as at the battle of Waxhaws, got out of hand was more so the result of unruly men under his command getting carried away than any inherent deviltry or sinister design on his part. And if Sherman's maxim that "war is cruelty, and you cannot refine it" has any truth to it, Tarleton's lapses, such as in his rampant burning of homes and executing civilians, if not excusable, were at least within the purview of his orders; nor were such practices unique to him. He was after all simply obeying and following directives, and if any blame is to be leveled, the *more* proper object should have been his superiors. In retrospect his unusually bad reputation seems to have been the largely result of Americans propaganda understandably seeking to demonize the British war effort by way of using a colorful figure for that purpose, and later as well some British apologists who resented his post war candor. It is also interesting to note in his favor that when at the time of the French Revolution Lafayette was imprisoned at Olmutz by Francis II of Austria, Tarleton, as a member of Parliament, seconded a motion (March 17, 1794) to have the British government seek the Marquis' release; but which was foolishly voted down by opposition led by, on that occasion, the short-sighted Edmund Burke.

What follows below are two contemporary assessments of Tarleton's *A History of the Campaigns of 1780 and 1781, in the Southern Provinces of North America* (1787). It should in fairness be noted that much of the negativity and derision directed at him, as evinced by these reviewers, stemmed in no little part from Tarleton's repeated, and not without justice, criticisms of Cornwallis' handling of the southern campaign, and, in turn, his alleged ingratitude of the latter's fatherly patronage. Per chance as well, personal jealousy may have been a further inducement of animosity. Included here in addition is a separate review of Roderick Mackenzie's no less acerbic *Strictures on Tarleton's History* (1787).

~~~***~~~

From *The Critical Review, or the Annals of Literature*, for Jan. 1787, volume 63, pp. 346-352.

A History of the Campaigns of 1780 end 1781, in the Southern Provinces of North America.
By Lieutenant-colonel Tarleton. 4to. 1L. 6s. Cadell.

THIS History is, in general, a compilation of the official letters of the British officers, both in the sea and land service; of the American and French commanders, which have appeared in the news-papers, with lord Rawdon's much admired campaign, from the *Remembrancer* and *Annual Register*. The military transactions are collected into a regular order: the author, lieutenant-colonel Tarleton, enters into a very minute detail of his own services, and makes a very free comment on those of others, and in particular of lord Cornwallis. His conclusions are not, however, always logically deduced, nor, as we conceive, warranted by military science. We must examine colonel Tarleton's opinions in general, and his criticisms on others, particularly on lord Rawdon and lord Cornwallis; for we do not find any information very interesting or uncommon in the transactions themselves. The plans are useful and correctly executed.

The detail of military actions is seldom of importance to any but those of the profession, and they necessarily make the greatest part of a publication of this nature. As an history, it ought to be authenticated by public papers, but, as a work of general information, it is not pleasing to hear the most trifling circumstances digested by a minute historian, and to read them again in the official letters of the commanders. As a specimen of our author's manner, and his reasoning, we shall select the passage commenting on the action of the Cowpens. Colonel Tarleton relates the history of the action, nearly as it is described in the marquis de Chastellux's *Travels*: if there had been an essential difference we should have pointed it out, according to our promise.
~~~

"On the 14th earl Cornwallis informed Tarleton that Leslie had surmounted his difficulties, and that he imagined the enemy would not pass the Broad-river, though it had fallen very much. Tarleton then answered, that he would try to cross the Pacolet, to force them, and desired earl Cornwallis to acquire as high a station as possible, in order to slop their retreat. No letter, order, or intelligence, from head-quarters reached Tarleton after this reply, previous to the defeat on the 17th, and after that event he found earl Cornwallis on Turkey-creek, near twenty-five miles below the place where the action had happened. The distance between Wynnesborough and King's-mountain, or Wynnesborough and Little Broad-river, which would have answered the same purpose, does not exceed sixty-five miles: earl Cornwallis commenced his march on the 7th or 8th of January. It would be mortifying to describe the advantages that might have resulted from his lordship's arrival at the concerted point, or to expatiate upon the calamities which were produced by this event.'

In this passage, we think we perceive a manifest contradiction. If no letter or order reached colonel Tarleton from lord Cornwallis, in answer to his proposal, there could be no point concerted for his lordship to arrive at and the reflections do not seem to accord, in the opinion of the best judges, with military propriety, as it is apparent, that he either should not have been detached from the main army, or, when detached, that he should have relied on the troops under his command for success.

Of the action, he says,

The disposition was planned with coolness, and executed without embarrassment. The defeat of the British must be ascribed either to the bravery or good conduct of the Americans; to the loose manner of forming which had always been practised by the king's troops in America; or to some unforeseen event, which may throw terror into the most disciplined soldiers, or counteract the best concerted designs. The extreme extension of the files always exposed the British regiments and corps, and would, before this unfortunate affair, have been attended with detrimental effect, had not the multiplicity of lines with which they generally fought rescued them from such imminent danger. If infantry who are formed very open, and only two deep, meet with opposition, they can have no liability: But when they experience an unexpected shock, confusion will ensue, and flight, without immediate support, must be the inevitable consequence."

These are principles on which common sense, the foundation; of all science, may, we think, decide. Military men may probably be induced to wish that they had been promulgated before the action of the Cowpens; and they will condemn the colonel for want of tactical knowledge, that might have led him to alter any interior arrangement which he thought erroneous, or for not suiting the general disposition of the troops to his own numbers.

Lord Cornwallis's support of lieutenant-colonel Tarleton, who, in consequence of his defeat, required his lordship's approbation of his proceedings, or his leave to retire, till enquiry could be instituted to investigate the merits of his conduct (p. 222), is fully expressed in a letter, which we transcribe with pleasure, as success is too often supposed to be an infallible criterion of desert.

"You have forfeited no part of my esteem as an officer by the unfortunate event of the action of the 17th: the means you used to bring the enemy to action were able and masterly, and must ever do you honour. Your disposition was unexceptionable; the total misbehaviour of the troops could alone have deprived you of the glory which was so justly your due."

We cannot agree in some of the political proposals of our author, particularly where, on the desertion of the militia, he thinks it would have been adviseable to incorporate them with the regular troops. Surely those who were remiss or treacherous in the lesser duties of the militia, could not have been brought to undergo the hardships, which this volume tells us were the lot of the king's troops.

Colonel Tarleton's remarks on lord Rawdon's conduct are, we think, also exceptionable. Previous to the battle of Camden, it appears that this nobleman, when general Gates advanced into South Carolina, took post at Lynche's Creek, 14 miles from Camden, and in Gates's road to that place.

"General Gates (says our author) advanced to the creek opposite to the British camp, and skirmishes ensued between the advanced parties of the two armies. The American commander discovered that Lord Rawdon's position was strong, and he declined an attack; but he had not sufficient penetration to conceive, that by a forced march up the creek, he could have passed Lord Rawdon's flank, and reached Camden; which would have been an easy conquest, and a fatal blow to the British."

This reflection must suppose a supineness in lord Rawdon, by no means consistent with his abilities and military talents, nor to the decision which this very movement illustrated. It seems to have been a part of that system, which, on Gates' moving in the line described by our historian, brought on the action and the victory. We need only transcribe colonel Tarleton's own reflections on the misconduct of Gates, for an illustration of this conjecture.

"On reviewing the striking circumstances preceding and during the battle, the conduct of earl Cornwallis cannot be placed in a clearer light than by contrasting it with that of his opponent. The faults committed by the American commander, during his short campaign at the head of the southern army, were neither unimportant in themselves, nor inconsiderable in number. The first misconception imputed to general Gates, was the not breaking in upon the British communications as soon as he arrived near Lynche's creek. The move up the creek, and from thence to Camden, was practicable and easy before the king's troops were concentered at that place; or he might, without the smallest difficulty, have occupied a strong position on Saunders' Creek, five miles from Camden, before earl Cornwallis joined the royal forces. His second error was moving an army, consisting of young corps and undisciplined militia, in the night: A manœuvre always to be avoided with troops of that description, in the neighbourhood of an enterprizing enemy; and only to be hazarded when regiments are perfectly officered, and well trained. His third mistake was in the disposition of his army before the action: if the militia had been formed into one line, in front of the continentals, they would have galled the British in the wood, when approaching to attack the main body: or, if the militia had been kept totally separate from the continentals, and too much confidence had not been placed in them, perhaps that confusion in part of the Maryland line, owing to the early flight of Caswell's brigade, had never happened. His last and greatest fault, was attempting to make an alteration in the disposition the instant the two armies were going to engage; which circumstance could not escape the notice of a vigilant enemy, who by a skilful and sudden attack threw the American left wing into a state of confusion, from which it never recovered. The favourable opportunities which presented themselves to earl Cornwallis during the march and the action, were seized with judgment, and prosecuted with vigour; a glorious victory crowned the designs of the general, and the exertions of the troops."

Our military historian is decidedly of opinion, that lord Cornwallis ought to have moved from Cross Creek to Camden, without going into Virginia. Speaking of the advantage gained by earl Cornwallis over the marquis de la Fayette, at the passage of James River, colonel Tarleton observes,

"The events of this day were particularly important, and claimed more attention than they obtained. The marquis de la Fayette had made a long march, in very sultry weather, with, about fifteen hundred continentals and one thousand militia, to strike at the rear of the British before they passed to James island: too great ardour, or false intelligence, which is most probable, for it is the only instance of this officer committing himself during a very difficult campaign, prompted him to cross a morass to attack earl Cornwallis, who routed him, took his cannon, and must inevitably have destroyed his army, if night had not intervened. His lordship might certainly have derived more advantage from this victory. If the two battalions of light infantry, the guards, and colonel Yorke's brigade, who had all been slightly engaged, or any other corps, and the cavalry, had been detached, without knapsacks, before dawn of day, to pursue the Americans, and push them to the utmost, the army of the marquis de la Fayette must have been annihilated. Such an exploit would have been easy, fortunate, and glorious, and would have prevented the combination which produced the fall of York Town, and Gloucester. It was suggested to earl Cornwallis, in opposition to the plan of pursuing the victory, that sir Henry Clinton's requisition for troops was a circumstance (hence of greater consequence, and more worthy of attention. This was allowed to be a strong and forcible reason; but at that same time it was represented, that the exertion of half, or two thirds of the British army, in pursuit of the Americans, would not occasion delay, or in the least derange the original design of proceeding to Portsmouth. Experience fully evinced and justified the propriety of this opinion.

"Lieutenant-colonel Tarleton, with two hundred dragoons, and eighty mounted infantry, was ordered to proceed after daybreak across the swamp, in pursuit of the enemy; and three Companies of light infantry were directed to take post beyond it, until he returned. Some wounded men, and deserters joined the British before they reached the Green Springs, where the marquis de la Fayette had rallied his troops after the action. The dragoons then struck into the road by which, about two hours before, the Americans had retreated, and they had not advanced four miles when they met a patrole of mounted riflemen. The captain who commanded it, and several of his men were killed or taken: The remainder were pursued into the marquis de la Fayette's army, who had been forced by extreme fatigue to repose themselves no more than six miles from the field of battle. In this situation they would have been an easy prey to a powerful detachment of the British, who could have marched into their rear by several roads, whilst the light troops amused them in front; or the infantry might have followed the route of the continentals in case they retreated, and the English dragoons and mounted infantry could have passed through the woods into their front, or on their flank, and have impeded and harassed them till the foot could force them to action. Either of these plans must have succeeded against a corps that was destitute of cavalry; that had made a forced march in very hot weather during the preceding day; that had been routed, and had retreated without refreshment or provisions. When the late defeat, the diminished force, and the bodily fatigue of the Americans arc contrasted with the recent success, the superior numbers, and the active vigour of the British, it may fairly be presumed, that less time than twelve hours would have given, without the smallest hazard, a decisive advantage to the king's troops."

Lieutenant-colonel Tarleton also accuses his general of neglect, in not attacking la Fayette before the junction of the French at Williamsburgh (p. 369). If we admit the propriety of this attempt, can we suppose it easy to surprise a distant enemy, whose obvious aim it was to avoid any contest, while he waited for the junction of other armies to strike a very important stroke. Our author also decidedly supports the construction which sir Henry Clinton placed on his own official letters; a construction which we find in lord Cornwallis's account of the correspondence, he did not admit; and, in a summary of the campaigns of 1780, and 1781, at the end of the volume, he says,

"A retrospective view of British operations plainly discovers that the march from Wilmington to Petersburg was formed and executed by earl Cornwallis without the knowledge or consent of sir Henry Clinton: That York Town and Gloucester were voluntarily occupied by his lordship, in preference to Old Point comfort, when a post for the protection of the navy was required: That as soon as sir Henry Clinton was apprized of the minister's wish to make a serious attempt upon Virginia, he committed as large a corps to earl Cornwallis in that province as was compatible with the safety of New York and its dependencies, during the vicinity of the French and American army: That every intelligence which could be obtained of the enemy's movements was transmitted by the commander in chief, who made all the efforts in his power to assist and relieve his lordship from the period that the French fleet entered the Chesapeak to the hour of the capitulation at York Town: And that earl Cornwallis may be said to incur the imputation of misconceiving his own danger, in not destroying la Fayette's detachment after the affair near James island; in not striking at the corps at Williamsburgh previous to the junction of Washington and Rochambeau; in quitting so early the outward for the inner position, where he was obliged to make proposals to surrender eight days after the enemy opened their batteries; and in not adopting sooner and more decidedly the measure of passing through the country. Some instances of oversight may, therefore, be attributed to his lordship, which precipitated, perhaps, the fate of his own army; but the genuine cause of the great national calamity, which put a period to the continental war, must by all ranks and descriptions of men be principally ascribed to the minister in England, or the admiral in the West Indies. The arrival of De Grasse in the Chesapeak equally animated the confidence of the allies, and destroyed all the British, hopes of conquest or of reconciliation in that quarter. The safety of earl Cornwailis's army, in all human probability, would only have procrastinated the evil day; for the past success of the campaign, and the future prospect of the king's troops, were counteracted by the formidable appearance of the French fleet. The superiority at sea proved the strength of the armies of Great Britain, deranged the plans of her generals, disheartened the courage of her friends, and finally confirmed the independency of America."

As there was little novelty in the facts, or the arrangement of this History, our quotations and remarks have been necessarily confined to the observations and reflections more peculiarly the author's own. It is unfortunate that we can so seldom agree with him, except in identical propositions, which, it was useless to select. It will be obvious, that colonel Tarleton it unfortunate in the period of his publication. The observations, whether just or unjust, are such as must have occurred to him on the spot, and previous to the conclusion of the war. If they were ever to have been made public, they mould have been so while earl Cornwallis was in England. Admitting that the accusations which a lieutenant-colonel brings against his general be true, the reader will reflect that the same want of discernment and ability will weaken the commander's uniform testimony to the merits of colonel Tarleton, and will greatly invalidate the force of that unqualified decision, which lord Cornwallis made in his favour, against the troops under his command, at the unfortunate action of the Cowpens. This was a decision which the noble earl made without any opportunity of personal observation, or exercising that deliberation which preceded all those measures, the propriety of which our historian has attacked.

On the whole, we cannot praise this *History*: it is diffuse, laboured, and tedious. The author appears every where, forward, on the canvas; and, when his importance is estimated by the weight of his own remarks, we are tempted frequently to remove him to the back-ground.

~~~***~~~

From *The English Review, or, An abstract of English and foreign literature*, vol. X, for December 1787, pp. 403-418.

Art. I. *A History of the Campaigns of 1780 and 1781, in. the Southern Provinces of North-America.* By Lieutenant Colonel Tarleton, Commandant of the late British Legion. 4to. 1l. 6s. Cadell.

IT is an opinion that has been carefully propagated of late years, especially by authors who were interested in its success, that little credit is to be given to historians who were contemporary with the agents and actions which they describe; that the truth of an historical narrative requires transactions to be reviewed in a remote light; and that the springs of human action, the policy of princes, and the secrets of cabinets, can only be developed by the research and discernment of succeeding centuries. In some cases this is true. When a civil war has shaken a state, or a revolution taken place in a kingdom, personal animosity and party resentment must be obliterated from the minds of men, and a nation recover from the shock of internal commotion, before many events can be traced to their just causes, or the characters of the principal agents be delineated in their true colours. There may, however, be enlightened individuals, who, when the fervid bustle of transactions is over in which they were engaged, may be extremely well qualified, if they possess a philosophical temper, to write the history of their own times. Cardinal de Retz, who happily saw his errors and survived his prejudices, delineates the troubles of the League with an impartial pen; and the philosopher faithfully exposes the errors of the politician. Clarendon and Burnet, though sometimes partial in their representation of characters, give a lively, and, in general, a just picture of cotemporary events; and we make no doubt but that Lord North, from his undoubted ability, his intimate acquaintance with the springs of action, and his calm and serene temper, could write a most incomparable history of the late American war.

But whatever objections may be made to a general history of one's own times, describing characters as well as events, and including the motives of actions as well as their consequences, no reasonable doubt can be entertained but that an intelligent officer, free from partiality and prejudice, is well qualified to write a narrative of the campaigns in which he served, and of the battles which he fought. With this view Lieutenant-Colonel Tarleton, well known in the martial, now enters the literary, world; wishes to associate the honours of Minerva with those of Mars; and to blend the laurels of eloquence with those of valour. Xenophon and Caesar, not to mention General Burgoyne, courted both Minervas successfully, and excelled equally in wielding the pen and the sword. Fired with enthusiastic admiration of these celebrated heroes and historians, why may not the commandant of the thundering legion cry out, like the Italian artist, "I too am a painter?"

Tentanda est via qua me quoque possim
~~~

Tollere humo, victorque virum volitare per ora.[63]

The history before us is confined to the campaigns of 1780 and 1781 in the southern provinces of North-America; and our author gives an additional interest to his narrative by recording in prose to the public what Aeneas recited in verse to Dido, events and transactions quorum pan magna suit. The exordium of our historian, like the march of a warrior, is brisk and spirited.

"This short history commences at a time when the whole aspect of the American war experienced a change the most critical and interesting; when prospects, big with the utmost importance, sprung up in a variety of shapes, and gave birth to those decisive events which so speedily followed. While several European powers privately assisted the colonies, in opposition to the mother country, they undoubtedly injured the interests of Great-Britain, without allowing her the advantage of reprisal; but when France and Spain threw off the mask, -- and openly embraced the cause of American independence, the nature Of the war underwent a manifest alteration. From that epoch, different political, as well as naval and military measures, might have been adopted. The magnitude of the confederacy was evident and fortunate would it have been for England had she attacked the vulnerable situation of her avowed enemies at that momentous and critical period. An immediate attention to the West-Indies, and an early evacuation of New-York, might have produced such important consequences as would, in all human probability, have given a different termination to the war: her blood and treasures might then have been saved; her natural enemies might then have been humbled; and America would have resorted again to the protection of her parent state, after Great-Britain had vindicated her own dignity, and established that preeminence, which me had acquired in her late contest with the house of Bourbon. But as it is intended only to enter into a detail of occurrences which took place in the southern provinces, during the campaigns of 1780 and 1781, and not to deviate into political disquisitions, it will be sufficient to point out the primary cause upon which the principal events were hinged, and then proceed to the narrative of military operations."

These observations are just and manly; they indicate a vigour of intellect, and an acquaintance with political affairs. There were two periods in the late unfortunate struggle with America, in which a line of conduct, different from that which was pursued, might have terminated favourably for this country. Before the European powers took a part in the quarrel, and when we had only to struggle with America, the object of British policy, if at that time there had been any policy in Britain, was to bring the contest to a sudden decision, and to break Washington's army in one great battle. Delays were fatal to us, but favourable to America. On various occasions this could have been easily effected. At one period there were nearly eighty thousand British and German troops in America a force which the colonies were not in a condition to resist. Washington's army, if once broken and dispersed, could never have recovered. America would have been struck with a panic, and returned to its allegiance. Instead of this we weakened our forces by spreading them over an immense surface; endeavoured to garrison towns and defend forts; and made war not on the Americans, but on America.

When France and Spain threw off the mask, and openly supported the cause of American rebellion, as our author justly observes, different political and military measures ought to have been adopted. To have withdrawn our troops from America, and bent our whole force to attack the vulnerable situation of our enemies, particularly in the West-Indies, might have humbled the pride of trance, and perhaps reduced our colonies to subjection to the mother-country.

Colonel Tarleton next proceeds to relate the effect of D'Estaing's attack upon Savannah, which he reckons the primary cause on which the principal events were hinged that took place during the campaigns of 1780 and 1781:

"In the autumn of the year 1779 congress was considerably advanced in credit and power by the military combination in Georgia. The appearance of the French, although the attack upon Savannah was not crowned with success, reanimated the expiring vigour of the desponding Americans, and confirmed the

[63] [*Edit. Note.* This quote from Vergil's *Georgics*, as translated by author William Sotheby (1757-1833), reads "I, too, will strive o'er earth my flight to raise, And wing'd by victory, catch the gale of praise."]

attachment of the unsteady. The loss of the naval superiority presented an unexpected scene to the British commander in chief, counteracted the promise of the minister, and equally deranged the intentions of both. After that event, administration could never hope for a fortunate period to the American, war, except in full confidence that the fleets of England could prevent the ships of France from giving interruption to the military operations in that quarter of the globe: and undoubtedly the success of the commander in chief on the western continent, and the future expectations of the loyalists, could only be sounded on the permanent superiority of the British navy."

These are very strange and unaccountable assertions, especially in the beginning of a work. The combination to which our author alludes was that of the French army under the Count d'Estaing with the Americans commanded by General Lincoln in September 1779. The army of the count, which amounted to five thousand regular troops, was joined by an equal number of Americans. This united force was repulsed, and totally routed by less than three thousand soldiers and seamen before the unfinished works of Savannah. It argues therefore a strange perversion of reason to infer that the cause of America could have derived support from such disaster and disgrace. Dr. [David] Ramsay, a member of the American congress, has lately published "A History of the Revolution of South-Carolina," in which he gives the fallowing account of the engagement at Savannah, and its consequences: "The siege being raised, the continental troops retreated over the river Savannah. A depression of spirits succeeded, much increased by the preceding elevation. The Georgian exiles, who had arrived from all quarters to repossess themselves of their estates, were a second time obliged to abandon their country, and seek refuge among strangers. The currency depreciated much faster than ever, and the most gloomy apprehensions respecting the southern states generally took possession of the minds of the people. The repulse at Savannah impressed the people with high ideas of the power of Britain."*[64]

So different are the accounts of the American and the Englishman! There are some very extraordinary incidents in the American war, but nothing so unaccountable as Colonel Tarleton's supposition that the power and credit of congress could strengthen, and the expiring vigour of the Americans revive, by the overthrow of their friends and allies.

The action at the Cowpens, conducted by Colonel Tarleton, which terminated unfavourably for the commander, and which gave a decided turn to the American cause, both in North and South-Carolina, occupies an important part in. these annals. As this is composed with great care, and written with spirit and elegance, we shall extract it as the most favourable specimen we have hitherto met with of Colonel Tarleton's literary abilities:

"'Lieutenant-Colonel Tarleton having attained a position, which he certainly might deem advantageous on account of the vulnerable situation of the enemy, and the supposed vicinity of the two British corps on the east and west of Broad River, did not hesitate to undertake those measures which the instructions of his commanding officer imposed, and his own judgment, under the present appearances, equally recommended. He ordered the legion dragoons to drive in the militia parties who covered the front, that General Morgan's disposition might be conveniently and distinctly inspected. He discovered that the American commander had formed a front line of about one thousand militia, and had composed his second line and reserve of five hundred continental light infantry, one hundred and twenty of Washington's cavalry, and three hundred back woodsmen. This accurate knowledge being obtained, Tarleton desired the British infantry to disencumber themselves of every thing, except their arms and ammunition: the light infantry were then ordered to file to the right till they became equal to the flank of the American front line: the legion infantry were added to their left and, under the fire of 2 three-pounders, this part of the British troops was instructed to advance within three hundred yards of the enemy. This situation being acquired, the seventh regiment was commanded to form upon the left of the legion infantry, and the other three-pounder was given to the right division of the seventh; a captain, with fifty dragoons, was placed on each flank of the corps, who formed the British front line, to protect their own, and threaten the flanks of the enemy; the first battalion of the seventy-first was desired to extend a little to the left of the seventh regiment, and to remain one hundred and fifty yards in the rear. This body of infantry, and near two

---

[64] [*Footnote in the original*] * Ramsay's Hist. Carolin, p. 41, 46.

hundred cavalry, composed the reserve. During the execution of these arrangements, the animation of the officers, and the alacrity of the soldiers, afforded the most promising assurances of success. The disposition being completed, the front line received orders to advance; a fire from some of the recruits of the seventh regiment was suppressed, and the troops moved on in as good a line as troops could move at open files; the militia, after a short contest, were dislodged, and the British approached the continentals. The fire on both sides was well supported, and produced much slaughter; the cavalry on the right were directed to charge the enemy's left; they executed the order with great gallantry, but were drove back by the fire of the reserve, and by a charge of Colonel Washington's cavalry.

"As the contest between the British infantry in the front line and the continentals seemed equally balanced, neither retreating, Lieutenant-Colonel Tarleton thought the advance of the seventy-first into line, and a movement of the cavalry in reserve to threaten the enemy's right flank, would put a victorious period to the action. No time was loll in performing this manœuvre. The seventy-first were desired to pass the seventh before they gave their fire, and were directed not to entangle their right flank with the left of the other battalion. The cavalry were ordered to incline to the left, and to form a line, which would embrace the whole of the enemy's right flank. Upon the advance of the seventy-first all the infantry again moved on; the continentals and back-woodsmen gave ground; the British rushed forwards; an order was dispatched to the cavalry to charge; an unexpected fire at this instant from the Americans, who came about as they were retreating, stopped the British, and threw them into confusion. Exertions to make them advance were useless. The part of the cavalry which had not been engaged fell likewise into disorder, and an unaccountable panic extended itself along the whole; line. The Americans, who before thought they had lost the action, taking advantage of the present situation, advanced upon the British troops, and augmented their astonishment. A general flight ensued. Tarleton sent directions to his cavalry to form about four hundred yards to the right of the enemy, in order to check them, whilst he endeavoured to rally the infantry to protect the guns. The cavalry did not comply with the order, and the effort to collect the infantry was ineffectual; neither promises nor threats could gain their attention; they surrendered or dispersed, and abandoned the guns to the artillery-men, who defended them for some time with exemplary resolution. In this last stage of defeat Lieutenant-Colonel Tarleton made another struggle to bring his cavalry to the. charge. The weight of such an attack might yet retrieve the day, the enemy being much broken by their late rapid advance; but all attempts to restore order, Collection, or courage, proved fruitless. Above two hundred dragoons forsook their leader, and left the field of battle. Fourteen officers and forty horsemen were, however, not unmindful of their own reputation, or the situation of their Commanding officer. Colonel "Washington's cavalry were charged, and driven back into the continental infantry by this handful of brave men. Another party of the Americans, who had seized upon the baggage of the British troops on the road from the late encampment, were dispersed, and this detachment retired towards Broad River unmolested. On the route Tarleton heard, with infinite grief and astonishment, that the main army had not advanced beyond Turkey Creek; he therefore directed his course to the south-east, in order to reach Hamilton's Ford, near the mouth of Bullock's Creek, whence he might communicate with Earl Cornwallis.

"The number of the killed and wounded, in the action at the Cowpens, amounted to near three hundred on both sides, officers and men inclusive: this loss was almost equally shared; but the Americans took two pieces of cannon, the colours of the seventh regiment, and near four hundred prisoners."

To this narrative, which is not deficient in artifice, bur author adds two observations, in which he endeavours to vindicate his own conduct with regard to the unhappy issue of this engagement, and imputes the blame of the overthrow at Cowpens to the total misbehaviour of the troops, and to the failure of Lord Cornwallis in arriving at a concerted point, and weakening the force of the enemy by co-operative movements. But an author, who served in the campaigns 1780 and 1781, and who has written "Strictures on Colonel Tarleton's History," has exposed the futility of his vindication. The opinion of Dr. Ramsay on the event of this engagement is worthy of attention: "Lieutenant-Colonel Tarleton had hitherto acquired distinguished reputation; but he was greatly indebted for his military fame to good fortune and accident. In all his previous engagements he either had the advantage of surprising an incautious enemy; of attacking them when panic-struck after recent defeats; or of being opposed to undisciplined militia. He had gathered no laurels by hard sighting against an equal force; his repulse on this occasion (Cowpens) did more essential injury to the British interest than was compensated by all his victories. Tarleton's defeat was the first link, in a grand chain of causes, which finally drew down ruin, both in North and South-Carolina, on the royal interests."*[65]

Upon the whole, "The History of the Campaigns in America of 1780 and 1781" is written with uncommon spirit and elegance for a temporary production, such as this undoubtedly will prove. But the author is too much the hero of his own tale, and brings his own figure too often into the foreground of the picture. In the history of events so recent and so important, Colonel Tarleton might have reflected that there were many military critics to dispute his pretended merits, and controvert his supposed facts. Both worlds indeed have given their evidence against him; the historians of America, as well as of Britain, contradict his rash narrative, and his unblushing assertions. His attacks on Lord Cornwallis, malignant, though concealed, will fall to the ground. That general was not without defects; but one of the chief of these was his partiality for Colonel Tarleton; a partiality which was, equally offensive to the English and to the loyal Americans.

As the compiler of a quarto volume, our author possesses no small share of discernment. He has republished in his appendix three letters from Lord Rawdon, three letters from General Green, one from Colonel Stuart, one from Colonel Balfour, and another from General Marion, which are well known in this country. The extracts from the *Remembrancer* and the *Annual Register* form also a copious part of this collection; as if the composer had supposed that a great volume necessarily indicates a great author. The style and manner of Julius Cesar in his Commentaries, which is imitated in this production, is amusing at first, but afterwards becomes offensive and disgusting. There is a remarkable difference between a hero and a mere adventurer; and Alexander the Great ought never to be confounded with Alexander, the Coppersmith.

Art. II. *Strictures on Lieutenant-Colonel, Tarleton's "History of the Campaigns of 1780 and 1781 in the Southern Provinces of North-America." Wherein military Characters and Corps are vindicated from injurious Aspersions, and several important Transactions placed in their proper Point of View, in a Series of Letters to a Friend. By Roderick Mackenzie, late Lieutenant in the Seventy-first Regiment. To which if added, a Detail of the Siege of Ninety Six, and the Recapture of the Island of New-Providence.* 8vo. As. boards. Faulder, London, 1787.

FRANCISCO Lopez de Gomara, the domestic chaplain of Cortez, published in 1554 a Chronicle of New Spain, the chief object of which was to celebrate the exploits, and magnify the merits, of his patron. When Bernal Diaz del Castillo found, on the perusal of the work, that neither he himself nor many of his fellow-soldiers were once mentioned, by Gomara, but that the fame of all their exploits was ascribed to Cortez, the gallant veteran laid hold of his pen with indignation, and, composed his true history of the conquest of New Spain, in which he does justice to himself and his brave associates. Although he possesses no remarkable skill in composition, and writes more like a soldier than a scholar, yet, as he relates transactions of which he was a witness, and in which he performed a considerable part, his accounts bear all the mark? of authenticity, and are accompanied with such a pleasant: *naivete*, and such interesting details, as render his book one of the most singular and curious that is to be found in any language. In like manner Mr. Mackenzie, (the author of the work before us) who served in Lord Cornwallis's army, and was wounded as the battle of Cowpens, struck with the many errors and misrepresentations contained in Tarleton's history, has seized the pen of retribution, and, with a manly spirit of truth, has detected the fallacy of the vain-glorious journalist, vindicated the injured honour pf his countrymen, and rendered justice to some of the first characters in the British army. Colonel Tarleton's memoirs have been read with an avidity proportionate to the ideas once formed of his military talents; and, as the public has been deceived by consummate artifice, it became necessary to detect the sophistry which produced the deception. After having exposed Colonel Tarleton's erroneous statement of the consequences which resulted from the successful defence of Savannah, Mr. Mackenzie attacks him in one of the leading principles of his book:

"It is generally admitted, that the love of fame is, or ought to be, the ruling passion of every soldier; and perhaps it has, in a greater or less degree, had a manifest influence in impelling this order of men to glorious actions, from a Leonidas at Thermopylæ to our immortal Wolfe at the Heights of Abraham.

---

[65] [*Footnote in the original*] * Ramsay's Hist. Carolin, Vol. II, p. 200.

Of this the Corsican chief Paoli, when defending his native island from the attacks of a mercenary republic, appeared truly sensible: 'He devised an excellent method of promoting bravery among his countrymen. He wrote a circular letter to the priests of every parish in the island, desiring a list to be made out of all those who had fallen in battle. No institution was better contrived; it might be adopted by every nation, as it would give double courage to soldiers, who would have their fame preserved, and at the same time leave to their relatives the valuable legacy of a claim to the kindness of the state.' In addition to this first principle, it certainly affords a melancholy satisfaction to find in the page of history that justice is done to the memory of the dead; it mingles sympathy with the tears of the widow and orphan; it may encourage future soldiers to emulate the actions of their predecessors, whose lives may have been sacrificed in the service of their country it also gives to the relations of these brave men that claim to the kindness of the state which the Corsican historian, has described. Liberal minds only are influenced by these exalted maxims. But let us consider the light in which they have been viewed by the journalist of the Southern American campaigns."

These observations do equal honour to the understanding and the heart of our author. But what has been the conduct: of Colonel Tarleton as a historian? Dazzled with his own merit, and having his attention entirely absorbed with his own exploits, he endeavours to cast a shade over those of others. He has passed over in silence some of the most distinguished examples of bravery in the campaigns which he records, and has not even mentioned the glorious death of many gallant officers who fell in the cause of their country. He has been equally indifferent to the fate of many American loyalists; men of incorruptible integrity and undaunted valour, who sacrificed their private interest to public good; and who, though they knew that the peace of their families was destroyed by the ravages of war, fought and bled with manly spirit, and maintained their allegiance to their latest moments.

No charge of omission, however, can be brought against him in relating his own achievements, and the adventures of his corps. Every horse that sickened or died makes a figure in his journal. In p. 17 we find "five *horses* killed and wounded." Page 20, "the British dragoons lost two men and four *horses*; and the same evening twenty horses expired with fatigue." Page 30, "thirty-one *horses* killed and wounded." Page 115, "twenty *horses* were killed and wounded." Page 180, "with thirty *horses* killed and three men wounded, and a few horses.'

An author bestowing a superior attention to the wounds and death of horses belonging to his own corps to the fall of OFFICERS of equal or superior merit to himself, presents us with the idea of a Yahoo writing the history of the Houyhnhnms.

The errors which Colonel Tarleton committed at the unfortunate engagement at Cowpens, and which seem to decide his *military* character, are judiciously pointed out by Mr. Mackenzie:

"The first error in judgment to be imputed to Lieutenant-Colonel Tarleton, on the morning of the 17th of January 1781, is, the not halting his troops before he engaged the enemy. Had he done so, it was evident that the following advantages would have been the result of his conduit: General Morgan's force and situation might have been distinctly viewed under cover of a very superior cavalry; the British infantry, fatigued with rapid marches, day and night, for some time past, as has been already observed, might have had rest and refreshment; a detachment from the several corps left with the baggage, together with battmen and officers servants, would have had time to come up and join in the action. The artillery all this time might have been playing upon the enemy's front, or either flank, without risk or insult; the commandants of regiments, Majors M'Arthur and Newmarsh, officers who held commissions long before our author was born, and who had reputations to this day unimpeached, might have been consulted; and, not to dwell on the enumeration of all the advantages which would have accrued from so judicious a delay, time would have been given for the approach of Earl Cornwallis to the preconcerted point, for the attainment of which he has been so much and so unjustly censured.

"The second error was, the unofficer-like impetuosity of directing the line to advance before it was properly formed, and before the reserve had taken its ground; in consequence of which, as might have been expected, the attack was premature, confused, and irregular.

"The third error in this ruinous business was, the omission of giving discretional powers to that judicious veteran M'Arthur to advance with the reserve at the time that the front line was in pursuit of the militia, by which means the connection, so necessary to troops engaged in the field, was not preserved.

"'His fourth error was, ordering Captain Ogilvie, with a troop consisting of no more than forty men, to charge before any impression was made on the continentals, and before Washington's cavalry had been engaged.

"The next, and the most destructive, for I will not pretend to follow him through all his errors, was in not bringing up a column of cavalry, and completing the route, which, by his own acknowledgement, had commenced through the whole American infantry."

Upon the whole, these "Strictures" are in the true spirit of military criticism. Mr. Mackenzie has drawn his pen, as he did his sword, for the honour of his country, and has vindicated eminent names that had been injured by misrepresentation. To render justice to great characters that have suffered from obloquy or detraction, is to partake of their glory; to rescue honourable achievements from oblivion, and place them in the fairest light, is next to the praise of performing them.

Our author modestly apologizes for his style, and inform the reader that he is not to expect elegant or polished diction. Plain observations, deduced from such stubborn facts as impress the mind with conviction, stand in need of no rhetorical ornaments. But in truth his composition requires no apology; and, notwithstanding some incorrect expressions, is manly, nervous, and animated. It possesses beauties which rhetoric cannot confer, the noble plainness of amiable sincerity,-and the honest warmth of undissembled probity.

To these Strictures are subjoined "A Detail of the Siege of Ninety-Six, and an Account of the Recapture of New Providence;" in which there is much curious and important information.

THE WOEFUL FATES OF THE CAVALRY

Light horsemen have traditionally acted as the eyes and ears of an army; it being among their duties and tasks to safe-guard and protect the forces to which they were attached from being snuck up on or taken unawares. It is no little remarkable then to learn that the cavalry of the Continental army itself had a somewhat embarrassing, and in some instances tragic record, even to the point of two outright (at least in result if not in premeditated intention) massacres, for being caught by surprise; demonstrating in an indirect yet most graphic manner the adage (mistakenly ascribed to Edmund Burke) that "the price of liberty is eternal vigilance." We witness this undoing of the American horsemen in the following actions:

* Sept. 28, 1778: Baylor's Massacre or Old Tappan (presently "Vale"), N.J.
Beware of a general whom others call "No flint" Grey; who in September by preconcerted ruse and subterfuge surprised Baylor's 3rd Continental Light Dragoons, catching the men asleep, and bayoneting and otherwise slaying most all of them -- some in their beds![66]

* Oct. 4-5, 1778 (also given in some sources mistakenly as 15 Oct.): Little Egg Harbor, or Little Neck, or Mincock, Isld., N.J.
In an amphibious night attack carried out against them, an entire infantry company of Pulaski's Legion was summarily slaughtered -- with fifty men admitted by the British themselves to have been killed -- after being caught off guard by a combined battalion of 250-300 of the 70th Regt. and New Jersey Volunteers, led by Capt. Patrick Ferguson (of the N.J. Vol. and *not* P.F. of King's Mountain.) Pulaski did, even so, later arrive in time with his cavalry and some additional Pulaski's Legion infantry to force Ferguson's retreat and inflict some losses on the British. (See Ward p. 617 and Boatner, 3rd ed., p. 638.)

* July 2, 1779: Pound Ridge, N.Y.
Although Sheldon's Connecticut light horse (i.e., the 2nd Continental Light Dragoons) had enough advance notice to evade the wily Tarleton; they are ignominiously lifted of some gear and equipment, including their standard, and which was with fanfare re-introduced to the world upon its auction by Tarleton's heirs only a few years ago. And it may, arguably, have been owing to the foreknowledge of Providence that spared the unit from the much and far worse that had befallen Baylor's and Pulaski's corps.

* April 13, 1780: Monck's Corner, S.C.
Bland's (the 1st CLD) and Baylor's Corps, this time under Colonels Anthony Walton White and William Washington respectively, as a result of some poor placement of night pickets, are among those routed by a raid carried on at Monck's Corner by Ferguson, Tarleton and the 17th Light Dragoons; the American cavalry alone incurring upwards of 30 cavalrymen killed and 70 taken prisoner; plus the loss of 83 dragoon horses.

* May 6, 1780: Lenud's Ferry, S.C.
Deaf to William Washington's earnest remonstrances to continue the crossing of the Santee with their remaining men, Anthony Walton White opted for a rest, and in a matter of time, without warning, was overcome by Tarleton on a forced march. What Americans weren't captured were compelled to swim the great river to escape.

Although no unit of British army dragoons was ever ambushed during the war, there were at least two notable instances where Provincial cavalry were.

* July 12, 1780: Huck's Defeat or Williamson's Plantation, S.C.
Partisan colonels Richard Winn and Edward Lacey surround a British Legion detachment under Capt. Christian Huik and kill or capture most of them, including Huik himself who is felled by musket and rifle balls.

---

[66] For an at length examination of this affair, see http://www.bergencountyhistory.org/Pages/baylormassacre.html ; with as well William Maurer's *Dragoon Diary: The History of the Third Continental Light Dragoons*, and "A Tale of Two Tappans: Desertion, Evasion, and Ill Will" by Todd Braisted in *Patriots of the Revolution Magazine*, May-June 2012, vol. 5, iss. 3.

* July 3, 1781: Armstrong's Capture or Congaree Creek, S.C.
A contingent of Lee's Legion cavalry under Capt. James Armstrong lays a trap and succeeds in taking prisoner some 47 (ostensibly) South Carolina Royalist cavalry, including 2 officers, that had been out foraging.

Aside from the incident at the Spread Eagle tavern in Philadelphia (20 Jan. 1778), but from which they actually emerged victorious, Lee's Legion itself was never found disconcerted, and lost very few men from ambushes in the course of the war (instances in which they did occurred in 1782 in South Carolina); for their commander understood well the importance of constant readiness and continual intelligence. Marion, of course, was among the greatest of all at eluding surprise, and what he knew about forestalling raids and staving off ambuscades he reportedly picked up from Indian fighting; and that is to punctually change one's camp location as frequently as possible; while making sure to constantly keep on disciplined watch *alert* and active sentinels.

"JAMES B. COOPER, A Hero of Two Wars Soldier in Revolutionary War; Sailor in War of 1812"

Although we don't customarily associate Lee's Legion with the Navy, one of it's members, James B. Cooper (1761-1854), from New Jersey, actually went on after the war to serve as an officer in that branch of the armed services, and even commanded some gunboats off the New Jersey coast during the War of 1812. Below is an unusual and interesting little sketch of Cooper's life by Wallace McGeorge, M. D.; as entered in *Notes On Old Gloucester County, New Jersey* (1917), compiled and edited by Frank H. Stewart, pp. 132-138:

~~~***~~~

James B. Cooper, or plain James Cooper as his name appears on the muster roll of the first troop, Lee's Legion, Continental Troops, Revolutionary War, was born at Cooper's Point, Camden, N. J., in 1761, and enlisted February 1, 1779, for three years.

In the archives of the Bureau of Pensions, it is recorded that "James B. Cooper enlisted in the Continental Line, and served to the end of the Revolutionary War, at which period he was a private in James Armstrong's First Troop of Colonel Lee's Partisans, Legion of Light Dragoons."

Lee's Legion was originally composed of Virginians, but while it was serving in the vicinity of Camden and Haddonfield, one hundred Jerseymen were enlisted and mustered into the Legion, two of whom, James B. Cooper and John Mapes, died in Haddonfield.

The commander of this Partisan Legion was Henry Lee, of Virginia. He entered the service in 1776, at the command of a company of Virginia volunteers, and had distinguished himself in scouting parties, and harrassing the enemy's pickets. His adventurous exploits soon won for him the popular appellation of "Light Horse Harry."

Environment had much to do with James Cooper's enlistment. Born a Friend [i.e. a Quaker], reared under Friends' influence, opposed to war and bloodshed, he was subject to many temptations to forego those principles of peace which had been instilled into him from early childhood.

Living at Cooper's Point, in Camden, N. J., directly opposite Philadelphia, where American or British soldiers were constantly to be seen, his father's house occupied either by the Continental or British forces all the earlier, it is no wonder that despite the commands of his father and the earnest and loving solicitations of his mother, he forsook the principles of Friends, choosing rather to serve his country as a soldier than to continue neutral and passive during the struggle for freedom. Although only a stripling in his eighteenth year, he ran away from home, enlisted and became a Dragoon.

Early in the summer, Lee's Legion was ordered to the northern part of this State and the river counties in New York, and in July, 1779, as a volunteer, he took part in the storming and capture of Stony Point, by Mad Anthony Wayne.

General Wayne was the officer picked out by Washington for this daring work, and he readily assented. It is a popular tradition that when Washington proposed to Wayne the storming of Stony Point, the reply was : "General, I'll storm hell, if you will only plan it." To which Washington is said to have replied, "Suppose you try Stony Point first."

One of the engagements in our State in which Lee's Legion was victorious was the capture of Paulus Hook, in what is now Jersey City. Major Lee in his scoutings had discovered that the British post at Paulus Hook, immediately opposite New York, was very negligently guarded. Paulus Hook at that time was a long, low point of the Jersey shore stretching into the Hudson, and connected to the mainland by a sandy isthmus. A fort had been erected on it, and it was garrisoned with five hundred men under Major
~~~

Sutherland. It was a strong position. A creek fordable only in two places rendered the Hook difficult of access. Lee had discovered these features, and he had proposed to Washington the daring plan of surprising the fort at night. The commander-in-chief was pleased with the project and consented to it, stipulating that Lee was to "surprise the post, bring off the garrison immediately and effect a retreat."

On August 18, 1779, Lee set out with three hundred of Lord Stirling's division and a troop of dismounted dragoons. Between two and three o'clock, on the morning of August 19, Lee arrived at the creek. It happened fortunately that the British commanders had the day before dispatched a foraging party to a part of the country called the English Neighborhood, and as Lee and his men approached they were mistaken by the sentinel for this party on its return. The darkness of the night favored the mistake, and our troops passed the creek and ditch, entered the works unmolested and had made themselves masters of the post before the garrison was well roused from sleep. Major Sutherland and about sixty Hessians threw themselves into a, small block house on the left of the fort and opened an irregular fire. To attempt to dislodge them would have cost too much time. Alarm guns from ships in the harbor, and the forts at New York, threatened speedy reinforcements to the enemy. Having captured one hundred and fifty-nine prisoners, Lee returned without trying to destroy either the barracks or artillery. He had achieved his object, a coup-de-main of signal audacity. Few of the enemy were slain for there was but little fighting and no massacre. His own loss was two men killed and three wounded. James Cooper was one of the dismounted dragoons. A beautiful monument in Jersey City marks the spot where this struggle occurred.

In 1781 General Washington removed General Gates from the command of the Southern army, and appointed General Nathaniel Greene in his place. "Light Horse Harry" with his legion were transferred from the Northern army and sent south to aid Greene in his arduous task and for the rest of the war the Legion was engaged in the wresting of the Southern States from the British army. Private Cooper took part in the battles of Guilford Court House and Eutaw Springs.

In the battle of Eutaw Springs, which was fought on September 8, 1781, Lee's Legion was assigned to the duty of covering the right flank, and Armstrong's troops, in which Cooper served, led the advance.

As the English retreated next day after destroying many of their stores the victory was considered to be ours. The American loss was very heavy in this prolonged battle and this may have been the place to which Captain Cooper referred when he told his friend John Redfield, of Gloucester, that he stood in the battle when every third man was killed.

During the entire Revolutionary War, Congress only voted six gold medals for bravery in action, and three of those were to General Wayne, for his storming of Stony Point; to Light Horse Harry for his surprise of Paulus Hook, and to General Greene for his victory at Eutaw Springs, and in each of these three engagements Private Cooper was one of the men who helped to win. Which only proves the statement that when a Quaker does fight, he fights well. What other private or officer had a better record in the entire war?

Prowell's History of Camden County says Cooper assisted in the storming of Forts Mott[e], Granby and Watson, all of which surrendered to Light Horse Harry. Private Cooper was once sent with dispatches to General Washington, and on another occasion with a flag of truce to the British commander, showing the esteem in which he was held by his leader.

After the Revolutionary War was over James B. Cooper adopted a seafaring life, and rose to the command of some fine ships sailing from Philadelphia.

In 1805 he organized a company of cavalry from the young men of Haddonfield and Woodbury, and was elected its captain. It was from this circumstance that Cooper got his title of Captain.

In the War of 1812 Cooper accepted the position of sailing master in the navy, and was in charge of the gun boats on the New Jersey coast, to guard against the depredations of the British cruisers. This was a dangerous task, for his vessel was inferior in guns, and it was his duty when he discovered the foe, by his superiority in sailing, to notify the American frigates so they could meet the enemy.

Through the Bureau of Navigation at Washington, I have been enabled to secure the following data as to Commander Cooper's services in the United States Navy:

1812, July 9. Warranted a sailing master in the Navy this date. Appointed from New Jersey.
1815, May 26. Promoted to Acting Lieutenant.
1816, Aug. 9. Ordered to report to Commodore Murray for duty.
1822, Jan. 10. Ordered to Philadelphia on duty.
1822, April 22. Promoted to Lieutenant from this date, and ordered to report for duty at Baltimore.
1832, July 5. Ordered to the Navy Yard, at New York.
1832, Nov. 5. Detached from the Navy Yard, New York, and granted two months' leave of absence.
1834, May 2. Appointed to the Naval Asylum, Philadelphia.
1838, Aug. 13. Granted three-months' leave, which was renewed Nov. 16, 1838; Feb. 22, 1839; May, 1839.
1839-1840-1841. He was granted six months' leave of absence continuously till September 8, 1841, when he was promoted to Commander from this date.
1854, Feb. 5. Died this day at Haddonfield, New Jersey.

On July 5, 1828, nearly fifty years after his enlistment in the Continental army, a pension was allowed him. After his retirement from the command of the Naval Asylum at Philadelphia, he returned to his home in Haddonfield, where he spent the remainder of his days. Captain James B. Cooper was the last survivor of Lee's Legion, dying seventy-five years and four days after he was mustered into the service of his country -- in his ninety-third year. In his death, as in his life, he was unfortunately the cause of the animadversion of Friends [i.e., the Quakers]. Having a son who was an Admiral in the Navy, and on account of his military and naval service in two wars, he was buried with military honors. Soldiers and sailors took part, the Naval Reserves coming from Philadelphia for this purpose. Here, again, there was a conflict between Church and State, or between principles and affection. The soldiers and sailors followed his remains on foot to the Friends' Meeting House Burying Ground, in Haddonfield, and fired a salute over his grave, to the horror of many Friends. What with flags flying and guns firing, it was a sorry day for many rigid orthodox Quakers. Even in his family there was a divided feeling. The widow, proud of her departed hero, acquiesced in the desire of his military and naval friends, and followed his remains to the grave in this military parade, while the widow's sister was so horrified at this vain pomp that she stayed at home, and would not even look upon this wicked show. Many young Friends and the world's people enjoyed this unusual spectacle as a mark of respect to this grand old man, and a grand-daughter, who was then only a little child, said she liked to see the soldiers and the flags, and thought it was just the thing. No stone marks the grave of this grand old man.

A SEA FIGHT TO REMEMBER: *The Randolph vs. The Yarmouth*

The son of a Philadelphia banker, Captain Nicholas Biddle has been described as one the finest sea captains the nascent U.S. Navy produced: perhaps matched only by John Paul Jones and Joshua Barney for both wits and rarely-equaled intrepidity. Prior to the Revolutionary War, he actually schooled and served in the Royal Navy as a midshipman alongside Horatio Nelson. When troubles began brewing to a heated pitch with the Mother country, however, Biddle resigned his commission, and later went on to officer ships of the Pennsylvania, and afterward Continental Navy.

On the moonlit night of March 7, 1778, his 36 gun frigate the U.S.S. *Randolph* -- armed mostly with 18 pounders; plus a flotilla of four smaller S.C. Navy ships not engaged -- encountered the H.M.S. *Yarmouth* of 64 guns (mostly 32 and some 42 pounders) east off Barbadoes. Writes James Fenimore Cooper in his *History of the Navy of the United States of America* (1839) that notwithstanding the marked superiority of his British foe: "we find it difficult, under the circumstances, to suppose that this gallant seaman [Biddle] did not actually contemplate carrying his powerful antagonist, most probably by boarding" (pp. 66-67, 1856 ed.)

Captain William Hall of the South Carolina sloop *Notre Dame*, 16 guns, who was a witness reported that the *Randolph* beat up on the *Yarmouth* "so roughly for 12 or 15 minutes [out of some 20 minutes in all after contact] that the British ship must shortly have struck, having lost her bowsprit and topmasts and being otherwise greatly shattered, while the Randolph had suffered very little; but in this moment of glory, as the Randolph was wearing to get on her quarter, she unfortunately blew up." ~ *Independent Chronicle*, August 13, 1778.

Yet the most detailed and full contemporary account of what occurred comes from the letter of Captain Nicholas Vincent, of the *Yarmouth*, to his superior Admiral Young, written on March 17th:

"On the 7th instant at half past five P.M. discovered six sail in the S.W. quarter, on a wind standing to the northward; two of them ships, three brigs and a schooner. We were then 50 leagues due east of this island. We immediately bore down upon them and about nine got close to the weather quarter of the largest and headmost ship. They had no colours hoisted and as ours were then up, I hailed her to hoist hers or I would fire into her; on which she hoisted American and immediately gave us her broadside, which we returned, and in about a quarter of an hour she blew up.

"It was fortunate for us that we were to windward of her; as it was, our ship was in a manner covered with parts of her. A great piece of a top timber, six feet long, fell on our poop; another large piece of timber stuck in our fore top-gallant sail, then upon the cap. An American ensign, rolled up, blown in upon the forecastle, not so much as singed.

"Immediately on her blowing up, the other four dispersed different ways. We chased a little while two that stood to the southward and afterwards another that bore away right before the wind, but they were soon out of sight, our sails being torn all to pieces in a most surprising manner. We had five men killed and twelve wounded.

"But what I am now going to mention is something very remarkable. The 12th following, being then in chase of a ship steering west, we discovered a piece of wreck with four men on it waving; we hauled up to it, got a boat out, and brought them on board. They proved to be four men who had been in the ship which blew up and who had nothing to subsist on from that time but by sucking the rain water that fell on a piece of blanket which they luckily had picked up."

~ *London Chronicle*, May 26,1778; Almon's *Remembrancer*, vi, 143; Brit. Adm. Rec., Captain's Logs, No. 1091 (log of the *Yarmouth*); Port Folio, October, 1809.

What must have been the thoughts, one wonders, of the four survivors -- out of a 315 man crew and which included a detachment of the 1st South Carolina regiment, under Capt. Joseph Joor, acting as

Marines -- after going through such an event; and which was the greatest loss of life in a single U.S. Navy ship up until Pearl Harbor.[67]

ON THE DEATH OF CAPTAIN NICHOLAS BIDDLE
Commander of the Randolph Frigate, Blown up near Barbadoes, 1776 (1781)

By Philip Freneau

What distant thunders rend the skies,
What clouds of smoke in columns rise,
What means this dreadful roar?
Is from his base Vesuvius thrown,
Is sky-topt Atlas tumbled down,
Or Etna's self no more!

Shock after shock torments my ear;
And lo!—two hostile ships appear,
Red lightnings round them glow:
The *Yarmouth* boasts of sixty-four,
The *Randolph* thirty-two—no more—
And will she fight this foe!

The *Randolph* soon on Stygian streams
Shall coast along the land of dreams,
The islands of the dead!
But Fate, that parts them on the deep,
May save the Briton yet to weep
His days of victory fled.

Say, who commands that dismal blaze,
Where yonder starry streamer plays?
Does Mars with Jove engage!
'Tis Biddle wings those angry fires,
Biddle, whose bosom Jove inspires,
With more than mortal rage.

Tremendous flash!—and hark, the ball
Drives through old *Yarmouth*, flames and all;
Her bravest sons expire;
Did Mars himself approach so nigh,
Even Mars, without disgrace, might fly
The *Randolph's* fiercer fire.

---

[67] With respect to the general subject of instances where defeat was snatched from the jaws of victory -- arguably due to a bizarre and unforseeable "act of god" -- there is, in again the annals of the Navy, the case of the U.S.S. frigate *Essex* versus the H.M.S. frigate *Phoebe* and the brig H.M.S. *C herub* that took place Mar. 28, 1814; in the Pacific Ocean just off Valparaiso, Chile. There Capt. David Porter, commanding the *Essex,* lost the main topmast owing to a sudden squall just when he was clear to make his escape from the two British vessels which had been sent in those far off waters to go after him, and which unforeseeable accident effectively caused the *Essex* to lie a sitting duck in the water. The story of that most dramatic engagement, and unusual circumstances leading up to, is the basis of the Patrick O'Brien's *The Far Side of the World* (later made into the film "Master and Commander" [2003]), and which, telling the story from the British viewpoint, has the *Essex* as a French ship. Porter's own frequently gripping narrative of his most enterprising and, but for his strange final undoing, *nearly* successful voyage is recounted in his memorable *Journal of a Cruise made to the Pacific Ocean by Captain David Porter, in the United States Frigate Essex, in the Years 1812, 1813, and 1814* (1815).*Note.* I use the title "U.S.S." retroactively when such designation was not formally adopted by United States Navy ships until 1907.

The Briton views his mangled crew,
"And shall we strike to thirty-two?—
(Said Hector, stained with gore)
"Shall Britain's flag to these descend—
"Rise, and the glorious conflict end,
"Britons, I ask no more!"

He spoke—they charged their cannon round,
Again the vaulted heavens resound,
The Randolph bore it all,
Then fixed her pointed cannons true—
Away the unwieldy vengeance flew;
Britain, thy warriors fall.

The *Yarmouth* saw, with dire dismay,
Her wounded hull, shrouds shot away,
Her boldest heroes dead—
She saw amidst her floating slain
The conquering *Randolph* stem the main—
She saw, she turned—and fled!

That hour, blest chief, had she been thine,
Dear Biddle, had the powers divine
Been kind as thou wert brave;
But Fate, who doomed thee to expire,
Prepared an arrow, tipt with fire,
And marked a watery grave.

And in that hour, when conquest came,
Winged at his ship a pointed flame,
That not even he could shun—
The battle ceased, the *Yarmouth* fled,
The bursting *Randolph* ruin spread,
And left her task undone!

EL LIBERATOR.

"My religious and filial devotion to General Washington could not be better recognized by his family than by [their] honoring me with the commission they have entrusted to me [i.e. sending Bolivar a portrait of Washington along with a lock of the latter's hair]...Of all men living, and even of all men in history, Bolivar is the very one to whom my paternal friend would have preferred to send this present. What else can I say to the great citizen whom South America has honored with the name of Liberator, confirmed in him by two worlds, a man endowed with an influence equal to his self-denial, who carries in his heart the sole love of freedom and of the republic?"
~ Lafayette in a letter to Bolivar, dated 13 Oct. 1825.

While Simon Bolivar (1783-1830) has been referred to as South America's George Washington, he could also be reasonably likened to Napoleon, James Madison, Francis Marion, and Abraham Lincoln! And a student who prides himself on our own American Revolution without some rudimentary knowledge of Bolivar's feats and achievements[68] risks making himself look quite foolish.

In addition to being a dogged and, usually, victorious military leader and strategist, Bolivar was an extraordinary intellect and well-read thinker. And if the only legacy he'd left us were his writings, both those penned by himself and those dictated to secretaries, he would still deserve to be famous internationally for these alone. Those not already acquainted with them will not fail to be impressed by the broad scope and depth of his scholarship, his fervid passion for freedom and improving the lot of the South American peoples, his learned insights on government, and the literary eloquence with which he expresses himself.

Here's a sample of what I mean by way of an excerpt from his Address to the Congress of Angostura, Feb. 15, 1819:

"The people of America having been held under the triple yoke of ignorance, tyranny and vice, have not been in a position to acquire either knowledge, power or virtue. Disciples of such pernicious masters, the lessons we have received and the examples we have studied, are most destructive. We have been governed more by deception than by force, and we have been degraded more by vice than by superstition. Slavery is the offspring of Darkness; an ignorant people is a blind tool, turned to its own destruction; ambition and intrigue exploit the credulity and inexperience of men foreign to all political, economical or civil knowledge; mere illusions are accepted as reality, license is taken for liberty, treachery for patriotism, revenge for justice. Even as a sturdy blind man who, relying on the feeling of his own strength, walks along with the assurance of the most wide awake man and, striking against all kinds of obstacles, can not steady his steps.

"A perverted people, should it attain its liberty, is bound to lose this very soon, because it would be useless to try to impress upon such people that happiness lies in the practice of righteousness; that the reign of law is more powerful than the reign of tyrants, who are more inflexible, and all ought to submit to the wholesome severity of the law; that good morals, and not force, are the pillars of the law and that the exercise of justice is the exercise of liberty. Thus, Legislators, your task is the more laborious because you are to deal with men misled by the illusions of error, and by civil incentives. Liberty, says Rousseau, is a succulent food, but difficult to digest. Our feeble fellow-citizens will have to strengthen their mind much before they will be ready to assimilate such wholesome nourishment. Their limbs made numb by their fetters, their eyesight weakened in the darkness of their dungeons and their forces wasted away through their foul servitude, will they be capable of inarching with a firm step towards the august temple of Liberty? Will they be capable of coming close to it, and admiring the light it sheds, and of breathing freely its pure air?

"Consider well your decision. Legislators. Do not forget that you are about to lay the foundations of a new people, which may some day rise to the heights that Nature has marked out for it, provided you

[68] Or for that matter those of Bolivar's predecessor Toussaint Louveture.

make those foundations proportionate to the lofty place which that people is to fill. If your selection be not made under the guidance of the Guardian Angel of Venezuela, who must inspire you with wisdom to choose the nature and form of government that you choose to adopt for the welfare of the people; if you should fail in this, I warn you, the end of our venture would be slavery.

"The annals of past ages display before you thousands of governments. Recall to mind the nations which have shone most highly on the earth and you will be grieved to see that almost the entire world has been, and still is, a victim of bad government. You will find many systems of governing men, but all are calculated to oppress them, and if the habit of seeing the human race, led by shepherds of peoples, did not dull the horror of such a revolting sight, we would be astonished to see our social species grazing on the surface of the globe, even as lowly herds destined to feed their cruel drivers.

"Nature, in truth, endows us at birth with the instinctive desire for liberty; but whether because of negligence, or because of an inclination inherent in humanity, it remains still under the bonds imposed on it. And as we see it in such a state of debasement we seem to have reason to be persuaded that the majority of men hold as a truth the humiliating principle that it is harder to maintain the balance of liberty than to endure the weight of tyranny. Would to God that this principle, contrary to the morals of Nature, were false! Would to God that this principle were not sanctioned by the indolence of man as regards his most sacred rights!"

~~~***~~~

With respect to his military career, Bolivar knew defeat as well as victory, and the troops of his Royal Spanish opponents were often capable as fighting as well or better than his own men, and most of the time he was heavily, sometimes absurdly, outnumbered. How then did he achieve ultimate victory? By having a iron-willed resolve, boldness, genius for leadership; a superior grasp of guerilla warfare, and a resilient steadfastness of purpose all of which his adversaries, generally, lacked. Moreover, he had lieutenants and allies, such as Paez, Sucre, and San Martin, no less lions in the field than himself.[69] It is instructive to observe that in the latter part of the South American Wars for independence that he was assisted by British veterans of the Peninsula War, up to a reported 6,000; who served in his army as volunteers and mercenaries. Ironically, the same Spanish Bolivar combated as foes had fought alongside the U.S. versus the British during the American Revolution; while the Peninsula War veterans themselves had, under Wellington, been with Spain against the French. To perhaps confuse matters further, in 1806-07 the British, in a fairly large scale invasion of Argentina, had attempted, to wrest that country from Spain (which was then allied with Napoleonic France) only to be defeated by a gallant and determined band of indigenous Argentines (without help from any Spanish troops) under Gen. Santiago de Liniers.

If, as is inevitably pointed out, Bolivar was by the end of his life disappointed in his political vision and goal for South America, this may be much *more* attributed to the exceedingly ambitious, and impractical grandeur of what he set out to do -- and *all at once* no less -- than, as he himself came to supposing, to cravenness and ineptitude on the part of the Latin American people of that time.

[69] Indeed, some experts praise San Martin as being a markedly superior general compared to Bolviar. For a summary overview and sketch of Bolivar's military activity, see: http://www.militaryheritage.com/bolivar.htm
~~~

CHARGE!!!

We don't ordinarily view the Revolutionary War as a contest involving formal, battlefield cavalry charges (as opposed to run on skirmishes and ambuscades involving swordsmen on horseback), yet there were actually several, and even as few and small in size as these were, say compared the Seven Years, French Revolutionary, or Napoleonic wars, a number of them were so decisive that at least one, namely that by the Virginia dragoons and South Carolina/Georgia partisans at Cowpens, could be said to have decided the fate of the war. This thought prompted me then to attempt to compile a list of mutually head-on confrontations where the dread command was given; with the below being the result of my readings, inquiries, and or reminders furnished by our internet community of historians.

Cavalry Charges by the British:

* White Plains, 28 Oct. 1776. Two hundred 17th Light Dragoons cause the precipitous rout of a large contingent of rebel militia; though are forestalled by reinforcing Continentals from turning it into a sanguine debacle.
* Waxhaws, 29 May 1780.
* Camden, 16 Aug. 1780. Tarleton's horsemen deliver the finalizing *coup de main* to Cornwallis' victory.
* Cowpens, 17 Jan. 1781. The ambushed and disconcerted assault on the flying militia by the 17th Regt. of Light Horse.
* Guilford Courthouse, 15 March 1781. Tarleton successfully essays Campbell's riflemen in the latter part of that engagement.
* Spencer's Ordinary, 26 June 1781. Simcoe's Queen's Rangers are succored by the surprise appearance of a troop of British Legion, under Capt. Ogelvey, and which disorders the Am. flank.
* Gloucester Point, 3 Oct. 1781. British counter the charge initiated by Duc de Lauzun's Volontaires Étrangers.

***By the Americans*:**
* Stono Ferry, 20 June 1779. Pulaski's Legion (though the Count himself was not present at the battle) check the advancing British with a gallant charge, thus permittting a safe American withdrawal.
* Cowpens, 17 Jan. 1781.
* Road from New Garden Meeting House, 15 March 1781. Tarleton himself describes the charge by Lee's Legion there as "spirited."
* Guilford Court House, 15 March 1781. William Washington's cavalry sends the British guards reeling.
* Hobkirk's Hill, 25 April 1781. Col. William Washington charges and routs the loyalist cavalry under Maj. John Coffin; thereby saving Gen. Greene's artillery from imminent capture.
* Quinby Bridge, 17 July 1781. A detachment of Lee's Legion cavalry under Capt. James Armstrong, and supported by some of Francis Marion's men, gallop precipitately over rickety Quinby Bridge; just in time to prevent it from being dismantled.
* Gloucester Point, 3 Oct. 1781. Lauzun's Legion spur forward, with pistols flashing, at the prone and ready Tarleton.

THE HOUSE OF NIGHT (1779, revised 1786)

A Vision

By Philip Freneau.

The son of a prosperous wine merchant of French extraction and a Scotch mother, Philip Freneau (1752-1832) graduated from Princeton, alongside fellows James Madison and Hugh Henry Brackenridge, with the class of 1771. It had originally been intended that he become a clergyman, but, caught up in the political and philosophical fervor of his times, he instead ended up turning to literary pursuits. After a few years working various jobs, including tutor on Long Island, and later some failed attempts at securing employment as a writer while in Maryland and Philadelphia, he set sail for the island of Santa Cruz in the West Indies in late Autumn of 1775. Why he left the country when it was just embarked upon that very struggle which he later, and with such passion and fervor, wrote on behalf of is a bit of a mystery.[70] In any event, while in Santa Cruz Freneau resided at the estate of a Captain Hansen, and having in the interim acquired some skill at both navigation and mastering a vessel, was occasionally hired by Hansen for purposes of making short voyages and running local errands by ship. In addition, he also spent some time composing verse, and it was while on the island he wrote three of his most original and creative poetical works: "Santa Cruz," "The Jamaica Funeral," and "The House of Night" -- the last perhaps having been first worked on as early as 1775. Finally returning to the United States in June 1779, he reunited in Philadelphia with his old comrade and classmate Brackenridge; who at the time was publishing the short-lived, yet revolutionary in its own right, *United States Magazine*, and to which Freneau became a contributor. It was in this periodical that same year, in August, that his "House of Night" first appeared, and which one learned critic, while emphatic as to its admitted defects, calls "the most remarkable poem written in America up to it's time;"[71] which, though an overstatement in view of the works of Anne Bradstreet and Edward Taylor, is not without its truth. Freneau subsequently expanded "House" to about twice its original size and published it again in 1786; then in the 1795 self-published edition of his verse included there a severely shortened version of the poem, "The Vision of Night -- A fragment;" yet which is so abridged as to bear only marginal similarity to prior drafts.

As well as being something of a harbinger of the gothic romantic verse of such as Coleridge and Poe (some stanzas resemble lines from "The Raven"), "House of Night" is unique for its liveliness and vigor, and is on occasion even stupefying in its stark imagery and dramatization of the dreary. At others time, it is unintentionally risible, indeed, laugh out-loud funny (e.g., the allusion to George III) – which ostensibly is why Freneau drastically reduced the poem in size in 1795. Yet as the critics agree, it is the crude and blunt earlier version (of 1786) that attracts the most interest. Drawing for inspiration evidently on Thomas Parnell "A Night-Piece on Death" (1714),[72] Edward Young's "Night Thoughts" (1742) and Robert Blair's "The Grave" (1743); with their being present also echoes of Dante, John Donne's apostrophizing of Death, *Paradise Lost*, and Thomson's "Winter," "House," nonetheless, is novel and inventive in its own right. At times, and again allowing for its deplorable lack of structural unity, "House" has an emotional penetration and force that it is not too much of an exaggeration to describe it as intoxicatingly brilliant; while being somewhat reminiscent of some of the better Elizabethan poets for its curious whimsy and flamboyant, if on occasion ludicrous and not a little morbid, flights of fancy.

---

[70] Though be it noted, earlier in 1775 Freneau had taken up his pen to write *and publish* (in New York and later as well Philadelphia) "American Liberty, A Poem;" "General Gage's Confession, Being the Substance of His Excellency's Last Conference, with His Ghostly Father, Friar Francis;" "The Last Dying Words, Dying speech and Confession of J----s R----g—n [James Rivington], P---t---r, Who was Executed at New Brunswick, In the Province of New Jersey, On the Thirteenth Day of April, 1775. Supposed to be written by himself the night preceding the day of his execution;" "On the Conqueror of America Shut Up in Boston, A Poem;" and "A Voyage to Boston, A Poem."

[71] Samuel Marion Tucker, in *The Cambridge History of American Literature*, vol. I, ch. IX, "The Beginnings of [Am.] Verse: 1610-1808," see p. 181.

[72] [72] While Parnell is usually given credit for inaugurating the gothic movement in 18th century English poetry, Shakespeare, of course, also has his share and moments of ghostly midnight and churchyard verses; while Virgil, for example in the opening to his version of the Orpheus tale in Book IV of the Georgics, could be said to be one of the actual inventors of gothic poetry. As for the brand of gothic heralded by Walpole's *Castle of Otranto* it seems reasonable to surmise that Congreve's tragedy of 1687 "The Mourning Bride" – an at one time extremely popular stage vehicle -- was also some kind of general influence on literary works.

Drawing then from Fred Lewis Pattee's comprehensive and thorough *The Poems of Philip Freneau* (1902), and without further ado, we reproduce this most imaginative and entertaining, if less than perfect, work for those who might else have missed.[73]

~~~***~~~

ADVERTISEMENT -- This Poem is founded upon the authority of Scripture, inasmuch as these sacred books assert, that the *last enemy that shall be conquered is Death*. For the purposes of poetry he is here personified, and represented as on his dying bed. The scene is laid at a solitary palace, (the time midnight) which, tho' before beautiful and joyous, is now become sad and gloomy, as being the abode and receptacle of Death. Its owner, an amiable, majestic youth, who had lately lost a beloved consort, nevertheless with a noble philosophical fortitude and humanity, entertains him in a friendly manner, and by employing Physicians, endeavours to restore him to health, altho' an enemy; convinced of the excellence and propriety of that divine precept, *If thine enemy hunger, feed him; if he thirst, give him drink.* He nevertheless, as if by a spirit of prophecy, informs this (fictitiously) wicked being of the certainty of his doom, and represents to him in a pathetic manner the vanity of his expectations, either of a reception into the abodes of the just, or continuing longer to make havock of mankind upon earth. The patient finding his end approaching, composes his epitaph, and orders it to be engraved on his tombstone, hinting to us thereby, that even Death and Distress have vanity; and would be remembered with honour after he is no more, altho' his whole life has been spent in deeds of devastation and murder. He dies at last in the utmost agonies of despair, after agreeing with an avaricious Undertaker to intomb his bones. This reflects upon the inhumanity of those men, who, not to mention an enemy, would scarcely cover a departed friend with a little dust, without certainty of reward for so doing. The circumstances of his funeral are then recited, and the visionary and fabulous part of the poem disappears. It concludes with a few reflexions on the impropriety of a too great attachment to the present life, and incentives to such moral virtue as may assist in conducting us to a better.

A VISION

Felix qui potuit rerum cognoscere causas,
Atque metus omnes et inexorabile Fatum
Subjecit pedibus, strepitumque Acherontis avari.[74]
Virg. Geog. II. v. 49

1

Trembling I write my dream, and recollect
A fearful vision at the midnight hour;
So late, Death o'er me spread his sable wings,
Painted with fancies of malignant power!

2

Such was the dream the sage Chaldean saw
Disclos'd to him that felt heav'n's vengeful rod,
Such was the ghost, who through deep silence cry'd,
Shall mortal man be juster than his God?

---

[73] The version Pattee reproduces is considerably longer, with 63 more stanzas, than and in some small portions different and emended from that which appeared in the Aug. 1779 issue of *United States Magazine*. Also, we include some of Freneau's original footnotes from the latter absent in Pattee's text, and marked here with a "#" at the end. The quote from *Georgics* as well is not in Pattee. For the 1779 version, see: https://archive.org/details/FreneauHouseOfNight1779

[74] [*Edit. Note.* "Happy he who could know the causes of things, and who subjects all fears and inexorable Fate, and the crash of greedy Acheron to his feet."]
~~~

3

Let others draw from smiling skies their theme,
And tell of climes that boast unfading light,
I draw a darker scene, replete with gloom,
I sing the horrors of the House of Night.

4

Stranger, believe the truth experience tells,
Poetic dreams are of a finer cast
Than those which o'er the sober brain diffus'd,
Are but a repetition of some action past.

5

Fancy, I own thy power -- when sunk in sleep
Thou play'st thy wild delusive part so well
You lift me into immortality,
Depict new heavens, or draw the scenes of hell.

6

By some sad means, when Reason holds no sway,
Lonely I rov'd at midnight o'er a plain
Where murmuring streams and mingling rivers flow
Far to their springs, or seek the sea again.

7

Sweet vernal May! Tho' then thy woods in bloom
Flourish'd, yet nought of this could Fancy see,
No wild pinks bless'd the meads, no green the fields,
And naked seem'd to stand each lifeless tree:

8

Dark was the sky, and not one friendly star
Shone from the zenith or horizon, clear,
Mist sate upon the woods, and darkness rode
In her black chariot, with a wild career.

9

And from the woods the late resounding note
Issued of the loquacious Whip-poor-will,*
Hoarse, howling dogs, and nightly roving wolves
Clamour'd from far off cliffs invisible.

[*A Bird peculiar to America, of a solitary nature, who never sings but in the night. Her note resembles the name given to her by the country people. – Freneau's note.]

10

Rude, from the wide extended Chesapeke
I heard the winds the dashing waves assail,
And saw from far, by picturing fancy form'd,
The black ship travelling through the noisy gale.

11

At last, by chance and guardian fancy led,
I reach'd a noble dome, rais'd fair and high,
And saw the light from upper windows flame,
Presage of mirth and hospitality.

12

And by that light around the dome appear'd
A mournful garden of autumnal hue,
Its lately pleasing flowers all drooping stood
Amidst high weeds that in rank plenty grew.

13

The Primrose there, the violet darkly blue,
Daisies and fair Narcissus ceas'd to rise,
Gay spotted pinks their charming bloom withdrew,
And Polyanthus quench'd its thousand dyes.

14

No pleasant fruit or blossom gaily smil'd,
Nought but unhappy plants or trees were seen,
The yew, the myrtle, and the church-yard elm,
The cypress, with its melancholy green.

15

There cedars dark, the osier, and the pine,
Shorn tamarisks, and weeping willows grew,
The poplar tall, the lotos, arid the lime,
And pyracantha did her leaves renew.

16

The poppy there, companion to repose,
Display'd her blossoms that began to fall,

And here the purple amaranthus rose
With mint strong-scented, for the funeral.

17

And here and there with laurel shrubs between
A tombstone lay, inscrib'd with strains of woe,
And stanzas sad, throughout the dismal green,
Lamented for the dead that slept below.

18

Peace to this awful dome! when strait I heard
The voice of men in a secluded room,
Much did they talk of death, and much of life,
Of coffins, shrouds, and horrors of a tomb.

19

Pathetic were their words, and well they aim'd
To explain the mystic paths of providence,
Learn'd were they all, but there remain'd not I
To hear the upshot of their conference.

20

Meantime from an adjoining chamber came
Confused murmurings, half distinguish'd sounds,
And as I nearer drew, disputes arose
Of surgery, and remedies for wounds.

21

Dull were their feuds, for they went on to talk
Of *Anchylosis** and the shoulder blade,
Os Femoris,* *Trochanters** -- and whate'er
Has been discuss'd by Cheselden or Meade:[75]

[* *Anchylosis* -- a morbid contraction of the joints. *Os Femoris* -- the thigh bone. *Trochanters* two processes in the upper part of the thigh bone, otherwise called *rotator major et minor*, in which the tendons of many muscles terminate. – Freneau's note.]

22

And often each, to prove his notion true,
Brought proofs from Galen or Hippocrates --
But fancy led me hence -- and left them so,
Firm at their points of hardy No and Yes.

---

[75] [*Two famous Anatomists* – Freneau's note #.]

23

Then up three winding stairs my feet were brought
To a high chamber, hung with mourning sad,
The unsnuff'd candles glar'd with visage dim,
'Midst grief, in ecstacy of woe run mad.

24

A wide leaf d table stood on either side,
Well fraught with phials, half their liquids spent,
And from a couch, behind the curtain's veil,
I heard a hollow voice of loud lament.

25

Turning to view the object whence it came,
My frighted eyes a horrid form survey'd;
Fancy, I own thy power -- Death on the couch,
With fleshless limbs, at rueful length, was laid.

26

And o'er his head flew jealousies and cares,
Ghosts, imps, and half the black Tartarian crew,
Arch-angels damn'd, nor was their Prince remote,
Borne on the vaporous wings of Stygian dew.

27

Around his bed, by the dull flambeaux' glare,
I saw pale phantoms -- Rage to madness vext,
Wan, wasting grief, and ever musing care,
Distressful pain, and poverty perplext.

28

Sad was his countenance, if we can call
That countenance, where only bones were seen
And eyes sunk in their sockets, dark and low,
And teeth, that only show'd themselves to grin.

29

Reft was his scull of hair, and no fresh bloom
Of chearful mirth sate on his visage hoar:
Sometimes he rais'd his head, while deep-drawn groans
Were mixt with words that did his fate deplore.

30

Oft did he wish to see the daylight spring,
And often toward the window lean'd to hear,
Fore-runner of the scarlet-mantled morn,
The early note of wakeful Chanticleer.

31

Thus he -- But at my hand a portly youth
Of comely countenance, began to tell,
"That this was Death upon his dying bed,
"Sullen, morose, and peevish to be well;

32

"Fixt is his doom -- the miscreant reigns no more
"The tyrant of the dying or the dead;
"This night concludes his all-consuming reign,
"Pour out, ye heav'ns, your vengeance on his head.

33

"But since, my friend (said he), chance leads you here
"With me this night upon the sick attend,
"You on this bed of death must watch, and I
"Will not be distant from the fretful fiend.

34

"Before he made this lofty pile his home,
"In undisturb'd repose I sweetly slept,
"But when he came to this sequester'd dome,
"'Twas then my troubles came, and then I wept:

35

"Twice three long nights, in this sad chamber, I,
"As though a brother languish'd in despair,
"Have 'tended faithful round his gloomy bed,
"Have been content to breathe this loathsome air.

36

"A while relieve the languors that I feel,
"Sleep's magic forces close my weary eyes;
"Soft o'er my soul unwonted slumbers steal,
"Aid the weak patient till you see me rise.

37

"But let no slumbers on your eye-lids fall,
"That if he ask for powder or for pill
"You may be ready at the word to start,
"And still seem anxious to perform his will.

38

"The bleeding Saviour of a world undone
"Bade thy compassion rise toward thy foe;
"Then, stranger, for the sake of Mary's son,
"Thy tears of pity on this wretch bestow.

39

"'Twas he that stole from my adoring arms
"Aspasia, she the loveliest of her kind,
"Lucretia's virtue, with a Helen's charms,
"Charms of the face, and beauties of the mind.

40

"The blushy cheek, the lively, beaming eye,
"The ruby lip, the flowing jetty hair,
"The stature tall, the aspect so divine,
"All beauty, you would think, had center'd there.

41

"Each future age her virtues shall extol,
"Nor the just tribute to her worth refuse;
"Fam'd, to the stars Urania bids her rise,
"Theme of the moral, and the tragic Muse.

42

"Sweet as the fragrance of the vernal morn,
"Nipt in its bloom this faded flower I see;
"The inspiring-angel from that breast is gone,
"And life's warm tide forever chill'd in thee!

43

"Such charms shall greet my longing soul no more,
"Her lively eyes are clos'd in endless shade,
"Torpid, she rests on yonder marble floor;
"Approach, and see what havock Death has made.

44

"Yet, stranger, hold -- her charms are so divine,
"Such tints of life still on her visage glow,
"That even in death this slumbering bride of mine
"May seize thy heart, and make thee wretched too.

45

"O shun the sight -- forbid thy trembling hand
"From her pale face to raise the enshrouding lawn --
"Death claims thy care, obey his stern command,
"Trim the dull tapers, for I see no dawn!"

46

So said, at Death's left side I sate me down,
The mourning youth toward his right reclin'd;
Death in the middle lay, with all his groans,
And much he toss'd and tumbled, sigh'd and pin'd.

47

But now this man of hell toward me turn'd,
And strait, in hideous tone, began to speak;
Long held he sage discourse, but I forebore
To answer him, much less his news to seek.

48

He talk'd of tomb-stones and of monuments,
Of Equinoctial climes and India shores,
He talk'd of stars that shed their influence,
Fevers and plagues, and all their noxious stores.

49

He mention'd, too, the guileful *calenture*,*
Tempting the sailor on the deep sea main,
That paints gay groves upon the ocean floor,
Beckoning her victim to the faithless scene.

[* *Calenture* -- an inflammatory fever, attended with a delirium, common in long voyages at sea, in which the diseased persons fancy the sea to be green fields and meadows, and, if they are not hindered, will leap overboard. – Freneau's note.]

50

Much spoke he of the myrtle and the yew,
Of ghosts that nightly walk the church-yard o'er,
Of storms that through the wint'ry ocean blow

And dash the well-mann'd galley on the shore,

51

Of broad-mouth'd cannons, and the thunderbolt,
Of sieges and convulsions, dearth and fire,
Of poisonous weeds -- but seem'd to sneer at these
Who by the laurel o'er him did aspire.

52

Then with a hollow voice thus went he on:
"Get up, and search, and bring, when found, to me,
"Some cordial, potion, or some pleasant draught,
"Sweet, slumb'rous poppy, or the mild Bohea.

53

"But hark, my pitying friend! -- and, if you can,
"Deceive the grim physician at the door
"Bring half the mountain springs -- ah! hither bring
"The cold rock water from the shady bower.

54

"For till this night such thirst did ne'er invade,
"A thirst provok'd by heav'n's avenging hand;
"Hence bear me, friends, to quaff, and quaff again
"The cool wave bubbling from the yellow sand.

55

"To these dark walls with stately step I came,
"Prepar'd your drugs and doses to defy;
"Smit with the love of never dying fame,
"I came, alas! to conquer -- not to die!"

56

Glad, from his side I sprang, and fetch'd the draught,
Which down his greedy throat he quickly swills,
Then on a second errand sent me strait,
To search in some dark corner for his pills.

57

Quoth he, "These pills have long compounded been,
"Of dead men's bones and bitter roots, I trow;
"But that I may to wonted health return,

“Throughout my lank veins shall their substance go.”

58

So down they went. -- He rais’d his fainting head
And oft in feeble tone essay’d to talk;
Quoth he, “Since remedies have small avail,
“Assist unhappy Death once more to walk.”

59

Then slowly rising from his loathsome bed,
On wasted legs the meagre monster stood,
Gap’d wide, and foam’d, and hungry seem’d to ask,
Tho’ sick, an endless quantity of food.

60

Said he, “The sweet melodious flute prepare,
“The anthem, and the organ’s solemn sound,
“Such as may strike my soul with ecstacy,
“Such as may from yon’ lofty wall rebound.

61

“Sweet music can the fiercest pains assuage,
“She bids the soul to heaven’s blest mansions rise,
“She calms despair, controuls infernal rage
“And deepest anguish, when it hears her, dies.

62

“And see, the mizzling, misty midnight reigns,
“And no soft dews are on my eye-lids sent!--
“Here, stranger, lend thy hand; assist me, pray,
“To walk a circuit of no large extent."--

63

On my prest shoulders leaning, round he went,
And could have made the boldest spectre flee,
I led him up stairs, and I led him down,
But not one moment’s rest from pain got he.

64

Then with his dart, its cusp unpointed now,
Thrice with main strength he smote the trembling floor;
The roof resounded to the fearful blow,

And Cleon started, doom'd to sleep no more.

65

When thus spoke Death, impatient of controul,
"Quick, move, and bring from yonder black bureau
"The sacred book that may preserve my soul
"From long damnation, and eternal woe.

66

"And with it bring -- for you may find them there,
"The works of holy authors, dead and gone,
"The sacred tome of moving Drelincourt, [76]
"Or what more solemn Sherlock mus'd upon:[77]

67

"And read, my Cleon, what these sages say,
"And what the sacred Penman hath declar'd,
"That when the wicked leaves his odious way,
"His sins shall vanish, and his soul be spar'd."

68

But he, unmindful of the vain command,
Reason'd with Death, nor were his reasonings few:
Quoth he "My Lord, what frenzy moves your brain,
"Pray, what, my Lord, can Sherlock be to you,

69

"Or all the sage divines that ever wrote,
"Grave Drelincourt, or heaven's unerring page;
"These point their arrows at your hostile breast,
"And raise new pains that time must ne'er assuage.

70

"And why should thus thy woe disturb my rest?
"Much of Theology I once did read,
"And there 'tis fixt, sure as my God is so,
"That Death shall perish, tho' a God should bleed.

---

[76] [*Drelincourt on death* – Freneau's note #.]

[77] [*Sherlock* – Freneau's note #.] [*Edit. Note*. Charles Drelincourt (1595-1669) author of *The Christian's Defence Against the Fears of Death; with Seasonable Directions How to Prepare Ourselves to Die Well* (1732), and William Sherlock (c.1641-1707) of *A Practical Discourse concerning Death* (1690).]

71

“The martyr, doom’d the pangs of fire to feel,
“Lives but a moment in the sultry blast;
“The victim groans, and dies beneath the steel,
“But thy severer pains shall always last.

72

“O miscreant vile, thy age has made thee doat --
“If peace, if sacred peace were found for you,
“Hell would cry out, and all the damn’d arise
“And, more deserving, seek for pity too.

73

“Seek not for Paradise -- ’tis not for thee,
“Where high in heaven its sweetest blossoms blow,
“Nor even where, gliding to the Persian main,
“Thy waves, Euphrates, through the garden flow!

74

“Bloody has been thy reign, O man of hell,
“Who sympathiz’d with no departing groan;
“Cruel wast thou, and hardly dost deserve
“To have *Hic Jacet* stampt upon thy stone.

75

“He that could build his mansion o’er the tombs,
“Depending still on sickness and decay,
“May dwell unmov’d amidst these drowsier glooms,
“May laugh the dullest of these shades away.

76

“Remember how with unrelenting ire
“You tore the infant from the unwilling breast --
“Aspasia fell, and Cleon must expire,
“Doom’d by the impartial God to endless rest:

77

“In vain with stars he deck’d yon’ spangled skies,
“And bade the mind to heaven’s bright regions soar,
“And brought so far to my admiring eyes
“A glimpse of glories that shall blaze no more!

78

"Even now, to glut thy devilish wrath, I see
"From eastern realms a wasteful army[78] rise:
"Why else those lights that tremble in the north?
"Why else yon' comet blazing through the skies?

79

"Rejoice, O fiend; Britannia's tyrant sends
"From German plains his myriads to our shore.
"The fierce Hibernian with the Briton join'd --
"Bring them, ye winds! but waft them back no more.

80

"To you, alas! the fates in wrath deny
"The comforts to our parting moments due,
"And leave you here to languish and to die,
"Your crimes too many, and your tears too few.

81

"No cheering voice to thee shall cry, Repent!
"As once it echoed through the wilderness --
"No patron died for thee – damn'd, damn'd art thou
"Like all the devils, nor one jot the less.

82

"A gloomy land, with sullen skies is thine,
"Where never rose or amaranthus grow,
"No daffodils, nor comely columbine,
"No hyacinths nor asphodels for you.

83

"The barren trees that flourish on the shore
"With leaves or fruit were never seen to bend,
"O'er languid waves unblossom'd branches hang,
"And every branch sustains some vagrant fiend.

84

"And now no more remains, but to prepare
"To take possession of thy punishment;
"That's thy inheritance, that thy domain,
"A land of bitter woe, and loud lament.

[78] [*British* – Freneau's note #. Also the adjective first used here instead of "wasteful" is "bloody."]

85

"And oh that He, who spread the universe,
"Would cast one pitying glance on thee below!
"Millions of years in torments thou might'st fry,
"But thy eternity! -- who can conceive its woe!"

86

He heard, and round with his black eye-balls gaz'd,
Full of despair, and curs'd, and rav'd, and swore:
"And since this is my doom," said he, "call up
"Your wood-mechanics[79] to my chamber door:

87

"Blame not on me the ravage to be made;
"Proclaim, even Death abhors such woe to see;
"I'll quit the world, while decently I can,
"And leave the work to George my deputy."

88

Up rush'd a band, with compasses and scales
To measure his slim carcase, long and lean --
"Be sure," said he, "to frame my coffin strong,
"You, master workman, and your men, I mean:

89

"For if the Devil, so late my trusty friend,
"Should get one hint where I am laid, from you,
"Not with my soul content, he'd seek to find
"That mouldering mass of bones, my body, too!

90

"Of hardest ebon let the plank be found,
"With clamps and ponderous bars secur'd around,
"That if the box by Satan should be storm'd,
"It may be able for resistance found."

91

"Yes," said the master workman, "noble Death,
"Your coffin shall be strong -- that leave to me --
"But who shall these your funeral dues discharge?

---

[79] [* Undertakers. – Freneau's note#..]

"Nor friends nor pence you have, that I can see."

92

To this said Death – "You might have ask'd me, too,
"Base caitiff, who are my executors,
"Where my estate, and who the men that shall
"Partake my substance, and be call'd my heirs.

93

"Know, then, that hell is my inheritance,
"The devil himself my funeral dues must pay --
"Go -- since you must be paid -- go, ask of him,
"For he has gold, as fabling poets say."

94

Strait they retir'd -- when thus he gave me charge,
Pointing from the light window to the west,
"Go three miles o'er the plain, and you shall see
"A burying-yard of sinners dead, unblest.

95

"Amid the graves a spiry building stands
"Whose solemn knell resounding through the gloom
"Shall call thee o'er the circumjacent lands
"To the dull mansion destin'd for my tomb.

96

"There, since 'tis dark, I'll plant a glimmering light
"Just snatch'd from hell, by whose reflected beams
"Thou shalt behold a tomb-stone, full eight feet,
"Fast by a grave, replete with ghosts and dreams.

97

"And on that stone engrave this epitaph,
"Since Death, it seems, must die like mortal men;
"Yes on that stone engrave this epitaph,
"Though all hell's furies aim to snatch the pen.

98

"Death in this tomb his weary bones hath laid,
"Sick of dominion o'er the human kind
"Behold what devastations he hath made,

"Survey the millions by his arm confin'd.

99

"Six thousand years has sovereign sway been mine,
"None, but myself, can real glory claim;
"Great Regent of the world I reign'd alone,
"And princes trembled when my mandate came.

100

"Vast and unmatched throughout the world, my fame
"Takes place of gods, and asks no mortal date --
"No; by myself, and by the heavens, I swear,
"Not Alexander's name is half so great.

101

"Nor swords nor darts my prowess could withstand,
"All quit their arms, and bow'd to my decree,
"Even mighty Julius died beneath my hand,
"For slaves and Caesars were the same to me!"

102

"Traveller, wouldst thou his noblest trophies seek,
"Search in no narrow spot obscure for those;
"The sea profound, the surface of all land
"Is moulded with the myriads of his foes."

103

Scarce had he spoke, when on the lofty dome
Rush'd from the clouds a hoarse resounding blast --
Round the four eaves so loud and sad it play'd
As though all musick were to breathe its last.

104

Warm was the gale, and such as travellers say
Sport with the winds on Zaara's barren waste;
Black was the sky, a mourning carpet spread,
Its azure blotted, and its stars o'ercast!

105

Lights in the air like burning stars were hurl'd,
Dogs howl'd, heaven mutter'd, and the tempest blew,
The red half-moon peeped from behind a cloud

As if in dread the amazing scene to view.

106

The mournful trees that in the garden stood
Bent to the tempest as it rush'd along,
The elm, the myrtle, and the cypress sad
More melancholy tun'd its bellowing song.

107

No more that elm its noble branches spread,
The yew, the cypress, or the myrtle tree,
Rent from the roots the tempest tore them down,
And all the grove in wild confusion lay.

108

Yet, mindful of his dread command, I part
Glad from the magic dome -- nor found relief;
Damps from the dead hung heavier round my heart,
While sad remembrance rous'd her stores of grief.

109

O'er a dark field I held my dubious way
Where Jack-a-lanthorn walk'd his lonely round,
Beneath my feet substantial darkness lay,
And screams were heard from the distemper'd ground,

110

Nor look'd I back, till to a far off wood,
Trembling with fear, my weary feet had sped --
Dark was the night, but at the inchanted dome
I saw the infernal windows flaming red.

111

And from within the howls of Death I heard,
Cursing the dismal night that gave him birth,
Damning his ancient sire, and mother sin,
Who at the gates of hell, accursed, brought him forth. [80]

112

[For fancy gave to my enraptur'd soul

---

[80] [* *See Paradise Lost, book II. v. 780.* – Freneau's note #.]

An eagle's eye, with keenest glance to see,
And bade those distant sounds distinctly roll,
Which, waking, never had affected me.]

113

Oft his pale breast with cruel hand he smote,
And tearing from his limbs a winding sheet,
Roar'd to the black skies, while the woods around,
As wicked as himself, his words repeat.

114

Thrice tow'rd the skies his meagre arms he rear'd,
Invok'd all hell, and thunders on his head,
Bid light'nings fly, earth yawn, and tempests roar,
And the sea wrap him in its oozy bed.

115

"My life for one cool draught! -- O, fetch your springs,
"Can one unfeeling to my woes be found!
"No friendly visage comes to my relief,
"But ghosts impend, and spectres hover round.

116

"Though humbled now, dishearten'd and distrest,
"Yet, when admitted to the peaceful ground,
"With heroes, kings, and conquerors I shall rest,
"Shall sleep as safely, and perhaps as sound."

117

Dim burnt the lamp, and now the phantom Death
Gave his last groans in horror and despair --
"All hell demands me hence," -- he said, and threw
The red lamp hissing through the midnight air.

118

Trembling, across the plain my course I held,
And found the grave-yard, loitering through the gloom,
And, in the midst, a hell-red, wandering light,
Walking in fiery circles round the tomb.

119

Among the graves a spiry building stood,

Whose tolling bell, resounding through the shade,
Sung doleful ditties to the adjacent wood,
And many a dismal drowsy thing it said.

120

This fabrick tall, with towers and chancels grac'd,
Was rais'd by sinners' hands, in ages fled;
The roof they painted, and the beams they brac'd,
And texts from scripture o'er the walls they spread:

121

But wicked were their hearts, for they refus'd
To aid the helpless orphan, when distrest,
The shivering, naked stranger they mis-us'd,
And banish'd from their doors the starving guest.

122

By laws protected, cruel and prophane,
The poor man's ox these monsters drove away; --
And left Distress to attend her infant train,
No friend to comfort, and no bread to stay.

123

But heaven look'd on with keen, resentful eye,
And doom'd them to perdition and the grave,
That as they felt not for the wretch distrest,
So heaven no pity on their souls would have.

124

In pride they rais'd this building tall and fair,
Their hearts were on perpetual mischief bent,
With pride they preach'd, and pride was in their prayer,
With pride they were deceiv'd, and so to hell they went.

125

At distance far approaching to the tomb,
By lamps and lanthorns guided through the shade,
A coal-black chariot hurried through the gloom,
Spectres attending, in black weeds array'd,

126

Whose woeful forms yet chill my soul with dread,

Each wore a vest in Stygian chambers wove,
Death's kindred all – Death's horses they bestrode,
And gallop'd fiercely, as the chariot drove.

127

Each horrid face a grizly mask conceal'd,
Their busy eyes shot terror to my soul
As now and then, by the pale lanthorn's glare,
I saw them for their parted friend condole.

128

Before the hearse Death's chaplain seem'd to go,
Who strove to comfort, what he could, the dead;
Talk'd much of Satan, and the land of woe,
And many a chapter from the scriptures read.

129

At last he rais'd the swelling anthem high,
In dismal numbers seem'd he to complain;
The captive tribes that by Euphrates wept,
Their song was jovial to his dreary strain.

130

That done, they plac'd the carcase in the tomb,
To dust and dull oblivion now resign'd,
Then turn'd the chariot tow'rd the House of Night,
Which soon flew off, and left no trace behind.

131

But as I stoop'd to write the appointed verse,
Swifter than thought the airy scene decay'd;
Blushing the morn arose, and from the east
With her gay streams of light dispell'd the shade.

132

What is this Death, ye deep read sophists, say? --
Death is no more than one unceasing change;
New forms arise, while other forms decay,
Yet all is Life throughout creation's range.

133

The towering Alps, the haughty Appenine,

The Andes, wrapt in everlasting snow,
The Apalachian and the Ararat
Sooner or later must to ruin go.

134

Hills sink to plains, and man returns to dust,
That dust supports a reptile or a flower;
Each changeful atom by some other nurs'd
Takes some new form, to perish in an hour.

135

Too nearly join'd to sickness, toils, and pains,
(Perhaps for former crimes imprison'd here)
True to itself the immortal soul remains,
And seeks new mansions in the starry sphere.

136

When Nature bids thee from the world retire,
With joy thy lodging leave a fated guest;
In Paradise, the land of thy desire,
Existing always, always to be blest.

WAR AND WASHINGTON

While "Yankee Doodle" is the tune most usually associated with the Revolutionary War, there is little record of its being actually much sung at *that* time -- certainly not in the army. Much more commonly heard in the American camps, taverns, homes, and on the march was Jonathan Mitchell Sewall's (1748-1808) "War and Washington."[81] The song, sung to the tune "The British Grenadiers," appeared at least as early as 1778 in Sewall's "Epilogue to Cato;" which latter was read at the Valley Forge encampment following a performance there, acted by army officers and staff, of Joseph Addison's acclaimed heroic tragedy of 1712.

It was and has been some point of amusement that the Rebels entertained the seemingly extravagant notion of taking and annexing Canada. Yet, as Seawell's popular song here shows, there were even such, and of such fervor, who did and would talk of conquering Britain itself, perhaps even all of Europe! Proud boast indeed. And whether "Washington" himself would have approved is open to question. But we can at least applaud the pluck and gumption of it; and which perhaps can serve as a useful reminder of potential benefit sometimes to be had in elevating one's sights and aspirations beyond conventional reckoning.

~~~***~~~

Vain Britons, boast no longer with proud indignity,
By land your conquering legions, your matchless strength at sea,
Since we, your braver sons incensed, our swords have girded on.
Huzza, huzza, huzza, huzza, for war and Washington.

Urged on by North and vengeance those valiant champions came,
Loud bellowing Tea and Treason, and George was all on flame,
Yet sacrilegious as it seems, we rebels still live on,
And laugh at all their empty puffs, huzza for Washington!
Still deaf to mild entreaties, still blind to England's good,
You have for thirty pieces betrayed your country's blood.
Like [A]Esop's greedy cur you'll gain a shadow for your bone.
Yet find us fearful shades indeed inspired by Washington.

Mysterious! unexampled! incomprehensible!
The blundering schemes of Britain their folly, pride, and zeal.
Like lions how ye growl and threat! mere asses have you shown,
And ye shall share an ass's fate, and drudge for Washington!

Your dark unfathomed councils our weakest heads defeat,
Our children rout your armies, our boats destroy your fleet,
And to complete the dire disgrace, cooped up within a town [Boston.]
You live the scorn of all our host, the slaves of Washington!

Great Heaven! is this the nation whose thundering arms were hurled.
Through Europe, Afric, India? whose navy ruled a world?
The lustre of your former deeds, whole ages of renown.
Lost in a moment, or transferred to us and Washington!

---

[81] See *The Private Soldier Under Washington* (1902) by Charles Knowles Bolton p. 240, and *The Revolutionary People at War: The Continental Army & American Character, 1775-1783* (1979) by Charles Royster p. 248. See also *A Narrative of Joshua Davis* (1811) by Joshua Davis, pp. 30-32. Respecting Seawell: "Jonathan Mitchell Sewall (1748-1808), a lawyer-poet of Portsmouth, New Hampshire, who versified *Washington's Farewell Address* and paraphrased parts of the Bible and of Ossian, contributed to [Joseph Dennie's] the *Port Folio* in 1801 a few short versions of Ossian. His *Eulogy on Washington* and *Poems* were published in 1801." *Joseph Dennie and his Circle* by Milton Ellis, Bulletin of the University of Texas, July 1915, no. 40, p. 166.
~~~

Yet think not thirst of glory unsheaths our vengeful swords,
To rend your bands asunder, or cast away your cords,
'T is heaven-born freedom fires us all, and strengthens each brave son.
From him who humbly guides the plough, to god-like Washington.

For this, oh could our wishes your ancient rage inspire.
Your armies should be doubled, in numbers, force, and fire.
Then might the glorious conflict prove which best deserved the boon,
America or Albion, a George or Washington!

Fired with the great idea, our Fathers' shades would rise,
To view the stern contention, the gods desert their skies;
And Wolfe, 'midst hosts of heroes, superior bending down,
Cry out with eager transport, God save great Washington!

Should George, too choice of Britons, to foreign realms apply,
And madly arm half Europe, yet still we would defy
Turk, Hessian, Jew, and Infidel, or all those powers in one,
While Adams guards our senate, our camp great Washington!

Should warlike weapons fail us, disdaining slavish fears,
To swords we'll beat our ploughshares, our pruning-hooks to spears,
And rush, all desperate, on our foe, nor breathe till battle won.
Then shout, and shout America! and conquering Washington!

Proud France should view with terror, and haughty Spain revere.
While every warlike nation would court alliance here;
And George, his minions trembling round, dismounting from his throne
Pay homage to America and glorious Washington!

MOHICANS IN THE REVOLUTION

"I am a dry tree. I will die here..." - Chief Daniel Nimham

We so take as a given the widespread involvement of Native Americans in the Revolutionary War. And yet might events have resolved themselves quite differently for the Indians (than they did) had they not been so actively enlisted into British service? For example, the mid-war invasions by the Iroquois (1778), the Cherokees and Creeks (1780-81) soon enough became a pretext for the Americans to subsequently and ruthlessly maul and devastate those nations; so that by the same token had these tribes not been used to attack, might they have ended up surviving the conflict much better than they did? Such a what-if cannot but prompt our wonder. But as is usual with such speculations our answers are or can at best only provide us with tentative surmises. Yet if we do assume an affirmative to the question, should then the Americans be blamed for not making much more of an effort to sway the Indians to their own side, or a least to a neutral one? The answer to this second question, may also very well, and tragically, be yes; with there being evidence to suggest as much. Notwithstanding, it may have been simply gold, or the lack of, that finally determined the matter, and in the contest of money the rebelling Americans were easily and hands down the losers.[82] On the other hand and in the final analysis, it can and will be argued, no amount of enlightened treatment by either or any government ever would have spared the natives the havoc and injustice bound ultimately to result from the unavoidable the deluge of Euro-American land seekers.

There were, despite this, a few Indians who did fight alongside Washington's army: most notably the Oneida, the Seneca, the Catawba,[83] and the Wappingers or Mahicans; and it might come as a surprise to some that the latter were not only not merely an invention of James Fenimore Cooper, but indeed a number of the descendants of that tribe are still much alive today -- thus happily making the title of Cooper's famous novel, in real-life, a misnomer. John Trumbull's painting "The Death of Montgomery" (1787) contains a figure wielding a tomahawk and scorning defeat who happens to be Iroquois chief Akiatonharónkwen, also known by Joseph Louis Cook, who subsequent to the 1775 assault on Quebec was formally commissioned by Congress a lieutenant colonel in the Continental Army; and who in that capacity served both diplomatically and militarily with honor and merit. Then there was as well Chief Hon Yerry (also "Hanyerry") of the Oneida who saw action alongside the Dutch New York militia at the particularly difficult and incarnadine battle of Oriskany, and who subsequently lost his life for the American cause in the Sullivan expedition of 1779; not to mention a sizable number of Oneida, some 50, who were part of Capt Allan McLane's active contingent of scouts, and skirmishers operating in the environs of Philadelphia in 1777. The British naturally had even more of a share of valiant Indian warriors serving with them; not least of which were Guristersigo of the Creeks (called "Emistessigo" by David Ramsay, and which *may* be more correct), Anthony Wayne's, bold adversary in Georgia in 1782, and, of course, the English educated, widely esteemed,[84] and redoubtable Joseph Brant. Esther Montour of Tioga or "Queen Esther" (1720-?), and on whom Brockden Brown evidently based Queen Mab of *Edgar Huntley* (1801), was another famous, or depending on your view infamous, scourge of the patriots.

---

[82] Some Americans were against or else reluctant to enlist the Indians; evidently, since doing so only gave the wealthier British an more of an excuse and pretext to do the same. See *American Archives*, Fourth Series, vol. 6, (1843), edited by Peter Force, pp. 1532, 1698, 1719. Burgoyne's invasion in 1777 is what more than anything else enlisted the Indians in large numbers into the war. Further, it was the Loyalist and Indian strategic set back at the battle of Oriskany that brought about major and subsequent forays, and that included the battle of Wyoming in July 1778. This was retaliated by the Americans with the fairly incredible raid of Col. Thomas Hartley in 1778 against the Indian towns of Onaquaga and Tioga. This in turn incited the notorious Cherry Valley attack in November. All of which then finally resulted in the Sullivan Expedition of 1779; that tragically decimated the Iroquois completely. Initially, many, probably most, of the Indians had wanted to stay out of the conflict entirely; with some such as the Oneida and Tuscaroras assisting the Americans when the Loyalists and other Iroquois went on the offensive in both in 1777 (at Oriskany) and in 1778 under Butler and Brant. But owing to the Senecas (based at Canandaigua, N.Y.) and a minority from some other tribes deciding to take part with the British; such neutrality was not to be; with the devastation then being made to be suffered by all. Without doubt, this is, in its implications, a surprising story that ought to be better known than it is. For how different might have been the resultant fate of *all* North American Indians had it been possible to keep the Iroquois neutral.

[83] Particularly deserving of our notice is that the 3rd Troop of Lee's Legion cavalry was originally composed entirely of Oneida Indians in the period from 1778 to 1779, and in the Guilford Court House campaign, the Catawba Indians (of South and North Carolina) fought alongside the Legion at the battle of Alamance, aka Clapp's Mill, N.C., on 2 March 1781.

[84] Though erroneously implicated by some in the Wyoming and Cherry Valley massacres.

To give us some introductory perspective on the Native Americans in the Revolutionary War, we have here two excerpts. The first of these is from James Kirke Paulding's serio-comic historical novel *Koningsmarke, the Long Finne* (1823), Book IV, ch. 2, pp. 192-198, and which provides a summary overview of the predicament besetting Indians generally in the face of early white encroachment; with Paulding using late 17th century Delaware and Pennsylvania as his setting. The second, and also a becoming and wry complement to the first text, comes from Loyalist and Provincial officer John Graves Simcoe's *A Journal of the Operations of the Queen's Rangers, from the End of the Year 1777 to the Conclusion of the Late American War* (1784),[85] and recounts from British-American eyes the last stand of the Stockbridge Indians, fighting on behalf of General Washington's army on August 31st, 1778; in an engagement that took place in the Bronx (lying then on the outskirts of the northern part of New York City.) While Chief Daniel Nimham features prominently in accounts of the battle, it was his son Captain Abraham Nimham who actually commanded the Wappinger forces.[86]

~~~***~~~

A Sketch of the Native of North America

By James Kirke Paulding (1778-1860)

...In the intermediate spaces, between these distant settlements [i.e., roughly in and between present-day western New Jersey, eastern Pennsylvania, and Delaware], resided various small tribes of Indians, who sometimes maintained friendly relations with their new neighbours, at others committed depredations and murders. The early settlers of this country were, perhaps, as extraordinary a race of people as ever existed. Totally unwarlike in their habits, they ventured upon a new world, and came, few in numbers, *fearlessly into the society and within the power of a numerous race of savages. The virtuous and illustrious William Penn, and his followers, whose principles and practice were those of non-resistance, and who held even self-defence unlawful, trusted themselves to the wilds, not with arms in their hands, to fight their way among the wild Indians, but with the olive branch, to interchange the peaceful relations of social life. There was in these adventurers generally, a degree of moral courage, faith, perseverance, hardihood, and love of independence, civil and religious, that enabled them to do with the most limited means, what, with the most ample, others have failed in achieving. We cannot read their early history, and dwell upon the patient endurance of labours and dangers on the part of the men, of heroic faith and constancy on that of the women, without feeling our eyes moisten, our hearts expand with affectionate admiration of these our noble ancestors, who watered the young tree of liberty with their tears, and secured to themselves and their posterity the noblest of all privileges, that of worshipping God according to their consciences, at the price of their blood.

The character of the Indian nations, which inhabited these portions of the country, and indeed that of all the various tribes of savages in North America, was pretty uniform. Like all ignorant people, they were very superstitious. When the great comet appeared in 1680, a Sachem was asked what he thought of its appearance. "It signifies," said he, "that we Indians shall melt away, and this country be inhabited by another people." They had a great veneration for their ancient burying-grounds; and when any of their friends or relatives died at a great distance, would bring his bones to be interred in the ancient cemetery of the tribe. Nothing, in after times, excited a deeper vengeance against the white people, than their ploughing up the ground where the bones of their fathers had been deposited. When well treated, they were kind and liberal to the strangers; but were naturally reserved, apt to resent, to conceal their resentment, and retain it a long time. But their remembrance of benefits was equally tenacious, and they never forgot the obligations of hospitality.

An old Indian used to visit the house of a worthy farmer at Middletown in New-Jersey, where he was always hospitably received and kindly entertained. One day the wife of the farmer observed the Indian to be more pensive than usual, and to sigh heavily at intervals. She inquired what was the matter, when he replied, that he had something to tell her, which, if it were known, would cost him his life. On being further

---

[85] Here reproduced from the 1844 edition, pp. 81-87.
[86] For more on Native Americans in the American Revolution, see: http://www.wampumchronicles.com
~~~

pressed, he disclosed a plot of the Indians, who were that night to surprise the village, and murder all the inhabitants. "I never yet deceived thee," cried the old man; "tell thy husband, that he may tell his white brothers; but let no one else know that I have seen thee to day." The husband collected the men of the village to watch that night. About twelve o'clock they heard the war-whoop; but the Indians, perceiving them on their guard, consented to a treaty of peace, which they never afterwards violated.

Their ideas of justice were nearly confined to the revenging of injuries; but an offender who was taken in attempting to escape the punishment of a crime, submitted to the will of his tribe, without a murmur. On one occasion, a chief named Tashyowican lost a sister by the small-pox, the introduction of which by the whites was one great occasion of the hostility of the Indians. "The Maneto [i.e. god] of the white man has killed my sister," said he, "and I will go kill the white man." Accordingly, taking a friend with him, they set upon and killed a settler of the name of Huggins. On receiving information of this outrage, the settlers demanded satisfaction of the tribe to which Tashyowican belonged, threatening severe retaliation if it were refused. The Sachems despatched two Indians to take him, dead or alive. On coming to his wigwam, Tashyowican, suspecting their designs, asked if they intended to kill him. They replied, "no -- but the Sachems have ordered you to die." "And what do you say, brothers?" replied he. "We say you must die," answered they. Tashyowican then covered his eyes, and cried out "kill me," upon which they shot him through the heart.

Previous to their intercourse with the whites, they had few vices, as their state of society furnished them with few temptations; and these vices were counterbalanced by many good, not to say great qualities. But, by degrees, they afterwards became corrupted by that universal curse of their race, spirituous liquors, the seductions of which the best and greatest of them could not resist. It is this which has caused their tribes to wither away, leaving nothing behind but a name, which will soon be forgotten, or, at best, but a miserable remnant of degenerate beings, whose minds are debased, and whose forms exhibit nothing of that tall and stately majesty which once characterized the monarchs of the forest.

But the most universal and remarkable trait in the character of the red-men of North America, was a gravity of deportment, almost approaching to melancholy. It seemed as if they had a presentiment of the fate which awaited them in the increasing numbers of the white strangers; and it is certain, that there were many traditions and prophecies among them, which seemed to indicate the final ruin and extinction of their race. Their faces bore the expression of habitual melancholy; and it was observed that they never laughed or were gay, except in their drunken feasts, which, however, generally ended in outrage and bloodshed. The little Christina [a fictional character in *Koningsmarke*] always called them THE SAD PEOPLE; and the phrase aptly expressed their peculiar character.

It is little to be wondered at, if two races of men, so totally distinct in habits, manners, and interests, and withal objects of mutual jealousy, suspicion and fear, should be oftener enemies than friends. Every little singularity observed in the actions and deportment of each other, accordingly gave rise to suspicion, often followed by outrage; and every little robbery committed on the property of either, was ascribed to the other party, so that the history of their early intercourse with each other, is little other than a narrative of bickerings and bloodshed. Thus they continued, until it finally happened in the new, as it hath always happened in the old world, that the "wise white-man" gained a final ascendency, and transmitted it to his posterity...

~~~***~~~

From ***Journal of the Queen's Rangers*** by John Graves Simcoe.

The Stockbridge Indians about sixty in number, excellent marksmen, had just joined Mr. Washington's army. Lt Col. Simcoe was describing a private road to Lt. Col. Tarleton: Wright, his orderly dragoon, alighted and took down a fence of Devou's farm yard, for them to pass through; around this farm the Indians were ambuscaded; Wright had scarce mounted his horse, when these officers, for some trivial reason, altered their intentions, and, spurring their horses, soon rode out of sight, and out of reach of the Indians. In a few days after, they had certain information of the ambuscade, which they so fortunately had escaped: in all probability, they owed their lives to the Indians' expectations of surrounding and taking
~~~

them prisoners. Good information was soon obtained, by Lt. Col. Simcoe, of General [Charles] Scott's situation, and character; and he desired Sir William Erskine would lay before the Conmander in Chief his request, that he would permit the York Volunteers to join him, for a week; that, during that time, he might attack Scott's camp: he particularly named the York Volunteers, as he wished to unite the Provincials in one enterprise; unfortunately, that regiment could not be spared, as it was ordered for embarkation. Scott soon altered his position; and the source of intelligence, relative to him, was destroyed.

The rebels had, in the day time, a guard of cavalry, near Marmaroneck, which was withdrawn at night: it was intended to cover the country, and protect some sick horses, turned into the salt marshes in the neighbourhood; Lt. Col. Simcoe determined to attempt its surprisal; General Scott's camp was not above three miles from it; and, in case of alarm, he had a shorter march to intercept the party, at Eastchester bridge, than it had to return there. The troops, consisting of the Queen's Rangers, and the cavalry of the Legion, marched at night; at Chester bridge, Captain [John] Saunders, an officer of great address and determination, was left in ambuscade in a wood, with a detachment of the Rangers, and in the rear of the post that the enemy would, probably, occupy, if they should attempt to cut off the party in its retreat. His directions were, to remain undiscovered; to let a patroles pass; and, in case the enemy should post themselves, to wait until the party, upon its return, should be engaged in forcing the passage, and then to sally upon their rear. The troops continued their march, passing the creek, higher up, with the greatest silence; they went through fields, obliterating every trace of their passage when they crossed roads, to avoid discovery from disaffected people, or the enemy's numerous patroles. When they arrived at their appointed station, Lt. Col. Tarleton, with the cavalry, ambuscaded the road, on which the enemy's guard was to approach; Lt. Col. Simcoe occupied the centre, with the infantry, in a wood, and Major Ross was posted on the right, to intercept whomsoever Lt. Col.Tarleton should let pass. Two or three commissaries, and others, who were on a fishing party, were taken. At six o'clock, as he was previously ordered, Lt. Col. Tarleton left his post, when the party of the enemy instantly appeared in his rear: they owed their safety to mere accident. The information that both the old and new piquet of the enemy generally arrived at this post at five o'clock, was true; a horse, belonging to a Serjeant, breaking loose, the officer chose to wait till it was caught, and this delayed them for a full hour. Three dragoons, who had previously advanced to a house within the ambuscade, were now taken, and about thirty or forty lame or sick horses. The troops, followed at a distance by the rebel dragoons, returned home without any accident. Scott, upon the alarm, ordered off his baggage ; and Washington sent cannon, and troops, to his assistance, and put his army under arms. Captain Saunders permitted two patroles to pass, having effectually concealed his party. The prisoners said, that, two mornings before. General Gates had been there fishing.

Lt. Col. Simcoe, returning from head quarters, the 20th of August, heard a firing, in front, and being informed that Lt. Col. Emmerick [Andreas Emmerich] had patrolled, he immediately marched to his assistance. He soon met him retreating; and Lt Col. Emmerick being of opinion the rebels were in such force, that it would be adviseable to return, he did so. Lt. Col. Simcoe understood that Nimham, an Indian chief, and some of his tribe, were with the enemy; and by his spies, who were excellent, he was informed that they were highly elated at the retreat of Emmerick's corps, and applied it to the whole of the light troops at Kingsbridge. Lt. Col. Simcoe took measures to increase their belief; and, ordering a day's provision to be cooked, marched the next morning, the 31st of August, a small distance in front of the post, and determined to wait there the whole day, in hopes of betraying the enemy into an ambuscade: the country was most favourable to it. His idea was, as the enemy moved upon the road which is delineated in the plan as intersecting the country, to advance from his flanks; this movement would be perfectly concealed by the fall of the ground upon his right, and by the woods upon the left; and he meant to gain the heights in the rear of the enemy, attacking whomsoever should be within by his cavalry and such infantry as might be necessary. In pursuance of these intentions, Lt. Col. Emmerick, with his corps, was detached from the Queen's Rangers, and Legion; as, Lt Col. Simcoe thought, fully instructed in the plan; however, he, most unfortunately, mistook the nearer house for one at a greater distance, the names being the same, and there he posted himself, and soon after sent from thence a patrole forward, upon the road, before Lt Col. Simcoe could have time to stop it. This patrole had no bad effect, not meeting with any enemy: had a single man of it deserted, or been taken, the whole attempt had, probably, been abortive. Lt. Col. Simcoe, who was half way up a tree, on the top of which was a drummer boy, saw a flanking party of the enemy approach. The troops had scarcely fallen into their ranks, when a smart firing was heard from the Indians, who had lined the fences of the road, and were exchanging shot with Lt. Col. Emmerick, whom they had discovered. The Queen's Rangers moved rapidly to gain the heights, and Lt. Col. Tarleton immediately advanced with the Huzzars, and the Legion cavalry: not being able to pass the fences in his front, he made a circuit to return further upon their right; which being reported to Lt. Col Simcoe, he broke from the column of the Rangers, with the grenadier company, and, directing Major Ross to conduct the corps to the heights, advanced to the road, and arrived, without being perceived, within ten yards of the Indians. They had been intent upon the attack of Emmerick's corps, and the Legion; they now gave a yell, and fired upon the grenadier company, wounding four of them, and Lt Col. Simcoe. They were driven from the fences; and Lt. Col. Tarleton, with the cavalry, got among them, and pursued them rapidly down Courtland's-ridge: that active officer had a narrow escape; in striking at one of the fugitives, he lost his balance and fell from his horse; luckily, the Indian had no bayonet, and his musket had been discharged. Lt Col. Simcoe joined the battalion, and seized the heights. A Captain of the rebel light infantry, and a few of his men, were taken; but a body of them, under Major Stewart, who afterwards was distinguished at Stony Point, left the Indians, and fled. Though this ambuscade, in its greater part, failed, it was of consequence. Near forty of the Indians were killed, or desperately wounded; among others, Nimham, a chieftain, who had been in England, and his son; and it was reported to have stopt a larger number of them, who were excellent marksmen, from joining General Washington's army. The Indian doctor was taken; and he said, that when Nimham saw the grenadiers close in his rear, he called out to his people to fly, "that he himself was old, and would die there;" he wounded] Lt. Col. Simcoe, and was killed by Wright, his orderly Huzzar. The Indians fought most gallantly; they pulled more than one of the cavalry from their horses; French, an active youth, bugle-horn to the Huzzars, struck at an Indian, but missed his blow; the man dragged him from his horse, and was searching for his knife to stab him, when, loosening French's hand, he luckily drew out a pocket-pistol, and shot the Indian through the head, in which situation he was found. One man of the Legion cavalry was killed, and one of them, and two of the Huzzars, wounded.[87]

[87] A further contemporary source for this battle is Johann Ewald's *Diary of the American War: A Hessian Journal*; translated and edited by Joseph P. Tustin. Yale University Press, New Haven and London, 1979. p. 145.

BLACK PATRIOTS FOR LIBERTY

It is a regrettable but true that Blacks during the Revolution were often the butt of scorn, derision and ridicule by many on both sides. Phrases like "boys, old men, and negroes,"[88] in describing some of the American rank and file were not intended as compliments. Although today we feel reassured in knowing that Blacks served as soldiers in the Continental Army, some even as NCOs, back then it was, as could be expected, a struggle gaining respect and due recognition. And yet it is, perhaps oddly enough, to its credit that war provided them with an opportunity to attempt to do so; and in this was one way in which the bitter and destructive conflict could be said to have produced beneficial results: not results that were *of themselves* broad and far reaching, but as seeds of later growth and development and which, as part of a process ongoing over the course of generations, did significantly help to raise the American Black male from his hitherto servile and subsidiary class status.

Pre-Civil War abolitionists were not at loss to play up the contribution of Blacks in the Revolutionary War, and William Cooper Nell's *The Colored Patriots of the American Revolution with Sketches of Several Distinguished Colored Persons* (1855), with introduction by Harriet Beecher Stowe, is one exemplary instance of such efforts. The ensuing is taken from pages 129-131 of that volume. The military action being described presumably refers to the battle at Newport, Rhode Island of 29 August 1778 in which the 1st Rhode Island Regiment gallantly distinguished themselves.[89]

~~~***~~~

[William Cooper Nell:] I have received from Mr. George E. Willis, of Providence, the following list of names, as among the colored soldiers in the Rhode Island Regiment during the Revolutionary War:--

SCIPIO BROWN,
PRINCE VAUGHN,
GUY WATSON,
PRIMUS RHODES,
PRINCE GREENE,
HENRY TABOR,
REUBEN ROBERTS,
CÆSAR POWER,
THOMAS BROWN,
SAMSON HAZZARD,
RICHARD RHODES,
CUFF GREENE,
CATO GREENE,
PRINCE JENKS,
PHILO PHILLIPS,
YORK CHAMPLIN,

[88] Orders of Gen. Washington, dated Head-Quarters, Cambridge, November 12, 1775. Initially, both Washington and the Continental Congress, evidently to avoid offending southern slave holder, discouraged the use of blacks as soldiers. But later in 1776, Washington was approached by black veterans, some of whom acquitted themselves as fighters in the siege of Boston, and who petitioned his continued support. For this and the obvious practical need of helping to keep the army manned, he came around to changing his position; ultimately persuading Congress to do the same. It thereafter became a common practice to enlist slaves or hire blacks as substitutes in order to meet a given individual's recruitment obligations.

[89] See the "Narrative of Boyrereau Brinch: An Enslaved African American in the Revolutionary Army, 1777-1783 (1810) – EXCERPTS" which gives one Black soldier's account of his experiences fighting in the American Army, and who by his own report also found himself within the thick of it; available at: http://nationalhumanitiescenter.org/pds/makingrev/war/text6/aframerbrinch.pdf For further reading, see *The Negro in the American Revolution* (1961) by Benjamin Quarles, and also "Black in Blue: African Americans in the Continental Army," *Patriots of the American Revolution* magazine, July/Aug. 2011, vol 4, issue 4, *and* "'They were good soldiers.' African– Americans Serving in the Continental Army," see https://www.scribd.com/doc/123231213/They-were-good-soldiers-African-Americans-Serving-in-the-Continental-Army -- both by John C, Rees
~~~

ICHABOD NORTHUP.
RICHARD COZZENS, a fifer in the Rhode Island Regiment, was born in Africa, and died in Providence. in 1829.

In this connection, the following extracts from an address delivered, in 1842, before the Congregational and Presbyterian Anti-Slavery Society, at Francestown, N. H., by Dr. HARRIS, a Revolutionary veteran, will be read with great interest:--

"I sympathize deeply," said Dr. Harris, "'in the objects of this Society. I fought, my hearers, for the liberty which you enjoy. It surprises me that every man does not rally at the sound of liberty, and array himself with those who are laboring to abolish slavery in our country. The very mention of it warms the blood in my veins, and, old as I am, makes me feel something of the spirit and impulses of '76.

"Then liberty meant something. Then, liberty, independence, freedom, were in every man's mouth. They were the sounds at which they rallied, and under which they fought and bled. They were the words which encouraged and cheered them through their hunger, and nakedness, and fatigue, in cold and in heat. The word slavery then filled their hearts with horror. They fought because they would not be slaves. Those whom liberty has cost nothing, do not know how to prize it.

"I served in the Revolution, in General Washington's army, three years under one enlistment. I have stood in battle, where balls, like hail, were flying all around me. The man standing next to me was shot by my side--his blood spouted upon my clothes, which I wore for weeks. My nearest blood, except that which runs in my veins, was shed for liberty. My only brother was shot dead instantly in the Revolution. Liberty is dear to my heart--I cannot endure the thought, that my countrymen should be slaves.

"When stationed in the State of Rhode Island, the regiment to which I belonged was once ordered to what was called a flanking position,--that is, upon a place which the enemy must pass in order to come round in our rear, to drive us from the fort. This pass was every thing, both to them and to us; of course, it was a post of imminent danger. They attacked us with great fury, but were repulsed. They reinforced, and attacked us again, with more vigor and determination, and again were repulsed. Again they reinforced, and attacked us the third time, with the most desperate courage and resolution, but a third time were repulsed. The contest was fearful. Our position was hotly disputed and as hotly maintained.

"But I have another object in view in stating these facts. I would not be trumpeting my own acts; the only reason why I have named myself in connection with this transaction is, to show that I know whereof I affirm. There was a black regiment in the same situation. Yes, a regiment of negroes, fighting for our liberty and independence,--not a white man among them but the officers,-- stationed in this same dangerous and responsible position. Had they been unfaithful, or given way before the enemy, all would have been lost. Three times in succession were they attacked, with most desperate valor and fury, by well disciplined and veteran troops, and three times did they successfully repel the assault, and thus preserve our army from capture. They fought through the war. They were brave, hardy troops. They helped to gain our liberty and independence.

"Now, the war is over, our freedom is gained--what is to be done with these colored soldiers, who have shed their best blood in its defence? Must they be sent off out of the country, because they are black? or must they be sent back into slavery, now they have risked their lives and shed their blood to secure the freedom of their masters? I ask, what became of these noble colored soldiers? Many of them, I fear, were taken back to the South, and doomed to the fetter and the chain.

"And why is it, that the colored inhabitants of our nation, born in this country, and entitled to all the rights of freemen, are held in slavery? Why, but because they are black? I have often thought, that, should God see fit, by a miracle, to change their color, straighten their hair, and give their features and complexion the appearance of the whites, slavery would not continue a year. No, you would then go and abolish it with the sword, if it were not speedily done without. But is it a suitable cause for making men slaves, because God has given them such a color, such hair and such features, as he saw fit?"

PAULUS: A MONODY

This enchanting and soulful poem, ostensibly inspired in part by Milton's "Lycidas," appears as part of (what amounts to) the appendix to Alexander Garden's *Anecdotes of the Revolutionary War*, second series (1828), pp. 236-238. The effective anonymity of both the subject and author of this "Monody" confers on it a brooding charm and poignancy, and which lend it the verve and air of a Romantic piece written decades later than when it actually was. Perhaps had the author lived, he might have become an American Cowper, Byron, or Shelley; any of whom some, on perusing this both melancholy and defiant effusion, will per chance be reminded of.

~~~***~~~

The Monody which follows, was written very shortly after the commencement of the war of the Revolution, by a young Irish student named DUNN, then attached to the Glasgow College. The name of the friend so pathetically lamented, was (to the best of my recollection) ROGERS, a native of Maryland, who, hastening homewards to assist in defending the liberties of his country, unhappily perished at sea.

PAULUS: A MONODY.

Upon a sea-girt rock Eugenius stood,
And viewed with stedfast eyes the rolling flood;
And still, in every passing wave
He sought his Paulus' watery grave,
And fancy oft the corse descry'd,
Wound in its billowy shroud, and floating with the tide.

But far on wide Atlantic's dreary coast,
Beneath a Promontory's shade,
The youth by pious hands is laid,
And vainly dost thou weep thy Paulus lost,
To distant shores and more inclement skies;
The faithless vessel yielded up her prize.

And are you then at rest,
The sport no longer of the watery waste;
An unprotected corse?
The swain is blest,
Who snatch'd thee from the surge's force,
And hallowed is the glebe that holds thy clay,
And blest the pious youth that sung thy funeral lay.

But ah! thy virtues could he tell,
Thy firm integrity above a price;
Thy warm devotion to the public weal;
Thy ardent friendship honour nice.
Courage with pity still allied,
And modesty that like a veil did all thy virtues hide.

Could he thy innocence declare,
A grace so rare,
When linked with knowledge, that it shone
Complete in thee alone.
Could he thy love of liberal arts proclaim.
Still guided to the noblest end,
Thy country's freedom to defend,
~~~

Not to achieve an empty name.
For this thou oft hast conn'd the historic page,
For this the jurist's knotty lore,
From Alfred's down to William s age,
Increasing still thy copious store,
A future gift for the Atlantic's shore.

Thine was the task her sacred rights to guard,
Her wide-spread States with friendly links to bind;
The happiness of millions thy reward,
Thy monument in every patriot mind.

Soon, as the tyrant spoke the word
'Be slaves! or dread the exterminating sword,'
Britannia's hated isles you fled,
And mourn d her antient spirit dead;
Your native woods you sought,
With Spartan virtue fraught;
That virtue which can fate defy,
Prepared to nobly live or bravely die.

Behold the wish'd for shore,
The tempest howls and Paulus is no more.
Whilst many a mercenary host,
Securely glides along the hapless coast
While safe the German transport bends its sails,
And Caledonia's slaves arrive with prosperous gales --

Yet shall thy country's liberties survive;
Yet shall she triumph o'er her ruthless foe.
And Paulus yet shall live,
Whilst tyrants sink beneath the avenging blow;
Short is the gloomy Despot's sway,
But freedom's radiant form shall never know decay,

Immortal Youth farewell, thy sorrowing friend
This last sad tribute to thy virtues pays,
Too true a mourner justly to commend,
And rich in reverence, though but poor in praise,
Yet shall Columbia oft thy worth rehearse,
When patriot virtue claims her poet's song,
Thy sorrowing friends repeat the solemn verse,
Thy native woods the solemn notes prolong.

THE AMERICAN CAVALRYMAN IN JAMES FENIMORE COOPER'S *THE SPY*

While we must be careful to take much of Fenimore Cooper's *The Spy: a Tale of Neutral Ground* (1821) as history with a grain of salt; still the emotional atmosphere he breathes into his prose, while undeniably larger than life, cannot but have an authentic basis; inasmuch as it is possible for a reader to palpably imbibe that spirit, and that would seem to have emanated as much from real and living persons as much as Cooper's imagination. As well as realistically portraying individuals, the novel delves as deeply, if at times with flamboyant hyperbole, in revealing the respective psychologies of combatant and non-combatant rebels and loyalists generally or on the group level, and this in a believable and convincing manner. Chapter 13, it might be further noted, contains an interesting and lively exchange between an American and British officer over the question of black slavery.

It will or might be of curious notice to some Lee's Legion scholars that the depiction of the Virginia light horsemen in Cooper's tale, and which takes place in Westchester County, N.Y, about 1778, is evidently and at least in significant part drawn from and modeled on Lee's Legion. One reason for surmising this is the apparent resemblance of Maj. Peyton Dunwoodie to Henry Lee (and or one of Lee's officers); at least more resembling of him than, say, other well known Virginia cavalry leaders; like the comparatively mild and less volatile in temper Theodorick Bland, George Baylor, or for that matter William Washington.

~~~***~~~

CHAPTER VII

The game's afoot;
Follow your spirit.
-- Shakespeare.

The rough and unimproved face of the country, the frequency of covers, together with the great distance from their own country, and the facilities afforded them for rapid movements to the different points of the war, by the undisputed command of the ocean, had united to deter the English from employing a heavy force in cavalry, in their early efforts to subdue the revolted colonies.

Only one regiment of regular horse was sent from the mother country, during the struggle [in fact, there were two sent -- the 16th and 17th Light Dragoons]. But legions and independent corps were formed in different places, as it best accorded with the views of the royal commanders, or suited the exigency of the times. These were not unfrequently composed of men raised in the colonies, and at other times drafts were had from the regiments of the line, and the soldiers were made to lay aside the musket and bayonet, and taught to wield the saber and carbine. One particular body of the subsidiary troops was included in this arrangement, and the Hessian yagers were transformed into a corps of heavy and inactive horse.

Opposed to them were the hardiest spirits of America. Most of the cavalry regiments of the continental army were led and officered by gentlemen from the South. The high and haughty courage of the commanders had communicated itself to the privates, who were men selected with care and great attention to the service they were intended to perform.

While the British were confined to their empty conquests in the possession of a few of the larger towns, or marched through counties that were swept of everything like military supplies, the light troops of their enemies had the range of the whole interior.

The sufferings of the line of the American army were great beyond example; but possessing the power, and feeling themselves engaged in a cause which justified severity, the cavalry officers were vigilant in providing for their wants, and the horse were well mounted, well fed, and consequently eminently effective. Perhaps the world could not furnish more brave, enterprising, and resistless corps of light cavalry, than a few that were in the continental service at the time of which we write...

~~~***~~~

CHAPTER VIII

...Dunwoodie had lingered in front of the cottage, after he paid his parting compliments, with an unwillingness to return, that he thought proceeded from his solicitude for his wounded friends. The heart which has not become callous, soon sickens with the glory that has been purchased with a waste of human life. Peyton Dunwoodie, left to himself, and no longer excited by the visions which youthful ardor had kept before him throughout the day, began to feel there were other ties than those which bound the soldier within the rigid rules of honor. He did not waver in his duty, yet he felt how strong was the temptation. His blood had ceased to flow with the impulse created by the battle. The stern expression of his eye gradually gave place to a look of softness; and his reflections on the victory brought with them no satisfaction that compensated for the sacrifices by which it had been purchased. While turning his last lingering gaze on the Locusts [home of the Wharton's], he remembered only that it contained all that he most valued. The friend of his youth was a prisoner [loyalist Capt. Henry Wharton], under circumstances that endangered both life and honor. The gentle companion of his toils, who could throw around the rude enjoyments of a soldier [Capt. Singleton, a youthful American cavalry officer who had been severely wounded] the graceful mildness of peace, lay a bleeding victim to his success. The image of the maid [Frances Wharton] who had held, during the day, a disputed sovereignty in his bosom, again rose to his view with a loveliness that banished her rival, glory, from his mind...

DID PULASKI NAP?

Acting as Brigadier General in the Continental army from 15 Sept. 1777 to his death on 11 Oct. 1779 at the unsuccessful siege of Savannah, Polish born Count Casimir Pulaski (1745-1779) holds the exceptional honor of being named "Father of the American Cavalry." It might seem odd that a foreigner should have been awarded such eminent distinction in the Continetal army's mounted arm. Yet it needs be understood that in the eighteenth century some of the very best cavalrymen came from central and eastern European countries such as Hungary[90] and Poland. Moreover, the young Pulaski had already earned fame fighting for liberty in his homeland (against, at that time, the Russians) prior to his arrival; when he came with the highly regarded (by Congress) recommendations of both Benjamin Franklin and Lafayette. And yet as such his appointed was in some measure diplomatic and political, and while in the army he not infrequently found himself at odds and disagreement with American officers who perhaps did not take kindly to preferment being granted to someone of his foreign, aristocratic, and occasionally exacting temperament. In consequence, as well as other reasons, no actual cavalry brigade was formed under him as was originally intended, and instead, he was effectually reduced to leading a single Legion; albeit the first one (Mar. 1778) and that preceded Lee's and Armand's. Some biographical accounts speak erroneously of his leading cavalry charges at Brandywine, Germantown and Savannah. The first two did not occur, and at Savannah, the advance on the Spring Hill Redoubt in which he was mortally felled was more an approach on enemy siege lines than a charge proper.

The following chapter (IV) from *American Catholic Historical Researches* (1910) by Martin J. Griffin (pp. 18-23) thoughtfully addresses a controversy in part of which it is claimed that Washington did not receive adequate warning or delay of the British counterattack at Germantown owing to Pulaski's having fallen -- literally -- to sleep. While no one for the moment questioned the valiant Pole's courage, there was some who believed, Col. Charles Cotesworh Pinckney in particular, that on the day of Germantown the Count manifested gross negligence. This chapter, but which can be read as an independent article, is singularly illuminating not so much for the specific point debated; for, after all, even if Pulaski had slumbered, we don't know the specific circumstances under which the somnolence was induced, or why an aide simply didn't rouse him. Of more interest is what the controversy reveals about the characters of some of the Continental army's officers, including in addition a large role played in this controversy by Nathanael Greene biographer William Johnson; as each endeavors to exonerate himself and or someone else from dreaded imputations of dishonor.

~~~***~~~

On October 4th [1777] the Battle of Germantown was fought. "The Divisions of Greene and Stephen were the last that retreated and these were covered by Count Pulaski and his Legion." [Lossing's *Field Book*, III, p. 318.]

[Benson J.] Lossing errs in saying "Legion," as it was not then organized. He meant "Cavalry."

"On the day of the battle of Germantown," says Lieutenant Bentalou, "Pulaski was sorely disappointed and mortified. There were but four regiments of horse raised, and not one of them completed. Three of them only, such as they were, had joined General Washington's army, and on the day of battle, guards were furnished out of those regiments, to attend on the Commander-in-Chief and on other Generals -- or employed in other service, so that Pulaski was left with so few men as not to have it in his power to undertake anything of importance. This was to him a matter of deep regret and bitter chagrin."

WAS PULASKI ASLEEP?

In 1822 Judge William Johnson, of Charleston, South Carolina, published *Sketches of Life and Correspondence of Nathaniel Greene, Major-General of the Armies of the Revolution*, in which, in relating about the Battle of Germantown, he stated:

---

[90] Michael Kovats de Fabriczy (1724-1779), a Hungarian cavalry officer who had served under *both* Maria Theresa and Frederick the Great, accompanied Pulaski to America, and was himself slain in fighting near Charleston, S.C. in May 1779.
~~~

"It is a melancholy fact, of which few were informed, that the celebrated Pulaski, who commanded the patrol, was found by General Washington himself asleep in a farm house. Policy only, and a regard to the rank and misfortunes of the offender, could have induced the General to suppress the fact. Yet to this circumstance, most probably, we are to attribute the success of the enemy's patrol in approaching near enough to discover the advance of the American column."

Lieutenant Paul Bentalou, one of Pulaski's surviving officers, "one," he said, "whose pride it shall ever be to have served his country under that celebrated commander—who was by his side when he received his mortal wound, and who attended him 'till the moment when his noble soul departed from the gangrened body, to reascend to its native heaven," issued a reply to Judge Johnson, entitled: *Pulaski Vindicated from an Unsupported Charge Inconsiderately or Malignantly Introduced in Judge Johnson's Sketches of the Life and Correspondence of Gen. Nathaniel Greene*, Baltimore, 1824.

PULASKI VINDICATED.

In this he said: "Those who know anything of Pulaski, may probably exclaim, upon being told of this unaccountable drowsiness, in the most watchful, the most indefatigable, the most active military commander that ever was: 'What! Pulaski asleep at such a moment! at the approach of a battle likely to prove bloody and decisive, and when so much depended on his vigilance! The thing is incredible!'"

The North American Review, No. 47 (1825), also resented the charge of Judge Johnson, whereupon the Judge issued *Remarks, Critical and Historical, on an Article in the Forty-Seventh Number of the North American Review Relating to General Pulaski*, in which he upheld his statement. In a Postscript he declared: "General Lafayette when lately in Columbia, declared it to be true of his own knowledge."

Bentalou in his reply to Johnson's *Remarks* related that when in 1824 Lafayette visited Baltimore he was asked by Bentalou, "whether he had heard Washington or anyone else, say Pulaski had been found asleep by Washington and that the ill success at Germantown was principally to be ascribed to that circumstance?" The inquiry actually caused him to start and he answered with vehemence, "No! Never!"On Lafayette's second visit to Baltimore the question was repeated in the presence of several witnesses and again the answer was "No! Never!" -- and Lafayette proceeded to speak of Pulaski in the highest terms. Hon. John Barney, Representative in Congress and son of Commodore [Joshua] Barney, who was present certified. "My impressions were that the memory of Pulaski was cherished by Lafayette, as a gallant soldier, who had devoted himself to the service of our country, and that he terminated his life without blemish or reproach." [P. 11.]

Judge Johnson in his *Remarks Critical and Historical*, issued in 1825 in reply to Bentalou says in answer to his denial of the truth of the statement of Johnson that Pulaski, being asleep, was the cause of the disaster to the Americans and asking, "Where was the necessity for relating this anecdote respecting Count Pulaski?" said "this is my answer: The question was whether it was or was not the pause at the Chew house which gave time to the enemy to advance and repel the assailants? My reply is that the halt there was but momentary and other causes operated to bring the enemy forward in time to support the party in Chew's house. That they had notice through their patrol of the advance of our army in time to make preparations to receive them." The reply is obvious "that our patrols, or at least one of them did not do their duty."

The British account is that the approach of the Americans was discovered by the British patrols. And Pulaski must have retired early, since the discovery was made at three o'clock, whereas the front of the right column, according to Mr. Marshall, did not encounter the British picket until sunrise.

"Why did not Washington publicly stigmatize Pulaski for the offence?" The Judge's reply is: "At the date of the battle it was all important to conciliate foreigners, forbearance in such a case became almost a duty. The crisis was one at which Washington might well exercise forbearance toward foreigners. He knew not at time of his report to Congress that his approach had been discovered and reported at three o'clock in the morning. Nor could he have known it until long after. He had therefore no specific injury to lay to the charge of Pulaski at the time."

The North American Review, April 1825, answers:

"The kind of 'policy' to which Washington's silence is here ascribed, was not that which became the Commander-in-Chief of a nation's forces, nor is it that which Washington was known in any other case to exercise. Such a policy, indeed, would have been little else than betraying the high trust confided to him, and a most unjustifiable breach of right conduct, in suffering the odious consequences of the neglect of one officer to be borne by those who had faithfully done their duty. Moreover, Washington afterwards recommended Pulaski to Congress, was instrumental in procuring him a very high and responsible appointment in the service and always treated him as an officer, whom he respected, and in whom he had the fullest confidence. These considerations alone are enough to destroy the force of the charge.

"It needs not to be inquired whether Pulaski was found in a farm house or what he did, or whether he did anything, at the battle of Germantown; it is enough to know, that Washington was acquainted with all his conduct there much better than any other person, and that he never lisped a whisper of censure for neglect of duty, but, on the contrary, aided in his future promotion. In short, we doubt not, Judge Johnson has been deceived, and that the authority on which he relied, from whatever source it came, is not entitled to credit; and every generous-minded citizen must lament, that he should have sanctioned, by his name, a charge calculated to reflect no honor on the character of Washington, and to cast reproach on the memory of a brave man, whose fame is so well earned, who devoted his best days to a defence of the rights of outraged humanity in his native land, and when exiled by the usurpers whom he could not conquer, gave the last years of his life, and the last drop of his blood, to the struggles for the liberties of America." In *The Charleston Courier*, April 4, 1825, is a communication signed "An Enemy to Persecution," though it reads as if Judge Johnson was the author. It states:

"It is literally true, as appears from a note voluntarily written by an officer of distinction who was at General Washington's side as his Aide-de-Camp when the discovery was made and heard him express all that indignation which the circumstance so naturally provoked."

The "officer of distinction" was General Charles Cotesworth Pinckney who, on returning to "An Enemy of Persecution" the pamphlet of Bentalou *Pulaski Vindicated,* said, the "author has uniformly attacked Judge Johnson for mentioning the truth about Pulaski."

Johnson declared, further, that Pinckney had "more than once in conversation with me," confirmed "the charge, that General Washington's silence at the time (except to those around him) had regard to the general merits of a brave foreigner whose own feelings, probably, inflicted sufficient punishment and evinced that his subsequent promotion was not likely to injure the service—nor did it. He fought nobly on many future occasions, and died nobly at the siege of Savannah; under circumstances, however, a little different from those stated by his Vindicator. The writer never thought of maliciously detracting from Pulaski's military virtues. It is indeed a false delicacy that would withhold from the public stock of information facts like this."

George Washington Park Custis, adopted son of General Washington, in his *Recollections* says:

"The celebrated Count Pulaski who was charged with the services of watching the enemy and gaining intelligence, was said to have been found asleep in a farm house. But although the gallant Pole might have been overtaken by slumber, from the great fatigue growing out of the duties of the advanced guard, yet no soldier was more wide awake in the moment of combat than the intrepid and chivalric Count Pulaski." [P. 195, Ed. 1860.]

Jared Sparks says, relative to the charge of sleeping:

"He has been charged by one writer with a delinquency at Germantown, in being off his guard at night, while he was in advance of the army, marching towards the enemy's lines. As no other writer has mentioned this circumstance, and as it was never made known to the public till more than forty years after it is said to have occurred, and as it is proved by the whole course of his life, that Pulaski's military fault, if he had one, was that of rushing with too much impetuosity upon the enemy, it seems both idle and unjust to entertain for a moment such a suspicion, especially when it is not pretended to rest on any better foundation than conjecture and hearsay." [*Am. Biog.*, XIV, 421.]

But it is nowhere claimed or shown that Pulaski's patrol was the one on whom the duty lay and in which it failed -- to warn of the presence nearby of the enemy. It is not shown that it was Pulaski's patrol that was at fault if any were. By the British account it would appear that it was the taking possession of the Chew house and the endeavor of the Americans to oust them therefrom that were the important factors in the failure of the Americans to win the battle.

The British Government must have considered the occupation of the Chew House as the cause of the disaster to the Americans. "It was six companies of the South Lancashire Regiment, 40th Regiment of Foot—now the Prince of Wales' Volunteers -- that seized the Chew House and turned the tide of the affray. For this act it was honored with the only medal given to any Regiment by the British government for deeds done in the Revolutionary War." [Taylor's *Valley Forge*, 107.]

Notwithstanding the affair at the Chew House "we ran away from the arms of Victory open to receive us," reported General Wayne.

Washington reported to Congress: "Our troops retreated at the instant when Victory was declaring herself in our favor. The tumult, disorder and despair which it seems had taken place in the British army were scarcely to be paralleled. I can discover no other cause for not improving this happy opportunity than the extreme haziness of the weather."

So even had Pulaski been caught asleep by Washington and he had allowed that delinquency to pass then and ever afterwards, and the affair at the Chew House had retarded operations, yet notwithstanding all these victory lessening factors, the testimony is that they did not seriously defeat the movements of Washington. At any rate whether an almost victory or an unexpected repulse when the news of the battle reached France, Vergennes, the Minister of Foreign Affairs, declared, "The brave Americans are worthy the aid of France." But a few months had to pass in the negotiations until February 6, 1778, when the Treaty of Alliance was signed.

WHAT THEY WERE READING...(in 1786)

What better way to get a sense of public thoughts and sentiments than to have a look over what people are or were reading? The following list consists of some titles, drawn from volume seven of Charles Evans' (1850-1935) irreplaceable catalog of early national literature *American Bibliography: 1639-1820*, of what was on the shelves of American bookstores in the year 1786. The *Cambridge History of American Literature* (1921), vol. III,[91] we might note states that James Buckland's *An Account of the Discovery of a Hermit, Who Lived about 200 Years in a Cave at the Foot of a Hill, 73 Days Journey Westward of the Great Alleghany Mountains* [92] was "probably the best domestic seller of 1786."

~~~*~~~

* AN ADDRESS DELIVERED AT MANCHESTER, [NH] IN THE PRESENCE OF THE OFFICERS AND BRETHREN OF THE NORTH STAR LODGE ON THE FESTIVAL OF ST. JOHN THE EVANGELIST, THE 29TH OF DECEMBER, 1785. By ONE OF THE BRETHREN.
Bennington, Vermont, Printed by Hastnell & Russell, 1786. pp. 17. 12mo.

* NEW SENTIMENTS, DIFFERENT FROM ANY YET PUBLISHED, UPON THE DOCTRINE OF UNIVERSAL SALVATION, AS CONNECTED WITH DOCTRINES GENERALLY APPROVED. REMARKS UPON THE FORCE OF DIVINE REVELATION. A GENERAL VIEW OF ANCIENT CHRISTIANITY COMPARED WITH MODERN. A SKETCH OF CHURCH HISTORY, AND RELIGION OF NATIONS. BY ADELOS. [Two lines from] MEN OF ATHENS.
Providence: Printed by Bennett Wheeler. 1786. pp. [62], (61-68). 8vo.

* THE ADVENTURES OF A HACKNEY COACH.
Philadelphia: Printed and sold by Enoch Story, 1786.

* ADVICE FROM A LADY OF QUALITY TO HER CHILDREN; IN THE LAST STAGE OF A LINGERING ILLNESS. TRANSLATED FROM THE FRENCH BY S. GLASSE, D. D. F. R. 8. CHAPLAIN IN ORDINARY TO HIS MAJESTY.
Philadelphia: Printed and sold by Young and M'Culloch, corner of Second and Chesnut-Streets. 1786. 2 vols. in one.

* SELECT FABLES OP AESOP AND OTHER FABULISTS. IN THREE BOOKS. CONTAINING FABLES FROM THE ANCIENTS, FABLES FROM THE MODERNS, in. ORIGINAL FABLES, NEWLY INVENTED. BY ROBERT DODSLEY.

* "PARADISE LOST." A NEW EDITION.
Philadelphia: Printed and sold by Joseph Crukshank, in Market-Street, between Second and Third-Streets. MDCCLXXXVI. pp. 228, (1), frontispiece. 12mo. AAS.

* A CONCISE DISCANT ON THE BEAUTIES OF THE SCRIPTURES. BY J. ALLEN, D. D. WITH THE REMARKABLE CONVERSION OF THE REV. MR. HART.
Philadelphia: Printed and sold by Enoch Story, 1786.

* A SERMON, DELIVERED THE NEXT SABBATH AFTER THE SUDDEN DEATH OF ELIPHALET KIMBALL, . . . WHO WAS DROWNED IN MERRIMACK RIVER, OCTOBER 24, 1785.
Newbury-Port : Printed by John Mycall. 1786.

* CHRIST IN THE CLOUDS COMING TO JUDGMENT; OR THE DISSOLUTION OF ALL THINGS. BY THE REV. ISAAC AMBROSE.
Boston: Printed and sold at John Boyle's Printing-Office, Marlborough- Street. [1786.] pp. 15. 16mo. AAS.

---

[91] p. 539.
[92] See *Continental Army Series*, vol. II, ch. 36.
~~~

* AMERICAN PHILOSOPHICAL SOCIETY. TRANSACTIONS OF THE AMERICAN PHILOSOPHICAL SOCIETY, HELD AT PHILADELPHIA, FOR PROMOTING USEFUL KNOWLEDGE. VOLUME II.
Philadelphia : Printed and sold by Robert Aitken, at Pope's Head in Market-Street. M.DCC.LXXXVI. pp. xxxii, 397, (10), plates, chart. 4to. AAS. Plates engraved by James Poupard. The Chart of the Gulf Stream is accompanied by Remark, by Dr. Franklin.

* THE AMERICAN PRICE-CURRENT, CONTAINING THE MARKET PRICE OF EVERY COMMODITY; ALSO, DUTIES, DRAWBACKS, PRICE OF AMERICAN STOCKS, MARINE LIST, SHIP NEWS, SALES AT AUCTION, PREMIUMS OF INSURANCE, COURSE OF EXCHANGE WITH EUROPE, &c., &c., WITH A VARIETY OF OTHER USEFUL INFORMATION. THE WHOLE REGULATED BY THE ASSISTANCE OF SEVERAL BROKERS AND FACTORS. NO. 1. MONDAY, MAY 1, [No. 14. MONDAY, JULY 31, 1786.]
New-York: Printed by Francis Childs, 1786. Sm. fol.

* ADDRESS TO THE PUBLIC, CONTAINING SOME REMARKS ON THE PRESENT POLITICAL STATE OF THE AMERICAN REPUBLICKS, &C. BY AMICUS REPUBLICS.
December 4, 1786. Exeter : Printed and sold by Lamson and Ranlet, at their office, near the Treasurer's. [1786.] pp. [36.] 12mo. HC. LOC. NYPL.

* A MIRROR, REPRESENTING SOME RELIGIOUS CHARACTERS OF THE PRESENT TIMES. BY MR. JOHN ANDERSON. [One line from] PHILIP, n. 21.
Philadelphia: Printed by Young, Stewart and M'Culloch, the corner of Chesnut and Second-Streets. M.DCC.LXXX.VI. pp. (2), 59. 8vo. AAS. CLS.

* ANDREWS'S SOUTH-CAROLINA AND GEORGIA ALMANACK AND EPHEMERIS, FOR THE YEAR OF OUR LORD 1787, BEING THE 3o AFTER BISSEXTILE OR LEAP YEAR.
Savannah: [Printed at Nassau, New-Providence, by John Wells.] Sold at the Printing-Office by N. Johnston, [1786.]

* AN ORATION DELIVERED JULY 4, 1786, AT THE REQUEST OF THE INHABITANTS OF THE TOWN OF BOSTON, IN CELEBRATION OF THE ANNIVERSARY OF AMERICAN INDEPENDENCE. BY JONATHAN L. AUSTIN, ESQ.
Boston: Printed by Peter Edes. [1786.] pp. 19. 4to. AAS. BA. LOC.

* THE VIRGINIA ALMANACK, FOR THE YEAR 1787. BEING THE THIRD AFTER BISSEXTILE OR LEAP YEAR. CALCULATED ACCORDING TO ART, AND WILL ANSWER EITHER VIRGINIA OR NORTH-CAROLINA.
Richmond: Printed by Augustine Davis. [1786.] pp. (36). 18mo. VSL.

* PLAY-BILL OF ISABELLA; AND THE LIAR. As PERFORMED BY THE OLD AMERICAN COMPANY AT ANNAPOLIS, [MD] DECEMBER, 5, 1786.
[Annapolis: Printed by F. and 8. Green, 1781.] Broadside.

* GRAMMATICAL INSTITUTES: OR AN EASY INTRODUCTION TO DR. LOWTH'S ENGLISH GRAMMAR: DESIGNED FOR THE USE OF SCHOOLS, AND TO LEAD YOUNG GENTLEMEN AND LADIES, INTO THE KNOWLEDGE OF THE FIRST PRINCIPLES OF THE ENGLISH LANGUAGE. BY JOHN ASH, L. L. D.
New-York: Printed and sold by Shepard Kollock, 1786.

* OBSERVATIONS ON THE PERNICIOUS PRACTICE OF THE LAW. PUBLISHED OCCASIONALLY IN THE INDEPENDENT CHRONICLE. BY HONESTUB.
Boston: Printed by Adams and Nourse, in Court-Street. M,DCC.LXXXVI.

* A SHORT TREATISE ON RICE MACHINERY; WITH A SCHEDULE OF THE EXPENSE. ALSO, THE CONSTRUCTION OF PUMPS. WITH PROPER TABLES, &C. BY J. B. ESQ; OF SOUTH-CAROLINA, 1786.
Charleston: Printed by Bowen and Maryland 1786.

* PLAY-BILL OF THE WONDER; AND THE DEUCE is IN HIM. SEPTEMBER 11, 1786.
[Baltimore: Printed by John Hayes 1786.] Broadside.

* DOCTOR WATTS'S IMITATION OF THE PSALMS OF DAVID, CORRECTED AND ENLARGED. BY JOEL BARLOW. TO WHICH IS ADDED A COLLECTION OF HYMNS; THE WHOLE APPLIED TO THE STATE OP THE CHRISTIAN CHURCH IN GENERAL. THE SECOND EDITION. LUKE xxiv.
Hartford: Printed by [Barlow and Babcock Hudson and Goodwin, and Nathaniel Patten. [With the privilege of copy-right.] [1786.]

* A WONDERFUL DISCOVERY OF A HERMIT! AND A MOST REMARKABLE NARRATIVE OF A CITIZEN OF LONDON, WHO LEFT HIS NATIVE COUNTRY ON ACCOUNT OF BEING CONNECTED WITH A NOBLEMAN'S DAUGHTER, AND SAILED IN A SHIP BOUND FOR ITALY; GIVING ALSO A PARTICULAR ACCOUNT OF HIS BEING BY MISFORTUNE SHIPWRECKED AND CAST ON THE AMERICAN SHORE IN THE YEAR 1580, AND LATELY FOUND WELL IN A CAVE BACK OF THE VIRGINIA MOUNTAINS, AGED TWO HUNDRED AND TWENTY-SEVEN YEARS, BY CAPT. JAMES BUCKLAND AND MR. JOHN FIELDING, TWO GENTLEMEN WHO IN JUNE, 1785, WERE RECONNOITERING THE BACK COUNTRY. CONTAINING ALSO A DETAIL OF THE TIME AND MANNER OF HIS COMING THERE; HIS WAY OF LIVING, &c.
[Boston : Printed by Ezekiel Russell and] Sold at the Office near Liberty Pole; where may be had, A Wonderful account of the death and burial of the above Hermit. [1786.] Broadside, fol. AAS.

* THE SEAMAN'S JOURNAL. BEING AN EASY AND CORRECT METHOD OF KEEPING THE DAILY RECKONING OF A SHIP DURING THE COURSE OF HER VOYAGE.
New-York: Printed and sold by Hugh Gaine, 1786.

* A SURPRIZING THOUGH TRUE ACCOUNT, OF THE STRANGE & WICKED LIFE, AND THE HAPPY CONVERSION, OF PHOEBE FIELDING, OF THE CITY OF LONDON, SHEWING THE ILL CONSEQUENCES OF BAD COMPANY TO YOUNG WOMEN, AND THE BAD TENDENCY OF THE CONDUCT OF PARENTS AND FRIENDS, IN DISCARDING DAUGHTERS OR RELATIONS, FOR ACCIDENTAL DEVIATIONS FROM THE PATHS OF VIRTUE. WRITTEN BY HERSELF. PUBLISHED FOR THE BENEFIT OF YOUNG PEOPLE IN THE YEAR 1785, BY PARTICULAR ORDER, AND AT THE PRIVATE EXPENCE OF THE BENEVOLENT SOCIETY IN LONDON; AND BY THEM EARNESTLY RECOMMENDED TO THE PERUSAL OF CHRISTIANS OF ALL DENOMINATIONS. [Signed, Phoebe Catherines.]
Re-printed in Bennington, in the State of Vermont, by Hancell & Russell, in the year of our Lord, M,DCC,LXXXVI. pp. 12. 12mo. AAS.

* THE CATHOLICK CHRISTIAN INSTRUCTED IN THE SACRAMENTS, SACRIFICE, CEREMONIES, AND OBSERVANCES OF THE CHURCH. BY THE LATE RT. REV. R. CHALLONER, D. D.
Philadelphia: Printed by and for C. Talbot, in Front-Street, Editor of Reeve's History of the Bible, 1786. pp. (4), 264. 12mo. AAS.

* GOD ADMONISHING HIS PEOPLE OF THEIR DUTY, AS PARENTS AND MASTERS. A SERMON, PREACHED AT NEW-LONDON, DECEMBER 20TH, 1786. OCCASIONED BY THE EXECUTION OF HANNAH OCUISH, A MULATTO GIRL, AGED 12 YEARS AND 9 MONTHS, FOR THE MURDER OF EUNICE BOLLES, AGED 6 YEARS AND 6 MONTHS. BY HENRY CHANNING, M. A.
New-London: Printed by T. Green. M,DCC,LXXXVI. pp. [31.] 8vo. AAS.

* CHILD'S DAILY PRESENT.
Philadelphia: Printed and sold by W. Spotswood, in Front-Street, 1786.

* CHILD'S PLAY THING, OH EASY SPELLING.
Philadelphia: Printed and sold by W. Spotswood, in Front-Street, 1786.

* CHILD'S POCKET COMPANION.
Philadelphia: Printed and sold by W. Spotswood, in Front-Street, 1786.

* CHRISTMAS RHYME, ON SWING SWANG, &C.
Philadelphia: Printed and told by W. Spotswood, in front-Street, 1786.

* A CIRCUMSTANTIAL NARRATIVE OF THE LOSS OF THE HALSEWELL, EAST-INDIAMAN, CAPT. RICHARD PIERCE, WHICH WAS UNFORTUNATELY WRECKED AT SEACOMB, IN THE ISLE OF PURBECK, ON THE COAST OF DORSETSHIRE, ON FRIDAY, JANUARY 6, 1786. WITH HER WERE LOST

TWO HUNDRED SOULS.
Springfield: Printed and sold by Stebbins and Russell 1786.

* AN INTRODUCTION TO THE MAKING OF LATIN. COMPOSING, AFTER AN EASY COMPENDIOUS METHOD, THE SUBSTANCE OF THE LATIN SYNTAX, WITH PROPER ENGLISH EXAMPLES, MOST OF THEM TRANSLATIONS FROM THE CLASSICS AUTHORS, IN ONE COLUMN, AND THE LATIN WORDS IN ANOTHER. To WHICH IS SUBJOINED, IN THE SAME METHOD, A SUCCINCT ACCOUNT OF THE AFFAIRS OF ANCIENT GREECE AND ROME, INTENDED AT ONCE TO BRING BOYS ACQUAINTED WITH HISTORY, AND THE IDIOM OF THE LATIN TONGUE. WITH RULES FOR THE GENDER OF NOUNS. BY JOHN CLARKE, LATE MASTER OF THE PUBLIC GRAMMAR SCHOOL IN HULL. THE FIRST WORCESTER EDITION; CAREFULLY CORRECTED; AND DILIGENTLY REVISED BY THE TWENTY-FOURTH LONDON EDITION.
Printed at Worcester, Massachusetts by Isaiah Thomas, . . . MDCC- LXXXVI. pp. xii, 276. 12mo. AAS. LOC.

* AN ESSAY ON THE SLAVERY AND COMMERCE OF THE HUMAN SPECIES, PARTICULARLY THE AFRICAN. TRANSLATED FROM A LATIN DISSERTATION, WHICH WAS HONOURED WITH THE FIRST PRIZE IN THE UNIVERSITY OF CAMBRIDGE, FOR THE YEAR 1785, WITH ADDITIONS. [One line of Latin from] LIVY.
London, Printed: Philadelphia: lie-printed by Joseph Crukshank, in Market-Street, between Second and Third-Streets. MDCCLXXXVI

* A COPY OF A LETTER, WRITTEN BY OUR BLESSED LORD AND SAVIOR, JESUS CHRIST, AND FOUND UNDER A GREAT STONE, 65 YEARS AFTER HIS CRUCIFIXION.
London, Printed: Botton, He-printed and told [by John Boyle] at the Printing-Office in Marlborough-Street. [1786.] pp. 8. 16mo. AAS.

* THE DEATH AND BURIAL OF COCK ROBIN; WITH THE TRAGICAL DEATH OF A. APPLE PYE.
Philadelphia: Printed and sold by W. Spotswood, in Front-Street, 1786.

* TRAVELS OF ROBINSON CRUSOE. WRITTEN BY HIMSELF.
Worcester, Massachusetts, Printed by Isaiah Thomas, MDCCLXXXVI.

* A BRIEF AND REMARKABLE NARRATIVE OF THE LIFE AND EXTREME SUFFERINGS OF BARNABAS DOWNS, JUN. WHO WAS AMONG THE NUMBER OF THOSE WHO ESCAPED DEATH ON BOARD THE PRIVATEER BRIG ARNOLD, JAMES MAYER, COMMANDER, WHICH WAS CAST AWAY NEAR PLYMOUTH-HARBOUR, IN A MOST TERRIBLE SNOW-STORM, DECEMBER 26, 1778, WHEN MORE THAN SIXTY PERSONS WERE FROZEN TO DEATH. CONTAINING ALSO A PARTICULAR ACCOUNT OF SAID SHIPWRECK.[93]
[Boston:] Printed by E. Russell, for the Author, 1786. pp. 16. 16mo. AAS.

* THE FAIRING; OR, GOLDEN TOY FOR CHILDREN OF ALL SIZES AND DENOMINATIONS, IN WHICH THEY CAN SEE ALL THE FUN IN THE FAIR, AND AT HOME BE AS HAPPY AS IF THEY WERE THERE. A BOOK OF GREAT CONSEQUENCE TO ALL WHOM IT MAY CONCERN.
Philadelphia : Printed and sold by W. Spots-wood, in Front-Street, 1786.

* A FAITHFUL NARRATIVE OF ELIZABETH WILSON, WHO WAS EXECUTED AT CHESTER, JANUARY 30, 1786, CHARGED WITH THE MURDER OF HER TWIN INFANTS. CONTAINING SOME ACCOUNT OF HER DYING SAYINGS; WITH SOME SERIOUS REFLECTIONS. DRAWN UP AT THE REQUEST OP A FRIEND

* A FEW SALUTARY HINTS, POINTING OUT THE POLICY AND CONSEQUENCES OF ADMITTING BRITISH SUBJECTS TO ENGROSS OUR TRADE AND BECOME OUR CITIZENS. ADDRESSED TO THOSE WHO EITHER RISQUED OR LOST THEIR ALL IN BRINGING ABOUT THE REVOLUTION. [Six lines from] ECCLESIASTICUS, CHAP. xn. VERSE
Charleston: Printed by Surd and Haswell, 1786. pp. 10. 12mo.

---

[93] See chapter 41 of *Continental Army Series*, volume II.

* THE FOLLOWING ODE, ON THE BIRTH-DAY OF HIS EXCELLENCY GENERAL WASHINGTON, CELEBRATED BY THE ADOPTED SONS, AT THE PENNSYLVANIA COFFEE-HOUSE IN PHILADELPHIA, WAS COMPOSED BY A MEMBER OP THE SOCIETY.
Philadelphia: Printed by M. Carey and Co. in Front-Street. 1786.

* THE NEW-YORK DIRECTORY. CONTAINING, A VALUABLE AND WELL CALCULATED ALMANACK; TABLES OF THE DIFFERENT COINS, SUITABLE FOR ANY STATE, AND DIGESTED IN SUCH ORDER, AS TO RENDER AN EXCHANGE BETWEEN ANY OF THE UNITED STATES PLAIN AND EASY. LIKEWISE, 1. THE NAMES OF ALL THE CITIZENS, THEIR OCCUPATIONS AND PLACES OF ABODE. 2. THE MEMBERS IN CONGRESS, FROM WHAT STATE, AND WHERE RESIDING. 3. GRAND DEPARTMENTS OF THE UNITED STATES FOR ADJUSTING PUBLIC ACCOUNTS, AND BY WHOM CON DUCTED. 4. MEMBERS IN SENATE AND ASSEMBLY, FHOM WHAT COUNTY, AND WHERE RESIDING. 5. JUDGES, ALDERMEN, AND OTHER CIVIL OFFICERS, WITH THEIR PLACES OF ABODE. 6. PUBLIC STATE-OFFICERS, AND BY WHOM KEPT. 7. COUNSELLORS AT LAW, AND WHERE RESIDING. 8. MINISTERS OF THE GOSPEL, WHERE RESIDING AND OF WHAT CHURCH. 9. PHYSICIAN, SURGEONS, AND THEIR PLACES OF ABODE. 10. PRESIDENT, DIRECTORS, DAYS, AND HOURS OF BUSINESS AT THE BANK. 11. PROFESSORS, &c. OF THE UNIVERSITY OF COLUMBIA COLLEGE. 12. RATES OF POSTAGE, AS BY LAW ESTABLISHED. 13. ARRIVALS AND DEPARTURES OF THE MAILS AT THE POST-OFFICE. BY DAVID FRANKS.
New-York: Printed by Shepard Kollock, corner of Wall and Water Streets, M,DCC,LXXX,VI.

* THE POEMS OF PHILIP FRENEAU. WRITTEN CHIEFLY DURING THE LATE WAR.
Philadelphia: Printed by Francis Bailey, at Yorick's Head, in Market- Street. MDCCLXXXVI. pp. vii, (1), 407. 8vo. BM. BPL. HSP. JOB. LOC. MHS. Reprinted in London in 1861.

* THE HISTORY OF LITTLE GOODY TWO-SHOES;[94] OTHERWISE CALLED MRS. MARGERY TWO-SHOES. WITH THE MEANS BY WHICH SHE ACQUIRED HER LEARNING AND WISDOM, AND IN CONSEQUENCE THEREOF HER ESTATE. SET FORTH AT LARGE FOR THE BENEFIT OF THOSE WHO FROM A STATE OF RAGS AND CARE, AND HAVING SHOES BUT HALF A PAIR; TITLES FORTUNE AND THEIR FAME WOULD FIX, AND GALLOP IN A COACH AND SIX. SEE THE ORIGINAL MANUSCRIPT IN THE VATICAN AT ROME, AND THE CUTS BY MICHAEL ANGELO. ILLUSTRATED WITH THE COMMENTS OF OUR GREAT MODERN CRITICS.
Philadelphia: Printed and sold by W. Spotswood, in Front-Street, 1786.

* THE HISTORY OF LITTLE KING PIPPIN, WITH AN ACCOUNT OF THE MELANCHOLY DEATH OF FOUR NAUGHTY BOYS, WHO WERE DEVOURED BY WILD BEASTS.
Philadelphia: Printed and sold by Young, Stewart and MCulloch, the corner of Chesnut and Second-Street, 1786.

* THE HISTORY OF THE HOLY JESUS, CONTAINING A BRIEF AND PLAIN ACCOUNT OF His BIRTH, LIFE, DEATH, RESURRECTION AND ASCENSION INTO HEAVEN; AND HIS COMING AGAIN AT THE CHEAT AND LAST DAY OF JUDGMENT. BEING A PLEASANT AND PROFITABLE COMPANION FOR CHILDREN; COMPOSED ON PURPOSE FOR THEIR USE. BY A LOVER OF THEIR PRECIOUS SOULS. THE FIRST WORCESTER EDITION. Worcester, (Massachusetts) Printed by Isaiah Thomas

* A DISCOURSE ON THE CAUSES OF NATIONAL PROSPERITY, ILLUSTRATED BY ANCIENT AND MODERN HISTORY, EXEMPLIFIED IN THE LATE AMERICAN REVOLUTION. ADDRESSED TO THE SOCIETY OF THE CINCINNATI, IN THE STATE OF RHODE-ISLAND, AT THEIR ANNUAL MEETING AT EAST-GREENWICH, JULY 4, 1786. BY ENOS HITCHCOCK, A. M. OF PROVIDENCE. [One line of Latin from] VIRGIL.
Providence: Printed by Bennett Wheeler. [1786.] pp.28. 8vo. AAS. BA.

---

[94] Commonly assumed to have been written by Oliver Goldsmith. See *Continetal Army Series...Odds and Ends*, p. 172.

THE AMERICAN WAR SERVICE OF LORD EDWARD FITZGERALD

Although the life of Irish peer and honored revolutionary Lord Edward Fitzgerald (1763-1798) was of a tragically brief span -- dieing valiantly at the age of 36 in a failed uprising attempt against British rule in Ireland in late May 1798 -- it managed to contain a remarkable amount of activity and travel for such a young man; including some years spent fighting on behalf *of the British in the American war for Independence, and where he crossed swords, perhaps literally, against Lee's Legion at the battle of Quinby Bridge, S.C., 17 July, 1781.*

The following is an extract describing his American Revolutionary War record taken from vol. I, pp. 17-28, of The Life and Death of Lord Edward Fitzgerald *(1831), written by renown and popular Irish poet and composer of songs, Thomas Moore (1779-1852). Moore, at one time a traveling companion and confidante of Lord Byron, though liked for his writings in this country, took a dim view of Jefferson's Democratic-Republican America when, in 1804, he made a tour of that took him from Norfolk, Virginia, (where he first disembarked) up finally into Canada. He composed several satirical poems on what he perceived to be ochlocracy and lack of culture in the newly established nation; and found himself most at home during his visit chiefly among Federalists and British sympathizers. Ironically, whether his radical idol Lord Edward would have shared his disdainful sentiments is understandably open to conjecture.*

~~~****~~~

At the beginning of June [1781], Lord Edward's regiment [the 19th Regt. of Foot], and the two others that sailed with it from Cork, landed at Charlestown. Their arrival at this crisis was an event most seasonable for the relief of the English forces acting in that quarter, who were, by the late turn of the campaign, placed in a situation of arduous difficulty. The corps under Lord Rawdon's command at Charlestown having been found hardly sufficient for the defence of that capital, he was unable, with any degree of safety, to detach from his already inadequate force such aid as, in more than one point, the perilous state of the province required. Post after post had fallen into the hands of the Americans, and the important fort called "Ninety-Six," which had been for some time invested by General Greene, was now also on the point of being lost for want of those succours which the straitened means of Lord Rawdon prevented him from affording.

In this juncture the three regiments from Ireland arrived, and gave an entirely new aspect to the face of affairs. Though destined originally to join Lord Cornwallis, they were, with a prompt sense of the exigencies of the moment, placed, by the officer who had the command of them, at the disposal of Lord Rawdon, and thus enabled his Lordship, not only to relieve the garrison of Ninety-Six, but also to follow up this impression with a degree of energy and confidence, of which even his enterprising gallantry would have been without such aid incapable. It was, indeed, supposed that the American general was not a little influenced in his movements by the intelligence which he had received, that the newly arrived troops were "particularly full of ardour for an opportunity of signalizing themselves."

That Lord Edward was among these impatient candidates for distinction can little be doubted; and it was but a short time after their joining he had the good fortune to achieve a service which was not only brilliant but useful, and brought him both honour and reward. The 19th regiment, being posted in the neighbourhood of a place called Mon[c]k's Corner, found itself menaced, one morning at daybreak, with an attack from Colonel Lee, one of the ablest and most enterprising of the American partisans. This officer having made some demonstrations, at the head of his cavalry, in front of the 19th, the colonel of that regiment (ignorant, as it appears, of the nature of American warfare), ordered a retreat; -- a movement wholly unnecessary, and rendered still more discreditable by the unmilitary manner in which it was effected: all the baggage, sick, medicines, and paymasters' chests being left in the rear of the column of march, where they were liable to be captured by any half-dozen stragglers. Fortunately, Lord Edward was upon the rear-guard, covering the retreat of the regiment, and, by the firm and determined countenance of his little party, and their animated fire, kept the American corps in check till he was able to break up a small wooden bridge over a creek which separated him from his pursuers, and which could not be crossed by the
~~~

enemy without making a long detour. Having secured safety so far, Lord Edward reported the state of affairs to the colonel; and, the disreputable panic being thus put an end to, the regiment resumed its original position.

Major Doyle, now General Sir John Doyle, -- an officer whom but to name is to call up in the minds of all who have the happiness of knowing him whatever is most estimable and amiable, both in the soldier and the man, -- was, at this time, at the head of Lord Rawdon's staff; and to him, acting as adjutant-general, the official report of the whole affair was made. Without delay he submitted it to his noble chief, who was so pleased with this readiness of resource, in. so young an officer, that he desired Major Doyle to write instantly to Lord Edward in his name, and offer him the situation of aide-de-camp on his staff.

This appointment was, in every respect, fortunate for the young soldier, as, besides bringing him into near relations with a nobleman so amiable, it placed him where he was enabled to gratify his military tastes by seeing war carried on upon a larger and more scientific scale, and, it may be added, under one of the very best masters. He accordingly repaired to head-quarters, and from thence accompanied Lord Rawdon in his rapid and successful movement for the relief of Ninety-Six.

It was in the course of this expedition that Lord Edward exhibited, -- or rather was detected in, -- a trait of personal courage, of that purely adventurous kind which is seldom found but in romance, and of which the following particulars have been related to me by the distinguished person then acting as adjutant-general.

"Among the varied duties which devolved upon me as chief of the staff, a most material one was obtaining intelligence. This was effected partly by the employment of intelligent spies in various directions, and partly by frequent reconnaissances; which last were not devoid of danger, from the superior knowledge of the country possessed by the enemy. Upon these occasions I constantly found Lord Edward by my side, with the permission of our noble chief, who wished our young friend to see every thing connected with real service. In fact the danger enhanced the value of the enterprise in the eyes of this brave young creature. In approaching the position of Ninety-Six, the enemy's light troops in advance became more numerous, and rendered more frequent patrols necessary upon our part.

"I was setting out upon a patrol, and sent to apprise Lord Edward; but he was nowhere to be found, and I proceeded without him, when, at the end of two miles, upon emerging from the forest, I found him engaged with two of the enemy's irregular horse: he had wounded one of his opponents, when his sword broke in the middle, and he must have soon fallen in the unequal contest, had not his enemies fled on perceiving the head of my column. I rated him most soundly, as you may imagine, for the undisciplined act of leaving the camp, at so critical a time, without the general's permission. He was, -- or pretended to be, -- very penitent, and compounded for my reporting him at the head-quarters, provided I would let him accompany me, in the hope of some other enterprise. It was impossible to refuse the fellow, whose frank, manly, and ingenuous manner would have won over even a greater tyrant than myself. In the course of the day we took some prisoners, which I made him convey to head-quarters, with a *Bellerophon* message, which he fairly delivered. Lord Moira gravely rebuked him; but I could never find that he lost *much ground* with his chief for his *chivalrous valour*."

After the relief of Ninety-Six, Lord Rawdon, whose health had suffered severely from the climate, found it advisable to return to England, in consequence of which Lord Edward rejoined his regiment.

The calm that succeeded Lord Rawdon's departure from South Carolina, owing to the activity with which he had retrieved the affairs of the royal forces, and thus established an equipoise of strength between the two parties, could be expected, of course, only to last till one of them had become powerful enough to disturb it. Accordingly, in the autumn, General Greene, having received reinforcements from another quarter, proceeded, with his accustomed vigour, to resume offensive operations; and, by his attack upon Colonel Stuart [Lieut. Col. Alexander Stewart], at Eutaw Springs, gave rise to one of the best fought actions that had occurred during the war. Though the meed of victory, on this occasion, was left doubtful between the claimants, that of honour is allowed to have been fairly the due of both. So close, indeed, and desperate was the encounter, that every officer engaged is said to have had, personally, and hand to hand, an opportunity of distinguishing himself; and Lord Edward, who, we may take for granted, was among the foremost in the strife, received a severe wound in the thigh, which left him insensible on the field.

In this helpless situation he was found by a poor negro, who carried him off on his back to his hut, and there nursed him most tenderly, till he was well enough of his wound to bear removing to Charlestown. This negro was no other than the "faithful Tony," whom, in gratitude for the honest creature's kindness, he now took into his service, and who continued devotedly attached to his noble master to the end of his career.

It had been intended that Major Doyle, on the departure of Lord Rawdon, should resume the station he had before held on the staff of Lord Cornwallis; but in consequence of this irruption of new forces into the province, he was requested by General Goold [Paston Gould], who had succeeded to the chief command, still to continue to him the aid of his local knowledge and experience, so as to avert the mischiefs which a total want of confidence in most of the persons newly appointed to command now threatened. Major Doyle therefore again took upon himself the duties of adjutant-general and public secretary, and proceeded, vested with full powers, to the scene of the late action, for the purpose both of ascertaining the true state of affairs, and of remedying the confusion into which they had been thrown. Here he found Lord Edward slowly recovering from his wound, and the following is the account which he gives of his young friend: -- "I am not sure that he was not then acting as aide-de-camp to Stuart, as the 19th, I think, was not there. At all events, he had been foremost in the melee, as usual, and received a very severe wound in the thigh. At this same time, Colonel Washington, a distinguished officer of the enemy's cavalry, was severely wounded and made prisoner; and while I was making preparations to send them down comfortably to Charlestown, Lord Edward, forgetting his own wound, offered his services to *take charge* of his gallant enemy. I saw him every day till he recovered, about which time I was sent to England with the public despatches [sic]."

To these notices of a part of his lordship's life, hitherto so little known, it would be unjust not to add the few words of comment, as eloquently as they are cordially expressed, with which the gallant writer closes his communication to me on the subject: --

"Of my lamented and ill-fated friend's excellent qualities I should never tire in speaking. I never knew so loveable a person, and every man in the army, from the general to the drummer, would cheer the expression. His frank and open manner, his universal benevolence, his *gaiete de coeur*, his valour almost chivalrous, and, above all, his unassuming tone, made him the idol of all who served with him. He had great animal spirits, which bore him up against all fatigue; but his courage was entirely independent of those spirits -- it was a valour *sui generis*.

"Had fortune happily placed him in a situation, however difficult, where he could *legitimately* have brought those varied qualities into play, I am confident he would have proved a proud ornament to his country."

It may not perhaps, though anticipating a period so much later, appear altogether ill-timed to mention in this place, that when Lord Edward lay suffering under the fatal wounds of which he died in 1798, a military man connected with government, who had known him at this time in Charlestown, happening to allude, during a visit to him in prison, to the circumstances under which they had first become acquainted, the gallant sufferer exclaimed -- "Ah! I was wounded then in a very different cause; -- that was in fighting against liberty -- this, in fighting for it."

It is, indeed, not a little striking that there should have been engaged at this time, on opposite sides, in America, two noble youths, Lafayette and Lord Edward Fitzgerald, whose political principles afterwards so entirely coincided; and that, while one of them was fated early to become the victim of an unsuccessful assertion of these principles, it has been the far brighter destiny of the other to contribute more than once, splendidly to their triumph.

TWO "CONNECTICUT WITS" – Joel Barlow and David Humphreys

Joel Barlow (1754-1812) was one of the "Connecticut Wits" -- along with Timothy Dwight, John Trumbull, David Humphreys, Lemuel Hopkins, and Richard Alsop -- and who gathered in the late 1780's in Hartford for purposes of showing, by way of verse and essays published in newspapers, high-minded support for Federalist-Nationalism; accompanied by a satirical contempt and ridiculing scorn for lawlessness and disorder, as manifested in Shays' rebellion, and mindless levelers, including ingratitude displayed by some citizens toward retiring Continental army officers with respect to the latter's receiving just reimbursement for their war service. In addition to at one time acting as chaplain for the 3rd Mass. brigade, and subsequently becoming lawyer, bookseller, land dealer, newspaper publisher, and European diplomat under Madison, Barlow was particularly conspicuous for being both a genuinely pious, if ad hoc (it took him six weeks to be ordained) clergyman, *and* flaming pro-French Revolutionary. Emory Elliott in his *Revolutionary Writers: Literature and Authority in the New Republic, 1725-1810* (1986) makes a point of demonstrating that several of the Connecticut Wits and other important writers of the early United States took up authorship as a substitute for and instead of addressing the public as orthodox preachers; religion having lost much of its earlier pervasive influence following the Revolutionary War. Certianly Barlow without is one good example of this transition. And yet we must not think of such writers as desiring to supplant and overthrow traditional religion; rather their purpose was speak in a language people would more readily listen to; while showing themselves possessed of modern minds capable of adapting to the ineluctable moral and social changes transpiring in both the former colonies and Europe.

Traditionally received as Barlow's fondest work is his light and humorous ode "Hasty Pudding" (1793); a tribute to corn flakes; written in the parodying manner of Samuel Butler, Alexander Pope, and fellow Hartford Wit John Trumbull; while he was in France observing the Revolution. Despite its overtly comical character, the poem contains occasionally beautiful lines respecting nature and rustic life not unlike something Wordsworth, himself a Revolutionary pilgrim in France at that same time, might have penned.

Yet more ambitiously, Barlow also composed two very grave and weighty epics, written in heroic couplets, centered on Columbus and the birth and hope of "America;" namely *The Vision of Columbus* (1787) and *The Columbiad*" (1807). While, as is routinely observed, these in totum are *too* laborious in size and scope to work as poetry, they are notwithstanding not occasionally golden and stirring in their visionary and optimistic flights of ecstasy. Moreover, the two are also wonderful historical curiosities in describing then relatively recent events -- including Revolutionary War battles, campaigns, and personalities -- *poetically*.

The following is a specimen from *The Vision of Columbus*, Book IX; which latter and early draft, as inspired and imaginative literature, is by many preferred over *The Columbiad*. And yet the admittedly more editorially contrived and self-conscious *Columbiad* can still be enjoyable and rousing in its own right as a nostalgic and in its way robust and likeable memento of the idealistic aspirations of the Revolutionary era.

At this blest period, when thy [Columbus'] peaceful race
Shall speak one language and one cause embrace,
Science and arts a speedier course shall find,
And open earlier on the infant mind,
No foreign terms shall crowd with barbarous rules,
The dull, unmeaning pageantry of schools;
Nor dark authorities, nor names unknown
Fill the learn'd head with ignorance not its own;
But truth's fair eye, with beams unclouded, shine,
And simplest rules her moral lights confine;
One living language, one unborrowed dress
Her boldest flights with happiest force express;
Triumphant virtue, in the garb of truth,
Win a pure passage to the heart of youth,

Pervade all climes, where suns or oceans roll,
And bid the gospel cheer the illumined whole,
As the glad day-star, on his golden throne,
Fair type of truth and promise of the sun,
Smiles up the orient, in his rosy way,
Illumines the front of heaven, and leads the day;
Thus soaring Science, daughter of the skies,
First o'er the nations bids her beauties rise,
Prepares the glorious way, to put abroad
The beams of Heaven's own morn, the splendors of a God.
Then blest Religion leads the raptured mind,
Thro' brighter fields and pleasures more refined;
Teaches the roving eye, at one broad view,
To glance o'er time and look Existence thro',
See worlds, and worlds, to Being's formless end,
With all their hosts, on One dread power depend,
Seraphs and suns and systems round him rise,
Live in his life and kindle from his eyes,
His boundless love, his all pervading soul
Illume, sublime, and harmonizes the whole;
Teaches the pride of man to fix its bound
In one small point of this amazing round;
To shrink and rest, where Heaven has fix'd its fate,
A line its space, a moment for its date;
Instructs the heart a nobler joy to taste,
And share its feelings with another's breast,
Extend its warmest wish for all mankind,
And catch the image of the Maker's mind;
While mutual love commands all strife to cease,
And earth join joyous in the songs of peace...

~~~***~~~

David Humphreys (1752-1818) was among the most versatile and scholarly of the "Connecticut Wits," and who in addition to sometime bard, served as of Washington's aide-de-camps, and indeed was one of the most liked and personally befriended of the General's staff. He was later U.S. plenipotentiary (under Washington) to the court of Spain, sheep breeder, industrialist, historian and biographer. Here is a sonnet of his, and a song (to the tune "Restoration March.")

ADDRESSED TO MY FRIENDS AT YALE COLLEGE, ON MY LEAVING THEM TO JOIN THE ARMY (1776)

ADIEU, thou Yale! where youthful poets dwell,
No more I linger by thy classic stream.
Inglorious ease and sportive songs farewell!
Thou startling clarion! break the sleeper's dream!
And sing, ye bards! the war-inspiring theme.
Heard ye the din of battle? clang of arms?
Saw ye the steel 'mid starry banners beam?
Quick throbs my breast at war's untried alarms,
Unknown pulsations stirr'd by glory's charms.
While dear Columbia calls, no danger awes,
Though certain death to threaten'd chains be join'd.
Though fails this flesh devote to freedom's cause,
Can death subdue th' unconquerable mind?
Or adamantine chains ethereal substance bind?
~~~

FREEDOM'S CALL

Though love's soft transports may
  A while allure the soul,
When Freedom calls to war,
  Those powers she will control;
When British bands in hostile arms,
  Indignantly we view,
What patriot's breast but throbs, to bid
  His love, and ease, adieu;
    In Freedom's all-inspiring cause,
      To fly alert to arms,
  And change his downy bed
    For Mars's dread alarms.

Then let not love's sweet bane
  Your gallant souls enthral,
But in your country's cause,
  Resolve to stand or fall;
And when by our united force
  We've drove the tyrants home,
With laurels, such as graced the brows
  Of sons of ancient Rome,
    We'll each return to his kind lass,
      Whose beauty soon shall prove
    That for the toils of war
      The best reward is love.

A "SILENCE DOGOOD" SAMPLER

Benjamin Franklin's "Silence Dogood" letters antedated his more famous *Poor Richard's Almanac;* indeed, are among his earliest known compositions. As his *Autobiography* recounts, they were submitted anonymously, using the female pseudonym "Silence Dogood," to his brother James' Boston weekly *The New-England Courant.* In them he touches on a broad range of topics, including manners, culture, fashion, literature, history, religion, and public improvement. While many know of Franklin's *reputation* for being witty and funny, what might come as a surprise to some was that he *actually was* and could be so -- even by much later standards. To have written the "Dogood" letters, and which were the literary ancestor of American humor writings of such as Francis Hopkinson, Hugh Henry Brackenridge, Philip Freneau, Royall Tyler, Washington Irving, James Kirke Paulding, Joseph Pendleton Kennedy, and leading up to Mark Twain would be a plum and honor for any author. Yet how much even more impressed must we be when we realize he was but a 16 year-old apprentice (to his brother) at the time he wrote them! He drew much of his model and inspiration from Addison and Steele's *Tatler* and *Spectator* essays, and which in quality of laughing humor (for instance in "Dogood" letter no. VII on New World poetry) he matches if not, necessarily, surpasses.

The proceeding is a selection from the "Dogood" letters; reproduced with spelling unchanged and as they first appeared in 1722.[95]

~~~***~~~

N° 39, From Monday April 23. to Monday April 30. 1722
To the Author of the New-England Courant.

Sir, No 3

It is undoubtedly the Duty of all Persons to serve the Country they live in, according to their Abilities; yet I sincerely acknowledge, that I have hitherto been very deficient in this Particular; whether it was for want of Will or Opportunity, I will not at present stand to determine: Let it suffice, that I now take up a Resolution, to do for the future all that *lies in my Way* for the Service of my Countrymen.

I HAVE from my Youth been indefatigably studious to gain and treasure up in my Mind all useful and desireable Knowledge, especially such as tends to improve the Mind, and enlarge the Understanding: And as I have found it very beneficial to me, I am not without Hopes, that communicating my small Stock in this Manner, by Peace-meal to the Publick, may be at least in some Measure useful.

I AM very sensible that it is impossible for me, or indeed any *one* Writer to please *all* Readers at once. Various Persons have different Sentiments; and that which is pleasant and delightful to one, gives another a Disgust. He that would (in this Way of Writing) please all, is under a Necessity to make his Themes almost as numerous as his Letters. He must one while be merry and diverting, then more solid and serious; one while sharp and satyrical, then (to mollify that) be sober and religious; at *one* Time let the Subject be Politicks, then let the next Theme be Love: Thus will every one, one Time or other find some thing agreeable to his own Fancy, and in his Turn be delighted.

ACCORDING to this Method I intend to proceed, bestowing now and then a few gentle Reproofs on those who deserve them, not forgetting at the same time to applaud those whose Actions merit Commendation. And here I must-not forget to invite the ingenious Part of your Readers, particularly those of my own Sex to enter into a Correspondence with me, assuring them, that their Condescension in this Particular shall be received as a Favour, and accordingly acknowledged.

I THINK I have now finish'd the Foundation, and I intend in my next to begin to raise the Building. Having nothing more to write at present, I must make the usual excuse in such Cases, of being in haste, assuring you that I speak from my Heart when I call my self, The most humble and obedient of all the Servants your Merits have acquir'd,

SILENCE DOGOOD

---

[95] The 18th century "f" however we have replaced with an "s."
~~~

Those who incline to favour Mrs. Dogood with their Correspondence, are desir'd to send their Letters (directed to her) to the Publishers of this Paper.

~~~* ~~~

N° 45
June 4. to Monday June 11. 1722.
Quem Dies videt veniens Superbum,
Hunc Dies vidit fugiens jacentem.[96]
~ Seneca.

To the Author of the New-England Courant.

SIR, [No VI.]

AMONG the many reigning Vices of the Town which may at any Tune come under my Consideration and Reprehension, there is none which I am more inclin'd to expose than that of *Pride*. It is acknowledg'd by all to be a Vice the most hateful to God and Man. Even those who nourish it in themselves, hate to see it in others. The proud Man aspires after Nothing less than an unlimited Superiority over his Fellow-Creatures. He has made himself a King in *Soliloquy*; fancies himself conquering the World, and the Inhabitants thereof consulting on proper Methods to acknowledge his Merit. I speak it to my Shame. I my self was a Queen from the Fourteenth to the Eighteenth Year of my Age, and govern'd the World all the Time of my being govern'd by my Master. But this speculative Pride may be the Subject of another Letter: I shall at present confine my Thoughts to what we call *Pride of Apparel*. This Sort of Pride has been growing upon us ever since we parted with our Homespun Cloaths for *Fourteen Penny Stuff*, &c. And the *Pride of Apparel* has begot and nourish'd in us a *Pride of Heart*, which portends the Ruin of Church and State. *Pride goeth before Destruction, and a haughty Spirit before a Fall*: And I remember my late Reverend Husband would often say upon this Text, That a Fall was the *natural Consequence*, as well as Punishment of Pride. Daily Experience is sufficient to evince the Truth of this Observation. Persons of small Fortune under the Dominion of this Vice, seldom consider their Inability to maintain themselves in it, but strive to imitate their Superiors in estate, or Equals in Folly, until one Misfortune comes upon the Neck of another, and every Step they take is a Step backwards. By striving to appear rich they become really poor, and deprive themselves of that Pity and Charity, which is due to the humble poor Man, who is made so more immediately by Providence. THIS Pride of Apparel will appear the more foolish, if we consider, that those airy Mortals, who have no other Way of making themselves considerable but by gorgeous Apparel, draw after them Crowds of Imitators, who hate each other while they endeavour after a Similitude of Manners. They destroy by Example, and envy one another's Destruction.

I CANNOT dismiss this Subject without some Observations on a particular Fashion now reigning among my own Sex, the most immodest and inconvenient of any the Art of Woman has invented, namely, that of *Hoop-Petticoats*. By these they are incommoded in their General and Particular Calling; and therefore they cannot answer the ends of either necessary or ornamental Apparel.

These monstrous topsy-turvy *Mortar-Pieces*, are neither fit for the Church, the Hall, or the Kitchen; and if a Number of them were well mounted on *Noddles-Island*, they would look more like Engines of War for bombarding the Town, than Ornaments of the Fair Sex. An honest Neighbour of mine, happening to be in Town some time since on a publick Day, inform'd me, that he saw four Gentlewomen with their Hoops half mounted in a Balcony, as they withdrew to the Wall, to the great Terror of the Militia, who (he thinks) might attribute their irregular Volleys to the formidable Appearance of the Ladies Petticoats.

I ASSURE you, Sir, I have but little Hopes of perswading my Sex, by this Letter, utterly to relinquish the extravagant Foolery, and Indication of Immodesty, in this monstrous Garb of their's; but I would at least desire them to lessen the Circumference of their Hoops, and leave it with them to consider, Whether they, who pay no Rates or Taxes, ought to take up more Room in the King's Highway, than the Men, who yearly contribute to the Support of the Government.

---

[96] [*Edit. Note.* "Who saw in vain pride the coming days, Now sees fleeing days thrown away."]
~~~

I am, Sir,
Your Humble Servant,
SILENCE DOGOOD.

~~~* ~~~

N° 47

June 18. to Monday June 25. 1722.

Give me the Muse, whose generous Force,
Impatient of the Reins,
Pursues an unattempted Course,
Breaks all the Criticks Iron Chains.
~ [Isaac] Watts.

To the Author of the New-England Courant.

SIR, [No VII.]

It has been the Complaint of many Ingenious Foreigners, who have travell'd amongst us, *That good Poetry is not to be expected in New-England.* I am apt to Fancy, the Reason is, not because our Countrymen are altogether void of a Poetical Genius, nor yet because we have not those Advantages of Education which other Countries have, but purely because we do not afford that Praise and Encouragement which is merited, when any thing extraordinary of this Kind is produc'd among us: Upon which Consideration I have determined, when I meet with a Good Piece of *New-England* Poetry, to give it a suitable Encomium, and thereby endeavour to discover to the World some of its Beautys, in order to encourage the Author to go on, and bless the World with more, and more Excellent Productions.

THERE has lately appear'd among us a most Excellent Piece of Poetry, entitled, *An Elegy upon the much Lamented Death of Mrs.* Mehitebell Kitel, *Wife of* Mr. John Kitel *of* Salem, Etc. It may justly be said in its Praise, without Flattery to the Author, that it is the most *Extraordinary* Piece that was ever wrote in *New-England.* The Language is so soft and Easy, the Expression so moving and pathetick, but above all, the Verse and Numbers so Charming and Natural, that it is almost beyond Comparison.

The Muse *disdains*
Those Links and Chains,
Measures and Rules of Vulgar Strains,
And o'er the Laws of Harmony a Sovereign Queen she reigns.

I FIND no English Author, Ancient or Modern, whose Elegies may be compar'd with this, in respect to the Elegance of Stile, or Smoothness of Rhime; and for the affecting Part, I will leave your Readers to judge, if ever they read any Lines, that would sooner make them *draw their Breath* and Sigh, if not shed Tears, than these following.

Come let us mourn, for we have lost a
Wife, a Daughter, and a Sister,
Who has lately taken Flight, and
greatly we have mist her.

In another place,

Some little Time *before she yielded up her Breath,*
She said, I ne'er shall hear one Sermon more on Earth.
She kist her Husband some little Time *before she expir'd,*
Then lean'd her Head the Pillow on, just out of Breath and
Tir'd.

BUT the Threefold Appellation in the first Line
— *a Wife, a Daughter, and a Sister,*
~~~

must not pass unobserved. That Line in the celebrated Watts,

GUNSTON *the Just, the Generous, and the Young*,

is nothing Comparable to it. The latter only mentions three Qualifications of *one* Person who was deceased, which therefore could raise Grief and Compassion but for *One*. Whereas the former, (*our most excellent Poet*) gives his Reader a Sort of an Idea of the Death of *Three Persons*, viz.

— a Wife, a Daughter, and a Sister,

which is *Three Times* as great a Loss as the Death of *One*, and consequently must raise *Three Times* as much Grief and Compassion in the Reader.

I SHOULD be very much straitened for Room, if I should attempt to discover even half the Excellencies of this Elegy which are obvious to me. Yet I cannot omit one Observation, which is, that the Author has (to his Honour) invented a new Species of Poetry, which wants a Name, and was never before known. His muse scorns to be confin'd to the old Measures and Limits, or to observe the dull Rules of Criticks;

Nor Rapin *gives her Rules to fly, nor* Purcell *Notes to Sing*.
~ Watts.

NOW 'tis Pity that such an Excellent Piece should not be dignify'd with a particular Name; and seeing it cannot justly be called, either *Epic, Sapphic, Lyric,* or *Pindaric*, nor any other Name yet invented, I presume it may, (in Honour and Remembrance of the Dead) be called the KITELIC. Thus much in the Praise of *Kitelic Poetry*.

IT is certain, that those Elegies which are of our own Growth, (and our Soil seldom produces any other sort of Poetry) are by far the greatest part, wretchedly Dull and Ridiculous. Now since it is imagin'd by many, that our Poets are honest, well-meaning Fellows, who do their best, and that if they had but some Instructions how to govern Fancy with Judgment, they would make indifferent good Elegies; I shall here subjoin a Receipt for that purpose, which was left me as a Legacy, (among other valuable Rarities) by my Reverend Husband. It is as follows,

A RECEIPT *to make* a New-England
Funeral ELEGY.

For the Title of your Elegy. *Of these you may have enough ready made to your Hands; but if you should chuse to make it your self, you must be sure not to omit the words* AEtatis Suae,[97] *which will Beautify it exceedingly.*

For the Subject of your Elegy. *Take one of your Neighbours who has lately departed this Life; it is no great matter at what Age the Party dy'd, but it will be best if he went away suddenly, being* Kill'd, Drown'd, *or* Frose to Death.

Having chose the Person, take all his Virtues, Excellencies, &c. and if he have not enough, you may borrow some to make up a sufficient Quantity: To these add his last Words, dying Expressions, &cs. if they are to be had; mix all these together, and be sure you strain them well. Then season all with a Handful or two of Melancholly Expressions, such as, Dreadful, Deadly, cruel cold Death, unhappy Fate, weeping Eyes, *&c. Have mixed all these Ingredients well, put them into the empty Scull of some* young Harvard; *(but in Case you have ne'er a One at Hand, you may use your own,) there let them Ferment for the Space of a Fortnight, and by that Time they will be incorporated into a Body, which take out, and having prepared a sufficient Quantity of double Rhimes, such as* Power, Flower; Quiver, Shiver; Grieve us, Leave us; tell you, excel you; Expeditions, Physicians; Fatigue him, Intrigue him; *&c. you must spread all upon Paper, and if you can procure a Scrap of Latin to put at the End, it will garnish it mightily; then having affixed your Name at the Bottom, with a* Moestus Composuit,[98] *you will have an Excellent Elegy.*

---

[97] [*Edit. Note*. "Man's life and estate."]
[98] [*Edit. Note*. "Sorrow brings (us) together."]

N. B. *This Receipt will serve when a Female is the Subject of your Elegy, provided you borrow a greater Quantity of Virtues, Excellencies, &c.*

SIR,
Your Servant,
SILENCE DOGOOD

P. S. I shall make no other Answer to *Hypercarpus's* Criticism on my last Letter than this, *Mater me genuit, peperit max filia matrem.*[99]

~~~* ~~~

N° 49

The New-England Courant.

From Monday July 2. to Monday July 9. 1722.

To the Author of the New-England Courant.

SIR, [No VIII.]

I PREFER the following Abstract from the London Journal to any Thing of my own, and therefore shall present it to your Readers this week without any further Preface.

'WITHOUT Freedom of Thought, there can be no such Thing as Wisdom; and no such Thing as publick Liberty, without Freedom of Speech; which is the Right of every Man, as far as by it, he does not hurt or controul the Right of another: And this is the only Check it ought to suffer, and 'the only Bounds it ought to Know.

'This sacred Privilege is so essential to free Governments, 'that the Security of Property, and the Freedom of Speech always go together; and in those wretched Countries where a Man cannot call his Tongue his own, he can scarce call any Thing else his own. Whoever would overthrow the Liberty of a Nation, must begin by subduing the Freeness of Speech; a *Thing* terrible to Publick Traytors.

'This Secret was so well known to the Court of *King Charles the First*, that his wicked Ministry procured a Proclamation, to forbid the People to talk of Parliaments, which those Traytors had laid aside. To assert the undoubted Right of the Subject, and defend his Majesty's legal Prerogative, was called Disaffection, and punished as Sedition. Nay, People were forbid to talk of Religion in their Families: For the Priests had combined with the Ministers to cook up Tyranny, and suppress Truth and the Law, while the late *King James*, when *Duke of York*, went avowedly to Mass, Men were fined, imprisoned and undone, for saying he was a Papist: And that *King Charles the Second* might live more securely a Papist, there was an Act of Parliament made, declaring it Treason to say that he was one.

'That Men ought to speak well of their *Governours* is true, while *their Governours* deserve to be well spoken of; but to do publick Mischief without hearing of it, is only the Prerogative and Felicity of Tyranny: A free People will be shewing that they are *so*, by their Freedom of Speech.

'The Administration of Government is nothing else but the Attendance of the *Trustees of the People* upon the Interest and Affairs of the People: And as it is the Part and Business of the People, for whose Sake alone all publick Matters are, or ought to be transacted, to see whether they be well or ill transacted; so it is the Interest, and ought to be the Ambition, to all honest Magistrates, to have their Deeds openly examined, and publickly scan'd: Only the *wicked Governours* of Men dread what is said of them; *Audivit* Tiberius *proba queis lacerabitur, atque* perculsus est.[100] The public Censure was true, else he had not felt it bitter. Freedom of Speech is ever the Symptom, as well as the Effect of a good Government. In old *Rome*, all was left to the Judgment and Pleasure of the People, who examined the publick Proceedings with such Discretion, & censured those who administred them with such Equity and Mildness, that in the space of Three Hundred Years, not five publick Ministers suffered unjustly. Indeed whenever the *Commons* proceeded to Violence, the great Ones had been the Agressors.

---

[99] [*Edit. Note.* "Mother begat me, the daughter flowered into a mother."]
[100] [*Edit. Note.* "So heard, Tiberius proof will rend and will overthrow."]
~~~

'GUILT only dreads Liberty of Speech, which drags it out of its lurking Holes, and exposes its Deformity and Horrour to Day-light. *Horatius, Valerius, Cincinnatus*, and other vertuous and undesigning Magistrates of the Roman Commonwealth, had nothing to fear from Liberty of Speech. *Their virtuous* Administration, the more it was examin'd, the more it brightned and gain'd by Enquiry. When *Valerius* in particular, was accused upon some flight grounds of affecting the Diadem; he who was the first Minister of *Rome*, does not accuse the People for examining his Conduct, but approved his Innocence in a Speech to them; and gave such Satisfaction to them, and gained such Popularity to himself, that they gave him a new Name; *inde cognomen factum Publicolae est*;[101] to denote that he was their Favourite and their Friend — *Latae deinde leges — Ante omnes de provocation* ADVERSUS MAGISTRATUS AD POPULUM,[102] Livii, lib. 2, Cap. 8.

'But Things afterwards took another Turn. *Rome* with the Loss of its Liberty, lost also its Freedom of Speech; then Men[']s Words began to be feared and watched; and then first began the *poysonous* Race of *Informers* banished indeed under the righteous Administration of *Titus, Narva* [Nerva], Trajan, Aurelius, &c. but encouraged and enriched under the *vile Ministry of Sejanus, Tigillinus, Pallas, and Cleander: Queri libet, quod in secreta nostra non inquirant principes, nisi quos Odimus,*[103] says *Pliny* to *Trajan*.

'The best Princes have ever encouraged and promoted Freedom of Speech; they know that upright Measures would defend themselves, and that all upright Men would defend them. *Tacitus*, speaking of the Reign of some of the Princes abovemention'd, says with Extasy, *Rara Temporum felicitate, ubi sentire qua, velis, & qua sentias dicere licet*: A blessed Time when you might think what you would, and speak what you thought.

'I doubt not but old *Spencer* and his *Son*, who were the *Chief Ministers* and *Betrayers* of *Edward the Second*, would have been very glad to have stopped the Mouths of all the honest Men in *England*. They dreaded to be called *Traytors*, because they were *Traytors*. And I dare say, Queen *Elizabeth's Walsingham*, who deserved no Reproaches, feared none. Misrepresentation of publick Measures is easily overthrown, by representing publick Measures truly; when they are honest, they ought to be publickly known, that they may be publickly commended; but if they are knavish or pernicious, they ought to be publickly detested.'

Yours, &c,
SILENCE DOGOOD.

~~~* ~~~

N° 51

From Monday July 16. to Monday July 23. 1722

Corruptio optimi eft pessima[104]

To the Author of the New-England Courant.

SIR, [No. IX]

It has been for some Time a Question with me, Whether a Commonwealth suffers more by hypocritical Pretenders to Religion, or by the openly Profane? But some late Thoughts of this Nature, have inclined me to think, that the Hypocrite is the most dangerous Person of the Two, especially if he sustains a Post in the Government, and we consider his Conduct as it regards the Publick. The first Artifice of a *State Hypocrite* is, by a few savoury Expressions which cost him Nothing, to betray the best Men in his Country into an Opinion of his Goodness; and if the Country wherein he lives is noted for the Purity of Religion, he the more easily gains his End, and consequently may more justly be expos'd and detested. A notoriously profane Person in a private Capacity, ruins himself, and perhaps the Destruction of a few of his Equals; but a publick Hypocrite every day deceives his betters, and makes them the Ignorant Trumpeters of his supposed Godliness: They take him for a Saint, and pass him for one, without considering that they are (as it were) the Instruments of publick Mischief out of Conscience, and ruin their Country for God's sake.

---

[101] [*Edit. Note.* " From thence surnames are made a family name."]
[102] [*Edit. Note.* "Carries then the laws before all opposition, the Master to the People."]
[103] [*Edit. Note.* "It is pleasing for us to complain, because they inquire not into our secrets first, but of those we hate."]
[104] [*Edit. Note.* "The corruption of the best is the worst."]
~~~

THIS Political Description of a Hypocrite, may (for ought I know) be taken for a new Doctrine by some of your Readers; but let them confider, that *a little Religion, and a little Honesty, goes a great way in Courts*. 'Tis not inconsistent with Charity to distrust a Religious Man in Power, tho' he may be a good Man; he has many Temptations "*to propagate public Destruction for Personal Advantages and Security:*" And if his Natural Temper be covetous, and his Actions often contradict his pious Discourse, we may with great Reason conclude that he has some other Design in his Religion besides barely getting to Heaven. But the most dangerous Hypocrite in a Common-Wealth, is one who *leaves the Gospel for the sake of the Law*: A Man compounded of Law and Gospel, is able to cheat a whole Country with his Religion, and then destroy them under *Colour of Law:* And here the Clergy are in great Danger of being deceiv'd, and the People of being deceiv'd by the Clergy, until the Monster arrives to such power and Wealth, that he is out of the reach of both, and can oppress the People without their own blind Assistance. And it is a sad Observation, that when the People too late see their Error, yet the Clergy still persist in their Encomiums on the Hypocrite; and when he happens to die *for the Good of his Country*, without leaving behind him the Memory of *one good Action*, he shall be sure to have his Funeral Sermon stuffed with *Pious Expressions* which he dropt at such a Time, and at such a Place, and on such an Occasion; than which nothing can be more prejudicial to the Interest of Religion, nor indeed to the Memory of the Person deceas'd, The Reason of this Blindness in the Clergy is, because they are honourably supported (as they ought to be) by their People, and see nor feel nothing of the Oppression which is obvious and burdensome to every one else.

But this Subject raises in me an Indignation not to be born; and if we have had, or are like to have any Instances of this Nature in *New-England*, we cannot better manifest our Love to Religion and the Country, than by setting the Deceivers in a true Light, and undeceiving the Deceived, however such Discoveries may be represented by the ignorant or designing Enemies of our Peace and Safety.

I shall conclude with a Paragraph or two from an ingenious Political Writer in the *London Journal*, the better to convince your Readers, that Publick Destruction may be easily carry'd on by *hypocritical Pretenders to Religion*.

"A raging Passion for immoderate Gain had made Men universally and intensely hard-hearted: They were every where devouring one another. And yet the Directors and their Accomplices, who were the acting Instruments of all "this outrageous Madness and Mischief, set up for wonderful pious Persons, while they were defying Almighty God, and plundering Men; and they set apart a Fund of Subscriptions for charitable Uses; that is, they mercilessly made a whole People Beggars, and charitably supported a few *necessitous* and *worthless* FAVOURITES. I doubt not, but if the Villany had gone on with Success, they would have had their Names handed down to Posterity with Encomiums; as the Names of other *publick Robbers*, have been! We have *Historians* and ODE MAKERS now living, very proper for such a Task. It is certain, that most People did, at one Time, believe the *Directors* to be *great and worthy Persons*. And an honest Country Clergy man told me last Summer, upon the Road, that *Sir John* was an excellent publick-spirited Person, for that he had beautified his Chancel.

"Upon the whole we must not judge of one another by their best Actions; since the worst Men do some Good, and all Men make fine Professions: But we must judge of Men by the whole of their Conduct, and Effects of it. Thorough Honesty requires great and long Proof, since many a Man, long thought honest, has at length proved a Knave. And it is from judging without Proof, or false Proof, that Mankind continue Unhappy."

I am, SIR,
your humble Servant,
SILENCE DOGOOD.

"LIBERTY OR DEATH": Extracts of Addison's "Cato, a Tragedy" (1712)

"...A day, an hour, of virtuous liberty,
Is worth a whole eternity in bondage."
~ Act II, scene 2.

By all accounts, it would seem a given that Joseph Addison's redoubtable "Cato" could fairly compete for the title of the most popular and influential stage play in all of recorded history. So much so that for many this theatrical drama became a real life blue-print -- if not interpreted as an out-and-out prophecy -- of subsequent and momentous historical events; And Life intentionally, and without embarrassment or apology, copied Art – indeed, went on to surpass in grandeur its fictional counterpart.

Quite what incited the impassioned sentiments Addison put forth is something of puzzle. Were they prompted merely by the Whig versus Tory politics of his day? These last seem to have been relatively tame compared to the vociferous, if not violent, wranglings of the politics of prior and subsequent British generations. In its lauding of Stoic virtues one does sense in Addison's work a Puritanical revulsion for and reaction to the profligacy or at least raciness of Restoration theater. This presumably must be taken as one contributing factor. Yet in championing strict morals Addison, like Milton, paradoxically uses excess to combat the excess of his cultural rivals. Noteworthy as well, "Cato" should be seen as an English entry into Corneille's dramatic school of uncompromising heroic virtue -- with Roman history more or less artificially drawn upon as a prop on which Addison could build on and explore his theme. At the same time, Addison drew his inspiration to use Cato as his hero from Plutarch and or the poet Lucan's Roman civil war epic *Pharsalia*; both of which were immediately familiar to many of his audience.

It is not a little peculiar that "Cato" was, at first at least, generally received and understood as a Whig literary triumph; the Whigs being, after all, the defunct Puritans in a revived and moderated form. And yet the historical Cato the Younger bore far greater resemblance to a conservative of Addison's time than the 18th century populist reformers we more commonly associate the Whigs with. And ironically, the Caesar so decried as tyrant in "Cato" had his most prominent predecessor in the reactionary and unscrupulous Sulla -- one of the greatest champions of that same status quo Roman conservatism Cato vied for politically. Also oddly, Addison himself, in *Spectator* essay no. 169, thought that Cato's dogged espousal of virtue in most any other would have been insufferable; while Caesar otherwise was easily the more likable man for his "goodness." At the same time, the Republic historical Cato represented was by that time oft dominated by corrupt and self-serving aristocrats, and who vied against the middle class, the remaining plebs, and proletariat; whom Caesar, like the Gracchi and Marius before him, took it upon himself to lead.

To say that "Cato's" later impact was striking to the point of incredible is no overstatement. Decades before young men slew themselves after reading *Young Werther*, Eustace Budgell (1686–1737), a son of Addison's cousin and an author and political activist in his own right, invoked "Cato" as a cue to throw himself into the Thames; while leaving behind as a suicide note: "What Cato did, and Addison approved, cannot be wrong."

In 1721, John Trenchard (1662-1723) and Thomas Gordon (c. 1692–1750) took the name for their "Cato Letters" from the play; and issued writings notable in their presaging the American Revolutionary aims and that took to wing in the 1770s.

It is possible that the very youthful George Washington acted in a performance of Addison's play at a private gathering in Virginia, [105] and his subsequent persona as morally prepossessed American commander-in-chief is uncannily mirrored in the stage Cato. In addition, he sometimes quoted from or made allusions to "Cato" in his wartime correspondence. In 1778, it was performed at the Valley Forge

[105] In a letter to Sally Fairfax of 25 Sept. 1758, he had written: "I should think our time more agreeably spent, believe me, in playing a part in Cato, with the company you mention, and myself doubly happy in being the Juba to such a Marcia, as you must make."

encampment; which was altogether fitting seeing how very much of the play distinctly echoes American Revolutionary events and personalities. For example, in Act II, scene 4, we find the lines:

> "It is not now time to talk of aught
> But chains or conquest, liberty or death."

Or in Act IV, scene 4:

> "What a pity it is
> That we can die but once to serve our country."[106]

Frequent references are made to the importance of subsisting on prudence, hardship and sobriety, or warnings against the dangers of mutiny -- themes and subjects familiar to Continental soldiers. Similarly and time and again, it is easy for us to spot parallels which the Valley Forge audience could themselves see and that correlated with their own imminent experience and situation. Cato speaking in Act II, scen. 5 must have called to mind to some, not least of which Washington himself, the American rout at the battle of Long Island. In addition, Sempronius, the scheming senatorial intriguer and false ally of Cato, makes almost a dead ringer for Arnold. Yet it would be two years after Valley Forge before the latter's treason.

Beyond the 18th century, such heady moralistic fervor became hard to maintain, and it can be forgiven the sons if they did not wildly take to "Cato" as their fathers did. The play has been subsequently and up unto our own time often treated in a shallow and frivolous way by some of the more confused members of left and right: the right clumsily finding "Cato" timely in the fashionable sense; and the left, in too ready to dismiss it as outdated, show themselves as having little sense of poetry or of things larger than life, and some will naturally feel the play obviously deserves better than that. Now if only someone would do a production reviving it!

Addison's stage verse, it should be understood, and for all its dated affectation has a musicality that transcends its mere surface message; and to that extent it is perhaps this, in addition to some individual memorable lines, which gives the play genuinely sustaining merit. Simply put, Addison method of dramatic delivery is enjoyable to mimic whether in a friendly or unfriendly way. And the artful attention to the sound, phrasing, and rhythm of words in "Cato" is sometimes half the fun; different yet not so very unlike the witty use of language by 18th century humorists such as John Gay, Smollet, Fielding, Goldsmith, and Joe Miller where sound and meaning are inseparable to the emotional effect intended or aimed at -- and which good fellows will recognize and appreciate. In this sense, "Cato" remains a play for good fellows. But as is only mete, no one can force another to be a good fellow; so that you either *get it* or you *don't*.

Here then are some sample scenes, dialogue, and speeches.

~~~***~~~

from Act I, scen. 1.

Portius.
The dawn is overcast, the morning low'rs,
And heavily in clouds brings on the day,
The great, th' important day, big with the fate
Of Cato and of Rome — Our father's death
Would fill up all the guilt of civil war,
And close the scene of blood. Already Caesar
Has Ravag'd more than half the globe, and sees

[106] Compare also to Herodotus, Book 9, 72: "These obtained the most renown of those who fought at Plataia, for as for Callicrates, the most beautiful who came to the camp, not of the Lacedemonians alone, but also of all the Hellenes of his time, he was not killed in the battle itself; but when Pausanias was offering sacrifice, he was wounded by an arrow in the side, as he was sitting down in his place in the ranks; and while the others were fighting, he having been carried out of the ranks was dying a lingering death: and he said to Arimnestos a Plataian that it did not grieve him to die for Hellas, but it grieved him only that he had not proved his strength of hand, and that no deed of valour had been displayed by him worthy of the spirit which he had in him to perform great deeds."
~~~

Mankind grown thin by his destructive sword:
Should he go farther, numbers would be wanting
To form new battles, and support his crimes.
Ye gods, what havoc does ambition make
Among your works! —….

Believe me, Marcus, 'tis an impious greatness,
And mix'd with too much horror to be envied:
How does the lustre of our father's actions,
Through the dark cloud of ills that cover him,
Break out, and burn with more triumphant brightness?
His sufferings shine, and spread a glory round him
Greatly unfortunate, he fights the cause
Of honour, virtue, liberty, and Rome.
His sword ne'er fell but on the guilty head;
Oppression, tyranny, and power usurp'd,
Draw all the vengeance of his arm upon them...

Well dost thou seem to check my ling'ring here
On this important hour — I'll straight away,
And while the fathers of the senate meet,
In close debate to weigh th' events of war,
I'll animate the soldiers' drooping courage,
With love of freedom, and contempt of life:
I'll thunder in their ears their country's cause,
And try to rouse up all that's Roman in them.
'Tis not in mortals to command success,
But we'll do more, Sempronius; we'll deserve it...

Sempronius, solus.
Curse on the stripling! how he apes his sire!
Ambitiously sententious! — but I wonder
Old Syphax comes not; his Numidian genius
Is well dispos'd to mischief, were he prompt
And eager on it; but he must be spurr'd,
And every moment quickened to the course.
— Cato has us'd me ill: he has refus'd
His daughter Marcia to my ardent vows.
Besides, his baffled arms, and ruin'd cause,
Are bars to my ambition. Caesar's favour,
That show'rs down greatness on his friends, will raise me
To Rome's first honours. If I give up Cato,
I claim in my reward his captive daughter.

----

from Act I, scen. 3.

Syphax.
— Sempronius, all is ready,
I've sounded my Numidians, man by man,
And find them ripe for a revolt: they all
Complain aloud of Cato's discipline,
And wait but the command to change their master.

Sempronius.
Believe me, Syphax, there's no time to waste;
Even whilst we speak our conqueror comes on,
And gathers ground upon us every moment.
Alas! thou know'st not Caesar's active soul,
With what a dreadful course he rushes on
From war to war: in vain has nature form'd
Mountains and oceans to oppose his passage;
He bounds o'er all, victorious in his march:
The Alps and Pyreneans sink before him,
Through winds and waves and storms he works his way,
Impatient for the battle: one day more
Will set the victor thundering at our gates.
But tell me, hast thou yet drawn o'er young Juba?
That still would recommend thee more to Caesar,
And challenge better terms.
----

from Act I, scen. 4

Syphax.
Gods! where's the worth that sets this people up
Above your own Numidia's tawny sons!
Do they with tougher sinews bend the bow?
Or flies the javelin swifter to its mark,
Lanch'd from the vigour of a Roman arm?
Who like our active African instructs
The fiery steed, and trains him to his hand?
Or guides in troops th' embattled elephant,
Loaden with war? These, these are arts, my prince,
In which your Zama does not stoop to Rome.

Juba.
These all are virtues of a meaner rank,
Perfections that are plac'd in bones and nerves.
A Roman soul is bent on higher views:
To civilize the rude unpolish'd world,
And lay it under the restraint of laws;
To make man mild, and sociable to man;
To cultivate the wild licentious savage
With wisdom, discipline, and liberal arts;
Th' embellishments of life: virtues like these
Make human nature shine, reform the soul,
And break our fierce barbarians into men...

...To strike thee dumb: turn up thy eyes to Cato!
There may'st thou see to what a godlike height
The Roman virtues lift up mortal man,
While good, and just, and anxious for his friends,
He's still severely bent against himself;
Renouncing sleep, and rest, and food, and ease,
He strives with thirst and hunger, toil and heat;
And when his fortune sets before him all
The pomps and pleasures that his soul can wish,
His rigid virtue will accept of none.

Syphax.
Believe me, prince, there's not an African
That traverses our vast Numidian deserts
In quest of prey, and lives upon his bow,
But better practises these boasted virtues.
Coarse are his meals, the fortune of the chase,
Amidst the running stream he slakes his thirst,
Toils all the day, and at th' approach of night
On the first friendly bank he throws him down,
Or rests his head upon a rock till morn:
Then rises fresh, pursues his wonted game,
And if the following day he chance to find
A new repast, or an untasted spring,
Blesses his stars, and thinks it luxury.

Juba.
Thy prejudices, Syphax, wont discern
What virtues grow from ignorance and choice,
Nor how the hero differs from the brute.
But grant that others could with equal glory
Look down on pleasures, and the baits of sense;
Where shall we find the man that bears affliction,
Great and majestic in his griefs, like Cato?
Heavens! With what strength, what steadiness of mind,
He triumphs in the midst of all his sufferings!
How does he rise against a load of woes,
And thank the gods that throw the weight upon him!

----

from Act II, scen. 1.

Sempronius.
— My voice is still for war.
Gods! Can a Roman senate long debate
Which of the two to choose, slavery or death!
No, let us rise at once, gird on our swords,
And, at the head of our remaining troops,
Attack the foe, break through the thick array
Of his throng'd legions, and charge home upon him.
Perhaps some arm, more lucky than the rest,
May reach his heart, and free the world from bondage.
Rise, fathers, rise! 'Tis Rome demands your help;
Rise, and revenge her slaughter'd citizens,
Or share their fate! the corps of half her senate
Manure the fields of Thessaly, while we
Sit here, deliberating in cold debates
If we should sacrifice our lives to honour,
Or wear them out in servitude and chains,
Rouse up, for shame! our brothers of Pharsalia
Point at their wounds, and cry aloud — To battle!
Great Pompey's shade complains that we are slow,
And Scipio's ghost walks unreveng'd amongst us!

Cato.
Let not a torrent of impetuous zeal

Transport thee thus beyond the bounds of reason:
True fortitude is seen in great exploits
That justice warrants, and that wisdom guides,
All else is towering phrenzy and distraction.
Are not the lives of those who draw the sword
In Rome's defence intrusted to our care!
Should we thus lead them to a field of slaughter,
Might not the impartial world with reason say
We lavish'd at our death the blood of thousands,
To grace our fall, and make our ruin glorious!
Lucius, we next would know what's your opinion?

----

from Act II, scen. 4.

Cato.
Dost thou love watchings, abstinence, and toil,
Laborious virtues all! learn them from Cato:
Success and fortune must thou learn from Caesar...

Adieu, young prince: I would not hear a word
Should lessen thee in my esteem: remember
The hand of fate is over us, and heav'n
Exacts severity from all our thoughts:
It is not now a time to talk of aught
But chains or conquest; liberty or death.

----

from Act II, scen. 1

Portius.
Marcus, the friendships of the world are oft
Confederacies in vice, or leagues of pleasure;
Ours has severest virtue for its basis,
And such a friendship ends not but with life.

----

from Act II, scen. 5.

Cato.
Perfidious men! and will you thus dishonour
Your past exploits, and sully all your wars?
Do you confess 'twas not a zeal for Rome,
Nor love of liberty, nor thirst of honour,
Drew you thus far; but hopes to share the spoil
Of conquer'd towns, and plunder'd provinces?
Fired with such motives you do well to join
With Cato's foes, and follow Caesar's banners.
Why did I 'scape th' envenom'd aspic's rage,
And all the fiery monsters of the desert,
To see this day! why could not Cato fall
Without your guilt? Behold, ungrateful men!
Behold my bosom naked to your swords,

And let the man that's injur'd strike the blow.
Which of you all suspects that he is wrong'd,
Or thinks he suffers greater ills than Cato?
Am I distinguish'd from you but by toils,
Superior toils, and heavier weight of cares!
Painful pre-eminence!...

Meanwhile we'll sacrifice to Liberty.
Remember, O my friends, the laws, the rights,
The generous plan of power deliver'd down,
From age to age, by your renown'd forefathers,
(So dearly bought, the price of so much blood)
O let it never perish in your hands!
But piously transmit it to your children.
Do thou, great Liberty, inspire our souls,
And make our lives in thy possession happy,
Or our deaths glorious in thy just defence.

----

from Act. IV, scen. 4.

Lucius.
I stand astonish'd! what, the bold Sempronius!
That still broke foremost through the crowd of patriots,
As with a hurricane of zeal transported,
And virtuous even to madness —

Cato.
— Trust me, Lucius,
Our civil discords have produced such crimes,
Such monstrous crimes, I am surprised at nothing.
— O Lucius, I am sick of this bad world!
The daylight and the sun grow painful to me.

----

from Act V, scen. 1.

Cato, solus, sitting in a thoughtful posture: in his hand Plato's book on the Immortality of the soul. A drawn sword on the table by him.

It must be so — Plato, thou reason'st well! —
Else whence this pleasing hope, this fond desire,
This longing after immortality?
Or whence this secret dread, and inward horror,
Of falling into naught? why shrinks the soul
Back on herself, and startles at destruction?
'Tis the divinity that stirs within us;
'Tis heaven itself, that points out an hereafter,
And intimates eternity to man.
Eternity? thou pleasing, dreadful, thought!
Through what variety of untried being,
Through what new scenes and changes must we pass?
The wide, th' unbounded prospect, lies before me;

But shadows, clouds, and darkness rest upon it.
Here will I hold. If there's a power above us,
(And that there is all nature cries aloud
Through all her works,) he must delight in virtue;
And that which he delights in, must be happy.
But when! or where! — This world was made for Caesar.
I'm weary of conjectures — This must end them.

[*Laying his hand on his sword.*]

Thus am I doubly arm'd: my death and life,
My bane and antidote are both before me:
This in a moment brings me to an end;
But this informs me I shall never die.
The soul, secured in her existence, smiles
At the drawn dagger, and defies its point.
The stars shall fade away, the sun himself
Grow dim with age, and nature sink in years;
But thou shalt flourish in immortal youth,
Unhurt amidst the wars of elements,
The wrecks of matter, and the crush of worlds.
What means this heaviness that hangs upon me?
This lethargy that creeps through all my senses?
Nature oppress'd, and harass'd out with care,
Sinks down to rest. This once I'll favour her,
That my awaken'd soul may take her flight,
Renewed in all her strength, and fresh with life,
An offering fit for heaven. Let guilt or fear
Disturb man's rest: Cato knows neither of them,
Indifferent in his choice to sleep or die.

"*FOR MARS AND HEARTH*":[107]

The 1st and 2nd Canadian Regiments
of Washington's Army.

In spite of the defeat of Montgomery and Arnold in the assault on Quebec on December 31st, 1775, and as long as the Americans fought the War for independence, Congress never gave a thought of relinquishing Canada. Up until finalization of the Treaty of Paris in 1783, Benjamin Franklin raised the American annexation of that (then) province as a point for negotiation with the British; while prior to that, plans for later invasions had been seriously tabled on several occasions; including one scheme drafted by the Board of War in 1778 in which Lafayette, with Conway second in command, and using both their fluency in the French language and Gallic affiliations, was to attempt to secure support of French-Canadians as a stepping stone to ultimate conquest. Lafayette, however, soon found himself not happy with the arrangement. He had wanted de Kalb as his second in place of Conway, but this request was denied. So that by February he ended up going only as far as Albany before giving the project up entirely and returning to Washington's army. As a result, the 1778 expedition to take Canada was called off.

It was, nevertheless, not without good reason that Congress had high hopes of French Canadian assistance. For in late 1775 and January 1776 successful efforts had been undertaken to raise Canadian regiments on the Continental establishment. Specifically, on Nov. 10th, 1775, Congress directed Gen. Schuyler to recruit and organize a Canadian battalion. And as early as the 23rd of December, 200 men for this purpose were raised by Amer-Canadian (with parents from New York) Col. James Livingston (1747–1832) -- many of whom, incidentally, were originally recruited by Ethan Allen just prior to his capture at Montreal. Then on January 20th, 1776, as part of a plan to arm 1,000 additional Canadians, Congress authorized a second regiment; with Col. (later Brig. Gen.) Moses Hazen (1733-1803) -- recommended to Congress by his associate Edward Antil; when the latter arrived in Philadelphia to report Montgomery's repulse at Quebec -- elected to command it. At first this unit numbered some 250, but for most of the subsequent fighting operated at an average strength of about 400-500. Hazen, originally from Haverhill, Mass., had been active in the French and Indian war where he had served as a captain in Rogers' Rangers; was at the 1758 taking of Louisbourg, the siege of Quebec (though not at the climactic battle there) and at the battle of Sainte-Foy. At the outbreak of the Revolution Hazen held a commission, for which he was receiving half-pay, as a lieutenant in the British 44th Regiment of Foot.

The Canadian regiments were not part of any state quota; were manned by officers directly under the auspices of Congress, and thus acquired the formally adopted nickname of "Congress' Own." Initially, they were formed from northern New Yorkers and sympathetic Canadians hailing from Montreal, Quebec and Acadia. In 1777, the 2nd Regt. was reorganized to include two companies from Maryland and one from Connecticut. Yet otherwise and later it became to a large extent manned by immigrant Europeans and non-natives; such that in a sense the Canadian regiments, particularly the 2nd, became the American and Revolutionary War equivalent of the French Foreign Legion, and ranked among the elite of Washington's army.

The 1st Canadian Regiment, though probably never at a time numbering more than a couple hundred, served gallantly at the siege of Quebec, Trois-Rivières (June 7th, 1776), the Siege of Fort Stanwix (Aug. 1777), *possibly* the battles of Saratoga (as part of Learned's brigade), and Rhode Island (Aug. 29th, 1778.) Thereafter, they essentially did garrison duty in the Hudson Highlands, and were broken up on Jan. 1, 1781; with what remained of them incorporated into the 2nd Regiment.

The 2nd for its part was at the siege of Quebec, the retreat across New Jersey in the Autumn of 1776, Sullivan's Staten Island Raid (Aug. 22nd, 1777), Brandywine (Sept. 11th, 1777), Germantown (Oct. 4th, 1777), and Yorktown where they played a conspicuous role in the American light infantry assault on Redoubt No. 10 -- all the more fitting as the 2nd was among the very first Continental Army units to include a formal light infantry company. Worth noting as well is that in almost all these actions, the 2nd under Hazen's command incurred relatively significant numbers of casualties in killed and wounded.

---

[107] From the units' motto "Pro Aris et Focis;" and which is also translated "for altars and hearths."

The following is Hazen's memorial as submitted to Gen. Washington on Nov. 30th, 1779:

To his Excellency George Washington, Esq, General and Commander in Chief of the American Army, &c, &c, &c.
Humbly sheweth,

That the Canadian Regiment your Excellency's Memorialist has the Hononr to Command, was by a Resolution of Congress of the 20th of January, 1776, ordered to be raised in Canada for one year or during the then present Disputes; to compose four Battalions of Two Hundred and Fifty Men each, as will, by said Resolution of Congress, more fully appear.

That Four Hundred and Seventy-seven Men only were inlisted for the Term of the War, mustered and carried into Service. The Want of Money to pay the Bounty ordered prevented the Regiment from being completely filled up at that Time, and in that Country.

That a Part of the Officers and Men raised in Canada retreated with Genl. [John] Sullivan's Army on the 17th of June, 1776, from that Country; and that on the 23d of October, in the same year, the Hon. Continental Congress was pleased to order that the said Regiment should remain on the Original Establishment thereof, and be recruited to its Original Complement in any of the Thirteen United States, as the said Regiment did not belong to any particular State, nor was there any Additional Expense in the Mode of Officering the same.

That by the Alacrity and great Attention of the Recruiting Officers, Seven Hundred and Twenty Men were brought into the Field on the opening of the Campaign in the year 1777.

That this Regiment has been employed on hard Services in the Course of this Contest; a Part of it was at the Blockade and Assault of Quebec; the Regiment was with Genl. Sullivan in the Action of Staten Island, of the 22d of August, 1777; at Brandywine the 11th of September, and Germantown the 4th of October following: In all which it has acquitted itself with Honour, and was at the last mentioned Engagement amongst the Troops that were rewarded with your Excellency's Public Thanks.

That in the three several last-mentioned Engagements were killed, wounded and taken Prisoners fifteen Commissioned Officers and One Hundred and Thirty-three Non-commissioned Officers and Private Men:—That detach'd Parties from this Regiment have frequently been in warm Skirmishes with the Enemy, which have been conducted to the Honour of the Officer who commanded, tho' attended with the Loss of many brave Men.

That on the 4th of November, 1778, the Hon. Continental Congress was pleased to order that the said Regiment should remain on its Original Establishment, and that no new Appointments or Promotions of Officers be made therein, until further Orders of Congress.

That on the 15th of March, 1779, the Hon. Continental Congress was pleased to order Returns to be made of this Regiment, and others, setting forth the different States in which the Officers were raised, or the Non-commissioned Officers and Soldiers recruited, and that the said States should have Credit for the Officers and Men so raised or recruited, as a Part of their Quotas to be kept up in the Field. This Resolution it is presumed was entered into as well to do Justice to the several States, in Point of raising their several Quotas of Men, as to leave it in their Power to take Care of and reward the Officers and Men in the same Manner as they might their own State Battalions, which however just the Intention it can never affect this Regiment, so as to do it Justice in every Part thereof; for as the Officers are raised and the Regiment recruited from North Carolina to Canada, it is impossible that the Officers and Men should have the Benefit of the several and respective State Stores, to which it seems it was intended they should have a Right to in common with their own Troops; nor have they ever received a Farthing value from any one State before or since that Resolution took Place; on the other Hand, sixteen Officers and One Hundred and eleven Non-commissioned Officers and Soldiers are returned Volunteers from Canada, and otherwise belonging to no one of the Thirteen United States, consequently no Kind of Provision is or has been attempted to be made for them : However hard their Case, their Services are deserving of Notice : That the Canadian Soldiers are not inferior to any in the Regiment, in Point of Morality, Bravery, or Attachment to the Cause and Service in which they are engaged; a Proof of which, one Canadian only has deserted since the Regiment retreated out of Canada : Nine different Detachments were sent into that Country the last Summer for Intelligence, and the greater Part of the other Canadians within Sight of and not more than .one Days march of their own Country, Families, Friends, Connections and Estates. -- Four Hundred and Seventy-one Noncommissioned Officers and Soldiers are now on the Muster Rolls and Returns, Four hundred and Sixty of which are inlisted during the War, on Twenty Dollars Bounty only; not a Man has ever received either a Town or State Bounty to the Knowledge of your Memorialist.

That neither Officer or Soldier in the Regiment has ever received a Farthing's Value of Cloathing, or other Supplies whatever, out of any State or Continental Store, otherwise than a Dividend of coarse Clothes, with the other Troops at Hartford, by Order of Genl. Gates, the whole of which did not compose an Assortment that would have made up one Regimental Coat: That under the present Hardships, and many Difficulties herein enumerated, it is impossible to expect this Regiment can continue in the service unless some proper Provision of Cloathing for the Officers and Supplies for them and the Men, may, by some Means or other, be obtained so as to leave this Regiment on a footing with the Army.

Your Memorialist has the Pleasure to assure your Excellency, That notwithstanding the different States, Countries and Nations from which this Regiment has been raised, yet a perfect Harmony and a general Unanimity has always subsisted amongst the Officers as well as a most passive obedience cultivated among the Soldiers: -- and further, your Memorialist begs Leave to assure your Excellency, that he should not do Justice to the Regiment, if he did not add on this Occasion, that he has the Honour to command as good a Corps as any in the American Army. It is hoped and really wished that the Period may not be far off when this Regiment may be adopted by their own -- a fourteenth State in America. -- Your Memorialist therefore humbly prays your Excellency will please to take the Case of this Regiment into Consideration, and direct or recommend to Congress a remedy by which the Officers and Soldiers may be on a footing with the Army.

That in Point of Clothing and Supplies for the Regiment your Memorialist begs Leave to propose,

That the Commanding Officer, Paymaster, or some other Person, may be empowered to purchase such Articles of Clothing and Supplies, or Refreshments as are or may be furnished to the other Troops, and in like Proportion, and that they may be issued out or delivered to the Officers and Men in the same Manner as have been, now are, or may hereafter be, to other Continental Troops, at the same or like Discounts; -- that the Extra Prices and Amount of all such Cloathing and Supplies may be paid from Time to Time from the Military Chest; -- that a particular Account may be kept of all such Issues or Deliveries, and rendered to such Persons, and as often, as may be directed, in order that the Amount of the Extra Cost of all such Goods so delivered may be by the Public a Charge against the several and respective States, as issued to the Officers and Men which they have Credit for in their several and respective Quotas; and that such a Part as may be issued and delivered to the Canadian Volunteers be a Charge against the Public at large until a final Settlement, which appears to your Memorialist the only Method by which common Justice may be dune to the whole, and that all the Soldiers of the Regiment may be served at one and the same Time with such Refreshment as may be allowed them, which will naturally tend to Quiet the Minds of the Soldiers, and promote Harmony in the Regiment; for Soldiers who serve together ought to serve on one and the same footing; any Thing to the contrary has been found by Experience to be Subversive of that good Order and Military Discipline which ought to be preserved; for these Reasons, your Excellency's Memorialist was obliged to stop, by the Advice of the Officers of the Regiment, four Months Pay to the Officers raised and Soldiers inlisted from Connecticut, and by the Legislative Body of that State ordered to be paid to them, which remains yet in the hands of the Paymaster. Your Excellency's Memorialist will, as in Duty bound, ever pray,

MOSES HAZEN.
Camp, Peeks-Kill, Nov 30th, 1779.

[As found in *The Pennsylvania Archives*, vol. VIII, edited by Samuel Hazard. Joseph Severns & Co., Philadelphia, 1853. pp. 17-20.]

~~~*~~~

For further on the Canadian Regiments --

The American Archives, 4th Series, Vols. IV and V, 1775-1776. contain items concerning the Canadian regiments, Colonel Hazen's regiment. ("Congress' Own," 1776-1783.) (In *Pennsylvania Archives*, 2d Series, Vol. XI, pp. 99-107. Harrisburg, 1880. 8vo.) Brief sketch of the regiment, with a list of the Pennsylvania members.

Colonel James Livingston. (In *Magazine of American History*, Vol. XXI, Jan., 1889, pp. 71-74.) From John Schuyler's "The Society of the Cincinnati."
~~~

Moses Hazen. "The memorial of Colonel Moses Hazen to General Washington, 1779." (In *Pennsylvania Archives*, Vol. VIII 1779-1781, pp. 17-19. Philadelphia, 1853. 8vo.)

Benson J. Lossing. *The Life and Times of Philip Schuyler*. New York: Sheldon & Company, 1873. 2 vols. 12mo. Moses Hazen at Montreal, Vol. II, p. 42; Letter of, Vol. II, pp. 46-47, 50.

Benjamin Movers. "Biography of Major-General Benjamin Movers of Plattsburg, Clinton County, N.Y., written, in 1833 by request of his son, Benjamin H. Movers." (In *Historical Magazine*, Vol. XXI, Feb., 1872, pp. 92-94.) "A detailed history of this regiment (Hazen's) written by its Adjutant."

Berg, Fred Anderson. *Encyclopedia of Continental Army Units*. Stackpole Books, Harrisburg, Pennsylvania, 1972.

Boogher, W. F., ed. "Captain James Ducnan's Diary of the Siege of Yorktown," *Magazine of History* (1905): 407-16

Everest, Allan S. *Moses Hazen and the Canadian Refugees in the American Revolution*. Syracuse, Syracuse University Press, 1976.

Griffin, Martin Ignatius Joseph Griffin. *Catholics and the American Revolution, Volume 3*.Self-published, Philadelphia, 1911.

Lanctot, Gustave. *Canada & the American Revolution 1774-1783*. Trans. Margaret M. Cameron. Cambridge, Mass, Harvard U.Press, 1967

Pearce, Stewart, ed. "Extract from the diary of Captan Andrew Lee." *Pennsylvania Magazine of History and Biography* (1879): 167-173

Reed, Adela Peltier.Memmoirs of Antone Paulint, Veteran of the Old French War 1755 to 1760, Captain in Hazen's 2nd Canadian, "Congress'sOwn" regiment 1775 to 1783, Brevet major at the close of The Revolutionary War. Los Angeles. Privately printed, 1940.

Schuyler, John. "Colonel James Livingston." *Magazine of American History,* Vol. XXI, Jan. 1889): pp. 71-74

Stanley, George F.G. *Canada Invaded 1775-1776*. Toronto; Hakkert, 1973.

United States. Continental Congress. *Journals of the Continental Congress, 1774-1789*. Edited from the original records in the Library of Congress by Worthington Chauncey Ford, Vols. IV-VI. Jan.-Dec., 1776. Washington: Government Printing Office, 1905-1906. 3 vols. 4to. Contains memorials and reports relating to the Canadian regiments.

Wright, Robert K., Jr. *The Continental Army*. Center of Military History United States Army, Washington, D.C., 1989.

Major Robert Rogers' "PONTEACH: Or the Savages of America. A Tragedy" (1766): Some Excerpts

"This Dream no doubt is full of some great Meaning,
And in it bears the Fate of your Design,
But whether good or ill, to me 's a Secret."
~ Act II, scene 2.

The influence of the Iroquois confederacy as a model for the United States form of government has to some extent been exaggerated by some; since those who framed our Constitution had other examples to draw on, such as the *United* Provinces of the Netherlands; not to mention several ancient, medieval,[108] and renaissance instances, of cities, (German) "electorates," multi-provinces, or states, based on suffrage, and leagued or joined together under one democratic, republican, or else princely rule.[109] On the other hand, it seems that less than fair credit has been awarded the Native Americans for helping to stir us to revolt and spurring us to independent mindedness by way of the uprising in 1763 of the Ottawa tribesman Chief Pontiac (1763-1766; also and more properly titled, Chief Obwandiyag); an event probably most well known by way of Francs Parkman's epic, if rather chauvinistic, chronicle *The Conspiracy of Pontiac* (1851). Among some of the noted personages who participated in the war with the Ottawa chief was Major Robert Rogers, of Rogers' Rangers fame.

Even more interesting than his fighting the Indians in the Pontiac uprising, Rogers (who'd personally known the great chief) afterwards in London in 1766 wrote and published a stage play portraying the rebelling natives in a sympathetic light, entitled "Ponteach Or the Savages of America. A Tragedy." Though some scholars assume, it would seem correctly, that Rogers only contributed rather than penned the entire play; there is little question about his being the guiding hand and overriding heart and spirit behind it; and a close inspection of the text by experts has revealed or suggested input based on his own personal experience with Indians and white settlers. Moreover, "Ponteach" was, of course, not Rogers' only literary work. In addition to his *Journal of the French and Indian War* (1765), he also wrote *A Concise Account of North America* (1765),[110] an eminently readable and capacious overview of Pre-War America from the perspective of a American royal subject -- but a royal subject who especially prizes and appreciates democratic assemblies and religious tolerance and freedom. In the same work, he as well provides some at length and detailed remarks delineating the Indians, their characters and customs (pp. 205-253); that are, not least of which given his intimate dealings and associations with them, valuable and insightful contributions on the subject.[111]

Though biographers are naturally prompted to give Rogers' life story, there is much about quite what happened to him that remains a substantial mystery and remains to be better and further elucidated. At one point, he ended up in debtor's prison in London; at another he was tried by the British for treason but was acquitted. Come time of the Revolution, he was offered a command by Congress and himself tendered his services to Washington. Moreover, Israel Putnam, John Stark and Moses Hazen numbered among his friends. Yet Washington not long after ordered him arrested, and it is believed by some (based on a report of a Loyalist) that Rogers had aided in the capture of Nathan Hale. As a matter of course then, he went to British for employment. Yet might Washington have been misinformed, or else was Rogers' alleged entrapment of Hale mistaken or fabricated? More than likely, his having been earlier accused of treason a few years earlier played some part in all this. As such and again, there is too much that we simply do not know otherwise. Poor Rogers! He is not little reminiscent of Capt. Robert Stobo (1727–1770) of Virginia,

---

[108] The Vatican, it is worth noting, was the first post-ancient European system of government to choose its head or monarch by formal electors, i.e., in having a majority of Cardinals appoint the pope. Christopher Brooke, *Europe in in the Central Middle Ages*, p. 205.

[109] And yet *prior* to the Revolutionary War, a number of colonial Americans, including Benjamin Franklin, were indeed deeply impressed by the Iroquois confederacy as a stimulus for and model on the basis of which the disparate colonies, so they argued, ought themselves to unite. For further, see *Seeds of Liberty* (1948) by Max Savelle, pp. 328-329.

[110] See http://www.archive.org/details/aconciseaccount00rogeuoft

[111] Among other points that might be noted in this regard, some of the Native American males evidently resembled Tacitus' Germans in dedicating their lives war and hunting; while (outside of harvesting) refusing to do any menial work of any sort; the last being deemed the proper province of women.

another French and Indian war officer and wartime acquaintance of Washington's; also of exceptional daring and martial escapades, but who subsequently took his own life in 1770.[112] Perhaps Rogers and Stobo were haunted, mayhap even literally, by a ghost who jealously resented their success. Certainly at least to this writer such speculation, and given their mutually strange biographies and lamentable demises, is perhaps not so far fetched as one might out of hand assume.

As to "Ponteach" itself and as stated, it would be very odd if Rogers did not receive some material assistance in writing it. Its hendecasyllabic verse is written in familiar 18th century stage idiom and has its fair share of anachronisms; such as references to "lions" and "tygers" [113] by Native American speakers; while in Act III, scen. 3, stage directions tell us that the *Indian War Song* is to be sung "to the tune 'Over the Hills and far away.'"

Yet, as mentioned, Rogers stamp is still clearly on the thing, and it was extremely radical of him to be speaking out so passionately on behalf of Pontiac and the Indians -- something, after all, which would not likely have found much favor with either many British or Americans at the time. But not least of the play's fascination, some of the speeches Rogers gives Ponteach could with small revision sound as though they came from a zealous American colonial revolutionary – all the more peculiar given and considering that come the Revolution he ended up a Loyalist.

~~~***~~~

from Act I, scen. 2.

Scene II. A Desart.

Enter Orsbourn and Honnyman, two English Hunters.

Orsbourn.
Long have we toil'd, and rang'd the Woods in vain,
No Game, nor Track, nor Sign of any Kind
Is to be seen; I swear I am discourag'd
And weary'd out with this long fruitless Hunt.
No Life on Earth besides is half so hard,
So full of Disappointments, as a Hunter's:
Each Morn he wakes he views the destin'd Prey,
And counts the Profits of th' ensuing Day;
Each Ev'ning at his curs'd ill Fortune pines,
And till next Day his Hope of Gain resigns.
By Jove, I'll from these Desarts hasten home,
And swear that never more I'll touch a Gun.

----

from Act. I, scen. 3.

Cockum.
What shall we do with these damn'd bawling Indians?
They're swarming every Day with their Complaints
Of Wrongs and Injuries, and God knows what—
I wish the Devil would take them to himself.

---

[112] See *The Memoirs of Major Robert Stobo* (1854), written by Stobo but not published till 1854; "The Fantastic Adventures of Captain Stobo," by Robert C. Alberts, *American Heritage Magazine*, August 1963, vol. 14, iss. 5 (available at http://www.americanheritage.com/content/fantastic-adventures-captain-stobo), and *The Most Extraordinary Adventures of Major Robert Stobo* (1965) also by Alberts.

[113] William Bartram, however, in his *Travels* (1791) perhaps offers us some explanation by his noting that what is called "Tiger" in the southern American states is denoted "Panther" in the northern. Part I, Ch. 4, p. 46 n.
~~~

Frisk.
Your Honour's right to wish the Devil his Due.
I'd send the noisy Hellhounds packing hence,
Nor spend a Moment in debating with them.
The more you give Attention to their Murmurs,
The more they'll plague and haunt you every Day,
Besides, their old King Ponteach grows damn'd saucy,
Talks of his Power, and threatens what he'll do.
Perdition to their faithless sooty Souls,
I'd let 'em know at once to keep their Distance.

Cockum.
Captain, You're right; their Insolence is such
As beats my Patience; cursed Miscreants!
They are encroaching; fain would be familiar:
I'll send their painted Heads to Hell with Thunder!
I swear I'll blow 'em hence with Cannon Ball,
And give the Devil an Hundred for his Supper.

----

from Act. I, scen. 3.

2nd Chief.
Frenchmen would always hear an Indian speak,
And answer fair, and make good Promises.

Cockum.
You may be d——d, and all your Frenchmen too.

Ponteach.
Be d——d! what's that? I do not understand.

Cockum.
The Devil teach you; he'll do it without a Fee.

Ponteach.
The Devil teach! I think you one great Fool.
Did your King tell you thus to treat the Indians?
Had he been such a Dunce he ne'er had conquer'd,
And made the running French for Quarter cry.
I always mind that such proud Fools are Cowards,
And never do aught that is great or good.

Cockum.
Forbear your Impudence, you curs'd old Thief;
This Moment leave my Fort, and to your Country.
Let me hear no more of your hellish Clamour,
Or to D——n I will blow you all,
And feast the Devil with one hearty Meal.

Ponteach.
So ho! Know you whose Country you are in?
Think you, because you have subdu'd the French,
That Indians too are now become your Slaves?
This Country's mine, and here I reign as King;

I value not your Threats, nor Forts, nor Guns;
I have got Warriors, Courage, Strength, and Skill.
Colonel, take care; the Wound is very deep,
Consider well, for it is hard to cure.

----

from Act. I, scen. 3.

Sharp.
There's good and bad, you know, in every Nation;
There's some good Indians, some are the reverse,
Whom you can't govern, and restrain from ill;
So there's some Englishmen that will be bad.
You must not mind the Conduct of a few,
Nor judge the rest by what you see of them.

Ponteach.
If you've some good, why don't you send them here?
These every one are Rogues, and Knaves, and Fools,
And think no more of Indians than of Dogs.
Your King had better send his good Men hither,
And keep his bad ones in some other Country;
Then you would find that Indians would do well,
Be peaceable, and honest in their Trade;
We'd love you, treat you, as our Friends and Brothers,
And Raise the Hatchet only in your Cause.

----

from Act I, scen. 3.

Ponteach.
Your King, I hear 's a good and upright Man,
True to his word, and friendly in his Heart;
Not proud and insolent, morose and sour,
Like these his petty Officers and Servants:
I want to see your King, and let him know
What must be done to keep the Hatchet dull,
And how the Path of Friendship, Peace, and Trade
May be kept clean and solid as a Rock.

Sharp.
Our King is distant over the great Lake,
But we can quickly send him your Requests;
To which he'll listen with attentive Ear,
And act as tho' you told him with your Tongue.

Ponteach.
Let him know then his People here are Rogues,
And cheat and wrong and use the Indians ill.
Tell him to send good Officers, and call
These proud ill-natur'd Fellows from my Country,
And keep his Hunters from my hunting Ground.
He must do this, and do it quickly too,
Or he will find the Path between us bloody.

----

from Act I, scen. 3.

Ponteach.
Indians a'n't Fools, if White Men think us so;
We see, we hear, we think as well as you;
We know there 're Lies, and Mischiefs in the World;
We don't know whom to trust, nor when to fear;
Men are uncertain, changing as the Wind,
Inconstant as the Waters of the Lakes,
Some smooth and fair, and pleasant as the Sun,
Some rough and boist'rous, like the Winter Storm;
Some are Insidious as the subtle Snake,
Some innocent, and harmless as the Dove;
Some like the Tyger raging, cruel, fierce,
Some like the Lamb, humble, submissive, mild,
And scarcely one is every Day the same;
But I call no Man bad, till such he's found,
Then I condemn and cast him from my Sight;
And no more trust him as a Friend and Brother.
I hope to find you honest Men and true.

Sharp.
Indeed you may depend upon our Honours,
We're faithful Servants of the best of Kings;
We scorn an Imposition on your Ignorance,
Abhor the Arts of Falsehood and Deceit.
These are the Presents our great Monarch sent,
He's of a bounteous, noble, princely Mind
And had he known the Numbers of your Chiefs,
Each would have largely shar'd his Royal Goodness;
But these are rich and worthy your Acceptance,
Few Kings on Earth can such as these bestow,
For Goodness, Beauty, Excellence, and Worth.

Ponteach.
The Presents from your Sovereign I accept,
His friendly Belts to us shall be preserved,
And in Return convey you those to him.
[Belts and furs.
Which let him know our Mind, and what we wish,
That we dislike his crusty Officers,
And wish the Path of Peace was made more plain,
The Calumet I do not choose to smoke,
Till I see further, and my other Chiefs
Have been consulted. Tell your King from me,
That first or last a Rogue will be detected,
That I have Warriors, am myself a King,
And will be honour'd and obey'd as such;
Tell him my Subjects shall not be oppress'd,
But I will seek Redress and take Revenge;
Tell your King this; I have no more to say.

----

from Act II, scen. 1.

[Sons of Ponteach -- Chekitan and Philip]

Chekitan.
Should War be wag'd, what Discords may we fear
Among ourselves? The powerful Mohawk King [King Hendrick]
Will ne'er consent to fight against the English,
Nay, more, will join them as firm Ally,
And influence other Chiefs by his Example,
To muster all their Strength against our Father.
Fathers perhaps will fight against their Sons,
And nearest Friends pursue each other's Lives;
Blood, Murder, Death, and Horror will be rife,
Where Peace and Love, and Friendship triumph now.

Philip.
Such stale Conjectures smell of Cowardice.
Our Father's Temper shews us the reverse:
All Danger he defies, and, once resolv'd,
No Arguments will move him to relent,
No Motives change his Purpose of Revenge,
No Prayers prevail upon him to delay
The Execution of his fix'd Design:
Like the starv'd Tyger in Pursuit of Prey,
No Opposition will retard his Course;
Like the wing'd Eagle that looks down on Clouds,
All Hindrances are little in his Eye,
And his great Mind knows not the Pain of Fear.

Chekitan.
Such Hurricanes of Courage often lead
To Shame and Disappointment in the End,
And tumble blindfold on their own Disgrace.
True Valour's slow, deliberate, and cool,
Considers well the End, the Way, the Means,
And weighs each Circumstance attending them.
Imaginary Dangers it detects,
And guards itself against all real Evils.
But here Tenesco comes with Speed important;
His Looks and Face presage us something new.

----

from Act II, scen. 2

Tenesco.
Spoke like yourselves, the Sons of Ponteach;
Strength, Courage, and Obedience form the Soldier,
And the firm Base of all true Greatness lay.

Ponteach.
Our Empire now is large, our Forces strong,
Our Chiefs are wise, our Warriors valiant Men;
We all are furnish'd with the best of Arms,
And all things requisite to curb a Foe;

And now's our Time, if ever, to secure
Our Country, Kindred, Empire, all that's dear,
From these Invaders of our Rights, the English,
And set their Bounds towards the rising Sun.
Long have I seen with a suspicious Eye
The Strength and growing Numbers of the French;
Their Forts and Settlements I've view'd as Snakes
Of mortal Bite, bound by the Winter Frost,
Which in some future warm reviving Day
Would stir and hiss, and spit their Poison forth,
And spread Destruction through our happy Land.
Where are we now? The French are all subdued,
But who are in their Stead become our Lords?
A proud, imperious, churlish, haughty Band.
The French familiarized themselves with us,
Studied our Tongue, and Manners, wore our Dress,
Married our Daughters, and our Sons their Maids,
Dealt honestly, and well supplied our Wants,
Used no One ill, and treated with Respect
Our Kings, our Captains, and our aged Men;
Call'd us their Friends, nay, what is more, their Children,
And seem'd like Fathers anxious for our Welfare.
Whom see we now? their haughty Conquerors
Possess'd of every Fort, and Lake, and Pass,
Big with their Victories so often gain'd;
On us they look with deep Contempt and Scorn,
Are false, deceitful, knavish, insolent;
Nay, think us conquered, and our Country theirs,
Without a Purchase, or ev'n asking for it.
With Pleasure I wou'd call their King my Friend,
Yea, honour and obey him as my Father;
I'd be content, would he keep his own Sea,
And leave these distant Lakes and Streams to us;
Nay, I would pay him Homage, if requested,
And furnish Warriors to support his Cause.
But thus to lose my Country and my Empire,
To be a Vassal to his low Commanders,
Treated with disrespect and public Scorn
By Knaves, by Miscreants, Creatures of his Power;
Can this become a King like Ponteach,
Whose Empire's measured only by the Sun?
No, I'll assert my Right, the Hatchet raise,
And drive these Britons hence like frighted Deer,
Destroy their Forts, and make them rue the Day
That to our fertile Land they found the Way.

----

from Act II, scen. 2

Chekitan.
Would you the Mohawk Emperor [King Hendrick] displease,
And wage a bloody War, by which you made
Him and his num'rous Tribes your certain Foes?

Ponteach.
Most of his Tribes will welcome the Proposal;
For long their galled Necks have felt the Yoke,
Long wish'd for Freedom from his partial Sway,
In favour of the proud incroaching Britons.
Nay, they have oft, in spite of his Displeasure,
Rush'd forth like Wolves upon their naked Borders,
And now, like Tygers broken from their Chains,
they'll glut themselves, and revel in their Blood.
----

from Act III, scene 3.

Ponteach.
Do what he will, 'tis this explains my Meaning;
[Taking up the hatchet.
You all are well appris'd of my Design,
Which every passing Moment but confirms:
Nay, my Heart's pain'd while I withhold my Hand
From Blood and Vengeance on our hated Foes.
Tho' I should stand alone, I'll try my Power
To punish their Encroachments, Frauds, and Pride;
Yet tho' I die, it is my Country's Cause,
'Tis better thus to die than be despis'd;
Better to die than be a Slave to Cowards,
Better to die than see my Friends abus'd;
The Aged scorn'd, the Young despis'd and spurn'd.
Better to die than see my Country ruin'd,
Myself, my Sons, my Friends reduc'd to Famine,
Expell'd from hence to barren Rocks and Mountains,
To curse our wretched Fate and pine in Want;
Our pleasant Lakes and Fertile Lands usurp'd
By Strangers, Ravagers, rapacious Christians.
Who is it don't prefer a Death in War
To this impending Wretchedness and Shame?
Who is it loves his Country, Friends, or Self,
And does not feel Resentment in his Soul?
Who is it sees their growing Strength and Power,
And how we waste and fail by swift Degrees,
That does not think it Time to rouse and arm,
And kill the Serpent ere we feel it sting,
And fall the Victims of its painful Poison?
Oh! could our Fathers from their Country see
Their ancient Rights encroach'd upon and ravag'd,
And we their Children slow, supine, and careless
To keep the Liberty and Land they left us,
And tamely fall a Sacrifice to Knaves!
How would their Bosoms glow with patriot Shame,
To see their Offspring so unlike themselves?
They dared all Dangers to defend their Rights,
Nor tamely bore an Insult from a Foe.
Their plain rough Souls were brave and full of Fire,
Lovers of War, nor knew the Pain of Fear.
Rouse, then, ye Sons of ancient Heroes, rouse,
Put on your Arms, and let us act a Part
Worthy the Sons of such renowned Chiefs.

Nor urge I you to Dangers that I shun,
Or mean to act my Part by Words alone;
This Hand shall wield the Hatchet in the Cause,
These Feet pursue the frighted running Foe,
This Body rush into the hottest Battle;
There should I fall, I shall secure my Honour,
And, dying, urge my Countrymen to Vengeance
With more Success than all the Force of Words.
Should I survive, I'll shed the foremost Tear
O'er my brave Countrymen that chance to fall;
I'll be the foremost to revenge their Blood,
And, while I live, honour both them and theirs,
I add no more, but wait to hear your Minds.

----

from Act III, scen. 3

The Bear.
What is the Greatness of their King to us?
What of his Strength or Wisdom? Shall we fear
A Lion chain'd, or in another World?
Or what avails his flowing Goodness to us?
Does not the ravenous Tyger feed her Young?
And the fierce Panther fawn upon his Mate?
Do not the Wolves defend and help their Fellows,
The poisonous Serpent feed her hissing Brood,
And open wide her Mouth for their Protection?
So this good King shows Kindness to his own,
And favours them, to make a Prey of others;
But at his Hands we may expect no Favour,
Look back, my Friends, to our Forefathers' Time,
Where is their Country? where their pleasant Haunts?
The running Streams and shady Forests where?
They chas'd the flying Game, and liv'd in Plenty.
Lo, these proud Strangers now possess the Whole;
Their Cities, Towns, and Villages arise,
Forests are spoil'd, the Haunts of Game destroy'd,
And all the Sea Coasts made one general Waste;
Between the Rivers Torrent-like they sweep,
And drive our Tribes toward the setting Sun.
They who once liv'd on yon delightful Plains
Are now no more, their very Name is lost.
The Sons of potent Kings, subdu'd and murder'd,
Are Vagrants, and unknown among their Neighbours.
Where will the Ravage stop? the Ruin where?
Does not the Torrent rush with growing Speed,
And hurry us to the same wretched End?
Let us grow wise then by our Fathers' Folly,
Unite our Strength, too long it's been divided,
And mutual Fears and Jealousies obtain'd:
This has encourag'd our encroaching Foes,
But we'll convince them, once, we dare oppose them.

The Wolf.
Yet we have Strength by which we may oppose,
But every Day this Strength declines and fails.
Our great Forefathers, ere these Strangers came,
Liv'd by the Chace, with Nature's Gifts content,
The cooling Fountain quench'd their raging Thirst.
Doctors, and Drugs, and Med'cines were unknown,
Even Age itself was free from Pain and Sickness.
Swift as the Wind, o'er Rocks and Hills they chas'd
The flying Game, the bounding Stag outwinded,
And tir'd the savage Bear, and tam'd the Tyger;
At Evening feasted on the past Day's Toil,
Nor then fatigu'd; the merry Dance and Song
Succeeded; still with every rising Sun
The Sport renew'd; or if some daring Foe
Provok'd their Wrath, they bent the hostile Bow,
Nor waited his Approach, but rush'd with Speed,
Fearless of Hunger, Thirst, Fatigue, or Death.
But we their soften'd Sons, a puny Race,
Are weak in Youth, fear Dangers where they're not;
Are weary'd with what was to them a Sport,
Panting and breathless in One short Hour's Chace;
And every Effort of our Strength is feeble.
We're poison'd with the Infection of our Foes,
Their very Looks and Actions are infectious,
And in deep Silence spread Destruction round them.
Bethink yourselves while any Strength remains;
Dare to be like your Fathers, brave and strong,
Nor further let the growing Poison spread.
And would you stop it, you must resolve to conquer,
Destroy their Forts and Bulwarks, burn their Towns,
And keep them at a greater Distance from us.
Oh! 'tis a Day I long have wish'd to see,
And, aged as I am, my Youth returns
To act with Vigour in so good a Cause.
Yes, you shall see the old Wolf will not fail
To head his Troops, and urge them on to Battle.

----

from Act IV, scen. 3.

Messenger.
Huzza! for our brave Warriors are return'd
Loaded with Plunder and the Scalps of Christians.

[Enter Warriors.

Ponteach.
What have you done? Why all this Noise and Shouting?

1st Warrior.
Three Forts are taken, all consum'd and plunder'd;
The English in them all destroy'd by Fire,
Except some few escap'd to die with Hunger.

2nd Warrior.
We've smok'd the Bear in spite of all his Craft,
Burnt up their Den, and made them take the Field:
The mighty Colonel Cockum and his Captain
Have dull'd our Tomhocks; here are both their Scalps:
[Holding out the two scalps.
Their Heads are split, our Dogs have eat their Brains.

Philip.
If that be all they've eat, the Hounds will starve.

3rd Warrior.
These are the scalps of those two famous Cheats
Who bought our Furs for Rum, and sold us Water.
[Holding out the scalps, which Ponteach takes.
Our Men are loaded with their Furs again,
And other Plunder from the Villains' Stores.

Ponteach.
All this is brave!
[Tossing up the scalps, which others catch, and toss and throw them about.
This Way we'll serve them all.

Philip.
We'll cover all our Cabins with their Scalps.

Warriors.
We'll fat our Dogs upon their Brains and Blood.

Ponteach.
Ere long we'll have their Governors in Play.

Philip.
And knock their grey-wig'd Scalps about this Way.

Ponteach.
The Game is started; Warriors, hunt away,
Nor let them find a Place to shun your Hatchets.

All Warriors.
We will: We will soon shew you other Scalps.

Philip.
Bring some alive; I long to see them dance
In Fire and Flames, it us'd to make them caper.

Warriors.
Such Sport enough you'll have before we've done.
[Exeunt.

Ponteach.
This still will help to move the Mohawk King [Hendrick].
Spare not to make the most of our Success.

Philip.
Trust me for that—Hark; there's another Shout;

[Shouting without.
A Shout for Prisoners—Now I have my Sport.

Ponteach.
It is indeed; and there's a Number too.

Enter Warriors.

1st Warrior.
We've broke the Barrier, burnt their Magazines,
Slew Hundreds of them, and pursu'd the rest
Quite to their Settlements.

2nd Warrior.
There we took
Their famous Hunters Honnyman and Orsbourn:
The last is slain, this is his bloody Scalp [of Orsbourn].
[Tossing it up.
With them we found the Guns of our lost Hunters,
And other Proofs that they're the Murderers;
Nay, Honnyman confesses the base Deed,
And, boasting, says, he's kill'd a Score of Indians.

3rd Warrior.
This is the bloody Hunter: This his Wife;
[Leading them forward, pinioned and tied together.
With two young Brats that will be like their Father.
We took them in their Nest, and spoil'd their Dreams.

Philip.
Oh I could eat their Hearts, and drink their Blood,
Were they not Poison, and unfit for Dogs.
Here, you Blood-hunter, have you lost your Feeling?
You Tygress Bitch! You Breeder up of Serpents!
[Slapping Honnyman in the face, and kicking his wife.

Ponteach.
Stop—We must first consult which way to torture.
And whether all shall die—We will retire.

Philip [going].
Take care they don't escape.

Warrior.
They're bound secure.
[Exeunt Indians; manent Prisoners.

----

from Act IV, scen. 4.

Honnyman.
I am indeed. I murder'd many of them,
And thought it not amiss, but now I fear.

Mrs. Honnyman.
O shocking Thought! Why have you let me know
Yourself thus guilty in the Eye of Heaven?
That I and my dear Babes were by you brought
To this Extreme of Wretchedness and Woe?
Why have you let me know the solemn Weight
Of horrid Guilt that lies upon us all?
To have died innocent, and seen these Babes
By savage Hands dash'd to immortal Rest,
This had been light, for this implies no Crime:
But now we die as guilty Murderers,
Not savage Indians, but just Heaven's Vengeance
Pursues our Lives with all these Pains and Tortures.
This is a Thought that points the keenest Sorrow,
And leaves no Room for Anguish to be heighten'd.

Honnyman.
Upbraid me not, nor lay my Guilt to Heart;
You and these Fruits of our past Morning Love
Are innocent. I feel the Smart and Anguish,
The Stings of Conscience, and my Soul on Fire.
There's not a Hell more painful than my Bosom,
Nor Torments for the Damn'd more keenly pointed.
How could I think to murder was no Sin?
Oh, my lost Neighbour! I seduc'd him too.
Now death with all its Terrors disappears,
And all I fear 's a dreadful Something-after;
My Mind forebodes a horrid, woful Scene,
Where Guilt is chain'd and tortur'd with Despair.

Mrs. Honnyman.
The Mind oppress'd with Guilt may find Relief.

Honnyman.
Oh, could I reach the pitying Ear of Heaven,
And all my Soul evaporate in Sound,
'T would ask Forgiveness! but I fear too late;
And next I'd ask that you and these dear Babes
Might bear no Part in my just Punishment.
Who knows but by pathetic Prayers and Tears
Their savage Bosoms may relent towards you,
And fix their Vengeance where just Heaven points it?
I still will hope, and every Motive urge.
Should I succeed, and melt their rocky Hearts,
I'd take it as a Presage of my Pardon,
And die with Comfort when I see you live.
[Death halloo is heard without.

Mrs. Honnyman.
Hark! they are coming—Hear that dreadful Halloo.

----

from Act V, scen. 5.

Ponteach
What are your Tidings?—I have no more Sons.

Tenesco.
But you have Subjects, and regard their Safety.
The treacherous Priest, intrusted with your Councils,
Has publish'd all, and added his own Falsehoods;
The Chiefs have all revolted from your Cause,
Patch'd up a Peace, and lend their Help no more.

Ponteach.
And is this all? we must defend ourselves,
Supply the Place of Numbers with our Courage,
And learn to conquer with our very Looks:
This is a Time that tries the Truth of Valour;
He shows his Courage that dares stem the Storm,
And live in spite of Violence and Fate.
Shall holy Perfidy and seeming Lies
Destroy our Purpose, sink us into Cowards?

Tenesco.
May your Hopes prosper! I'll excite the Troops
By your Example still to keep the Field.
[Exit.

Ponteach.
'Tis coming on. Thus Wave succeeds to Wave,
Till the Storm's spent, then all subsides again—
The Chiefs revolted:—My Design betray'd:—
May he that trusts a Christian meet the same;
They have no Faith, no Honesty, no God,
And cannot merit Confidence from Men.
Were I alone the boist'rous Tempest's Sport,
I'd quickly move my shatter'd, trembling Bark,
And follow my departed Sons to Rest.
But my brave Countrymen, my Friends, my Subjects,
Demand my Care: I'll not desert the Helm,
Nor leave a dang'rous Station in Distress;
Yes, I will live, in spite of Fate I'll live;
Was I not Ponteach, was I not a King,
Such Giant Mischiefs would not gather round me.
And since I'm Ponteach, since I am a King,
I'll shew myself Superior to them all;
I'll rise above this Hurricane of Fate,
And shew my Courage to the Gods themselves.

[Enter Tenesco, surprised and pausing.]

I am prepar'd, be not afraid to tell;
You cannot speak what Ponteach dare not hear.

Tenesco.
Our bravest Troops are slain, the rest pursu'd;
All is Disorder, Tumult, and Rebellion.

Those that remain insist on speedy Flight;
You must attend them, or be left alone
Unto the Fury of a conquering Foe,
Nor will they long expect your Royal Pleasure.

Ponteach.
Will they desert their King in such an Hour,
When Pity might induce them to protect him?
Kings like the Gods are valued and ador'd,
When Men expect their Bounties in Return,
Place them in Want, destroy the giving Power,
All Sacrifices and Regards will cease.
Go, tell my Friends that I'll attend their Call.
[Rising. Exit Tenesco.
I will not fear—but must obey my Stars:
[Looking round.

Ye fertile Fields and glad'ning Streams, adieu;
Ye Fountains that have quench'd my scorching Thirst,
Ye Shades that hid the Sun-beams from my Head,
Ye Groves and Hills that yielded me the Chace,
Ye flow'ry Meads, and Banks, and bending Trees,
And thou proud Earth, made drunk with Royal Blood,
I am no more your Owner and your King.
But witness for me to your new base Lords,
That my unconquer'd Mind defies them still;
And though I fly, 'tis on the Wings of Hope.
Yes, I will hence where there's no British Foe,
And wait a Respite from this Storm of Woe;
Beget more Sons, fresh Troops collect and arm,
And other Schemes of future Greatness form;
Britons may boast, the Gods may have their Will,
Ponteach I am, and shall be Ponteach still.

Finis.

"THE ADVENTURE OF MAJOR LEE."

The ensuing anecdote concerning "Lighthorse Harry" Lee is found on page 164 of Henry C. Watson's *Yankee Tea-Party; or, Boston in 1773* (Lindsay & Blakiston, Phil., 1851); which book appeared as part of the "Young American's Library;" a contemporary advertisement for which series reads "Each of these volumes is well written, in a high, moral tone by responsible authors, and contains numerous anecdotes, illustrative of the early and latter history of our country. The compact style in which these works are written, as well as their low price, make them well adapted for Family, School, or District Libraries."

The truth of this action-packed escapade (reportedly) involving Henry Lee has yet, by myself at any rate, to be established. Nevertheless, Watson's *Tea-Party* anecdotes are elsewhere and essentially based on accurately grounded fact; so this bodes well in favor of this particular story's historicity. What's more, the details are both so specific and the circumstances so startling that it would be more strange if it should prove to be a mere yarn. Inasmuch as Generals Moses Hazen and Benjamin Lincoln act key parts in the drama, per chance somewhere in their respective correspondence of the time (evidently 1777) a clue or lead may be present to get to the bottom of this perhaps not insoluble question. In any case, and whether true or no, Watson serves up a thrill filled and action packed instance of early American story-telling.

~~~***~~~

"If courage and resolution make up the hero, our country didn't hunger for 'em during the Revolution," said Davenport.

"Yes, it's a difficult and nice matter to say who bears away the palm. But I do not believe that Col. M'Lean was surpassed," said Kinnison. "Col. Henry Lee was a man of the same mould," added Colson.

"Aye, he was; and that reminds me of an adventure of his which displays his courage and resolution," replied Kinnison.

THE ADVENTURE OF MAJOR LEE.

"In the Revolution, a prison was erected at Lancaster, Pennsylvania, for those red-coats who fell into our hands. The prisoners were confined in barracks, enclosed with a stockade and vigilantly guarded; but in spite of all precautions, they often disappeared in an unaccountable manner, and nothing was heard of them until they resumed their places in the British army. It was presumed that they were aided by American tories, but where suspicion should fall, no one could conjecture. Gen. [Moses] Hazen had charge of the post. He devised a stratagem for detecting the culprits, and selected Capt. Lee, afterwards Maj. Lee, a distinguished partisan officer, to carry out his plan. It was given out that Lee had left the post on furlough. He, however, having disguised himself as a British prisoner, was thrown into the prison with the others. So complete was the disguise, that even the intendant, familiar with him from long daily intercourse, did not penetrate it. Had his fellow-prisoners detected him, his history might have been embraced in the proverb, 'Dead men tell no tales.'

"For many days he remained in this situation, making no discoveries whatever. He thought he perceived at times signs of intelligence between the prisoners and an old woman who was allowed to bring fruit for sale within the enclosure: She was known to be deaf and half-witted, and was therefore no object of suspicion. It was known that her son had been disgraced and punished in the American army, but she had never betrayed any malice on that account, and no one dreamed that she could have the power to do injury if she possessed the will. Lee matched her closely, but saw nothing to confirm his suspicions. Her dwelling was about a mile distant, in a wild retreat, where she shared her miserable quarters with a dog and cat.

"One dark stormy night in autumn, Lee was lying awake at midnight. All at once the door was gently opened, and a figure moved silently into the room. It was too dark to observe its motions narrowly, but he could see that it stooped towards one of the sleepers, who immediately rose. Next it approached and touched him on the shoulder. Lee immediately started up. The figure then allowed a slight gleam from a
~~~

dark lantern to pass over his face, and as it did so whispered, impatiently, 'Not the man -- but come!' It then occurred to Lee that it was the opportunity he desired. The unknown whispered to him to keep his place till another man was called; but just at that moment something disturbed him, and making a signal to Lee to follow, he moved silently out of the room. They found the door of the house unbarred, and a small part of the fence removed, where they passed out without molestation. The sentry had retired to a shelter, where he thought he could guard his post without suffering from the rain; but Lee saw his conductors put themselves in preparation to silence him if he should happen to address them. Just without the fence appeared a stooping figure, wrapped in a red cloak, and supporting itself with a large stick, which Lee at once perceived could be no other than the old fruit-woman. But the most profound silence was observed: a man came out from a thicket at a little distance and joined them, and the whole party moved onward by the guidance of the old woman. At first they frequently stopped to listen, but having heard the sentinel cry, 'All's well!' they seemed reassured, and moved with more confidence than before.

"They soon came to her cottage. A table was spread with some coarse provisions upon it, and a large jug, which one of the soldiers was about to seize, when the man who conducted them withheld him. 'No,' said he, 'we must first proceed to business.'

"The conductor, a middle-aged, harsh-looking man, was here about to require all present, before he could conduct them farther, to swear upon the Scriptures not to make the least attempt at escape, and never to reveal the circumstances or agents in the proceeding, whatever might befall them. But before they had time to take the oath, their practised ears detected the sound of the alarm-gun; and the conductor, directing the party to follow him in close order, immediately left the house, taking with him a dark lantern. Lee's reflections were not now the most agreeable. If he were to be compelled to accompany his party to the British lines in New York, he would be detected and hanged as a spy; and he saw that the conductor had prepared arms for them, which they were to use in taking the life of any one who should attempt to escape. They went on with great despatch, but not without difficulty. Lee might now have deserted, in this hurry and alarm; but he had made no discovery, and he could not bear to confess that he had not nerve enough to carry him through. They went on, and were concealed in a barn the whole of the next day. Provisions were brought, and low whistles and other signs showed that the owner of the barn was in collusion with his secret guests. The barn was attached to a small farm-house. Lee was so near the house that he could overhear the conversation which was carried on about the door. The morning rose clear, and it was evident from the inquiries of horsemen, who occasionally galloped up to the door, that the country was alarmed. The farmer gave short and surly replies, as if unwilling to be taken off from his labour; but the other inmates of the house were eager in their questions; and, from the answers, Lee gathered that the means by which he and his companions had escaped were as mysterious as ever. The next night, when all was quiet, they resumed their march, and explained to Lee that, as he was not with them in their conspiracy, and was accidentally associated with them in their escape, they should take the precaution to keep him before them, just behind the guide. He submitted without opposition, though the arrangement considerably lessened his chances of escape.

"For several nights they went on in this manner, being delivered over to different persons from time to time; and, as Lee could gather from their whispering conversations, they were regularly employed on occasions like the present, and well rewarded by the British for their services. Their employment was full of danger; and though they seemed like desperate men, he could observe that they never remitted their precautions. They were concealed days in barns, cellars, caves made for the purpose, and similar retreats; and one day was passed in a tomb, the dimensions of which had been enlarged, and the inmates, if there had been any, banished to make room for the living. The burying-grounds were a favourite retreat, and on more occasions than one they were obliged to resort to superstitious alarms to remove intruders upon their path. Their success fully justified the experiment; and unpleasantly situated as he was, in the prospect of soon being a ghost himself, he could not avoid laughing at the expedition with which old and young fled from the fancied apparitions.

"Though the distance of the Delaware was not great, they had now been twelve days on the road, and such was the vigilance and suspicion prevailing throughout the country, that they almost despaired of effecting their object. The conductor grew impatient, and Lee's companions, at least one of them, became ferocious. There was, as we have said, something unpleasant to him in the glances of this fellow towards him, which became more and more fierce as they went on; but it did not appear whether it was owing to circumstances, or actual suspicion. It so happened that, on the twelfth night, Lee was placed in a barn, while the rest of the party sheltered themselves in the cellar of a little stone church, where they could talk and act with more freedom; both because the solitude of the church was not often disturbed even on the Sabbath, and because even the proprietors did not know that illegal hands had added a cellar to the conveniences of the building.

"Here they were smoking pipes with great diligence, and, at intervals not distant, applying a huge canteen to their mouths, from which they drank with upturned faces, expressive of solemn satisfaction. While they were thus engaged, the short soldier asked them, in a careless way, if they knew whom they had in their party. The others started, and took their pipes from their mouths to ask him what he meant. 'I mean,' said he, 'that we are honoured with the company of Capt. Lee, of the rebel army. The rascal once punished me, and I never mistook my man when I had a debt of that kind to pay.'

"The others expressed their disgust at his ferocity, saying that if, as he said, their companion was an American officer, all they had to do was to watch him closely. As he had come among them uninvited, he must go with them to New York, and take the consequences; but meantime it was their interest not to seem to suspect him, otherwise he might give an alarm—whereas it was evidently his intention to go with them till they were ready to embark for New York. The other person persisted in saying that he would have his revenge with his own hand; upon which the conductor, drawing a pistol, declared to him that if he saw the least attempt to injure Capt. Lee, or any conduct which would lead him to suspect that his disguise was discovered, he would that moment shoot him through the head. The soldier put his hand upon his knife, with an ominous scowl upon his conductor; but he restrained himself.

"The next night they went on as usual, but the manner of their conductor showed that there was more danger than before; in fact, he explained to the party that they were now not far from the Delaware, and hoped to reach it before midnight. They occasionally heard the report of a musket, which seemed to indicate that some movement was going on in the country.

"When they came to the bank there were no traces of a boat on the waters. Their conductor stood still for a moment in dismay; but, recollecting himself, he said it was possible it might have been secured lower down the stream; and forgetting every thing else, he directed the larger soldier to accompany him. Giving a pistol to the other, he whispered, 'If the rebel officer attempts to betray us, shoot him; if not, you will not, for your own sake, make any noise to show where we are.' In the same instant they departed, and Lee was left alone with the ruffian.

"He had before suspected that the fellow knew him, and now doubts were changed to certainty at once. Dark as it was, it seemed as if fire flashed from his eye, now he felt that revenge was within his power. Lee was as brave as any officer in the army; but he was unarmed; and though he was strong, his adversary was still more powerful. While he stood, uncertain what to do, the fellow seemed enjoying the prospect of revenge, as he looked on him with a steady eye. Though the officer stood to appearance unmoved, the sweat rolled in heavy drops from his brow. Lee soon took his resolution, and sprang upon his adversary with the intention of wresting the pistol from his hand; but the other was upon his guard, and aimed with such precision that, had the pistol been charged with a bullet, that moment would have been his last. But it seemed that the conductor had trusted to the sight of his weapons to render them unnecessary, and had therefore only loaded them with powder. As it was, the shock threw Lee to the ground; but fortunately, as the fellow dropped the pistol, it fell where Lee reached it; and as his adversary stooped, and was drawing his knife from his bosom, Lee was able to give him a stunning blow. He immediately threw himself upon the assassin, and a long and bloody struggle began. They were so nearly matched in strength and advantage, that neither dared unclench his hold for the sake of grasping the knife. The blood gushed from their mouths, and the combat would have probably ended in favour of the assassin -- when steps and voices were heard advancing, and they found themselves in the hands of a party of countrymen, who were armed for the occasion, and were scouring the banks of the river. They were forcibly torn apart, but so exhausted and breathless that neither could make an explanation; and they submitted quietly to their captors.

"The party of the armed countrymen, though they had succeeded in their attempt, and were sufficiently triumphant on the occasion, were sorely perplexed how to dispose of their prisoners. After some discussion, one of them proposed to throw the decision upon the wisdom of the nearest magistrate. They accordingly proceeded with their prisoners to his mansion, about two miles distant, and called upon him to rise and attend to business. A window was hastily thrown up, and the justice put forth his night-capped head, and with more wrath than became his dignity, ordered them off; and in requital for their calling him out of bed in the cold, generously wished them in the warmest place. However, resistance was vain: he was compelled to rise; and as soon as the prisoners were brought before him, he ordered them to be taken in irons to the prison at Philadelphia. Lee improved the opportunity to take the old gentleman aside, and told him who he was, and why he was thus disguised. The justice only interrupted him with the occasional inquiry, 'Most done?' When he had finished, the magistrate told him that his story was very well made, and told in a manner very creditable to his address; and that he should give it all the weight it seemed to require. And Lee's remonstrances were unavailing.

"As soon as they were fairly lodged in the prison, Lee prevailed on the jailor to carry a note to Gen. Lincoln, informing him of his condition. The general received it as he was dressing in the morning, and immediately sent one of his aids to the jail. That officer could not believe his eyes that he saw Capt. Lee. His uniform, worn-out when he assumed it, was now hanging in rags about him; and he had not been shaved for a fortnight. He wished, very naturally, to improve his appearance before presenting himself before the secretary of war; but the orders were peremptory to bring him as he was. The general loved a joke full well: his laughter was hardly exceeded by the report of his own cannon; and long and loud did he laugh that day.

"When Capt. Lee returned to Lancaster, he immediately attempted to retrace the ground; and so accurate, under all the unfavourable circumstances, had been his investigation, that he brought to justice fifteen persons who had aided the escape of British prisoners. It is hardly necessary to say, to you who know the fate of revolutionary officers, that he received, for his hazardous and effectual service, no reward whatever."

"A perilous adventure," observed Warner, as Kinnison concluded his narrative.

"It was," replied Davenport. "It seems rather strange how Capt. Lee could so disguise himself and impose upon the enemy. But he knew a thing or two more than common men, and I shouldn't wonder."

"The British had many useful friends in every part of the country, during the war, and were enabled to do many such deeds," remarked Colson.

"Fill up, my friends, another glass of ale, and drink the health of Capt. Lee!" added Hand, rising. The company filled their glasses and drank the toast. The veterans were not as deep drinkers as their young and vigorous friends, and therefore they merely sipped their ale and sat it aside.

A SKETCH OF ALLAN MCLANE (1828)
By Alexander Garden, of Lee's Legion.

"...from the time of his joining the Continental army, I can testify, that he [McLane] *distinguished himself highly, as a brave and enterprising officer..."*
~ Gen.George Washington, 1783.

What is specifically is true, or is not quite true, about Delaware's (but Philadelphia born) Captain Allan McLane's (1746–1829) colorful wartime exploits and adventures is not always so easy offhand to conclude. Yet even the most skeptical and jaded observer of human nature will have to concede that the sheer number of daring-do stories pertaining to him attest to their being, on the whole, a substantial plausibility to them. At one time later in his life, McLane seriously contemplated writing and publishing his memoirs, but, regrettably for us, he ultimately decided against it.[114] Although we can't speak to the particulars as to exactly why he declined to do so, it seems not unlikely that the reason was owing to his having done or been a part of so *many* heroic, pivotal events and hair-breadth scrapes, battles,[115] and encounters, that he must have feared being charged with either too much boasting and or else blatant fibbing. His reluctance to record in print his personal history in any case turns out to be very unfortunate in retrospect; since there are a number of details we would have liked to have had filled out for us; such as, *for example*, did he indeed use all or near all of his patrimony, some $15,000, to raise a company of Delaware light infantry? What other units were with his company in the several famous battles at which he was present? Was he really instrumental in saving Lafayette's corps at Barren Hill? (20 May 1778, for if so he might be said to have spared the Americans a severe and *decisive* defeat in the war.) How enlisted and from where did the 50 Oneida Indians come from who sometimes assisted him and Lee's Legion in their operations around Philadelphia in early 1778 and elsewhere? Who led and what became of them? Why and how were so many of Lee and McLane's men insubordinate in retreating from the Paulus Hook raid so early and soon as they did?[116] What were and how amicable were his relations with other members of Lee's Legion (including Lee himself?)[117] What special and unusual events and activities (if any) transpired when he served as Speaker of the Delaware State House of Representatives, or as one the Justice Department's very first U.S. Marshals?

While there as yet is no full-length biography, possibly the best single, non-contemporary account of McLane's life at the moment is Fred J. Cook's article for *American Heritage Magazine,* October, 1956, Vol. 7, Iss. 6.[118] In supplement to that piece, we present here Alexander Garden's (1757-1829) sketch from *Anecdotes of the American Revolution: Illustrative of the Talents and Virtues of the Heroes of the Revolution, Who Acted the Most Conspicuous Parts Therein* -- Second Series. A.E. Miller, Charleston, 1828; pp. 76-83.

~~~***~~~

[114] About a year after writing this, I learned from Michael Cecere's biography of Henry Lee *Wedded to My Sword* (2012), pp. 140n, 289, that at least some remnants of a memoir by McLane survive and can be found in the McLane Papers housed at the New York Historical Society. There is, incidentally as well, more information about McLane in Watson's *Annals of Philadelphia* (1857), vol. 2, pt. 2, ch, 13.

[115] McClane was present at Long Island, White Plains, Trenton, Princeton, Brandywine, Germantown, and Monmouth.

[116] Thus incurring the scorn and derision of Sir Henry Clinton (See Lord Mahon's *History of England*, vol. VI, 1774-1780 (1851). In the same volume, Mahon quotes Lee writing in a confidential missive to President Joseph Reed of Pennsylvania: "In my report to General Washington, I passed the usual general compliments on the troops under my command. I did not tell the world that near one half of my countrymen left me!" *Life of Reed*, vol. ii, p. 126.

[117] Historian Michael Cecere reports (*Wedded to My Sword*, pp. 139-140, 140n) McClane's declaiming bitterly against Lee's obstructing his advancing in rank in the Legion. And yet Washington's response (dated 30 Jan. 1780 Morristown) to a letter of Lee's perhaps suggests that the latter may rather have tried to help secure McLane's promotion. Wrote Washington: "I have received your favor of the 26th. inclosing one from Capn. McLane to you of the 15th. However Capn. McLane[']s services may entitle him to consideration, yet he is neither singular in his sacrifices nor situation. There are numbers in the line, who have been as long Captains and without promotion as himself. This is one of those circumstances incidental to all services. But with regard to his request the formation of new corps rests by no means with me, nor if it did I could not recommend the proposal to Congress at a time when the separate corps now in service experience so many inconveniencies, and are supposed too numerous. Capn. McLane however may be assured that my opinion of his military merits would induce me to do every thing in his favor consistent with propriety."

[118] See: http://www.americanheritage.com/content/allan-mclane-unknown-hero-revolution
~~~

ALLEN M'LEAN, OF DELAWARE.

I know of no individual, of his rank in the army, who engaged in such a variety of perilous adventures, or who, so invariably brought them to a happy issue, as Allen M'Lean [sic[119]]. A brief statement of his services, will best demonstrate his merits as a soldier, and claims to public favour as a zealous and inflexible patriot. At the commencement of the Revolution, he possessed a comfortable independency, holding in the city of Philadelphia, in houses and lots, property, equal in value to fifteen thousand dollars, the whole of which he sacrificed in the service of his country.[120] At the very commencement of hostilities, we find him stepping forward as a volunteer. Persuaded, from the ardent temper and strong prejudices of Lord Dunmore, that an appeal to arms would speedily occur in Virginia, he particularly directed his attention to that quarter, and witnessed the repulse of the British at the Great Bridge.[121] This early dawn of success giving increase to his military ardour, his utmost efforts were exerted to fit himself for command, and in 1775, a lieutenant's commission was presented to him, in a Militia Regiment, commanded by the Hon. Caesar Rodney, of Delaware. In 1776, he joined the army under General Washington, near New-York. The battle of Long Island speedily occurring, afforded an opportunity, which lie eagerly embraced, to acquire distinction. Observing the exposed situation of a British party, he obtained from Lord Sterling [Stirling] the aid of a small detachment from the Delaware Regiment, made a lieutenant and eighteen privates, prisoners, and though surrounded by the enemy, led them off in safety. He was present at the battle of the White Plains witnessed the capture of the Hessians at Trenton, and at Princeton, by his good conduct and exemplary gallantry, so particularly attracted the attention of General Washington, to be immediately appointed to a Captaincy in a Continental Regiment. Sent into Delaware to recruit, he speedily rejoined the army with ninety-four men, raised at his own expense, every shilling of the bounty-money being drawn from his pocket. On the march of the British army from the head of Elk, the particular duty assigned him was, to annoy them, which he did with effect, but at the expense of a lieutenant killed, and a considerable number of his men. Philadelphia being possessed by the British, after the battles of Brandywine and Germantown, the important duty was assigned to him by the Commander-in-chief, to watch the movements of the enemy, to protect the whig inhabitants, (as much as practicable) residing near the lines, and to prevent the disaffected from carrying supplies to the city. The results evinced the prudence of the measure. M'Lean was vigilant and active, and remarkably prudent, though possessed of the most dauntless intrepidity. On the very first night of service, he took three spies, fifteen British soldiers who had quitted the city in search of plunder, and twelve tories, carrying in supplies to the enemy. A discovery of the highest importance immediately followed. On the 3d of December, 1777, intelligence was communicated to him by a female, who, under some frivolous pretext, had passed the British lines, "that the enemy were to leave the city on the ensuing night, in hopes to surprise the Camp of General Washington, at White Marsh." Prompt in communicating this information to the Commander-in-chief, his immediate care was to intercept the progress of the foe. A position was accordingly taken near Germantown; when, so well-directed a fire was opened upon their front, that the British, supposing a considerable force at hand, desisted in the attempt to proceed further, and immediately formed a line of battle. Recovering, however, from their first surprize, they moved on in three columns, and about dav-dawn appeared in front of the American encampment. For two days they occupied this position, when Gen. Morgan, driving in their pickets on the right, and General Washington, making arrangements for a general attack, they struck their tents and precipitately returned to the city.

The service rendered to the Marquis De La Fayette, in the following month of May, was no less important. Entrusted by General Washington with a separate command, that aspiring soldier had taken post at Barren Hill Church. A traitor giving intelligence of his situation to General Howe, the Generals, Grant and Erskine, with five thousand picked men, were ordered to gain his rear, while General Grey, marched forward to attack him in front, and prevent his crossing the Schuylkill. The capture of two Grenadiers brought to M'Lean the first intelligence of the movement, which left no doubt on his mind, but that to strike at the Marquis, was the object of the expedition. Grant, accomplished his object, but finding his troops much fatigued by a night-march of twenty miles in a few hours, thought proper to wait the approach of

[119] [*Edit. Note.* "M'Lean" is apparently an earlier spelling; later formally changed.]
[120] [*Edit.* Henry Lee likewise spent not inconsiderable sums forming and equipping his Virginia cavalry that became the 5th troop of the 1st Continental Light Dragoons; and for which, as with McLane, he never sought nor received remuneration.]
[121] [*Edit.* Sometimes spoken of as Virginia's "Bunker Hill," 9 Dec. 1775.]

Grey. M'Lean reached Barren Hill about day-break, and imparted his apprehensions to General La Fayette, who could scarcely credit the report; but it was speedily confirmed from many quarters, and particularly by Captain Stone, of the Militia, who, hearing the British as they passed his dwelling, leaped from a window, and ran naked across the country towards Barren Hill, till perfectly exhausted, he met a friend, who took up the report and speedily conveyed it to the Marquis. There was no time for deliberation. The army was immediately led across the river at Marston's Ford. But, had Grant, in the first instance, pushed forward and occupied the strong grounds at the Ford, it is presumable that the command of the Marquis, not half as numerous as his own, must have surrendered, or been destroyed.

While General Washington lay at Valley Forge, M'Lean passed into the State of Delaware by his order, and rendered essential service by collecting supplies for the army, which could not otherwise have been obtained. Resuming his command before Philadelphia, in 1778, he never failed to vex and harass the enemy, till they evacuated the city, and hanging on their rear at the moment of embarkation, made one captain, a provost-marshall, three sergeants, two corporals, and thirty-four privates, prisoners. During their retreat through the Jerseys, he never ceased to annoy them, and by his activity at Monmouth, gave increase to his well-earned reputation.

He served under Major Lee,[122] both at the reduction of Paulus Hook, at which last named post, fifty prisoners were taken, and a gang of counterfeiters, who had imitated the Continental money, so exactly, that at the treasury the false could not be distinguished from the genuine bills.

His conduct at the reduction of Stoney [Stony] Point, deserves to be more particularly mentioned. Being ordered with a flag of truce, to conduct a Mrs. Smith to the post at Stoney Point, that lady having quitted it for the purpose of carrying some necessaries to her sons in New-York; he assumed the appearance of a simple countryman, and being politely received by the British officers, did not fail, while conversing with them, to examine with a soldier s eye, the strength of the position, and the points at which it would be assailable, with the best prospects of success. His split shirt, and rifle accoutrements, appear to have particularly attracted the attention of a young officer, who said to him "Well Captain, what do you think of our fortress is it strong enough to keep Mister Washington out?" "I know nothing of these matters," replied M Lean, "I am but a woodsman, and can only use my rifle; but, I guess the General (not Mister Washington, if you please) would be likely to think a bit, before he would run his head against such works as these. If I was a General, sure I am that I would not attempt to take it, though I had fifty thousand men." "And if," rejoined the officer, "General Washington, since you insist on his being styled General, should ever have the presumption to attempt it, he will have cause to rue his rashness, for this post is the Gibraltar of America, and defended by British valour, must be deemed impregnable." "No doubt, no doubt," replied M'Lean, "but, trust me, we are not such dolts as to attempt impossibilities, so that, as far as we are concerned, you may sleep in security." On the night subsequent to this conversation, the post was attacked and carried. Colonel M'Lean assured me, that when recognized by the officer, it would have been impossible to give a just idea of his surprise and confusion. The folly of his former boasting, appeared to rush on his mind with a peculiarly distressing effect, and he hastily retired, overwhelmed with shame arid mortification.

In June, 1781, entrusted with despatches of the highest importance by General Washington, to the Count de Grasse, he took the command of the Marines on board of the ship *Congress*, mounting twenty guns, and one hundred and forty men, and arrived at Cape Francais [François, Haiti] in July; there he found the Count holding a Council of War, the object of which was, to fix on proper measures for an immediate attack on the Island of Jamaica. But, before any definite arrangements could be made, the presence of M'Lean was called for, that he might be examined relative to the preparations made in America, for a combined attack by the Allies and American army, on the British force in the Chesapeake. To the

[122] [*Edit. Note.* Before being assigned by Congress to the 2nd Partisan Corps on July 13th, 1779, McLane's Delaware company had been a component of Patton's Additional Regiment; the latter comprised of soldiers from Pennsylvania, New Jersey, and Delaware. Additional and Extra regiments were units formed, on the proposal of Washington and approved by Congress, in late 1776 and mustered (typically headed by and named after wealthy, influential, and or prominent citizens) in early 1777 to compensate for insufficiently filled state quotas. The Additional and Extra regiments, of which there were six, were the solely the responsibility of Congress, and, unlike most regular Continentals, received no administrative supervision by, or pay from, a particular state.]

interrogatories proposed, he gave such satisfactory answers, and developed such cheering prospects of success, that he was informed by the Count, soon as the Council broke up, that he would immediately proceed to America, and act as circumstances might require, until the hurricane months should have passed over. Returning home with this pleasing intelligence, the *Congress* [24 guns] fell in with the British sloop of war *Savage*, of twenty guns [or 16 guns according to other sources], and one hundred and forty men, engaged her, and after a desperate action of five glasses, succeeded in capturing her. The *Congress* lost her boatswain, carpenter, two masters mates, and fifteen of her crew; the *Savage*, her sailing master, two midshipmen, and twenty-five of her crew. The victory, so honourable to the flag of the United States, was attributed, in a great degree, to the constant and well-directed fire of the marines.[123]

He was next ordered to take post near Sandy Hook, and being furnished with a barge to visit Long Island, was directed to communicate with persons from New-York, and having received from them the private signals of the British fleet sailing for the Chesapeake, for the relief of Lord Cornwallis, returned to the Jersey shore, embarked in a pilot-boat, arid delivered them safely to the Count de Grasse. He then took his station on the lines before York, till the garrison surrendered.

I could detail many other anecdotes relative to M'Lean, but what I have already written, is, in my estimation, amply sufficient to prove, that he was much relied on for his judgment, courage and integrity; that he retained the confidence of the Commander-in-chief, the Board of War, and the General officers he acted with, to the end; that he was in all the principal battles fought in the States of New-York, New-Jersey, Pennsylvania, Maryland, and Virginia; that he served his country faithfully on water as well as land; and, that although frequently contending with superior numbers, and exposed to every peril, he still extricated himself from difficulty, by the superiority of his courage and presence of mind, with distinguished eclat.

I annex a copy of the Certificate of Service, presented to him at the conclusion of the war, by General Washington:

"Allen M'Lean, Esq., was appointed a Captain, in one of the additional Continental Regiments of foot, in 1777, and by activity and industry, soon joined the army, with a Free Company. He commanded a party of observation, under my instructions, until July, 1779, when he was annexed, by a resolution of the Honourable Continental Congress, to Major Lee's Legion, to command the Infantry. From the certificate, which Major M'Lean is possessed of, it appears that he was early active in the cause of his country, and from the time of his joining the Continental army, I can testify, that he distinguished himself highly, as a brave and enterprising officer. Previously to the siege of York, he was employed to watch the motions of the British army, near New-York, as well as in Virginia, and was entrusted with dispatches of the first importance to His Excellency, Count De Grasse, which commission he executed with great celerity, and was afterwards very serviceable in reconnoitering and bringing intelligence of the strength and disposition of the British army and fleet in the Chesapeake.

"Given under my hand and seal, at Rocky Hill, near Princeton, November 4th, 1783.

GEORGE WASHINGTON."

On one occasion, doing duty near the British lines, finding his horse greatly fatigued, and himself much in want of rest and refreshment, he was retiring towards Germantown, when the enemy's cavalry appeared in view, and advancing with a rapidity that threatened to cut off the possibility of a retreat. The Commander of the British forces, perceiving that pursuit as a body would impede the celerity of movement, essential to success, selected two of his best mounted troopers, and ordered them to continue the chace [sic], and use every possible exertion to make him their prisoner. The first of these approaching very near, called to M Lean by name, and ordered him to surrender, but he, preserving his presence of mind, drew forth the only pistol he possessed, and leveling it with effect, laid his adversary prostrate in the dust. The second now coming up, was, in turn, eagerly charged, and being struck from his horse by the butt-end of

[123] [*Edit. Note.* Regarding this action between the *Congress* and the *Savage*, see James Fenimore Cooper's *History of the Navy of the United States* (1839), Vol. 1, ch. 11, pp. 255-257.]

the pistol that had disabled his companion, was incapacitated from using any further exertion, M'Lean, continuing his route, sought shelter in a swamp, where he remained in security, till the evening afforded him an opportunity of rejoining his command.

My wish on the present occasion is, to speak only of the occurrences of the Revolutionary war, but I have in my possession, an interesting memoir from the pen of Colonel M'Lean, relative to the proceeding of the Army before Washington [during the War of 1812], when taken and pillaged by Ross, the British General, that fills me both with grief and astonishment. Briefly to notice it, the Colonel says: --

"All was confusion nothing like spirit nothing like subordination universal complaint for the want of food, the Militia going off in every direction to seek it. Men, badly armed, being, in many instances, without flints in their muskets, and so completely without discipline, as to exhibit a far greater resemblance to an armed mob, than an organized army. I most religiously believe, that if I had been at the head of three hundred men, such as I led on to the attack of Paulas [sic] Hook, or such as I had under my command, during the war of our Independence, I should have defeated General Ross, when he pressed General Winder over the Eastern Branch. Confident I am, that the enemy would never have reached Washington, and America been spared the disgrace of beholding the British triumphantly possessing the Capital."

STAYING AT PEACE IN WARTIME

The Moravians were, and are, a Protestant evangelical and pietist sect or denomination, that was formed in 15th century in Bohemia (in what is now Czechoslovakia), followers of John Hus and who predated even the Lutherans, and who held strict pacifism in the highest regard. In about the mid 18th century Congregations of their followers came to Pennsylvania and, more to our own purpose here, the present day Winston-Salem area in North Carolina, and founded three settlements the latter province, specifically: Salem, Bethabara, and Bethania. These clean, well run and administered, and prosperous towns often acted as both supply and wayfaring points for both American and British forces during the Revolutionary War. And while both sides for the most part, respected the settlements' conscientious neutrality, the Moravians were hard pressed keeping the combatants housed and fed when occasion arose, most notably during the hot and heavy fighting in late 1780 and early 1781; while, simultaneously, attempting to remain above and apart from the fray.

The records of the congregations' minutes from those times provides an unusual and sometimes facetious picture of these Christian, and predominantly, but not exclusively, German, settlements striving, not without difficulty, to stay aloof from the partisanship of the conflict; while, simultaneously, endeavoring to care and provide for soldiers of opposing sides. The following, taken from *Records of the Moravians in North Carolina, Vol. IV: 1780-1783*, edited by Adelaide L. Fries (Edwards & Broughton Company, Raleigh: 1930) are some revealing, and at times comical, passages selected from those records. [124]

~~~***~~~

~ from minutes of the Salem Congregation

Aug. 22. [1780] Toward noon Colonel [John] Armstrong and his brother the Major arrived. They had been in the battle [i.e. the Battle of Camden, Aug. 16, 1780], and through them we heard that Brigadier [Griffith] Rutherford was taken prisoner. An attempt will be made to gather the scattered troops, and half the militia are to be called out. The people are in extreme fright because of the English... [125]

Aug. 26. This morning Col. Armstrong and Mr. Sheppard and Mr. Commans [Cummings] arrived, on their way to Hillsborough. The first-named told Br. [Brother] Bagge confidentially that men were speaking angrily against us as Tories, from whom an uprising might be expected from Virginia, who were known to deal sharply with such people. He promised to give the necessary orders for our protection, for he did not consider us Tories... [126]

Aug. 28. ...We hear that a company of light-horse, under Captain Caldwell, are on a Tory hunt in the neighborhood. They have beaten several men, and threatened Br. Steiner, claiming that he had spoken against *Liberty*. May the Lord mercifully turn this aside from us... [127]

Sept. 5. ...There is much distress in Bethabara, for 300 soldiers from Virginia are there, who have camped in the orchard, where they do as they please... [128]

Oct. 9. ...Andreas Volk's son came for the doctor for his brother-in-law Johann Krause, who was shot in the leg yesterday while standing guard at Richmond, which was again visited by a strong party of Tories under Gideon Wright. The bullet had remained in his limbs; Joseph Dixon was sent to bind up the wound. The Tories had expressed sympathy for the injured man, saying the ball had not been meant for him but for some one else, and so on. What consequences this may have remains to be seen... [129]

---

[124] On a related note, the Marquis de Chastellux writes at some length about the people and customs of the Moravians of Bethlehem, Pennsylvania; see his *Travels in North-America, in the Years 1780, 1781, and 1782* (1787), Part I, ch. II.
[125] *Records of the Moravians in North Carolina, Vol. IV: 1780-1783*, p. 1560.
[126] *Ibid.* p. 1561.
[127] *Ibid.* p. 1561.
[128] *Ibid.* p. 1563.
[129] *Ibid.* p. 1571.
~~~

Oct. 19. ...A Proclamation of [Maj.] General [William] Smallwood had been published, in which he stated that any soldier caught robbing would be brought to the camp and hanged. This order will have a good effect, for barbarous and unjust treatment has driven many to the Tories who would gladly have remained peaceful.[130]

~~~***~~~

~from minutes of the Bethabara Congregation

Feb. 6. [1781] During last night [Brig.] General [Andrew] Pickens arrived with his men and something over twenty wagons. Corn, hay, bread, and brandy were given to him at his request. He kept good order among his men. His manner was fatherly and mild, and he voted his belief that we would take no part in anything that was partisan or low. In the afternoon Colonel [Elijah] Clark arrived with more than fifty horse-men, and another company passed by the mill, all hurrying after General Pickens. So it went all day, partly with the passing of militia, partly with people fleeing from the war.[131]

Feb. 9. We expected the return of our guests of yesterday, but instead about eleven o'clock, a company of English dragoons arrived, bringing an order from Lord Cornwallis, for brandy, meat, meal and bread, and instructions that our mill should grind all it could, and that in the afternoon our wagon should take it to Bethania, where there were more than seven thousand men. In the afternoon the Commissary came for 100 gallons of brandy, more than 300 lbs. Of bread, and all the meal that was ready...Then came a company of German Tories, with an order for cattle for the army, -- just now the question is not who are friends of the land but who are friends of the king. The last named company seized several travelers here, and took them to Bethania, to the main camp.[132]

Feb. 16. The company in the tavern was called out at three o'clock this morning. The guard hailed some one, who replied: *Good Friend.* To the question: *Whose friend?* Came the answer: *King George's*.
Then it was quiet until nearly four o'clock when the advance guard of General Pickens company arrived with orders for meat, corn and meal...The General and his officers were polite and courteous, and assured us that no damage should be done; and as it would be necessary for our wagon to take the meat and meal to the camp late in the evening they promised that it should not be pressed. Our supply of bread was all taken, largely without pay. The company that was here last night returned, and it was in all respects a much disturbed time.[133]

March 10. The above-mentioned guests remained until noon. Last night they broke into the spring-house; and they took all the eggs, even from geese that were setting. We were glad that no more damage was done by these people, who have been robbing and plundering wherever they go. Several Brethren went from here to the election of new members of the Assembly. Colonel [William] Preston and Colonel [Walter] Crocket[t] arrived and spent the night. The fire from General Pickens' camp, between Rank's and the lower meadow, broke out, and before it could be extinguished a hundred rails were burned. The fence was probably set on fire, for it was discovered after they left.[134]

---

[130] *Ibid.* p. 1572.
[131] *Ibid.* p. 1741.
[132] *Ibid.* p. 1742.
[133] *Ibid.* p. 1743.
[134] *Ibid.* p. 1747.
~~~

ALMOST A TRAITOR: The Strange Case of Silas Deane

From very early on in the Revolutionary War, Sileas Deane (1737-1789) played nothing short of a crucial and pivotal role in securing for America invaluable foreign aid and supplies from Europe. Notwithstanding such auspicious beginnings, he was later accused by colleagues and members of Congress of using his position to make illicit, or at least inordinate, profits in financial speculation. These informal allegations were pressed on Deane when he returned to the United States in 1778 and subsequently brought about his dismissal by Congress from his post as envoy in France. Insofar as we later know, these charges turned out to be largely false. Despite the suspicions and acrimony of some members of Congress, such as Deane's own former diplomatic associate Arthur Lee, he afterward tried to solicit reimbursement for personal money losses he incurred in the course of his seeking and procuring munitions, clothing and other subsidies vital to the American war effort; only to have Congress summarily reject those claims.[135]

In late 1781, following Yorktown and after returning to France to settle some personal matters, a cache of personal letters he had written to his brother, and some others, were captured at sea by the British, and published in the loyalist New York newspaper *Rivington's Gazette.* In this correspondence, he expatiated on his despairing of the American military situation; the ineptitude of Congress to govern; a strong disapproval of the French, and a desire to settle for an honorable and amicable reconciliation with Britain. Although the publication of these letters did little to bolster British aims or change the course of the Revolution, they did prove an indelible scandal and embarrassment to Deane; who defended his writings as being nothing more than expressions of his private opinion at the time. Few then accepted this as an excuse; and he thereafter in some eyes suffered the ignominy of being lumped with Arnold.

It is not all that implausible that Deane may have been placed under enticements, temptations, and inimical pressures not unlike what Benedict Arnold was subject to; only while fellow Connecticut native Arnold actually turned coat, Deane only went so far as to consider doing so -- but went no further. Nonetheless, this was more than enough to condemn him in the view of many. One piece of evidence that suggests his being so tempted is Deane's argument against the French; saying that they had allied themselves with America only to get even with Britain and had no real sympathy with American ideals. This, after all, seems a very silly complaint, coming from an experienced and savvy ambassador no less; when even if true, the French could hardly be blamed for such a motive; nor should it have come as a surprise that the *Bourbon* court might look askance at *Revolutionary* goals and aspirations. That Deane should propose such an argument suggests that he was using it as an excuse to cover his resentment of Congress', and presumably also the French court's mistreatment of him. Like Arnold, therefore, it seems possible that Deane may, over time, have been deliberately probed, provoked, and antagonized by *someone* in order to push him to the brink. But again, unlike Arnold, Deane only neared the brink and it was *not* possible, as it turned out, to actually thrust him over it.[136]

This seems further supported by Arnold's bizarre and persistent effort when in London to become friendly to and make Deane's association -- which Deane took great pains to avoid, as shown in this letter he wrote to Benjamin Franklin:

"London,October19th,1783
"Sir,-I am informed by Col. Wadsworth and others lately from Paris that it was currently reported of me that I was intimate with General Arnold, and that a pamphlet lately published by Lord Sheffield owed to me most of the facts and observations contained in it. I have found by experience that from the moment a man becomes unpopular every report which any way tends to his prejudice is but too readily credited without the least examination or proof, and that for him to attempt to contradict them in public is like an attack on

---

[135] Years after his, Deane was vindicated in this last, with the United States awarding his heirs a large amount in compensation. He'd died in 1789, somewhat mysteriously, while still in England and *immediately* prior to a prospective voyage homeward.

[136] Deane, by theway, was implicated by the death-row testimony of arsonist and saboteur "John the Painter" (John Aitkens), in being one of the latter's sponsors and abettors. Among other reasons that might be educed in his defense, that Deane should subsequently show a leaning toward Britain, makes "the Painter's" charge appear less trustworthy. *Perhaps*, however, all might be explained by positing someone having pretended to Aitkens that he was "Deane."

the hydra; for every falsehood detected and calumny obviated several new ones of the same family come forward. This has well nigh rendered me callous to the attacks made on me in this way; yet it is impossible for me not to wish to stand fair in the opinion of those with whom I formerly acted, with whose confidence and friendship I have been more particularly honored, and this occasions me troubling you with this letter. Though you have condemned me of giving been guilty of great imprudence (and that justly), yet I have the satisfaction to know that you are still convinced of my integrity and fidelity whilst in the service of my country, and whilst I had the honor of being your colleague; and I wish to remove from your mind, if possible, every idea of my having acted an unfriendly part toward the interest of my country, or of my having countenanced so notorious an enemy as General Arnold by associating with him since my arrival in this city. The next day after my being in London, when I had no reason to suspect that any one knew any thing of me save those to whom I had sent notice of my being in town, and of my lodgings, I was surprized to find General Arnold introduced into my chamber without being announced by my landlord until he opened the door (my circumstances do not permit me to keep a servant). Several gentlemen were with me, and among others Mr. Hodge of Philadelphia. I can most sincerely say that I never was more embarrassed; and after a few questions on either part, and as cold a civility as I could use consistent with common decency, he took his leave. You well know that he is one who never wanted for assurance or address, and, as if we had been on our former footing, he urged me, at parting, to dine with him, which I civilly declined. The next day I changed my lodgings, and received from him repeatedly cards of invitation to his house, which I declined accepting, and in a few days he again called on me, at my new lodgings, in the same unceremonious manner as before. A gentleman from America was then with me, and remained in my chamber until he left me. On my parting with him on the stairs, I told him very freely that his visits were disagreeable to me, and could be of no service to him; that I could not return them, except that I might call with Mr. Sebor some evening to pay our respects to Mrs. Arnold, from whom I had received so many civilities in Philadelphia. This we did a few evenings after, and from that time, now more than five months since, I have not seen him, except in his carriage, passing me in the street."[137]

As for Arnold himself, Hessian officer Johannes Ewald, who ended up serving under him in Virginia for a spell in early 1781, left us this additional description:

"He was a man of medium size, well built, with lively eyes and fine features. He could be very polite and agreeable, especially at the table, but if one stayed too long in his company, then the apothecary and horse trader [his pre-war employments] showed through the general. He spoke a great deal about his heroic deeds on the other side, and frequently mentioned his ingenious trick at West Point, a story which he could make ridiculous with much wit.

"In his military actions he constantly displayed his former resolution, which, however, was mixed with a cautious concern due to his fear of the gallows if he fell into the hands of his countrymen. He always carried a pair of small pistols in his pocket as a last resource to escape being hanged. I have watched him very closely, and I found him very restless on the day the Americans threatened to take Portsmouth with a coup de main. On that day, he was not the 'American Hannibal.'

"His dishonorable undertaking, which, had it succeeded, could have actually turned the war more favorably for England, nevertheless cannot be justified, for surely self-gain alone had guided him, and not remorse for having taken the other side. If he really felt in his conscience that he had done wrong in siding against his mother country, he should have sheathed his sword and served no more, and then made known in writing his opinions and reasons. This would have gained more proselytes than his shameful enterprise, which every man of honor and fine feelings -- whether he be friend or foe of the common cause -- must loathe."[138]

True, Arnold, by his cynical and mercenary betrayal, while risking the lives of innocents in the process, did in fact do an undeniably sinister thing. Yet what emerges in retrospect, and as illustrated by the above quoted passage, is that his error was, after all, really that of a buffoon, and that, further, he was

---

[137] "The Deane Papers," vol. V, 1782-1790; found in *Collections of the New York Historical Society* (1890), pp. 212-215.
[138] Capt. Johann Ewald, *Diary of the American War: A Hessian Journal*, trans. and edit. by Joseph P. Tustin, pp. 294-296.

brought to the pass of making his fatal error maybe as a direct result of someone else clearly understanding how to exploit his weakness. Such as Arnold, or for that matter some of the more famous dictators of the 20th century, were, it could be argued, not themselves intrinsically bad people, but really only frail and foolish ones; but whose foolishness was used by someone who was (and presumably still is) evil. This is not to exonerate Arnold, etc. of their responsibility to do right and avoid wrong, or absolve them of the moral obligation not to be a great bane or curse to the world. The point is merely one of bringing attention to what seems to be the distinct possibility of a mysterious figure in the shadows isolating, guiding and luring such dupes onto villainous acts; while to ignore this only increases the likelihood of our misunderstanding what might actually have taken place; thus perhaps putting more blame, or at least opprobrium, on Arnold than was *all told* duly his. [139]

[139] For further on the Deane controversy see:
Paris papers; or Mr. Silas Deane's late intercepted letters, to his brothers, and other intimate friends, in America. To which are annexed for comparison, the Congressional declaration of indepedendency in July 1776, and that now inculating [sic] among the revolted provinces, with the never-to-be-forgotten orders of the rebel general in August 1776, for preventing a pacification (1782), at: http://quod.lib.umich.edu/e/evans/N13851.0001.001?view=toc
and
"An address to the free and independant [sic] citizens of the United States of North-America". By Silas Deane, Esquire (1784), at: http://quod.lib.umich.edu/e/evans/N14546.0001.001?view=toc

"...AND HEAVENLY FREEDOM SPREAD HER GOLDEN RAY":
The Revolutionary War Poetry of PHILLIS WHEATLEY PETERS.

The girl who was to become Phillis Wheatley Peters[140] (1753-1784) first arrived at 7 years old on a slave ship from Africa, and was purchased at a Boson slave auction by Susannah Wheatley, wife of John Wheatley a well-to-do Boston tailor. When Mrs. Wheatley saw Phillis' interest in writing she encouraged it, and moreover sought to furnish her with a quality religious and literary education. On Sarah's death in 1773, Phillis, at 20 years of age, was emancipated; had by that time had become something of a local sensation for her writing ability, and in the same year, under sponsorship of the Wheatleys, published her first volume of poetry. Living where and when she did, what might have been her thoughts and feelings, one wonders, regarding events such as the Boston Massacre, the Boston Tea Party, Lexington and Concord, and Bunker Hill -- which latter she was likely at the time in the vicinity of and able to view from a distance?

Phillis was not the first African-American poet of note; sharing honors as she did for that title with Jupiter Hammon (1711-1806)[141] and Lucy Terry (c.1730-1821)[142]; yet of the three she was and is certainly the most well-known. Benson J. Lossing, for instance, felt it only appropriate to write a sympathetic and dignified sketch of her in his *Field Book of the Revolution* (1850, vol. I, pp. 256-267), and later mentions Phillis as a sort of celebrity among celebrities who contributed out of their own pockets to the American War effort:

"In the summer of 1780 the distress of the American army was very great, on account of the scarcity of clothing, and the inadequate means possessed by the commissary department to afford a supply. The generous sympathies of the ladies of Philadelphia were aroused, and they formed an association for the purpose of affording relief to the poor soldiers. Never was the energy of genuine sympathy more nobly exercised than by the patriotic women who joined hands in this holy endeavor....

"Mrs. Sarah Bache, daughter of Dr. Franklin, was also a conspicuous actor in the formation of the association, and in carrying out its plans. All classes became interested, and the result was glorious. 'All ranks of society seemed to have joined in the liberal effort, from Phillis, the colored woman, with her humble seven shillings and sixpence, to the Marchioness De La Fayette, who contributed one hundred guineas in specie, and the Countess De Luzerne, who gave six thousand dollars in Continental paper. Those who had no money to contribute gave the service of their hands in plying the needle, and in almost every house the good work went on. It was charity in its genuine form, and from its purest source -- the voluntary outpourings from the heart. It was not stimulated by the excitements of our day -- neither fancy fairs or bazars; but the American women met, and, seeing the necessity that asked interposition, relieved it. They solicited money and other contributions directly and for a precise and avowed object. They labored with their needles, and sacrificed their trinkets and jewelry.'" (1851, vol. II, p. 106.)

Living at one of the most epochal times in American history, Phillis is uniquely representative of the Anglo to American transition period, of the old and new age, that spanned her own life, and exhibits in her work both pre-war and wartime attitudes and sensibilities. Most of Phillis' compositions tend to be rather stiff and conventional stichics; framed in heroic couplets in some ways imitative of Augustan verse writers. Thomas Jefferson, in his *Notes on the State of Virginia* (1781-1782), Query 14, disparagingly remarked of her talent:

"Misery is often the parent of the most affecting touches in poetry. Among the blacks is misery enough, God knows, but not poetry. Love is the peculiar oestrum of the poet. Their love is ardent, but it kindles the senses only, not the imagination. Religion, indeed, has produced a Phillis Wheatley; but it could not produce a poet."

---

[140] (1753–1784) She was married to free black John Peters in 1778.

[141] And who penned the in retrospect poignant line: "If we should ever get to Heaven, we shall find nobody to reproach us for being black, or for being slaves." *Hammon Address* (1786).

[142] Terry's son Cesar, incidentally, from Vermont fought with alongside the patriots" in the War for Independence.

This, on the other hand, is a rather harsh assessment, and indicates that she probably suffered ridicule from others; including some who did not believe she was actually the author of her writings. Yet despite and whatever her perceived shortcomings as a poet, there is nevertheless a rich purity to her vision. Meanwhile, she shows herself capable every now and then of a fine turn of phrase and of rendering sublime sentiments in a sincere and occasionally moving manner. And when further we take into account that she only survived to the age of 31, having often lived under circumstances sharply challenging and difficult, her achievement in retrospect is rightly be seen as something both touching and not a little short of astounding and marvelous.

What follows are some of Phillis' Revolutionary war pieces.

~~~***~~~

To His Excellency
George Washington

Sir,

I have taken the freedom to address your Excellency in the enclosed poem, and entreat your acceptance, though I am not insensible of its inaccuracies. Your being appointed by the Grand Continental Congress to be Generalissimo of the armies of North America, together with the fame of your virtues, excite sensations not easy to suppress. Your generosity, therefore, I presume, will pardon the attempt. Wishing your Excellency all possible success in the great cause you are so generously engaged in. I am,

Your Excellency's most obedient humble servant,
Phillis Wheatley
1776

TO HIS EXCELLENCY, GENERAL WASHINGTON (1776)

Celestial choir! enthron'd in realms of light,
Columbia's scenes of glorious toils I write.
While freedom's cause her anxious breast alarms,
She flashes dreadful in refulgent arms.
See mother earth her offspring's fate bemoan,
And nations gaze at scenes before unknown!
See the bright beams of heaven's revolving light
Involved in sorrows and veil of night!
   The goddess comes, she moves divinely fair,
Olive and laurel bind her golden hair:
Wherever shines this native of the skies,
Unnumber'd charms and recent graces rise.
   Muse! bow propitious while my pen relates
How pour her armies through a thousand gates,
As when Eolus heaven's fair face deforms,
Enwrapp'd in tempest and a night of storms;
Astonish'd ocean feels the wild uproar,
The refluent surges beat the sounding shore;
Or thick as leaves in Autumn's golden reign,
Such, and so many, moves the warrior's train.
In bright array they seek the work of war,
Where high unfurl'd the ensign waves in air.
Shall I to Washington their praise recite?
Enough thou know'st them in the fields of fight.
Thee, first in peace and honours, -- we demand
The grace and glory of thy martial band.
Fam'd for thy valour, for thy virtues more,
~~~

Hear every tongue thy guardian aid implore!
   One century scarce perform'd its destined round,
When Gallic powers Columbia's fury found;
And so may you, whoever dares disgrace
The land of freedom's heaven-defended race!
Fix'd are the eyes of nations on the scales,
For in their hopes Columbia's arm prevails.
Anon Britannia droops the pensive head,
While round increase the rising hills of dead.
Ah! cruel blindness to Columbia's state!
Lament thy thirst of boundless power too late.
   Proceed, great chief, with virtue on thy side,
Thy ev'ry action let the goddess guide.
A crown, a mansion, and a throne that shine,
With gold unfading, WASHINGTON! be thine.[143]

~~~***~~~

ON THE CAPTURE OF GENERAL LEE[144] (1776)

The deed perfidious, and the Hero's fate,
In tender strains, celestial Muse! relate.
The latent foe to friendship makes pretence
The name assumes without the sacred sense!
He, with a rapture well dissembl'd, press'd
The hero's hand, and fraudful, thus address'd.
   "O friend belov'd! may heaven its aid afford,
"And spread yon troops beneath thy conquering sword!
"Grant to America's united prayer
"A glorious conquest on the field of war.
"But thou indulgent to my warm request
"Vouchsafe thy presence as my honour'd guest:
"From martial cares a space unbend thy soul
"In social banquet, and the sprightly bowl."

---

[143] *Washington wrote in reply*:

"Cambridge, February 28, 1776.

Mrs. Phillis,

Your favour of the 26th of October did not reach my hands 'till the middle of December. Time enough, you will say, to have given an answer ere this. Granted. But a variety of important occurrences, continually interposing to distract the mind and withdraw the attention, I hope will apologize for the delay, and plead my excuse for the seeming, but not real neglect.

I thank you most sincerely for your polite notice of me, in the elegant Lines you enclosed; and however undeserving I may be of such encomium and panegyrick, the style and manner exhibit a striking proof of your great poetical Talents. In honour of which, and as a tribute justly due to you, I would have published the Poem, had I not been apprehensive, that, while I only meant to give the World this new instance of your genius, I might have incurred the imputation of Vanity. This and nothing else, determined me not to give it place in the public Prints.

If you should ever come to Cambridge, or near Head Quarters, I shall be happy to see a person so favoured by the Muses, and to whom Nature has been so liberal and beneficent in her dispensations.

I am, with great Respect, etc."

John C. Fitzpatrick, ed., *The Writings of George Washington*, 1745-1799, vol. IV, pp. 360-361.

[144] Maj. General Charles Lee. His capture was ostensibly less glorious and heroic than the poem implies; and it would seem more than probable that Phillis herself was unacquainted with the details. Nonetheless, the tribute is particularly of value in helping to now bring alive the high enthusiasm and regard some at one time held for him. Although, as is well known, following the battle of Monmouth he came under a cloud and was force to leave the army, possibly Lee's most positive contribution to the American cause was his reassuring confidence that helped instill in the colonial soldiers the notion that the British could both be fought and beaten; including among such fighting men William Moultrie; who, in his memoirs, cites Lee's encouragement of morale as instrumental in aiding the famous victory of the Revolutionaries at Charleston harbor in June 1776. As far as Monmouth goes, Lee cannot really be faulted militarily for falling back as he did; indeed, it can be convincingly argued that he rescued his detachment from almost certain destruction by his withdrawal. His actual blame (of significance) then -- if any -- lay in his undiplomatic squabbling with fellow officers about the matter afterward.
~~~

Thus spoke the foe; and warlike Lee reply'd,
"Ill fits it me, who such an army guide;
"To whom his conduct each brave soldier owes
"To waste an hour in banquets or repose:
"This day important, with loud voice demands
"Our wisest Counsels, and our bravest hands."
Thus having said he heav'd a boding sigh.
The hour approach'd that damps Columbia's Joy.
Inform'd, conducted, by the treach'rous friend
With winged speed the adverse train attend
Ascend the Dome, and seize with frantic air
The self surrender'd glorious prize of war!
On sixty coursers, swifter than the wind
They fly, and reach the British camp assign'd.
Arriv'd, what transport touch'd their leader's breast!
Who thus deriding, the brave Chief address'd.
"Say, art thou he, beneath whose vengeful hands
"Our best of heroes grasp'd in death the sands?
"One fierce regard of thine indignant eye
"Turn'd Brittain pale, and made her armies fly;
"But Oh! how chang'd! a prisoner in our arms
"Till martial honour, dreadful in her charms,
"Shall grace Britannia at her sons' return,
"And widow'd thousands in our triumphs mourn."
While thus he spoke, the hero of renown
Survey'd the boaster with a gloomy frown
And stern reply'd. "Oh arrogrance of tongue!
"And wild ambition, ever prone to wrong!
"Believ'st thou Chief, that armies such as thine
"Can stretch in dust that heaven-defended line?
"In vain allies may swarm from distant lands
"And demons aid in formidable bands.
"Great as thou art, thou shun'st the field of fame
"Disgrace to Brittain, and the British name!
"When offer'd combat by the noble foe,
"(Foe to mis-rule,) why did thy sword forgo
"The easy conquest of the rebel-land?
"Perhaps too easy for thy martial hand.
"What various causes to the field invite!
"For plunder you, and we for freedom fight:
"Her cause divine with generous ardor fires,
"And every bosom glows as she inspires!
"Already, thousands of your troops are fled
"To the drear mansions of the silent dead:
"Columbia too, beholds with streaming eyes
"Her heroes fall -- 'tis freedom's sacrifice!
"So wills the Power who with convulsive storms
"Shakes impious realms, and nature's face deforms.
"Yet those brave troops innum'rous as the sands
"One soul inspires, one General Chief commands
"Find in your train of boasted heroes, one
"To match the praise of Godlike Washington.
"Thrice happy Chief! in whom the virtues join,
"And heaven-taught prudence speaks the man divine!"
He ceas'd. Amazement struck the warrior-train,
And doubt of conquest, on the hostile plain.

BOSTON. Dec.r 30, 1776

~~~***~~~

ON THE DEATH OF GENERAL WOOSTER[145] (1778)

From this the muse rich consolation draws
He nobly perish'd in his Country's cause
His Country's Cause that ever fir'd his mind
Where martial flames, and Christian virtues join'd.
How shall my pen his warlike deeds proclaim
Or paint them fairer on the list of Fame --
Enough great Chief -- now wrapt in shades around
Thy grateful Country shall thy praise resound
Tho' not with mortals' empty praise elate
That vainest vapour to th' immortal State
Inly serene the expiring hero lies
And thus (while heav'nward roll his swimming eyes)
Permit, great power while yet my fleeting breath
And Spirits wander to the verge of Death --
Permit me yet to paint fair freedom's charms
For her the Continent shines bright in arms
By thy high will, celestial prize she came --
For her we combat on the field of fame
Without her presence vice maintains full sway
And social love and virtue wing their way
O still propitious be thy guardian care
And lead Columbia thro' the toils of war.
With thine own hand conduct them and defend
And bring the dreadful contest to an end --
For ever grateful let them live to thee
And keep them ever virtuous, brave, and free --
But how, presumptuous shall we hope to find
Divine acceptance with th' Almighty mind --
While yet (O deed ungenerous!) they disgrace
And hold in bondage Afric's blameless race?
Let virtue reign—And thou accord our prayers
Be victory our's, and generous freedom theirs.

The hero pray'd -- the wond'ring Spirit fled
And Sought the unknown regions of the dead --
Tis thine fair partner of his life, to find
His virtuous path and follow close behind --
A little moment steals him from thy Sight
He waits thy coming to the realms of light
Freed from his labours in the ethereal Skies
Where in Succession endless pleasures rise!

Phillis Wheatley
Queenstreet Boston July -- 15th 1778

---

[145] Brig. Gen. David Wooster (1711-1777), a distinguished French and Indian War veteran from New Haven Conn., succeeded to command of the American forces collecting for and besieging Quebec following the death of General Montgomery. He himself was mortally wounded at the battle of Ridgefield (27 April 1777) as part of an effort to thwart a British raid on Danbury, Conn. Evidently, Phillis, as an acquaintance, had met or otherwise had known Wooster, an anti-black slavery supporter, personally.
~~~

~~~***~~~

LIBERTY AND PEACE (1784)

LO! Freedom comes. Th' prescient Muse foretold,
All Eyes th' accomplish'd Prophecy behold:
Her Port describ'd, *"She moves divinely fair,*
"Olive and Laurel bind her golden Hair."
She, the bright Progeny of Heaven, descends,
And every Grace her sovereign Step attends;
For now kind Heaven, indulgent to our Prayer,
In smiling *Peace* resolves the Din of *War.*
Fix'd in *Columbia* her illustrious Line,
And bids in thee her future Councils shine.
To every Realm her Portals open'd wide,
Receives from each the full commercial Tide.
Each Art and Science now with rising Charms
Th' expanding Heart with Emulation warms.
E'en great *Britannia* sees with dread Surprize,
And from the dazzling Splendor turns her Eyes!
Britain, whose Navies swept th' *Atlantic* o'er,
And Thunder sent to every distant Shore;
E'en thou, in Manners cruel as thou art,
The Sword resign'd, resume the friendly Part!
For *Galia's* Power espous'd *Columbia's* Cause,
And new-born *Rome* shall give *Britannia* Law,
Nor unremember'd in the grateful Strain,
Shall princely *Louis'* friendly Deeds remain;
The generous Prince th' impending Vengeance eye's,
Sees the fierce Wrong, and to the rescue flies.
Perish that Thirst of boundless Power, that drew
On *Albion's* Head the Curse to Tyrants due.
But thou appeas'd submit to Heaven's decree,
That bids this Realm of Freedom rival thee!
Now sheathe the Sword that bade the Brave attone
With guiltless Blood for Madness not their own.
Sent from th' Enjoyment of their native Shore
Ill-fated -- never to behold her more!
From every Kingdom on *Europa's* Coast
Throng'd various Troops, their Glory, Strength and Boast.
With heart-felt pity fair *Hibernia* saw
Columbia menac'd by the Tyrant's Law:
On hostile Fields fraternal Arms engage,
And mutual Deaths, all dealt with mutual Rage:
The Muse's Ear hears mother Earth deplore
Her ample Surface smoak with kindred Gore:
The hostile Field destroys the social Ties,
And every-lasting Slumber seals their Eyes.
Columbia mourns, the haughty Foes deride,
Her Treasures plunder'd, and her Towns destroy'd:
Witness how *Charlestown's* curling Smoaks arise,
In sable Columns to the clouded Skies!
The ample Dome, high-wrought with curious Toil,
In one sad Hour the savage Troops despoil.
Descending *Peace* and Power of War confounds;
~~~

From every Tongue celestial *Peace* resounds:
As for the East th' illustrious King of Day,
With rising Radiance drives the Shades away,
So Freedom comes array'd with Charms divine,
And in her Train Commerce and Plenty shine.
Britannia owns her Independent Reign,
Hibernia, *Scotia*, and the Realms of *Spain*;
And great Germania's ample Coast admires
The generous Spirit that *Columbia* fires.
Auspicious Heaven shall fill with fav'ring Gales,
Where e'er Columbia spreads her swelling Sails:
To every Realm shall *Peace* her Charms display,
And Heavenly *Freedom* spread her golden Ray.

FRIEDRICH VON STEUBEN: Savior of the Army

"Savior of the Army" may indeed sound hyperbolic. Yet such title that we here adopt, while adding to it that of *Trainer-in-Chief*, is not that far removed from the truth. Along with such as William Cadogan, Berthier, Gneisenau, John Rawlins, Ludendorff, Freddie de Guingand, Hans Speidel, Grigorii M. Shtern, and George C. Marshall, Friedrich Wilhelm von Steuben (1730-1794) can be ranked as one of the best and most exemplary military chiefs of staff[146] of modern history, in that it could be reasonably said they were indispensable in making possible the success of those much more famous commanders whom they served.

As well as being perspicacious at spotting what needed to be done and a strict disciplinarian intolerant of incompetence, Steuben evinced an insightful understanding of human nature. Furthermore, he possessed a good sense humor; which latter gift served him remarkably well with both Americans and Europeans during the Revolution; such that perhaps not due credit has been granted him also as a diplomat. When Lafayette was chosen to supercede him in Virginia in 1781, rather than pout and murmur as some other generals might have done, Steuben served humbly and dutifully; and fought his first Revolutionary War battles as a field commander leading lowly militia and Continental recruits. Prior to that time, whether in Europe or America, almost all his military service had been as staff or administrator. In addition to skirmishing the invading British in Virginia, he, along with (Danish born) Col. Christian Febiger in Philadelphia, worked harder and more tirelessly than probably anyone else in the army in endeavoring to keep supplies and men coming to Greene's distraught southern command. Although much has been made of his spurious titles he used both as "Baron," which he himself maintained, and "Lieutenant General," conferred on him by Benjamin Franklin (in order to better sell him to Congress), he had in fact had experience as an officer on Frederick the Great's general staff. And it was this professional experience and education that made him most invaluable. For this reason and through Von Steuben, it could be said that Frederick, the British army, and the Native American Indian warrior (the latter with his own peculiar brand of war college that left *its* unique and signal impact) were, as it were, joint grandsires of the United States Army. An American soldier trained by Von Steuben was not unlike a musician learning from a technically proficient master, but who previously had to rely largely (with a few exceptions) on amateurs and self-made men for his instruction.

Yet oddly enough, the German mercenaries (aside from the jaegers) that fought in North America were noted to adhere to rigid military ways and tactics that usually ill suited the topography and circumstances of warfare that prevailed in America. And yet these mercenaries too were children of the Frederickean system. What then accounts for the discrepancy? The difference was that Frederick's method worked best on grand and spacious 18th century European battlefields. Von Steuben, on the other hand, adapted that system and method to the American personality and heavily forested environment; removing what didn't suit while being open to implement new approaches that did; and which most notably included the greater emphasis and reliance on light infantry troops espoused by Maurice de Saxe. Moreover, Steuben reduced the number of steps for loading and firing, and in this and similar way streamlined European methods and regulations that they more easily might be grasp and taken up by Continental Army soldiers.

He brought an orderliness and uniformity to the army (which included standardization of formations, drills, army field exercises, camp routine, inspections, and paperwork) that enhanced readiness and compatibility of troop movement (both before and on the battlefield),[147] hygiene, and discipline. As well he encouraged officer's to have a care and concern for the needs and welfare of the individual soldiers. But perhaps even more, Von Steuben freed the American army from *always* having to copy the British;

[146] As Inspector General, he was in effect, if not in name, Washington and the Continental Army's chief of staff.

[147] "Steuben produced a simple but efficient method for maneuvering on the battlefield. Like Guibert and other French theoreticians, he used both column and line to achieve tactical flexibility. Divisions and brigades marched in closed columns for speed and control and rapidly deployed into line for musket fire or bayonet charge. Skirmishers, either light infantry or details from line units, covered the columns during advance or withdrawal. They kept one hundred yards (the effective range of a musket) from the column to prevent enemy harassment of the main body. As soon as the column deployed into line, the skirmishers withdrew through gaps and re-formed. The men maintained silence when marching." Robert K. Wright, *The Continental Army*, pp. 140-141.

thereby instilling national pride that provided Washington's soldiers with a more independently based sense of their own military stature and significance.

His *Regulations for the Order and Discipline of the Troops of the United States* (1779), also known as the "Blue Book"(due to the light blue color of its cover) was the first United States Army field manual and standard for the service up until the War of 1812. It's written in a concise, thorough, and lucid manner and format; with something in it for all ranks to especially read and attend to -- from commanding general all the way through to private. While technical manuals understandably leave something to be desired when used as a source for winning literary extracts, here, nonetheless, are some selections from the Blue Book to furnish us with some insight into Steuben's outlook and method: [148]

~~~***~~~

CHAPTER III

OF THE FORMATION OF A COMPANY

A company is to be formed in two ranks, at one pace distance, with the tallest men in the rear, and both ranks sized, with the shortest men of each in the center. A company thus drawn up is to be divided into two sections or platoons; the captain to take post on the right of the first platoon, covered by a sergeant; the lieutenant on the right of the second platoon, also covered by a sergeant; the ensign four paces behind the center of the company; the first sergeant two paces behind the centre of the first platoon, and the eldest corporal two paces behind the second platoon; the other two corporals are to be on the flanks of the front rank.

CHAPTER IV

OF THE FORMATION OF A REGIMENT

A Regiment is to consist of eight companies, which are to be posted in the following order from right to left.

First Captain's

Colonel's

Fourth Captain's

Major's

Third Captain's

Lieutenant colonel's

Fifth captain's

Second captain's

For the greater facility in maneuvering, each regiment consisting of more than one hundred and sixty files, is to be formed in two battalions, with an interval of twenty paces between them, and one color posted in the center of each battalion; the colonel fifteen paces before the center of the first battalion; the

---

[148] Steuben also authored the sixteen page "A Letter on the Subject of an Established Militia, and Military Establishments, Addressed to the Inhabitants of the United States," and published in New York by J. M'Lean and Co. in 1784; which Washington essentially approved and formally replied to; notwithstanding the Baron's plan specifically excluded Negroes and Mulattoes from the 700 man (in total size) standing army. For the two texts in question, see: http://www.history.army.mil/books/revwar/ss/peacedoc.htm
~~~

lieutenant-colonel fifteen paces before the center of the second battalion; the major fifteen paces behind the interval of the two battalions; the adjutant two paces from the major; the drum and fife major two paces behind the center of the first battalion; their places behind the second battalion being supplied by a drum and fife; and the other drums and fifes equally divided on the wings of each battalion.

When a regiment is reduced to one hundred and sixty files, it is to be formed in one battalion, with both colours in the centre; the colonel sixteen paces before the colours; the lieutenant colonel eight paces behind the colonel; the major fifteen paces behind the centre of the battalion, having the adjutant at his side; the drum and fife major two paces behind the centre of the battalion; and the drums and fifes equally divided on the wings.

Every battalion, whether it compose the whole, or only half of a regiment, is to be divided into four divisions and eight platoons; no platoon to consist of less than ten files; so that a regiment consisting of less than eighty files cannot form battalions, but must be incorporated with some other, or employed on detachment.

In case of absence of any field officer, his place is to be filled by the officer next in rank in the regiment; and in order that the officers may remain with their respective companies, if any company officer is absent, his place shall be supplied by the officer next in rank in the same company; but should it happen that a company is left without an officer, the colonel or commanding officer may order an officer of another company to take the command, as well for the exercise as for the discipline and police of the company in camp.

When the light company is with the regiment it must be formed twenty paces on the right on the parade, but must not interfere with the exercise of the battalion, but exercise by itself; and when the light infantry are embodied, every four companies will form a battalion, and exercise in the same manner as the battalion in the line. [149]

~~~***~~~

CHAPTER V

OF THE INSTRUCTION OF RECRUITS

The commanding officers of each company is charged with the instruction of his recruits; and as that is a service that requires not only experience, but a patience and temper not met with in every officer, he is to make choice of an officer, sergeant, and one or two corporals of his company, who, being approved of by the colonel, are to attend particularly to that business: but in case of the arrival of a great number of recruits, every officer without distinction is to be employed on that service. The commanding officer of each regiment will fix on some place for the exercise of his recruits, where himself or some field officer must attend, to overlook their instruction.

The recruits must be taken singly, and first taught to put on their accoutrements, and carry themselves properly.

The position of a Soldier without Arms.

"He is to stand straight and firm upon his legs, with the head turned to the right so far as to bring the left eye over the waistcoat buttons; the heels two inches apart; the toes turned out; the belly drawn in a little, but without constraint; the breast a little projected; the shoulders square to the front, and kept back; and the hands hanging down the sides, with the palms close to the thighs.

Attention!

---

[149] The modern U.S. army quick step is still the same of 120 a minute rate but at 30 inches per step; while double time is 180 feet in a minute; see U.S. Army Field Manual FM 3-21.5. Similarly some other rules, standards and or regulations inaugurated by Von Steuben apply or are still in use today.
~~~

At this word the soldier must be silent, stand firm and steady, moving neither hand nor foot, (except as ordered) but attend carefully to the words of command.

This attention of the soldier must be observed in the strictest manner, till he receives the word

Rest!

At which he may refresh himself, by moving his hands or feet; but must not then sit down or quit his place, unless permitted so to do.

Attention! To the Left- Dress!

At this word the soldier turns his head briskly to the left, so as to bring his right eye in the direction of his waistcoat buttons.

To the Right- Dress!

The soldier dresses again to the right, as before.

The recruit must then be taught

The Facings…." [etc., pp. 6-12]

~~~***~~~

The Quick Step

Is also two feet, but about one hundred and twenty in a minute, and is performed on the same principle as the other. [p. 13]
~~~

AT HOME WITH GEORGE WASHINGTON

Among the earliest and most noteworthy accounts of the life of George Washington are those by David Humphreys (in 1789), Mason Locke "Parson" Weems (1800), David Ramsay (1807), and John Marshall (1805-1807). These were followed later in the mid 19th century with works by two of America's most acclaimed literary lights, James Kirke Paulding (1835), and Paulding's "Salmagundi" (1807-1808) collaborator and long-time friend Washington Irving (1855-1859). Of all these Washington biographies, Paulding's is one of the least familiar; possibly because his, as he described it himself, was "principally prepared for the use of the More Youthful class of readers." Yet despite its expressly juvenile character, the book is still valuable on a number of other levels, including, among other reasons that might be adduced, some little known private anecdotes and vignettes about the General -- furnished Paulding by several of Washington's intimate family and closest associates -- a few of which then are presented here.

~~~***~~~

[Washington's] marriage took place in the winter of 1759, but at what precise date is not to be found in any record, nor is it, I believe, within the recollection of any person living. I have in my possession a manuscript containing the particulars of various conversations with old Jeremy, Washington's black servant, who was with him at Braddock's defeat, and accompanied him on his wedding expedition to the White House. Old Jeremy is still living, while I am now writing, and in full possession of his faculties. His memory is most especially preserved, and, as might be expected, he delights to talk of Massa George. The whole series of conversations was taken down verbatim, in the peculiar phraseology of the old man, and it is quite impossible to read the record of this living chronicle of the early days of Washington, without receiving the full conviction of its perfect truth.

From this period Washington resided constantly at Mount Vernon, one of the most beautiful situations in the world. A wood-crowned bluff of considerable height projects out into the Potomac, here one of the most capacious and noble of rivers, affording an extensive view both above and below. A fine lawn slopes gracefully from the piazza in front of the house to the brow of the hill, where, high above the wave, you stand and view a wide prospect of great variety and interest. The house was at the time of his marriage of indifferent size and convenience, but was shortly improved into a capacious and imposing mansion. The place is worthy of him with whose memory it is inseparably associated, and long may it appertain to the family and name of Washington.

He here put in practice that system of regularity and of temperance in every species of indulgence and of labour, which he persevered in, as far as was consistent with his circumstances and situation, during the remainder of his life. His moments were numbered, and divided, and devoted to his various objects and pursuits. His hours of rising and going to bed were the same throughout every season of the year. He always shaved, dressed himself, and answered his letters by candle-light in summer and winter; and his time for retiring to rest was nine o' clock, whether he had company or not. He breakfasted at seven o' clock in summer, and eight in winter; dined at two, and drank his tea, of which he was very fond, early in the evening, never taking any supper. His breakfast always consisted of four small corn-cakes, split, buttered, and divided into quarters, with two small- sized cups of tea. At dinner he ate with a good appetite, but was not choice of his food; drank small-beer at his meals, and two glasses of old Madeira after the cloth was removed. He scarcely ever exceeded that quantity. The kernels of two or three black-walnuts completed the repast. He was very kind, affectionate, and attentive to his family, scrupulously observant of every thing relating to the comfort, as well as the deportment and manners, of the younger members.

His habits of military command produced a similar system with regard to his servants, of whom he exacted prompt attention and obedience. These conditions complied with, and they were sure of never being subjected to caprice or passion. Neglect or ill-conduct was promptly noticed, for the eye of the master was everywhere, and nothing connected with the economy of his estate escaped him. He knew the value of independence, and the mode by which it is obtained and preserved. With him idleness was an object of contempt, and prodigality of aversion. He never murdered an hour in wilful indolence, or wasted a dollar in
~~~

worthless enjoyment. He was as free from extravagance as from meanness or parsimony, and never in the whole course of his life did he turn his back on a friend, or trifle with a creditor.

In an old Virginia almanack of 1762, belonging to Washington, and now before me, interleaved with blank sheets, are various memoranda relating to rural affairs, all in his own hand-writing, a few of which I shall extract, for the purpose of showing my youthful readers that an attention to his private affairs was not considered beneath the dignity of the man destined to wield the fortunes of his country.

"April 5. Sowed timothy-seed in the old apple-orchard below the hill.
7th. Sowed, or rather sprinkled a little of ditto on the oats.
26th. Began to plant corn at all my plantations.
May 4. Finished planting corn at all my plantations."

Thus, in the dignified simplicity of usefulness did this great and good man employ himself during the years which elapsed between the period of his retirement after the expulsion of the French from the Ohio, until the commencement of the troubles which preceded the Revolution. His occupation was husbandry the noblest of all others; his principal amusement was hunting the deer, which at that time abounded in the forests of the Potomac. Here his skill in horsemanship rendered him conspicuous above all his competitors. He also read much, and his hour was early in the morning.

His custom was to retire to a private room, where no one was permitted to interrupt him. Much curiosity prevailed among the servants to know what he was about, and old Jeremy relates that, in order to gratify it, he one morning entered the room under pretence of bringing a pair of boots. Washington, who was reading, raised his eyes from the book, and getting quietly up "I tell you," said Jeremy, "I go out of de room faster dan I come in!"

[*Life of Washington*, ch. V, pp.62-64]

~~~***~~~

During the period which elapsed between his retirement from the presidency, and the lamented death of Washington, his days were happily and usefully occupied in rural pursuits and domestic enjoyments. Influenced by those great motives of patriotism which governed all his public acts, he indeed accepted the command of the army of the United States, in a season when it was believed the authority of his name would operate beneficially to his country. But he was never again called into action, and the few remaining years of his life were passed away in peaceful occupations, and in the bosom of repose. Mount Vernon was, of course, thronged with visitors; it was the shrine where his countrymen came to pay their devotions, and where distinguished foreigners thronged from all parts of Europe, to behold and to converse with the man who, after delivering a nation from foreign oppression, had left it in possession of the freedom he had won; the man who twice abdicated a power for which thousands and tens of thousands of vulgar heroes had sacrificed themselves and their country.

He exhibited the same wise economy of time, that same attention to his domestic affairs and rural occupations, the same cheerfulness in hours of relaxation, and the same attention to the happiness of those around him. He always rose at, or before dawn, lighted his candle, and entered his study, where he remained a considerable time, as was supposed, at his devotions. But no one ever knew, for none ever intruded on his sacred privacy. When his occupation was finished, he rung for his boots, and walked or rode out to pursue his morning exercise and avocations. Visitors did not interfere in the least with his course of life; they were made welcome, by permission to do as they pleased, and being convinced by all they saw that they interfered not in the least with the economy of the household, or the pleasures of others.

Like all truly great men, the manners of Washington, though eminently dignified, were adorned by the most unaffected simplicity. He relished the innocent gaiety of youth, the sprightly gambols of children, and enjoyed a decorous jest or humorous anecdote with a peculiar relish. If, while perusing a book or newspaper in the domestic circle, he met with any thing amusing or remarkable, he would read it aloud for their entertainment, and never failed to participate in every innocent or sportive frolic that was going on around him. His dignity was not that of pride or moroseness, but of intellect and virtue; and among those he loved, he laughed and joked like others. He was accustomed sometimes to tell the following story:
~~~

On one occasion, during a visit he paid to Mount Vernon, while president, he had invited the company of two distinguished lawyers, each of whom afterwards attained to the highest judicial situations in this country. They came on horseback, and, for convenience, or some other purpose, had bestowed their ward-robe in the same pair of saddle-bags, each one occupying his side. On their arrival, wet to the skin by a shower of rain, they were shown into a chamber to change their garments. One unlocked his side of the bag, and the first thing he drew forth was a black bottle of whiskey. He insisted that this was his companion s repository; but on unlocking the other, there was found a huge twist of tobacco, a few pieces of corn-bread, and the complete equipment of a, waggoner's pack-saddle. They had exchanged saddle-bags with some traveller by the way, and finally made their appearance in borrowed clothes, which fitted them most ludicrously. The general was highly diverted, and amused him self with anticipating the dismay of the waggoner, when he discovered this oversight of the men of law. It was during this visit that Washington prevailed on one his guests to enter into public life, and thus secured to his country the services of one of the most distinguished magistrates of this or any other age.

Another anecdote, of a more touching character, is derived from a source which, if I were permitted to mention, would not only vouch for its truth, but give it additional value and interest. When Washington retired from public life, his name and fame excited in the hearts of the people at large, and most especially the more youthful portion, a degree of reverence which, by checking their vivacity or awing them into silence, often gave him great pain. Being once on a visit to Colonel Blackburn, ancestor to the exemplary matron who now possesses Mount Vernon, a large company of young-people were assembled to welcome his arrival, or on some other festive occasion. The general was unusually cheerful and animated, but he observed that whenever he made his appearance, the dance lost its vivacity, the little gossipings [sic] in corners ceased, and a solemn silence prevailed, as at the presence of one they either feared or reverenced too much to permit them to enjoy themselves. He strove to remove this restraint by mixing familiarly among them, and chat ting with unaffected hilarity. But it was all in vain; there was a spell on the little circle, and he retired among the elders in an adjoining room, appearing to be much pained at the restraint his presence inspired. When, however, the young people had again become animated, he arose cautiously from his seat, walked on tip-toe to the door, which was ajar, and stood contemplating the scene for nearly a quarter of an hour, with a look of genuine and benevolent pleasure, that went to the hearts of the parents who were observing.

As illustrating his character and affording an example of his great self-command, the following anecdote is appropriate to my purpose. It is derived from Judge Breckenridge [Hugh Henry Brackenridge (1748–1816), Pennsylvania jurist and author of *Modern Chivalry* (1792 & 1815)] himself, who used often to tell the story. The judge was an inimitable humourist, and, on a particular occasion, fell in with Washington at a public house, where a large company had gathered together for the purpose of discussing the subject of improving the navigation of the Potomac. They supped at the same table, and Mr. Breckenridge essayed all his powers of humour to divert the general ; but in vain. He seemed aware of his purpose, and listened with a smile. However, it so happened that the chambers of Washington and Breckenridge adjoined, and were only separated from each other by a thin partition of pine boards. The general had retired first, and when the judge entered his own room, he was delighted to hear Washington, who was already in bed, laughing to himself with infinite glee, no doubt at the recollection of his stories.

The constitution of Washington was naturally strong, and though a life of labour, anxieties, and hardships had occasion ally impaired his health, still his equanimity, his temperance, and his constant exercise on horseback promised a green and vigorous old age. But it would appear that this great and good man, great in what he performed, but still greater in what he resisted, having finished the work for which he seems to have been expressly designed, was to be suddenly called away, lest, in the weakness of old age, he might possibly do something that would diminish the force of his own invaluable example, and thus deprive posterity of its most perfect model. He enjoyed his last retirement but two or three years, when he was called away to heaven.

I shall describe the last parting with one of his favourite nephews, as received from his own mouth.

“During this, my last visit to the general, we walked together about the grounds, and talked of various improvements he had in contemplation. The lawn was to be extended down to the river in the direction of the old vault, which was to be removed on account of the inroads made by the roots of the trees, with which it is crowned, which caused it to leak. I intend to place it there, said he, pointing to the spot where the new vault now stands. First of all, I shall make this change; for, after all, I may require it before the rest.

“When I parted from him, he stood on the steps of the front door, where he took leave of myself and another, and wished us a pleasant journey, as I was going to Westmoreland on business. It was a bright frosty morning, he had taken his usual ride, and the clear healthy flush on his cheek, and his sprightly manner, brought the remark from both of us that we had never seen the general look so well. I have sometimes thought him decidedly the handsomest man I ever saw; and when in a lively mood, so full of pleasantry, so agreeable to all with whom he associated, that I could hardly realize that he was the same Washington whose dignity awed all who approached him.

“A few days afterwards, being on my way home in company with others, while we were conversing about Washington, I saw a servant rapidly riding towards us. On his near approach, I recognized him as belonging to Mount Vernon. He rode up his countenance told the story he handed me a letter. Washington was dead!”

The old gentleman, for he is now very aged, was overcome by the recollection of that moment. Every circumstance connected with the departure of him whose life was one series of virtuous usefulness, and whose death was mourned by the tears of a whole nation, must be interesting to my young readers. They may learn from the example of Washington, that he whose conscience is void of reproach will always die without fear.

[*Ibid*, ch. XI, pp. 259-264]

DUPES OF THE PRETERNATURAL?

Some thoughts on André, Arnold, and Aaron Burr.

As some of you my esteemed and *patient* readers are or might be aware, in my sundry writings I have written on spirit people, that is to say *the unearthly*; having in some measure alluded to the same in my earlier Continental Army series pieces on Silas Deane, i.e., "Almost a Traitor -- The Strange Case of Silas Deane," and the one on Maj. Robert Rogers' "Ponteach." Although I take for granted that some do or would look askance on such conjectures and view such with matter of fact skepticism, I nevertheless am strongly convinced of the possibility that such claim can, when all is said and done, be empirically established and proven. This said, although I would not belabor the subject of just here, I did think it worth sharing, for purposes disinterested pondering purposes, some jottings and musings of mine on the ghosts or specters who *may* have *haunted the Revolution.* I reproduce these vignettes then as they originated from my personal journals; so that in any case you at minimum have the opportunity to judge for yourself. I'm sorry (due to exigencies somewhat beyond my control) I could not do this article up as a more formally developed composition. Yet since I have a mind to *possibly* adding to it at some later time, I thought it just as well to defer attempting too much here; thereby leaving more room and energy for that as yet uncertain eventuality. My assumptions are profuse and which I concede only makes the brief and perfunctory nature of these sketches all the more to be regretted. Even so, I do write considerably more on the topic of spirit people elsewhere, and which, if one is interested, can find be found at my website at http://www.gunjones.com

~~~***~~~

A most engaging account of the Arnold treason plot and resultant execution of André is given in Charles Stedman's *History of the Origins, Progress and Termination of the American War*, vol. II, pp. 247-253; the "what ifs" of that famous intrigue being no little stimulating of curious speculation. What if, for instance, the *Vulture,* André contact and pre-arranged vessel for evacuation, had not been fired upon by the Americans, and its retreat forced? It makes one think that *if there were* a spirit-person/devil who was personally inimical and somehow jealously had it out for André, such might have indirectly brought about the withdrawal of the *Vulture* to pass (say, by alerting the Americans.) Someone might object, even granting your assumption, why would a supposed "devil" do that rather than assist Arnold and Clinton? To which I would respond -- perhaps, it was seen at the last that that bringing about the scheme successfully was too fraught with complications and risky ramifications. At the same time, doing-in a handsome and dashing figure like André would or might be viewed as a great feather in a devil's cap. Also, if we look for who was most to blame for André's ignoble capture, was it not after all Arnold for instructing him to act as his prisoner? Perhaps, as something we might consider, Arnold originally obtained the idea and suggestion from *someone else*. The very difficulties Arnold is described as having found himself beset with were as likely as not fiendishly fomented or orchestrated taunts designed to get him to react -- certain such would be very in keeping with a literal devil's manner and mode of doing things.

As to André's sentence, I personally don't believe great fault, if any, can be found in it on technical or legal grounds such as Stedman or others argue; all the less so given the gravity of the danger his actions posed the Americans.[150] Respecting Arnold, Washington himself in later years thought it no

---

[150] In a footnote, vol. I, pp.208-209, to his *Life and Correspondence of Nathanael of Greene* (1822), Judge William Johnson relates the following concerning André:

"The following facts may be relied upon. Let them weigh with the reader for what they are worth.

"It was an universal belief, as well in the British army as in the city of Charleston after its fall, that Andre had been in the city in the character of a spy, during the siege. There is now living in the place a respectable citizen, who acted in the commissary department in the British army, during and after the siege; and another of equal respectability, and whose means of information were much greater, who was in Charleston during the siege, and remained in it until the evacuation, who will testify to the truth of this assertion. And this opinion is corroborated by the following fact. There were two brothers of the name of S. S. and E. S. both well known as men of property and respectable standing in society. The former was, to the last, faithfully devoted to the cause of the country, the other was disaffected. During the siege, S. S. being taken sick, was permitted to go to his brother's house to be better attended. There, he was introduced to, and repeatedly saw a young man, in a homespun dress, who was introduced to him by his brother as a Virginian, connected with the line of that state then in the city. After the fall of Charleston, S. S. was introduced to Major André, at his brother's house, and in him recognized the person of the Virginian whom he had seen during the siege. This he remarked to his brother, who acknowledged that he was the same, asserting his own ignorance of it at the time. S. S. related these facts to many persons in his
~~~

small proof of the former's aggravated perfidy that the former had taken prisoner the poor, deceived boatmen who were only obeying the orders given them by an (one-time) American general.[151] And yet, in fairness, was Arnold's villainy *wholly* of his own prompting and doing?

~~~***~~~

[Stedman] Whilst general Washington was absent from his army upon this service, a deep-laid scheme was formed by one of his own officers, one of general for delivering up to sir Henry Clinton the strong post of West Point, in the high lands upon the North River, the possession of which would have nearly cut off all communication between the northern important post into the and middle colonies. The officer engaged in this design was the hands of the famous general Arnold, whose services in the cause of America had been of the most meritorious kind, and whose brilliant actions in the field justly raised him to superior notice and regard. After the evacuation of Philadelphia by the British troops in the year 1778, he was appointed to command the American garrison that took possession of it; and while he acted in that capacity had the misfortune to disgust many of the inhabitants, and even to fall under the displeasure of congress. He lived expensively, and, as was supposed, considerably beyond his stated income; but he was at the fame time concerned in trading speculations, and had shares in several privateers; and upon the profits expected from those adventures, he probably relied, as a means of enabling him to keep up the state and style of life he had assumed. He had also claims against the public to a considerable amount; and upon the payment of them he depended as a fund to satisfy the immediate demands of his creditors, who were beginning to become importunate. But the trading speculations in which he had engaged proved unproductive; his privateers were unsuccessful; and a considerable portion of his demand against the public was cut off, by the commissioners appointed to examine his accounts. From the decision of the commissioners, general Arnold appealed to the congress, who appointed a committee of their own members to revise the sentence: But the committee of congress were even less favourable to his views than the commissioners, from whose decision he had appealed. They reported that the balance already allowed by the commissioners was more than general Arnold was entitled to receive.

So many disappointments could not fail to ruffle a temper less irritable than general Arnold's: Recollecting his former services, he gave full scope to his resentment, and complained of ill-usage and ingratitude in terms better calculated to provoke than to mollify, and such as were peculiarly offensive to congress. His enemies availed themselves of his indiscretion to swell the tide of popular clamour which already ran strongly against him. A court-martial was appointed to examine into his conduct during his command in Philadelphia, and by the sentence of that board it was in general terms reprehended, and himself subjected to the mortification of receiving a reprimand from general Washington.

---

lifetime, and his veracity was unquestionable. Another citizen, Mr. W. J., at the time of André's capture, a prisoner at St. Augustine, also saw the supposed Virginian at the house of E. S. while S. S. lay sick, and his recollection of the fact was revived by S. S. soon after he had made the discovery of his real character. It is also known that the life of E. S. was afterwards assiduously sought after by Marion's men, on the charge of his treachery."

[151] As recorded at Mount Vernon by his secretary Tobias Lear, in Lear's diary entry for 22 Oct. 1786: "...—I orderd Col. Hamilton to mount his horse & proceed with the greatest dispatch to a post on the river about <illegible>, papers found upon him [André] were in his possession. Colo. Jemmisson [John Jameson], when Andre was taken with these papers, could not beleive that Arnold was a traitor but rather thought it was an imposition of the British in order to destroy our Confidence in Arnold. he, however, immediately upon their being taken, dispatched an express after me, ordering him to ride night & day till he came up with me. the express went the lower road [(]which was the road by which I had gone to Connecticut) expecting that I should return by the same rout & that he sho'd meet me, but before he had proceeded far he was informed that I was returning by the upper road. he then cut across the Country & followed in my tract till I arrived at W[es]t Point. he arrived about 2 hours after & brot the above <paqe mutilated Arnold gave orders illegible> he ordered his men (who were very cleaver fellows & some of the better sort of soldiery) to proceed immediately on board the Vulture Sloop of war (as a flag) which was lying down the river, saying that they must be very expeditious as he must return in a short time to meet me, & promised them 2 Gallons of rum if they wou'd exert themselves. they did accordingly; but when they got on board the ship, instead of their two Gals. of rum, he ordered the Cockswain to be called down into the Cabin & informed him that he & the men must consider themselves as prisoners. the Cocksman was very much astonished, told him that they came on board under sanction of a flag. he answd that was nothing to the purpose—they were prisoners; but the Captain had more generosity than this mean, pittiful scoundrel & told the Cocksman that he would take his parole for him to go on shore & get cloaths, & whatever else was wanted for him & his compannions. he accordingly came, got his cloths &c. & returned on board; when they got to New York, General Clinton, ashamed of so low & mean an action, set them all at Liberty." For further, see: William Moultrie to Washington, 30 July 1786. *The Papers of George Washington* Digital Edition, ed. Theodore J. Crackel. Charlottesville: University of Virginia Press, Rotunda, 2008; Confederation Series (1 January 1784–23 September 1788), Volume 4 (2 April 1786–31 January 1787.
~~~

From this moment it is supposed that Arnold formed the design of quitting the American service and joining the British; and only delayed the execution of his purpose until an opportunity should offer of performing some essential service to the power which he was about to join, that might render his accession of more importance. A correspondence was opened with sir Henry Clinton: The a delivering up the post at West Point, where Arnold, now commanded, was the service he proposed to perform; and the interval of general Washington's absence, when he went to confer with the French commanders, was the time appointed for finishing the negotiation. To facilitate the means of carrying on the previous correspondence, the *Vulture* sloop of war was stationed in the North River, at such a distance from West Point as to excite no suspicion, but near enough to serve for the intended communication; and as general Arnold required a confidential person to treat with, major André, aid-du-camp to sir Henry Clinton, and adjutant-general of the British army, undertook to confer with him, and bring the British negotiation to a conclusion. For this purpose he repaired on board the *Vulture* sloop. At night, in pursuance of a previous arrangement, a boat from the shore carried him to the beach, where he met general Arnold; and day-light approaching before the business on which they had met was finally adjusted, major André was told that he must be conducted to a place of safety, and lie concealed until the following night, when he might return on board the *Vulture* without the danger of being discovered. The beach where the first conference was held was without, but the place of safety to which major André was conducted to lie concealed during the day, was within the American out-posts, against his intention, and with out his knowledge. Here, however, he remained with general Arnold during the day; and at night, the boatmen refusing to carry him on board the *Vulture*, because she had shifted her position during the day, in consequence of a gun being brought to bear upon her from the shore, he was reduced to the necessity of endeavouring to make his way to New York by land. Laying aside his regimentals, which he had hitherto worn, he put on a plain suit of clothes; and receiving a pass from general Arnold, under the assumed name of John Anderson, as if he had been sent down the country on public business, he set out on his return to New York. His pas port secured him from interruption at the American out-posts; and he had already passed them all, and thought himself out of danger, when three American militia-men, who had been sent out to patrol near the road along which he travelled, suddenly springing from the woods, seized the bridle of his horse and stopped him. The suddenness of the surprise seems to have deprived major André of his wonted presence of mind; and, although a man of the greatest address, he was entrapped by the rude simplicity of clowns. Having inquired from whence they were, and being answered, 'From below;' 'And so,' said he, 'am I.' It was not long before he discovered his mistake; but too late, it would appear, to remove the impression which his first answer had made. The men who had made him prisoners searched him for papers, and having taken from his boot a packet, in the hand-writing of general Arnold, determined to carry him without delay to their commanding officer. It was in vain that he offered them a purse of gold and his watch, to suffer him to pass: His promises of an ample provision, and getting them promotion, if they would accompany him to New York, were equally unavailing. The unfortunate André, after these efforts to regain his liberty, seems to have been regardless of what might be his own fate, and was only anxious to save general Arnold. Before the commanding officer of the militia he continued to perforate the supposed John Anderson, and requested that a messenger might be sent to general Arnold to acquaint him with his detention. A messenger being accordingly dispatched, and sufficient time having elapsed for general Arnold to make his escape, he no longer disguised his real name, and avowed himself to be major André, adjutant-general of the British army: He also wrote a letter to general Washington, in his real name, acquainting him that he was his prisoner, and accounting for the disguise which necessity had obliged him film to assume. The message sent to general Arnold, announcing the detention of John Anderson, was sufficient notice to him to provide for his own safety: He quitted West Point without delay, got on board the *Vulture* sloop, and in her proceeded to New York.

In the mean time general Washington returned from his interview with the French commanders, and being informed of what had patted during his absence, together with Arnold's escape, he reinforced the garrison of West Point with a strong detachment from his army, and appointed a board of general officers, to inquire into and report upon the cafe of major André. The candid, open, manly, and ingenuous explanation of his conduct, given by major André, before the board of officers, impressed with admiration and esteem even his enemies who were about to shed his blood. Dismissing from his thoughts all personal considerations of danger, he was only anxious that the transaction in which he had been engaged, shaded as it was by the intervention of unfortunate circumstances, might be cleared from obscurity, and appear in its genuine colours, at least with respect to his intention, which was incapable of swerving from the paths of honour. But the board of officers fixing their attention upon the naked fact of his being in disguise within their lines, without perhaps duly considering the unfortunate train of incidents which unexpectedly, and almost unavoidably, led him into that situation, were of opinion that he came under the description, and ought to suffer the punishment, of a spy.

The concern felt at New York, in consequence of the capture of major André, was in the mean time inconceivably great: His gallantry as an officer, and amiable demeanour as a man, had gained him not only the admiration, but the affection, of the whole army; and the uncertainty of his fate filled them with the deepest anxiety. Sir Henry Clinton, whose esteem and regard he enjoyed in an eminent degree, immediately opened a correspondence with general Washington, by means of a flag of truce, and urged every motive which justice, policy, or humanity, could suggest, to induce a remission of the sentence. Finding his letters ineffectual, he sent out general Robertson, with a flag, to confer upon the subject with any officer that should be appointed by general Washington. An inter-view took place between general Robertson and general Green[e], who had been president of the court-martial. But all efforts to save the unfortunate André were unavailing: His doom was irrevocably fixed. The greatness of the danger which the American army had escaped by the discovery of Arnold's plot before it was ripe for execution, seems to have extinguished in the breath of the inexorable Washington, every spark of humanity that remained. Although entreated by a most pathetic letter from major André, written on the day previous to his execution, to change the mode of his death from that of a common malefactor to one more correspondent to the feelings of a soldier, he would not condescend to grant even this inconsiderable boon to the supplication of his unfortunate prisoner: And on the second day of October this accomplished young officer met his fate, in the manner prescribed by his sentence, with a composure serenity, and fortitude, which astonished the beholders, and excited those emotions of sympathy that would have been more honourably and humanely exercised in averting than lamenting his fate.

Thus fell the unfortunate André. If intention is necessary to constitute guilt; and if guilt alone merits punishment, some doubt may be entertained with respect to the sentence of the board of officers. Major André did not, at first, knowingly enter within the American lines: He was then also in his regimentals: And when he actually found himself within those lines, contrarily to his intention, whatever he afterwards did, in order to extricate himself, by assuming a disguise, and using a feigned passport, ought rather to be ascribed to the imposed necessity of his situation than to choice. But, even if the sentence pronounced against him should be found agreeable to the letter of the law of nations, so unsuitable is the exercise of extreme justice to our imperfect state, that we turn with disgust from those transactions, in which the finer feelings of humanity have been sacrificed to its rigour. Bright as the fame of Washington shall shine in the annals of America, as one of the most illustrious supporters of her independence, the sons of freedom will lament the cold insensibility, that did not suffer him to interpose, in order to rescue from his fate so gallant an officer, and even could withhold from him the poor consolation of meeting death like a soldier; whilst a glance of indignation shall dart from the eyes of her fair and compassionate daughters, softened only by the tear of pity for the fate of the accomplished André.

~~~***~~~

Without question Aaron Burr stands as one of the most enigmatic and strangest characters in early United States history, and it is somewhat of a marvel why he was both *so* lionized and vilified in his time, and yet in retrospect did not accomplish anything as a public office holder that was especially noteworthy; while, outside of hearsay, was actually found guilty of palpably little. True, we learn later that according to the then British ambassador, Anthony Merry, he reportedly sought British aid in his scheme to betray the United States[152] -- but was this his real intention? And yet if betraying the United States was his goal, i.e., as the result of founding a breakaway kingdom in the west, how could he have imagined the United States would sit idly by and be so rudely used and insulted? Likewise (and based on what we read), Burr's incomprehensible foolishness revealed itself most glaringly in that his scheme relied so heavily on Wilkinson as the commander of American forces at New Orleans, whether to assist him in attacking Florida, Mexico, or else founding a new state. And yet Wilkinson, as it turned out, was in the secret pay of the Spaniards. What then was it that made him think Wilkinson could be relied upon in so crucial a role?

[152] See Henry Adams' *History of the United States during the Administration of Thomas Jefferson*, pp. 571, 576.
~~~

To compound the distortion and nonsense, some have tried to come to Burr's defense by defaming Hamilton or Jefferson, but this seems a poor explanation of the former's seemingly mad and mysterious actions.

In perusing a diversity of materials on Burr, one is inclined to think he (and also the perhaps overly condemned, or at least misunderstood, Wilkinson) was a target of spirit people hoodwinking and using him as the object of what amounted to a grandiose practical joke. Respecting the famous Weehawken duel, it seems not at all implausible that both Burr and Hamilton were in some ways victims of the same shadowy personage. The trick pistol, for instance, Hamilton (is said to have) brought to the duel may have been planted by someone else (whether before or after the event), and which seems more likely than to assume Hamilton would be such roguish cheat. And not least fiedishly of all, not merely Hamilton but Burr himself was done in by the duel.[153]

Burr's hounded life, including the very cruel views others had of him, despite the subsequent sympathy he received from such as John Adams and Washington Irving and the Irving brothers generally, and the bizarre and almost occult-like disappearance and loss of Burr's daughter, further possibly suggest that he was in some manner persecuted by spirit people (and their henchmen.) This is by no means to say that Burr was a complete innocent, but that a very little he was truly guilty of may have been extravagantly spun out by someone else to trip him up to his ruin.[154] Probably and more than anything else, it was his womanizing that was his chief undoing; a weakness an envious devil predictably delights in tormenting, exploiting, and charging for. In respect of his alleged conspiracy to seize power in the West, he seems more to blame for being ridiculous than malevolent. Although there is much circumstantial evidence, there is simply not enough conclusive proof as to his ultimate motives there.

That he was a grandson of Jonathan Edwards may also have been a contributing factor; insofar as that well-meaning divine, some of whose views -- such as predestination;[155] a favorite doctrine of devils; insofar that by means of it they can plausibly argue they are divinely impelled to do wrong – perhaps bordered, albeit unintentionally, on the diabolical, as a result drew mischievous spirit people to him, and plausibly in turn to some of his family. Alternatively, we might also say some of his family was beset and afflicted because Edwards himself was such a champion for good. Either way or both, I offer such comments as mere speculation, not irrefragable fact, yet speculation not perhaps without its potential as, ultimately, verifiable truth.[156]

---

[153] We still don't know with certainty what caused the Burr-Hamilton feud. However two facts which stand out in the controversy is that 1) Hamilton cost Burr the presidential election of 1800, and 2) the Federalists turned their back on Hamilton to support Burr in the New York gubernatorial election, probably because Hamilton, although avowedly anti-democratic, was adamantly pro-Union in the face of the then nascent New England secession movement, and Burr by contrast, and in his antipathy toward Jefferson and the Virginia dynasty, was perhaps more malleable and open-minded towards the New England confederates.

[154] During the Revolutionary War, Burr's own men "thought him a kind of necromancer, or magician." James Parton, *The Life and Times of Aaron Burr* (1888), vol. 1, p. 100.

[155] Edwards' ideas on predestination were of a qualified sort; by which he said, in effect, that man has free will, but that God knows a man's choices in advance. Such an interpretation of the question is a more than reasonable compromise; so that if, as I hypothecated when this was originally written by me, devils were encouraged by him due to his views on predestination, they were encouraged in error.

[156] In a letter to his son-in-law, Gov. Joseph Alston of South Carolina, written from New York on 20 Nov. 1815, Burr made these illuminating, albeit not a little politically motivated, comments regarding James Monroe; which provide unusual insight into some notable Revolutionary War figures (Burr himself included.)

"Independently of the manner of the nomination and the location of the candidate, the man himself [James Monroe] is one of the most improper and incompetent that could be selected. Naturally dull and stupid; extremely illiterate; indecisive to a degree that would be incredible to one who did not know him; pusillanimous, and, of course, hypocritical; has no opinion on any subject, and will be always under the government of the worst men; pretends, as I am told, to some knowledge of military matters, but never commanded a platoon, nor was ever fit to command one. ' -- He served in the Revolutionary War! --' that is, he acted a short time as aid-de-camp to Lord Stirling, who was regularly ********. Monroe's whole duty was to fill his lordship's tankard, and hear, with indications of admiration, his lordship's long stories about himself. Such is Monroe's military experience. I was with my regiment in the same division at the time. As a lawyer, Monroe was far below mediocrity.

"He never rose to the honour of trying a cause of the value of a hundred pounds. This is a character exactly suited to the views of the Virginia junto."

In the interest of bi-partisan fairness, here are Thomas Jefferson's views of Burr and Monroe:

[RE. Burr] "A great man in little things, he is really small in great ones." (To G. Hay, 1807.)

"I have had, and still have, such entire confidence in the late and present Presidents [Madison and Monroe], that I willingly put both soul and body into their pockets." (T`o N. Macon, 1819.)

“AMERICA, A Prophecy” (1793)
by William Blake

While for most of the conflict, the majority of the British public supported the war against the colonies, there were also many who sympathized with the Americans. There were yet others more or less neutral, and who sought, to their credit, to approach matters from a Christian and humanitarian outlook; and which included providing charity to victims of the war, such as American soldiers and sailors held as prisoners[157] or homeless and exiled Loyalists. Ethan Allen’s view of the British, as expressed in his *Narrative* (1779) is edifying on this question of British perspective of the conflict because although on one hand he manifests implacable hatred of “Britons” and British tyranny, he also shows a liking and affection for individual British people who displayed benevolence and understanding of the American’s or an individual American’s predicament.

And yet despite the obvious appeal of such British altruism and impartiality to us today, it was not always so easy a thing for a serving British army or naval officer to show himself as being too kindly. For he risked the disdain and contempt of combatants on both sides; from fellow British for lack of loyalty, and from Americans, in a kind of reverse psychology (that perhaps we might attribute to man’s fallen nature), who might construe his friendliness as a sign of weakness. For this reason, it seems all the more incumbent on us now to appreciate and respect those officers, soldiers and sailors who were just minded and charitably disposed; since it was often they who served to make the war more humane and less bitter between the contending parties than it might otherwise have been.[158]

Surely one of the most curious reactions by a Briton to the American war was that of artist, poet and visionary William Blake. In his “America: A Prophecy” (1793), one among a number of his twelve “Continental Prophecies,” by means of verse and pictorial illuminations, he depicts both Britain and America as being governed and impelled by gargantuan or global “myth-like” spirits or spiritual personages; themselves driven by passionate impulses desiring freedom and or else the enslavement of someone else. I use the term “myth-like” because for Blake these were not mythical beings as we might ordinarily conceive them to be, but in some spiritual and imaginative sense quite palpable and real forces directing and shaping great and international events. Yet how and to what extent *real* and in quite what way (perhaps psychological?) readers of Blake will have to interpret and decide for themselves. Those unfamiliar with his “prophecy” will be confused as to “America’s” meaning and symbolism. Unfortunately, it exceeds our present means and the constraints of these monographs to begin attempting an exegesis here; except to note that in the “Visions of the Daughters of Albion” (1793) the character Oothon, described as the “soft, soul of America,” is brutalized by one Bromion, and subsequently abandoned by Theotormon whom she loves. This said, those who *are* desirous or interested can naturally find thoughtful attempts at interpretation and explanation in critical books and essays, in particular those of Kathleen Raine, on Blake’s work.

~~~***~~~

PRELUDIUM

The shadowy Daughter of Urthona stood before red Orc,
When fourteen suns had faintly journey’d o’er his dark abode:
His food she brought in iron baskets, his drink in cups of iron.
Crown’d with a helmet and dark hair the nameless Female stood;
A quiver with its burning stores, a bow like that of night,

Monroe, also and incidentally, had been seriously wounded in the shoulder at the battle of Trenton while leading an attack there, and later served as a lieutenant colonel in the Virginia militia under Brig. Gen. Robert Lawson in Lafayette’s campaign against Cornwallis in 1781.

[157] “The committee in London for raising and applying monies for the relief of the American prisoners [of war], began in March [1780] to call upon the public afresh for new subscriptions, as the war continued beyond expectation: the same were readily made. Many individuals exhibited a compassion and liberality to the Americans, that does honor to human nature.” Rev. William Gordon, *The history of the rise progress and establishment of the independence of the United States of America* (1788), vol. III, pp. 416-417.

[158] Regarding whom and specifically see, for example, Allen’s *Narrative*, and Alexander Garden’s *Anecdotes*, 1st series (1822) p. 71n, and 2nd series (1828) pp. 109-111.
~~~

When pestilence is shot from heaven: no other arms she need!
Invulnerable tho' naked, save where clouds roll round her loins
Their awful folds in the dark air: silent she stood as night;
For never from her iron tongue could voice or sound arise,
But dumb till that dread day when Orc assay'd his fierce embrace.

"Dark Virgin," said the hairy Youth, "thy father stern, abhorr'd,
Rivets my tenfold chains, while still on high my spirit soars;
Sometimes an eagle screaming in the sky, sometimes a lion
Stalking upon the mountains, and sometimes a whale, I lash
The raging fathomless abyss; anon a serpent folding
Around the pillars of Urthona, and round thy dark limbs
On the Canadian wilds I fold; feeble my spirit folds;
For chain'd beneath I rend these caverns: when thou bringest food
I howl my joy, and my red eyes seek to behold thy face --
In vain! these clouds roll to and fro, and hide thee from my sight."

Silent as despairing love, and strong as jealousy,
The hairy shoulders rend the links; free are the wrists of fire;
Round the terrific loins he seiz'd the panting, struggling womb;
It joy'd: she put aside her clouds and smilèd her first-born smile,
As when a black cloud shows its lightnings to the silent deep.

Soon as she saw the Terrible Boy, then burst the virgin cry:

"I know thee, I have found thee, and I will not let thee go:
Thou art the image of God who dwells in darkness of Africa,
And thou art fall'n to give me life in regions of dark death.
On my American plains I feel the struggling afflictions
Endur'd by roots that writhe their arms into the nether deep.
I see a Serpent in Canada who courts me to his love,
In Mexico an Eagle, and a Lion in Peru;
I see a Whale in the South Sea, drinking my soul away.
O what limb-rending pains I feel! thy fire and my frost
Mingle in howling pains, in furrows by thy lightnings rent.
This is Eternal Death, and this the torment long foretold!"

A PROPHECY

The Guardian Prince of Albion burns in his nightly tent:
Sullen fires across the Atlantic glow to America's shore,
Piercing the souls of warlike men, who rise in silent night.
Washington, Franklin, Paine, & Warren, Gates, Hancock & Green;
Meet on the coast glowing with blood from Albion's fiery Prince.

Washington spoke: "Friends of America! look over the Atlantic sea;
A bended bow is lifted in heaven, & a heavy iron chain
Descends link by link from Albion's cliffs across the sea to bind
Brothers & sons of America, till our faces pale and yellow;
Heads deprest, voices weak, eyes downcast, hands work-bruis'd,
Feet bleeding on the sultry sands, and the furrows of the whip
Descend to generations that in future times forget."

The strong voice ceas'd; for a terrible blast swept over the heaving sea;
The eastern cloud rent; on his cliffs stood Albion's wrathful Prince

A dragon form clashing his scales at midnight he arose,
And flam'd red meteors round the land of Albion beneath.
His voice, his locks, his awful shoulders, and his glowing eyes,
Appear to the Americans upon the cloudy night.
Solemn heave the Atlantic waves between the gloomy nations,
Swelling, belching from its deeps red clouds & raging Fires!
Albion is sick. America faints! enrag'd the Zenith grew.
As human blood shooting its veins all round the orbed heaven
Red rose the clouds from the Atlantic in vast wheels of blood
And in the red clouds rose a Wonder o'er the Atlantic sea;
Intense! naked! a Human fire fierce glowing, as the wedge
Of iron heated in the furnace; his terrible limbs were fire
With myriads of cloudy terrors banners dark & towers
Surrounded: heat but not light went thro' the murky atmosphere.

The King of England looking westward trembles at the vision.

Albion's Angel stood beside the Stone of night, and saw
The terror like a comet, or more like the planet red
That once inclos'd the terrible wandering comets in its sphere.
Then Mars thou wast our center, & the planets three flew round
Thy crimson disk: so e'er the Sun was rent from thy red sphere;
The Spectre glowd his horrid length staining the temple long
With beams of blood; & thus a voice came forth, and shook the temple:

"The morning comes, the night decays, the watchmen leave their stations;
The grave is burst, the spices shed, the linen wrapped up;
The bones of death, the cov'ring clay, the sinews shrunk & dry'd.
Reviving shake, inspiring move, breathing! awakening!
Spring like redeemed captives when their bonds & bars are burst.
Let the slave grinding at the mill, run out into the field:
Let him look up into the heavens & laugh in the bright air;
Let the inchained soul shut up in darkness and in sighing,
Whose face has never seen a smile in thirty weary years,
Rise and look out, his chains are loose, his dungeon doors are open.
And let his wife and children return from the oppressors scourge.
They look behind at every step & believe it is a dream,
Singing. 'The Sun has left his blackness, & has found a fresher morning,
And the fair Moon rejoices in the clear & cloudless night;
For Empire is no more, and now the Lion & Wolf shall cease.'"

In thunders ends the voice. Then Albion's Angel wrathful burnt
Beside the Stone of Night; and like the Eternal Lion's howl
In famine & war, reply'd. "Art thou not Orc, who serpent-form'd
Stands at the gate of Enitharmon to devour her children;
Blasphemous Demon, Antichrist, hater of Dignities;
Lover of wild rebellion, and transgressor of God's Law;
Why dost thou come to Angels eyes in this terrific form?"

The terror answer'd: "I am Orc, wreath'd round the accursed tree:
The times are ended; shadows pass the morning gins to break;
The fiery joy, that Urizen perverted to ten commands,
What night he led the starry hosts thro' the wide wilderness:
That stony law I stamp to dust: and scatter religion abroad
To the four winds as a torn book, & none shall gather the leaves;
But they shall rot on desart sands, & consume in bottomless deeps;

To make the desarts blossom, & the deeps shrink to their fountains,
And to renew the fiery joy, and burst the stony roof.
That pale religious letchery, seeking Virginity,
May find it in a harlot, and in coarse-clad honesty
The undefil'd tho' ravish'd in her cradle night and morn:
For every thing that lives is holy, life delights in life;
Because the soul of sweet delight can never be defil'd.
Fires inwrap the earthly globe, yet man is not consum'd;
Amidst the lustful fires he walks; his feet become like brass,
His knees and thighs like silver, & his breast and head like gold."

"Sound! sound! my loud war-trumpets & alarm my Thirteen Angels!
Loud howls the eternal Wolf! the eternal Lion lashes his tail!
America is darken'd; and my punishing Demons terrified
Crouch howling before their caverns deep like skins dry'd in the wind.
They cannot smite the wheat, nor quench the fatness of the earth.
They cannot smite with sorrows, nor subdue the plow and spade.
They cannot wall the city, nor moat round the castle of princes.
They cannot bring the stubbed oak to overgrow the hills.
For terrible men stand on the shores, & in their robes I see
Children take shelter from the lightnings, there stands Washington
And Paine and Warren with their foreheads rear'd toward the east.
But clouds obscure my aged sight. A vision from afar!
Sound! sound! my loud war-trumpets & alarm my thirteen Angels!
Ah vision from afar! Ah rebel form that rent the ancient
Heavens; Eternal Viper self-renew'd, rolling in clouds,
I see thee in thick clouds and darkness on America's shore,
Writhing in pangs of abhorred birth; red flames the crest rebellious
And eyes of death; the harlot womb oft opened in vain
Heaves in enormous circles, now the times are return'd upon thee,
Devourer of thy parent, now thy unutterable torment renews.
Sound! sound! my loud war trumpets & alarm my thirteen Angels!
Ah terrible birth! a young one bursting! where is the weeping mouth?
And where the mothers milk? instead those ever-hissing jaws
And parched lips drop with fresh gore; now roll thou in the clouds
Thy mother lays her length outstretch'd upon the shore beneath.
Sound! sound! my loud war-trumpets & alarm my thirteen Angels!
Loud howls the eternal Wolf: the eternal Lion lashes his tail!"

Thus wept the Angel voice & as he wept the terrible blasts
Of trumpets, blew a loud alarm across the Atlantic deep.
No trumpets answer; no reply of clarions or of fifes,
Silent the Colonies remain and refuse the loud alarm.

On those vast shady hills between America & Albion's shore;
Now barr'd out by the Atlantic sea: call'd Atlantean hills:
Because from their bright summits you may pass to the Golden world
An ancient palace, archetype of mighty Emperies,
Rears its immortal pinnacles, built in the forest of God
By Ariston the king of beauty for his stolen bride.

Here on their magic seats the thirteen Angels sat perturb'd
For clouds from the Atlantic hover o'er the solemn roof.

Fiery the Angels rose, & as they rose deep thunder roll'd
Around their shores: indignant burning with the fires of Orc

And Boston's Angel cried aloud as they flew thro' the dark night.

He cried: "Why trembles honesty and like a murderer,
Why seeks he refuge from the frowns of his immortal station!
Must the generous tremble & leave his joy, to the idle: to the pestilence!
That mock him? who commanded this? what God? what Angel!
To keep the gen'rous from experience till the ungenerous
Are unrestrain'd performers of the energies of nature;
Till pity is become a trade, and generosity a science,
That men get rich by, & the sandy desart is giv'n to the strong
What God is he, writes laws of peace, & clothes him in a tempest
What pitying Angel lusts for tears, and fans himself with sighs
What crawling villain preaches abstinence & wraps himself
In fat of lambs? no more I follow, no more obedience pay!"

So cried he, rending off his robe & throwing down his scepter.
In sight of Albion's Guardian, and all the thirteen Angels
Rent off their robes to the hungry wind, & threw their golden scepters
Down on the land of America. indignant they descended
Headlong from out their heav'nly heights, descending swift as fires
Over the land; naked & flaming are their lineaments seen
In the deep gloom, by Washington & Paine & Warren they stood
And the flame folded roaring fierce within the pitchy night
Before the Demon red, who burnt towards America,
In black smoke thunders and loud winds rejoicing in its terror
Breaking in smoky wreaths from the wild deep, & gath'ring thick
In flames as of a furnace on the land from North to South
What time the thirteen Governors that England sent convene
In Bernard's house; the flames cover'd the land, they rouze they cry
Shaking their mental chains they rush in fury to the sea
To quench their anguish; at the feet of Washington down fall'n
They grovel on the sand and writhing lie, while all
The British soldiers thro' the thirteen states sent up a howl
Of anguish: threw their swords & muskets to the earth & ran
From their encampments and dark castles seeking where to hide
From the grim flames; and from the visions of Orc; in sight
Of Albion's Angel; who enrag'd his secret clouds open'd
From north to south, and burnt outstretchd on wings of wrath cov'ring
The eastern sky, spreading his awful wings across the heavens;
Beneath him roll'd his num'rous hosts, all Albion's Angels camp'd
Darken'd the Atlantic mountains & their trumpets shook the valleys
Arm'd with diseases of the earth to cast upon the Abyss,
Their numbers forty millions, must'ring in the eastern sky.

In the flames stood & view'd the armies drawn out in the sky
Washington, Franklin, Paine, & Warren, Allen, Gates, & Lee,
And heard the voice of Albion's Angel give the thunderous command;
His plagues obedient to his voice flew forth out of their clouds,
Falling upon America, as a storm to cut them off,
As a blight cuts the tender corn when it begins to appear.
Dark is the heaven above, & cold & hard the earth beneath:
And as a plague wind fill'd with insects cuts off man & beast,
And as a sea o'erwhelms a land in the day of an earthquake,
Fury! rage! madness! in a wind swept through America;
And the red flames of Orc that folded roaring fierce around
The angry shores, and the fierce rushing of th' inhabitants together!

The citizens of New-York close their books & lock their chests;
The mariners of Boston drop their anchors and unlade;
The scribe of Pensylvania casts his pen upon the earth;
he builder of Virginia throws his hammer down in fear.

Then had America been lost, o'erwhelm'd by the Atlantic,
And Earth had lost another portion of the infinite,
But all rush together in the night in wrath and raging fire
The red fires rag'd! the plagues recoil'd! then roll'd they back with fury
On Albion's Angels; then the Pestilence began in streaks of red
Across the limbs of Albion's Guardian, the spotted plague smote Bristol's
And the Leprosy London's Spirit, sickening all their bands:
The millions sent up a howl of anguish and threw off their hammer'd mail,
And cast their swords & spears to earth, & stood a naked multitude:
Albion's Guardian writhed in torment on the eastern sky,
Pale quivring toward the brain his glimmering eyes, teeth chattering,
Howling & shuddering his legs quivering; convuls'd each muscle & sinew:
Sick'ning lay London's Guardian, and the ancient miter'd York,
Their heads on snowy hills, their ensigns sick'ning in the sky.
The plagues creep on the burning winds driven by flames of Orc,
And by the fierce Americans rushing together in the night,
Driven o'er the Guardians of Ireland and Scotland and Wales.
They spotted with plagues forsook the frontiers & their banners sear'd
With fires of hell, deform their ancient heavens with shame & woe.
Hid in his caves the Bard of Albion felt the enormous plagues.
And a cowl of flesh grew o'er his head & scales on his back & ribs;
And rough with black scales all his Angels fright their ancient heavens.
The doors of marriage are open, and the Priests in rustling scales
Rush into reptile coverts, hiding from the fires of Orc,
That play around the golden roofs in wreaths of fierce desire,
Leaving the females naked and glowing with the lusts of youth.

For the female spirits of the dead pining in bonds of religion,
Run from their fetters reddening, & in long drawn arches sitting,
They feel the nerves of youth renew, and desires of ancient times
Over their pale limbs as a vine when the tender grape appears.

Over the hills, the vales, the cities, rage the red flames fierce:
The Heavens melted from north to south; and Urizen who sat
Above all heavens in thunders wrap'd, emerg'd his leprous head
From out his holy shrine, his tears in deluge piteous
Falling into the deep sublime! flag'd with grey-brow'd snows
And thunderous visages, his jealous wings wav'd over the deep;
Weeping in dismal howling woe he dark descended howling
Around the smitten bands, clothed in tears & trembling shudd'ring cold.
His stored snows he poured forth, and his icy magazines
He open'd on the deep, and on the Atlantic sea white shiv'ring.
Leprous his limbs, all over white, and hoary was his visage.
Weeping in dismal howlings before the stern Americans,
Hiding the Demon red with clouds & cold mists from the earth;
Till Angels & weak men twelve years should govern o'er the strong:
And then their end should come, when France reciev'd the Demon's light.

Stiff shudderings shook the heav'nly thrones! France Spain & Italy,
In terror view'd the bands of Albion, and the ancient Guardians
Fainting upon the elements, smitten with their own plagues.

They slow advance to shut the five gates of their law-built heaven,
Filled with blasting fancies and with mildews of despair,
With fierce disease and lust, unable to stem the fires of Orc.
But the five gates were consum'd, & their bolts and hinges melted
And the fierce flames burnt round the heavens, & round the abodes of men.

WILLIAM GILMORE SIMMS' *YEMASSEE* (1835): An excerpt.

One is hard put now to make apologies for William Gilmore Simms' (1806-1870) racism as an ante-bellum, pro-slavery southerner. Yet his skill and virtue as a thoughtful and erudite author otherwise will redeem him nevertheless to those who can appreciate such gifts and merit. In addition, had he the hindsight we have at a later point in history, it is no strain to envision his finally getting around to changing his tune. Because he was at heart a kind and gracious man, not above self-criticism; who combined a very earthy and visceral sensibility with, by contrast, a profound seeking of excellence and the sublime. Looking back himself on his career in his later years, he came to express the view, in reference to his writings, that he would have done and penned some things differently than he did, and which second thoughts it is not unthinkable he would or might have applied to his views on political and controversial subjects as well.

In addition to novels, Simms authored histories, including biographies on Francis Marion and Nathanael Greene, as well not a little poetry; as an example of the latter, his "Atalantis: A Story of the Sea" (1832) is a gripping and imaginative, if admittedly sometimes desultory and chaotic, opus deserving of more recognition than it has received. Yet it is his novels and as the southern counterpart of James Fenimore Cooper, that he is best remembered, and rightly so. Like most 19th century novelists (whether American or European) following in the wake of Sir Walter Scott, he tends to be excessively verbose; expressing in a few pages what might just as soon have been said in an effectively worded paragraph or two. However, in fairness to such novelists, it is important to remember that such prolixity not infrequently stemmed from the insistence of publishers for longer works; claiming they needed to meet public demand. Whether such was actually public demand, or else motivated by a desire to trivialize literature in the interest of pandering to (perceived) popular dullness and a crude desire for size may be open to question. What ever the real reason, reading Simms' novels is sometimes not unlike making one's way through a flooded Carolina swamp; that is to say be warned of turgid, as in verbose, obstructions and digressive sink holes that occur up in the course of the narrative journey. But if you are patient, you will before long come upon the solid land you're seeking. For myself, most entertaining are his Revolutionary war novels, particularly *The Forayers* (1855) and *Eutaw* (1856), and which, incidentally, properly abridged and edited would make good movies if anyone ever got around to doing such a thing. The *full* list of these, in their fictional chronological sequence, are:

* *The Cassique of Kiawah, a Colonial Romance* (1859) -- While not actually set in the Revolutionary war, lays the groundwork and backdrop for the following that are.
* *Joscelyn, A Tale of the Revolution* (1867)
* *The Partisan, A Tale of the Revolution* (1835)
* *Mellichampe, A Legend of the Santee* (1836)
* *Katherine Walton, or The Rebel of Dorchester* (1850)
* *The Scout* (aka as *The Kinsman*), *or Black Riders of the Congaree* (1841)
* *The Forayers, or The Raid of the Dog-Days* (1855)
* *Eutaw, A Sequel to the Forayers* (1856)
* *Woodcraft* (aka *The Sword and the Distaff*), *or Hawks About the Dovecoat* (1852, 1854)

Granted, the corniness of Simms' characters, dialogue, and plot situations, like those of the worthy Cooper, are sometimes enough to elicit an unintended laugh or groan. Yet also like Cooper's, his writings *more* frequently display a uncommon knack for depicting the genuinely tender and sentimental;[159] as well as being plentiful in color; inventive in their wording; moving in descriptions, and no little ingenious in eliciting poetry from odd and mundane circumstances. And yet possibly Simms greatest strength is in delivering up exciting action sequences, and no writer yet has yet to excel him in "blood and thunder" and the "rip-roaring." As a sample of this latter, the following comes from chapter XXXIV of *Yemassee* (1835); which tells the tragic tale of the revolt of South Carolina's indigenous natives in the early 18th century (1715-1717).

~~~***~~~

[159] Chapter XX from *Yemassee* being one offhand and good instance of such.
~~~

"And war is the great Moloch; for his feast,
Gather the human victims he requires,
With an unglutted appetite. He makes
Earth his grand table, spread with winding-sheets,
Man his attendant, who, with madness fit,
Serves his own brother up, nor heeds the prayer,
Groaned by a kindred nature, for reprieve."

BLOOD makes the taste for blood -- we teach the hound to hunt the victim, for whose entrails he acquires an appetite. We acquire such tastes ourselves from like indulgences. There is a sort of intoxicating restlessness in crime that seldom suffers it to stop at a solitary excess. It craves repetition -- and the relish so expands with indulgence, that exaggeration becomes essential to make it a stimulant. Until we have created this appetite, we sicken at its bare contemplation. But once created, it is impatient of employ, and it is wonderful to note its progress. Thus, the young Nero wept when first called upon to sign the warrant commanding the execution of a criminal. But the ice once broken, he never suffered it to close again. Murder was his companion -- blood his banquet -- his chief stimulant licentiousness – horrible licentiousness. He had found out a new luxury.

The philosophy which teaches this is common to experience all the world over. It was not unknown to the Yemassees. Distrusting the strength of their hostility to the English, the chief instigators of the proposed insurrection, as we have seen deemed it necessary to appeal to this appetite, along with a native superstition. Their battle-god called for a victim, and the prophet promulgated the decree. A chosen band of warriors was despatched [sic] to secure a white man; and in subjecting him to the fire-torture, the Yemassees were to feel the provocation of that thirsting impulse which craves a continual renewal of its stimulating indulgence. Perhaps one of the most natural and necessary agents of man, in his progress through life, is the desire to destroy. It is this which subjects the enemy -- it is this that prompts him to adventure -- which enables him to contend with danger, and to flout at death -- which carries him into the interminable forests, and impels the ingenuity into exercise, which furnishes him with a weapon to contend with its savage possessors. It is not surprising, if prompted by dangerous influences, in our ignorance, we pamper this natural agent into a disease, which preys at length upon ourselves.

The party despatched for this victim had been successful. The peculiar cry was heard indicating their success; and as it rung through the wide area, the crowd gave way and parted for the new comers, who were hailed with a degree of satisfaction, extravagant enough, unless we consider the importance generally attached to their enterprise. On their procuring this victim alive, depended their hope of victory in the approaching conflict. Such was the prediction of the prophet -- such the decree of their god of war -- and for the due celebration of this terrible sacrifice, the preparatory ceremonies had been delayed.

They were delayed no longer. With shrill cries and the most savage contortions, not to say convulsions of body, the assembled multitude hailed the entree of the detachment sent forth upon this expedition. They had been eminently successful; having taken their captive, without themselves losing a drop of blood. Upon this, the prediction had founded their success.

Not so the prisoner. Though unarmed he had fought desperately, and his enemies were compelled to wound in order to secure him. He was only overcome by numbers, and the sheer physical weight of their crowding bodies.

They dragged him into the ring, the war-dance all the time going on around him. From the copse, close at hand, in which he lay concealed, Harrison [the novel's white hero, an Englishman] could distinguish, at intervals, the features of the captive. He knew him at a glance, as a poor labourer, named Macnamara, an Irishman, who had gone jobbing about, in various ways, throughout the settlement. He was a fine-looking, fresh, muscular man -- not more than thirty -- and sustaining well, amid that fierce assemblage, surrounded with foes, and threatened with a torture to which European ingenuity could not often attain, unless in the Inquisitoral dungeons, the fearless character, which is a distinguishing feature with his countrymen. His long, black hair, deeply saturated and matted with his blood, which oozed out from sundry bludgeon-wounds upon the head, was wildly distributed in masses over his face and forehead.

His full, round cheeks, were marked by knife-wounds, also the result of his fierce defence against his captors. His hands were bound, but his tongue was unfettered; and as they danced and howled about him, his eye gleamed forth in fury and derision, while his words were those of defiance and contempt.

"Ay -- screech and scream, ye red divils – ye'd be after seeing how a jontleman would burn in the fire, would ye, for your idification and delight. But its not Tedd Macnamara, that your fires and your arrows will scare, ye divils; so begin, boys, as soon as ye've a mind to, and don't be too dilicate in your doings."

He spoke a language, so far as they understood it, perfectly congenial with their notion of what should become a warrior. His fearless contempt of death, his haughty defiance of their skill in the arts of torture -- his insolent abuse -- were all so much in his favour. They were proofs of the true brave, and they found, under the bias of their habits and education, an added pleasure in the belief, that he would stand well the torture, and afford them a protracted enjoyment of it. His execrations, poured forth freely as they forced him into the area, were equivalent to one of their own death-songs, and they regarded it as his.

He was not so easily compelled in the required direction. Unable in any other way to oppose them, he gave them as much trouble as he could, and in no way sought to promote his locomotion. This was good policy, perhaps, for this passive resistance -- the most annoying of all its forms, -- was not unlikely to bring about an impatient blow, which might save him from the torture. In another case, such might have been the result of the course taken by Macnamara; but now, the prophecy was the object, and though roughly handled enough, his captors yet forbore any excessive violence. Under a shower of kicks, cuffs, and blows from every quarter, the poor fellow, still cursing them to the last, hissing at and spitting upon them, was forced to a tree; and in a few moments tightly lashed back against it. A thick cord secured him around the body to its overgrown trunk, while his hands, forced up in a direct line above his head, were fastened to the tree with withes -- the two palms turned outwards, nearly meeting, and so well corded as to be perfectly immovable.

A cold chill ran through all the veins of Harrison and he grasped his knife with a clutch as tenacious as that of his fast-clinched teeth, while he looked, from his place of concealment, upon these dreadful preparations for the Indian torture. The captive was seemingly less sensible of its terrors. All the while, with a tongue that seemed determined to supply, so far as it might, the forced inactivity of all other members, he shouted forth his scorn and execrations.

"The pale-face will sing his death-song," -- in his own language cried a young warrior.

"Ay, ye miserable red nagers, -- ye don't frighten Tedd Macnamara now so aisily," he replied, though without comprehending what they said, yet complying as it were with their demand; for his shout was now a scream, and his words were those of exulting superiority.

"It aint your bows and your arrows, ye nagers, nor your knives, nor your hatchets, that's going to make Teddy beg your pardon, and ax for your mercies. I don't care for your knives, and your hatchets, at all at all, ye red divils. Not I -- by my faith, and my own ould father, that was Teddy before me."

They took him at his word, and their preparations were soon made for the torture. A hundred torches of the gummy pine were placed to kindle in a neighbouring fire -- a hundred old women stood ready to employ them. These were to be applied as a sort of cautery, to the arrow and knife-wounds which the more youthful savages were expected, in their sports, to inflict. It was upon their captives in this manner, that the youth of the nation was practised [sic]. It was in this school that the boys were prepared to become men -- to inflict pain as well as to submit to it. To these two classes, -- for this was one of the peculiar features of the Indian torture, -- the fire-sacrifice, in its initial penalties, was commonly assigned; and both of them were ready at hand to commence it. How beat the heart of Harrison with conflicting emotions, in the shelter of the adjacent bush, as he surveyed each step in the prosecution of these horrors.

They began. A dozen youth, none over sixteen, came forward and ranged themselves in front of the prisoner.

"And what for do ye face me down after that sort, ye little red nagers?" cried the sanguine prisoner.

They answered him with a whoop -- a single shriek -- and the face paled then, with that mimicry of war, of the man, who had been fearless throughout the real strife, and amid the many terrors which preceded it. The whoop was followed by a simultaneous discharge of all their arrows, aimed, as would appear from the result, at those portions of his person which were not vital.

This was the common exercise, and their adroitness was wonderful. They placed the shaft where they pleased. Thus, the arrow of one penetrated one palm, while that of another, almost at the same instant, was driven deep into the other. One cheek was grazed by a third, while a fourth scarified the opposite. A blunted shaft struck him full in the mouth, and arrested, in the middle his usual execration – "You bloody red nagers," and there never were fingers of a hand so evenly separated one from the other, as those of Macnamara, by the admirably-aimed arrows of those embryo warriors. But the endurance of the captive was proof against all their torture; and while every member of his person attested the felicity of their aim, he still continued to shout his abuse, not only to his immediate assailants, but to the old warriors, and the assembled multitude, gathering around, and looking composedly on -- now approving this or that peculiar hit, and encouraging the young beginner with a cheer. He stood all, with the most unflinching fortitude, and a courage that, extorting their freest admiration, was quite as much the subject of cheer with the warriors as were the arrow-shots which sometimes provoked its exhibition.

At length, throwing aside the one instrument, they came forward with the tomahawk. They were far more cautious with this fatal weapon, for, as their present object was not less the prolonging of their own exercises than of the prisoner's tortures, it was their wish to avoid wounding fatally or even severely. Their chief delight was in stinging the captive into an exhibition of imbecile and fruitless anger, or terrifying him into ludicrous apprehensions. They had no hope of the latter source of amusement from the firmness of the victim before them; and to rouse his impotent rage, was the study in their thought.

With words of mutual encouragement, and boasting, garrulously enough, each of his superior skill, they strove to rival one another in the nicety of their aim and execution. The chief object was barely to miss the part at which they aimed. One planted the tomahawk in the tree so directly over the head of his captive, as to divide the huge tuft of hair which grew massively in that quarter; and great was their exultation and loud their laughter, when the head thus jeoparded, very naturally, under the momentary impulse, was writhed about from the stroke, just at the moment when another aimed to lie on one side of his cheek, clove the ear which it would have barely escaped had the captive continued immoveable. Bleeding and suffering as he must have been with such infliction, not a solitary groan however escaped him. The stout-hearted Irishman continued to defy and to denounce his tormentors in language which, if only partially comprehended by his enemies, was yet illustrated with sufficient animation by the fierce light gleaming from his eye with a blaze like that of madness, and in the unblenching firmness of his cheek.

"And what for do ye howl, ye red-skinned divils, as if ye never seed a jontleman in your born days before? Be aisy, now, and shoot away with your piinted sticks, ye nagers, -- shoot away and be cursed to ye; sure it isn't Tedd Macnamara that's afeard of what ye can do, ye divils. If it's the fun ye're after now, honeys, -- the sport that's something like -- why, put your knife over this thong, and help this dilicate little fist to one of the bit shilalahs yonder. Do now, pretty crathers, do -- and see what fun will come out of it. Ye'll not be after loving it at all at all, I'm a thinking, ye monkeys, and ye alligators, and ye red nagers, and them's the best names for ye, ye ragamuffin divils that ye are."

It happened, however, as it would seem in compliance with a part of one of his demands, that one of the tomahawks, thrown so as to rest between the two uplifted palms of the captive, fell short, and striking the hide, a few inches below, which fastened his wrists to the tree, entirely separated it, and gave freedom to his arms. Though still incapable of any effort for his release, as the thongs tightly girdled his body, and were connected on the other side of the tree, the fearless sufferer, with his emancipated fingers, proceeded to pluck from his hands, amid a shower of darts, the arrows which had penetrated them deeply. These with a shout of defiance, he hurled back upon his assailants, they answering in similar style with another shout and a new discharge of arrows, which penetrated his person in every direction, inflicting the greatest pain, though carefully avoiding any vital region. And now, as if impatient of their forbearance, the boys were made to give way, and each armed with her hissing and resinous torch, the old women approached, howling and dancing, with shrill voices and an action of body frightfully demoniac. One after another they rushed up to the prisoner, and with fiendish fervour, thrust the blazing torches to his shrinking body, wherever a knife, an arrow, or a tomahawk had left a wound. The torture of this infliction greatly exceeded all to which he had been previously subjected; and with a howl, the unavoidable acknowledgment forced from nature by the extremity of pain, scarcely less horrible than that which they unitedly sent up around him, the captive dashed out his hands, and grasping one of the most forward among his unsexed tormentors, he firmly held her with one hand, while with the other he possessed himself of the blazing torch she bore. Hurling her backward, in the next moment, among the crowd of his enemies, with a resolution from despair, he applied the torch to the thongs which bound him to the tree, and while his garments shrivelled and flamed, and while the flesh blistered and burned with the terrible application, resolute as desperate, he maintained it on the spot, until the withes crackled, blazed, and separated.

His limbs were free -- a convulsion of joy actually rushed through his heart, and he shouted with a new tone, the result of a new and unimagined sensation. He leaped forward, and though the flames grasped and gathered in a thick volume, rushing from his waist to his extremities, completely enveloping him in their embrace, they offered no obstacle to the fresh impulse which possessed him. He bounded onward, with that over-head-and-heel evolution which is called the somerset [somersault], and which carried him, a broad column of fire, into the very thickest of the crowd. They gave way to him on every side -- they shrunk from that living flame, which mingled the power of the imperial element with the will of its superior, man. Panic-stricken for a few moments at the novel spectacle, they shrunk away on either hand before the blazing body, and offered no obstacle to his flight.

But the old warriors now took up the matter. They had suffered the game to go on as was their usage, for the tutoring of the youthful savage in those arts which are to be the employment of his life. But their own appetite now gave them speed, and they soon gathered upon the heels of the fugitive. Fortunately, he was still vigorous, and his hurts were those only of the flesh. His tortures only stimulated him into a daring disregard of any fate which might follow, and, looking once over his shoulder, and with a halloo not unlike their own whoop, Macnamara bounded forward directly upon the coppice which concealed Harrison. The latter saw his danger from this approach, but it was too late to retreat. He drew his knife and kept close to the cover of the fallen tree alongside of which he had laid himself down. Had the flying Macnamara seen this tree so as to have avoided it, Harrison might still have maintained his concealment. But the fugitive, unhappily, looked out for no such obstruction. He thought only of flight, and his legs were exercised at the expense of his eyes. A long-extended branch, shooting from the tree, interposed, and he saw it not. His feet were suddenly entangled, and he fell between the arm and the trunk of the tree. Before he could rise or recover, his pursuers were upon him. He had half gained his feet, and one of his hands, in promoting this object, rested upon the tree itself, on the opposite side of which Harrison lay quiet, while the head of Macnamara was just rising above it. At that moment a tall chief of the Seratees, with a huge club, dashed the now visible scull down upon the trunk. The blow was fatal -- the victim uttered not even a groan, and the spattering brains were driven wide, and into the upturned face of Harrison.

There was no more concealment for him after that, and starting to his feet, in another moment his knife was thrust deep into the bosom of the astonished Seratee before he had resumed the swing of his ponderous weapon. The Indian sunk back, with a single cry, upon those who followed him -- half paralyzed, with himself, at the new enemy whom they had conjured up. But their panic was momentary, and the next instant saw fifty of them crowding upon the Englishman. He placed himself against a tree, hopeless, but determined to struggle to the last. But he was surrounded in a moment -- his arms pinioned from behind, and knives from all quarters glittering around him, and aiming at his breast. What might have been his fate under the excitement of the scene and circumstances could well be said; for, already, the brother chief of the Seratee had rushed forward with his uplifted mace, and as he had the distinct claim to revenge, there was no interference. Fortunately, however, for the captive, the blow was stricken aside and intercepted by the huge staff of no less a person than the prophet.

"He is mine -- the ghost of Chaharattee, my brother, is waiting for that of his murderer. I must hang his teeth on my neck," was the fierce cry, in his own language, of the surviving Seratee, when his blow was thus arrested. But the prophet had his answer in a sense not to be withstood by the superstitious savage.

"Does the prophet speak for himself or for Manneyto? Is Manneyto a woman that we may say, Wherefore thy word to the prophet? Has not Manneyto spoken, and will not the chief obey? Lo! this is our victim, and the words of Manneyto are truth. He hath said one victim -- one English for the sacrifice, -- and but one before we sing the battle-song -- before we go on the war-path of our enemies. Is not his word truth? This blood says it is truth. We may not slay another, but on the red trail of the English. The knife must be drawn and the tomahawk lifted on the ground of the enemy, but the land of Manneyto is holy, save for his sacrifice. Thou must not strike the captive. He is captive to the Yemassee."

"He is the captive to the brown lynx of Seratee -- is he not under his club?" was the fierce reply.

"Will the Seratee stand up against Manneyto? Hear! That is his voice of thunder, and see, the eye which he sends forth in the lightning!"

Thus confirmed in his words by the solemn auguries to which he referred, and which, just at that moment came, as if in fulfillment and support of his decision, the Seratee obeyed, while all around grew silent and serious. But he insisted that, though compelled to forbear his blood, he was at least his captive. This, too, the prophet denied. The prisoner was made such upon the sacred ground of the Yemassees, and was, therefore, doubly their captive. He was reserved for sacrifice to the Manneyto at the conclusion of their present enterprise, when his doom would add to the solemnity of their thanksgiving for the anticipated victory.

EULOGIUM ON MAJOR-GENERAL GREENE

Presented to the Society of Cincinnati on July 4th 1789

by Alexander Hamilton.

"It is impossible to review this active and interesting campaign without feeling that much is due to General Greene; and that he amply justified the favourable opinion of the Commander-in-chief. He found the country completely conquered, and defended by a regular army estimated at four thousand men. The inhabitants were so divided, as to leave it doubtful to which side the majority was attached. At no time did the effective continental force which he could bring into the field, amount to two thousand men; and of these a considerable part were raw troops. Yet he could keep the field without being forced into action; and by a course of judicious movement, and of hardy enterprise, in which invincible constancy was displayed, and in which courage was happily tempered with prudence, he recovered the southern states. It is a singular fact, well worthy of notice, which marks impressively the soundness of his judgment, that although he never gained a decisive victory, he obtained, to a considerable extent, even when defeated, the object for which he fought.

"A just portion of the praise deserved by these achievements, is unquestionably due to the troops he commanded. These real patriots bore every hardship and privation with a degree of patience and constancy which can not be sufficiently admired. And never was a general better supported by his inferior officers. Not shackled by men who, without merit, held stations of high rank obtained by political influence, he commanded young men of equal spirit and intelligence, formed under the eye of Washington, and trained in the school furnished in the severe service of the north, to all the hardships and dangers of war."

~ John Marshall, *The Life of George Washington*, vol. IV, ch. 1.

Three months after the United States Constitution went into effect (on March 4, 1789) and which he strove vigorously to have adopted -- as much, if not more so, as he had fought with distinguished ardor and zeal during the war -- Alexander Hamilton[160] delivered to a July 4th gathering of the Society of Cincinnati an oration in commemoration of the late Maj. Gen. Nathanael Greene.[161] The address is of especial significance due both to its author and the then recent cast of the person and events being recollected. Much of his knowledge of Greene's southern campaign could only have come to Hamilton second-hand, and there is relatively little in his comments and observations that is original; using language that at times is perhaps inflated and overly formal, if well-meaning. Notwithstanding, he does strike a more personal note in warmly recalling individual officers; while characterizing Greene himself as a father figure who furnished encouragement and instilled inspiration in younger officers, and to whom many owed much of their own success; not least of which in benefiting from Greene as a model of command and leadership – that is, at least, after Greene himself had adequate time (that is, by about the date of the battle of Trenton) to more properly learn the ropes of his profession.

~~~***~~~

There is no duty that could have been assigned to me by this Society which I should execute with greater alacrity than the one I am now called upon to perform. All the motives capable of interesting an ingenuous and feeling mind conspire to prompt me to its execution. To commemorate the talents, virtues, and exploits of great and good men, is at all times a pleasing task to those who know how to esteem them. But when such men, to the title of superior merit, join that of having been the defenders and guardians of our country; when they have been connected with us as companions in the same dangers, sufferings, misfortunes, and triumphs; when they have been allied to us in the still more endearing character of friends, we recall the ideas of their worth with sensations that affect us yet more nearly, and feel an involuntary

---

160 And who later became Washington's Secretary of the Treasury on 11 Sept.1789. Also of note, in 1798 during the Quasi-War with France, President John Adams, under pressure from former Pres. Washington, with some reluctance appointed Hamilton Major General; effectively making him second only to Adams as head of the United States Army; hence we come across later contemporary references to "General Hamilton."

161 Greene had died reportedly of sunstroke, on the 19th of June 1786 at his Georgia home "Mulberry Grove," situated fourteen miles above Savannah.
~~~

propensity to consider their fame as our own. We seem to appropriate to ourselves the good they have done, to take a personal interest in the glory they have acquired, and to share in the very praise we bestow.

In entering upon a subject in which your feelings as well as my own are so deeply concerned, however it might become me to follow examples of humility, I shall refrain from a practice perhaps not less laudable than it is common. I cannot prevail upon myself to check the current of your sensibility by the cold formalities of an apology for the defects of the speaker. These can neither be concealed nor extenuated by the affectation of diffidence, nor even by the genuine concessions of conscious inability. 'Tis your command, and the reverence we all bear to the memory of him of whom I am to speak, that must constitute my excuse, and my claim to your indulgence. Did I even possess the powers of oratory, I should with reluctance attempt to employ them upon the present occasion. The native brilliancy of the diamond needs not the polish of art; the conspicuous features of pre-eminent merit need not the coloring pencil of imagination, nor the florid decorations of rhetoric.

From you who knew and loved him, I fear not the imputation of flattery, or enthusiasm, when I indulge an expectation, that the name of Greene will at once awaken in your minds the images of whatever is noble and estimable in human nature. The fidelity of the portrait I shall draw will therefore have nothing to apprehend from your sentence. But I dare not hope that it will meet with equal justice from all others, or that it will entirely escape the cavils of ignorance and the shafts of envy. For high as this great man stood in the estimation of his country, the whole extent of his worth was little known. The situations in which he has appeared, though such as would have measured the faculties and exhausted the resources of men who might justly challenge the epithet of great, were yet incompetent to the full display of those various, rare, and exalted endowments with which nature only now and then decorates a favorite, as if with intention to astonish mankind.

As a man, the virtues of Greene are admitted; as a patriot, he holds a place in the foremost rank; as a statesman, he is praised; as a soldier, he is admired. But in the two last characters, especially in the last but one, his reputation falls far below his desert. It required a longer life, and still greater opportunities, to have enabled him to exhibit, in full day, the vast, I had almost said the enormous, powers of his mind.

The termination of the American war -- not too soon for his wishes, nor for the welfare of his country, but too soon for his glory -- put an end to his military career. The sudden termination of his life cut him off from those scenes which the progress of a new, immense, and unsettled empire could not fail to open to the complete exertion of that universal and pervading genius which qualified him not less for the senate than for the field.

In forming our estimate, nevertheless, of his character, we are not left to supposition and conjecture. We are not left to vague indications or uncertain appearances, which partiality might varnish or prejudice discolor. We have a succession of deeds, as glorious as they are unequivocal, to attest his greatness and perpetuate the honors of his name.

It is an observation, as just as it is common, that in those great revolutions which occasionally convulse society, human nature never fails to be brought forward in its brightest as well as in its blackest colors; and it has very properly been ranked not among the least of the advantages which compensate for the evils they produce that they serve to bring to light, talents and virtues, which might otherwise have languished in obscurity, or only shot forth a few scattered and wandering rays.

NATHANIEL [sic] GREENE, descended from reputable parents, but not placed by birth in that elevated rank which, under a monarchy, is the only sure road to those employments that give activity and scope to abilities, must, in all probability, have contented himself with the humble lot of a private citizen, or, at most, with the contracted sphere of an elective office, in a colonial and dependent government, scarcely conscious of the resources of his own mind, had not the violated rights of his country called him to act a part on a more splendid and more ample theatre.

Happily for America, he hesitated not to obey the call. The vigor of his genius, corresponding with the importance of the prize to be contended for, overcame the natural moderation of his temper; and though not hurried on by enthusiasm, but animated by an enlightened sense of the value of free government, he cheerfully resolved to stake his fortune, his hopes, his life, and his honor upon an enterprise, of the danger of which he knew the whole magnitude; in a cause, which was worthy of the toils and of the blood of heroes.

The sword having been appealed to, at Lexington, as the arbiter of the controversy between Great Britain and America, Greene, shortly after, marched, at the head of a regiment, to join the American forces at Cambridge; determined to abide the awful decision.

He was not long there before the discerning eye of the American Fabius[162] marked him out as the object of his confidence.

His abilities entitled him to a pre-eminent share in the councils of his Chief. He gained it, and he preserved it, amidst all the *checkered varieties* of military vicissitude, and in defiance of all the intrigues of jealous and aspiring rivals.

As long as the measures which conducted us safely through the first most critical stages of the war shall be remembered with approbation; as long as the enterprises of Trenton and Princeton shall be regarded as the dawnings of that bright day which afterwards broke forth with such resplendent lustre; as long as the almost magic operations of the remainder of that memorable winter, distinguished not more by these events than by the extraordinary spectacle of a powerful army straitened within narrow limits by the phantom of a military force, and never permitted to transgress those limits with impunity, in which skill supplied the place of means, and disposition was the substitute for an army -- as long, I say, as these operations shall continue to be the objects of curiosity and wonder, so long ought the name of Greene to be revered by a grateful country. To attribute to him a portion of the praise which is due, as well to the formation as to the execution of the plans that effected these important ends, can be no derogation from that wisdom and magnanimity which knew how to select and embrace counsels worthy of being pursued.

The laurels of a Henry were never tarnished by the obligations he owed and acknowledged to a Sully.[163]

It would be an unpleasing task, and therefore I forbear to lift the veil from off those impotent councils, which, by a formal vote, had decreed an undisturbed passage to an enemy returning from the fairest fruits of his victories, to seek an asylum from impending danger, disheartened by retreat, dispirited by desertion, broken by fatigue, retiring through woods, defiles, morasses, in which his discipline was useless, in the face of an army superior in numbers, elated by pursuit, and ardent to signalize their courage. 'Tis enough for the honor of Greene to say, that he left nothing unessayed to avert and to frustrate so degrading a resolution. And it was happy for America, that the man, whose reputation could not be wounded without wounding the cause of his country, had the noble fortitude to rescue himself, and the army he commanded, from the disgrace with which they were both menaced by the characteristic imbecility of a council of war.

Unwilling to do more than merely to glance at a scene in which the meritorious might be involved with the guilty, in promiscuous censure, here let me drop the curtain, and invite you to accompany me to the Heights of Monmouth. There let me recall to your indignant view, the flower of the American infantry flying before an enemy that scarcely dared to pursue -- vanquished without a blow -- vanquished by their obedience to the commands of a leader who meditated their disgrace. Let me contrast with this the conduct of your Greene; the calm intrepidity and unshaken presence of mind with which he seconded the dispositions of his General, to arrest the progress of the disorder and retrieve the fortune of the day. Let me recall to your recollection that well-timed and happy movement on the left of the enemy, by which he so materially contributed to deciding the dubious event of the conflict, and turning the hesitating scale of victory.

---

[162] [*Edit. Note*. Gen. Washington.]

[163] [*Edit. Note*. Maximilien de Béthune, duc de Sully (1560–1641), Marshal of France, and prime minister and close advisor to Henry IV of France.]

From the Heights of Monmouth I might lead you to the Plains of Springfield, there to behold the veteran Knyphausen, at the head of a veteran army, baffled and almost beaten by a general without an army -- aided, or rather embarrassed, by small fugitive bodies of volunteer militia, the mimicry of soldiership!

But it would ill become me to detain you in the contemplation of objects diminutive in comparison with those that are to succeed.

Hitherto, we have seen the illustrious Greene acting in a subordinate capacity, the faint glimmerings of his fame absorbed and lost in the superior rays of a Washington. Happy was it for him to have been called to a more explicit station. Had this never been the case, the future historian, perplexed between the panegyric of friends and the satire of enemies, might have doubted in what colors to draw his true character. Accident, alone, saved a Greene from so equivocal a fate; a reflection which might damp the noble ardor of emulation, and check the towering flight of conscious merit.

The defeat of Camden, and the misfortune of Gates, opened the career of victory and of glory to Greene. Congress having resolved upon a successor to the former, the choice was left to the Commander-in-Chief, and fell upon the latter. In this destination, honorable in proportion as it was critical, he acquiesced with the mingled emotions of a great mind -- impelled by a sense of duty -- allured by the hope of fame -- apprised of the danger and precariousness of the situation, yet confident of its own strength, and animated by the magnitude of the object for which it was to be exerted.

Henceforth we are to view him on a more exalted eminence. He is no longer to figure in an ambiguous or secondary light; he is to shine forth the artificer of his own glory -- the leader of armies and the deliverer of States!

To estimate properly the value of his services, it is necessary to recur to the situation of the southern extremity of the Union at the time he entered upon the command in that quarter. Georgia and South Carolina subdued and overrun; the spirit of their people dejected and intimidated; the flame of resistance scarcely kept alive by the transient gleams of a few expiring embers; North Carolina distracted by the still recent effects of internal commotion, dreading the hostility of a considerable part of its own citizens, and depending, for its exertions, on the tried valor and patriotism of the rest, more than on the energy of a feeble and ill-organized government; Virginia, debilitated by the excessive efforts of its early zeal, and by the dissipation of its revenues and forces, in Indian hostilities, in domestic projects, encumbered by a numerous body of slaves, bound by all the laws of degraded humanity to hate their masters; deficient in order and vigor in its administration, and relying wholly, for immediate defence against threatened invasion, on the resources of a country, extensive, populous, and fertile, to be put in motion by the same ardent and magnanimous spirit which first lighted up the opposition to Great Britain, and set the glorious example of resistance to America. In such a situation what was to be hoped? What was to be hoped from a general without troops, without magazines, without money? A man of less depth of penetration or force of soul than Greene, would have recoiled at the prospect; but he, far from desponding, undertook the arduous task with firmness -- with a firmness which was the result of a well-informed estimate of a situation perilous but not desperate. He knew how much was to be expected from the efforts of men contending for the rights of man. He knew how much was to be performed by capacity, courage, and perseverance.

Not to be disconcerted by the most complicated embarrassments, nor the most discouraging prospects, he began, before he entered upon the duties of the field, by adjusting the outlines of the plan which was to regulate his future conduct; a plan conceived with as much wisdom, and so perfect a judgment of circumstances, that he never had occasion to depart from it in the progress of his subsequent operations. This alone might suffice to form the eulogium of his genius, and to demonstrate that he was an accomplished master in the science of military command.

His next care was to endeavor to impress the neighboring States with a proper sense of their situation, in order to induce them, with system and effect, to furnish the succors of which he stood in need. To urge the collection and accelerate the arrival of these, as well as to repel any invasion to which the State might be exposed, he stationed, in Virginia, the Baron de Steuben, an officer who merited and justified his confidence; and having made these preliminary arrangements, he hastened to put himself at the head of the inconsiderable remains of the southern army, which he joined at Charlotte, on the borders of North Carolina, destitute of every thing but courage, and an unconquerable attachment to the cause they had espoused.

To enter into a particular detail of the operations by which the Southern States were rescued from conquest and desolation, and the last project of Britain for the subjugation of America frustrated, would be to assume the province of the historian. This, neither the occasion, nor any reasonable claim to your indulgence, would justify. A general sketch is all that can, with propriety, be attempted, and shall limit my endeavors. To supply a necessitous army by coercion, and yet maintain the confidence and good-will of the coerced; this was among the first and not the least of the difficulties to be surmounted. But delicate and difficult as was the task, it was, nevertheless, accomplished. Conducted with system, moderation, and equity, even *military exactions* lost their rigor, and freemen venerated the hand that reluctantly stripped them of their property for their preservation.

Having concerted the arrangements requisite to this end, Greene, without further delay, entered upon that busy, complicated, and extraordinary scene, which may truly be said to form a phenomenon in war -- a scene which almost continually presents us, on the one hand, with victories ruinous to the victors; on the other, with retreats beneficial to the vanquished; which exhibits to our admiration a commander almost constantly obliged to relinquish the field to his adversary, yet as constantly making acquisitions upon him; beaten to-day; to-morrow, without a blow, compelling the conqueror to renounce the very object for which he had conquered, and, in a manner, to fly from the very foe he had subdued. Too weak, with his collected strength, to dispute the field with an enemy superior both in numbers and discipline, and urged by the necessity of giving activity to the natural force of the country, by rousing the inhabitants from the state of despondency into which they had sunk, with the prospect of succor and protection, Greene divided his little army into two parts: one of which he sent, under Morgan, into the western extremities of North Carolina; and, with the other, marched to Hicks' Creek.

This movement had the desired effect. The appearance of aid, magnified by advantages opportunely gained (though unimportant in themselves), rekindled the ardor of patriotic hope in the breasts of many who had begun to despair, and emboldened them to resume their arms, and again to repair to the standard of liberty.

Sensible of the importance of counteracting this policy of the American general, the British commander hesitated not about the part he should act. Directing his first attention towards the detachment under Morgan, and meditating a decisive blow against that corps, he committed the execution of the enterprise to Lieutenant-Colonel Tarleton, at the head of a thousand veterans. Tarleton, hitherto not less the favorite of fortune than of his chief, hastened to perform the welcome duty; anticipating an easy triumph over foes inferior both in numbers and discipline; and dreaming not of the reverse which was destined to confound his hopes, and even to sully the lustre of his former fame. In the very grasp of victory, when not to combat but to slaughter seemed all that remained to be done, the forward intrepidity of a [Lieut. Col. William] Washington, seconded by the cool, determined bravery of a [Lieut. Col. John Eager] Howard, snatched the trophy from his too eager and too exulting hand. He was discomfited and routed. The greater part of his followers were either killed or taken; and the remaining few, with himself, were glad to find safety in flight.

Here first the bright dawn of prosperity began to dispel that gloomy cloud which had for some time lowered over the Southern horizon! Thunderstruck at so unexpected a disaster, and ill able to spare so considerable a part of his force, Cornwallis resolved, at every sacrifice, to attempt the recovery of his captive troops. The trial of skilful exertion between the generals and of patient fortitude between the troops, to which that attempt gave occasion, was such as to render it difficult to pronounce to whom the palm of merit ought to be decreed. Abandoning whatever might impede the celerity of his motions, Cornwallis began and urged the pursuit of the detachment under Morgan, with a rapidity seldom equalled, never surpassed; while, on the other hand, the provident and active Greene spared no exertion to disappoint his enterprising adversary.

Anxious for the security of that detachment, with their prisoners, and desirous of affecting a reunion of his forces, now rendered necessary by a change of circumstances, he gave instant orders for the march of the body under his immediate command to Guilford Court-House; and hastened, in person, through the country, a hundred and fifty miles, to join General Morgan, whom he came up with on the banks of the Catawba. Thus, placed in front of the enemy, he was the better able to counteract their immediate design, and to direct the co-operation necessary to the intended junction. So well were his measures taken, that he succeeded in both objects. The prisoners were carried off in safety; and Guilford Court-House, the destined place of rendezvous, received and reunited the two divisions of the American army. Still, however, too weak to keep the field in the face of his enemy, a further retreat became inevitable. A resolution was accordingly taken to retire beyond the Dan. Here a new and not less arduous trial of skill ensued. To get between the American army and Virginia, intercept their supplies and reinforcements, and oblige them to fight on disadvantageous terms -- this now became the object of Cornwallis. With this view he directed his march into the upper country, where the rivers were fordable with facility; flattering himself that the depth of the waters below, and the want of boats, would oppose insuperable obstacles to the expeditious passage of the American troops. To retard the progress of the British army was, of course, an indispensable policy on the part of Greene. For this purpose, he practised every expedient which a mind, fertile in resource, could devise. And so efficacious were the expedients he adopted, that, surmounting all the impediments in his way, he completed his retreat across the Dan, without loss of men, baggage, or stores.

Such, nevertheless, was the energy of the pursuit, that in crossing the three principal rivers, the Catawba, the Yadkin, and the Dan, the British troops, in a manner, trod upon the heels of the American. In the passage of the last of the three, the van of the enemy's army reached one shore, almost at the very moment that the rear of ours landed on the opposite.

Cornwallis, upon this occasion, imitating Charles the Twelfth of Sweden, when the celebrated Schulenburgh made good his retreat across the Oder, in spite of the utmost efforts of that vigorous and enterprising monarch, might, with propriety, have exclaimed, This day, at least, Greene has conquered me! The art of retreating is perhaps the most difficult in the art of war. To have effected a retreat in the face of so ardent a pursuit, through so great an extent of country; through a country offering every obstacle, affording scarcely any resource; with troops destitute of every thing, who a great part of the way left the vestiges of their march in their own blood; -- to have done all this, I say, without loss of any kind may, without exaggeration, be denominated a masterpiece of military skill and exertion. Disappointed at his first aim, Cornwallis now retired from the Dan to Guilford Court-House. Having driven the American army out of North Carolina, he flattered himself that his efforts would at least be productive of the advantage of an accession of force, by encouraging the numerous royalists of that State to repair to his standard. Greene, not without apprehensions that the hopes of his competitor, in this respect, might be realized, lost not a moment, after receiving a small reinforcement from Virginia, in recrossing the Dan, to take post in the vicinity of the British army, and interrupt their communication with the country. Three weeks passed in a constant scene of military manoeuvre: Cornwallis, equally striving to bring his antagonist to an action; and Greene, adroitly endeavoring to elude it, yet without renouncing such a position as would enable him to prevent both supplies and reinforcements. On this occasion he played the part of Turenne; and he played it with complete success. The relative position which he took and maintained, and the tragical fate of a body of royalists, intercepted in their way to the British army, destroyed every prospect of that aid which they, not without reason, had promised themselves from their adherents in North Carolina.

Virginia, in the meantime, awakened by the presence of danger, exerted herself to reinforce the American army. Greene, speedily finding himself in a condition to outnumber his adversary, resolved to offer that battle which he had hitherto declined. He considered that, in the existing circumstances, a defeat must be, to the enemy, absolute ruin; while to him, from his superiority in cavalry, united with other advantages, it could be nothing more than a partial misfortune, and must be compensated at a price which the enemy could not afford to pay for it.

The two armies, now equally willing to try the fortune of a battle, met and engaged near Guilford Court-House. All that could be expected from able disposition towards insuring success, promised a favorable issue to the American arms. But superior discipline carried it against superior numbers and superior skill. Victory decreed the glory of the combat to the Britons; but Heaven, confirming the hopes of Greene, decreed the advantage of it to the Americans. Greene retired; Cornwallis kept the field. But Greene retired only three miles; and Cornwallis, in three days, abandoning the place where the laurels he had gained were a slender compensation for the loss he had suffered, withdrew to Wilmington on the sea-coast.

This victory cost him a large proportion of the flower of his army; and it cost him a [Lieut. Col. James] Webster.

Here occurred the problem, on the right solution of which depended the fame of Greene and the fate of the Southern States. There was every probability that the next movement of Cornwallis would be towards a junction with Arnold for the invasion of Virginia. Was the American general to keep pace with his adversary in his northern career, in order to resist his future enterprises? Or, was he to return into the field he had lately left, to endeavor to regain what had been there lost? The first, as the most obvious, and, in a personal light, the least perilous course, would have been thought the most eligible by an ordinary mind. But the last, as the wisest, though, to his own reputation, the most hazardous, appeared preferable to the comprehensive eye and adventurous spirit of a Greene.

On the one hand, he concluded, justly, that Virginia might safely be trusted to her own strength and resources, and to the aid which, if necessary, she might derive from the North, against all the force which the enemy were then able to employ in that quarter. On the other hand, he foresaw, that if South Carolina and Georgia should be abandoned to the situation in which they then were, they would quickly have abandoned themselves to despair; would have lost even the spirit of opposition; and might have been rendered, in several respects, subservient to the future progress of their conqueror. Under these impressions, he determined to return into South Carolina, to attempt the recovery of that and its neighboring State.

This was one of those strokes that denote superior genius, and constitute the sublime of war. 'Twas Scipio leaving Hannibal in Italy, to overcome him at Carthage!

The success was answerable to the judicious boldness of the design. The enemy were divested of their acquisitions in South Carolina and Georgia, with a rapidity which, if not ascertained, would scarcely be credible. In the short space of two months, all their posts in the interior of the country were reduced. The perseverance, courage, enterprise, and resource, displayed by the American general in the course of these events, commanded the admiration even of his enemies. In vain was he defeated in one mode of obtaining his object: another was instantly substituted that answered the end. In vain was he repulsed from before a besieged fortress: he immediately found other means of compelling its defenders to relinquish their stronghold. Where force failed, address and stratagem still won the prize.

Having deprived the enemy of all their posts in the interior of the country, and having wasted their forces in a variety of ways, Greene now thought himself in a condition to aim a decisive blow at the mutilated remains of the British army, and, at least, to oblige them to take refuge within the lines of Charleston. With this view he collected his forces into one body, and marched to give battle to the enemy, then stationed at the Springs of the Eutaw.

A general action took place. Animated, obstinate, and bloody was the contest. The front line of the American army, consisting of militia, after beginning a brisk attack, began to give way. At this critical and inauspicious juncture, Greene, with that collected intrepidity which never forsook him, gave orders to the second line, composed of Continentals, to advance to the charge with trailed arms. This order, enforced by example and executed with matchless composure and constancy, could not fail of success. The British veterans shrunk from the American bayonet. They were routed and pursued a considerable distance. Numbers of them fell into the hands of their pursuers, and the remainder were threatened with a similar fate; when, arriving at a position which, with peculiar advantages, invited to a fresh stand, they rallied and renewed the action. In vain did the intrepid [William] Washington, at the head of the pursuing detachment, redouble the efforts of his valor, to dislodge them from this new station. He was himself wounded and made a prisoner, and his followers, in their turn, compelled to retire.

But though the enemy, by an exertion of bravery which demands our esteem, saved themselves from the total ruin which was ready to overwhelm them, they had, nevertheless, received too severe a blow to attempt any longer to maintain a footing in the open country. They, accordingly, the day following, retreated towards Charleston, leaving behind them their wounded and a considerable quantity of arms. Here ended all serious offensive operations in the South! The predatory excursions which intervened between the battle of the Eutaw and the evacuation of Charleston and Savannah, deserve not a place in the catalogue of military achievements. But before we take leave of a scene as honorable as it was advantageous to the American arms, it behooves us to stop for a moment, to pay the tribute of merited applause to the memory of that gallant officer [Lieut. Col. Richard Campbell], who, at the head of the Virginia line, fell in this memorable conflict. More anxious, to the last, about his country than himself, in the very agonies of departing life, he eagerly inquired which of the contending parties prevailed; and having learned that his countrymen were victorious, he, like another Epaminondas,[164] yielded up his last breath in this noble exclamation: "*Then do I die contented*." Heroic Campbell! How enviable was such a death!

The evacuation of the two capitals of South Carolina and Georgia entirely restored those States to their own governments and laws. They now hailed the illustrious Greene as their defender and deliverer. Their gratitude was proportioned to the extent of the benefits resulting from his services; nor did it show itself in words only, but was manifested by acts that did honor to their generosity. Consecrated in the affections of their citizens to the remotest posterity, the fame of Greene will ever find in them a more durable, as well as a more flattering, memorial, than in the proudest monuments of marble or brass.

But where, alas, is now this consummate General; this brave Soldier; this discerning Statesman; this steady Patriot; this virtuous Citizen; this amiable Man? Why could not so many talents, so many virtues, so many bright and useful qualities, shield him from a premature grave? Why was he not longer spared to a country he so dearly loved; which he was so well able to serve; which still seems so much to stand in need of his services? Why was he only allowed to assist in laying the foundation, and not permitted to aid in rearing the superstructure, of American greatness? Such are the inquiries which our friendly, yet short-sighted, regrets would naturally suggest. But inquiries like these are to be discarded as presumptuous. 'Tis not for us to scan, but to submit, to the dispensations of Heaven. Let us content ourselves with revering the memory, imitating the virtues, and, as far as we dare, emulating the glory of the man, whom neither our warmest admiration, nor our fondest predilection, could protect from the fatal shaft. And as often as we indulge our sorrow for his loss, let us not fail to mingle the reflection, that he has left behind him, offspring who are the heirs to the friendship which we bore to the father, and who have a claim from many, if not from all of us, to cares not less than parental.

[164] [*Edit. Note.* (418-362 B.C.) Greek military innovator and victor of Leuctra (371 B.C.)]

THE BEST OF BURGOYNE

It is not a little ironic that one who so aspired to literary grace and popularity, and punctiliously sought positive public acceptance generally, should have been so roundly despised by some in consequence of his role in the Revolutionary War. Yet had Sir John Burgoyne, General, Member of Parliament (for Preston), and celebrated author, not participated in that conflict, it is more than likely that he, like Richard Brinsley Sheridan, would have come to be known to posterity as one of England's most beloved playwrights of his era. As it is the *Oxford Dictionary of Quotations* cites but one line from him, and which limiting would seem to more in consequence of Saratoga than his literary merit. For in truth, "Gentleman Johnny's" works, in all, hold up quite exquisitely, and he had a singular talent for composing enjoyable songs and lyrics; as well as a keen sense of the risible. Indeed, it is no little wonder his forbidding proclamation that inaugurated the upstate New York campaign (dated Camp Bouquet Ferry, June 20th, 1777) instantly invited satirical responses by the Americans, including a poem parody by Francis Hopkinson entitled "The Proclamation":[165] not only because of the incendiary nature of the thing, but because it contrasted with and acted as an ironic reminder of his efforts in stage comedy and operetta.

Even after leaving the war in America, he resumed his stage vocation with substantial success. Yet despite this, Saratoga had largely undone his literary career; just as it had utterly vanquished his one in the military. Which, again with regard to the former, is altogether unjust and a great shame; for here are dramatic writings suffused with of wit, humor, revelry, and pleasant sentiment – polished and not at all amateur or hack work. Of Burgoyne's play "The Heiress" (1786), Horace Walpole, who had hotly criticized the general during the war, stated: "Burgoyne's battles and speeches will be forgotten; but his delicious comedy...still continues the delight of the stage, and one of the most pleasing domestic compositions."

The title of this article is a bit tongue-in-cheek. Yet we thought we *would* try to present a sampling of Burgoyne's plays that will help give readers new to them a rudimentary idea of what they are like and about. For this reason, different extracts from the identical works might better have been selected. At the same time, the task of attempting to distill dramatic works by means of excerpts is sometimes a precarious venture and that typically leaves much to be desired. Moreover, Burgoyne wrote other, non-stage pieces that might also have been quoted from and included. This said, we hope the following provides readers with at least near as much and immense pleasure as we first had in discovering and reading them ourselves.

Finally there would seem to be some indirect yet deliberate references in the post-1777 plays to his military failure in America, and which latter apparently and not surprisingly had caused him no little personal grief. But respecting Saratoga, could not Howe, after all, have supported him much better than he did?

~~~***~~~

"THE MAID OF OAKS" (1774)

from Act I, scen. 1

Sir Harry. My own principle will answer my purpose just as well; with that perspective I have looked through the woman, and discovered the angel; and you will do the same when you see her, or never brag of your eyesight more.

Dupeley. Rhapsody and enthusiasm! -- I should as soon discover Mahomet's seventh heaven; but what says your uncle, Old Groveby, to this match?

Sir Harry. Faith I have asked him no questions, and why should I? when I know what must be his answer.

[165] At least that verse is ascribed to Hopkinson -- or alternatively, according to some sources, Gov. William Livingston of New Jersey. Hopkinson did in any event also write a prose satire on the same theme, and which is included in volume 1 of his *Miscellaneous Essays and Occasional Writings*, pp. 146-150.
~~~

Dupeley. Oh, he can never disapprove a passion that soars above the stars!

Sir Harry. He has all the prejudices of his years, and worldly knowledge; the common old gentleman's character -- You may see it in every drama from the days of Terence to those of Congreve; though not perhaps with quite so much good humour, and so little obstinacy as my uncle shews. He is ever most impetuous, when most kind; and I dare trust his resentment will end with a dramatic forgiveness. Should it not, I may have pride in the sacrifice of his estate, but no regret -- So much forfortune, Charles -- are there any other means to reconcile me to your approbation?

Dupeley. 'Gad I know but one more -- Have you laid any plan for succeeding at the divorce-shop next winter? It would be some comfort to your friends, to see you had a retreat in your head.

Sir Harry. Charles, I have listened to your raillery with more patience than it deserves, and should at last be out of humour with such an importation of conceit and affectation, if I was not sure our good sense would soon get the better of it. This is called knowing the world -- to form notions without, perhaps, ever seeing a man in his natural character, or conversing with a woman of principle; and then, for fear of being imposed upon, be really dup'd out of the most valuable feelings in human nature, confidence in friendship, and esteem in love.

----

from Act I, scen.2.

An outside Building, Workmen of all sorts passing to-and-fro.

Architect. [*As speaking to persons at work behind the side-scene*.] Come, bustle away, my lads, strike the scaffold, and then for the twelve o'clock tankard; up with the rest of the festoons there on the top of the columns.

First Gardener. Holloa! you sir, where are you running with those flowers?

Second Gardener. They're wanted for the Arcades; we can have no deceit there -- if you want store here, you may make them of paper -- anything will go off by candle-light.

First Lamp-lighter. [*Running*.] They want above a hundred more lamps yonder, for the illumination of the portico.

Second Lamp-lighter. Then they may get tallow-candles; I shan't have enough to make the sky clear in the saloon -- that damn'd Irish painter has made his ground so dingy, one might as soon make his head transparent as his portico.

Enter Irish Painter.

Painter. Arrah! what is that you say of my head, Mr. Lamp-lighter?

Second Lamp-lighter. I say you have spoil'd the transparency, by putting black where you should have put blue.

Painter. [*Dabbing his brush across his face*.] There's a black eye for you; and you may be thankful you got it so easily -- Trot away with your ladder upon your shoulder, or the devil fire we but you shall have black and blue both, my dear.

Architect. [*Returning*.] Good words, good words, gentlemen; no quarrelling -- Your servant, Mr. O'Daub; upon my word you have hit off those ornaments very well -- the first painter we have here could not have done better.

Painter. No, faith, I believe not, for all his hard name; sure O'Daub was a scene-painter before he was born, though I believe he is older than I too.

Architect. You a scene-painter!

Painter. Ay, by my soul was I, and for foreign countries too.

Architect. Where was that pray?

Painter. Faith, I painted a whole set for the Swish, who carries the Temple of Jerusalem about upon his back, and it made his fortune, though he got but a halfpenny a-piece for his show.

Architect. [*Ironically.*] I wish we had known your merits, you should certainly have been employ'd in greater parts of the work.

Painter. And, by my soul, it would have been better for you if you had -- I would have put out Mr. Lanterbug's stars with one dash of my pencil, by making them five times more bright -- Ho! if you had seen the sign of a setting sun, that I painted for a linendraper, in Bread-Street, in Dublin -- Devil burn me but the Auroree of O'Guide was a fool to it.

Architect. O'Guide! -- Who is he? Guid-o, I suppose you mean.

Painter. And if he has an O to his name, what signifies whether it comes before or behind -- Faith, I put it like my own of O'Daub, on the right side, to make him sound more like a gentleman -- besides it is more melodious in the mouth, honey.

Architect. Rest you merry, Master Carpenter -- take a draught of the 'Squire's liquor, and welcome, you shall swim in it, when all is over.

Painter. Faith let me have one merry quarter of an hour before we at it again, and it will be no loss of time neither -- we will make the next quarter after, as good as an hour -- and so his honour and the *sham-peter* will gain by the loss.

First Gardener. Well said, O'Daub! and if you will give us the song you made, the quarter of an hour will be merrier still.

Architect. Can you rhyme, O'Daub?

Painter. Yes, faith, as well as paint -- all the difference is, I do one with a brush, and t' other with a pen; I do one with my head, and both with my hands -- and if any of the poets of 'em all can produce better rhymes and raisins too within the gardens, I'll be content to have one of my own brushes ramm'd down my throat, and so spoil me for a singer as well as a poet hereafter.

Architect. Well said, Master Painter!

----

from Act II, scen.1.

Lady Bab.... -- Well, Mr. Oldworth, I am delighted with the idea of your Fête; it is so novel, so French, so expressive of what every body understands, and no body can explain; then there is something so spirited in an undertaking of expence, where a shower of rain would spoil it all.

Oldworth. I did not expect to escape from so fine a lady, but you and the world have free leave to comment upon all you see here.

'Laugh where you must, be candid where you can.'

I only hope that to celebrate a joyful event upon any plan, that neither hurts the morals nor politeness of the company, and at the same time sets thousands of the industrious to work, cannot be thought blame-worthy.

Lady Bab. Oh, quite the contrary, and I am sure it will have a run; a force upon the seasons and the manners is the true test of a refined taste, and it holds good from a cucumber at Christmas, to an Italian opera.

Maria. Is the rule the same among the ladies, Lady Bab? Is it also a definition of their refinement to act in all things contrary to nature?

Lady Bab. Not absolutely in all things, though more so than people are apt to imagine; for even in circumstances that seem most natural, fashion prompts ten times, where inclination prompts once; and there would be an end of gallantry at once in this country, if it was not for the sake of reputation.

Oldworth. What do you mean?

Lady Bab. Why, that a woman without a connection grows every day a more awkward personage; one might as well go into company without powder -- if one does not really despise old vulgar prejudices, it is absolutely necessary to affect it, or one must sit at home alone.

Oldworth. Indeed!

Lady Bab. Yes, like Lady Sprose, and talk morals to the parrot.

Maria. This is new, indeed; I always supposed that in places where freedom of manners was most countenanced, a woman pf unimpeached conduct carried a certain respect.

Lady Bab. Only fit for sheep-walks and *Oakeries* -- I beg your pardon, Mr. Oldworth -- in town it would just raise you to the whist-party of old Lady Cypher, Mrs. Squabble, and Lord Flimzey; and at every public place, you would stand amongst the footmen to call your own chair, while all the macaronies passed by, whistling a song through their tooth-picks, and giving a shrug -- 'Dem it, 'tis a pity that so fine a woman shou'd be lost to all common decency.'

Maria. [*Smiling*.] I believe I had better stay in the Oakery, as you call it; for I am afraid I shall never procure any *civility* in town, upon the terms required.

Lady Bab. Oh, my dear, yon have chose a horrid word to express the intercourse of the bon ton; *civility* may be very proper in a mercer, when one is choosing a silk, but familiarity is the life of good company. I believe this is quite new since your time, Mr. Oldworth, but 'tis by far the greatest improvement the beau monde ever made.

Oldworth. A certain ease was always an essential part of good breeding; but Lady Bab must explain her meaning a little further, before we can decide upon the improvement.

Lady Bab. I mean that participation of society, in which the French used to excel, and we have now so much outdone our models -- I maintain, that among the *superior set* -- mind, I only speak of them -- our men and women are put more upon a footing together in London, than they ever were before in any age or country.

Oldworth. And pray how has this happy revolution been effected ?

Lady Bab. By the most charging of all institutions, wherein we shew the world, that liberty is as well understood by our women as by our men; we have our *Bill of Rights* and our *Constitution* too, as well as they -- we drop in at all hours, play at all parties, pay our own reckonings, and in every circumstance (petticoats excepted) are true, lively jolly fellows.

----

from Act II, scen.1.

Enter first SHEPHERD, *very gaily, followed by a group of Shepherds and Shepherdesses.*

SONG.

Shepherd.

Hither, ye swains, with dance and song,
      Join your bands in sportive measure;
Hither, ye swains, with dance and song,
      Merrily, merrily, trip it along:
'Tis holiday, lads, from the cares of your tillage,
Life, health, and joy, to the lord of the village.
            Scenes of delight,
            Round you invite,
      Harmony, beauty, love, and pleasure:
Hither, ye swains, with dance and song.
      Join your bands in sportive measure,
Chorus. -- Hither ye swains, &c.

Shepherdess.

Hither, ye nymphs, and scatter around
      Every sweet the spring discloses;
Hither, ye nymphs, and scatter them round.
      With the bloom of the hour enamel the ground:
The feast of the day is devoted to beauty.
Sorrow is treason, and pleasure a duty:
            Love shall preside,
            Sovereign guide!
      Fetter his winks with links of roses:
Hither, ye nymphs, and scatter around
      Every sweet the spring discloses.
            Chorus. -- Hither ye nymphs, &c.

Both.

Lasses and lads, with dance and song.
      Join your bands in sportive measure:
Lasses and lads, with dance and song,
      Merrily, merrily trip it along:
An hour of youth is worth ages of reason,
'Tis the sunshine of life, take the gift of the season;
            Scenes of delight,
            Round you invite.
      Harmony, beauty, love, and pleasure.
            Chorus. -- Lasses and lads, &c.

Hurry. So much for singing, and now for dancing; pray give 'em room, ladies and gentlemen.

[*Here a grand dance of Shepherds and Shepherdesses.*

----

from Act III, scen 3.

SCENE III. *A Flower Garden.*

Enter Lady Bab, dressed as a Shepherdess, passing over the Stage, Oldworth *following.*

Oldworth. Hist, hist. Lady Bab. Here comes your prize ; for the sake of mirth, and the revenge of your sex, don't miss the opportunity.

Lady Bab. Not for the world; you see I am dress'd for the purpose. I have been out of my wits this half hour, for fear the scene should be lost, by interruption of the company -- what, is that he?

Oldworth. Yes, he is looking out for us.

Lady Bab. Step behind that stump of shrubs, and you shall see what an excellent actress I should have made, if fortune had not luckily brought me into the world an earl's daughter.

Oldworth. Don't be too hasty, for it is a pity Sir, Harry should not be a witness; he owes him vengeance too.

Lady Bab. Away, away.

[*Exit Oldworth. -- Lady Bab retires to a corner of the stage.*

Enter Dupeley.

Dupeley. Where the devil is Sir Harry? this is certainly the place where I was appointed to find him; but I suppose I shall spring him and his bride from under a rose-bush by and by, like two pheasants in pairing-time -- [*Observing Lady Bab.*] Hah! I wish that was a piece of game, she should not want a mate: is that a dress now for the day, or is she one of the natives of this extraordinary region? -- Oh! I see now, it is all pure Arcadian; her eyes have been used to nothing but daisy hunting; they are as awkward to her, when she looks at a man, as her elbows would be in a French Berline.

Lady Bab. [*Aside.*] My spark does not seem to want observation, he is only deficient in expression; but I will help him to that presently. Now to my character. [*Settles herself.*

Dupeley. [*Aside.*] What a neck she has! how beautifully nature works, when she is not spoil'd by a damn'd town stay-maker; what a pity she is so awkward! I hope she is not foolish.

[*During this observation, he keeps his eye fixed upon her neck; Lady Bab looks first at him, then at herself; unpins her nose-gay, and with an air of the most perfect naiveté; presents it to him.*

Lady Bab. You seem to wish for my nosegay, sir, it is much at your service.

[*Offers the flower and curtseys awkwardly.*

Dupeley. Oh, the charming innocent! -- my wishes extend a little further. A thousand thanks, my fair one; I accept it as a faint image of your own sweets. To whom am I so much obliged?

Lady Bab. To the garden-man, to be sure; he has made flowers to grow all over the garden, and they smell so sweet; pray smell 'em, they are charming sweet I assure you, and have such fine colours -- law! you are a fine nosegay yourself, I think. [*Simpers and looks at him*.

Dupeley. Exquisite simplicity! [*Half aside*.] sweet contrast to fashionable affectation -- Ah, I knew at first glance you were a compound of innocence and sensibility.

Lady Bab. Lack-a-dazy heart! how could you hit upon my temper so exactly?

Dupeley. By a certain instinct I have; for I have seen few, or none of the sort before; but, my dear girl, what is your name and situation?

Lady Bab. Situation!

Dupeley. Ay, what are you?

Lady Bab. I am a bridemaid [sic].

Dupeley. But, my sweet image of simplicity, when you are not a bridemaid, what is your way of life? how do you pass your time?

Lady Bab. I rise with the lark, keep my hands always employed, dance upon a holiday, and eat brown bread with content. [*With an innocent curtsey*.

Dupeley. O, the delicious description ! -- beachen shades, bleating flocks, and pipes, and pastorals. [*Aside*.] What an acquisition to my fame, as well as pleasure, to carry off this quintessence of Champétre! -- 'tis but an annuity job -- I'll do it.

[*During this soliloquy she examines him round and round*.

Lady Bab. And pray, what may you be? for I never saw any thing so out of the way in all my life! -- he, he, he! [*Simpering*.

Dupeley. Me, my dear -- I am a gentleman.

----

from Act V, scen 1.

[*Short flourish of instruments*.

VAUDEVILLE.

SHEPHERD.

Ye fine fangled folks, who from cities and courts,
    By your presence enliven the fields,
Accept for your welcome the innocent sports,
    And the fruits that our industry yields.
        Chorus. -- Ye fine fangled folks, &c.

No temple we raise to the idol of wealth,
    No altar to interest smokes,
To the blessings of love, kind seasons and health
    Is devoted the Feast of the Oaks.

Chorus. -- No temple we raise, &c.

SHEPHERDESS.

From the thicket and plain, each favourite haunt.
The villagers hasten away.
Your encouraging smile is the bounty they want.
To compensate the toils of the day.
Chorus. -- From the thicket, &c.

The milk-maid abandons her pail and her cow,
In the furrow the ploughman unyokes,
From the valley and meadow all press to the brow,
To assist at the Feast of the Oaks.
Chorus. -- The milk-maid, &c.

SHEPHERD.

The precept we teach b contentment and truth.
That our girls may not learn to beguile,
By reason to govern the pleasures of youth,
And decorate age with a smile.
Chorus. -- The precept we teach, &c.

No serpent approaches with venomous tooth.
No raven with ominous croaks,
Nor rancorous critic, more fatal than both.
Shall poison the Feast of the Oaks.
Chorus. --- No serpent approaches, &c.

SHEPHERDESS.

Bring roses and myrtles, new circlets to weave.
Ply the flutes in new measures to move,
And lengthen the song to the star of the eve,
The favouring planet of love.
Chorus. -- Bring roses and myrtles, &c.

Oh, Venus! propitious attend to the lay,
Each shepherd the blessing invokes;
May he who is true, like the youth of to-day,
Find a prize like the Maid of the Oaks.
Chorus. -- Oh, Venus! propitious, &c.

Druid. [*Stopping the Musicians.*]

Yet hold -- though Druid now no more,
He's wrong who thinks my spells are o'er,
Thus midst you all I throw them round,
Oh, may they fell on genial ground!
May ev'ry breast their influence prove!
The magic lies in truth of Love.
'Tis that irradiates ev'ry scene,
Restores from clouds the blue serene,
And makes, without a regal dome,
A palace of each humble home.

[*The whole finishes with* -- A Grand Dance.

~~~***~~~

"THE LORD OF THE MANOR" (1780)

from Act I, scen. 1

Rashly. Our claims were upon the *virtues*, not the weaknesses of the heart; and when they failed, obscurity was not only choice but prudence. Why give our children the name and knowledge of a rank, that might alienate their minds from the humble life to which they were destined?

Rental. What a sacrifice! how strange this situation must have appeared to you at first!

Rashly. My Anna was equally fitted for a cottage or a court. Her person, her accomplishments, her temper -- the universal charm of her society, made our new life a constant source of delight --

..............'The desert smil'd.
And Paradise was open'd in the wild.'

Encompass'd in an angel's frame.
    An angel's virtues lay;
Too soon did heav'n assert the claim,
    And call its own away.

My Anna's worth, my Anna's charms,
    Must never more return!
What now shall fill these widow'd arms?
    Ah, me I my Anna's urn!

Rental. Not so, my good sir, you have two living images of her; and for their sakes you must try to work upon this old obdurate -- Heaven has sent you together for that purpose.

Rashly. No, my friend; he is inflexibility itself -- I mean to fly him -- it must be your part to dispose of my farm and little property.

Rental. Your intention is too hasty -- I pretend to no skill in plotting, but I think I see my way clearly in your case -- dear sir, be advised by me --

----

from Act I, scen. 2

Annette. Dear sister, sing the song my father made upon a butterfly -- I have laugh'd at the insect ever since.

[Sophia *sings*]

Hence, reveller of tinsel wing.
Insipid, senseless, trifling thing;
Light spendthrift of thy single day.
Pert insignificance, away!

How joyless to thy touch or taste
Seems all the spring's profuse repast;
~~~

Thy busy, restless varied range
Can only pall the sense by change.

----

from Act I, scen. 3

SCENE III. *The Outside of the House*.

Enter Contrast, La Nippe, *and Huntsmen*.

La Nippe. The huntsmen, sir, have been practising a new chorus song; will you hear it?

Contrast. A hunting song quite breaks my ears, it is a continued yell of *horn* and *morn*, *wake the day* and *hark away* -- but they may begin; I shall hear enough as I walk off.

When the orient beam first pierces the dawn.
And printless yet glistens the dew on the lawn.
We rise to the call of the horn and the hound,
And Nature herself seems to live in the sound.

CHORUS.

Repeat it, quick Echo, the cry is begun,
The game is on foot, boys, we'll hunt down the
sun.

The Chase of old Britons was ever the care,
Their sinews it brac'd, 'twas the image of war.
Like theirs shall our vigour by exercise grow,
Till we turn our pursuit to our country's foe.

CHORUS.

Repeat it, shrill Echo, the war is begun.
The foe is on foot, boys, we'll fight down the
sun.

With spirits thus fir'd, to sleep were a shame,
Night only approaches to alter the game.
Diana's bright crescent fair Venus shall grace.
And from a new goddess invite a new chase.

CHORUS.

Be silent, fond Echo, the whisper's begun,
The game is on foot, boys, we want not the sun.

[*Exeunt*.

----

from Act II, scen. 1

SCENE I. *A Shrubbery*.
Enter Sophia *and* Annette, *arm in arm*.

Sophia. I CONFESS, Annette, you are a very forward scholar in affairs of the heart: but would you really persuade me, that the women in France scorn to be in love?

Annette. Just the contrary. Love, there, is the passion of all ages. One learns to lisp it in the cradle; and they will trifle with it at the brink of the grave; but it is always the cherup [sic] of life, not the moping malady, as it is here.

Sophia. And according to the notions of that fantastical people, how is the passion to be shewn?

Annette. Oh! in a woman, by any thing but confessing it.

Sophia. Surely, Annette, you must now be wrong: insincerity and artifice may, for aught I know, be the vices of fine folks in courts and cities; but in the rural scenes, where you as well as myself have been bred, I am persuaded the tongue and the heart go together in all countries alike.

Annette. So they may too: it would be wrong if the tongue told fibs of the heart; but what occasion for telling *all* the truth? -- I wish you saw a girl in Provence as she trips down the mountain with a basket of grapes upon her head, and all her swains about her, with a glance at one, and a nod at another, and a tap to a third -- 'till up rises the moon, and up strikes the tabor and pipe -- away go the baskets – *'Adieu panniers, Vendage est faite!'* -- her heart dances faster than her feet, and she makes ten lads happy instead of one, by each thinking himself the favourite.

Sophia. But the real favourite is not to be in suspense for ever?

Annette. No, no; she solves the mystery at last, but in a lively key. -- [*"A short French song."*]

Sophia. I admire your vivacity, Annette; but I dislike your maxims. For my part, I scorn even the shadow of deceit towards the man I love, and would sooner die than give him pain.

Annette. So wou'd I too, dear sister -- but why not bestow pleasures with a smile?

Sophia. Giddy girl -- you know not love.

Annette. Oh ! but you are mistaken -- I understand sentiment perfectly, and could act It to admiration. I cou'd gaze at the moon, prattle to the evening breeze, and make a companion of a rose for hours together -- "only I don't like to prick my fingers "with it" – *à propos* now; here's a charming bush in full blow, and you shall hear me address it exactly in your character -- [*Sings to a rose.*

Rest, beauteous flow'r, and bloom anew,
  To court my passing love;
Glow in his eyes with brighter hue.
  And all thy form improve.

And while thy balmy odours steal
  To meet his equal breath.
Let thy soft blush for mine reveal
  The imprinted kiss beneath.

Sophia. Get you gone, you trifler -- you'll make me angry.

Annette. Well, I'll only stroll with you as far as yonder great tree, and leave you to kiss the rest of the roses to the same tune. [*Exeunt.*

Sophia. Sir, I have tried while I could to treat you with some degree of respect -- you put it out of my power -- resentment and contempt are the only --

Contrast. Clarissa Harlow[166] in her altitudes! -- what circulating library has supplied you with language and action upon this occasion? or has your antiquated father instructed you, as he has me, in the mode of his days? -- Things are reversed, my dear -- when we fellows of superior class shew ourselves, the women throw themselves at us; and happy is she we deign to catch in our arms. [*Offers to take hold of her.*

Sophia. [*Enraged; and at last bursting into a passion of tears.*] Unheard-of assurance! What do you see m me to encourage such insolence? Or is it the very baseness of your nature, that insults a woman because she has no protector? [*Breaks from him -- at the instant,*

Enter Trumore.

Trumore. Protection is not so distant as you imagined -- compose yourself, my Sophia -- I have heard all -- cleave to me to settle the difference with this unworthy ruffian.

Contrast. Way-laid, by all that's desperate -- a rustic bully -- but I must submit, for I conclude he has a forest mob within call.

Trumore. A mob to encounter thee! -- a mob of fleas -- of gnats -- of pismires -- a wasp would be a sure assassin. -- But to be serious, sir -- though the brutality of your behaviour calls for chastisement, the meanness of it places you beneath resentment.

Contrast. How he assumes! because I know as little of a quarter-staff, as he of the weapons of a gentleman.

Trumore. It would indeed be profanation of English oak to put it into such hands -- thou outside without a heart -- when the mind is nerveless, the figure of a man may be cudgelled with a nettle.

Sophia. For heaven's sake, Trumore, be not violent, you make me tremble -- no further quarrel.

Trumore. Another word, sir, and no more -- could I suppose you a real sample of our fashionable youth, I should think my country indeed degraded -- but it cannot be -- away! -- and tell your few fellows, if even few exist, that there is still spirit enough among common people to defend beauty and innocence; and when such as you dare affronts like these, it is not rank nor estate, nor even effeminacy, that shall save them.

Contrast. Very sententious truly -- quite Rashly's flourish, -- In Italy now I could have this fellow put under ground for a sequin -- in this damned country, we can do nothing but despise him. Boxing was once genteel; but till the fashion returns, it would be as low to accept the challenge of a vulgar as to refuse it to an equal. [*Exit.*

Trumore. How is my Sophia? happy, happy moment that brought me to your rescue!

Sophia. If the thoughts you most wish I should entertain of my deliverer can repay you, trace them by your own heart, Trumore; they will harmonize with its tenderest emotions.

Trumore. Oh, the rapture of my Sophia's preference! thus let me pour forth my gratitude.
[*Kneeling y and kissing her hand.*

----

[166] [*Edit. Note.* In reference to the central character of Samuel Richardson's widely popular and influential novel, *Clarissa* (1748).]

from Act II, scen. 2

Rashly. Be comforted, Sophia, with the reflection, that I lament, and do not blame your attachment; you know I agree, both upon experience and principle, that the only basis for happiness in every station of life is disinterested love.

When first this humble roof I knew.
With various cares I strove;
My grain was scarce, my sheep were few,
My all of wealth was love.

By mutual toil our board was dress'd ;
The stream our drink bestow'd ;
But, when her lips tlie brim had press*d,
The cup with Nectar flow'd.

Content and Peace the dwelling shar'd,
No other guest came nigh,
In them was given, though gold was spar'd.
What gold could never buy.

No value has a splendid lot
But as the means to prove,
That from the castle to the cot
The all of life was love.

----

from Act III, scen. 2

Rental. By your dress you should belong to the army; pray, sir, what is your real business?

Trepan. I am a manufacturer of honour and glory -- vulgarly call'd a recruiting dealer -- or, more vulgarly still, a skin merchant. I come to a country wake as to a good market -- a little patience, and you shall see my practice -- come, paste up more bills -- and the devices -- they are not half thick enough – where's the lion rampant, with a grenadier's cap upon his head?

First Workman. Here, sir, here.

Trepan. And the marine device?

Second Workman. Here it is -- done to life -- the prize boarded; the decks running with arrack punch, and dammed up with gold dust.

Trepan. Right, lad, place that next the lion. I don't see the London tailor with his foot upon the neck of the French king.

Third Workman. Here he is in all his glory.

Trepan. Paste him up on the other flank of the lion -- so, so, pretty well -- what have you left for the corner?

Fourth Workman. The East-Indies, Captain, a nabob in triumph, throwing rough diamonds to the young fifers to play at marbles..

Trepan. [*To Rental*.] Very well, very well -- sir, how do you like my shop? "the wall" -- See how my new Colonels stand over the old ones, with their names in capitals as tall as their spontoons.

Rental. Arranged with a great deal of fancy indeed.

Trepan. Aye, and meaning too -- I can tell you -- but do only look at my recruits -- do but look at them -- [*Crimp gives the word March*.] there's stuff for all work -- southern rangers, and northern hunters -- lowlanders and highlanders, and loyals and royals, and chasseurs and dasheurs -- I suppose now you would like such a fellow as that. [*Pointing at a smart recruit*.

Rental. It is a thousand pities he should be shot at.

Trepan. Be in no apprehension, he'll never die by powder.

Rental. What do you mean?

Trepan. Lord help you! how you might be imposed upon -- he's my decoy-duck -- mere shew goods for the shop-window -- not an inch of wear and tear in the whole piece. The dog inherited desertion from his family. His brother was called Quicksilver Jack, he was hanged at last at Berlin, after having served six different princes in the same pair of shoes.

Crimp. [*To Trepan*.] Here's a fine set of country fellows getting round us, a march and a song might do well.

Trepan. [*Aside*.] You are right! -- [*Aloud*.] Come, my lads, we'll give you a taste of a soldier's life. Corporal Snap, give them the song our officers used to be so fond of; it will please their sweet-hearts as well as themselves -- strike up drums.

[*Corporal Snap sings*.]

Gallant comrades of the blade,
   Pay your vows to beauty;
Mars's [sic] toils are best repaid
   In the arms of beauty.

With the myrtle mix the vine,
   Round the laurel let them twine;
Then to glory, love, and wine
   Pay alternate duty.

CHORUS.

Gallant comrades, &c.

----

from Act III, scen. 3.

Sophia. Oh my fears! what means that ribband in your hat?

Trumore. The ensign of honour, when worn upon true principles, A passion for our country is the only one that ought to have competition with virtuous love -- when they unite in the heart our actions are inspiration.

From thine eyes imbibing fire,
   I a conqueror mean to prove;
Or with brighter fame expire.
   For my country and my love:

But ambition's promise over.
   One from thee I still shall crave;
Light the turf my head shall cover
   With thy pity on my grave.

Sophia. Trumore, this is too much for me -- heaven knows how little I am formed for the relish of ambition -- these heroic notions, how often do they lead to the misery of ourselves! -- of those we leave! --I claim no merit in my apprehensions -- alas they are too selfish.

~~~***~~~

"THE HEIRESS" (1786)

from Act 1, scen. 1.

Blandish. Thank you, my dear Letty; this is not the only tap you have hit me to-day, and you are right; for if you and I did not sometimes speak truth to each other, we should forget there was such a quality incident to the human mind. [*Exeunt.*

----

from Act 1, scen. 2.

SCENE II. -- *Lord Gayville's Apartment.*

Lord Gayville. She [i.e., Miss Alton] has never known me, but by the name of Mr. Heartly. Since my ambition has been to be loved for my own sake, I have been jealous of my title.

Enter Prompt.
[*Starts at seeing his master.*

Lord Gayville. Don't be afraid, Prompt -- your peace is made.

Prompt. Then there is my return for your lordship's goodness. [*Giving the letter.*] This letter was just now brought to the place appointed, by a porter.

Lord Gayville. By a cupid, honest Prompt, and these characters were engraved by the point of his arrow! [*Kissing the superscription.*] "To -- Heartly, Esq." Blandish, did you ever see any thing like it?

Blandish. If her style be equal to her hand-writing

Lord Gayville. If it be equal! -- Infidel! you shall have proof directly. [*Opens the letter precipitately.*] Hey-day! what the devil's here? my bills again, and no line -- not a word -- Death and disappointment, what's this!

Prompt. 'Gad, it's well if she is not off again -- 'faith, I never asked where the letter came from.

Lord Gayville. Should you know the messenger again?
~~~

Prompt. I believe I should, my lord. For a cupid he was somewhat in years, about six feet high, and a nose rather given to purple.

Lord Gayville. Spare your wit, sir, till you find him.

Prompt. I have a shorter way -- my life upon it I start her myself.

Blandish. And what is your device, sirrah?

Prompt. Lord, sir, nothing so easy as to bring every living creature in this town to the window: a tame bear, or a mad ox; two men, or two dogs fighting; a balloon in the air -- (or tied up to the ceiling, 'tis the same thing) -- make but noise enough, and out they come, first and second childhood, and every thing between -- I am sure I shall know her by inspiration.

Lord Gayville. Shall I describe her to you?

Prompt. No, my lord, time is too precious—I'll be at her last lodgings, and afterwards half the town over, before your lordship will travel from her forehead to her chin.

Lord Gayville. Away, then, my good fellow. He cannot mistake her; for when she was formed, nature broke the mould. [*Exit Prompt*.

----

from Act II, scen. 1.

Sir Clement. Emily, I protest you seem to study after me; proceed, child, and we will read together every character that comes in our way.

Lady Emily. Read one's acquaintance -- delightful! What romances, novels, satires, and mock heroics present themselves to my imagination! Our young men are flimsy essays; old ones, political pamphlets; coquets, fugitive pieces; and fashionable beauties, a compilation of advertised perfumery, essence of pearl, milk of roses, and Olympian dew. Lord, I should now and then though turn over an acquaintance with a sort of fear and trembling.

Clifford. How so?

Lady Emily. Lest one should pop unaware upon something one should not, like a naughty speech in an old comedy; but it is only skipping what would make one blush.

Sir Clement. Or if you did not skip, when a woman reads by herself, and to herself, there are wicked philosophers, who doubt whether her blushes are very troublesome.

Lady Emily. [*To Sir Clement*.] Do you know now that for that speech of yours -- and for that saucy smile of yours. [*To Clifford*.] I am strongly tempted to read you both aloud!

Sir Clement. Come try I'll be the first to open the book.

Lady Emily. A treatise of the Houyhnhnms, after the manner of Swift, tending to make us odious to ourselves, and to extract morose mirth from our imperfections. -- [*Turning to Clifford*.] Contrasted with an exposition of ancient morality addressed to the moderns: a chimerical attempt upon an obsolete subject.

Sir Clement. We must double down that page. And now we'll have a specimen of her ladyship.

Lady Emily. I'll give it you myself, and with justice; which is more than either of you would.

Sir Clement. And without skipping.

Sir Clement. But your uncle, the present lord, made amends?

Clifford. Amply. He offered to send me from Cambridge to an academy in Germany, to fit me for foreign service: well judging that a cannon ball was a fair and quick provision for a poor relation.

Sir Clement. Upon my word I have known uncles less considerate.

Sir Clement. You need not go out of the room for that purpose. The schedule of an heiress's fortune is a compendium of her merits, and the true security for marriage happiness.

Lady Emily. I am sure I guess at your system -- That union must be most wise, which has wealth to support it, and no affections to disturb it. Sir Clement. Right.

Lady Emily. That makes a divorce the first promise of wedlock; and widowhood the best blessing of life; that separates the interest of husband, wife, and child

Sir Clement. To establish the independent comfort of all --

Lady Emily. Upon the broad basis of family hatred. Excellent, my dear uncle, excellent indeed; and upon that principle, though the lady is likely to be your niece, and my sister, I am sure you will have no objection to my laughing at her a little.

Sir Clement. You'll be puzzled to make her more ridiculous than I think her. What is your plan?

Lady Emily. Why, though her pride is to be thought a leader in fashions, she is sometimes a servile copyist. Blandish tells me I am her principal model; and what is most provoking, she is intent upon catching my manner as well as my dress, which she exaggerates to an excess that vexes me. Now if she will take me in shade, I'll give her a new outline, I am resolved; and if I do not make her a caricature for a printshop.

Sir Clement. Well, Clifford! What do you think of her [i.e., Lady Emily]?

Clifford. That when she professes ill-temper, she. is a very awkward counterfeit.

Sir Clement. But her beauty, her wit, her improvement, since you went abroad? I expected from a man of your age and taste, something more than a cold compliment upon her temper. Could not you, compatibly with the immaculate sincerity you profess, venture as far as admiration?

Clifford. I admire her, sir, as I do a bright star in the firmament, and consider the distance of both as equally immeasurable.

Sir Clement. [*Aside*.] Specious rogue! [To him.] Well, leave Emily then to be winked at through telescopes; and now to a matter of nearer observation. What is Gayville doing?

----

from Act III, scen. 1.

Miss Alton. [*Aside*.] A very strange old man. [*To him, more confused*.] Sir, you'll pardon me, I believe Miss Alscrip is waiting.

Alscrip. Don't be afraid, my dear, enchanting diffident (zounds, what a flutter am I in!) don't be afraid -- my disposition, to be sure, is too susceptible; but then it is likewise so dove-like, so tender, and so innocent. Come, play me that tune, and enchant my ear, as you have done my eye.

Miss Alton. Sir, I wish to be excused, indeed it does not deserve your attention.

Alscrip. Not deserve it! I had rather hear you, than all the signoritininies together. -- These are the strings to which my senses shall dance. [*Sets the harp.*

Miss Alton. Sir, it is to avoid the affectation of refusing what is so little worth asking for.

[*Takes the harp and plays a few bars of a lively air. Alscrip kisses her fingers with rapture.*

Alscrip. Oh ! the sweet little twiddle-diddles!

Miss Alton. For shame, sir, what do you mean?

[*Alscrip gets hold of both her hands and continues kissing her fingers.*

Miss Alton. [*Struggling.*] Help!

Enter Miss Alscrip.

Miss Alscrip. I wonder what my papa is doing all this time?

[*A short pause --Miss Alscrip surprised -- Miss Alton confused. -- Alscrip puts his hand to his eye.*

Alscrip. Oh, child! I have got something in my eye, that makes me almost mad. -- A little midge -- I believe. -- 'Gad, I caught hold of this young lady's hand in one of my twitches, and her nerves were as much in a flutter as if I had bit her.

Miss Alscrip. [*Significantly.*] Yes, my dear papa, I perceive you have something in your eye, and I'll do my best to take it out immediately Miss Alton, will you do me the favour to walk into the drawing room?

Miss Alton. I hope, madam, you will permit me, at a proper opportunity, to give my explanation of what has passed? [*Retires.*

Miss Alscrip. There's no occasion -- Let it rest among the catalogue of wonders, like the Glastonbury thorn, that blooms at Christmas. To be serious, papa, though I carried off your behaviour as well as I could, I am really shocked at it -- A man of your years, and of a profession where the opinion of the world is of such consequence!

Alscrip. My dear Molly, have not I quitted the practice of attorney, and turned fine gentleman, to laugh at the world's opinion; or, had I not, do you suppose the kiss of a pretty wench would hurt a lawyer? My dear Molly, if the fraternity had no other reflections to be afraid of!

Miss Alscrip. Oh! hideous; Molly indeed! you ought to have forgot I had a christened name long ago; am not I going to be a countess? If you did not stint my fortune, by squand'ring yours away upon dirty trulls, I might be called your grace.

Alscrip. Spare your lectures, and you shall be called your highness, if you please.

----

from Act III, scen. 2.

Lady Emily. Do you know there is more than one duchess who has been seen in the same carriage with her husband -- like two doves in a basket, in the print of Conjugal Felicity; and another has been detected -- I almost blush to name it

Mrs. Blandish. Bless us! where? and how? and how?

Lady Emily. In nursing her own child![167]

Miss Alscrip. Oh, barbarism! -- For heaven's sake let us change the subject. You were mentioning a revived cap, Lady Emily; any thing of the Henry Quatre?

Lady Emily. Quite different. An English mob under the chin, and artless ringlets, in natural colour, that shall restore an admiration for Prior's Nut-brown Maid.

Miss Alscrip. Horrid! shocking!

Lady Emily. Absolutely necessary. To be different from the rest of the world, we must now revert to nature: make haste, or you have so much to undo, you will be left behind.

Miss Alscrip. I dare say so. But who can vulgarise all at once? What will the French say?

Lady Emily. Oh, we shall have a new treaty for the interchange of fashions and follies, and then say, they will complain, as they do of other treaties, that we out manufactured them.

Miss Alscrip. Fashions and follies! O, what a charming contention!

Lady Emily. Yes, and one, thank heaven, so perfectly well understood on both sides, that no counter declaration will be wanted to explain it.

Miss Alscrip. [*With an affected drop of her lip in her laugh*.] He! he! he! he! he! he!

Lady Emily. My dear Miss Alscrip, what are you doing? I must correct you as I love you. Sure you must have observed the drop of the under-lip is exploded since Lady Simpermode broke a tooth -- [*Sets her mouth affectedly*.] -- I am preparing the cast of the lips for the ensuing winter thus -- It is to be called the Paphian Mimp.

Miss Alscrip. [*Imitating*.] I swear I think it pretty -- I must try to get it.

Lady Emily. Nothing so easy. It is done by one cabalistical word, like a metamorphosis in the fairy tales. You have only, when before your glass, to keep pronouncing to yourself nimini-pimini -- the lips cannot fail taking their ply.

Miss Alscrip. Nimini—pimini—imini, mimini—oh! it's delightfully infantine -- and so innocent, to be kissing one's own lips.

Lady Emily. You have it to a charm—does it not become her infinitely, Mrs. Blandish?

Mrs. Blandish. Our friend's features must succeed in every grace! but never so much as in a quick change of extremes.

---

[167] [*Edit. Note*. The allusion here and in what follows is to "natural" ways and approaches to living as were propounded by Jean Jacques Rousseau.]

from Act III, scen. 3.

Rightly. No, Mr. Alscrip; though I acknowledge your skill, I do not subscribe to your doctrine. The English law is the finest system of ethics, as well as government, that ever the world produced, and it cannot be too generally understood.

Alscrip. Law understood! Zounds! would you destroy the profession?

Rightly. No, I would raise it. Had every man of sense the knowledge of the theory, to which he is competent; the practice would revert to the purity of its institution, maintain the rights, and not promote the knavery, of mankind.

Alscrip. [*Aside*.] Plaguy odd maxims! Sure he means to try me. -- [*To him*.] Brother Rightly, we know the world, and are alone -- I have locked the door.

----

from Act IV, scen. 1

Enter Sir Clement.

Sir Clement. Well, Clifford, what do you think of her?

Clifford. Make yourself perfectly easy, sir: this girl, when known, can make no impression on Lord Gayville's mind; and I doubt not but a silk gown and a lottery ticket, had they been offered as an ultimatum, would have purchased her person.

Sir Clement. [*With a dry sneer*.] Don't you sometimes, Clifford, form erroneous opinions of people's pretensions? Interest and foolish passion inspire strange notions -- as one or the other prevails, we are brought to look so low, or so high --

Clifford. [*With emotion*.] That we are compelled to call reason and honour to our aid.

Sir Clement. And then?

Clifford. We lose the intemperance of our inclinations in the sense of what is right.

Sir Clement. [*Aside*.] Sententious impostor! -- [*To him*.] But to the point.

Clifford. Sir, I would please you if I could -- I am thinking of a scheme to restore Lord Gayville to his senses, without violence or injury to any one of the parties.

Sir Clement. Let me hear it.

Clifford. Why, the wench being cut short of marketing by word of mouth, desired me to write proposals. I am inclined to do so. We will show the answer to Lord Gayville, and, depend upon it, there will be character enough displayed to cure him of the sentimental part of his attachment.

----

from Act V, scen. 2

SCENE II. -- *Hyde Park. Enter Lord Gayville impetuously, looking at his watch.*

Lord Gayville. Not here! I am sure I marked the hour as well as the place, precisely in my note. [*Walks about.*] Had I been told three days ago, that I should have been the appellant in a premeditated duel, I should have thought it an insult upon my principles -- That Clifford should be the cause of my transgressing the legal and sacred duties, we have ever both maintained -- oh, it would have seemed a visionary impossibility -- But he comes to cut reflections short.

Enter Clifford.

Lord Gayville. I waited for you, sir.

Clifford. [Bows in silence.]

Lord Gayville. That ceremonial would grace an encounter of punctilio, but applies ill to the terms upon which I have called you here.

Clifford. What terms are those, my lord?

Lord Gayville. Vengeance! Ample, final vengeance! Draw, sir.

Clifford. No, my lord; my sword is reserved for more becoming purposes: it is not the instrument of passion; and has yet been untried in a dispute with my friend.

Lord Gayville. But why is it not ready for a different trial, the vindication of perfidy, the blackest species of perfidy, that ever the malignant enemy of mankind infused into the human breast -- perfidy to the friend who loved and trusted you, and in the nearest interests of his heart.

Clifford. Take care, my lord; should my blood boil like yours, and it is rising fast, you know not the punishment that awaits you. I came temperate, your gross provocation and thirst of blood make temperance appear disgrace -- I am tempted to take a revenge.

Lord Gayville. [*Draws.*] The means are ready. Come, sir, you are to give an example of qualities generally held incompatible -- bravery and dishonour.

Clifford. Another such a word, and by heaven! -- How have I deserved this opinion?

Lord Gayville. Ask your conscience -- Under the mask of friendship you have held a secret intercourse with the woman I adore; you have supplanted me iiv her affections, you have robbed me of the very charm of my life -- can you deny it?

Clifford. I avow it all.

Lord Gayville. Unparalleled insolence of guilt!

Clifford. Are you sure there is nothing within the scope of possibility that would excuse or atone

Lord Gayville. Death -- Death only -- no abject submission -- no compromise for infamy -- choose instantly -- and save yourself from the only stretch of baseness left -- the invention of falsehood to palliate --

Clifford. [*In the utmost agitation, and drawing his sword.*] Falsehood! -- You shall have no other explanation. -- [*After a struggle within himself, Clifford drops the point, and exposes his breast.*]

Lord Gayville. Stand upon your defence, sir – What do you mean?

Clifford. You said nothing but my life would satisfy you, take it, and remember me.

Lord Gayville. I say so still -- but upon an equal pledge -- I am no assassin.

Clifford. [*With great emotion.*] If to strike at the heart of your friend, more deeply than that poor instrument in your hand could do, makes an assassin, you have been one already.

Lord Gayville. That look, that tone, how like to innocence! Had he not avowed such abominable practices

Clifford. I avow them again: I have rivalled you in the love of the woman you adore -- her affections are rivetted -- to me. I have removed her from your sight; secured her from your recovery

Lord Gayville. D—nation!

Clifford. I have done it to save unguarded beauty; to save unprotected innocence; to save -- a sister.

Lord Gayville. A sister!

Clifford. [*With exultation.*] Vengeance! Ample, final vengeance! [*A pause.*] It is accomplished -- over him -- and over myself -- my victory is complete.

Lord Gayville. Where shall I hide my shame!

Clifford. We'll share it, and forget it here. [*Embraces.*

Lord Gayville. Why did you keep the secret from me?

Clifford. I knew it not myself, till the strange concurrence of circumstances, to which you were in part witness a few hours since, brought it to light. I meant to impart to you the discovery, when my temper took fire -- Let us bury our mutual errors in the thought, that we now for life are friends.

Lord Gayville. Brothers, Clifford -- Let us interchange that title, and doubly, doubly ratify it. Unite me to your charming sister; accept the hand of Lady Emily in return -- her heart I have discovered to be yours. We'll leave the world to the sordid and the tasteless; let an Alscrip, or a Sir Clement Flint, wander after the phantom of happiness, we shall find her real retreat, and hold her by the bonds she covets, virtue, love, and friendship.

Clifford. Not a word more, my lord, the bars against your proposal are insuperable.

Lord Gayville. What bars? Clifford. Honour, propriety -- and pride.

Lord Gayville. Pride, Clifford!

Clifford. Yes, my lord; Harriet Clifford shall not steal the hand of a prince; nor will I -- though doting on Lady Emily with a passion like your own, bear the idea of a clandestine union in a family, to whom I am bound by obligation and trust. Indeed, my lord, without Sir Clement's consent, you must think no more of my sister.

[*Editor's Note.* After some at length legal surprises that follow in the concluding scene, it turns out that not only is Miss Alston in truth Clifford's sister, Harriet, but also a rich heiress. *Finis.*]

~~~***~~~

"RICHARD COEUR DE LION" (1786)

from Act I, scen. 1.
~~~

Mathew. You love dancing, Antonio?

Song -- Antonio.

The merry dance I dearly love.
  For then Collette thy hand I seize.
  And press it too whene'er I please,
And none can see, and none reprove;
  Then on thy cheek quick blushes glow,
  And then we whisper soft and low,
Oh! how I grieve! you ne'er her charms can know.

II.

She's sweet fifteen, I'm one year more,
  Yet still we are too young, they say.
  But we know better, sure, than they,
Youth should not listen to threescore;
  And I'm resolv'd I'll tell her so,
  When next we whisper soft and low.
Oh! how I grieve! you ne'er her charms can know.
[*Exit.*

Song.

Oh, Richard! oh, my love!
  By the faithless world forgot ;
I alone in exile rove,
  To lament thy hapless lot.
I alone of all remain
To unbind thy cruel chain,
  By the faithless world forgot;
I, whose bosom sunk in grief,
Least have strength to yield relief.

Delusive glory! faithless pow'r
  Thus the valiant you repay,
In disasters heavy hour,
  Faithless friendihip's [sic] far away.
      Yet, royal youth,
One faithful heart,
      From tenderest truth,
Tho' hopeless, never shall depart.

Oh, Richard! oh, my love!
  By the faithless world forgot ;
I alone in exile rove,
  To lament thy hapless lot.

----

from Act I, scen. 2.

Air -- Matilda *and* Lauretta.

Mat.
The god of love a bandeau wears,
Wou'd you know what it declares,
    And why his eyes are clouded ;
'Tis to shew us that his pow'r
Is ne'er so fatal, ne'er so sure,
    As when in darkness shrowded.

Laur.
Good Sir, repeat that pretty strain,
Pray again, again.
A lesson kind it does impart,
To guard against a lover's art.

Mat..........With all my heart.

----

from Act I, scen. 3.

[Richard.]

Song.

Lost to the world, forgot, forlorn.
In vain to me returns the morn
    That brings no more my glorious toils,
Yet bless the beams that give to sight
This image of my soul's delight,
    This heaven of soothing smiles.
Vain is the thought of former power
To sooth the present mournful hour:
O Death! be thou my friend;
Hopeless I live, my sorrows end.

SCENES FROM THE LIFE OF GOLDSMITH

"...Thine, Freedom, thine the blessings pictured here,
Thine are those charms that dazzle and endear:
Too blest indeed were such without alloy;
But fostered even by freedom, ills annoy.
That independence Britons prize too high,
Keeps man from man, and breaks the social tie;
The self-dependent lordlings stand alone,
All claims that bind and sweeten life unknown.
Here, by the bonds of nature feebly held,
Minds combat minds repelling and repellled;
Ferments arise, imprisoned factions roar,
Represt ambition struggles round her shore;
Till, over-wrought, the general system feels
Its motions stop, or frenzy fire the wheels.

"Nor this the worst. As nature's ties decay,
As duty, love, and honor, fail to sway,
Fictitious bonds, the bonds of wealth and law,
Still gather strength, and force unwilling awe.
Hence all obedience bows to these alone,
And talent sinks, and merit weeps unknown;
Till time may come, when, stript of all her charms,
The land of scholars, and the nurse of arms,
Where noble stems transmit the patriot flame,
Where kings have toiled, and poets wrote for fame,
One sink of level avarice shall lie,
And scholars, soldiers, kings, unhonored die..."
~ from "The Traveller" (1764) [lines 335-360.]

Our present topic does not fit what has hitherto been the general run of titles in our "Continental Army series" -- being neither tied in or focused on matters and or personages of a military or political sort. Unless, that is, we include the American struggle for *literary autonomy*; that ensued shortly after America's "second war for independence," i.e., the War of 1812; and in which *cultural* struggle the *Edinburgh Review, Quarterly Review* and British dominance in literature generally might symbolically or euphemistically -- at least in the mind of certain American authors and readers of the time -- be seen as the literary equivalent of military forces of Howe, Clinton, and Cornwallis; nefariously bent on intellectual subjugation of the infant nation. And yet just as American swords and arms were furnished by and or had their start based on British models; so, not surprisingly, did American pens. You are probably familiar with how Sir Walter Scott served as a direct influence on and inspiration to Fenimore Cooper and Gilmore Simms.[168] But are you aware also that Oliver Goldsmith, in conjunction with Joseph Addison, also served a comparable role with respect to Irving and Paulding? Not only can one find obvious echoes, borrowed notions, and stylistic imitations of the Irish poet, novelist, and playwright in these American humorists, but they made open avowals of their debt to and admiration of him. Goldsmith, like the Americans, was, and for all his personal association with such as Johnson, Joshua Reynolds, and Edmund Burke, a bit of an outsider to high British culture and yet competed successfully with them; moreover he appealed to sentiments of common people and the domestic foibles and felicity of such, and which struck a ready chord with Irving and Paulding. And like Irving and Paulding, Goldsmith's humor is rarely laugh out-loud provoking and more than pleasantly mirthful. And it's fair to say that all three authors are more well known for their proclivity for the merrily sentimental, including an attachment to the loving qualities of ordinary folk, than for riotous comedy per se.

In 1840, Irving, in tribute to his literary mentor, published a biography of Goldsmith, and which is a surprise minor masterpiece of psychological study that reveals and examines multiple facets of Goldsmith's personality and of those he knew. Practically no one goes unpraised or unscathed in his study, and Irving's candid impartiality evinces a scholarly professionalism and sense of justice that does him credit as a serious historian.

---

[168] Scott had not insignificant impact on Irving and Paulding as well.

On a personal level, we find Goldsmith was rather an odd fish in London society, and there are aspects to his real life character that resemble Rip Van Winkle and Ichabod Crane -- in the case of Rip, Goldsmith's sometimes foolish spendthrift generosity, and regarding Ichabod, his often cutting an absurd social figure and being made the butt of not infrequent practical jokes. Possibly Goldmsith's worst misfortune, strange as it may sound, was that he became a major public figure of sorts during his life -- when it might have been best -- at least for his writings -- if only these last actually survived him, rather than his biography. For his life story is in many way a both pathetic and ludicrous one, and that is at somewhat embarrassing odds with the sometimes lofty and elegant quality of his literary works -- a discrepancy which, even in his lifetime, cast him, no doubt unfairly, in a farcical light.

In Whig versus Tory politics, Goldsmith steered a carefully neutral course, and dieing suddenly as he died of rather amorphous causes in 1774, we can little guess quite how he would have reacted to the revolt of the colonies. For this reason he stands as someone who perhaps appears friendly to both sides -- without it ever having become necessary for him to publicly choose between them; as doubtless would have been the case, as with Johnson, had he lived.[169]

The following then are some notable passages from Irving's warm yet astute biography.

~~~***~~~

"My father," says the 'Man in Black' [quoting from Goldsmith's *The Citizen of the World* (1762)], who, in some respects, is a counterpart of Goldsmith himself, "my father, the younger son of a good family, was possessed of a small living in the church. His education was above his fortune, and his generosity greater than his education. Poor as he was, he had his flatterers poorer than himself; for every dinner he gave them, they returned him an equivalent in praise; and this was all he wanted. The same ambition that actuates a monarch at the head of his army influenced my father at the head of his table: he told the story of the ivy-tree, and that was laughed at; he repeated the jest of the two scholars and one pair of breeches, and the company laughed at that; but the story of Taffy in the sedan chair was sure to set the table in a roar. Thus his pleasure increased in proportion to the pleasure he gave; he loved all the world, and he fancied all the world loved him.

"As his fortune was but small, he lived up to the very extent of it; he had no intention of leaving his children money, for that was dross; he resolved they should have learning, for learning, he used to observe, was better than silver or gold. For this purpose he undertook to instruct us himself, and took as much care to form our morals as to improve our understanding. We were told that universal benevolence was what first cemented society; we were taught to consider all the wants of mankind as our own; to regard the *human face divine* with affection and esteem; he wound us up to be mere machines of pity, and rendered us incapable of withstanding the slightest impulse made either by real or fictitious distress. In a word, we were perfectly instructed in the art of giving away thousands before we were taught the necessary qualifications of getting a farthing."

In the Deserted Village we have another picture of his father and his father's fireside:

"His house was known to all the vagrant train,
He chid their wanderings, but relieved their pain;
The long-remembered beggar was his guest,
Whose beard, descending, swept his aged breast;

[169] "Johnson [quoting Dryden]...:
'For colleges on bounteous kings depend,
And never rebel was to arts a friend.'
General Paoli observed, that successful rebels might [i.e., might be a friend.] Martinelli: 'Happy rebellions.' Goldsmith: 'We have no such phrase.' General Paoli: 'But have you not the thing?' Goldsmith: 'Yes, all our happy revolutions. They have hurt our constitution, and will hurt it, till we mend it by another HAPPY REVOLUTION.' I never before discovered that my friend Goldsmith had so much of the old prejudice in him." ~ From the 1773 section of Boswell's *Life of Johnson*. Goldsmith's ideas on politics and government are nowhere better expressed than in chapter 19 of *The Vicar of Wakefield*, and from which we might reasonably infer that his views were nearer those of Johnson than Thomas Paine.
~~~

The ruin'd spendthrift, now no longer proud
Claim'd kindred there, and had his claims allow'd;
The broken soldier, kindly bade to stay.
Sat by his fire, and talk'd the night away;
Wept o'er his wounds, or tales of sorrow done,
Shoulder'd his crutch, and show'd how fields were won.
Pleased with his guests, the good man learned to glow
And quite forgot their vices in their woe;
Careless their merits or their faults to scan,
His pity gave ere charity began." [ch. 1]

Among the most cordial of Goldsmith's intimates in London during this time of precarious struggle were certain of his former fellow-students in Edinburgh. One of these was the son of a Dr. Milner, a dissenting minister, who kept a classical school of eminence at Peckham, in Surrey. Young Milner had a favorable opinion of Goldsmith's abilities and attainments, and cherished for him that good will which his genial nature seems ever to have inspired among his school and college associates. His father falling ill, the young man negotiated with Goldsmith to take temporary charge of the school. The latter readily consented; for he was discouraged by the slow growth of medical reputation and practice, and as yet had no confidence in the coy smiles of the muse. Laying by his wig and cane, therefore, and once more wielding the ferule, he resumed the character of the pedagogue, and for some time reigned as vicegerent over the academy at Peckham. He appears to have been well treated by both Dr. Milner and his wife, and became a favorite with the scholars from his easy, indulgent good nature. He mingled in their sports, told them droll stories, played on the flute for their amusement, and spent his money in treating them to sweetmeats and other schoolboy dainties. His familiarity was sometimes carried too far; he indulged in boyish pranks and practical jokes, and drew upon himself retorts in kind, which, however, he bore with great good humor. Once, indeed, he was touched to the quick by a piece of schoolboy pertness. After playing on the flute, he spoke with enthusiasm of music, as delightful in itself, and as a valuable accomplishment for a gentleman, whereupon a youngster, with a glance at his ungainly person, wished to know if he considered himself a gentleman. Poor Goldsmith, feelingly alive to the awkwardness of his appearance and the humility of his situation, winced at this unthinking sneer, which long rankled in his mind. [ch.7]

A still more congenial intimacy of the kind was that contracted by Goldsmith with Mr. afterward Sir Joshua Reynolds. The latter was now about forty years of age, a few years older than the poet, whom he charmed by the blandness and benignity of his manners, and the nobleness and generosity of his disposition, as much as he did by the graces of his pencil and the magic of his coloring. They were men of kindred genius, excelling in corresponding qualities of their several arts, for style in writing is what color is in painting; both are innate endowments, and equally magical in their effects. Certain graces and harmonies of both may be acquired by diligent study and imitation, but only in a limited degree; whereas by their natural possessors they are exercised spontaneously, almost unconsciously, and with ever-varying fascination. Reynolds soon understood and appreciated the merits of Goldsmith, and a sincere and lasting friendship ensued between them. [ch. 14]

Goldsmith had, as yet, produced nothing of moment in poetry. Among his literary jobs, it is true, was an oratorio entitled The Captivity, founded on the bondage of the Israelites in Babylon. It was one of those unhappy offsprings of the muse ushered into existence amid the distortions of music. Most of the oratorio has passed into oblivion; but the following song from it will never die:

"The wretch condemned from life to part,
Still, still on hope relies,
And every pang that rends the heart
Bids expectation rise.

"Hope, like the glimmering taper's light,
  Illumes and cheers our way;
 And still, as darker grows the night,
  Emits a brighter ray."

Goldsmith distrusted his qualifications to succeed in poetry, and doubted the disposition of the public mind in regard to it. "I fear," said he, "I have come too late into the world; Pope and other poets have taken up the places in the temple of Fame; and as few at any period can possess poetical reputation, a man of genius can now hardly acquire it." Again, on another occasion, he observes: "Of all kinds of ambition, as things are now circumstanced, perhaps that which pursues poetical fame is the wildest. What from the increased refinement of the tunes, from the diversity of judgment produced by opposing systems of criticism, and from the more prevalent divisions of opinion influenced by party, the strongest and happiest efforts can expect to please but in a very narrow circle." [ch. 15]

Sixty guineas for the Vicar of Wakefield! and this could be pronounced *no mean* price by Dr. Johnson, at that time the arbiter of British talent, and who had had an opportunity of witnessing the effect of the work upon the public mind; for its success was immediate. It came out on the 27th of March, 1766; before the end of May a second edition was called for; in three months more a third; and so it went on, widening in a popularity that has never flagged. Rogers, the Nestor of British literature, whose refined purity of taste and exquisite mental organization rendered him eminently calculated to appreciate a work of the kind, declared that of all the books which, through the fitful changes of three generations, he had seen rise and fall, the charm of the Vicar of Wakefield had alone continued as at first; and could he revisit the world after an interval of many more generations, he should as surely look to find it undiminished. Nor has its celebrity been confined to Great Britain. Though so exclusively a picture of British scenes and manners, it has been translated into almost every language, and everywhere its charm has been the same. Goethe, the great genius of Germany, declared in his eighty-first year that it was his delight at the age of twenty, that it had in a manner formed a part of his education, influencing his taste and feelings throughout life, and that he had recently read it again from beginning to end--with renewed delight, and with a grateful sense of the early benefit derived from it.[170]

It is needless to expatiate upon the qualities of a work which has thus passed from country to country, and language to language, until it is now known throughout the whole reading world, and is become a household book in every hand. The secret of its universal and enduring popularity is undoubtedly its truth to nature, but to nature of the most amiable kind; to nature such as Goldsmith saw it. The author, as we have occasionally shown in the course of this memoir, took his scenes and characters in this as in his other writings, from originals in his own motley experience; but he has given them as seen through the medium of his own indulgent eye, and has set them forth with the colorings of his own good head and heart. Yet how contradictory it seems that this, one of the most delightful pictures of home and homefelt happiness, should be drawn by a homeless man; that the most amiable picture of domestic virtue and all the endearments of the married state should be drawn by a bachelor, who had been severed from domestic life almost from boyhood; that one of the most tender, touching, and affecting appeals on behalf of female loveliness should have been made by a man whose deficiency in all the graces of person and manner seemed to mark him out for a cynical disparager of the sex.

We cannot refrain from transcribing from the work a short passage illustrative of what we have said, and which within a wonderfully small compass comprises a world of beauty of imagery, tenderness of feeling, delicacy and refinement of thought, and matchless purity of style. The two stanzas which conclude

[170] [*Edit. Note.* "'It is essential,' continued Goethe, 'that you build up capital that will not be exhausted. This will accomplish this with the studies you have begun in the English language and literature. Hold yourself to these and profit by every hour of the excellent opportunity provided by the young Englishmen...And don't forget, our own literature has for the most part come from theirs...Our novels, our tragedies, where have they come from but Goldsmith, Fielding, and Shakespeare? And still today, where can you find in Germany three great literary figures to equal Lord Byron, Moore, and Walter Scott? Therefore, I say again, strengthen your English..." 3 Dec. 1814, *Conversations with Goethe* by Eckermann, Gisela C. O'Brien trans.]

it, in which are told a whole history of woman's wrongs and sufferings, is, for pathos, simplicity, and euphony, a gem in the language. The scene depicted is where the poor Vicar is gathering around him the wrecks of his shattered family, and endeavoring to rally them back to happiness.

"The next morning the sun arose with peculiar warmth for the season, so that we agreed to breakfast together on the honeysuckle bank; where, while we sat, my youngest daughter at my request joined her voice to the concert on the trees about us. It was in this place my poor Olivia first met her seducer, and every object served to recall her sadness. But that melancholy which is excited by objects of pleasure, or inspired by sounds of harmony, soothes the heart instead of corroding it. Her mother, too, upon this occasion, felt a pleasing distress, and wept, and loved her daughter as before. 'Do, my pretty Olivia,' cried she, 'let us have that melancholy air your father was so fond of; your sister Sophy has already obliged us. Do, child; it will please your old father.' She complied in a manner so exquisitely pathetic as moved me.

"'When lovely woman stoops to folly,
And finds too late that men betray,
What charm can soothe her melancholy.
What art can wash her guilt away?

"'The only art her guilt to cover,
To hide her shame from every eye,
To give repentance to her lover,
And wring his bosom -- is to die.'" [ch. 17]

THE social position of Goldsmith had undergone a material change since the publication of The Traveler [sic]. Before that event he was but partially known as the author of some clever anonymous writings, and had been a tolerated member of the club and the Johnson circle, without much being expected from him. Now he had suddenly risen to literary fame, and become one of the *lions* of the day. The highest regions of intellectual society were now open to him; but he was not prepared to move in them with confidence and success. Ballymahon had not been a good school of manners at the outset of life; nor had his experience as a "poor student" at colleges and medical schools contributed to give him the polish of society. He had brought from Ireland, as he said, nothing but his "brogue and his blunders," and they had never left him. He had traveled, it is true; but the Continental tour which in those days gave the finishing grace to the education of a patrician youth, had, with poor Goldsmith, been little better than a course of literary vagabondizing. It had enriched his mind, deepened and widened the benevolence of his heart, and filled his memory with enchanting pictures, but it had contributed little to disciplining him for the polite intercourse of the world. His life in London had hitherto been a struggle with sordid cares and sad humiliations. "You scarcely can conceive," wrote he some time previously to his brother, "how much eight years of disappointment, anguish, and study have worn me down." Several more years had since been added to the term during which he had trod the lowly walks of life. He had been a tutor, an apothecary's drudge, a petty physician of the suburbs, a bookseller's hack, drudging for daily bread. Each separate walk had been beset by its peculiar thorns and humiliations. It is wonderful how his heart retained its gentleness and kindness through all these trials; how his mind rose above the "meannesses of poverty," to which, as he says, he was compelled to submit; but it would be still more wonderful, had his manners acquired a tone corresponding to the innate grace and refinement of his intellect. He was near forty years of age when he published The Traveler, and was lifted by it into celebrity. As is beautifully said of him by one of his biographers, "he has fought his way to consideration and esteem; but he bears upon him the scars of his twelve years' conflict; of the mean sorrows through which he has passed; and of the cheap indulgences he has sought relief and help from. There is nothing plastic in his nature now. His manners and habits are completely formed; and in them any further success can make little favorable change, whatever it may effect for his mind or genius"...

It may not have been disgrace that he feared, but rudeness. The great lexicographer [Johnson], spoiled by the homage of society, was still more prone than himself to lose temper when the argument went against him. He could not brook appearing to be worsted; but would attempt to bear down his adversary by the rolling thunder of his periods; and when that failed, would become downright insulting. Boswell called it "having recourse to some sudden mode of robust sophistry"; but Goldsmith designated it much more happily. "There is no arguing with Johnson," said he, "*for when his pistol misses fire,he knocks you down with the butt end of it.*" [ch. 18]

After all, it was honest pride, not vanity, in Goldsmith, that was gratified at seeing his portrait deemed worthy of being perpetuated by the classic pencil of Reynolds, and "hung up in history," beside that of his revered friend, Johnson. Even the great moralist himself was not insensible to a feeling of this kind. Walking one day with Goldsmith, in Westminster Abbey, among the tombs of monarchs, warriors, and statesmen, they came to the sculptured mementos of literary worthies in Poets' Corner. Casting his eye round upon these memorials of genius, Johnson muttered in a low tone to his companion,

"Forsitan et nostrum nomen miscebitur istis"[171]

Goldsmith treasured up the intimated hope, and shortly afterward, as they were passing by Temple bar, where the heads of Jacobite[172] rebels, executed for treason, were mouldering aloft on spikes, pointed up to the grizzly mementos, and echoed the intimation,

"*Forsitan et nostrum nomen miscebitur istis*" [ch. 27]

"He always wore a wig, a peculiarity which those who judge of his appearance only from the fine poetical head of Reynolds would not suspect; and on one occasion some person contrived seriously to injure this important adjunct to dress. It was the only one he had in the country, and the misfortune seemed irreparable until the services of Mr. Bunbury's valet were called in, who, however, performed his functions so indifferently that poor Goldsmith's appearance became the signal for a general smile."

This was wicked waggery, especially when it was directed to mar all the attempts of the unfortunate poet to improve his personal appearance, about which he was at all times dubiously sensitive, and particularly when among the ladies. [ch. 32]

Near to his rural retreat at Edgeware, a Mr. Seguin, an Irish merchant, of literary tastes, had country quarters for his family, where Goldsmith was always welcome.

In this family he would indulge in playful and even grotesque humor, and was ready for anything--conversation, music, or a game of romps. He prided himself upon his dancing, and would walk a minuet with Mrs. Seguin, to the infinite amusement of herself and the children, whose shouts of laughter he bore with perfect good-humor. He would sing Irish songs, and the Scotch ballad of Johnny Armstrong. He took the lead in the children's sports of blind man's buff, hunt the slipper, etc., or in their games at cards, and was the most noisy of the party, affecting to cheat and to be excessively eager to win; while with children of smaller size he would turn the hind part of his wig before, and play all kinds of tricks to amuse them.

One word as to his musical skill and his performance on the flute, which comes up so invariably in all his fireside revels. He really knew nothing of music scientifically; he had a good ear, and may have played sweetly; but we are told he could not read a note of music. Roubillac, the statuary, once played a trick upon him in this respect. He pretended to score down an air as the poet played it, but put down

---

[171] [*Edit. Note.* "And perhaps our name(s) will be mingled with these."]

[172] [*Edit. Note.* "James" is an Anglicization (based on Latin) of "Jacob," and originally "Jacobite" referred to the followers of James II, of the Stuarts, and who was overthrown by William and Mary in England's Dutch-aided Glorious Revolution of 1788. Prior to the French Revolution, "Jacobite" in England meant someone who espoused the cause to secure the British throne for heirs of the Stuart family line, such as, for example, "Bonnie Prince Charlie" in 1745, and came to have the connotation of *anarchist*; hence the later (of course, many years after Goldsmith and Johnson) and extended application of the term "Jacobite" to French Revolutionaries.]

crotchets and semi-breves at random. When he had finished, Goldsmith cast his eyes over it and pronounced it correct! It is possible that his execution in music was like his style in writing; in sweetness and melody he may have snatched a grace beyond the reach of art!

He was at all times a capital companion for children, and knew how to fall in with their humors. "I little thought," said Miss Hawkins, the woman grown, "what I should have to boast, when Goldsmith taught me to play Jack and Jill by two bits of paper on his fingers." He entertained Mrs. Garrick, we are told, with a whole budget of stories and songs; delivered the Chimney Sweep with exquisite taste as a solo; and performed a duet with Garrick of Old Rose and Burn the Bellows.

"I was only five years old," says the late George Colman, "when Goldsmith one evening, when drinking coffee with my father, took me on his knee and began to play with me, which amiable act I returned with a very smart slap in the face; it must have been a tingler, for I left the marks of my little spiteful paw upon his cheek. This infantile outrage was followed by summary justice, and I was locked up by my father in an adjoining room, to undergo solitary imprisonment in the dark. Here I began to howl and scream most abominably. At length a friend appeared to extricate me from jeopardy; it was the good-natured doctor himself, with a lighted candle in his hand, and a smile upon his countenance, which was still partially red from the effects of my petulance. I sulked and sobbed, and he fondled and soothed until I began to brighten. He seized the propitious moment, placed three hats upon the carpet, and a shilling under each; the shillings, he told me, were England, France, and Spain. 'Hey, presto, cockolorum!' cried the doctor, and, lo! on uncovering the shillings, they were all found congregated under one. I was no politician at the time, and therefore might not have wondered at the sudden revolution which brought England, France, and Spain all under one crown; but, as I was also no conjurer, it amazed me beyond measure. From that time, whenever the doctor came to visit my father,

"I pluck'd his gown to share the good man's smile; a game of romps constantly ensued, and we were always cordial friends and merry playfellows." [ch. 34]

"Thwarted in the plans and disappointed in the hopes which had recently cheered and animated him, Goldsmith found the labor at his half-finished tasks doubly irksome from the consciousness that the completion of them could not relieve him from his pecuniary embarrassments. His impaired health, also, rendered him less capable than formerly of sedentary application, and continual perplexities disturbed the flow of thought necessary for original composition. He lost his usual gayety and good-humor, and became, at times, peevish and irritable. Too proud of spirit to seek sympathy or relief from his friends, for the pecuniary difficulties he had brought upon himself by his errors and extravagance; and unwilling, perhaps, to make known their amount, he buried his cares and anxieties in his own bosom, and endeavored in company to keep up his usual air of gayety and unconcern. This gave his conduct an appearance of fitfulness and caprice, varying suddenly from moodiness to mirth, and from silent gravity to shallow laughter; causing surprise and ridicule in those who were not aware of the sickness of heart which lay beneath.

His poetical reputation, too, was sometimes a disadvantage to him; it drew upon him a notoriety which he was not always in the mood or the vein to act up to. "Good heavens, Mr. Foote," exclaimed an actress at the Haymarket Theater, "what a humdrum kind of man Dr. Goldsmith appears in our green-room compared with the figure he makes in his poetry!" "The reason of that, madam," replied Foote, "is because the muses are better company than the players."....

On the 4th of August we find them together at Vauxhall; at that time a place in high vogue, and which had once been to Goldsmith a scene of Oriental splendor and delight. We have, in fact, in the Citizen of the World, a picture of it as it had struck him in former years and in his happier moods. "Upon entering the gardens," says the Chinese philosopher, "I found every sense occupied with more than expected pleasure; the lights everywhere glimmering through the scarcely-moving trees; the full-bodied concert bursting on the stillness of the night; the natural concert of the birds in the more retired part of the grove, vying with that which was formed by art; the company gayly dressed, looking satisfaction, and the tables spread with various delicacies, all conspired to fill my imagination with the visionary happiness of the Arabian lawgiver, and lifted me into an ecstasy of admiration. [*Citizen of the World*, Letter xxi]" [ch. 43]

He belonged to a temporary association of men of talent, some of them members of the Literary Club, who dined together occasionally at the St. James' Coffee-house. At these dinners, as usual, he was one of the last to arrive. On one occasion, when he was more dilatory than usual, a whim seized the company to write epitaphs on him, as "The late Dr. Goldsmith," and several were thrown off in a playful vein, hitting off his peculiarities. The only one extant was written by Garrick, and has been preserved, very probably, by its pungency:

"Here lies poet Goldsmith, for shortness called Noll,
Who wrote like an angel, but talked like poor poll." [ch. 44]

Never was the trite, because sage apothegm, that "The child is father to the man" [Wordsworth], more fully verified than in the case of Goldsmith. He is shy, awkward, and blundering in childhood, yet full of sensibility; he is a butt for the jeers and jokes of his companions, but apt to surprise and confound them by sudden and witty repartees; he is dull and stupid at his tasks, yet an eager and intelligent devourer of the traveling tales and campaigning stories of his half military pedagogue; he may be a dunce, but he is already a rhymer; and his early scintillations of poetry awaken the expectations of his friends. He seems from infancy to have been compounded of two natures, one bright, the other blundering; or to have had fairy gifts laid in his cradle by the "good people" who haunted his birthplace, the old goblin mansion on the banks of the Inny.

He carries with him the wayward elfin spirit, if we may so term it, throughout his career. His fairy gifts are of no avail at school, academy, or college; they unfit him for close study and practical science, and render him heedless of everything that does not address itself to his poetical imagination and genial and festive feelings; they dispose him to break away from restraint, to stroll about hedges, green lanes, and haunted streams, to revel with jovial companions, or to rove the country like a gypsy in quest of odd adventures.

As if confiding in these delusive gifts, he takes no heed of the present nor care for the future, lays no regular and solid foundation of knowledge, follows out no plan, adopts and discards those recommended by his friends, at one time prepares for the ministry, next turns to the law, and then fixes upon medicine. He repairs to Edinburgh, the great emporium of medical science, but the fairy gifts accompany him; he idles and frolics away his time there, imbibing only such knowledge as is agreeable to him; makes an excursion to the poetical regions of the Highlands; and having walked the hospitals for the customary time, sets off to ramble over the Continent, in quest of novelty rather than knowledge. His whole tour is a poetical one. He fancies he is playing the philosopher while he is really playing the poet; and though professedly he attends lectures and visits foreign universities, so deficient is he on his return, in the studies for which he set out, that he fails in an examination as a surgeon's mate; and while figuring as a doctor of medicine, is outvied on a point of practice by his apothecary. Baffled in every regular pursuit, after trying in vain some of the humbler callings of commonplace life, he is driven almost by chance to the exercise of his pen, and here the fairy gifts come to his assistance. For a long time, however, he seems unaware of the magic properties of that pen; he uses it only as a makeshift until he can find a *legitimate* means of support. He is not a learned man, and can write but meagerly and at second-hand on learned subjects; but he has a quick convertible talent that seizes lightly on the points of knowledge necessary to the illustration of a theme; his writings for a time are desultory, the fruits of what he has seen and felt, or what he has recently and hastily read; but his gifted pen transmutes everything into gold, and his own genial nature reflects its sunshine through his pages.

Still unaware of his powers he throws off his writings anonymously, to go with the writings of less favored men; and it is a long time, and after a bitter struggle with poverty and humiliation, before he acquires confidence in his literary talent as a means of support, and begins to dream of reputation.

From this time his pen is a wand of power in his hand, and he has only to use it discreetly, to make it competent to all his wants. But discretion is not a part of Goldsmith's nature; and it seems the property of these fairy gifts to be accompanied by moods and temperaments to render their effect precarious. The heedlessness of his early days; his disposition for social enjoyment; his habit of throwing the present on the neck of the future, still continue. His expenses forerun his means; he incurs debts on the faith of what his magic pen is to produce, and then, under the pressure of his debts, sacrifices its productions for prices far below their value. It is a redeeming circumstance in his prodigality, that it is lavished oftener upon others than upon himself; he gives without thought or stint, and is the continual dupe of his benevolence and his trustfulness in human nature.

We may say of him as he says of one of his heroes, "He could not stifle the natural impulse which he had to do good, but frequently borrowed money to relieve the distressed; and when he knew not conveniently where to borrow, he has been observed to shed tears as he passed through the wretched suppliants who attended his gate"...

"His simplicity in trusting persons whom he had no previous reasons to place confidence in, seems to be one of those lights of his character which, while they impeach his understanding, do honor to his benevolence. The low and the timid are ever suspicious; but a heart impressed with honorable sentiments expects from others sympathetic sincerity." [Goldsmith's *Life of Nashe.*]

His heedlessness in pecuniary matters, which had rendered his life a struggle with poverty even in the days of his obscurity, rendered the struggle still more intense when his fairy gifts had elevated him into the society of the wealthy and luxurious, and imposed on his simple and generous spirit fancied obligations to a more ample and bounteous display.

"How comes it," says a recent and ingenious critic, "that in all the miry paths of life which he had trod, no speck ever sullied the robe of his modest and graceful muse. How amid all that love of inferior company, which never to the last forsook him, did he keep his genius so free from every touch of vulgarity?"

We answer that it was owing to the innate purity and goodness of his nature; there was nothing in it that assimilated to vice and vulgarity. Though his circumstances often compelled him to associate with the poor, they never could betray him into companionship with the depraved. His relish for humor and for the study of character, as we have before observed, brought him often into convivial company of a vulgar kind; but he discriminated between their vulgarity and their amusing qualities, or rather wrought from the whole those familiar features of life which form the staple of his most popular writings.

Much, too, of this intact purity of heart may be ascribed to the lessons of his infancy under the paternal roof; to the gentle, benevolent, elevated, unworldly maxims of his father, who "passing rich with forty pounds a year," infused a spirit into his child which riches could not deprave nor poverty degrade. Much of his boyhood, too, had been passed in the household of his uncle, the amiable and generous Contarine; where he talked of literature with the good pastor, and practiced music with his daughter, and delighted them both by his juvenile attempts at poetry. These early associations breathed a grace and refinement into his mind and tuned it up, after the rough sports on the green, or the frolics at the tavern. These led him to turn from the roaring glees of the club, to listen to the harp of his cousin Jane; and from the rustic triumph of 'throwing sledge," to a stroll with his flute along the pastoral banks of the Inny.

The gentle spirit of his father walked with him through life, a pure and virtuous monitor; and in all the vicissitudes of his career we find him ever more chastened in mind by the sweet and holy recollections of the home of his infancy.

It has been questioned whether he really had any religious feeling. Those who raise the question have never considered well his writings; his Vicar of Wakefield, and his pictures of the Village Pastor, present religion under its most endearing forms, and with a feeling that could only flow from the deep convictions of the heart. When his fair traveling companions at Paris urged him to read the Church Service on a Sunday, he replied that "he was not worthy to do it." He had seen in early life the sacred offices performed by his father and his brother, with a solemnity which had sanctified them in his memory; how could he presume to undertake such functions? His religion has been called in question by Johnson and by Boswell; he certainly had not the gloomy hypochondriacal piety of the one, nor the babbling mouth-piety of the other; but the spirit of Christian charity breathed forth in his writings and illustrated in his conduct give us reason to believe he had the indwelling religion of the soul.

We have made sufficient comments in the preceding chapters on his conduct in elevated circles of literature and fashion. The fairy gifts which took him there were not accompanied by the gifts and graces necessary to sustain him in that artificial sphere. He can neither play the learned sage with Johnson, nor the fine gentleman with Beauclerc, though he has a mind replete with wisdom and natural shrewdness, and a spirit free from vulgarity. The blunders of a fertile but hurried intellect, and the awkward display of the student assuming the man of fashion, fix on him a character for absurdity and vanity which, like the charge of lunacy, it is hard to disprove, however weak the grounds of the charge and strong the facts in opposition to it.

In truth, he is never truly in his place in these learned and fashionable circles, which talk and live for display. It is not the kind of society he craves. His heart yearns for domestic life; it craves familiar, confiding intercourse, family firesides, the guileless and happy company of children; these bring out the heartiest and sweetest sympathies of his nature.

"Had it been his fate," says the critic we have already quoted, "to meet a woman who could have loved him, despite his faults, and respected him despite his foibles, we cannot but think that his life and his genius would have been much more harmonious; his desultory affections would have been concentered, his craving self-love appeased, his pursuits more settled, his character more solid. A nature like Goldsmith's, so affectionate, so confiding -- so susceptible to simple, innocent enjoyments -- so dependent on others for the sunshine of existence, does not flower if deprived of the atmosphere of home."

The cravings of his heart in this respect are evident, we think, throughout his career; and if we have dwelt with more significancy than others upon his intercourse with the beautiful Horneck family, it is because we fancied we could detect, amid his playful attentions to one of its members, a lurking sentiment of tenderness, kept down by conscious poverty and a humiliating idea of personal defects. A hopeless feeling of this kind -- the last a man would communicate to his friends -- might account for much of that fitfulness of conduct, and that gathering melancholy, remarked, but not comprehended by his associates, during the last year or two of his life; and may have been one of the troubles of the mind which aggravated his last illness, and only terminated with his death.

We shall conclude these desultory remarks with a few which have been used by us on a former occasion. From the general tone of Goldsmith's biography, it is evident that his faults, at the worst, were but negative, while his merits were great and decided. He was no one's enemy but his own; his errors, in the main, inflicted evil on none but himself, and were so blended with humorous, and even affecting circumstances, as to disarm anger and conciliate kindness. Where eminent talent is united to spotless virtue, we are awed and dazzled into admiration, but our admiration is apt to be cold and reverential; while there is something in the harmless infirmities of a good and great, but erring individual, that pleads touchingly to our nature; and we turn more kindly toward the object of our idolatry, when we find that, like ourselves, he is mortal and is frail. The epithet so often heard, and in such kindly tones, of "Poor Goldsmith," speaks volumes. Few who consider the real compound of admirable and whimsical qualities which form his character would wish to prune away its eccentricities, trim its grotesque luxuriance, and clip it down to the decent formalities of rigid virtue. "Let not his frailties be remembered," said Johnson; "he was a very great man." But, for our part, we rather say "Let them be remembered," since their tendency is to endear; and we question whether he himself would not feel gratified in hearing his reader, after dwelling with admiration on the proofs of his greatness, close the volume with the kind-hearted phrase,
so fondly and familiarly ejaculated, of "POOR GOLDSMITH." [ch. 45]

NEW JERSEY REBELS:

The Evolution of a Revolution 1765-1776

New Jersey is not one of the colonies, like Massachusetts or Virginia, that first comes to mind when we think of the outbreak of revolt in 1775, and or the stirring events leading up to. And yet without the united and unanimous involvement of *all* the colonies, presumably, the independence movement could not but have fallen significantly short of its aim. It only makes sense then to join to our knowledge of the Boson Tea Party, Patrick Henry, and Lexington a better sense and idea than what is commonly had of what was going on elsewhere in the thirteen colonies – in, for example, such an one as New Jersey. Indeed, until Howe invaded (and, without himself quite intending to, ravaged) the state in late 1776, consensus in New Jersey was far from an obviously settled matter. And even after Washington's startling victories of Trenton and Princeton, the state remained an important source for loyalist soldiers; furnishing as it did one of the British army's most notable and (relatively) full strength Provincial regiments, the New Jersey Volunteers.

By way of selected extracts then from the dated and catalogued entries found in the *Analytical Index to the Colonial Documents of New Jersey, In the State Paper Offices of England* (1858)[173] compiled by Henry Stevens, it is possible to compose and present an informative and edifying picture of how the Revolutionary cause evolved in that state. It is then with this object in mind that we submit the following pertinent portions of Stevens' compendium to you our readers. If granted this presentation is, as we frankly concede in advance, much less than perfect, not thoroughly meticulous, or on all points exact, it does have the merit of being a brief and digestible summary. And despite unavoidable gaps in the record (whether here or in Stevens' work as a whole), these entries manage to vividly impart no little of the drama of the times; accompanied by lively, albeit terse, vignettes and sketches of a number of that drama's leading participants. Those entries in square brackets refer to items or material included as added documents not formally a part of the Royal and official correspondence itself of which this outline is chiefly comprised and in reference to. One thing that becomes apparent in perusing such a record as this is that "taxation without representation" was merely one of a number of issues which set the colonies and Britain at loggerheads. And just as or of more concern to the colonists was the interference with the crown in the power of the colonial assemblies -- including in one instance insisting that *country coroners* be royally appointed rather than chosen by the provincial legislatures.

Most of the footnotes and citations in Stevens' original text have been omitted; while in the meantime we've inserted mention of important events and dates in the general chronology to help the reader better follow what was transpiring from the larger view.

~~~***~~~

1764

[April 5, 1764 - The Sugar Act]

Aug. 11. St. James'. Circular Letter from the Secr. of State to the Governors in North America, desiring them from to time to transmit such information as they may procure relative to the illicit trade within their respective Governments -- the method in which it is conducted, the commodities in which it is concerned, the extent to which it is carried, and the means of preventing the same.

Aug. 11. St. James'. Circular Letter from the Secr. of State to the Governors in North America, desiring them that the conveyance of letters, by the post, should be facilitated and extended throughout the Colonies.

[Aug. 24. Elizabethtown. Letter from Robert Ogden to Cortlandt Skinner -- Encloses a copy of resolutions received from the Committee of Correspondence of Massachusetts Assembly, for his perusal and advice -- all the Colonies should unite and exert themselves to keep off the threatened blow of imposing taxes, duties, &c., -- an Assembly having been called in New York, suggests that Gov'r [William] Franklin[174] be requested to call the New Jersey Assembly at an early day.]

[173] Found in *Collections of the New Jersey Historical Society* (1858), Volume 5.
[174] Loyalist son of Benjamin Franklin.
~~~

[Mr. Ogden was delegate from New Jersey to the Congress which met in New York, Oct. 7, 1765, and shared with Mr. Ruggles, of Massachusetts, the unenviable distinction of having dissented from the action of the Congress and withdrawn from its deliberations. Being Speaker of the New Jersey Assembly, a meeting of that body was called at his request on 27th Nov., and the next day he resigned that position and his seat as a member from Essex Co., and an indirect censure was passed upon him by resolutions thanking his associates in the Congress for the "faithful and judicious discharge of the trust reposed in them."]

[Sept. 1, 1764 - The Currency Act]

1765

Feb. 9. St. James'. Circular Letter from the Earl of Halifax to the Governors in North America, transmitting some explanatory orders relative to the command of the troops stationed in their respective Governments.

[March 22, 1765 - The Stamp Act]

[March 24, 1765 - The Quartering Act]

June 20. Burlington.[175] Letter from the Speaker of the Assembly of New Jersey to the Speaker of the Massachusetts Bay Assembly -- Though the people of New Jersey are not without "a just sensibility" respecting the Stamp Act, yet they are against uniting on the present occasion, and only wish the other Colonies success they can "loyally and reasonably desire."

Sept. 14. Burlington. Letter from Gov'r Franklin to General [Thomas] Gage -- The Distributor of Stamps in New Jersey having resigned his office on account of the intimations he had received, and having refused to take the charge of the said stamps, Gov'r Franklin is desirous to be informed whether he could have the aid of the military in case he should find it necessary to call upon them.

Sept. 16. New York. Letter from Gen. Gage to Gov'r Franklin, informing him that he may depend upon having one hundred men, with proper officers, ready to march to New Jersey at his requisition, to preserve good order in that Province.

Sept. 23. Burlington. Letter from Gov'r Franklin to the R't Hon. H. S. Conway, Secr. of State -- Congratulates upon his appointment to the Secretaryship -- the principal matter which agitates the minds of the people of New Jersey, is the Act of Parliament for establishing a stamp duty in America -- the Distributor of Stamps resigned his office -- Gen. Gage has promised the aid of the military if it should be necessary -- he, the Governor, will appoint a person to distribute the stamps until he receives further commands on the subject from home.

Oct. 10. Burlington. Letter from Gov'r Franklin to the Board of Trade -- Notwithstanding the many inflammatory publications which have been circulated against the Stamp Act, from the neighbouring Provinces, peace and order prevails throughout New Jersey -- the Distributor of Stamps resigned his office through timidity -- the stamps are removed on board the King's ship Sardine -- there will be a great difficulty to find any gentleman in the Province who can give security, and be willing to undertake the office of Distributor of Stamps.

Nov. 13. Burlington. Letter from Gov'r Franklin to the Board of Trade -- Received no instructions to carry the Stamp Act into execution -- transmits a copy of the Minutes of Council, with their advice on the subject -- the seditious spirit from the neighbouring Colonies is beginning to appear in New Jersey -- the people of that Province are sure to follow the example set to them by their neighbours -- at the last Supreme Court only criminal matters were transacted -- the lawyers have entered into an agreement not to act under the Stamp Law.

[175] New Jersey then was divided in two halves, and had two capitals: Burlington in the west and Perth Amboy in the east.

Nov. 30. Burlington. Letter from Gov'r Franklin to Secr. Conway -- The infection, with regard to the Stamp Act, has spread from the neighbouring Colonies to N. Jersey -- they committed no riots as yet, but the most prudent management is necessary to prevent them -- the Minutes of Council and Votes of Assembly are sent to enable to form a true judgment of the situation of the Province.

[Dec. 9. Letter from the Committee of Correspondence of the New Jersey Assembly to Joseph Sherwood, the agent of the Province, in London -- Transmitting copies of the petitions to the King and both Houses of Parliament, agreed to by the Congress in New York -- the Minutes of the House of Assembly, relating to the resignation of the Speaker, (Robert Ogden,) and communicating their views upon the exciting topics of the day.]

1766

[March 18, 1766 - The Declaratory Act]

1767

[June 29, 1767 - The Townshend (Revenue) Act. Other Townshend Acts later included in the same year were the Indemnity Act, the Commissioners of Customs Act, the Vice Admiralty Court Act, and the New York Restraining Act.]

July 18. Whitehall. Letter from Secr. Shelburne to Gov'r Franklin -- Conveying the King's displeasure at the Assembly of N. Jersey for having avoided a complete obedience to an Act of the British Parliament, for rendering more effectual in America, an Act for punishing mutiny and desertion.

Aug. 7. Letter from the Secr. of State to Gov'r Franklin, enclosing an Order in Council repealing an Act passed in the Province of New Jersey, for supplying the barracks with furniture and other necessaries for the King's troops, and copy of the representation from the Board of Trade upon said Act.

Aug. 22. Burlington. Letter from Gov'r Franklin to Secr. Shelburne -- Sends Minutes of Council and Assembly, and copies of twelve Acts passed at the last session -- the Assembly of New Jersey made provision for supplying the King's troops, quartered in that Colony, with all the necessaries required by Act of Parliament.

(Oct.) 22. Burlington. Letter from Gov'r Franklin to Secr. Shelburne -- The inequality of the expense in quartering troops causes dissatisfaction in the Colonies -- suggests a plan to obviate this, by appropriating some of the Crown revenue in America, for the defraying of those expenses for the future.

1768

Jan. 23. Whitehall. Circular Letter from the Earl of Hillsborough to all the Governors in North America and the West Indies, desiring them to transmit a complete collection, either in manuscript or print, of the laws of each Colony.

Feb. 20. Whitehall. Circular Letter from the Earl of Hillsborough to all the Governors in North America, transmitting a duplicate of the Address of the House of Commons to the King, of the 27th March, 1766, and desiring the Governors to pay exact obedience to the said Address.

Feb. 23. Whitehall. Letter from the Earl of Hillsborough, Secr. of State, to Gov'r Franklin -- The law passed in New Jersey for making provision for quartering the King's troops is referred to the Board of Trade -- the King received the greatest satisfaction from the submission and obedience of the Colonies, to the laws and authority of the Mother Country -- his, the Governor's, plan for regulating the expenses in the

Colonies for quartering the King's troops, will have a proper attention paid to it -- any irregularities and improper behaviour of the officers or soldiers ought to be severely punished.

[April 4. Great Barrington, Mass. Rev. Samuel Hopkins to Rev. Mr. Bellamy -- The Rev. Jeremiah Halsey of Lamington, N. J., preached the public Lecture for Mr. Foxcraft, in Boston -- he greatly disobliged every clergyman in town, except one or two -- his theme Was: 'Tis impossible for an impenitent to believe on Christ -- and one inference was, that faith is not the first act of the renewed soul -- Dr. Chauncy says he is astonished at the man's impudence -- the Clergy in Boston are greatly displeased with the letter wrote by the Convention of Clergy at Elizabethtown, in which they repeatedly declare they have nothing against a Bishop's being sent to America, if by an Act of Parliament he may be confined wholly to the people of his own denomination, and excluded from all civil authority, &c., -- they say this gives up the whole, even all they desire -- such an Act of Parliament may be made, but will soon be repealed, when a Bishop has once got footing in America, &c., &c.]

April 30. Whitehall. Circular Letter from the Earl of Hillsborough to all the Governors on the Continent of America, directing them to take all legal measures for the apprehending of Melchisedeck Kinsman, charged with murder of one William Odgers, a Custom Officer, who sailed from Falmouth in one of the N. York packets about three weeks ago.

May 7. New Jersey. The Humble Address and Petition of the Assembly of New Jersey to the King, praying relief from some of the late Acts of Parliament imposing a duty on them for the express purpose of raising a revenue.
N. B.-- This Address was not delivered until after the 15th Nov., 1768. See the E. of H.'s letter to Gov'r Franklin of that date.

May 9. Virginia. Letter from Payton [Peyton] Randolph, Speaker of the House of Burgesses of Virginia, to the Speaker of the Assembly of New Jersey, calling upon the said Assembly to join the union, in order to take every regular step to assert their constitutional liberty, of which the late Acts of the British Parliament manifestly tend to deprive them of.
Enclosed in letter from Gov'r Franklin to the Earl of Holdernesse, Jan. 28, 1769.

May 14. Whitehall. Letter from Secretary Lord Hillsborough to the Governor of New Jersey -- Requesting him to give all the assistance and support in his power to the Officers of Customs in the discharge of their duties.

July 11. Burlington. Letter from Gov'r Franklin to Secr. Hillsborough -- The Assembly of New Jersey sent an answer to the letter from the Speaker of the Massachusetts Bay, but no notice of it was taken on their Minutes, which induced him to believe they had not -- the answer was printed in "The Pennsylvania Chronicle and Universal Advertiser" of 4th July, 1768, No. 24, of Vol. II., a copy of which is herewith enclosed -- the Assembly of New Jersey have been dissolved, and a new one elected -- sends an anonymous pamphlet, published first in New York, and reprinted in Philadelphia.

Enclosing the Pennsylvania Chronicle and Universal Advertiser, July 11, 1768, and "The Power and Grandeur of G't Br., &c.," (a pamphlet.).

--------- Philadelphia. A pamphlet entitled "The Power and Grandeur of Great Britain, founded on the liberty of the Colonies, and the mischiefs attending the taxing them by Act of Parliament, demonstrated" --- Philadelphia, printed and sold by Wm. Goddard, at the new Printing Office in Market Street. MDCCLXVIII.
Enclosed in foregoing letter of Gov'r Franklin.

[Aug. 1, 1768 - Boston Non-Importation Agreement]

August 25. Burlington. Letter from Gov'r Franklin to the Earl of Hillsborough -- Received copies of several papers relative to the murder of William Odgers, one of the Officers of the Customs in Cornwall -- every step will be taken to secure the murderer if he should be found within the Government of N. J.

Aug. 25. Burlington. Letter from Gov'r Franklin to the Earl of Hillsborough, in answer to the complaint made by the Commissioners of Customs in America to the King -- There has been but one instance in N. Jersey when one of the Custom Officers was obstructed in the execution of his duty; but Mr. Hatton, the Collector of Salem, had exceedingly misbehaved himself, being "a man of a most unhappy temper."

1769

May 13. Whitehall. Letter from Secr. Lord Hillsborough to the Governor of New Jersey -- Encloses the King's speech to Parliament -- His Majesty's present Government have at no time entertained a design to propose laying any further taxes on America, for the purpose of raising a revenue -- their intention to propose the taking off duties upon glass, paper and colours, such duties having been laid contrary to the true principles of commerce -- reliance upon his prudence to explain such measures, which may tend to remove prejudices and re-establish mutual confidence and affection.

1770

[Jan. 28. New York. Gov'r Franklin to Cortlandt Skinner -- The riotous proceedings at Monmouth of so alarming a nature that he had thought it necessary to summon a meeting of the Council at Amboy on 7th Feb., and to require the attendance of the Sheriff and Justices of the County present at the riot -- the affair such an audacious insult to the Government, that let the consequences be what they might, the offenders should be punished in the most exemplary manner.]

[March 5, 1770 - The Boston Massacre]

[April 12, 1770 – Parliament repeals Townshend Acts]

April 28. Burlington. Letter from Gov'r Franklin to the Earl of Hillsborough -- The mandamus appointing Mr. Stephen Skinner of the Council of N. Jersey received -- the Assembly was called on account of the riots committed by the "Sons of Liberty' in the counties of Monmouth and Essex, but the rioters are entirely quelled and humbled -- observations upon an Act against excessive costs in the recovery of debts under £50 -- the Assembly are pressing the Governor to give up the appointment of Coroners, and to let them for the future be entirely elected by the people as in the counties in England.

June 6. St. James'. Order of Council, disallowing two Acts of the Assembly of New Jersey passed in 1769, viz., an Act for striking £100,000 in bills of credit, and a supplementary Act for settling the common lands of the township of Bergen.

June 12. Whitehall. Letter from the Earl of Hillsborough to Gov'r Franklin, desiring him to take the proper steps for promulgating His Majesty's Royal disallowance of two Acts of the Province of New Jersey.

July 6. Whitehall. Letter from the Earl of Hillsborough to Gov'r Franklin -- The Acts of the Assembly of New Jersey are communicated to the Board of Trade -- the activity and zeal of the Council and Civil Magistrates to suppress the riots in the counties of Monmouth and Essex highly commended -- the King approves Gov'r Franklin's conduct in not giving up the power of appointing Coroners.

Sept. 29. Perth Amboy. Letter from Gov'r Franklin to the Earl of Hillsborough -- The members of the Assembly of New Jersey are greatly displeased at the disallowance of the paper money Act, and it is to be feared that a party among them will take the advantage of the ill-humor, and prevail on the Assembly not to grant any money for the support of the King's troops stationed in that Province.

Nov. 5. Burlington. Letter from Gov'r Franklin to the Earl of Hillsborough -- The session of the Assembly of New Jersey lasted until the 27th of Oct. -- they came to a resolution that no further provision should be made for the supply of the troops, but the matter was reconsidered, and they granted £500 currency for that purpose, which will last until April -- the Assembly have left the appointment of the barrack masters entirely to the Governor -- the masters nominated by the Assembly greatly imposed upon and defrauded the Province.

Nov. 15. Whitehall. Letter from Secr. Lord Hillsborough to the Governor of New Jersey -- The King's pleasure that he should, without delay, with the advice of his Council and Assembly, fall upon some means to put Indian affairs under such regulations as may have the effect of preventing abuses of trade and violences, &c., which the Indians so justly complain of.

Dec. 11. Whitehall. Circular Letter from the Earl of Hillsborough to the Governors in North America and West Indies, directing them to give every assistance to the King's Officers to raise such a number of recruits as shall be necessary for augmenting the battalions now serving in America.

Dec. 11. Whitehall. Letter from the Earl of Hillsborough to Governor Franklin -- Transmits two Orders of Council; one disallowing an Act of New Jersey for regulating the practice of the law, another confirming an Act for choosing Representatives in the counties of Morris, Cumberland, and Sussex -- observations upon the said Acts.

Dec. 19. Whitehall. Representation from the Board of Trade to the King, recommending the repeal of an Act of the Assembly of New Jersey, passed there in November, 1769, entitled "An Act to erect courts in the several counties in this Colony for the trial of causes of ten pounds and under."

1771.

Jan. 2. Whitehall. Letter from the Earl of Hillsborough to Gov'r Franklin -- Nothing would have been more unbecoming than the New Jersey Assembly's refusal to provide for the King's troops -- it gives great pleasure to find they had receded from so indecent a resolution.

[March 30. Burlington. Letter from Governor Franklin to Lieutenant Arthur Wadman, 26th Regiment -- Promising all the assistance in his power in furthering the recruiting of men in New Jersey -- Lieut. W. having arrived in the Province for the purpose, and made New Brunswick his headquarters -- had issued a proclamation to all magistrates and other civil officers to aid and assist.]

May 4. Whitehall. Letter from the Earl of Hillsborough to Gov'r Franklin -- The King doubts not but the people of New Jersey will put themselves in a state of defence in case of a war with Spain -- His Lordship is aware of the difficulties that will attend making a general regulation for the Indian trade, and cannot but lament the obstacles which have been thrown in the way of establishing a general superintending power over all the British' Dominions in America -- the King has been pleased to approve Mr. D. Coxe for the vacancy in the Council of New Jersey, occasioned by the death of Mr. John Ladd.

June 1. Burlington. Letter from Gov'r Franklin to the Earl of Hillsborough -- The Assembly of New Jersey still refuse to grant any money for the supply of the King's troops stationed there -- the reasons why they should not be dissolved -- they will be prorogued from time to time, until the orders from the King shall arrive what is to be done in this matter.

June 7. St. James'. Order of Council disallowing an Act of the Assembly of New Jersey, passed in March, 1770, entitled "An Act to explain and amend an Act for the relief of insolvent debtors."

June 7. St. James'. Order of Council disallowing an Act of the Assembly of New Jersey, passed in November, 1769, entitled an Act to erect Courts in the several counties in this Colony for the trial of causes of ten pounds and under.

Oct. 21. Burlington. Letter from Gov'r Franklin to the Earl of Hillsborough -- Mr. Lawrence thankful for the honor of being appointed to the Council Board of New Jersey -- the meeting of the Assembly will take place on the 20th November, when he will not fail to renew his endeavours to persuade the Assembly to provide for the King's troops -- is surprised to find that the Commissioners of the Customs at Boston have transmitted to the Treasury Board the complaint of Hatton, whom they knew to have before acted "as a villain in his office."

Dec. 27. Burlington. Letter from Gov'r Franklin to the Earl of Hillsborough -- The Assembly was prevailed upon to provide for the arrears due to the troops stationed in New Jersey -- the debt of the Colony incurred during the late war, about £200,000 currency, is to be paid off annually until 1783, at £15,000 a-year -- observations on this subject -- the matter of appointment of an Agent is also settled agreeably to the wishes of the Board of Trade.

1772

Feb. 8. Whitehall. Circular Letter from the Earl of Hillsborough to all the Governors in America, informing them of the death of the Princess Dowager of Wales, which took place on that day in the morning. Enclosing. Circular about the mourning, and Circular about the alteration of the Form of prayer for the Royal Family.

Feb. 13. Whitehall. Representation from the Board of Trade to the King -- Enclosing drafts of an additional instruction for the Governors in America, relating to the alteration in the prayers for the Royal Family.

March 4. Whitehall. Letter from the Earl of Hillsborough to Gov'r Franklin -- The King approves of the zeal and attention shown for his service in obtaining the provision for his troops lately stationed in New Jersey.

[June 9, 1772 - The burning of the *Gaspee*]

June 24. Burlington. Letter from Gov'r Franklin to the Earl of Hillsborough -- Glad to hear that his success to obtain a provision for the troops has been so satisfactory to the King -- the Assembly are called for the 19th of Aug.

Sept. 4. Letter from the Earl of Dartmouth to the Chief Justices of New York, New Jersey, Massachusetts, and the Judge of the Vice Admiralty Court at Boston, informing of their being appointed Commissioners for inquiring into and making report to the King of all the circumstances relative to the attacking, plundering and burning the *Gaspee* schooner within the Colony of Rhode Island.

Sept. 4. Whitehall. Letter from the Earl of Dartmouth (Secr. of State) to Gov'r Franklin -- In consequence of the daring insult offered to His Majesty's Commission, in the plundering and burning the *Gaspee* schooner in the River of Narraganset, within the Colony of Rhode Island, the Chief Justice of N. Jersey is directed with all convenient despatch to repair thither, in order to the carrying the issued Commission into execution.

Sept. 5. Whitehall. Letter from the Earl of Dartmouth to the Chief Justices of New York, New Jersey, Massachusetts, and the Judge of the Vice Admiralty Court at Boston, enclosing copy of a despatch received from R. Ad. Montague, with the list of the names of persons stated to have been. ringleaders in the attack and burning of the *Gaspee* schooner in Rhode Island.

Oct. 5. Burlington. Letter from Gov'r Franklin to the Earl of Hillsborough -- The Assembly of New Jersey (notwithstanding all the resolutions of the late House to the contrary) granted a sum of money for the support of the King's troops.

Oct. 5. Amboy, N. J. Letter from Mr. Smyth, Chief Justice of New Jersey, to the (Earl of Hillsborough) -- Arrived at N. York on the 22d of Sept., -- on his coming to New Jersey he found the Governor and Assembly engaged in a violent contest on the subject of the Treasurer of the Province, who about four years ago was robbed of £6000 of public money -- the opinion of the people in general on the subject of the new projected Government on the Ohio is very unfavorable -- desires to be allowed to receive a certain sum of money that may be granted by the Assembly for his travelling expenses on the Circuit -- the demand for the British goods in the Colonies is very brisk.

1773

Feb. 8. New York. Letter from Frederick Smyth, Esq., Chief Justice of New Jersey, to the Earl of Dartmouth, upon his return from Rhode Island, where he went to assist in carrying on an inquiry into the circumstance relative to the plundering and burning the schooner *Gaspee* -- gives a particular account of the disposition of the inhabitants of that and the neighbouring Provinces, and expresses his fears that the intention of the Government will be defeated, and the offenders screened from the hand of justice.

[May 10, 1773 - The Tea Act]

[Dec. 16 1773 - Boston Tea Party]

1774

March 10. Whitehall. Circular Letter from Mr. Pownall, by order of the Earl of Dartmouth, to all the Governors in America, enclosing copies of the King's Message to both Houses of Parliament, relative to the disturbances in America, and the resolutions of both Houses which followed thereupon.

[March 31, 1774 - Boston Port Act]

April 6. Whitehall. Circular Letter from Mr. Pownall, by direction of the Earl of Dartmouth, to all the Governors in America, enclosing copy of an Act of Parliament to prevent the landing of goods in the harbour of Boston.

[May 20, 1774 - Administration of Justice Act and Massachusetts Government Act]

May 31. Burlington. Letter from Gov'r Franklin to the Earl of Dartmouth -- The people of New Jersey are not concerned in carrying on any commerce with the Massachusetts Bay -- the merchants of Philadelphia and New York are inclined to assist those of Boston -- a Congress of members of the several Houses of Assembly proposed -- the people of New Jersey joined in the scheme, as they did not choose to appear singular -- the measure is absurd, if not unconstitutional -- he will endeavour to keep the Province quiet, and no attachment nor connections shall ever make him swerve from the duty of his station -- as the times are likely to be more and more difficult, the Seat of Government will be removed to Amboy, where a Council can be assembled with greater ease than at Burlington.

June. 1. Whitehall. Circular Letter from Mr. Knox, by order of the Earl of Dartmouth, to all the Governors in America, (except Massachusetts Bay,) transmitting copies of two Acts of Parliament, viz. -- An Act for the impartial administration of justice in the cases of persons questioned for any acts done by them in the execution of the law, or for the suppression of the riots and tumults in Mass'ts Bay; and an Act for better regulating the Government of the Province of Mass'ts Bay, in New England -- directing the said Acts to be made public in each colony.

[June 2, 1774 - (2nd) Quartering Act]

[June 13. Elizabethtown. Letter from the Committee of the people of Essex County to the inhabitants of Monmouth County -- "Friends to the liberties and privileges of the American Colonies" -- commenting upon the events at Boston, and recommending a general meeting at New Brunswick, July 21.]

[June 22, 1774 - Quebec Act]

July 6. Whitehall. Letter from the Earl of Dartmouth to Gov'r Franklin -- It could hardly be expected that the Assembly of New Jersey would resist appointing a Committee of Correspondence -- the King approves the removal of the Government Seat from Burlington to Amboy.

Sept. 3 & 5. Philadelphia. Extracts of two (secret and confidential) letters from one of the Delegates for the Congress at Philaphia [sic] to Gov'r Franklin -- Giving an account of the temper of the Delegates, their first day's proceedings, individual description of some of them -- the resolves, &c.
Enclosed in Gov'r Franklin's letter to the Earl of Dartmouth of 6th September, 1774.

[Sept. 5-Oct. 26 - Meeting of the First Continental Congress in Philadelphia]

Sept. 6. Burlington. Letter from Gov'r Franklin to the Earl of Dartmouth -- There has been a general meeting at New Brunswick, when they came to resolutions similar to those of the other Colonies a copy of which is contained in the enclosed -- "The Pennsylvania Gazette" [July 27, No. 2379] -- transmits copies of two letters from a member of the Congress, containing an account of their first two days' proceedings, with the request that they should be kept secret [dated Sept. 3 and Sept. 5] -- the same gentleman wrote a pamphlet, entitled "Arguments on both Sides, &c.," which is already printed, and a copy herewith transmitted, but is doubtful whether it will be of any use to make it public.
-- A printed Pamphlet, but it is very doubtful if ever it was circulated, entitled "Arguments on both sides in the dispute between G't Britain and her Colonies," -- In which those in favor of the power of Parliament to bind the Colonies are stated and answered, and the rights of the Colonists explained and asserted on new and just principles -- by a sincere friend to both countries -- to which is added, Lord N.'s [North's] Political Creed with respect to America -- printed in the year 1774.
Enclosed in Gov'r Franklin's letter to the Earl of Dartmouth, of 6th Sept., 1774.

Sept. 7. Whitehall. Letter from the Earl of Dartmouth to Gov'r Franklin -- Acknowledges the receipt of several public papers -- the King is very much concerned about the nomination of Deputies from the different Colonies to meet in general Congress at Philadelphia -- the complaints of grievances coming from each Colony separately, would have much greater weight than from a channel, of the propriety and legality of which there may be much doubt -- the measure is gone too far to encourage any hope of its being retracted.

Oct. 19. Whitehall. Circular Letter from the Earl of Dartmouth to all the Governors in America -- Enclosing King's order for arresting and securing any gunpowder, arms or ammunition, which might be imported from England to the Colonies, except the Master of the ship will show a license for so doing.

Oct. 29. New York. Letter from Gov'r Franklin to the Earl of Dartmouth -- Transmits a pamphlet, published by the Congress at Philadelphia, containing their resolutions, &c.

Oct. Philadelphia. Petition of the members of the Congress at Philadelphia to the King, praying the redress of the grievances -- fifty-one original signatures, among which are Samuel and John Adams, General Washington, and other eminent men.

Nov. 2. Whitehall. Letter from the Earl of Dartmouth to Gov'r Franklin -- The King approves his conduct in transmitting the papers in his despatch of the 6th of September -- every information with regard to the state of North America would be very useful -- it will be kept most secret.

Dec. 6. Perth Amboy. Letter from Gov'r Franklin to the Earl of Dartmouth -- Although the proceedings of the Congress are not altogether satisfactory, yet the terms of association (non-import) will be generally carried into execution -- the opinion of the moderate men is, that the mother country must either consent to what must appear humiliating in the eyes of all Europe, or to compel obedience to her laws by a military force -- a plan of constitutional union with Great Britain was proposed and even entered on their Minutes, with an order referring it to further consideration, but the plan and order was afterward erased from the Minutes -- copy of the "plan of constitutional union with |the mother country is herewith transmitted."

Dec. 10. Whitehall. Circular Letter from Earl of Dartmouth to all the Governors in America, transmitting to them copies of the King's speech to both Houses of Parliament, their Addresses, and the King's declaration of his determination to withstand every attempt to weaken his authority over the Colonies.

[Dec. 22. New Jersey citizens of the town of Greenwich dressed as Indians, and emulating those of Boston, seized tea from the British brig *Greyhound*, moored on Cohansey Creek (a tributary of the Delaware River), and burned its cargo. This event came to be known as "The New Jersey Tea Party."]

1775.

Jan. 4. Whitehall. Circular Letter from the Earl of Dartmouth to the Governors in North America, directing them to prevent the choice of Deputies to attend the Continental Congress, and to exhort all persons from such unjustifiable proceedings.

[Jan. 5. Shrewsbury. Advertisement calling a meeting of the inhabitants of Shrewsbury for the 17th Jan., to choose a Committee in accordance with the recommendations of the Continental Congress.]

Jan. 7. Whitehall. Letter from the Earl of Dartmouth to Gov'r Franklin -- The despatch of the 6th of Dec., and the plan of a proposed Union was received -- the Parliament at the next sitting will come to some final decision with regard to the Colonies -- the disapprobation of the proceedings of the Congress from the higher class of men in New York and New Jersey, must have an influence upon the minds of unprejudiced persons.

Feb. 1. Perth Amboy. Letter from Gov'r Franklin to the (Earl of Dartmouth) -- The Assembly of New Jersey met on the 1lth of Jan., and have approved the proceedings of the Congress at Philadelphia -- transmits public papers -- observations on the Assembly's Address.

Feb. 13. New Jersey. Address of the Assembly of New Jersey to the King -- Recapitulating their grievances, and praying for the redress of them.

Feb. 18. Perth Amboy. Letter from Gov'r Franklin to the Earl of Dartmouth -- Notice is given to all the officers of the Customs in New Jersey, to seize all arms and ammunition which may be imported into that Province, without a license from the King or the Privy Council.

Feb. 22. Whitehall. Circular Letter from the Earl of Dartmouth to the Governors of New York, N. Jersey, New Hampshire and Pennsylvania, enclosing the Addresses of both Houses of Parliament to the King, with regard to the state of the American Colonies -- a bill brought to the House of Commons for restraining the trade and fisheries to the four New England Governments, and a copy of a resolution declaratory of the sense of Parliament upon the subject of taxation -- it is hoped that the last-named resolution will produce such a conduct on the part of the Colonies as shall lead to a restoration of the public tranquility.

March 3. Whitehall. Circular Letter from the Earl of Dartmouth to the Governors in North America -- Enclosing copy of a resolution of the House of Commons, (27th Feb.) which resolution the King approves entirely, and hopes that the Colonies will handsomely provide for the Civil Government -- but every attempt to violate the rights of Parliament, to distress and obstruct the lawful commerce of his subjects, and to encourage in the Colonies ideas of independence, he will resist with firmness.

April 3. Perth Amboy. Letter from Gov'r Franklin to the Earl of Dartmouth -- Desires that all the intelligence which he communicates may be kept as secret as possible -- transmits extracts of several letters, giving an account of the disposition of the people of New Jersey -- Mr. Galloway has published a pamphlet containing his plan of a proposed union between Great Britain and the Colonies, with reasons in support of it -- is very much concerned to find that his letter of the 29th of Oct. was not delivered -- the Assembly had resolved upon appointing members for the intended general Congress in May -- all the

Circular Letters sent to the Governors are published in Rhode Island newspapers, with some innocent remarks.

April 5. Whitehall. Circular Letter from Mr. Pownall, by order of the Earl of Dartmouth, to all the Governors in North America -- Enclosing copy of an Act of Parliament for restraining the trade and commerce of the four New England Colonies.

April 5. Whitehall. Circular Letter from Mr. Pownall to all the Governors in America -- Enclosing a Gazette containing a Proclamation issued by order of the States General, prohibiting the exportation of arms and ammunition from their dominions.
Enclosing the London Gazette from March 28 to April 1, 1775. No. 11548.

April 15. Whitehall. Circular Letter from the Earl of Dartmouth to the several Governors in North America -- Acquainting them with the King's pleasure that the orders of the Commander-in-Chief of the forces in America shall be supreme, and be obeyed accordingly.

[April 19 1775 - Battles of Lexington and Concord]

May 6. Perth Amboy. Letter from Gov'r Franklin to the Earl of Dartmouth -- The reconciliation with the people was totally defeated by the proceedings of the King's troops at Concord -- the people of N. J. are alarmed—they are arming themselves -- attempt to carry the treasury chest and the records away -- they are entering into associations similar to that of New York, to obey their Congress -- observations on Gen. Gage's measures -- the impropriety of publishing the Governor's correspondence, by order of the House of Commons.

May 22. Whitehall. Letter from Secr. Lord Dartmouth to the Governor of New Jersey -- Acquainting him with the death of the Queen of Denmark, the King's sister, and enclosing the Gazette containing the orders for mourning.

June 5. Perth Amboy. Letter from Gov'r Franklin to the Earl of Dartmouth -- Incorporated the whole letter of the 3d of March into his speech at the opening of the session in New Jersey -- It is whispered that the Assembly intend to propose some other terms of accommodation -- opinions on the Governor's speech -- since the affair at Lexington the Colonies have been in the utmost commotion -- proceedings in New Jersey -- the militia officers send their resignations-- the paper money could not be sunk -- the Assembly took notice of the extracts from his despatches, published in Almon's Parliamentary Register, and have entered it on their Minutes -- encloses several printed and MS. papers.

June 7. Whitehall. Letter from the Earl of Dartmouth to Gov'r Franklin -- Every intelligence received from him will be kept secret -- it is evident now that the appointment of the Delegates to the Congress could not have been prevented by any measures -- received an unfavorable account of a conflict between the King's troops and some of the Provincials, but receiving no intelligence from Gen. Gage, no reliance can be placed upon the truth of it.

[July - Congress offers King George the "Olive Branch" petitition, but which he refuses even to read.]

July 4. Perth Amboy. Letter from Gov'r Franklin to the Earl of Dartmouth -- Intelligence of the movements of the Provincial troops in New Jersey and Philadelphia -- sends Minutes of the Council and Journals of the Assembly.

July 4. Whitehall. Letter from the Earl of Dartmouth to Gov'r Franklin -- Gen. Gage's attempt at Concord had a fatal effect upon the mind of the people, and frustrated the object for which the Circular Letter of the 3d of March was sent to the Governor -- no hope of a reconciliation -- the King is firmly resolved to crush the rebellion -- Gen. Gage and Admiral Graves have orders to exert the most vigorous efforts for suppressing the rebellion.

July 5. Perth Amboy. Letter from Gov'r Franklin to the Earl of Dartmouth -- Major [Philip] Skene arrested in Philadelphia -- Copies of the order of the Congress for the arrest of Maj. Skene -- his letter to Gov'r Penn, and the Governor's answer transmitted.
[Major Skene arrived in Philadelphia from London with some other officers on 7th June. He had been appointed Governor of the Forts at Ticonderoga and Crown Point. His papers were examined, and he sent a prisoner to Connecticut. On July 24th, 1776, Gen. Washington was authorized to consent to his exchange.]

July 12. Whitehall. Letter from the Earl of Dartmouth to Gov'r Franklin -- His speech to the Assembly of New Jersey on the 16th of May is highly approved -- the Assembly felt the force of it, only withheld their concurrence from the fear of the consequences that would follow from the appearance of separating from the other Colonies -- the notice which the Assembly has taken of the publication in the Parliamentary Register of one of his letters, is illiberal and unjust.

Aug. 2. Perth Amboy. Letter from Gov'r Franklin to the Earl of Dartmouth -- A formal Declaration has been published by Congress, and every preparation is made for carrying on war -- sends a copy of that declaration, and a letter from Col. Coxe to Mr. Skinner -- the latter shows the critical situation of the Government officers -- the leaders of the people are aiming to establish a Republic.

Sept. 1. Petition of the Congress to the King, signed by 48 members from the different Colonies -- those of New Jersey were Wil. Livingston, John De Hart and Richard Smith -- praying His Majesty to adopt measures of reconciliation—delivered to the Earl of Dartmouth by Messrs. Penn and Lee.

Sept. 5. Perth Amboy. Letter from Gov'r Franklin to the Earl of Dartmouth -- The despatch of the 7th of June came to him opened at the Post Office at New York -- orders should be given to the Captains of the packets to deliver despatches to the Captain of the man-of-war stationed in New York -- an account of the proceedings of the people -- he is loth to desert his station, but it would mortify him extremely to be led like a " bear" through the country to some place of confinement in New England like Gov'r Skeene -- the Government officers in New Jersey are not protected -- the Provincial Congress at Trenton took upon them the entire command of the militia -- no prospect of the salaries being paid to the King's officers.

Sept. 6. Whitehall. Circular Letter from Mr. Pownall, by order of the Earl of Dartmouth, to all the Governors in America, enclosing the King's Proclamation of the 23d of Aug., for suppressing rebellion and sedition.

Oct. 3. Perth Amboy. Letter from Gov'r Franklin to the Earl of Dartmouth -- The matters are now carried so far that unless some propositions should come from Great Britain, there seems little probability of a change of conduct among the people -- suggests the expediency of his speech being published in England -- suspects that his despatches were opened either in London, Falmouth, or some intermediate office -- John Adams avowed that the letters published in Draper's Mass. Gazette to Gen. Gage were his -- Lord Stirling, (Mr. Alexander,) one of the Council of New Jersey, accepted a Colonel's Commission from the Provincial Congress[176] -- Samuel Smith, Esq., on account of his age and infirmities, has resigned his seat at the Board, but no gentleman as yet would consent to be nominated -- the Courts are still open -- the Council advised calling the Assembly on the 15th of next month, but there is a doubt if they will meet.

Oct. 28. Whitehall. Circular Letter from the Earl of Dartmouth to all the Governors in America, except Massachusetts Bay and North Carolina, enclosing the King's speech and the address, in order to convince the rebellious inhabitants of the Colonies of the firm resolution of every branch of the Legislature to maintain the dignity and authority of Parliament, as well as their desire at reconciliation.

Nov. 1. Perth Amboy. Letter from Gov'r Franklin to the Earl of Dartmouth -- Some of the despatches were miscarried -- by order of the Continental Congress, two battalions are to be raised in New Jersey -- unless the army under Schuyler or Washington be defeated, there seems every probability of the inhabitants following the Congress implicitly -- sends some newspapers containing various intelligence -- one Dr. Church arrested by Washington, and accused of acting as a spy in his camp -- encloses copy of Dr.

[176] William Alexander, i.e., "Lord Stirlng," of course, would later become a Major General in the Continental Army.

Church's letter to Major Kane at Boston, intercepted at Rhode Island, and delivered to Washington -- the fate of transport from Boston to New York -- the uncertainty of conveyance of letters prevents writing more particularly.

Nov. 8. Whitehall. Circular Letter from the Earl of Dartmouth to the several Governors in North America, directing them to inform all the King's officers in their respective Governments, that they are at liberty to withdraw themselves from the Colony whenever their personal safety shall make it necessary for them so to do.

Dec. 3. Burlington. Letter from Gov'r Franklin to the Earl of Dartmouth -- Transmits copies of his Speech at the opening of the session, the Council and Assembly's Addresses and his Answer; also a Message to them on the support of Government, and a proclamation for suppressing rebellion and sedition, &c., which will give an idea of the present state of affairs.

Dec. 23. Whitehall. Letter from Lord George Germain to Gov'r- Franklin -- The King is very much concerned that the people of New Jersey have submitted to the Congress -- the King approves of his conduct, and relies upon his fidelity.

Dec. 23. Whitehall. Circular Letter from Lord George Germain to all the Governors in America, except Connecticut and Rhode Island -- Enclosing an Act of Parliament appointing Commission to enquire into the state of the Colonies, in order to restore tranquillity, and to establish a permanent union with the mother country.

1776.

[Perth Amboy? Draft of a pledge for .the signature of Royalists, written in a feigned hand -- Arms to be provided, and they to hold themselves in readiness three times a week for instruction in their use, to enable them "the better to defend our constitutional rights, maintain the laws, support the magistrates, and protect ourselves and fellow-subjects from violence and injury"-- allegiance to King George the Third to be faithfully borne, &c.]

Jan. 5. Perth Amboy. Secret and confidential letter from Governor Franklin to the Earl of Dartmouth -- Several petitions presented to the Assembly to discourage any attempt to promote an independency of Great Britain -- majority of people in New Jersey and Pennsylvania averse to it -- danger seems to be that the design will be carried by degrees -- Assembly granted the usual support to Government, but they evaded complying with His Majesty's requisition -- their intention to petition the King on the present unhappy disputes prevented by a Committee of the General Congress at Philadelphia -- has reason to believe that some of the Council are strongly inclined to favor the measures of Congress -- two Judges and one Justice of the Peace have been seized for refusing to sign associations, and speaking against proceedings of Congress -- William Stirling, commonly called Earl of Stirling, he has suspended from the Council -- generally believed that Congress will have assistance from France, if not from Spain -- French fleet expected in the St. Lawrence, and French troops have already arrived in the West Indies -- the Tories (as they are called) in Sussex County have furnished themselves with arms -- two of the New Jersey Delegates to Congress have resigned their seats, &c.

Jan. 8. Perth Amboy. Letter from Gov'r Franklin to Secretary Lord Dartmouth -- That Lieut.-Col. Wm. Winds, with a party of Provincials, surrounded his house at two o'clock in the morning, and presented his servant with a letter demanding that on account of his letters, that were intercepted, having been sent to the Continental Congress, he was to give his word and honor that he would not leave the Province till the issue were known -- his reply, that he did not intend to do so -- Mr. Skinner's house was also invested, but he had previously escaped, and believes he is safe on board one of the King's ships at New York -- Lord Stirling alone is to blame for these transactions, who seized his despatch of the 5th instant -- finds it is conjectured the Congress will order him to be seized and sent to the interior of the country, so that he may not have any opportunity of transmitting any further intelligence to His Lordship -- whatever may happen will not swerve him in the least from his loyalty.

[Feb. 9. Commission of Elias Dayton to be Colonel of third battalion of the New Jersey troops, signed by John Hancock.]

[March 17. Lord Stirling to the New Jersey Committee of Safety -- Relating to the necessity for suspending the operation of the civil law during the campaign.]

March 28. Perth Amboy. Letter from Governor Franklin to Secretary Lord George Germain -- A full account of being seized prisoner in his own house, by Lord Stirling's orders, with the intention of conveying him to Elizabethtown, which was however prevented by the interference of the Chief Justice, who went to Lord Stirling -- the proceedings, as he has heard, have been disapproved of by the Continental Congress -- remarks on same -- regrets the absence of Mr. Cortlandt.

Skinner, the Attorney General and Speaker of the Assembly, on board a man-of-war with Governor Tryon, whose services would, as always, have been of great assistance -- he has left a wife and thirteen children depending on him for support -- recommends his case to the King -- anticipates some difference with the Council at their next meeting -- has been told that a majority of the Provincial Congress which lately met at Brunswick, appeared inclined to adopt an independency -- encloses printed pamphlets and newspapers, with articles touching the seizing the Commissioners immediately on their arrival -- fears their labours will be comparatively useless -- many represent "reconciliation and ruin as nearly related" -- encloses public papers.

[July 3. John Witherspoon to President of Congress -- Expressing his surprise that Governor Franklin had not yet been carried further than Hackensack.[177]]

[For particulars of Gov'r Franklin's arrest, see *Contributions to East Jersey History*, pp. 194-199. Capt. Kinney, who commanded the Escort having him in charge, was cited before the Provincial Congress to account for his "loitering on the way" to Connecticut.]

[177] The arrested Governor was being sent to Connecticut for confinement there.

ELOQUENCE OF CHIEFS

It has been a long-standing criticism of James Fenimore Cooper's *Leather Stocking* novels that he romanticized and exaggerated the virtues of Indians.[178] Upon reflection, this comes as a somewhat curious charge; seeing how just about no one appears to have faulted him for romanticizing whites as well. Yet the plain and simple truth seems to be that every now and then there are, indeed, wise, honorable and heroic people in real life -- even if more rarely than one could wish; and who and what Cooper wrote about did have some fair basis in fact. Furthermore, it was often observed in the rising decades of the Republic how the Natives had become much degraded following the successive incursions of white settlers, culture, and ways of living (not least of which the imbibing of alcohol) onto what were once Indian lands. How very ironic it is then to reflect on how many modern whites have, in some respects, significantly declined from what *their* ancestors once were.

In the interest of giving our readers of what the *authentic* Noble Savage of old was actually like, we reproduce here five speeches given by chiefs from the 17th and 18th centuries as recorded by American chroniclers and amateur anthropologists. The first three of these occur as appendices to "A Discourse Delivered Before the New-York Historical Society, on 6th December, 1811"[179] by DeWitt Clinton (1769–1828), son of Maj. Gen. James Clinton and nephew of Gov. George Clinton of N.Y., himself Mayor of New York City (establishing the New York Historical Society in 1804 while serving in that office); Lieutenant Governor of N.Y.; anti-war candidate for President against James Madison in 1812, and finally Governor of N.Y. His "Discourse" is itself informative and stimulating (if at certain times dubious in its facts and inadequately weighed assertions) as both a reflection of contemporary sensitivity to Indian concerns and as one of the earliest survey histories of the Five Nations;[180] which latter tribes Clinton extols as being superior, not least of which in their eloquence, compared to other Natives and for the decidedly Republican character of the Iroquois' joint-tribal government.

~~~***~~~

Monsieur De La Barre's Speech, addressed to Garangula, an Onondaga Chief, the Indians and French officers at the same time forming a circle round about him.

"The king, my master, being informed that the Five Nations have often infringed the peace, has ordered me to come hither with a guard, and to send Obguesse to the Onondagas, to bring the chief sachems to my camp. The intention of the great king is, that you and I may smoke the calumet of peace together; but on this condition, that you promise me, in the name of the Senecas, Cayugas, Onondagas, and Mohawks, to give entire satisfaction and reparation to his subjects, and for the future never to molest them.

"The Senecas, Cayugas, Onondagas, Oneidas, and Mohawks, have robbed and abused all the traders that were passing to the Illinois and Miamies, and other Indian nations, the children of my king; they have acted, on these occasions, contrary to the treaty of peace with my predecessor. I am ordered, therefore, to demand satisfaction; and to tell them, that in case of refusal, or their plundering us any more, that I have express orders to declare war. This belt confirms my words. The warriors of the Five Nations have conducted the English into the lakes, which belong to the king, my master, and brought the English among the nations that are his children to destroy the trade of his subjects, and to withdraw these nations from him. They have carried the English thither, notwithstanding the prohibition of the late governor of New-York, who foresaw the risk that both they and you would run. I am willing to forget those things; but if ever the like should happen for the future, I have express orders to declare war against you. This belt confirms my words. Your warriors have made several, barbarous incursions on the Illinois and Miamies. They have massacred men, women, and children; they have made many of these nations prisoners, who thought themselves safe in their villages in time of peace. These people, who are my king's children, must not be your slaves: you must give them their liberty, and send them back into their own country. If the Five

---

178 One of the first to have imputed this charge being author-frontiersman William Joseph Snelling (1804-1848) in his *Tales of the Northwest; or, Sketches of Indian Life and Character* (1830). Cooper, incidentally, gives less romanticized portrayals of Indians in his later *Wyandotte* (1843) and *The Oak Openings* (1848).

179 *Collections of New York Historical Society* (1814), vol. 2, pp. 37-98; available at http://www.archive.org/details/collectionsnewy02socigoog

180 The first was *The History of the Five Indian Nations of Canada, Which are dependent on the Province of New York, etc.* (1747) by New York physicist, scientist, farmer, colonial envoy to the Indians, and Lieutenant-Governor Cadwallader Colden (1688-1776). Colden was also a stern Deist, and scientific correspondent and colleague of Franklin and Alexander Garden, Sr.
~~~

Nations shall refuse to do this, I have express orders to declare war against them. This belt confirms my words.

"This is what I have to say to Garangula, that he may carry to the Senecas, Onondagas, Oneidas, Cayugas, and Mohawks, the declaration which the king, my master, has commanded me to make. He doth not wish them to force him to send a great army to Cadarackui fort, to begin a war, which must be fatal to them. He would be sorry that this fort, that was the work of peace, should become the prison of your warriors. We must endeavour on both sides to prevent such misfortunes. The French, who are the brethren and friends of the Five Nations, will never trouble their repose, provided that the satisfaction which I demand be given; and that the treaties of peace be hereafter observed. I shall be extremely grieved if my words do not produce the effect which I expect from them; for then I shall be obliged to join with the governor of New York, who is commanded by his master to assist me, and burn the castles of the Five Nations, and destroy you. This belt confirms my words."

Garangula, after walking five or six times round the circle, answered the French governor, who sat in an elbow chair, in the following strain:

"YONNONDIO,

"I honour you, and the warriors that are with me likewise honour you. Your interpreter has finished your speech: I now begin mine. My words make haste to reach your ears; hearken to them.

"Yonnondio, you must have believed, when you left Quebec, that the sun had burnt up all the forests, which render our country inaccessible to the French, or that the lakes had so far overflown the banks, that they had surrounded our castles, and that it was impossible for us to get out of them. Yes, Yonnondio, surely you must have dreamt so; and the curiosity of seeing so great a wonder, has brought you so far. Now you are undeceived, since that I and the warriors here present, are come to assure you that the Senecas, Cayugas, Onondagas, Oneidas, and Mohawks, are yet alive. I thank you in their name for bringing back into their country the calumet which your predecessor received from their hands. It was happy for you that you left under ground that murdering hatchet which has been so often died in the blood of the French. Hear, Yonnondio; I do not sleep; I have my eyes open, and the sun which enlightens me, discovers to me a great captain at the head of a company of soldiers, who speaks as if he were dreaming. He says that he only came to the lake to smoke on the great calumet with the Onondagas; but Garangula says that he sees the contrary; that it was to knock them on the head, if sickness had not weakened the arms of the French.

"I see Yonnodio raving in a camp of sick men, whose lives the great spirit has saved by inflicting this sickness on them. Hear, Yonnondio: our women had taken their clubs; our children and old men had carried their bows and arrows into the heart of your camp, if our warriors had not disarmed them, and kept them back, when your messenger Ohguesse came to our castles. It is done, and I have said it. Hear, Yonnondio; we plundered none of the French but those that carried guns, powder and ball to the Twightwies and Chictaghicks, because those arms might have cost us our lives. Herein we follow the example of the Jesuits, who stave all the kegs of rum brought to our castles, lest the drunken Indians should knock them on the head. Our warriors have not beaver enough to pay for all these arms that they have taken; and our old men are not afraid of the war. This belt preserves my words.

"We carried the English into our lakes to trade there with the Utawawas and Quatoghies as the Andirondocks brought the French to our castles to carry on a trade, which the English say is theirs. We are born free. We neither depend on Yonnondio nor Corlear.

"We may go where we please, and carry with us whom we please. If your allies be your slaves, use them as such. Command them to receive no other but your people. This belt preserves my words.

"We knocked the Twightwies and Chictaghicks on the head because they had cut down the trees of peace, which were the limits of our country. They have hunted beavers on our land. They had acted contrary to the customs of all Indians; for they left none of the beavers alive: they killed both male and female. They brought the Satanas into the country to take part with them after they had concerted ill designs against us. We have done less than either the English or French, that have usurped the lands of so many Indian nations, and chased them from their own country. This belt preserves my words.

"Hear, Yonnondio; what I say is the voice of all the Five Nations: hear what they answer. Open your ears to what they speak. The Senecas, Cayugas, Onondagas, Oneidas, and the Mohawks, say, that when they buried the hatchet at the Cadarackui (in the presence of your predecessor) in the middle of the fort, they planted the tree of peace in the same place, to be there carefully preserved, that in place of a retreat for

soldiers, that fort might be a rendezvous for merchants; that in place of arms and ammunition of war, beavers and merchandize should only enter there.
"Hear, Yonnondio; take care for the future, that so great a number of soldiers as appear there do not choke the tree of peace planted in so small a fort It will be a great loss, if after it had so easily taken root, you should stop its growth, and prevent its covering your country and ours with its branches. I assure you, in the name of the Five Nations, that our warriors shall dance to the calumet of peace under its leaves, and shall remain quiet on their mats, and shall never dig up the hatchet till their brother, Yonnondio, or Corlear, shall, either jointly or separately, endeavor to attack the country, which the great spirit has given to our ancestors. This belt preserves my words; and this other, the authority which the Five Nations have given me."

Then Garangula, addressing himself to Monsieur La Main, said, "take courage, Ohguesse, you have spirit, speak -- explain my words; forget nothing; tell all that your brethren and friends say to Yonnondio, your governor, by the mouth of Garangula, who loves you, and desires you to accept of this present of beaver, and take part with me in my feast to which I invite you. This present of beaver is sent to Yonnondio on the part of the Five Nations."

[*Collections of New York Historical Society* (1814), vol. 2, pp. 99-104]

~~~***~~~

Speech of the Mohawk Chiefs to the Magistrates of Albany, on the 25th of March, 1689-90,[181] *after the destruction of Schenectady.*

"Brethren,
"The murder of our brethren at Schenectady by the French, grieves us as much as if it had been done to ourselves, for we are in the same chain; and no doubt our brethren of New England will be likewise sadly affected with this cruel action of the French. The French on this occasion have not acted like brave men, but like thieves and robbers. Be not therefore discouraged. We give this belt to wipe away your tears.

"Brethren,
"We lament the death of so many of our brethren, whose blood has been shed at Schenectady. We don't think that what the French have done can be called a victory, it is only a farther proof of their cruel deceit The governor of Canada sends to Onondaga, and talks to us of peace with our whole house, but war was in his heart, as you may now see by woeful experience. He did the same formerly at Cadarackui, and in the Senecas country. This is the third time he has acted so deceitfully. He has broken open our house at both ends, formerly in the Senecas country, and now here. We hope, however, to be revenged of them. One hundred of our bravest young men are in pursuit of them; they are brisk fellows, and they will follow the French to their doors. We will beset them so closely, that not a man in Canada shall dare to step out of doors to cut a stick of wood; but now we gather up our dead to bury them, by this second belt

"Brethren,
"We came from our castles with tears in our eyes, to bemoan the blood shed at Schenectady by the perfidious French. While we bury our dead murdered at Schenectady, we know not what may have befallen our own people, that are in pursuit of the enemy: they may be dead. What has befallen you may happen to us; and therefore we come to bury our brethren at Schenectady with this third belt.
"Great and sudden is the mischief, as if it had fallen from Heaven upon us. Our forefathers taught us to go with all speed to bemoan and lament with our brethren, when any disaster or misfortune happens to any in our chain. Take this belt of vigilance, that you may be more watchful for the future. We give our brethren eye water to make them sharp sighted. (Giving a fourth belt.)
"We now come to the house where we usually renew the chain; but alas! We find the house polluted with blood. All the Five Nations have heard of this, and we are come to wipe away the blood, and clean the house. We come to invite Corlear, and every one of you, and Quider, (calling to every one of the principal men present by their names) to be revenged of the enemy, by this fifth belt.

[181] [*Edit. Note.* The massacre and burning of Schenectady, carried out by French and Indian raiders, occurred on Feb. 8-9, 1690.]
~~~

"Brethren,
"Be not discouraged; we are strong enough. This is the beginning of your war, and the whole house have their eyes fixed upon you at this time, to observe your behaviour. They wait your motion, and are ready to join in any resolute measures.
"Our chain is a strong chain; it is a silver chain; it can neither rust nor be broken. We, as to our parts, are resolute to continue the war.
"We will never desist, so long as a man of us remains. Take heart; do not pack up and away;*[182] this will give heart to a dastardly enemy. We are of the race of the bear; and a bear, you know, never yields, while one drop of blood is left. We must all be bears. (Giving a sixth belt)

"Brethren,
"Be patient; this disaster is an affliction which has fallen from Heaven upon us. The sun, which hath been cloudy, and sent this disaster, will shine again with its pleasant beams. Take courage, courage -- (Repeating the word several times as they gave a seventh belt)

(*To the English*)

"Brethren,
"Three years ago we were engaged in a bloody war with the French, and you encouraged us to proceed in it. Our success answered our expectation; but we were not well begun, when Corlear stopped us from going on. Had you permitted us to go on, the French would not now have been able to do us the mischief they have done -- we would have prevented their sowing, planting, or reaping.
"We would have humbled them effectually, but now we die. The obstructions you then made now ruin us. Let us after this be steady, and take no such false measures for the future, but prosecute the war vigorously. (Giving a beaver skin.)
"The brethren must keep good watch, and if the enemy come again, send more speedily to us. Don't desert Schenectady. The enemy will glory in seeing it desolate. It will give them courage that had none before. Fortify the place; it is not well fortified now: The stockades are too short; the Indians can jump over them. (Gave a beaver skin.)

"Brethren,
"The mischief done at Schenectady cannot be helped now; but for the future, when the enemy appears any where, let nothing hinder your sending to us by expresses, and fire great guns, that all may be alarmed. We advise you to bring all the River Indians under your subjection to live near Albany, to be ready on all occasions.
"Send to New-England; tell them what has happened to you. They will undoubtedly awake, and send us their helping hand. It is their interest, as much as ours, to push the war to a speedy conclusion. Be not discouraged; the French are not so numerous as some people talk. If we but heartily unite to push on the war, and mind our business, the French will soon be subdued.
"The magistrates having returned an answer on the twenty-seventh, to the satisfaction of the Indians, they repeated it all over, word by word, to let the magistrates see how carefully they minded, and then added.

"Brethren,
"We are glad to find you are not discouraged. The best and wisest men sometimes make mistakes. Let us now pursue the war vigorously. We have a hundred men out; they are good scouts. We expect to meet all the sachems of the other nations, as they come to condole with you. You need not fear our being ready at the first notice. Our ax[e] is always in our hands; but take care that you be timely ready. Your ships, that must do the principal work, are long a fitting out. We do not design to go out with a small company, or in skulking parties; but as soon as the nations can meet, we shall be ready with our whole force. If you would bring this war to a happy issue, you must begin soon, before the French can recover the losses they have received from us, and get new vigour and life, therefore send in all haste to New-England. Neither you nor we can continue long in the condition we are now in: we must order matters so that the French be kept in continual fear and alarm at home; for this is the only way to be secure, and in peace here.

---

[182] * [*DeWitt Clinton's note:*] This was spoken to the English who were about removing from Albany.

"The Scatikok Indians, in our opinion, are well placed where they are (to the northward of Albany;) they are a good out-guard; they are our children, and we must take care that they do their duty: but you must take care of the Indians below the town; place them near the town, so as they may be of more service to you."

[*Collections of New York Historical Society* (1814), vol. 2, pp 105-109]

~~~***~~~

Substance of the Speech of Good Peter[183] *to Governor* [George] *Clinton and the Commissioners of Indian Affairs at Albany, on the occasion referred to in the discourse.*

Brother Governor of the State of New-York, and all the other great chiefs of the state of New-York, open your ears, and all you chiefs of the Wife Nations here assembled, open your cars.

The business we have now met about is of the greatest importance: how happy must we all be if we can arrange it for our mutual good.

We have this day assembled, and smoked our pipes in peace. That you may know the reason of my addressing you, I would inform you that my brethren, the Cayugas, and my children, the Senecas, requested me to be their mouth on this solemn occasion, and understanding that it is agreeable to the great chief of New-York, I now stand here. You will possess your minds in peace, for I have no disposition to oppose you in any respect, but shall move forward in the strait path.

Brother Chief,
In the first place, I would inform you, that last spring we were invited to a treaty at Muskingum -- where your voice also called upon us to attend -- some of our nation went there, and have not yet returned.

When our uncles, the chiefs, left our council fire, their only business at Muskingum, was the establishment of a good peace. This mission was agreeable to us all -- even the warriors; for although the clouds blacken in the south, and the winds sometimes blow, yet as long as our sachems labour for a peace, the minds of our young men are composed.

This, great chief, I only observe to open the way for what is to follow. Shortly after, the cloud from the south began to rise; we again saw the effulgence of the sun; but as soon as we saw it, an evil spirit commenced its work, threatening the annihilation of our territory.

Brother Governor,
Although I observed to you, that an evil spirit had invaded our peace, yet do not suppose that the Five Nations were disposed to cherish this enemy; we were deceived: we believed it to be a good spirit, sent by the great council of the state, and we thought that we should not injure ourselves by opening our ears to their voice. This was indeed new to us, for never before had the Five Nations such a meeting with any of our brethren of this island. We had invariably conferred together according to ancient and settled usage.

It would be tedious to go into detail, and state at large the means by which we were misled. We cannot see but a small depth into the heart of men, and can only discover the work of his tongue, it appears that you then sensibly sympathized with us in our situation, and looking back to ancient times, endeavoured to discover a method of recovering our sinking territory.

Soon after this the Oneida nation heard your voice. Although it was small at first, yet it gave us life, to find that you would extend your arm, and save our country. It informed us, that you would kindle a council fire at Fort Stanwix, inform us of our situation, and relieve us from our difficulties. It also directed us to send it

[183] [*Edit. Note.* Peter was a chief of the Oneidas. Although Peter was not himself a warrior, the tribe had sided and fought side by side with the Americans in the Revolutionary War; most notably at the battle of Oriskany in 1777.]
~~~

on to the other nations, which we did. At the council fire at Fort Stanwix, but one nation, the Onondagas, attended; there was a strange bird that flew about your voice, and related strange stories. This bird kept flying about while you held this council fire. After your patience had been exhausted in waiting several days, you then determined to take us, one by one, as we came to the council fire; and with this we were content.

When you had finished with the Onondagas, you then showed the agreement to us, the Oneidas, pointed out the true path, and opened our eyes. We then comprehended your sentiments as they were laid before us. You raised us from sinking into an unfathomable gulph, and placed us on a high mountain; you erected a fortification around us, so that no evil spirits, or strange birds, could fly over and disturb us; you completed an agreement to our mutual satisfaction: it is firm and unalterable; no evil spirit shall be able to erase the lines. We are now fixed, and dwell in peace.

I need not enlarge upon the council, at Fort Stanwix, and the proceedings at that place. You remember you saw a few Senecas there. You welcomed them, although they were neither invited, nor sachems, but little children; they then told you with what difficulty they leaped over the mound at Canasake.

You also remember, that when those Seneca young men left you, you gave them good advice. As your patience was not yet exhausted, and your love for the Five Nations continued in full force, you invited the Senecas, through them, to meet you at Albanv this winter, to consult upon subjects connected with their welfare. You also requested their attendance from the remotest parts of the nation. They again heard your voice: you opened their eyes; and it pierced them to the heart to see their territory sinking, and that by and by the warriors would not be at liberty to hurt upon their land, and to provide for their women and children.

Soon after this, the headmen and warriors deliberated on our message, and determined that it would be for the good of the Five Nations, and prevent our utter destruction, to repair to this place. Although some of our sachems have not returned from the southward, yet we are persuaded that our deliberations and proceedings will meet their approbation.

After frequent conferences with our brethren, the Senecas, we determined to repair to this ancient council fire; we thought it agreeable to ancient usage to take with us two brothers of the Onondagas and Oneidas, as witnesses, to this place, where our ancestors kindled their council fires; the smoke of which reached the heavens, and round which they sat and talked of peace. I observed at first, that I should only touch upon one event after another. But need I call your attention to the councils and treaties held here by your and our forefathers. They then had but one head and one heart; the chain of friendship was made of silver, so that it could not rust Our ancestors, you know, frequently met to brighten this chain, with a design to see whether any evil spirit that disturbs the peace of brethren, shook it or sat upon it.

But I must leave this pleasant subject, the paths of our ancestors. You have seen some of our brethren of the Five Nations, the Cayugas; you have opened your mind, and encouraged us to believe that you can save our sinking country; and that if any of your people have overleaped the bounds prescribed, you can erase the lines. This has given us great encouragement and universal pleasure.

Brother Governor,
The Cayugas and Senecas, here present, thank you from the bottom of our hearts, that you have communicated freely with us. When we heard your first and second voice we were glad; but now we are quite rejoiced. It convinces us that you remembered and cherished the treaties between you and our forefathers. The great spirit gave our ancestors and us this island; and we know that you are anxious to promote his design, that we should have a place whereon to live. We love our country, and our fathers loved their country.

We said we were glad to meet you and hear your voice, and to feel assured that you are able to save our sinking territory; we now put it all under your power; put your hands over the whole, reserving to us such a dish as you shall prescribe for us. This is perfectly agreeable to the usages of our ancestors, who loved peace, and loved their land; and why? Because they loved their women and their children; and while they loved peace and their land, they enjoyed happy days.

We repeat that we rejoice in this meeting, and in these proceedings. Those we have left behind, and those that will return from the south, will also rejoice at the result of our conferences. Our little ones can now look with pleasure for fish in the streams, and our warriors can hunt for wild beasts in the woods, and feel confident that they will not be driven from their country. (A string of black wampum with six rows.)

Brother,
I have repeatedly said, that I was glad to hear your mind; your words have sunk deep into my heart, and have raised up my land and country, that were about to sink. I entreat you, by this string, to keep firm to your word, and to reach out your hand over my country. Our dish we will reserve. This transaction will rejoice, not only our absent friends, but our children's children, to the latest generation. They will declare with joy, that Aquilanda,*[184] the governor of New York, has rescued their country from destruction. (A string of white wampum with six rows.)

You have heard our voice; we now entreat you to open your ears, and hear a speech from our sisters, the governesses.

Brother,
Our ancestors considered it a great offence to reject the counsels of their women, particularly of the female governesses. They were esteemed the mistresses of the soil. *Who*, said our forefathers bring us into being -- *Who* cultivate our lands, kindle our fires, and boil our pots, but the women?
Our women say, that they are apprehensive their uncles have lost the power of huntings as they were about destroying their country; but they take this opportunity of thanking you for preventing their fall down the precipice, to which their uncles had brought them.
They entreat that the veneration of their ancestors, in favour of women, be not disregarded, and that they may not be despised: the great spirit is their maker.

The female governesses beg leave to speak, with that freedom allowed to women, and agreeable to the spirit of our ancestors. They entreat the great chief to put forth his strength, and preserve them in peace; for they are the life of the nation; your power cannot be disputed. Those that disturb them are your subjects, and you can punish them. They rejoice, that while their counsellors are settling a peace at Muskingum, and you are here labouring for their good, tranquillity will be spread over the whole country, (Six strings of wampum.)

Then Good Peter added.

Brother,
Possess your mind in peace. You are sensible that in affairs of importance, omissions may be made, and that a person is allowed afterward to correct them.
You have greatly encouraged us, by promising to watch over our peace, and to provide for our welfare. It is probable, that when we have completed our business here, some bad men may break over the fence you have set around us. There are, excuse us brother, some bad men among the white people of this island; they may not hear your voice as far as our country: we therefore propose that Peter Ryckman, our child, may live among us in your behalf, look at our affairs, and watch over our interests.
You have now heard our minds, and the resolutions we had formed before we left our country. I only act here as an agent, by the request of my brothers, the Cayugas, and I am now released from my engagements.

[*Collections of New York Historical Society* (1814), vol. 2, pp. 110-116]

~~~***~~~

The following comes from Thomas Jefferson's Notes on the State of Virginia *(1781-1782), Query 6.*

"Of their [Native American] eminence in oratory we have fewer examples, because it is displayed chiefly in their own councils. Some, however, we have of very superior lustre. I may challenge the whole orations of Demosthenes and Cicero, and of any more eminent orator, if Europe has furnished more

[184] * [*DeWitt Clinton's note:*] An Indian name given to Governor Clinton, which signifies *rising sun*.
~~~

eminent, to produce a single passage, superior to the speech of Logan [Tah-gah-jute], a Mingo chief,[185] to Lord Dunmore, when governor of this state. And, as a testimony of their talents in this line, I beg leave to introduce it, first stating the incidents necessary for understanding it. In the spring of the year 1774, a robbery and murder were committed on an inhabitant of the frontiers of Virginia, by two Indians of the Shawanee tribe. The neighbouring whites, according to their custom, undertook to punish this outrage in a summary way. Col. Cresap, a man infamous for the many murders he had committed on those much-injured people, collected a party, and proceeded down the Kanhaway in quest of vengeance. Unfortunately a canoe of women and children, with one man only, was seen coming from the opposite shore, unarmed, and unsuspecting an hostile attack from the whites. Cresap and his party concealed themselves on the bank of the river, and the moment the canoe reached the shore, singled out their objects, and, at one fire, killed every person in it. This happened to be the family of Logan, who had long been distinguished as a friend of the whites. This unworthy return provoked his vengeance. He accordingly signalized himself in the war which ensued. In the autumn of the same year, a decisive battle was fought at the mouth of the Great Kanhaway, between the collected forces of the Shawanees, Mingoes, and Delawares, and a detachment of the Virginia militia. The Indians were defeated, and sued for peace. Logan however disdained to be seen among the suppliants. But, lest the sincerity of a treaty should be distrusted, from which so distinguished a chief absented himself, he sent by a messenger the following speech to be delivered to Lord Dunmore.

"I appeal to any white man to say, if ever he entered Logan's cabin hungry, and he gave him not meat; if ever he came cold and naked, and he clothed him not. During the course of the last long and bloody war, Logan remained idle in his cabin, an advocate for peace. Such was my love for the whites, that my countrymen pointed as they passed, and said, 'Logan is the friend of white men.' I had even thought to have lived with you, but for the injuries of one man. Col. Cresap, the last spring, in cold blood, and unprovoked, murdered all the relations of Logan, not sparing even my women and children. There runs not a drop of my blood in the veins of any living creature. This called on me for revenge. I have sought it: I have killed many: I have fully glutted my vengeance. For my country, I rejoice at the beams of peace. But do not harbour a thought that mine is the joy of fear. Logan never felt fear. He will not turn on his heel to save his life. Who is there to mourn for Logan? -- Not one."

~~~***~~~

Red Jacket (c. 1752-1830), also known as Sagoyewatha after 1780, was a Seneca who allied with the British in the Revolutionary war, but afterward made his peace with the Americans, including being received by Presidents Washington and John Adams. Of all the speeches reproduced here by us, this, in which he addresses some missionaries, is possibly the most famous and well known; and can be found in The Life and Times of Red Jacket (1841) by W. L. Stone. Although some might loosely interpret Red Jacket's address as a wholesale rejection of Christianity, this is evidently mistaken as he seems more correctly to find blame with certain kinds of hypocrites, well meaning or otherwise, instead. Indeed, it is perhaps a little touching how in the use of the titles "Brethren" and "Brother" (found in most of these speeches), Christianity would appear to have helped play a positive role in bringing whites and Indians together in peace. That certain putative members failed to live up to the basic tenets of their faith, or else worse used it for ulterior ends, of course will surprise no one.

FRIEND AND BROTHER -- It was the will of the Great Spirit that we should meet together this day. He orders all things, and has given us a fine day for our council. He has taken his garment from before the sun, and caused it to shine with brightness upon us. Our eyes are opened, that we see clearly; our ears are unstopped, that we have been able to hear distinctly the words you have spoken. For all these favors we thank the Great Spirit; and him only.

Brother: This council fire was kindled by you. It was at your request that we came together at this time. We have listened with attention to what you have said. You requested us to speak our minds freely. This gives us great joy; for we now consider that we stand upright before you, and can speak what we think. All have heard your voice, and all speak to you now as one man. Our minds are agreed.

---

[185] [*Edit. Note.* Believed actually to have been of Cayuga/Iroquois origin.]
~~~

Brother: You say you want an answer to your talk before you leave this place. It is right you should have one, as you are a great distance from home, and we do not wish to detain you. But we will first look back a little, and tell you what our fathers have told us, and what we have heard from the white people.

Brother: Listen to what we say. There was a time when our forefathers owned this great island. Their seats extended from the rising to the setting sun. The Great Spirit had made it for the use of Indians. He had created the buffalo, the deer, and other animals for food. He had made the bear and the beaver. Their skins served us for clothing. He had scattered them over the country, and taught us how to take them. He had caused the earth to produce corn for bread. All this He had done for his red children, because He loved them. If we had some disputes about our hunting ground, they were generally settled without the shedding of much blood. But an evil day came upon us. Your forefathers crossed the great water, and landed on this island. Their numbers were small. They found friends and not enemies. They told us they had fled from their own country for fear of wicked men, and had come here to enjoy their religion. They asked for a small seat. We took pity on them; granted their request; and they sat down amongst us. We gave them corn and meat; they gave us poison in return.
The white people, brother, had now found our country. Tidings were carried back, and more came amongst us. Yet we did not fear them. We took them to be friends. They called us brothers. We believed them, and gave them a larger seat At length their numbers had greatly increased. They wanted more land; they wanted our country. Our eyes were opened, and our minds became uneasy. Wars took place. Indians were hired to fight against Indians, and many of our people were destroyed. They also brought strong liquor amongst us. It was strong and powerful, and has slain thousands.

Brother: Our seats were once large, and yours were small. You have now become a great people, and we have scarcely a place left to spread our blankets. You have got our country, but are not satisfied; you want to force your religion upon us.

Brother: Continue to listen. You say that you are sent to instruct us how to worship the Great Spirit agreeably to his mind; and, if we do not take hold of the religion which you white people teach, we shall be unhappy hereafter. You say that you are right, and we are lost. How do we know this to be true? We understand that your religion is written in a book. If it was intended for us as well as you, why has not the Great Spirit given to us, and not only to us, but why did He not give to our forefathers, the knowledge of that book, with the means of understanding it rightly? We only know what you tell us about it. How shall we know when to believe, being so often deceived by the white people?

Brother: You say there is but one way to worship and serve the Great Spirit. If there is but one religion, why do you white people differ so much about it? Why not all agreed, as you can all read the book?

Brother: We do not understand these things. We are told that your religion was given to your forefathers, and has been handed down from father to son. We also have a religion, which was given to our forefathers, and has been handed down to us, their children. We worship in that way. It teaches us to be thankful for all the favors we receive; to love each other, and to be united. We never quarrel about religion.

Brother: The Great Spirit has made us all, but He has made a great difference between his white and red children. He has given us different complexions and different customs. To you He has given the arts. To these He has not opened our eyes. We know these things to be true. Since He has made so great a difference between us in other things, why may we not conclude that He has given us a different religion according to our understanding? The Great Spirit does right He knows what is best for his children; we are satisfied.

Brother: We do not wish to destroy your religion, or take it from you. We only want to enjoy our own.

Brother: You say you have not come to get our land or our money, but to enlighten our minds. I will now tell you that I have been at your meetings, and saw you collect money from the meeting. I cannot tell what this money was intended for, but suppose that it was for your minister, and if we should conform to your way of thinking, perhaps you may want some from us.

Brother: We are told that you have been preaching to the white people in this place. These people are our neighbors. We are acquainted with them. We will wait a little while, and see what effect your preaching has upon them. If we find it does them good, makes them honest, and less disposed to cheat Indians, we will then consider again of what you have said.

Brother: You have now heard our answer to your talk, and this is all we have to say at present as we are going to part, we will come and take you by the hand, and hope the Great Spirit will protect you on your journey, and return you safe to your friends.

FLAMBOROUGH HEAD REVISITED

In preparing an article pertaining to Israel Potter, made famous by Herman Melville's fictionalized account of him, I originally contemplated presenting a selection of passages from Potter's 1824 memoir *Life and remarkable adventures of Israel R. Potter, (a native of Cranston, Rhode-Island.)*, co-written with Henry Trumbull, a Providence author and publisher. Yet for two reasons I decided against this. For one, and the lesser of the two reasons, there are grounds for believing that there *may* be much more to the historical Potter than he himself admitted to; with, for instance, allegations that he did not nearly tell the full story; including his *possibly* having acted as a double agent during the Revolutionary War; as averred, *correctly or no*, in "Israel Potter: Genesis of a Legend" by David Chacko and Alexander Kulcsar (see *The William and Mary Quarterly*, 3rd Series, Vol. 41, No. 3, July 1984.) My second inducement, even if the first didn't suffice, is that the more moving portions of Potter's account deal less with his Revolutionary war experiences than with his Dickensian life of extreme poverty in London after the war. While not without its relevance or human interest value, providing as it does glimpses of lives and fates of poor soldiers in England after the great wars (both Revolutionary and Napoleonic), the affect on a reader is rather dismal and depressing; making Potter's ordeal almost existential and more emotionally akin to Melville's "Bartleby, The Scrivener" than his fictional Israel Potter. No doubt for the same cause, Melville devotes *much* less space proportionally to Potter's post-war experiences in his 1854-1855 serialized novelette than does Potter himself in the original memoir, saying:

"But these experiences, both from their intensity and his solitude, were necessarily squalid. Best not enlarge upon them. For just as extreme suffering, without hope, is intolerable to the victim, so, to others, is its depiction without some corresponding delusive mitigation. The gloomiest and truthfulest dramatist seldom chooses for his theme the calamities, however extraordinary, of inferior and private persons; least of all, the pauper's; admonished by the fact, that to the craped palace of the king lying in state, thousands of starers shall throng; but few feel enticed to the shanty, where, like a pealed knuckle-bone, grins the unupholstered corpse of the beggar." [ch. 26]

What Melville then opted to do instead is use Potter's narrative as the basis of a usually rollicking picaresque novel along the lines of Le Sage, Fielding and Smollett. At the same time, he takes Potter's story and turns it into a kind of *Bildungsroman* or novel of formation in order to give it some depth. As Melville's own father died when he was but twelve years old,[186] he seemed when he was growing up to have been on the look-out for an uncle, such as Roderick Random had, to serve as a substitute; and judging by *White Jacket* (1850) and *Potter*, he apparently found one or more when serving as a sailor. For it most likely would have been from such a fatherly surrogate that Melville acquired some of that kindly, yet no-nonsense, paternal affection and outlook he adopts in raising and caring for the youthful characters of his stories.

Although unfairly denigrated by some as essentially a piece of hired work written purely for money making, this assessment of *Potter* is a gross distortion. As well as eminently enjoyable, in parts it contains some of Melville's most virile prose and life observations. If it is less than it might have been this is because the novel is simply less structured and fully developed than it might potentially have been. Otherwise it has worthwhile commentary and a lesson to relate regarding the common folk, that is to say *the pawns*, of great historical events, and a story sufficiently entertaining to carry and render amusing the lesson. Perhaps its most inexcusable flaw is the inclusion of an anachronistic episode involving Ethan Allen as an afterthought, and which in terms of chronological sequence is glaringly out of place; thus overtly bringing out the limitations Melville labored under while writing it. While the historical Potter did not cross paths with either Ethan Allen or John Paul Jones, he did reportedly meet George III, Benjamin Franklin, and Henry Laurens (though Melville makes no mention at all of the latter.)

Yet it is probably in the mostly fictional chapters dealing with the historical John Paul Jones that Melville's novel most takes wing; which conclusion doubtless fans of Defoe, Smollett, Cooper, Marryat, C.S. Forester, Adam Hardy (pen name of Kenneth Bulmer), or Alexander Kent (Douglas Reeman) -- some

---

[186] Melville's grand-father, on his mother's side, incidentally was Col. Peter Gansevoort, the heroic defender of Fort Stanwix during the Saratoga campaign.

of *my* favorite naval novelists -- will doubtless readily concur with. Further, John Paul Jones is easily the novel's most effulgent and memorable character.

Even so, due credit naturally must be granted poor Potter himself, and his like, whose curious adventures furnished Melville something to hang his humor and musings on, and whose real life experiences, requiring much sacrifice and suffering, made it all possible -- not only for Jones and Melville, but ourselves as free citizens who ultimately benefited by their service to our country. Here then to give you a sample of Melville at some of his best is chapter 19 recounting, with literary drama and excitement unsurpassed by *any* author, the encounter between the *Bonhomme Richard* and the *Serapis*.

~~~~****~~~~

The battle between the Bon Homme Richard and the Serapis stands in history as the first signal collision on the sea between the Englishman and the American. For obstinacy, mutual hatred, and courage, it is without precedent or subsequent in the story of ocean. The strife long hung undetermined, but the English flag struck in the end.

There would seem to be something singularly indicatory I in this engagement. It may involve at once a type, a parallel, and a prophecy. Sharing the same blood with England, and yet her proved foe in two wars--not wholly inclined at bottom to forget an old grudge--intrepid, unprincipled, reckless, predatory, with boundless ambition, civilized in externals but a savage at heart, America is, or may yet be, the Paul Jones of nations.

Regarded in this indicatory light, the battle between the Bon Homme Richard and the Serapis--in itself so curious--may well enlist our interest.

Never was there a fight so snarled. The intricacy of those incidents which defy the narrator's extrication, is not illy figured in that bewildering intertanglement of all the yards and anchors of the two ships, which confounded them for the time in one chaos of devastation.

Elsewhere than here the reader must go who seeks an elaborate version of the fight, or, indeed, much of any regular account of it whatever. The writer is but brought to mention the battle because he must needs follow, in all events, the fortunes of the humble adventurer whose life lie records. Yet this necessarily involves some general view of each conspicuous incident in which he shares.

Several circumstances of the place and time served to invest the fight with a certain scenic atmosphere casting a light almost poetic over the wild gloom of its tragic results. The battle was fought between the hours of seven and ten at night; the height of it was under a full harvest moon, in view of thousands of distant spectators crowning the high cliffs of Yorkshire.

From the Tees to the Humber, the eastern coast of Britain, for the most part, wears a savage, melancholy, and Calabrian aspect. It is in course of incessant decay. Every year the isle which repulses nearly all other foes, succumbs to the Attila assaults of the deep. Here and there the base of the cliffs is strewn with masses of rock, undermined by the waves, and tumbled headlong below, where, sometimes, the water completely surrounds them, showing in shattered confusion detached rocks, pyramids, and obelisks, rising half-revealed from the surf -- the Tadmores of the wasteful desert of the sea. Nowhere is this desolation more marked than for those fifty miles of coast between Flamborough Head and the Spurm.

Weathering out the gale which had driven them from Leith, Paul's [i.e., Paul Jones'] ships for a few days were employed in giving chase to various merchantmen and colliers; capturing some, sinking others, and putting the rest to flight. Off the mouth of the Humber they ineffectually manoeuvred with a view of drawing out a king's frigate, reported to be lying at anchor within. At another time a large fleet was encountered, under convoy of some ships of force. But their panic caused the fleet to hug the edge of perilous shoals very nigh the land, where, by reason of his having no competent pilot, Paul durst not approach to molest them. The same night he saw two strangers further out at sea, and chased them until three in the morning, when, getting pretty nigh, ho surmised that they must needs be vessels of his own
~~~~

squadron, which, previous to his entering the Firth of Forth, had separated from his command. Daylight proved this supposition correct. Five vessels of the original squadron were now once more in company. About noon a fleet of forty merchantmen appeared coming round Flamborough Head, protected by two English man-of-war, the Serapis and Countess of Scarborough. Descrying the five cruisers sailing down, the forty sail, like forty chickens, fluttered in a panic under the wing of the shore. Their armed protectors bravely steered from the land, making the disposition for battle. Promptly accepting the challenge, Paul, giving the signal to his consorts, earnestly pressed forward. But, earnest as he was, it was seven in the evening ere the encounter began. Meantime his comrades, heedless of his signals, sailed independently along. Dismissing them from present consideration, we confine ourselves, for a while, to the Richard and the Serapis, the grand duellists of the fight.

The Richard carried a motley, crew, to keep whom in order one hundred and thirty-five soldiers--themselves a hybrid band--had been put on board, commanded by French officers of inferior rank. Her armament was similarly heterogeneous; guns of all sorts and calibres; but about equal on the whole to those of a thirty-two-gun frigate. The spirit of baneful intermixture pervaded this craft throughout.

The Serapis was a frigate of fifty guns, more than half of which individually exceeded in calibre any one gun of the Richard. She had a crew of some three hundred and twenty trained man-of-war's men.

There is something in a naval engagement which radically distinguishes it from one on the land. The ocean, at times, has what is called its *sea* and its *trough of the sea*; but it has neither rivers, woods, banks, towns, nor mountains. In mild weather it is one hammered plain. Stratagems, like those of disciplined armies--ambuscades, like those of Indians, are impossible. All is clear, open, fluent. The very element which sustains the combatants, yields at the stroke of a feather. One wind and one tide at one time operate upon all who here engage. This simplicity renders a battle between two men-of-war, with their huge white wings, more akin to the Miltonic contests of archangels than to *the comparatively squalid* tussles of earth.

As the ships neared, a hazy darkness overspread the water. The moon was not yet risen. Objects were perceived with difficulty. Borne by a soft moist breeze over gentle waves, they came within pistol-shot. Owing to the obscurity, and the known neighborhood of other vessels, the Serapis was uncertain who the Richard was. Through the dim mist each ship loomed forth to the other vast, but indistinct, as the ghost of Morven. Sounds of the trampling of resolute men echoed from either hull, whose tight decks dully resounded like drum-heads in a funeral march.

The Serapis hailed. She was answered by a broadside. For half an hour the combatants deliberately manoeuvred, continually changing their position, but always within shot fire. The. Serapis--the better sailer of the two--kept critically circling the Richard, making lounging advances now and then, and as suddenly steering off; hate causing her to act not unlike a wheeling cock about a hen, when stirred by the contrary passion. Meantime, though within easy speaking distance, no further syllable was exchanged; but an incessant cannonade was kept up.

At this point, a third party, the Scarborough, drew near, seemingly desirous of giving assistance to her consort. But thick smoke was now added to the night's natural obscurity. The Scarborough imperfectly discerned two ships, and plainly saw the common fire they made; but which was which, she could not tell. Eager to befriend the Serapis, she durst not fire a gun, lest she might unwittingly act the part of a foe. As when a hawk and a crow are clawing and beaking high in the air, a second crow flying near, will seek to join the battle, but finding no fair chance to engage, at last flies away to the woods; just so did the Scarborough now. Prudence dictated the step; because several chance shot--from which of the combatants could not be known--had already struck the Scarborough. So, unwilling uselessly to expose herself, off went for the present this baffled and ineffectual friend.

Not long after, an invisible hand came and set down a great yellow lamp in the east. The hand reached up unseen from below the horizon, and set the lamp down right on the rim of the horizon, as on a threshold; as much as to say, Gentlemen warriors, permit me a little to light up this rather gloomy looking subject. The lamp was the round harvest moon; the one solitary foot-light of the scene. But scarcely did the rays from the lamp pierce that languid haze. Objects before perceived with difficulty, now glimmered ambiguously. Bedded in strange vapors, the great foot-light cast a dubious, half demoniac glare across the waters, like the phantasmagoric stream sent athwart a London flagging in a night-rain from an apothecary's blue and green window. Through this sardonical mist, the face of the Man-in-the-Moon--looking right towards the combatants, as if he were standing in a trap-door of the sea, leaning forward leisurely with his arms complacently folded over upon the edge of the horizon--this queer face wore a serious, apishly self-satisfied leer, as if the Man-in-the-Moon had somehow secretly put up the ships to their contest, and in the depths of his malignant old soul was not unpleased to see how well his charms worked. There stood the grinning Man-in-the-Moon, his head just dodging into view over the rim of the sea:--Mephistopheles prompter of the stage.

Aided now a little by the planet, one of the consorts of the Richard, the Pallas, hovering far outside the fight, dimly discerned the suspicious form of a lonely vessel unknown to her. She resolved to engage it, if it proved a foe. But ere they joined, the unknown ship--which proved to be the Scarborough--received a broadside at long gun's distance from another consort of the Richard the Alliance. The shot whizzed across the broad interval like shuttlecocks across a great hall. Presently the battledores of both batteries were at work, and rapid compliments of shuttlecocks were very promptly exchanged. The adverse consorts of the two main belligerents fought with all the rage of those fiery seconds who in some desperate duels make their principal's quarrel their own. Diverted from the Richard and the Serapis by this little by-play, the Man-in-the-Moon, all eager to see what it was, somewhat raised himself from his trap-door with an added grin on his face. By this time, off sneaked the Alliance, and down swept the Pallas, at close quarters engaging the Scarborough; an encounter destined in less than an hour to end in the latter ship's striking her flag.

Compared to the Serapis and the Richard, the Pallas and the Scarborough were as two pages to two knights. In their immature way they showed the same traits as their fully developed superiors.

The Man-in-the-Moon now raised himself still higher to obtain a better view of affairs.

But the Man-in-the-Moon was not the only spectator. From the high cliffs of the shore, and especially from the great promontory of Flamborough Head, the scene was witnessed by crowds of the islanders. Any rustic might be pardoned his curiosity in view of the spectacle, presented. Far in the indistinct distance fleets of frightened merchantmen filled the lower air with their sails, as flakes of snow in a snow-storm by night. Hovering undeterminedly, in another direction, were several of the scattered consorts of Paul, taking no part in the fray. Nearer, was an isolated mist, investing the Pallas and Scarborough--a mist slowly adrift on the sea, like a floating isle, and at intervals irradiated with sparkles of fire and resonant with the boom of cannon. Further away, in the deeper water, was a lurid cloud, incessantly torn in shreds of lightning, then fusing together again, once more to be rent. As yet this lurid cloud was neither stationary nor slowly adrift, like the first-mentioned one; but, instinct with chaotic vitality, shifted hither and thither, foaming with fire, like a valiant water-spout careering off the coast of Malabar.

To get some idea of the events enacting in that cloud, it will be necessary to enter it; to go and possess it, as a ghost may rush into a body, or the devils into the swine, which running down the steep place perished in the sea; just as the Richard is yet to do.

Thus far the Serapis and the Richard had been manoeuvring and chasing to each other like partners in a cotillion, all the time indulging in rapid repartee.

But finding at last that the superior managableness of the enemy's ship enabled him to get the better of the clumsy old Indiaman, the Richard, in taking position, Paul, with his wonted resolution, at once sought to neutralize this, by hugging him close. But the attempt to lay the Richard right across the head of the Serapis ended quite otherwise, in sending the enemy's jib-boom just over the Richard's great tower of Pisa, where Israel was stationed; who, catching it eagerly, stood for an instant holding to the slack of the sail, like one grasping a horse by the mane prior to vaulting into the saddle.

“Aye, hold hard, lad,” cried Paul, springing to his side with a coil of rigging. With a few rapid turns he knitted himself to his foe. The wind now acting on the sails of the Serapis forced her, heel and point, her entire length, cheek by jowl, alongside the Richard. The projecting cannon scraped; the yards interlocked; but the hulls did not touch. A long lane of darkling water lay wedged between, like that narrow canal in Venice which dozes between two shadowy piles, and high in air is secretly crossed by the Bridge of Sighs. But where the six yard-arms reciprocally arched overhead, three bridges of sighs were both seen and heard, as the moon and wind kept rising.

Into that Lethean canal--pond-like in its smoothness as compared with the sea without--fell many a poor soul that night; fell, forever forgotten.

As some heaving rent coinciding with a disputed frontier on a volcanic plain, that boundary abyss was the jaws of death to both sides. So contracted was it, that in many cases the gun-rammers had to be thrust into the opposite ports, in order to enter to muzzles of their own cannon. It seemed more an intestine feud, than a fight between strangers. Or, rather, it was as if the Siamese Twins, oblivious of their fraternal bond, should rage in unnatural fight.

Ere long, a horrible explosion was heard, drowning for the instant the cannonade. Two of the old eighteen-pounders--before spoken of, as having been hurriedly set up below the main deck of the Richard--burst all to pieces, killing the sailors who worked them, and shattering all that part of the hull, as if two exploded steam-boilers had shot out of its opposite sides. The effect was like the fall of the walls of a house. Little now upheld the great tower of Pisa but a few naked crow stanchions. Thenceforth, not a few balls from the Serapis must have passed straight through the Richard without grazing her. It was like firing buck-shot through the ribs of a skeleton.

But, further forward, so deadly was the broadside from the heavy batteries of the Serapis--levelled point-blank, and right down the throat and bowels, as it were, of the Richard--that it cleared everything before it. The men on the Richard’s covered gun-deck ran above, like miners from the fire-damp. Collecting on the forecastle, they continued to fight with grenades and muskets. The soldiers also were in the lofty tops, whence they kept up incessant volleys, cascading their fire down as pouring lava from cliffs.

The position of the men in the two ships was now exactly reversed. For while the Serapis was tearing the Richard all to pieces below deck, and had swept that covered part almost of the last man, the Richard's crowd of musketry had complete control of the upper deck of the Serapis, where it was almost impossible for man to remain unless as a corpse. Though in the beginning, the tops of the Serapis had not been unsupplied with marksmen, yet they had long since been cleared by the overmastering musketry of the Richard. Several, with leg or arm broken by a ball, had been seen going dimly downward from their giddy perch, like falling pigeons shot on the wing.

As busy swallows about barn-eaves and ridge-poles, some of the Richard’s marksmen, quitting their tops, now went far out on their yard-arms, where they overhung the Serapis. From thence they dropped hand-grenades upon her decks, like apples, which growing in one field fall over the fence into another. Others of their band flung the same sour fruit into the open ports of the Serapis. A hail-storm of aerial combustion descended and slanted on the Serapis, while horizontal thunderbolts rolled crosswise through the subterranean vaults of the Richard. The belligerents were no longer, in the ordinary sense of things, an English ship and an American ship. It was a co-partnership and joint-stock combustion-company of both ships; yet divided, even in participation. The two vessels were as two houses, through whose party-wall doors have been cut; one family (the Guelphs) occupying the whole lower story; another family (the Ghibelines) the whole upper story.

Meanwhile, determined Paul flew hither and thither like the meteoric corposant-ball, which shiftingly dances on the tips and verges of ships’ rigging in storms. Wherever he went, he seemed to cast a pale light on all faces. Blacked and burnt, his Scotch bonnet was compressed to a gun-wad on his head. His Parisian coat, with its gold-laced sleeve laid aside, disclosed to the full the blue tattooing on his arm, which sometimes in fierce gestures streamed in the haze of the cannonade, cabalistically terrific as the charmed standard of Satan. Yet his frenzied manner was less a testimony of his internal commotion than intended to inspirit and madden his men, some of whom seeing him, in transports of intrepidity stripped themselves to their trowsers, exposing their naked bodies to the as naked shot The same was done on the Serapis, where several guns were seen surrounded by their buff crews as by fauns and satyrs.

At the beginning of the fray, before the ships interlocked, in the intervals of smoke which swept over the ships as mist over mountain-tops, affording open rents here and there--the gun-deck of the Serapis, at certain points, showed, congealed for the instant in all attitudes of dauntlessness, a gallery of marble statues—fighting gladiators.

Stooping low and intent, with one braced leg thrust behind, and one arm thrust forward, curling round towards the muzzle of the gun, there was seen the *loader*, performing his allotted part; on the other side of the carriage, in the same stooping posture, but with both hands holding his long black pole, pike-wise, ready for instant use--stood the eager *rammer and sponger*; while at the breech, crouched the wary *captain of the gun*, his keen eye, like the watching leopard's, burning along the range; and behind all, tall and erect, the Egyptian symbol of death, stood the *matchman*, immovable for the moment, his long-handled match reversed. Up to their two long death-dealing batteries, the trained men of the Serapis stood and toiled in mechanical magic of discipline. They tended those rows of guns, as Lowell girls the rows of looms in a cotton factory. The Parcae were not more methodical; Atropos not more fatal; the automaton chess-player not more irresponsible.

"Look, lad; I want a grenade, now, thrown down their main hatchway. I saw long piles of cartridges there. The powder monkeys have brought them up faster than they can be used. Take a bucket of combustibles, and let's hear from you presently."

These words were spoken by Paul to Israel. Israel did as ordered. In a few minutes, bucket in hand, begrimed with powder, sixty feet in air, he hung like Apollyon from the extreme tip of the yard over the fated abyss of the hatchway. As he looked down between the eddies of smoke into that slaughterous pit, it was like looking from the verge of a cataract down into the yeasty pool at its base. Watching, his chance, he dropped one grenade with such faultless precision, that, striking its mark, an explosion rent the Serapis like a volcano. The long row of heaped cartridges was ignited. The fire ran horizontally, like an express on a railway. More than twenty men were instantly killed: nearly forty wounded. This blow restored the chances of battle, before in favor of the Serapis.

But the drooping spirits of the English were suddenly revived, by an event which crowned the scene by an act on the part of one of the consorts of the Richard, the incredible atrocity of which has induced all humane minds to impute it rather to some incomprehensible mistake than to the malignant madness of the perpetrator.

The cautious approach and retreat of a consort of the Serapis, the Scarborough, before the moon rose, has already been mentioned. It is now to be related how that, when the moon was more than an hour high, a consort of the Richard, the Alliance, likewise approached and retreated. This ship, commanded by a Frenchman, infamous in his own navy, and obnoxious in the service to which he at present belonged; this ship, foremost in insurgency to Paul hitherto, and which, for the most part, had crept like a poltroon from the fray; the Alliance now was at hand. Seeing her, Paul deemed the battle at an end. But to his horror, the Alliance threw a broadside full into the stern of the Richard, without touching the Serapis. Paul called to her, for God's sake to forbear destroying the Richard. The reply was, a second, a third, a fourth broadside, striking the Richard ahead, astern, and amidships. One of the volleys killed several men and one officer. Meantime, like carpenters' augers, and the sea-worm called Remora, the guns of the Serapis were drilling away at the same doomed hull. After performing her nameless exploit, the Alliance sailed away, and did no more. She was like the great fire of London, breaking out on the heel of the great Plague. By this time, the Richard had so many shot-holes low down in her hull, that like a sieve she began to settle.

"Do you strike?" cried the English captain.

"I have not yet begun to fight," howled sinking Paul.

This summons and response were whirled on eddies of smoke and flame. Both vessels were now on fire. The men of either knew hardly which to do; strive to destroy the enemy, or save themselves. In the midst of this, one hundred human beings, hitherto invisible strangers, were suddenly added to the rest. Five score English prisoners, till now confined in the Richard's hold, liberated in his consternation by the master at arms, burst up the hatchways. One of them, the captain of a letter of marque, captured by Paul, off the Scottish coast, crawled through a port, as a burglar through a window, from the one ship to the other, and reported affairs to the English captain.

While Paul and his lieutenants were confronting these prisoners, the gunner, running up from below, and not perceiving his official superiors, and deeming them dead, believing himself now left sole surviving officer, ran to the tower of Pisa to haul down the colors. But they were already shot down and trailing in the water astern, like a sailor's towing shirt. Seeing the gunner there, groping about in the smoke, Israel asked what he wanted.

At this moment the gunner, rushing to the rail, shouted "Quarter! quarter!" to the Serapis.

"I'll quarter ye," yelled Israel, smiting the gunner with the flat of his cutlass.

"Do you strike?" now came from the Serapis.

"Aye, aye, aye!" involuntarily cried Israel, fetching the gunner a shower of blows.

"Do you strike?" again was repeated from the Serapis; whose captain, judging from the augmented confusion on board the Richard, owing to the escape of the prisoners, and also influenced by the report made to him by his late guest of the port-hole, doubted not that the enemy must needs be about surrendering.

"Do you strike?"

"Aye!--I strike *back*" roared Paul, for the first time now hearing the summons.

But judging this frantic response to come, like the others, from some unauthorized source, the English captain directed his boarders to be called, some of whom presently leaped on the Richard's rail, but, throwing out his tattooed arm at them, with a sabre at the end of it, Paul showed them how boarders repelled boarders. The English retreated, but not before they had been thinned out again, like spring radishes, by the unfaltering fire from the Richard's tops.

An officer of the Richard, seeing the mass of prisoners delirious with sudden liberty and fright, pricked them with his sword to the pumps, thus keeping the ship afloat by the very blunder which had promised to have been fatal. The vessels now blazed so in the rigging that both parties desisted from hostilities to subdue the common foe.

When some faint order was again restored upon the Richard her chances of victory increased, while those of the English, driven under cover, proportionally waned. Early in the contest, Paul, with his own hand, had brought one of his largest guns to bear against the enemy's mainmast. That shot had hit. The mast now plainly tottered. Nevertheless, it seemed as if, in this fight, neither party could be victor. Mutual obliteration from the face of the waters seemed the only natural sequel to hostilities like these. It is, therefore, honor to him as a man, and not reproach to him as an officer, that, to stay such carnage, Captain Pearson, of the Serapis, with his own hands hauled down his colors. But just as an officer from the Richard swung himself on board the Serapis, and accosted the English captain, the first lieutenant of the Serapis came up from below inquiring whether the Richard had struck, since her fire had ceased.

So equal was the conflict that, even after the surrender, it could be, and was, a question to one of the warriors engaged (who had not happened to see the English flag hauled down) whether the Serapis had struck to the Richard, or the Richard to the Serapis. Nay, while the Richard's officer was still amicably conversing with the English captain, a midshipman of the Richard, in act of following his superior on board the surrendered vessel, was run through the thigh by a pike in the hand of an ignorant boarder of the Serapis. While, equally ignorant, the cannons below deck were still thundering away at the nominal conqueror from the batteries of the nominally conquered ship.

But though the Serapis had submitted, there were two misanthropical foes on board the Richard which would not so easily succumb--fire and water. All night the victors were engaged in suppressing the flames. Not until daylight were the flames got under; but though the pumps were kept continually going, the water in the hold still gained. A few hours after sunrise the Richard was deserted for the Serapis and the other vessels of the squadron of Paul. About ten o'clock the Richard, gorged with slaughter, wallowed heavily, gave a long roll, and blasted by tornadoes of sulphur, slowly sunk, like Gomorrah, out of sight.

The loss of life in the two ships was about equal; one-half of the total number of those engaged being either killed or wounded.

In view of this battle one may ask--What separates the enlightened man from the savage? Is civilization a thing distinct, or is it an advanced stage of barbarism?

~~~~~~******~~~~~~

Notice appearing in the *New York Journal and Daily Patriotic Register* (N.Y.C.), Feb. 27, 1788:

PRIZE - MONEY

Of the Squadron under John Paul Jones, Efquire.

NOTICE is hereby given to thofe
Officers and men of the Frigates Alliance and
Bon homme Richard, who are entitled to a fhare
In the prizes taken by the fquadron under the com-
mand of John Paul Jones, Efq. That a divifion has
been made of the proceeds of fuch prizes as were
sold in France, and that the fhares will be paid to
The refpective claimants on their legal reprefenta-
tives, on their producing, at this office, fufficient
proof that they are the perfons, or are empowered
By the perfons actually entitled to the fhares they
refpectively claim.
Benjamin Walker, Commiffioner.
Office of accounts, Marine department.
~~~~~~

THE JILTED MUSE:

A Chance Smattering of Choice Francis Hopkinson.

Signer of the Declaration of Independence for New Jersey; purported designer of the first United States flag; devisor the Great Seal of the United States, and was the first known *American born* musical composer (of a *written* composition);[187] as well as, along with John Trumbull (the poet), Freneau, and Brackenridge, one of the most noted satirists the Revolutionary War era produced -- are just a few of the honors and credits for which Francs Hopkinson (1737–1791) receives recognition. And yet these are merely the conspicuous surface of his many accomplishments. For Hopkinson, like Franklin and Jefferson (with whom he was friends as well as political associates), was one of those renaissance men of colonial America whose desire for learning and intellectual self-improvement scarce knew bounds. Scientist, mechanic, minor inventor, chemist, draughtsman, sketch artist,[188] psychologist, poet, lyricist, composer, keyboard musician (harpsichord and organ), essayist, humorist, lawyer, legislator, and judge are all occupations in which he exhibited proficient or better competence and expertise. Granted, as he would himself doubtless concede, in most of these fields he was but a dabbling, if avid, amateur. Yet endowed with an encyclopedic perspective combined with an intelligent and insatiable proclivity for nearly all branches of fashionable and higher learning, Hopkinson ranks as one of early America's bona fide polymaths and intellect liberating enlightenment thinkers.

Yet such a vastly broad scope of endeavor comes not without its cost, and Hopkinson usually knew or was aware of his intrinsic and otherwise unavoidable limitations; at one point stating:

"I have been long urged by an invincible property to attempt some thing for the public good, or public convenience, so as to render my name famous amongst the benefactors of mankind. As my desire is much stronger than my abilities, I am obliged to be content with humble attempts at discoveries of limited importance; for I confess that my genius is not of the highest rank."[189]

For over-extending himself as he did, Hopkinson did not always achieve results proportionate with his ability, and had he narrowed his focus and energies to a few areas rather than to so many, he might, for instance, have garnered fame as an author or musical composer of the first rate. As it was, however, his literary and musical works, although displaying a commendable appreciation for grace and refinement, are generally, and rightly, accorded at best a second class standing; so that, all in all, they tend to be more of pronounced historical and curiosity interest than illustrious specimens of Western culture and art; indeed, several of writings and compositions hardly merit even third rank status; with his satires, for example, at times verging on the inane and sophomoric.

But again this was evidently much more the result of attempting too much rather than lack of talent or inspiration. For while such as Brockden Brown, Joseph Dennie, Irving, and Bryant forsook Law for the Muse, Hopkinson conversely forsook the Muse for the Law -- and it very much often shows in the *variety*[190] of his literary and musical productions.

This fortunately is not the case with *all* he did, and in addition to his famous "The Battle of the Kegs" (1778),[191] some of his compositions (including those musical) evince a promise that we can only deeply regret was not better realized than it might have been. To give you instances of such, here are samples in the way of extracts of poetry most of them written in his youth (at the time of the French and Indian War), and a humorous essay he penned much later.[192] Though these are the exception rather than the

[187] Hopkinson's son Joseph (1770-1842), incidentally, was the author of the lyrics to "Hail, Columbia," the United States' first unofficial national anthem; set to the music of German-American composer Philip Phile (c.1734–1793).

[188] Having at one time received personal instruction from Benjamin West.

[189] From his essay "Surveying," see *The Miscellaneous Essays and Occasional Writings of Francis Hopkinson, Esq.* (1792), Vol. 2, p. 127.

[190] Along with "various," an oft used and favorite word of Hopkinson's.

[191] Lampooning Howe's troops waging war on explosive kegs, or mines, set afloat in the Delaware River. These miniature mines, by the way, were conceived and designed by submarine inventor David Bushnell.

[192] In poetry and or song his influences were Milton, Dryden, Pope, Shenstone, Thomson, Young, Gay, and Prior; while with regard to satire Samuel Butler, The Spectator, Swift, and Sterne would appear to have been among his favorites.

rule as applied to his writings as a whole, there are further and other such pieces that we might have included, not least of which his forays into questions of government and jurisprudence. Yet in the interest of brevity and convenience, we've relegated this introductory presentation to some of his poetry and humorous prose. For more (and from which the following are taken), see the three volume and posthumously published *The Miscellaneous Essays and Occasional Writings of Francis Hopkinson, Esq.* (1792).

~~~***~~~

ODE on MUSIC

Hark! hark! the sweet vibrating lyre
Sets my attentive soul on fire;
Thro' all my frame what pleasures thrill
Whilst the loud treble warbles shrill,
And the more slow and solemn bass
Adds charm to charm and grace to grace.

Sometimes in sweetly languid strains
The guilty trembling string complains:
How it delights may ravished ear
When the expiring notes I hear
Vanish distant and decay! --
They steal my yielding soul away.

Neatly trip the merry dance,
And lightly touch and swiftly glance;
Let boundless transport laugh aloud
Sounds madly ramble mix and crowd,
Till all in one loud rapture rise,
Spread thro' the air and reach the skies.

But when you touch the solemn air,
Oh! swell each note distinct and clear;
In ev'ry strain let sorrow sigh,
Languish soft and sweetly die.

So shall th' admir'd celestial art,
Raise and transport my ravish'd heart
Exalt my soul, and give my mind
Ideas of sublimer kind.
So great the bliss it seems to prove
There must be music too above.
That from the trumpets silver sound
Of wing'd arch-angels plac'd around
Thy burning throne -- Oh! king of Heaven!
Most perfect harmony is giv'n:
Whilst happy saints in concert join
To make the music more divine,
And with immortal voices sing
HOSANNAHS to their glorious KING.

~~~***~~~

SONG.

Beauty and merit now are join'd,
An angel's form, an angel's mind

Are sweetly met *in thee*,
Thy soul, which all the virtues grace,
Shines forth with lustre in thy face,
From affectation free.

II.

Who in thy form, too lovely maid!
Can read thy temper there display'd;
Can look and calmly see?
The face that with such beauty charms,
The breast which so much virtue warms,
Is sure too much for me!

~~~***~~~

from ADVICE To AMANDA.

...III.

When next you see your faithful swain,
Your Strephon at your feet;
When next you hear him sigh his pain
And tend'rest vows repeat.

IV.

Then think 'tis fit a love so true
Should meet a kind regard;
And think 'tis given alone to you
His virtue to reward...

~~~***~~~

from L'ALLEGRO.

...'Where the linnet's warbling lay
Still attends my flow'ry way;
And the lark's melodious song
Charms me as I go along:
Or let me pause and view the scene,
The blooming vales, the hillocks green;
The stream, that winding in meanders,
Thro' the tufted meadow wanders;
The fields where flocks in safety stray,
And harmless lambkins sport and play.

Behold far off, with roaming eye,
Between two oaks a cot I spy,
Where Darby sits beside the door,
Nor envies kings their royal store:
Whilst Joan, a matron staid and lage,
Remains the comfort of his age;
And Phillis near, with voice so sweet,
Phillis their hand-maid, spruce and neat,
Cheers their old hearts with merry song,
And spins and sings the whole day long...

...But hark! the music's sudden sound
Spreads universal gladness round;
Joy lightens quick in ev'ry face,
An instant buz fills all the place:
And now prepared on either hand,
The beaux and belles in order stand:
And now they trip the merry dance,
And to quick movements smoothly glance.
Each fair her partner leads astray,
Thro' a long labyrinthian way;
Each swain his flying fair pursues,
Who still the pleasing toil renews.

Me the shrill soaring sounds inspire,
With transports that can rise no higher;
My body skims along the floor,
I feel my willing feet no more:
The music lends me wings; and I
In waving motions seem to fly:
And beaux and belles and tapers bright,
Swim undistinguish'd in my sight.

If such thy pleasures, smiling joy,
Oh! may'st thou e'er my mind employ;
Dawn in my breast perpetual day,
And chase intruding care away.

~~~***~~~

from IL PENSEROSO.

...Whilst thus the elements engage,
And with encreasing fury rage;
Oh! let me find some stony shed,
Where I may safely lodge my head,
T' enjoy the horrors of the storm,
And to its God due rites perform.
Beneath yon rock, whose mossy side
With fearful bend o'erhangs the tide,
Grotesque and wild, a cave I spy,
And to its shelter quickly fly.
But as I climb the grass-grown steep,
Whose darksome height juts o'er the deep;
Sent from aloft, with startled ear,
A sudden voice of woe I hear --

"Rage on thou tempest of the sky,
"Your fiercest vengeance I defy:
"A ruder storm whirls in my breast,
"And death alone can give me rest;
"My sorrows in this stream shall steep,
"And I" -- then plunges in the deep.
Nature a-while yet fond of life
Maintains with death an equal strife;
The lover strives to gain the shore,
But sinks, alas! to rise no more.
~~~

Save me, ye powers, from scenes so sad,
Scenes not of melancholy bred;
But sprung from furious wild despair,
In Stygian cell begot of care.

But might I hear true love complain,
In a more mild and temp'rate strain;
Then let my frequent feet be seen
On yonder steep romantic green;
Along whose yellow gravelly side,
Schuylkill sweeps his lucid tide:
*[193]Where waters fall with constant roar,
Re-bellowing down the rocky shore.
Where nightly at the turf-clad grave,
In concert with the bird of eve;
Beneath the glimpses of the moon,
The hermit mourns *Amelia* gone:

Till reason lifts his eye to heav'n,
And mild submitting thoughts are given.

Thus, melancholy, shalt thou please,
If thou wilt find me scenes like these:
Thus may'st thou e'er my mind employ,
And banish ev'ry lighter joy.

But when the summer scenes are lost,
Welcome winter! welcome frost!
Then I'll spend the long, long night,
By the lamp's pale and glimm'ring light:
Creeping nigher still and nigher
To the half extinguish'd fire,
Where midst the glowing coals I view
Lambent flames of livid blue:
Or listen to the crackling tread
Of heavy foot on snowy bed:
While howling blasts around me rage,
And wind, and snow, and hail, engage;
And through a crevice in the wall,
Boreas whistles shrill and small;
And the doors, by time grown weak,
On their iron hinges creak:
There I'll muse on stories old,
By a toothless matron told;
Of a tall, wan, and slender sp'rit,
Stalking in the dead of night;
Whose long trailing winding sheet
Flows luxuriant round his feet:
Gaping wounds all o'er him bleed,
To disclose some horrid deed:
With beck'ning hands he seems to say,
"Haste to my grave, come, come away!"

---

[193] [*Hopkinson's note*] *Alluding to the affecting story of Theodore and Amelia, in the first number of the Hermit. – Vide Amer. Mag. for October, 1757.

Thus should my fancy ever find
Some dreary scene to sill my mind;
And thus I'd sit with fixed eye,
To see the crumbling embers die,
Fearing to turn to either side,
Lest there the horned spectres glide:
Till morn, slow peeping from on high,
Should twinkle with unwelcome eye;
Then would I shun th' intruding ray,
And hide me from the garish day;
Darkling to bed would silent creep,
Hush'd by the howling winds to sleep.

~~~***~~~

from AN EVENING HYMN.

...When mortal pangs his frame shall seize,
And the chill'd blood begins to freeze;
When my fixt eyes must roll no more,
And life escapes thro' ev'ry pore.

Ah! what shall cheer my drooping heart.
Shall worldly honours joy impart?
Can sensual pleasure sweeten death,
Or wealth redeem one parting breath?

Therefore, my soul, thy thoughts employ,
On *God*, thy *Glory, wealth* and joy:
Virtue alone is stable here,
Nought but religion is sincere.

~~~***~~~

from EXTEMPORE VERSES FROM The Top Of MOUNT PARNASSUS, A Lofty Hill In Lancaster County.

...With anxious care, let others strive
Uncertain bliss to find,
And for expected wealth and fame
Resign their peace of mind.

In some such blest retreat as this,
Let me my hours employ,
And *Rosalinda* still be near,
To Brighten ev'ry joy.

~~~***~~~

from A SENTIMENT:

Occasioned by a conversation with Mr. P-- M--, one of the principal men among the Christian Society, called Dunkars, at EPHRATA, in the province of Pennsylvania.

...Each may be right in their peculiar way,
If proper motives mould their worship sway:
If but the *love divine of God* is there,
The spirit genuine of unfeigned pray'r;
Tis true devotion; and the Lord of love
Such pray'rs and praises kindly will approve.
~~~

Whether from golden altars they should rise,
And wrapt in sound, roll to the lofty skies,
Or from Ephrata's seat, so meek, so low,
The soft and silent aspirations flow...

~~~***~~~

SONG I. [From Hopkinson's "Seven Songs"[194] (1759-1760)]

I.

Come, fair Rosina, come away,
Long since stern Winter's storms have ceas'd;
See! Nature, in her best array,
Invites us to her rural feast:
The season shall her treasure spread,
Her mellow fruits and harvests brown,
Her flowers their richest odours shed,
And ev'ry breeze pour fragrance down.

II.

At noon we'll seek the wild wood's shade,
And o'er the pathless verdure rove;
Or, near a mossy fountain laid,
Attend the music of the groves;
At eve, the sloping mead invites
'Midst lowing herds and flocks to stray;
Each hour shall furnish new delights,
And love and joy (hall crown the day.

~~~***~~~

SONG III.

I.

Beneath a weeping willow's shade
She sat and sang alone;
Her hand upon her heart she laid
And plaintive was her moan.
The mock bird fat upon a bough
And list'ned to her lay,
Then to the distant hills he bore
The dulcet notes away.

II.

Fond echo to her strains reply'd,
The winds her sorrows bore;
Adieu! dear youth—adieu! she cry'd,
I ne'er shall see thee more.
The mock-bird sat upon a bough
And list'ned to her lay,

[194] [*Edit. Note.* Actually eight songs; as another was added before publication.]

Then to the distant hills he bore
The dulcet notes away.

~~~***~~~

SONG VIII.

I.

The traveller benighted and lost,
O'er the mountains pursues his lone way;
The stream is all candy'd with frost
And the icicle hangs on the spray,
He wanders in hope some kind shelter to find
"Whilst thro' the sharp hawthorn keen blows the cold wind."

II.

The tempest howls dreary around
And rends the tall oak in its flight;
Fast falls the cold snow on the ground,
And dark is the gloom of the night.
Lone wanders the trav'ler a shelter to find,
"Whilst thro' the sharp hawthorn still blows the cold wind."

III.

No comfort the wild woods afford,
No shelter the trav'ler can see—
Far off are his bed and his board
And his home, where he wishes to be.
His hearth's cheerful blaze still engages his mind
"Whilst thro' the sharp hawthorn keen blows the cold wind."

N. B. The last eight Songs were set to Music by the Author.[195]

~~~***~~~

*[196] For the Pennsylvania Packet.

A Man who is *disposed* to be entertained may find amusement in the mod common occurrences of life. Objects strike the eye, and incidents affect the mind, very differently in different persons. Some men accustom themselves to see every thing in a ludicrous point of view; others, in a serious light; and the multitude are content with mere perception; that is, barely seeing and hearing, without making any other further use of their senses.

This diversity of disposition is founded in the original constitutions of the parties. The *humorist* was funny and roguish when a boy; following the propensity of his nature, he acquires an habitual facility in associating ludicrous ideas with the most ordinary, and seemingly the most barren incidents of life. His eye immediately discovers any Angularity of countenance, or manner, because he is always looking for Angularities; and he finds something to divert him in the mod common transactions, because he is always hunting for diversion.

[195] [*Edit. Note*. The above verse and airs can be found in volume 3 of *The Miscellaneous Essays, etc.*]
[196] [*Hopkinson's note*] * Some personal altercations in the public papers occasioned this piece of ridicule.

I have myself, some tincture of this disposition; and, when disengaged from more serious business, I sally forth with a design to seek for entertainment. A variety of sources immediately present. For instance: it requires no great effort of imagination to suppose that the major part of the inhabitants of this great city [Philadelphia] are actually *mad.* Impressed with this idea, I observe the countenance, gait, and manner of every one I meet, and endeavour to class my lunatics under different species of frenzy.

One fellow drives along with such heedless impetuosity, that he treads in the gutters instead of stepping over them, and runs against the [lamp] posts, which he might easily avoid. Another, has such strong marks of anxiety, expressed in every feature of his face, that his whole soul seems to be absorbed in some sale, purchase, or other pursuit. A third, is haranguing with great vehemence to two or three ignoramuses who devour his politics with open ears. And, I see a fourth, in a violent passion, cursing and swearing like a sailor in a storm. But there is no end to the variety of characters that present, and consequently no end to this source of observation and entertainment.

At another time, I apply to the streets for a different species of diversion. I walk round a square, and attend to all the scraps and fragments of conversation I can pick up *en passant*. When I return home I write these on separate pieces of paper: and then amuse myself with arranging them in such order as to produce, if possible some apparent connection. If this cannot be done, I make another excursion, and collect more materials, till out of a great number, I am enabled to accomplish my purpose. For example --

{What's the price of butter to-day?
{It will fell for 4/. per gallon by the hogshead.

{Is your cousin married?
{She will be launched next Thursday.

{She is a good beast, and will carry you through thick and thin.
{Ay! to be sure we mud support the constitution.

{Do you think *the funding bill**[197] will pass?
{No friend. The insurers must bear the loss: we have nothing to do with it.

{They say *Longchamp**[198] will be given up.
{That's my man -- no, its mine -- I swear its mine: it rolled into the gutter; it struck against that gentleman's foot, and he kicked it into the gutter. -- Didn't it Tom? Didn't it jack? -- You lie! I say it didn't. -- Did it Cuff? Did it Pompey? And here a boxing match.

But my present fancy is to suppose the public newspapers to be so many real theatres, on which some comedy or farce is daily exhibited for my entertainment. About nine o'clock the packet of the day is brought in: I take my feat: the curtain rides, and the play begins.

For instance:

Scene -- Philadelphia.

Enter a doctor of divinity,
and a doctor of medicine.*[199]

---

[197] [*Hopkinson's note*] * A bill for funding the public debt was at this time before the house. Those who had contributed nothing in the late war, were unwilling to be taxed for the payment of interest on the funds lent to government for carrying it on: and therefore opposed the bill.

[198] [*Hopkinson's note*] A Frenchman who had insulted the consul and minister of France, and immediately took the oath of allegiance to the date of Pennsylvania, and claimed protection as a citizen of the common-wealth: but the minister of France demanded him as a French subject, and a deserter from the army. This matter occasioned a great deal of confusion, and much trouble to government.

[199] [*Hopkinson's note*] * A warm controversy between Dr. E-- and Dr. R-- , respecting the *university of Pennsylvania*, and the *college at Carlisle*: in which the broad bottom of the university was too frequently mentioned to pass unnoticed.

A very familiar dialogue commences, in which each performer endeavours to display the character of his antagonist in as striking a manner as possible to my great satisfaction. I imagine I see the professional battle. The divine throws text off scripture in the face of his adversary, and hampers him with the cords of logical conclusions; whilst the physician squirts clysters at the divine, and claps cantharides on his back.

But the most comical part of the scene is this. The learned divine *hoists* the university, and exposing its naked flesh, exclaims with admiration -- "Oh, charming! behold and see what a broad bottom is here!" Whereupon the physician immediately *hoists Dickenson college*, and with equal eloquence descants upon its *narrow bottom* -- "Look, says the divine, on this capacious disk -- on the one side sits the *pope*; on the other side sits Luther; and see how snug: *Calvin* lies between them both." "Its all wrong, replies the physician, *Calvin* has no business there: he will be choaked -- he will be suffocated -- he will be squeezed to death -- here is a fine narrow bottom more fit for his accommodation. He can have it all to himself -- he is a *usurper* there, but this is his own flesh and blood." From words they proceed to blows. The divine is heated with zeal seven times hotter than Nebuchadnezzar's furnace: he vociferates -- "The sword of the Lord and of Gideon!" and forthwith flogs away on the narrow bottom of poor Carlisle. The physician is also enraged. "By the bones oi Boerhaave, and the dust of Hypocrates, says he, I will be even with you:" and without further prelude, falls to scourging the pope, Luther, and Calvin all at once upon the broad bottom of the university. But the scene changes ---

Enter two musicians.

(Another battle.)

*[200] Mr. *Tweedledum* begins the attack with a full *discord* in a sharp third, and leaves it *unresolved*, which to be sure is very shocking. Mr. *Tweedle-dee*[201] replies in the *natural key*; but in a *sharp third* also. *Tweedledum* then changes the modulation, and after running a rapid division, closes with a chromatic arp[p]egio in a flat third. There is no bearing this. The parties are enraged -- *Tweedledum* seizes the diapason pipe of an organ -- *Twee-dledee* defends himself with a silver mounted flute: and to it they go -- blasting away at each other with astonishing vigour and dexterity. Methinks I hear the shrill tones of the flute, now ranging through the upper octave, and maintaining acknowledged superiority; and now descending into the flowery plains of the fruitful tenor, and yielding to the powerful vibrations of the dreadful organ pipe.

Thus it is, that by the help of imagination, and a talent for considering circumstances in a Angular point of view, I am enabled to find entertainment in occurrences which are scarcely noticed by others. But I never make sport of matters really serious. The miseries, misfortunes, and sufferings of our fellow creatures can never be proper subjects of ridicule; but the passions, follies, and absurdities of mankind are surely lawful occasions of laughter.

A.B.

March, 1785.[202]

---

[200] [*Hopkinson's note*] * A dispute between Mr. Brown, an eminent performer on the flute, and Mr. Bentley, an organist.

[201] [*Edit. Note.* The use of the comical names "Tweedle-dum" and "Tweedle-dee" is traditionally first ascribed to a satirical epigram by English poet John Byrom (1692–1763); with those titles referring respectively to rival composers George Frederic Handel and Giovanni Battista Bononcini.]

[202] *Ibid.* Vol. 2, p. 138.

"...YOUR DUTIFUL SON, JOHN LAURENS"

"Nature had adorned him [John Laurens] with a profusion of her choicest gifts, to which a well-conducted education had added its most useful as well as its most elegant improvements. Though his fortune and family entitled him to pre-eminence, yet he was the warm friend of republican equality. Generous and liberal, his heart expanded with genuine philanthropy. Zealous for the rights of humanity, he contended that personal liberty was the birth-right of every human being, however diversified by country, colour or capacity. His insinuating address, won the hearts of all his acquaintances: his sincerity and virtue secured their lasting esteem. Acting from the most honourable principles -- uniting the bravery and other talents of a great officer with the knowledge of a complete scholar, and the engaging manner of a well-bred gentleman, he was the idol of his country -- the glory of the army -- and an ornament of human nature. His abilities shone in the legislature and in the cabinet, as well as in the field, and were equal to the highest stations. His admiring country, sensible of his rising merit, stood prepared to confer on him her most distinguished honours. Cut down in the midst of all these prospects, he has left mankind to deplore the calamities of war, which in the twenty-seventh year of his life, deprived society of so valuable a citizen."
~ David Ramsay, *History of the Revolution of South Carolina* (1785), vol. II, pp. 374-375.

A person who takes the trouble to learn about the life of Col. John Laurens (1754-1782), from South Carolina, in detail will find him a far more extraordinary figure than commonly hurried generalizations make him out to be. Had he survived the war, he very well might have attained a Founding Father status similar to that of his fellow Aide-de-camp Alexander Hamilton. For like Hamilton, he was in many ways a far sighted progressive, highly intelligent, outspoken, brave, charming, and personable. But also like Hamilton, Laurens' signal frailty was youthful rashness and impetuosity. And yet, ironically, that same apparent and oft lamented defect, which ultimately cost both men their lives, could be said to have been instrumental in Laurens' case in securing from Louis XVI emergency funds and supplies for the American finances and war effort when, in the summer of 1781, they were most urgently required -- a feat probably no one else,[203] not even the adroit Dr. Franklin, could have accomplished. Likewise who else but the audacious Laurens, accompanied by the Viscount de Noailles, could have demanded harsh surrender terms of the British at Yorktown?

From his own writings and others' accounts of him, Laurens comes across and leaves the impression of having been of those rare souls who believed that if you can't champion and stand up for the weak -- or doggedly stand up for higher principle (which devotion is typically among mortals itself often deemed a form of weakness) -- you must yourself (at bottom) be weak. Not that Laurens was a saint -- he wasn't. And, we might add, when he joined Greene in 1782 to lead in the southern army, he encountered dissatisfaction from fellow officers, including Lee; who distrusted his ability as a military strategist and tactician. Yet in his full-hearted idealism he came almost as close to being a saint as any other of America's revolutionaries. And for the same reason, to come away from learning his life story is, at least for those who feel, a rather sad experience. As with Alexander Scammell and several others, such scarcely matched hope and promise was pointlessly terminated in the fervid flush of youth; and with the end of the war -- and victory -- so breathlessly close at hand. In addition, it is not so very improbable that had he lived the entire course of American history, including the fate of Black Americans, might have been significantly altered. Why this is so you will see presently in some of the following extracts taken from letters written to his father and President of Congress (1777-1778) Henry Laurens and that appear in *The Army Correspondence of Colonel John Laurens in the Years 1777-8, with a Memoir by William Gilmore Simms* (1867). My choice of subjects which Laurens addresses in these letters is rather un-uniform, but the diversity of selection I hope is helpful in providing a more full portrait of Laurens and his era.

~~~***~~~

[203] That is aside perhaps from Lafayette.
~~~

HEAD QUARTERS - Whitemarsh Camp [outside Philadelphia],
5th November, 1777

My Dear Father:*

...I could recollect and commit hastily to paper, and what will be a treasure to him as a Newsmonger, Humphrey's *Gazette* of the 25th. I expected to have been able to procure another for you, but have been disappointed.

The light manner in which Count [Carl von] Donop[']s affair is related[204] -- Sr[205] Wm Howe's Kitean harangue to such he would delude into the loyal corps of which he has reserved to himself the Colonelcy and other little anecdotes, may make it acceptable even a day or two hence, if you have not already seen it, and in that time I may get it from some one whose curiosity and that of his circle is satisfied or called off to some thing more recent.

A day or two ago, Capt [Henry] Lee of the light horse with twelve of his troops, dispersed a foraging party on the other side Schuylkill, took a Captain of the Queen's Rangers (this is the name given to the new levies of provincial troops), and seven privates, two of whom were marines. [p.68]

~~~***~~~

HEAD QUARTERS,
7th November, 1777.

...Our anxiety had been raised in camp, by a report that a heavy firing of musquetry had been heard for a considerable time on the evening of the same day -- it turns out to be nothing more than a few single guns which Potter's militia and the enemy's detachment on Province Island make a practice of firing at each other without com[mittin]g to any action. Four deserters from the enemy brought in this morning, say that the militia men call'd to the British soldiers and invited them to go over, promising them beef and flour the red-coats in return ask'd them to come and partake of their salt that from raillery they proceeded to abuse -- and at length to discharging their pieces at each other, without any other effect as far as they know than wounding a Hessian yager... [pp. 70-71]

~~~***~~~

HEAD QUARTERS,
3d December, 1777.

...If the majority of the people in each state, or only the majority of the states, can he persuaded that it is a religious duty, as was the case of the Greeks with respect to the Amphictionic League,[206] or a duty to themselves as most favouring their private and political interests to maintain the confederation, it will he established upon the most permanent basis that human affairs admit of, and the opinion propagated by education will pass to remote posterity. I shall study these laws with the greatest attention in my retirement.

We have received several accounts from outposts within a few days past intimating that an attack upon us was meditated. We have in consequence prepared ourselves, paraded our men so as to make them acquainted with their ground and its advantages; but the enemy have remained within their works. Many are of opinion that Sr Wm Howe will not suffer any thing but mere necessity, or a very tempting prospect of decisive success, to call him from good winter quarters. Others say that from past experience he knows

---

204 [*Edit. Note.* Donop was mortally wounded in the attack on Fort Mercer, 22 Oct. 1777.]

205 [*Edit. Note.* "Sr" meaning of course "Sir;" with like use of abbreviations for personal titles used in Laurens correspondence generally.]

206 [*Edit. Note.* Or Amphictyonic League, an alliance or confederation of Hellenic city *states* (rather than mere *cities*), such as Athens, Sparta, Boetia, Thessaly, Locri, Delphi, etc.; established prior to the days of the polis. It was organized in various forms and members from the time after the Trojan war up until the 2nd century A.D.; usually bound by sacred and religious ties to one or more gods and important temples dedicated to such deities.]

the vicinity of the Continental army to be exceedingly troublesome, and that it is his interest to drive us to a more respectable distance. In the mean time the season advances in which armies in general are forced to repair to more substantial shelter than tents, and whose inclemency is more particularly grievous to our ill-clothed soldiers. The question is whether we are to go into remote winter quarters, and form a chain of cantonments in the interior part of the country; leaving a vast extent of territory exposed to the devastation of an enraged unsparing enemy; leaving inhabitants who will be partly seduced by the expectation of gold, or more generally compell'd to fill the traitorous provincial corps now raising; leaving plentiful granaries and large stocks of cattle, ample means for subsisting the troops and Tory citizens in Philadelphia, and for victualling transports that may carry home Mr. Burgoyne and his army; leaving the well affected to fall a sacrifice, and deplore our abandonment of them and the country; or, whether we shall take a position more honourable, more military, more republican, more consonant to the popular wish -- in a proper situation for covering the country, or at least so much of it as circumstances will permit -- and for distressing and annoying the Enemy?

Winter campaigns it is said are ominous to the best appointed and best disciplined armies. The misery incident to them occasions desertion and sickness which waste their numbers. Our army in particular requires exemption from fatigue in order to compensate for their want of clothing.

Relaxation from the duties of a campaign, in order to allow them an opportunity of being disciplined and instructed; warm quarters, that it may appear in the spring with undiminished numbers and in the full prowess of health, &ca. Besides it is urged that the hardships which our soldiers undergo discourage men from enlisting. The answers that might be given in our particular circumstances to these general objections against winter campaigns are only for your private ear, and not to be trusted in a letter to the possibility of miscarriage; besides, we may take a position which will not absolutely expose us to a winter campaign, but furnish us excellent quarters for men at the same time that it leaves us within distance for taking considerable advantages of the enemy, and cover a valuable and extensive country. [pp. 90-92]

~~~***~~~

HEAD QUARTERS,
23d Jan., 1778.

...You asked me, my dear father, what bounds I have set to my desire of serving my country in the military line? I answer glorious death, or the triumph of the cause in which we are engaged.

I must not conclude without giving you a short account of a brilliant defence lately made by a few of Capt. [Henry] Lee's troop [of the 1st Continental Light Dragoons]. Near two hundred of the enemy's light dragoons made an attempt to surprise the captain in his quarters. They concealed their march by a circuitous road, and arrived at the house a little after day-break conducted by an intelligent guide. Lee had at the time with him only his lieutenant, Mr. [William] Lindsay, a corporal and four privates, and Major [John] Jameson of the same regiment who happen'd to be there on a visit. They posted themselves in the house and made the necessary preparations for defence. Capt. Delancy [James, or possibly Oliver, Delancey], who commanded the enemy's advanced guard, led it on bravely till he arrived under cover of the eves, while the main body kept up a constant fire from a distance on the windows. After repeated efforts had been made to enter the house, the party repulsed made an attempt to seize the horses which were in the stable, but such a well directed constant fire was kept up from the house that the bravest dragoon did not venture to dismount. The loss of the enemy was one commissioned officer and three or four privates. The party in its retreat picked up a quarter-master's serjeant and a couple of videttes. Lieutenant Lindsay was wounded in the hand. Too much praise cannot be bestowed upon the officers and men who had the honor of forcing such an incomparable superiority of numbers to a shameful retreat. Capt. Nichols was at Lee's quarters in his way from Philadelphia during the action, and gives our little party great applause as I have been told.

We have some as brave individuals among our officers as any that exist. Our men are the best crude materials for soldiers I believe in the world, for they possess a docility and patience which astonish foreigners. With a little more discipline we should drive the haughty Briton to his ships... [pp. 110-112]
~~~

~~~***~~~

HEAD QUARTERS,
2d Feb., 1778.

The more I reflect upon the difficulties and delays which are likely to attend the completing our Continental regiments, the more anxiously is my mind bent upon the scheme, which I lately communicated to you. The obstacles to the execution of it had presented themselves to me, but by no means appeared insurmountable. I was aware of having that monstrous popular prejudice, open-mouthed against me, of under taking to transform beings almost irrational, into well disciplined soldiers, of being obliged to combat the arguments, and perhaps the intrigues, of interested persons. But zeal for the public service, and an ardent desire to assert the rights of humanity, determined me to engage in this arduous business, with the sanction of your consent. My own perseverance, aided by the countenance of a few virtuous men, will, I hope, enable me to accomplish it.

You seem to think, my dear father, that men reconciled by long habit to the miseries of their condition, would prefer their ignominious bonds to the untasted sweets of liberty, especially when offer'd upon the terms which I propose.

I confess, indeed, that the minds of this unhappy species must be debased by a servitude, from which they can hope for no relief but death, and that every motive to action but fear, must be nearly extinguished in them. But do you think they are so perfectly moulded to their state as to be insensible that a better exists? Will the galling comparison between them selves and their masters leave them unenlightened in this respect? Can their self love be so totally annihilated as not frequently to induce ardent wishes for a change?

You will accuse me, perhaps, my dearest friend, of consulting my own feelings too much; but I am tempted to believe that this trampled people have so much human left in them, as to be capable of aspiring to the rights of men by noble exertions, if some friend to mankind would point the road, and give them a prospect of success. If I am mistaken in this, I would avail myself, even of their weakness, and, conquering one fear by another, produce equal good to the public. You will ask in this view, how do you consult the benefit of the slaves? I answer, that like other men, they are the creatures of habit. Their cowardly ideas will be gradually effaced, and they will be modified anew. Their being rescued from a state of perpetual humiliation, and being advanced, as it were, in the scale of being, will compensate the dangers incident to their new state.

The hope that will spring in each man's mind, respecting his own escape, will prevent his being miserable. Those who fall in battle will not lose much; those who survive will obtain their reward. Habits of subordination, patience under fatigues, sufferings and privations of every kind, are soldierly qualifications, which these men possess in an eminent degree.

Upon the whole, my dearest friend and father, I hope that my plan for serving my country and the oppressed negro race will not appear to you the chimera of a young mind, deceived by a false appearance of moral beauty, but a laudable sacrifice of private interest, to justice and the public good.

You say, that my resources would be small, on account of the proportion of women and children. I do not know whether I am right, for I speak from impulse, and have not reasoned upon the matter. I say, altho my plan is at once to give freedom to the negroes, and gain soldiers to the states; in case of concurrence, I sh'd sacrifice the former interest, and therefore w'd change the women and children for able-bodied men. The more of these I could obtain, the better; but forty might be a good foundation to begin upon.

It is a pity that some such plan as I propose could not be more extensively executed by public authority. A well chosen body of 5,000 black men, properly officer'd, to act as light troops, in addition to our present establishment, might give us decisive success in the next campaign.
~~~

I have long deplored the wretched state of these men, and considered in their history, the bloody wars excited in Africa, to furnish America with slaves the groans of despairing multitudes, toiling for the luxuries of merciless tyrants.

I have had the pleasure of conversing with you, sometimes, upon the means of restoring them to their rights. When can it be better done, than when their enfranchisement may be made conducive to the public good, and be modified, as not to overpower their weak minds?

You ask, what is the general's opinion, upon this subject? He is convinced, that the numerous tribes of blacks in the southern parts of the continent, offer a resource to us that should not be neglected. With respect to my particular plan, he only objects to it, with the arguments of pity for a man who would be less rich than he might be...[207] [pp. 114-118]

~~~***~~~

HEAD QUARTERS,
17th Feb., 1778.

...We have lately been in a most alarming situation for want of provisions. The soldiers were scarcely restrained from mutiny by the eloquence and management of our officers. Those who are employed to feed us, either for want of knowledge or for want of activity or both, never furnish supplies adequate to our wants.

I have more than once mentioned to you that we have been obliged to renounce the most important enterprises, delay the most critical marches, by the delinquency of commissaries. Here of late it has reduced us almost to the point of disbanding. The head of the department is a stationary attendant on Congress; what he might do if he had views sufficiently extensive, by a proper employment of agents, I know not; but as the case is at present, he seems to be almost useless. I have heard it asserted by more than one sensible, disinterested man, that the removal of Mr. [Joseph] Trumbull from that office has been the source of all our misfortunes. He had considerable connections and influence in a great meat country, and had laid such a train for supplying the army, as in all probability would have put us out of the reach of bad weather, difficult roads and other common accidents. Certain it is that the want of providence, or want of ability in the present managers, has brought us to the brink of ruin. By extraordinary exertions, by scraping from distant scanty magazines and collecting with parties, we have obtained a temporary relief; and have hopes that the representation of our late distress to several persons of influence and authority in different states, will procure us such farther supplies as will save us from the disagreeable necessity of dividing the army into cantonments.

To the ill offices of Trumbull's friends we may attribute perhaps a part of our distress. The increasing number of privateers in the New England states, the subsistence of the convention troops, and an expedition now on foot, will greatly diminish the meat resources of the country on which we principally depend. The carcasses of horses about the camp, and the deplorable leanness of those which still crawl in existence, speak the want of forage equal to that of human food. General Greene with a party of two thousand, is now foraging, but will be able to collect only the gleanings of a country over which an unsparing enemy has passed.

A small detachment from his party under the command of Major Billiard, made an attempt to surprise the enemy's picket near their bridge. The design was discovered and the picket had time to post

---

[207] [*Edit. Note.* Such was wealthy S.C. plantation owner Henry Laurens' closeness to his son, combined with rising misgivings of his own respecting the institution of slavery, that in the face of much conventional wisdom, he took John's proposal quite in earnest. Raising the point of enlisting Blacks in large numbers with Washington, the latter, from Middle brook, N.J. on March 20, 1779, replied: "...The policy of our arming Slaves is, in my opinion, a moot point, unless the enemy set the example; for should we begin to form battalions of them, I have not the smallest doubt (if the War is to be prosecuted) of their following us in it, and justifying the measure upon our own ground; the upshot then must be, who can arm fastest, and where are our Arms? Besides, I am not clear that a discrimination will not render Slavery more irksome to those who remain in it; most of the good and evil things of this life are judged of by comparison; and I fear a comparison in this case will be productive of much discontent in those who are held in servitude; but as this is a subject that has never employed much of my thoughts, these are no more than the first crude Ideas that have struck me upon the occasion..."]
~~~

itself in a stone house, at the distance of 500 yards. Our men were saluted with a general discharge; they marched forward and returned the lire, and would have proceeded to storming the house, but it was thought more advisable to retire. Our party had five men slightly wounded; the enemy's loss was one Hessian killed, and another mortally wounded.

Gen'l. Wayne is detached by Gen'l Greene to cross the Delaware at Wilmington, for the purpose of destroying all the hay on the Jersey shore which we cannot secure for our own use, and which may fall into the enemy's hands, and with a view of driving all the cattle from the neighborhood of the river, by a circuitous road to camp. If he finds it practicable to cross the river and carry that plan into execution, he is to make a large sweep and return here with what ever he can collect by the way of Gorshen.

The disaffected inhabitants find means to conceal their teams and cattle, so that the country appears more naked than it really is.

Deserters from the enemy inform us that they are preparing for a grand forage, and that they will probably make it in Bucks county. We have the same business in contemplation in the same place.

I must not omit informing you of a gallant defence made by a justice of the peace in Philadelphia county (on the other side of the Schuylkill), known by the appellation of Squire Knox. This gentleman's house was surrounded early in the morning some days ago by a party of traitors, lately distinguished by the title of royal refugees; he was in bed in a lower room, and upon their demanding admittance, was going to open to them, when his son who was above, and perceiving from the window fixed bayonets, call'd to him to keep his door shut and warned him of danger. The villains in the mean time pressed against the door; the old man armed himself with his cutlass, and his son descended with a gun. The door was at length forced half open by one of the most enterprising; the father kept it in that position with his left hand, and employed his right in defending the passage. After some vigorous strokes, his cutlass broke; the bad condition of the son's fusil had prevented his tiring till this moment. He was now prepared to salute the assailants, but the old man thinking all was lost by the failure of his weapon, called to him not to fire; upon farther examination, however, he says he found that by being shortened, it was only better adapted to close quarters, and renewed the fight.

The villains fired seven shots through the door, one of which grazed the squire's knee, which was all the damage done. They then threw down their arms and took to their heels; they were pursued by the Knoxes and a family of militia, and one of them who was concealed in a cellar was taken.

The besetting Mr. Knox's house is a matter of civil cognizance, but it appears that the prisoner has held correspondence with the enemy, and supplied them with provisions, and he will probably suffer death for those offences by sentence of court-martial... [pp. 125-129]

~~~***~~~

HEAD QUARTERS,
9th March, 1778.

...The number of men unfit for duty by reason of their nakedness, the number sick in hospitals, and present under innoculation [sic], certainly emaciate the effective column in our returns.

Similar causes, added to the severity of the season, have prevented our completing the works of the camp, in such a manner as would have been indispensably necessary if we had been engaged with a more alert and enterprising antagonist...

It is a very bad principle, to trust to the usual sluggishness and inactivity of the enemy. But when I reflect upon the great indulgence of Gen'l Howe, I draw some consolation from hoping that he will not do violence to his nature by any extraordinary exertions at the present moment, but postpone his visit till we be
~~~

better prepared for receiving him. These truths are deposited in the breasts of a few, and must be deplored in silence. But every prudent method and general argument should be used to stimulate the different states to the immediate completion of their regiments.

I am truly sensible of your kindness on the subject of my black battalion. Nothing would tempt me to quit my present station, but a prospect of being more useful in another.

The ambition of serving my country, and desire of gaining fame, leads me to wish for the command of men. I would cherish those dear, ragged Continentals, whose patience will be the admiration of future ages, and glory in bleeding with them... [pp. 135-136]

~~~***~~~

HEAD QUARTERS,
11th April, 1778.

...If we were as virtuous as we ought to be, we should have those who are enriching themselves by commerce, privateering and farming, supplying the army with every necessary convenience at a moderate rate; but as experience proves that it is in vain to expect this, all I would demand of Congress, is that they would contrive some means of furnishing us with articles which nature cannot forego, and which are useful in giving respectability to the military state, at such prices as bear some proportion to our pay.

I would wish to see the military state rendered honorable, and all odious distinctions of jealousy laid aside, for we are all citizens, and have no separate interests. If mediocrity could be established generally, by any means, it would be well; it would ensure us virtue and render our independency permanent. But there never will be virtue in the poor, when there are rich in the same community. By imperceptible and indirect methods, we should labour to establish and maintain equality of fortunes as much as possible, if we would continue to be free.

It is a fact that our officers cannot satisfy the simple wants of nature, much less make that appearance which is annexed to the military state, with their pay. It is no less a fact that in every town on the continent, luxury nourishes as it would among a people who had conquered the world, and were about to pay for their victories, by their decline. This I hope Congress will take seriously into consideration.

I would by no means wish our pay to be increased, but I would wish to see temptations to peculation in weak men removed, and the honest man delivered from the necessity of reducing himself to beggary. This will best be effected by a public establishment for supplying wants at a moderate price... [pp. 157-158]

~~~***~~~

HEAD QUARTERS,
27th April, 1778.

...And if our men in power, and men of influence, will redouble their exertions instead of being lulled into security, the new and artful attack of the British minister, will be foiled and expose him to contempt. He will be obliged to with draw his troops -- I mean as many of them as we suffer to escape -- and tacitly to acknowledge what he will be afterwards forced explicitly to ratify -- our independence. At the same time, if no secret alliance has been entered into on our part with France, our agents at that court need not represent it as an impossible event, that a treaty should take place between Great Britain and America, from the degree of affection which may still remain between the two nations and the propensity to a connexion which arises from the identity of habits and language.

I have been informed that the tone of our ambassadors was infinitely too modest to produce the effects which we had a right to expect... [p. 163]

~~~***~~~

HEAD QUARTERS,
1st May, 1778.

I snatch a minute to congratulate my dear father, upon the important intelligence from France. As the matter is represented she seems to have acted with politic generosity towards us, and to have timed her declaration in our favour most admirably for her own interests, and the abasement of her ancient rival. If the general languor can be shaken off, and that this event instead of increasing our supineness stimulates us to vigorous exertions, we may close the war with great eclat, provided General Howe does not receive timely orders to collect his force and secure a retreat. France might give a mortal blow to the English naval force in its present scattered state... [pp. 165-166]

~~~***~~~

HEAD QUARTERS, ENGLISH TOWN,
30th June, 1778.

I was exceedingly chagrined that public business prevented my writing to you from the field of battle, when the General sent his dispatches to Congress. The delay, however, will be attended with this advantage, that I shall be better able to give you an account of the enemy's loss; tho' I must now content myself with a very succinct relation of this affair. The situation of the two armies on Sunday was as follows: Gen'l Washington, with the main body of our army, was at 4 miles distance from English Town. Gen'l [Charles] Lee, with a chosen advanced corps, was at that town. The enemy were retreating down the road which leads to Middle Town; their flying army composed (as it was said), of 2 batallions of British grenadiers, 1 Hessian grend'rs, 1 batallion of light infantry, 1 regiment of guards, 2 brigades of foot, 1 regt. of dragoons and a number of mounted and dismounted Jagers. The enemy's rear was preparing to leave Monmouth village, which is 6 miles from this place, when our advanced corps was marching towards them. The militia of the country kept up a random running fire with the Hessian Jagers; no mischief was done on either side. I was with a small party of horse, reconnoitering the enemy, in an open space before Monmouth, when I perceived two parties of the enemy advancing by files in the woods on our right and left, with a view, as I imagined, of enveloping our small party, or preparing a way for a skirmish of their horse. I immediately wrote an account of what I had seen to the General, and expressed my anxiety on account of the languid appearance of the Continental troops under Gen'l Lee.

Some person in the mean time reported to Gen'l Lee that the enemy were advancing upon us in two columns, and I was informed that he had, in consequence, ordered Varnum's brigade, which was in front, to repass a bridge which it had passed. I went myself, and assured him of the real state of the case; his reply to me was, that his accounts had been so contradictory, that he was utterly at a loss what part to take. I repeated my account to him in positive distinct terms, and returned to make farther discoveries. I found that the two parties had been withdrawn from the wood, and that the enemy were preparing to leave Monmouth. I wrote a second time to Gen'l Washington. Gen'l Lee at length gave orders to advance. The enemy were forming themselves on the Middle Town road, with their light infantry in front, and cavalry on the left flank, while a scattering, distant fire was commenced between our flanking parties and theirs. I was impatient and uneasy at seeing that no disposition was made, and endeavoured to find out Gen'l Lee to inform him of what was doing, and know what was his disposition. He told me that he was going to order some troops to march below the enemy and cut oft their retreat. Two pieces of artillery were posted on our right without a single foot soldier to support them. Our men were formed piecemeal in front of the enemy, and there appeared to be no general plan or disposition calculated on that of the enemy; the nature of the ground, or any of the other principles which generally govern in these cases.

The enemy began a cannonade from two parts of their line; their whole body of horse made a furious charge upon a small party of our cavalry and dissipated them, and drove them till the appearance of our infantry, and a judicious discharge or two of artillery made them retire precipitately. Three regiments of ours that had advanced in a plain open country towards the enemy's left flank, were ordered by Gen'l Lee to retire and occupy the village of Monmouth. They were no sooner formed there, than they were ordered to quit that post and gain the woods. One order succeeded another with a rapidity and indecision calculated to ruin us. The enemy had changed their front and were advancing in full march towards us; our men were fatigued with the excessive heat. The artillery horses were not in condition to make a brisk retreat. A new position was ordered, but not generally communicated, for part of the troops were forming on the right of the ground, while others were marching away, and all the artillery driving off. The enemy, after a short halt, resumed their pursuit; no cannon was left to check their progress. A regiment was ordered to form behind a fence, and as speedily commanded to retire. All this disgraceful retreating, passed without the firing of a musket, over ground which might have been disputed inch by inch. We passed a defile and arrived at an eminence beyond, which was defended on one hand by an impracticable fen, on the other by thick woods where our men would have fought to advantage. Here, fortunately for the honour of the army, and the welfare of America, Gen'l Washington met the troops retreating in disorder, and without any plan to make an opposition. He ordered some pieces of artillery to be brought up to defend the pass, and some troops to form and defend the pieces. The artillery was too distant to be brought up readily, so that there was but little opposition given here. A few shot though, and a little skirmishing in the wood checked the enemy's career. The Gen'l expressed his astonishment at this unaccountable retreat. Mr. Lee indecently replied that the attack was contrary to his advice and opinion in council. We were obliged to retire to a position, which, though hastily reconnoitered, proved an excellent one. Two regiments were formed behind a fence in front of the position. The enemy's horse advanced in full charge with admirable bravery to the distance of forty paces, when a general discharge from these two regiments did great execution among them, and made them fly with the greatest precipitation. The grenadiers succeeded to the attack. At this time my horse was killed under me. In this spot the action was hottest, and there was considerable slaughter of British grenadiers. The General ordered Woodford's brigade with some artillery to take possession of an eminence on the enemy's left, and cannonade from thence. This produced an excellent effect. The enemy were prevented from advancing on us, and confined themselves to cannonade with a show of turning our left flank. Our artillery answered theirs with the greatest vigour. The General seeing that our left flank was secure, as the ground was open and commanded by it, so that the enemy could not attempt to turn it without exposing their own flank to a heavy fire from our artillery, and causing to pass in review before us, the force employed for turning us. In the mean time, Gen'l Lee continued retreating. Baron Steuben was order'd to form the broken troops in the rear. The cannonade was incessant and the General ordered parties to advance from time to time and engage the British grenadiers and guards. The horse shewed themselves no more. The grenadiers showed their backs and retreated every where with precipitation. They returned, however, again to the charge, and were again repulsed. They finally retreated and got over the strong pass, where, as I mentioned before, Gen'l Washington first rallied the troops. We advanced in force and continued masters of the ground; the standards of liberty were planted in triumph on the field of battle. We remained looking at each other, with the defile between us, till dark, and they stole off in silence at midnight. We have buried of the enemy's slain, 233, principally grenadiers; forty odd of their wounded whom they left at Monmouth, fell into our hands. Several officers are our prisoners. Among their killed are Co'l Moncton, a captain of the guards, and several captains of grenadiers. We have taken but a very inconsiderable number of prisoners, for want of a good body of horse. Deserters are coming in as usual. Our officers and men behaved with that bravery which becomes freemen, and have convinced the world that they can beat British grenadiers. To name any one in particular w'd be a kind of injustice to the rest. There are some, however, who came more immediately under my view, whom I will mention that you may know them. B. Gen'l Wayne, Col. Barber, Col. Stewart, Col. Livingston, Col. Oswald of the artillery, Capt. Doughty deserve well of their country, and distinguished themselves nobly.

The enemy buried many of their dead that are not accounted for above, and carried off a great number of wounded. I have written diffusely, and yet I have not told you all. Gen'l Lee, I think, must be tried for misconduct. However, as this is a matter not generally known, tho' it seems almost universally wished for, I would beg you, my dear father, to say nothing of it.... [pp. 193-199]

~~~***~~~

HEAD QUARTERS (on the lovely banks of the Raritan, opposite New Brunswick),
2d July, 1778.

I had the pleasure of writing to you the day before yesterday, from English Town, but through some mistake my letter was not delivered to the express, altho' it was written in a hurry. I recollect no
~~~

circumstance in it relative to our late engagement, which farther inquiry and consideration do not confirm. From a second view of the ground, as well as the accounts I have since had of the enemy's strength and designs, it is evident to me that Mr. Clinton's whole flying army would have fallen into our hands, but for a defect of abilities or good will in the commanding officer of our advanced corps. His precipitate retreat spread a baneful influence every where. The most sanguine hope scarcely extended farther, when the Commander in chief rallied his troops, than to an orderly retreat; but by his intrepidity and presence of mind, a firm line of troops was formed on a good position, from whence he cannonaded with advantage, and detached light parties in front, who drove the enemy from the field. Gen'l Clinton arid Lord Cornwallis were both present at the action.

The reason for not pursuing them farther with the main body of our army was, that people well acquainted with the country said, that the strength of the ground would render it impracticable for us to injure them essentially; and that the sandy, parched soil, together with the heat of the sun, would probably occasion us considerable loss. From the specimen of yesterday's march we have reason to think it fortunate that we took the part we have done; the heat of the weather, thirsty soil, and heavy sand, reduced us to the necessity of bringing on many of our weaker men in waggons.

We are now arrived in a delightful country where we shall halt and refresh ourselves. Bathing in the Raritan, and the good living of the country will speedily refresh us. I wish, my dear father, that you could ride along the banks of this delightful river. Your zeal for the public service will not at this time permit it. But the inward satisfaction which you must feel from a patriotic discharge of your duty, is infinitely superior to the delights of retirement and ease. I admire your constant virtue, and will imitate your example...

...I have seen the General much embarrassed this day, on the subject of those who distinguished them selves in the battle of Monmouth. To name a few, and be silent with regard to many of equal-merit w'd be an injustice to the latter; to pass the whole over unnoticed w'd be an unpardonable slight; indiscriminate praise of the whole w'd be an unfair distribution of rewards; and yet, when men generally conducted themselves so well as our officers did, this matter is allowable and is eligible, because least liable to give offence.

The merit of restoring the day, is due to the General; and his conduct was such throughout the affair as has greatly increased my love and esteem for him. My three brother aid[e]s [to Gen. Washington] gained themselves great applause by their activity and bravery, while the three secretaries acted as military men on this occasion, and proved themselves as worthy to wield the sword as the pen.

Gen'l Steuben, his aids and your son, narrowly escaped being surrounded by the British horse, early on the morning of the action. We reconnoitered them rather too nearly, and L'd Cornwallis sent the dragoons of his guard to make us prisoners. Gen'l Clinton saw[208] the Baron's star,[209] and the whole pursuit was directed at him; but we all escaped, the dragoons fearing an ambuscade of infantry.

We have buried Col. Moncton with the honours of war.[210] [pp. 200-203]

~~~***~~~

---

208 [*Laurens' note.*] "A dragoon deserter from the enemy just informs us of this. He says three others came off with him, and that the Hessians are deserting amazingly."

209 [*Edit. Note.* The Star of the Order of Fidelity, often seen in portraits of Von Steuben, was an honorary knighthood bestowed on him in 1769 by William, Margrave of Baden-Durlach.]

210 [*Edit. Note.* Lieut. Col. Henry Monckton (1740-1778) of the British 45th Regt. of Foot.]
~~~

Laurens' own gravestone
at Monck's Corner, S.C. and which reads:

Sacred to the Memory of
John Laurens
Son of
Henry and Eleanor
Laurens
Born 28th October 1754
Died 27th August 1782
"Dulce et decorum est
pro patria mori"

~~~***~~~

Some other topics mentioned or discussed in Laurens' 1777-78 letters to his father:
* Battle of Red Bank (Fort Mercer), 22 Oct. 1777: pp. 70, 73-74, 78
* Chevalier Capt. Thomas-Antoine de Mauduit du Plessis (also given as "Plessis-Mauduit"), hero of Red Bank: pp. 106-, 233-234
* Controversial promotion of James Wilkinson to Brig. Gen. following Saratoga: p. 83
* Valley Forge: pp. 91-92, 97-98, 182
* Thomas Conway and the "Conway Cabal," pp. 100-102, 137, 180
* Projected invasion of Canada. This was scrapped due largely to Lafayette's objection to Conway's involvement in the plan, but also owing in part to Laurens advisement and dissuasion of Lafayette: pp. 112-113
* Foraging by Howe's and Washington's forces: pp. 126-128
* Baron Von Steuben: pp. 131-133, 137, 146-147, 160, 186-187, 202-203
* Capt. John Barry: pp. 139, 232-233
* Count Brig. Gen. Casmir Pulaski, also his legion: pp. 141-142
* News of France's alliance with the Americans: pp. 167-170, 171-172
* Relations and protocol between Congress and Washington: p. 170
* Battle of Barren Hill, 20 May 1778: pp. 174-175, 187-189
* Evacuation of Philadelphia by the British: pp. 176-178, 180, 183-184, 187, 191-192
* British peace Commissioners in Philadelphia: pp. 178-179, 181-182, 184-185, 187
* Prospect of reforming and reorganizing the Cont. army; which John Laurens advocates: pp. 186, 190-191
* Arrival of Admiral D'Estaing: pp. 207-208, 210-211
* Aborted Franco-American assault on Newport, Rhode Island, July-Aug. 1778: pp. 210-223
* Laurens on France, Britain, and the greater strategic picture: pp. 225-229
* Lafayette, somewhat strangely, revives idea of taking Canada, which Laurens dissuades him from: pp. 230-231
~~~

THE VIEW FROM STRAWBERRY HILL:
Horace Walpole and the American Revolution

The era of Horace Walpole's father, Prime Minister Robert Walpole (in office 1721–1742) and the decades immediately leading up to, in terms of peace, prosperity, and general social improvement could, relatively speaking, be considered one of the most halcyon periods in British history. And that so few are acquainted with it -- outside of, say, the specific biography of Marlborough or else some literary, artistic, musical, or scientific giant like Defoe,[211] Addison, Pope, Hogarth, Handel, and Newton -- is perhaps as sure proof as any of the truth of this assertion

What is more, and oddly enough, the revolt of American the whigs in 1776 was in a sense of a conservative nature inasmuch as it sought to bring back those times which many knew from living memory; when crown and colonies peaceably co-existed: without taxation or unfriendly coercion; when America was proud of her parentage and the American colonies were not yet so wealthy as to command more than casual or curious attention of the British themselves.[212] The Americans had come to view William and Mary's, Walpole's, and Pitt the elder's eras as being the proper measure of the status quo. Yet all changed when following the brilliantly successful Seven Years/French and Indian War, the spirit of the nation seemed to turn from an attitude of domestic self-improvement and cultural refinement and excellence to that of a robust commercial imperialism, accompanied by a fast rising and unparalleled economic supremacy among the states of Europe.[213] The British empire was, after all, a commercial, not miltary empre. As the 1770's developed, well then might many colonists have viewed the reigning powers-that-be as wrongful usurpers of those earlier, more tranquil times; all the more so as growing economies on both sides of the Atlantic provided greater opportunity for greed and avarice to play more intrusive and potent roles in people's lives and communities in both America and England and America. Ironically, the refractory revolutionaries were in their own eyes the true conservatives; while for some vociferous few within the mother country itself, Britain's soul was battling for its very life. And in Horace Walpole's case, with a breadth of vision that transcended thoughtless acquiescence to changing times, he felt this struggle most acutely.

It is a fact no little familiar to many of us that in the competition for goods and the control of prosperity, orchestrated and methodical criminality (not least of which such criminality that refuses to stop short of murder) will often, if not always, prevail over idealism and brotherly good will. And it was in the former, sinister light that the more ardent Whigs, rightly or wrongly, came to see the presiding Tories and their allies; such that as events came to reach a heated pitch in the American War, the defeat of Lord North's Ministry and what it represented was deemed the defeat of folly and crime.

Yet were such as Lords Bute,[214] Grenville, Wedderburn, North, or Germain the actual culprits or only stand-ins for un-public, unaccountable others lying in the shadows? For most people, in the haze of

---

[211] Quite in the spirit of many of the later Revolutionaries, Robinson Crusoe's father admonishes his son to eschew the extravagance of the rich and titled elite, and shun the hardships and ignominy of poverty; advising instead to steer an economically middle class course in his life. Defoe also, it should be noted, was (in effect) the inventor and part inspiration for for Richard Steele's *Tatler* (1709, and subsequently Addison and Steele's *Spectator* of 1711) essays; that is, articles intended as light "diversions" and as supplements and in contrast to serious analysis and addressing of political and economic affairs.

[212] "When Sir Robert Walpole was minister in the Spanish war, a scheme was mentioned to him of taxing the American colonies. He smiled, and said, 'I will leave that for some of my successors who may have more courage than I have, and less a friend to commerce than I am.' He added, 'It has been a maxim with me during my administration to encourage the trade of the American colonies in their utmost latitude (nay, it has been necessary to pass over some irregularities in their trade with Europe), for by encouraging them to an extensive growing foreign commerce, if they gain 500,000 *l.* I am convinced that in two years afterwards full 250,000 *l.* of their gain will be in his Majesty's Exchequer.' He ended with saying, 'This is a taxing them more agreeable, both to their own constitution and to ours.'" *Gentleman's Magazine* for 1765, p. 500.

[213] Samuel Johnson in *Lives on the Poets* (1779): "Riches were not [i.e., in Dryden's time] become familiar to us, nor had the nation yet learned to be liberal [in its spending habits.]"

"The appetite of England had been whetted by the rapid commercial expansion. A world of never-ending luxury could be won by vigorous and aggressive action against her competitors; so it seemed to many of the London merchants. That war would bring commercial wealth was a deep-seated belief which influenced English politics profoundly."

~ J.H. Plumb, *England in the Eighteenth Century* (1950), ch. 2, p. 27.

[214] Although it is now generally agreed by historians that what remained of Bute's power in the early 1770s was *at that time* greatly exaggerated and misunderstood, Frederick the Great for one, in his *Memoir of the Peace* (*Works* vol. IV, p. 172), wrote "The Scotch

comprehending wide and far flung worldly affairs, it wasn't always easy or even exactly necessary to say. What mattered was that regardless of who specifically was most at fault, something clearly was wrong -- and that things came to blows is matter of fact confirmation of this. And yet bitterly critical as he is in his famous letters, Walpole was hesitant to dwell for more than a spell on one or two individuals that might be considered most blameworthy, and rather makes use of colorfully varied illustrations and examples to argue his point. His support of the Americans arguably had its roots in his antipathy for the Tories who both ousted his father and then came to dominate Parliament. But as he himself makes plain, even if party affiliation is construed to be an important motivating factor, he still feels it is still necessary to adduce sound and objective reasons (not merely rhetorical or political ones) for the inflammatory minority opinion (in Britain) he espouses.

As well as a foremost connoisseur of (literal) *belle lettres*, imaginative aesthete, and meticulous antiquarian, Walpole became the Samuel Pepys of his generation, and his correspondence is a treasure trove in its addressing numerous and diverse subjects; not least of which the American Revolutionary War as seen from one Englishman's eyes. Selections and collections made from it, while having the practical advantage of brevity, unfortunately cannot begin to do the entire corpus of Walpole's chatty missives justice; other than to serve as a sampler to encourage a reader to seek out more. The following then, with the aforesaid caveat, is one such unavoidably handicapped set of selections. Our title itself *technically* is a misnomer, as not all the letters from which the ensuing extracts are taken were written at Strawberry Hill. But we so liked the sound and appositeness otherwise, we retained it all the same.

~~~***~~~

To Sir Horace Mann
From Paris, Feb. 29, 1766.

...The Duke of Richmond has been gone to England this fortnight; he had a great deal of business, besides engagements here; and if he has failed writing, at least I believe he received yours. Mr. Conway, I suppose, has received them too, but not to my knowledge; for I have received but one from him this age. He has had something else to do than to think of Pretenders, and pretenders to pretensions. It has been a question (and a question scarcely decided yet) not only whether he and his friends should remain Ministers, but whether we should not draw the sword on our colonies, and provoke them and the manufacturers at home to rebellion. The goodness of Providence, or Fortune by its permission, has interposed, and I hope prevented blood; though George Grenville and the Duke of Bedford, who so mercifully checked our victories, in compassion to France, grew heroes the moment there was an opportunity of conquering our own brethren. It was actually moved by them and their banditti to send troops to America. The stout Earl of Bute, who is never afraid when not personally in danger, joined his troops to his ancient friends, late foes, and now new allies. Yet this second race of Spaniards, so fond of gold and thirsting after American blood, were routed by 274; their whole force amounting but to 134. The Earl, astonished at this defeat, had recourse to that kind of policy which Machiavel recommends in his chapter of *back-stairs*. Caesar himself disavowed his Ministers, and declared he had not been for the repeal, and that his servants had used his name without his permission. A paper was produced to his eyes, which proved this denial an equivocation. The Ministers, instead of tossing their places into the middle of the closet, as I should have done, had the courage and virtue to stand firm, and save both Europe and America from destruction... [*The Letters of Horace Walpole*, edited by Peter Cunningham, Vol. IV, p. 479]

~~~***~~~

To Sir Horace Mann
From Strawberry Hill, May 6, 1770.

---

earl governed the king and the kingdom. Resembling those malignant spirits of which we continually speak, but which we never see, he concealed both himself and his operations in deep darkness. His emissaries, his creatures, were engines by which he moved the political machine, according to his will. His system of politics was that of the old Tories, who maintained that the happiness of England required that the king should enjoy despotic power."

...In Parliament their numbers are shrunk to nothing, and the session is ending very triumphantly for the Court. But there is another scene opened of a very different aspect. You have seen the accounts from Boston. The tocsin seems to be sounded to America. I have many visions about that country, and fancy I see twenty empires and republics forming upon vast scales over all that continent, which is growing too mighty to be kept in subjection to half a dozen exhausted nations in Europe. As the latter sinks, and the others rise, they who live between the eras will be a sort of Noahs, witnesses to the period of the old world and origin of the new. I entertain myself with the idea of a future senate in Carolina and Virginia, where their future patriots will harangue on the austere and incorruptible virtue of the ancient English! will tell their auditors of our disinterestedness and scorn of bribes and pensions, and make us blush in our graves at their ridiculous panegyrics. Who knows but even our Indian usurpations and villanies may become topics of praise to American schoolboys? As I believe our virtues are extremely like those of our predecessors the Romans, so I am sure our luxury and extravagance are too…[Vol. V, p. 235]

~~~***~~~

To Sir Horace Mann
From Strawberry Hill, Oct. 6, 1774.

...We have a new famous Bill, devised by the late Mr. Grenville, that has its first operation now; and what changes it may occasion, nobody can yet foresee. The first symptoms are not favourable to the Court; the great towns are casting off submission, and declaring for popular members. London, Westminster, Middlesex, seem to have no monarch but Wilkes, who is at the same time pushing for the Mayoralty of London, with hitherto a majority on the poll. It is strange how this man, like a phoenix, always revives from his embers! America, I doubt, is still more unpromising. There are whispers of their having assembled an armed force, and of earnest supplications arrived for succours of men and ships. A civil war is no trifle; and how we are to suppress or pursue in such a vast region, with a handful of men, I am not an Alexander to guess; and for the fleet, can we put it upon casters and wheel it from Hudson's Bay to Florida? But I am an ignorant soul, and neither pretend to knowledge nor foreknowledge. All I perceive already is, that our Parliaments are subjected to America and India, and must be influenced by their politics; yet I do not believe our senators are more universal than formerly... [Vol. VI p. 128]

~~~***~~~

To the Countess of Ailesbury.
From Strawberry Hill, Nov. 7, 1774.

...Expectation hangs on America. The result of the general assembly is expected in four or five days. If one may believe the papers, which one should not believe, the other side of the waterists are not *doux comme des moutons*, and yet we do intend to eat them…[Vol. VI, p 141]

~~~***~~~

To Sir Horace Mann
From Strawberry Hill, Nov. 24, 1774.

...Don't tell me I am grown old and peevish and supercilious -- name the geniuses of 1774, and I submit. The next Augustan age will dawn on the other side of the Atlantic. There will, perhaps, be a Thucydides at Boston, a Xenophon at New York, and, in time, a Virgil at Mexico, and a Newton at Peru. At last, some curious traveller from Lima will visit England and give a description of the ruins of St. Paul's, like the editions of Balbec and Palmyra; but am I not prophesying, contrary to my consummate prudence, and casting horoscopes of empires like Rousseau? Yes; well, I will go and dream of my visions... [Vol. VI, p 152]

~~~***~~~

To Henry Seymour Conway
From Arlington Street, Nov. 27, 1774.

...America is still more refractory, and I doubt will outvote the ministry. They have picked General Gage's pocket of three pieces of cannon,[215] and intercepted some troops that were going to him. Sir William Draper is writing plans of pacification in our newspapers; and Lord Chatham flatters himself that he shall be sent for when the patient is given over; which I don't think at all unlikely to happen. My poor nephew is very political too: so we shall not want mad doctors. Apropos, I hear Wilkes says he will propose Macreth for Speaker... [Vol. VI, p 152]

~~~***~~~

To Henry Seymour Conway
From Arlington Street, Dec. 15, 1774.

...The long expected sloop is arrived at last, and is indeed a man of war! The General Congress have voted a non-importation, a non-exportation, a non-consumption; that, in case of hostilities committed by the troops at Boston, the several provinces will march to the assistance of their countrymen; that the cargoes of ships now at sea shall be sold on their arrival, and the money arising thence given to the poor at Boston; that a letter, in the nature of a petition of rights, shall be sent to the King; another to the House of Commons; a third to the people of England; a demand of repeal of all the acts of Parliament affecting North America passed during this reign, as also of the Quebec-bill: and these resolutions not to be altered till such repeal is obtained.

Well, I believe you do not regret being neither in parliament nor in administration! As you are an idle man, and have nothing else to do, you may sit down and tell one a remedy for all this. Perhaps you will give yourself airs, and say you was a prophet, and that prophets are not honoured in their own country. Yet, if you have any inspiration about you, I assure you it will be of great service -- we are at our wit's end -- which was no great journey. Oh! you conclude Lord Chatham's crutch will be supposed a wand, and be sent for. They might as well send for my crutch; and they should not have it; the stile is a little too high to help them over. His Lordship is a little fitter for raising a storm than laying one, and of late seems to have lost both virtues. The Americans at least have acted like men, gone to the bottom at once, and set the whole upon the whole. Our conduct has been that of pert children: we have thrown a pebble at a mastiff, and are surprised that it was not frightened. Now we must kill the guardian of the house which will be plundered the moment little master has nothing but the old nurse to defend it. But I have done with reflections; you will be fuller of them than I... [Vol. VI, p 158]

~~~***~~~

To Henry Seymour Conway
From Arlington Street, Dec. 26, 1774.

...It is supposed here, that the new proceedings of the French Parliament will produce great effects: I don't suppose any such thing. What America will produce I know still less; but certainly something very serious. The merchants have summoned a meeting for the second of next month, and the petition from the Congress to the King is arrived. The heads have been shown to Lord Dartmouth; but I hear one of the agents is again presenting it; yet it is thought it will be delivered, and then be ordered to be laid before Parliament. The whole affair has already been talked of there on the army and navy-days; and Burke, they say, has shone with amazing Wit and ridicule on the late inactivity of Gage, and his losing his cannon and straw; on his being entrenched in a town with an army of observation; with that army being, as Sir William Meredith had said, an asylum for magistrates, and to secure the port. Burke said, he had heard of an asylum for debtors and whores, never for magistrates; and of ships never of armies securing a port... [Vol. VI, p 159]

[215] [*Edit. Note.* A pre-war raid by some Massachusetts militia of a British stores depot near Portsmouth (now N.H.)]

~~~***~~~

To Henry Seymour Conway
From Arlington Street, Jan, 15, 1775.

You have made me very happy by saying your journey to Naples is laid aside. Perhaps it made too great an impression on me; but you must reflect, that all my life I have satisfied myself with your being perfect, instead of trying to be so myself. I don't ask you to return, though I wish it: in truth there is nothing to invite you. I don't want you to come and breathe fire and sword against the Bostonians, like that second Duke of Alva, the inflexible Lord George Germain; or to anathematize the court and its works, like the incorruptible Burke, who scorns lucre, except when he can buy a hundred thousand acres from naked Caribs for a song. I don't want you to do any thing like a party-man. I trust you think of every party as I do, with contempt, from Lord Chatham's mustard-bowl down to Lord Rockingham's hartshorn. All, perhaps, will be tried in their turns, and yet, if they had genius, might not be Mighty enough to save us. From some ruin or other I think nobody can, and what signifies an option of mischiefs? An account is come of the Bostonians having voted an army of sixteen thousand men, who are to be called minute-men, as they are to be ready at a minute's warning. Two directors or commissioners, I don't know what they are called, are appointed. There has been too a kind of mutiny in the fifth regiment. A soldier was found drunk on his post. Gage, in his time of danger, thought vigour necessary, and sent the fellow to a court-martial. They ordered two hundred lashes. The general ordered them to improve their sentence. Next day it was published in the *Boston Gazette*. He called them before him, and required them on oath to abjure the communication, three officers refused. Poor Gage is to be scape-goat, not for this, but for what was a reason against employing him, incapacity. I wonder at the precedent! Howe is talked of for his successor. Well, I have done with you! -- Now I shall go gossip with Lady Ailesbury... [Vol. VI, p 169]

~~~***~~~

To Henry Seymour Conway
From Arlington Street, Jan. 22, 1775.

After the magnificent overture for peace from Lord Chatham, that I announced to Madame du Deffand, you will be most impatient for my letter. *Ohime'*! you will be sadly disappointed. Instead of drawing a circle with his wand round the House of Lords, and ordering them to pacify America, on the terms he prescribed before they ventured to quit the circumference of his commands, he brought a ridiculous, uncommunicated, unconsulted motion for addressing the King immediately to withdraw the troops from Boston, as an earnest of lenient measures. The Opposition stared and shrugged; the courtiers stared and laughed. His own two or three adherents left him, except Lord Camden and Lord Shelburne, and except Lord Temple, who is not his adherent and was not there. Himself was not much animated, but very hostile; particularly on Lord Mansfield, who had taken care not to be there. He talked of three millions of Whigs in America, and told the ministers they were checkmated and had not a move left to make. Lord Camden was as strong. Lord Suffolk was thought to do better than ever, and Lord Lyttelton's declamation was commended as usual. At last, Lord Rockingham, very punily, and the Duke of Richmond joined and supported the motion; but at eight at night it was rejected by 68 to 18, though the Duke of Cumberland voted for it.

This interlude would be only entertaining, if the scene was not so totally gloomy. The cabinet have determined on civil war, and regiments are going from Ireland and our West Indian islands. On Thursday the plan of the war is to be laid before both Houses. To-morrow the merchants carry their petition; which, I suppose, will be coolly received, since, if I hear true, the system is to cut off all traffic with America at present -- as, you know, we can revive it when we please. There! there is food for meditation! Your reflections, as you understand the subject better than I do, will go further than mine could. Will the French you converse with be civil and keep their countenances?... [Vol. VI, p 180]

~~~***~~~
~~~

To Dr. Gem.
From Arlington Street, April 4, 1776.

...I beg your pardon, Sir, for giving you this long trouble; but I could not help venting myself, when shocked to find such renegade conduct in a Parliament that I was rejoiced had been restored. Poor human kind! is it always to breed serpents from its own bowels? In one country, it chooses its representatives, and they sell it and themselves -- in others, it exalts despots -- in another, it resists the despot when he consults the good of his people! Can we wonder mankind is wretched, when men are such beings? Parliaments run wild with loyalty, when America is to be enslaved or butchered. They rebel, when their country is to be set free! I am not surprised at the idea of the devil being always at our elbows. They who invented him, no doubt could not conceive how men could be so atrocious to one another, without the intervention of a fiend. Don't you think, if he had never been heard of before, that he would have been invented on the late partition of Poland! Adieu, dear Sir. Yours most sincerely. [Vol. VI, p. 320]

~~~***~~~

To Henry Seymour Conway
From Strawberry Hill, June 30, 1776.

...I can neither walk nor sing -- nor, indeed, am fit for any thing but to amuse myself in a sedentary trifling way. What I have most certainly not been doing, is writing any thing: a truth I say to you, but do not desire you to repeat. I deign to satisfy scarce any body else. Whoever reported that I was writing any thing, must have been so totally unfounded, that they either blundered by guessing without reason, or knew they lied -- and that could not be with any kind intention; though saying I am going to do what I am not going to do, is wretched enough. Whatever is said of me without truth, any body is welcome to believe that pleases. In fact, though I have scarce a settled purpose about any thing, I think I shall never write any more. I have written a great deal too much, unless I had written better, and I know I should now only write still worse. One's talent, whatever it is, does not improve at sixty -- yet, if I liked it, I dare say a good reason would not stop my inclination; -- but I am grown most indolent in that respect, and most absolutely indifferent to every purpose of vanity. Yet without vanity I am become still prouder and more contemptuous. I have a contempt for my countrymen that makes me despise their approbation. The applause of slaves and of the foolish mad is below ambition. Mine is the haughtiness of an ancient Briton, that cannot write what would please this age, and would not, if he could. Whatever happens in America this country is undone. I desire to be reckoned of the last age, and to be thought to have lived to be superannuated, preserving my senses only for myself and for the few I value... [Vol. VI, p. 352]

~~~***~~~

To Henry Seymour Conway
From Strawberry Hill, Thursday, Oct. 31, 1776.

...Here is a solution of the Americans declaring themselves independent. Oh! the folly, the madness, the guilt of having plunged us into this abyss! Were we and a few more endued with any uncommon penetration? No: they who did not see as far, would not. I am impatient to hear the complexion of to-day. I suppose it will, on the part of administration, have been a wretched farce of fear, daubed over with airs of bullying. You, I do not doubt, have acted like yourself, feeling for our situation, above insulting, and unprovoked but at the criminality that has brought us to this pass. Pursue your own path, nor lean to the court that may be paid to you on either side, as I am sure you will not regard their being displeased that you do not go as far as their interested views may wish. If the court should receive any more of what they call good news, I think the war with France will be unavoidable. It was the victory at Long Island and the frantic presumption it occasioned, that has ripened France's measures -- And now we are to awe them by pressing -- an act that speaks our impotence! -- which France did not want to learn!... [Vol. VI, p 386]

~~~***~~~
~~~

To Sir Horace Mann.
From Arlington Street, Jan. 24, 1777.

...The tide of victories continues: Fort Washington was taken at the end of the year, and Rhode Island since. A great deal is still to do, and not much less if the war was over. It does not appear yet that Dr. Franklin has persuaded Franco to espouse America openly. One hears a great deal of underhand support, and in general the disposition of the French is for war with us; but I never believe but on facts, seldom reports, and seldomer prophecies and conjectures; chance being the great mistress of human affairs in the *dernier ressort*... [Vol. X, p. 7]

~~~***~~~

To the Rev. William Mason
From Arlington Street, Feb. 17, 1777.

...The news from America are, as usual, difficult to be fathomed. The court denies being certain of the discomfit of the Hessians, yet their runners pretend that the Hessian prisoners have been retaken. It is fact that the royalists have neither yet taken Providence nor the American ships: the other side believe that Lord Cornwallis has received a check at the Jerseys. [Am. major general Charles] Lee is certainly taken by the poltroonery of his own men, of whom he had eighteen to Colonel Harcourt's fourteen. He has written a short letter in which he himself says so, and adds that he submits to his fate, only regretting that liberty will no longer enjoy a foot of earth...[Vol. X, p. 14]

~~~***~~~

To the Rev. William Mason.
From Arlington Street, Feb. 27, 1777.

...The capture of the Hessians is confirmed with circumstances somewhat untoward, for they were not surprised, and yet all laid down their arras as if they liked lands in America better than the wretched pittance they are to receive out of the Landgrave's dole.

It is now the fashion to cry up the manoeuvre of General Washington in this action, who has beaten two English regiments, too, and obliged General Howe to contract his quarters -- in short, the campaign has by no means been wound up to content... [Vol. X, p. 20]

~~~***~~~

To Sir Horace Mann.
From Arlington Street, March 5, 1777.

...I have kept my sentiments pretty much to myself, but nothing has made me change my opinion. At present, the aspect is not as if I had been totally in the wrong. The campaign in America has lost a great deal of its florid complexion, and General Washington is allowed by both sides not to be the worst general in the field. The stocks are grown positive that we shall have a French war. That was so self-evident, that I should be ashamed of bragging I had always foreseen it. A child might foretell many of the consequences. I leave it to those who would not foresee to excuse themselves as they can.

The *Gazettes* will tell you as much as you are allowed to know or believe. If you do not understand them, you will not be singular. The time is coming, I doubt, when truth will write a more legible hand. In one word, the retreat of the Americans seems to have been wise; you will find they will flight and have fought, and that, when we believed Philadelphia was gone, General Howe has been obliged to contract hs quarters. I should think less than *unlimited submission* would content us at present; and I leave you to judge whether France will be omitted in the negotiation, and whether she will enjoin the Congress to be very tractable. I hope there will be a little more wisdom in making the peace than there was in making the
~~~

war; *but they who make the one, do not always consider that they may not be equally wasters to make the other*... [Vol. X, p. 23]

~~~***~~~

To Sir Horace Mann.
From Strawberry Hill, April 3, 1777.

...I have nothing very new to tell you on public affairs, especially as I can know nothing more than you see in the papers. It is my opinion that the King's affairs are in a very bad position in America. I do not say that his armies may not gain advantages again; though I believe there has been as much design as cowardice in the behaviour of the provincials, who seem to have been apprised that protraction of the war would be more certainly advantageous to them than heroism. Washington, the dictator, has shown himself both a Fabius and a Camillus. His march through our lines is allowed a prodigy of generalship. In one word, I look upon a great part of America as lost to this country! It is not less deplorable, that, between art and contention, such an inveteracy has been sown between the two countries as will probably outlast even the war! Supposing this unnatural enmity should not soon involve us in other wars, which would be extraordinary indeed, what a difference, in a future war with France and Spain, to have the colonies in the opposite scale, instead of being in ours! What politicians are those who have preferred the empty name of sovereignty to that of alliance, and forced subsidies to the golden ocean of commerce!

Alas! the trade of America is not all we shall lose! The ocean of commerce wafted us wealth at the return of regular tides: but we had acquired an empire too, in whose plains the beggars we sent out as labourers could reap sacks of gold in three or four harvests; and who with their sickles and reaping-hooks have robbed and cut the throats of those who sowed the grain. These rapacious foragers have fallen together by the ears; and our Indian affairs, I suppose, will soon be in as desperate a state as our American, Lord Pigot has been treacherously and violently imprisoned, and the Company here has voted his restoration. I know nothing of the merits of the cause on either side: I dare to say both are very blamable. I look only to the consequences, which I do not doubt will precipitate the loss of our acquisitions there; the title to which I never admired, and the possession of which I always regarded as a transitory vision. If we could keep it, we should certainly plunder it, till the expense of maintaining would overbalance the returns; and, though it has rendered a little more than the holy city of Jerusalem, I look on such distant conquests as more destructive than beneficial; and, whether we are martyrs or banditti, whether we fight for the Holy Sepulchre or for lacks of rupees, I detest invasions of quiet kingdoms, both for their sakes and for our own; and it is happy for the former, that the latter are never permanently benefited... [Vol. X, p. 31]

~~~***~~~

To the Countess of Upper Ossory
From Strawberry Hill, June 15 1777

...Have you got through Dr. Robertson, Madam? I am not enchanted. There is a great affectation of philosophizing without much success. But there is one character that charms me, besides Las Casas, at whom the good doctor rather sneers; it is that of Pedro di Gasca, who was disinterested enough to make ten Parliaments blush. Do but imagine the satisfaction with which he must have retired with his poverty, after the great things he had done, when every other of his countrymen were cutting the throats of Americans for gold! He did not want to be Treasurer of the Navy, as well as general and pacificator. I am delighted too with the ingratitude of the Spanish monarchs to all their heroic assassins. How fortunate the Otaheitans, to have no gold mines in their country! [Vol. X, p. 61]

~~~***~~~

To the Countess of Upper Ossory.
From Strawberry Hill, Aug. 8, 1777.

...Have you read General Burgoyne's rhodomontade [i.e., Burgoyne's proclamation to the Americans prior to his invasion proper of New York], in which he almost promises to cross America in a
~~~

hop, step, and a jump? I thought we were cured of hyperboles. He has sent over, too, a copy of his talk with the Indians, which they say is still more supernatural. I own I prefer General Howe's taciturnity, who at least, if he does nothing, does not break his word. It is supposed the latter is sailed to Boston, and that the former has kicked Ticonderoga into one of the lakes -- I don't know which, I am no geographer... [Vol. X, p. 91]

~~~***~~~

To Sir Horace Mann.
From Strawberry Hill, Aug. 11, 1777.

...The conquest of America is put off to the millennium. It is hoped, and thence supposed, that General Howe is gone to take some place, or beat some army, that is more practicable than dislodging Washington. Burgoyne has sent over a manifesto, that, if he was to overrun ten provinces, would appear too pompous; and yet, let him achieve ever so little, it will be sure of not being depreciated; so great is the want of something to keep up the spirits of the people, who stare a little at being bullied on their own coasts, after being told that five thousand men would overrun all America. France sits by and laughs, receives our remonstrances, sends us an ambassadress, and winks on Dr. Franklin, that it is all the comfort she will give us. -- I believe you will not wish me to expatiate more on that chapter... [Vol. X, p. 94]

~~~***~~~

To Sir Horace Mann
From Arlington Street, Oct. 26, 1777.

It is past my usual period of writing to you; which would not have happened but from an uncommon, and indeed, considering the moment, an extraordinary dearth of matter. I could have done nothing but describe suspense, and every newspaper told you that. Still we know nothing certain of the state of affairs in America; the very existence where, of the Howes, is a mystery. The General is said to have beaten Washington, Clinton to have repulsed three attacks, and Burgoyne to be beaten. The second alone is credited. Impatience is very high, and uneasiness increases with every day. There is no sanguine face anywhere, but many alarmed ones. The pains taken, by circulating false reports, to keep up some confidence, only increase the dissatisfaction by disappointing. Some advantage gained may put off clamour for some months: but I think, the longer it is suspended, the more terrible it will be; and how the war should end but in ruin, I am not wise enough to conjecture. France suspends the blow, to make it more inevitable. She has suffered us to undo ourselves: will she allow us time to recover? We have begged her indulgence in the first: will she grant the second prayer?... [Vol. X, p. 143]

~~~***~~~

To the Countess of Upper Ossory.
From Strawberry Hill, Monday night, Nov. 3, 1777.

St. John is a false prophet, and of the house of Bolingbroke; the angel of the Church of Philadelphia is a blind buzzard, and cannot see a yard beyond his nose. A heathen Cupid, with a bandage over his eyes, is worth a hundred of such blundering cherubim, that, like bats, fly about in the dark, and take a farthing candle for the sun. There, my Lady, there's Washington beaten, and Philadelphia taken! Commend me to Revelations! If your angel would be seeing, why did not he put on his spectacles and hover over Arnold, who has beaten the vapouring Burgoyne, and destroyed his magazines? Carleton, who was set aside for General Hurlothrumbo, is gone to save him and the remains of his army, if he can. On Saturday night, not a minister but was packing up: yesterday morning, they ran about, shouting and huzzaing, like madmen!... [Vol. X, p. 148]

~~~***~~~

To Sir Horace Mann.
From Arlington Street, Dec. 4, 1777.

...General Clinton has marched to relieve or find Burgoyne, but was forced to be content with taking two forts [on the Hudson River, below Albany], and showing uncommon valour. The next paragraph will tell you why his expedition was unnecessary.

On Tuesday night came news from Carleton at Quebec, which indeed had come from France earlier, announcing the total annihilation (as to America) of Burgoyne's army. Carleton declares he has no authentic information; but from all the intelligence he can get, and which he believes, Burgoyne, after dispatching Colonel Fraser [i.e., Brig. Gen. Simon Fraser] with 1,000 men to seek provisions, which whole body with their commander was cut off, fought desperately to extricate himself; but, numbers increasing and pouring upon him, he had been forced to lay down his arms, and the whole remaining army, which some say still consisted of 5,000, but probably were reduced much lower, surrendered themselves prisoners, and are to be transported to England, on parole of not serving more in America -- no bad circumstance for us, if they were but here? Burgoyne is said to be wounded in three places; his vanquisher Arnold is supposed to be dead of his wounds. [Vol. X, p. 160]

~~~***~~~

To the Countess of Upper Ossory
From Arlington Street, Friday night, late, Dec. 5, 1777.

...I must own I had not sorted my feelings into different drawers, and therefore cannot one day pull out one, and grieve for burning a town, or destroying a beautiful province; and the next day take out an assortment of compassion for an army that marched under such a savage proclamation as Burgoyne's. The accounts that are come, own that the provincials have treated him and his fellow-prisoners with the utmost humanity. On the other hand, I must contradict myself, and do justice to General Clinton, who spared all he could when he took the two forts. We have been horribly the aggressors; and I must rejoice that the Americans are to be free, as they had a right to be, and as I am sure they have shown they deserve to be. I cannot answer for what our troops would have done, had they conquered; and less what the spirit would have done that sent them. Lord Chatham is an Irishman: he would recall the troops and deny the independence of the Americans. He is in the right to recall an army that cannot conquer it; but a country that will not be conquered, and that cannot be, is but in an odd sort of state of dependence. He seems to be afraid of their condescending even to trade with us. No, Madam, we do not want ministers that would protract our difficulties. I look on them but as beginning now, and am far from thinking that there is any man, or set of men, able enough to extricate us. I own there are very able Englishmen left, but they happen to be on t' other side of the Atlantic. If his Majesty hopes to find them here, I doubt he will be mistaken: it is not worth his while to change hands... [Vol. X, p. 163]

~~~***~~~

To the Rev. William Mason
From Arlington Street, Feb. 18, 1778

...The faults of the administration, according to their own calculation, are *two*: one of being misinformed, the other of persisting in a mere point of honour. Some will perhaps think they have been guilty of two more; -- the destruction of twenty-four thousand lives on their own side, and Lord knows how many thousands on t'other, with the burning of towns, desolation of the country, and the expense of above thirty millions of money; the second consists of two parts -- rejection of all proposals of accommodation offered by the opposition, and the delay of offering terms themselves till they knew it was too late; for Lord North was asked if he did not know that the treaty between the Americans and France is signed? He would not answer till Sir George Saville hallooed out, 'An answer, an answer, an answer!' His Lordship then rose, could not deny the fact, but said he did not know it officially; that is, I suppose, it does not stand on the votes of the Parliament at Paris...

A night's rest has not dissipated the astonishment of mankind. Everybody that comes in stares, and cannot express himself. Who can at once reconcile a supplication of alliance with the high and mighty

States of America, with a total improbability of obtaining it? and the faintest hope of peace, with a prospect of a war with France? How, an acknowledgement of independence, with a pretension of supplies, or a suspension of the war for a year and a half, with any intention of renewing it, when the Americans shall have had time to settle their government and recruit? but who can digest all the contradictions into which the Government plunges every day?... [Vol. X, p. 189]

~~~***~~~

To Sir Horace Mann
From Arlington Street, Feb. 18, 1778.

I DO not know how to word the following letter; how to gain credit with you! How shall I intimate to you, that you must lower your topsails, waive your imperial dignity, and strike to the colours of the thirteen United Provinces of America? Do not tremble, and imagine that Washington has defeated General Howe, and driven him out of Philadelphia; or that Gates has taken another army; or that Portsmouth is invested by an American fleet. No: no military new event has occasioned this revolution. The sacrifice has been made on the altar of peace. Stop again: peace is not made, it is only implored, -- and, I fear only on this side of the Atlantic. In short, yesterday, February 17th, a most memorable era, Lord North opened his conciliatory plan, -- no partial, no collusive one. In as few words as I can use, it solicits peace with the States of America: it haggles on no terms; it acknowledges the Congress, or anybody that pleases to treat; it confesses errors, misinformation, ill-success, and impossibility of conquest; it disclaims taxation, desires commerce, hopes for assistance, allows the independence of America, not verbally, yet virtually, and suspends hostilities till June 1779. It does a little more: not *verbally*, but *virtually*, it confesses that the opposition have been in the right from the beginning to the end.

The warmest American cannot deny but these gracious condescensions are ample enough to content that whole continent; and yet, my friend, such accommodating facility had one defect, -- it came too late. The treaty between the high and mighty States and France is signed; and instead of peace, we must expect war with the high allies. The French array is come to the coast, and their officers here are recalled...

I have lived long, but never saw such a day as last Tuesday! From the first, I augured ill of this American war; yet do not suppose that I boast of my penetration. Far was I from expecting such a conclusion! Conclusion!...

[The same letter to Rev. Mason resumed on Feb. 20, 1778.]

...Acts of Parliament have made a war, but cannot repeal one. They have provoked -- not terrified; and Washington and Gates have respected the Speaker's mace no more than Oliver Cromwell did... [Vol. X, p. 193]

~~~***~~~

To Sir Horace Mann.
From Strawberry Hill, March 27, 1778.

...No more troops are to go to America; we are collecting our whole force; the new-raised regiments will have been an advantageous addition, as they were not embarked; and the militia, which is complete in every county but two, is to take the field. As to America, it will certainly retain its seat amongst the sovereignties of this world: so, Columbus's invasion begins to be set aside; and one quarter of the globe will not be held *in commendam* by another! Imagination could expatiate widely on that chapter -- but what have I to do with a new era in the annals of mankind?... [Vol. X, p. 211]

~~~***~~~

To Sir Horace Mann
From Strawberry Hill, May 31, 1778.
~~~

...General Burgoyne has succeeded and been the topic, and for two days engrossed the attention of the House of Commons; and probably will be heard of no more. He was even forgotten for three hours while he was on the *tapis*, by a violent quarrel between Temple Luttrell (a brother of the Duchess of Cumberland) and Lord George Germaine; but the public has taken affection for neither them nor the General: being much more disposed at present to hate than to love -- except the dead. It will be well if the ill-humour, which increases, does not break out into overt acts…[Vol. X, p. 257]

~~~***~~~

To the Rev. William Mason
From Strawberry Hill, July 4, 1778.

Children break their playthings to see the inside of them. Pope thought superior beings looked on Newton but as a monkey of uncommon parts: would not he think that we have been like babies smashing an empire to see what it was made of? Truly I doubt whether there will be a whole piece left in three months: the conduct bears due proportion to the incapacity -- you ought to be on the spot to believe it...

...General Howe is arrived and was graciously received. The agreeable news he brought is, that Clinton for want of provisions has abandoned Philadelphia and marched through the Jerseys to New York without molestation, on condition of not destroying Philadelphia. The Congress has ratified the treaty with France, and intend to treat the Commissioners[216] *de haut en bas*, unless you choose to believe the *Morning Post*, who says five provinces declare for peace. I told you lately my curiosity to know what is to be left to us at a general peace. The wisest thing the ministers could do would be to ask that question incontinently. I am persuaded in the present apathy that the nation would be perfectly pleased, let the terms be what they would. A series of disasters may spoil this good humour, and there often wants but a man to fling a stone to spread a conflagration…

…Our writers have been disputing for these hundred and sixty-six years on Whig and Tory principles. Their successors, who I suppose will continue the controversy, will please to allow at least that if the ministers of both parties were equally complaisant when in power, the splendour of the crown (I say nothing of the happiness of the people, which is never taken into the account) has constantly been augmented by Whig administrations, and has faded (and then and now a little more) when Tories have governed! The reason is as plain: Whig principles are founded on sense; a Whig may be a fool, a Tory must be so: the consequence is plain; a Whig when a minister may abandon his principles, but he will retain his sense and will therefore not risk the felicity of his posterity by sacrificing everything to selfish views. A Tory attaining power hurries to establish despotism: the honour, the trade, the wealth, the peace of the nation, all are little to him in comparison of the despotic will of his master, but are not you glad I write on small paper? [Vol. X, p. 270]

~~~***~~~

To the Rev. Mr. Cole
From Strawberry Hill, July 12, 1778.

....Has not this Indian summer dispersed your complaints? We are told we are to be invaded. Our Abbots and Whitgifts now see with what successes and consequences their preaching up a crusade against America has been crowned! Archbishop Markham may have an opportunity of exercising his martial prowess. I doubt he would resemble Bishop Crewe more than good Mr. Baker. Let us respect those only who are Israelites indeed. I surrender Dr. Abbot to you. Church and presbytery are terms for monopolies, Exalted notions of church matters are contradictions in terms to the lowliness and humility of the gospel. There is nothing sublime but the Divinity. Nothing is sacred but as His work. A tree or a brute stone is more respectable as such, than a mortal called an Archbishop, or an edifice called a Church, which are the puny and perishable productions of men. Calvin and Wesley had just the same views as the Pope; power

[216] [*Edit. Note.* The British peace commissioners sent to Philadelphia in early 1778 and lead by Lord Carlisle.]

and wealth their objects. I abhor both, and admire Mr. Baker. Let us respect only those that are Israelites indeed. I surrender Dr. Abbot to you. Church and presbytery are human nonsense, invented by knaves to govern fools. Church and Kirk are terms for monopolies. *Exalted notions of Church matters* are contradictions in terms to the lowliness and humility of the Gospel. There is nothing sublime but the Divinity. Nothing is sacred but as His work. A tree or a brute stone is more respectable as such, than a mortal called an Archbishop, or an edifice called a Church, which are the puny and perishable productions of men. Calvin and Wesley had just the same views as the Popes; power and wealth their objects. I abhor both, and admire Mr. Baker.

P.S. I like Popery as well as you, and have shown I do. I like it as I like chivalry and romance. They all furnish one with ideas and visions, which presbyterianism does not. A Gothic church or a convent fills one with romantic dreams -- but for the mysterious, the Church in the abstract, it is a jargon that means nothing, or a great deal too much, and I reject it and its apostles, from Athanasius to Bishop Keene. [Vol. X, p. 278]

~~~***~~~

To the Rev. William Mason
From Strawberry Hill, July 18, 1778.

...Well; war proclaimed! [with France] and I am near sixty-one. Shall I live to see peace again? and what a peace! I endeavour to compose my mind, and call in every collateral aid. I condemn my countrymen, but cannot, would not divest myself of my love to my country. I enjoy the disappointment of the Scots, who had prepared the yoke for the Americans and for our necks too. I cannot blame the French whom we have tempted to ruin us: yet, to be ruined by France! -- there the Englishman in me feels again. My chief comfort is in talking to you, though you do not answer me. I write to vent my thoughts, as it is easier than brooding over them, but allow that it is difficult to be very tranquil when the navy of England is at stake. That thought annihilates resentment. I wish for nothing but victory and then peace, yet what lives must victory cost! Nor will one victory purchase it. The nation is so frantic that success would intoxicate us more; yet calamity, that alone could sober us, is too near our doors. Resignation to the will of Heaven is the language of reason as well as of religion, when one knows not what would be best for us. It is a dilemma to which the honest are reduced: our gamesters are in a worse situation. The best they can hope for is to sit down with the debris of an empire. What a line they have drawn between them and Lord Chatham! I believe it was modesty made them not attend his funeral. Will the house of Brunswick listen again to the flatterers of prerogative?

My time of life, that ought to give me philosophy, dispirits me. I cannot expect to live to see England revive. I shall leave it at best an insignificant island. Its genius is vanished like its glories; one sees nor hero nor statesman arise to flatter hope. Dr. Franklin, thanks to Mr. Wedderburn, is at Paris. Every way I turn my thoughts, the returns are irksome. What is the history of a fallen empire? A transient satire on the vices and follies that hurried it to dissolution. The protest of a few that foretold it is not registered. The names of Jefferies and two or three principals satisfy the sage moralist who hurries to more agreeable times. I will go to bed and sleep, if I can. Pray write to me; tell me how you reconcile your mind to our situation -- I cannot. Two years ago I meditated leaving England if it was enslaved. I have no such thought now. I will steal into its bosom when my hour comes, and love it to the last. [Vol. X, p. 283]

~~~***~~~

To Henry Seymour Conway
From Strawberry Hill, June 16, 1779.

...Well! here we are, *aris et focis* and all at stake! What can we be meaning? Unable to conquer America before she was assisted -- scarce able to keep France at bay -- are we a match for both, and Spain too? What can be our view? nay, what can be Our expectation? I sometimes think we reckon it will be more creditable to be forced by France and Spain to give up America, than to have the merit with the latter of doing it with grace. -- But, as [Addison's] Cato says,

"I'm weary of conjectures -- this must end them;"

that is, the sword: -- and never, I believe, did a Country Plunge itself into such difficulties step by step, and for six years, together, without once recollecting that each foreign war rendered the object of the civil war more unattainable; and that in both the foreign wars we have not an object in prospect. Unable to recruit our remnant of an army in America, are we to make conquests on France and Spain? They may choose their attacks: we can scarce choose what we will defend... [Vol. X, p. 422]

~~~***~~~

To Sir Horace Mann.
From Strawberry Hill, June 16, 1779.

...I shall not boast of having been a better soothsayer than you, when I foretold that the American war would not be of short duration. It is a trist honour to be verified a prophet of woes. Were I vain of the character, a Spanish war, added to an American and to a French one, wore a fine field; but I do not ambition being a Jeremiah, though my countrymen are so like the Jews. Nor does it require inspiration to prophesy, when one has nothing to do but to calculate. Were you here, you would not be alarmed. You would see no panic; you would hoar of nothing but diversions. The ministers affirm the majority of America is with us, and it is credited. Were they to tell us half the Spanish fleet would come over to us, it would be credited too. When it does not, perhaps they will tell us it has. -- Well! what is most to be dreaded is the dissipation of our delusion. When the *reveil* comes, it will be serious indeed!... [Vol. X, p. 425]

~~~***~~~

To The Countess of Ailesbury
Saturday night, July 10, 1779.
From Strawberry Hill

...We could not Conquer America when it stood alone; then France supported it, and we did not mend the matter. To make it still easier, we have driven Spain into the alliance. Is this wisdom? Would it be presumption, even if one were single, to think that we must have the worst in such a contest? Shall I be like the mob, and expect to conquer France and Spain, and then thunder upon America? Nay, but the higher mob do not expect such success. They would not be so angry at the house of Bourbon, if not morally certain that those kings destroy all our passionate desire and expectation of conquering America. We bullied, and threatened, and begged, and nothing would do. Yet independence was still the word. Now we rail at the two monarchs -- and when they have banged us, we shall sue to them as humbly as we did to the Congress. All this my senses, such as they are, tell me has been and will be the case. What is worse, all Europe is of the same opinion; and though forty thousand *baronesses* may be ever so angry, I venture to prophesy that we shall make but a very foolish figure whenever we are so lucky as to obtain a peace; and posterity, that may have prejudices of its own, will still take the liberty to pronounce, that its ancestors were a wo[e]ful set of politicians from the year 1774 to -- I wish I knew when... [Vol. X, p. 446]

~~~***~~~

To Sir Horace Mann
From Strawberry Hill, Sept. 16, 1779.

...Nature gave to mankind a beautiful world, and larger than it could occupy, -- for, as to the eruption of Goths and Vandals occasioned by excess of population, I very much doubt it; and mankind prefers deforming the ready Paradise, to improving and enjoying it. Ambition and mischief, which one should not think were natural appetites, seem almost as much so as the impulse to propagation; and those pious rogues, the clergy, preach against what Nature forces us to practise (or she could not carry on her system), and not twice in a century say a syllable against the Lust of Destruction! Oh! one is lost in moralising, as one is in astronomy! In the ordinance and preservation of the great universal system one sees the Divine Artificer, but our intellects are too bounded to comprehend anything more... [Vol. XI, p. 25]

~~~***~~~

To Sir Horace Mann
From Berkeley Square, Jan. 13, 1780

...What might have been expected much sooner, appears at last -- a good deal of discontent; but chiefly where it was not much expected. The country gentlemen, after encouraging the Court to war with America, now, not very decently, are angry at the expense. As they have long seen the profusion, it would have been happy had they murmured sooner. Very serious associations are forming in many counties; and orders, under the title of petitions, coming to Parliament for correcting abuses. They talk of the waste of money; are silent on the thousands of lives that have been sacrificed -- but when are human lives counted by any side?... [Vol. XI, p. 101]

~~~***~~~

To Sir Horace Mann,
From Berkeley Square, May 18, 1780.

...America has begun to announce itself for a successor to old Europe, but I already doubt whether it will replace its predecessors; genius does not seem to make great shoots there. Buffon says that European animals degenerate across the Atlantic; perhaps its migrating inhabitants may be in the same predicament. If my reveries are true, what pity that the world will not retire into itself and enjoy a calm old age!... [Vol. XI, p. 172]

~~~***~~~

To the Countess of Upper Ossory.
From Berkeley Square, at night, June 16, 1780

...The conquest of Charleston is a great event at the present moment: not a good one if it ensanguines us against peace. I neither understand military details nor love them for that reason. But this success is coupled with a very remarkable event. A Colonel Scott, I think a prisoner, says the Americans are sick of the war, but have been buoyed up by Spanish gold, and by *French promises of the conflagration of London* -- a hellish sort of war, but who set the precedent? The court talk much of a plot, and this anecdote is corroborative. Indeed I cannot at all agree with Mr. F.[217] in wishing Lord George Gordon may not be found guilty. He is so black in my eyes already, that though I have infinite compassion for criminals, I never heard of one I should pity less. If he is the source of our being ruled by an army, I shall abhor him still more. Have you heard, Madam, that the common soldiers style one another *your worship*, as being the only Justices of Peace?... [Vol. XI, p. 225]

~~~***~~~

To Sir Horace Mann.
From Berkeley Square, Oct. 4, 1780.

....General Dalrymple is arrived from Sir Henry Clinton, with heavy baggage indeed, full of bad news! The *Gazette* has produced only samples strewed over with fine sugar, to make it as palatable and little bitter as possible; but the sum total is, that adieu to America I All the visions that mounted in fumes into our heads from the capture of Charleston are turned to smoke; and it were well if it would rest there. To be cured of that dream would be no calamity; but I wish we may have no collateral losses! I fear we ache in some islands, and are not quite without twitches on the continent of America. Well! as I was right in foreseeing some miserable issue from the American war, I have a mind to try my skill in foretelling peace. 'Tis sure I wish it most fervently... [Vol. XI, p. 291]

~~~***~~~

To Sir Horace Mann.
From Strawberry Hill, Oct. 9, 1780 [resumed from a Oct. 7 letter]

---

[217] [*Edit. Note*. Richard Fitzpatrick, brother-in-law of Lady Ossory.]

...I have just heard some news that you will like to hear, and which will make you hold up your head again a little *vis-a'-vis M.de Barbantane*. An express arrived to-day from Lord Cornwallis who with two thousand men has attacked General Gates in Carolina at the head of seven thousand, and entirely defeated him, killed nine hundred, and taken one thousand prisoners; and there has since been a little codicil, of all which you will see the particulars in the to-morrow's Gazette. But it is very late, and this must go to town early in the morning. I allow you to triumph, though Gates is my godson, and your namesake...[218] [Vol. XI, p. 294]

~~~***~~~

To the Countess of Upper Ossory
From Berkeley Square, Nov. 16, 1780.

...A good courtier, yesterday, sang the praises to me of that atrocious villain, Arnold, who, he said, till he heard of André's execution, would not discover the persons at New York, with whom Washington was in secret correspondence; then indeed he did. Only think of the monster! I hope he will be a Privy Councillor I betraying to Sir Harry Clinton, in the height of his indignation for André the wretched poor souls cooped up in New York, who are guilty of that correspondence. When I expressed my horror at such bloody treachery, and said I did not doubt but Lord Cornwallis's savage executions had hurried on André's fate, and were, besides cruel, indiscreet; the same apologist said, 'Oh, we have more prisoners of theirs than they have of ours.' How tender to their *own friends*, who they do not care if hanged, provided they can spill more buckets of blood! I know nothing of poor André; he is much commended, but so he would be if as black as Arnold... [Vol. XI, p. 316]

~~~***~~~

To Henry Seymour Conway
From Berkeley Square, Jan. 3, 1781.

...I sit and gaze with astonishment at our frenzy. Yet why? Are not nations as liable to intoxication as individuals? Are not predictions founded on calculation oftener rejected than the prophecies of dreamers? Do we not act precisely like Charles Fox, who thought he had discovered a new truth in figures, when he preached that wise doctrine, that nobody could want money that would pay enough for it? The consequence was, that in two years he left himself without the possibility of borrowing a shilling. I am not surprised at the spirits of a boy of parts; I am not surprised at the people; I do wonder at government, that games away its consequence. For what are we now really at war with America, France, Spain, and Holland! -- Not with hopes of reconquering America; not with the smallest prospect of conquering a foot of land from France, Spain, or Holland. No; we are at war on the defensive to protect what is left, or more truly to stave off, for a year perhaps, a peace that must proclaim our nakedness and impotence... [Vol. XI, p. 357]

~~~***~~~

To the Countess of Upper Ossory
From Berkeley Square, Jan. 4, 1781.

...In good truth, I was glad of anything that would occupy me, and turn my attention from all the horrors one hears or apprehends. I am sorry I have read the devastation of Barbadoes and Jamaica, &c, &c.; when one can do no good, can neither prevent nor redress^ nor has any personal share, by oneself or one's friends, is it not excusable to steep one's attention in anything? I fear, Madam, you and Lord Ossory have a suffering friend: poor Mr. James, I hear, is totally ruined -- his whole property swept away! There is another dreadful history, less known: the expedition sent against the Spanish settlements is cut off by the climate, and not a single being is left alive. The Duchess of Bedford told me last night that the poor soldiers were so averse, that they were driven to the march by the point of the bayonet, and that, beside the men, twenty-five officers have perished.

---

[218] [*Letters of Horace Walpole*, vol. XI, editor's note (p. 295): "Horatio Gates, the American general, was son of an inferior officer of the revenue in England, who married a housekeeper of the second Duke of Leeds. Mrs. Gates was very intimate with the woman of Lady Walpole, Mr. H. W.'s mother, which occasioned his being godfather, about twelve years old, to her son..."]
~~~

Lord Cornwallis and his tiny army are scarce in a more prosperous way. On this dismal canvas a fourth war is embroidered; and what, I think, threatens still more, the French administration is changed, and likely to be composed of more active men, and much more hostile to England. Our ruin seems to me inevitable. Nay, I know those who smile in the Drawing-room, that groan by their fireside: they own we have no more men to send to America, and think our credit almost as nearly exhausted. Can you wonder, then, Madam, if I am glad to play with Quipos -- Oh, no! nor can I be sorry to be on the verge -- does one wish to live to weep over the ruins of Carthage?... [Vol. XI, p. 359]

~~~***~~~

To the Rev. William Mason
From Berkeley Square, Thursday night late, Jan. 4, 1781.

...This good town is quite happy, for it has gotten a new plaything, a Dutch War; and the folks that are to gain by Privateering, have persuaded those who are to pay the piper, to dance for joy. In the midst of this exultation came accounts that would make any body shudder, but an overgrown capital, who care for nothing but their daily bread, news, and *circenses*. All Barbadoes and half Jamaica are annihilated. The inhabitants are buried or famishing. The shipping too has suffered deplorably. The events in America are not more flattering. Leslie, who had taken a walk into two or three open towns, one of which was Norfolk, that we burnt three or four years ago, has been recalled and is re embarked, to try to save Lord Cornwallis, who has found the country as hostile as it was proclaimed to be friendly, and is in great danger too from five thousand men dispatched by Washington to strengthen Gates. An expedition sent against the Spanish settlements has been so totally destroyed by the climate that not a single man is left alive. The officers to the number of twenty-five are all dead too. My pen revolts at detailing such horrors! If I turn from them I have nothing else to tell you. I used to write of books as well as news, I have not seen one. Raspe's book indeed is in the press and will appear in February; I have been correcting the second sheet this evening... [Vol. XI, p. 362]

~~~***~~~

To Sir Horace Mann.
From Berkeley Square, March 30, 1781.

I WROTE a letter to you for your messenger the moment he arrived, but he was detained here so long that it must have reached you antiquated. He found us exulting for the capture of St. Eustatia: the scene is a little changed since, both in West and East. America is once more not quite ready to be conquered, though every now and then we fancy it is. Tarleton is defeated. Lord Cornwallis is checked, and Arnold not sure of having betrayed his friends to much purpose. If we are less certain of recovering what we have thrown away, we are in still as much danger of losing what we acquired, not more creditably, at the other end of the world. Hyder Ally, an Indian potentate, thinking he has as much right to the diamonds of his won country as the Rumbolds and Sykes's, who were originally waiters in a tavern, has given us a blow, and his not done [i.e., "has not done doing so"]… [Vol. XI, p. 419]

~~~***~~~

To Sir Horace Mann.
From Berkeley Square, Nov. 26, 1781.

...An account came yesterday that could not but be expected, that Washington and the French have made Lord Cornwallis and his whole army prisoners. I do not know what others think, but to me it seems fortunate that they were not all cut to pieces. It is not heroic perhaps, but I am glad that this disaster arriving before our fleet reached the Chesapeak, it turned back to New York without attacking the French fleet who are above three to two, thirty-seven to twenty-three. This is all I know yet; and yet this comes at an untoward moment; for the Parliament meets to-morrow, and it puts the Speech and speeches a little into disorder.

I cannot put on the face of the day, and act grief. Whatever puts an end to the American war will save the lives of thousands -- millions of money too. If glory compensates such sacrifices, I have never heard that disgraces and disappointments were palliatives; but I will not descant, nor is it right to vaunt of
~~~

having been in the right when one's country's shame is the solution of one's prophecy, nor would one join in the triumph of her enemies. Details you will hear from France sooner than I can send them; but I will write again the moment I know anything material. I am sorry your nephew is not arrived; who, by being in Parliament and in the world, would be sooner and better informed than I, who stir little out of my own house, and have no political connections, nor scarce a wish but to die in peace.... [Vol. XII, p. 102]

ROYALL TYLER & THE BIRTH OF AMERICAN STAGE COMEDY (1787)

"And last Miss Fortune, whimpering came,
Cured me of love's tormenting flame,
And all my beau pretences.
In widow's weeds, the prude appears;
See now -- she drowns me with her tears,
With bony fist, now slaps my ears,
And brings me to my senses."
~ from Tyler's poem "My Mistress"

In an effort to further enhance moral unanimity, civic mindedness, and individual sobriety, the Continental Congress on Oct 24th 1774 passed a resolution that proclaimed a blunt disapproval of idle pastimes such as gaming, horse racing, and theater. It buttressed its continued commitment to this measure later in Oct. 1778 by issuing two additional resolutions, the second of which, i.e., of Oct. 16th, read:

"Whereas: Frequenting playhouses and theatrical entertainments has a fatal tendency to divert the minds of the people from a due attention to the means necessary for the defence of their country and the preservation of their liberties, -- Resolved: That every person holding an office under the United States, who shall act, promote, encourage, or attend such plays, shall be deemed unworthy to hold such office, and shall be accordingly dismissed."

While time of war was a reasonable justification for such a policy, it was of course by no means without precedent in the colonies. Boston, as early as 1750 had forbade plays and other theatrical entertainments in the city; which statute remained on the books till 1793. Even Philadelphia, in April 1775, placed a ban on theater that was only rescinded in 1789. Other major cities, like Newport, Baltimore, Charleston, largely observed the wishes of Congress; although by as early as June 1781 amateur and semi-amateur shows put on by small groups, some of which included former Continental officers and soldiers, and which exhibited songs, recitations, and individual dramatic scenes began appearing in Baltimore and Annapolis. In occupied New York, however, the theater thrived, and plays were acted and directed there by British officers till the war's close.[219]

Yet it is worth observing that often drama tells the truth that cannot otherwise be said; but which *if said* is derided as *mere drama* or make-believe. Hence, there was perhaps more sense than we give credit to for banning theater during the age of Oliver Cromwell, or in America during colonial and Revolutionary times; namely, that such a ban arguably made it *more possible* to believe *truths* that else would be deemed or thought of as *unbelievable*.[220]

Enter Boston Harvard educated lawyer Royall Tyler. While serving (at the rank of Major) as aide to Maj. Gen. Benjamin Lincoln in the suppression of Shays' Rebellion in 1787, he was dispatched to New York City to enlist the support of New York in that cause; all the more necessary in view of the leader of the insurgents having left Massachusetts and retreated into New York state for refuge. With his mission to secure New York aid fulfilled, Tyler, while sojourning in Gotham's metropolis, managed to make the acquaintance of "The American Company" -- a troupe of English players, domiciling themselves at the John Street Theater; who sought to revive theater life in the city; in spite of the Puritanical and Quaker

[219] See *With An Air Debonair: Musical Theatre In America 1785-1815* by Susan L. Porter; a positively delightful and superb book on its subject.

[220] For further, see "Another High Road to Hell. An Essay on the Pernicious Nature and Destructive Effects of the Modern Entertainments from the Pulpit" (1768, Boston) by John Chater, and "Extracts from the Writings of Divers Eminent Authors, of Different Religious Denominations; and at Various Periods of Time, Representing the Evils and Pernicious Effects of Stage Plays, and Other Vain Amusements" (1789) issued by the Evangelical Lutheran Church in North America, and "The Rights of the Drama: or, An Inquiry Into the Origin, Principles, and Consequences of Theatrical Entertainments" (1792, Boston) by Philo Dramatis.

attitudes, not to mention the aforesaid Congressional edicts, disapproving of such efforts and still prevalent at large. Although Tyler had never actually seen a professionally done stage play in his life, he took it upon himself to write one. And, as it happened, the company, knowing a good thing when they saw it, kindly received his work, "The Contrast," and agreed to stage it. Opening on April 16, 1787, the modest sized -- in terms of number of players, props, and simple backdrops -- production scored a resounding success, and subsequently went on to be acted in Philadelphia, Baltimore, and Boston with equally propitious response. In addition to being the first ever professionally produced comedy play written by an American author,[221] "The Contrast" played an influential part in helping to lessen public prejudice and distrust of serious theater -- as opposed to more commonly accepted forms of entertainment; such as pantomimes, harlequinades, and circus acts.

While "The Contrast" is conspicuously short on plot development, it was, for its day, strikingly innovative in its cast of characters, particularly in the case of Col. Henry Manly, a former Continental army officer, and his "waiter" Jonathan. It was also shrewdly written inasmuch as it used such personages to appeal to patriotic and moral values; while implicitly arguing that theater was and could in fact be of benefit to society if approached and utilized wisely and responsibly.

Manly embodies the selfless and disinterested virtues and ideals of Washington and the Society of Cincinnati. At the same time, he is an altruistic sort who looks to giving to and aiding those in need. Not perhaps least remarkable of his adeptness in handling the character, Tyler presents him in a convincing and believable manner. Meanwhile, the character of the rustic Jonathan struck even more of a note of affinity with audiences, and was the first of a long line of like comic stage and film characters, and which include Colonel Nimrod Wildfire (from Paulding's play "Lion of the West" [1831]) up unto the Beverly Hillbillies; which is to say a self-confident yokel whose humor lies in his (or hers) naively misinterpreting the ways of culture and urban society. Contrary to the assertion of some scholars, Jonathan was not a pure invention of Tyler's, and we see some of this same kind of personality in the joking, down to earth Ethan Allen, as revealed in the latter's 1779 *Narrative*. In fact, "The Contrast" makes an allusion to Allen (Act I, sc. 1) in the way of mentioning a General from Vermont. As well, it should be noted, country Irishmen and Englishmen of course long and traditionally played a like role in British farces and comedies.

Yet, rather strangely, the play, even by later standards, in its sexual references and innuendos, borders on racy; and here Tyler may have been impacted by Restoration comedies. Moreover, it would seem Tyler in his earlier life bore a greater resemblance to Billy Dimple, the play's dissipatious rake, than to Manly. Indeed, Tyler later lost out -- much to his genuine grief and sorrow -- on the hand in marriage to Nabby Adams, daughter of John and Abigail; exactly because her parents with, at that time, some good reason did not think him a reliable and propitious match for her.[222] Much distraught, Tyler sought ever afterward to rehabilitate has character and reputation whenever he could; finally settling down as respected judge; and ultimately coming to preside as a Justice on the Supreme Court of the state of Vermont. And though remaining a virile and outspoken humorist, he became a living illustration of the reformed Prodigal Son, including writing not a few works of a religious nature while decrying and warning against profligate sensuality.

For those without the leisure at present moment to sit and read the entire thing, and or who would otherwise much prefer to see it performed, we submit for your perusal this abridgment of Tyler's comedic triumph.

~~~***~~~

---

[221] The first stage *drama* penned by a native North American and to be performed in the colonies (in 1767) was "The Prince of Parthia;"written by Thomas Godfrey (1736-63).

[222] Col, William Stephens Smith (1775-1816), who Nabby ended up marrying and who also happened to have been one of Gen. Washington aides in the war, has been characterized as an alcoholic and spendthrift, and consequently, it is concluded, was a far worse match than Tyler would have been. In fairness to Smith, however, it may be unjust to too readily accept this interpretation of him; if for no other reason that it is among a historians most difficult and delicate tasks to delve into and be able to accurately assess someone's private life, including the sort of pressures they were under. Such, at any rate, are my own feelings on the subject.
~~~

from Act I, scene 1

Scene, an Apartment at CHARLOTTE'S
CHARLOTTE and LETITIA discovered...

LETITIA
...I hear that Mr. Dimple and Maria are soon to be married.

CHARLOTTE[223]
You hear true. I was consulted in the choice of the wedding clothes. She is to be married in a delicate white sattin, and has a monstrous pretty brocaded lutestring for the second day. It would have done you good to have seen with what an affected indifference the dear sentimentalist turned over a thousand pretty things, just as if her heart did not palpitate with her approaching happiness, and at last made her choice and arranged her dress with such apathy as if she did not know that plain white sattin and a simple blond lace would shew her clear skin and dark hair to the greatest advantage.

LETITIA
But they say her indifference to dress, and even to the gentleman himself, is not entirely affected.

CHARLOTTE
How?

LETITIA
It is whispered that if Maria gives her hand to Mr. Dimple, it will be without her heart.

CHARLOTTE
Though the giving the heart is one of the last of all laughable considerations in the marriage of a girl of spirit, yet I should like to hear what antiquated notions the dear little piece of old-fashioned prudery has got in her head.

LETITIA
Why, you know that old Mr. John-Richard-Robert-Jacob-Isaac-Abraham-Cornelius Van Dumpling, Billy Dimple's father (for he has thought fit to soften his name, as well as manners, during his English tour), was the most intimate friend of Maria's father. The old folks, about a year before Mr. Van Dumpling's death, proposed this match: the young folks were accordingly introduced, and told they must love one another. Billy was then a good-natured, decent-dressing young fellow, with a little dash of the coxcomb, such as our young fellows of fortune usually have. At this time, I really believe she thought she loved him; and had they been married, I doubt not they might have jogged on, to the end of the chapter, a good kind of a sing-song lack-a-daysaical life, as other honest married folks do.

CHARLOTTE
Why did they not then marry?

LETITIA
Upon the death of his father, Billy went to England to see the world and rub off a little of the patroon rust. During his absence, Maria, like a good girl, to keep herself constant to her [k]nown true-love, avoided company, and betook herself, for her amusement, to her books, and her dear Billy's letters. But, alas! how many ways has the mischievous demon of inconstancy of stealing into a woman's heart! Her love was destroyed by the very means she took to support it.

---

[223] [*Edit. Note.* Sister of Col. Henry Manly.]

CHARLOTTE
How? -- Oh! I have it--some likely young beau found the way to her study.

LETITIA
Be patient, Charlotte; your head so runs upon beaux. Why, she read Sir Charles Grandison, Clarissa Harlow, Shenstone, and the Sentimental Journey; and between whiles, as I said, Billy's letters. But, as her taste improved, her love declined. The contrast was so striking betwixt the good sense of her books and the flimsiness of her love-letters, that she discovered she had unthinkingly engaged her hand without her heart; and then the whole transaction, managed by the old folks, now appeared so unsentimental, and looked so like bargaining for a bale of goods, that she found she ought to have rejected, according to every rule of romance, even the man of her choice, if imposed upon her in that manner. Clary Harlow would have scorned such a match.

CHARLOTTE
Well, how was it on Mr. Dimple's return? Did he meet a more favourable reception than his letters?

LETITIA
Much the same. She spoke of him with respect abroad, and with contempt in her closet. She watched his conduct and conversation, and found that he had by travelling, acquired the wickedness of Lovelace without his wit, and the politeness of Sir Charles Grandison without his generosity. The ruddy youth, who washed his face at the cistern every morning, and swore and looked eternal love and constancy, was now metamorphosed into a flippant, palid, polite beau, who devotes the morning to his toilet, reads a few pages of Chesterfield's letters, and then minces out, to put the infamous principles in practice upon every woman he meets.

CHARLOTTE
But, if she is so apt at conjuring up these sentimental bugbears, why does she not discard him at once?

LETITIA
Why, she thinks her word too sacred to be trifled with. Besides, her father, who has a great respect for the memory of his deceased friend, is ever telling her how he shall renew his years in their union, and repeating the dying injunctions of old Van Dumpling…

----

from Act II, scene 2

A Room in VAN ROUGH'S House
MARIA sitting disconsolate at a Table, with Books, &c.

SONG.

I.
The sun sets in night, and the stars shun the day;
But glory remains when their lights fade away!
Begin, ye tormentors! your threats are in vain,
For the son of Alknomook shall never complain.

II.
Remember the arrows he shot from his bow;

Remember your chiefs by his hatchet laid low:
Why so slow? -- do you wait till I shrink from the pain?
No -- the son of Alknomook will never complain.

III.
Remember the wood where in ambush we lay,
And the scalps which we bore from your nation away:
Now the flame rises fast, you exult in my pain;
But the son of Alknomook can never complain.

IV.
I go to the land where my father is gone;
His ghost shall rejoice in the fame of his son:
Death comes like a friend, he relieves me from pain;
And thy son, Oh Alknomook! has scorn'd to complain.

There is something in this song which ever calls forth my affections. The manly virtue of courage, that fortitude which steels the heart against the keenest misfortunes, which interweaves the laurel of glory amidst the instruments of torture and death, displays something so noble, so exalted, that in despite of the prejudices of education I cannot but admire it, even in a savage. The prepossession which our sex is supposed to entertain for the character of a soldier is, I know, a standing piece of raillery among the wits. A cockade, a lapell'd coat, and a feather, they will tell you, are irresistible by a female heart. Let it be so. Who is it that considers the helpless situation of our sex, that does not see that we each moment stand in need of a protector, and that a brave one too? Formed of the more delicate materials of nature, endowed only with the softer passions, incapable, from our ignorance of the world, to guard against the wiles of mankind, our security for happiness often depends upon their generosity and courage. Alas! how little of the former do we find! How inconsistent! that man should be leagued to destroy that honour upon which solely rests his respect and esteem. Ten thousand temptations allure us, ten thousand passions betray us; yet the smallest deviation from the path of rectitude is followed by the contempt and insult of man, and the more remorseless pity of woman; years of penitence and tears cannot wash away the stain, nor a life of virtue obliterate its remembrance. Reputation is the life of woman; yet courage to protect it is masculine and disgusting; and the only safe asylum a woman of delicacy can find is in the arms of a man of honour. How naturally, then, should we love the brave and the generous; how gratefully should we bless the arm raised for our protection, when nerv'd by virtue and directed by honour! Heaven grant that the man with whom I may be connected -- may be connected! Whither has my imagination transported me -- whither does it now lead me? Am I not indissolubly engaged, "by every obligation of honour which my own consent and my father's approbation can give," to a man who can never share my affections, and whom a few days hence it will be criminal for me to disapprove -- to disapprove! would to heaven that were all -- to despise. For, can the most frivolous manners, actuated by the most depraved heart, meet, or merit, anything but contempt from every woman of delicacy and sentiment?

----

from Act II, scene 1

CHARLOTTE
As I hope to be married, my brother Henry is in the city.

LETITIA
What, your brother, Colonel Manly?

CHARLOTTE
Yes, my dear; the only brother I have in the world.

LETITIA
Was he never in this city?

CHARLOTTE
Never nearer than Harlem Heights, where he lay with his regiment.

LETITIA
What sort of a being is this brother of yours? If he is as chatty, as pretty, as sprightly as you, half the belles in the city will be pulling caps for him.

CHARLOTTE
My brother is the very counterpart and reverse of me: I am gay, he is grave; I am airy, he is solid; I am ever selecting the most pleasing objects for my laughter, he has a tear for every pitiful one. And thus, whilst he is plucking the briars and thorns from the path of the unfortunate, I am strewing my own path with roses.

LETITIA
My sweet friend, not quite so poetical, and a little more particular.

CHARLOTTE
Hands off, Letitia. I feel the rage of simile upon me; I can't talk to you in any other way. My brother has a heart replete with the noblest sentiments, but then, it is like -- it is like -- Oh! you provoking girl, you have deranged all my ideas -- it is like -- Oh! I have it -- his heart is like an old maiden lady's bandbox; it contains many costly things, arranged with the most scrupulous nicety, yet the misfortune is that they are too delicate, costly, and antiquated for common use.

LETITIA
By what I can pick out of your flowery description, your brother is no beau.

CHARLOTTE
No, indeed; he makes no pretension to the character. He'd ride, or rather fly, an hundred miles to relieve a distressed object, or to do a gallant act in the service of his country; but should you drop your fan or bouquet in his presence, it is ten to one that some beau at the farther end of the room would have the honour of presenting it to you before he had observed that it fell. I'll tell you one of his antiquated, anti-gallant notions. He said once in my presence, in a room full of company, -- would you believe it? -- in a large circle of ladies, that the best evidence a gentleman could give a young lady of his respect and affection was to endeavour in a friendly manner to rectify her foibles. I protest I was crimson to the eyes, upon reflecting that I was known as his sister.

LETITIA
Insupportable creature! tell a lady of her faults! if he is so grave, I fear I have no chance of captivating him.

CHARLOTTE
His conversation is like a rich, old-fashioned brocade, -- it will stand alone; every sentence is a sentiment. Now you may judge what a time I had with him, in my twelve months' visit to my father. He read me such lectures, out of pure brotherly affection, against the extremes of fashion, dress, flirting, and coquetry, and all the other dear things which he knows I doat upon, that I protest his conversation made me as melancholy as if I had been at church; and heaven knows, though I never prayed to go there but on one occasion, yet I would have exchanged his conversation for a psalm and a sermon.

Church is rather melancholy, to be sure; but then I can ogle the beaux, and be regaled with "here endeth the first lesson," but his brotherly here, you would think had no end. You captivate him! Why, my dear, he would as soon fall in love with a box of Italian flowers. There is Maria, now, if she were not engaged, she might do something. Oh! how I should like to see that pair of pensorosos together, looking as grave as two sailors' wives of a stormy night, with a flow of sentiment meandering through their conversation like purling streams in modern poetry…

----

from Act III, scene 1

DIMPLE'S Room.

DIMPLE discovered at a Toilet, Reading.

…Now, did not my lord expressly say that it was unbecoming a well-bred man to be in a passion, I confess I should be ruffled. [Reads.] "There is no accident so unfortunate, which a wise man may not turn to his advantage; nor any accident so fortunate, which a fool will not turn to his disadvantage." True, my lord; but how advantage can be derived from this I can't see. Chesterfield himself, who made, however, the worst practice of the most excellent precepts, was never in so embarrassing a situation. I love the person of Charlotte, and it is necessary I should command the fortune of Letitia. As to Maria! -- I doubt not by my sang-froid behaviour I shall compel her to decline the match; but the blame must not fall upon me. A prudent man, as my lord says, should take all the credit of a good action to himself, and throw the discredit of a bad one upon others. I must break with Maria, marry Letitia, and as for Charlotte -- why, Charlotte must be a companion to my wife. -- Here, Jessamy![224]…

----

from Act III, scene 1

JESSAMY
Stay here one moment, and I will call him. -- Jonathan! -- Mr. Jonathan! -- [Calls.]

JONATHAN [within]
Holla! there.--[Enters.] You promise to stand by me -- six bows you say. [Bows.]

JESSAMY
Mrs. Jenny, I have the honour of presenting Mr. Jonathan, Colonel Manly's waiter, to you. I am extremely happy that I have it in my power to make two worthy people acquainted with each other's merits.

JENNY
So, Mr. Jonathan, I hear you were at the play last night.

JONATHAN
At the play! why, did you think I went to the devil's drawing-room?

JENNY
The devil's drawing-room!

[224] [*Edit. Note.* Dimple's manservant and Jonathan's moral counterpart.]

JONATHAN
Yes; why an't cards and dice the devil's device, and the play-house the shop where the devil hangs out the vanities of the world upon the tenter-hooks of temptation? I believe you have not heard how they were acting the old boy one night, and the wicked one came among them sure enough, and went right off in a storm, and carried one quarter of the play-house with him. Oh! no, no, no! you won't catch me at a play-house, I warrant you.

JENNY
Well, Mr. Jonathan, though I don't scruple your veracity, I have some reasons for believing you were there: pray, where were you about six o'clock?

JONATHAN
Why, I went to see one Mr. Morrison, the hocus pocus man; they said as how he could eat a case knife.

JENNY
Well, and how did you find the place?

JONATHAN
As I was going about here and there, to and again, to find it, I saw a great crowd of folks going into a long entry that had lantherns over the door; so I asked a man whether that was not the place where they played hocus pocus? He was a very civil, kind man, though he did speak like the Hessians; he lifted up his eyes and said, "They play hocus pocus tricks enough there, Got knows, mine friend."

JENNY
Well --

JONATHAN
So I went right in, and they shewed me away, clean up to the garret, just like meeting-house gallery. And so I saw a bower of topping folks, all sitting round in little cabbins, "just like father's corn-cribs"; and then there was such a squeaking with the fiddles, and such a tarnal blaze with the lights, my head was near turned. At last the people that sat near me set up such a hissing -- hiss -- like so many mad cats; and then they went thump, thump, thump, just like our Peleg threshing wheat, and stampt away, just like the nation; and called out for one Mr. Langolee,--I suppose he helps act the tricks.

JENNY
Well, and what did you do all this time?

JONATHAN
Gor, I--I liked the fun, and so I thumpt away, and hiss'd as lustily as the best of 'em. One sailor-looking man that sat by me, seeing me stamp, and knowing I was a cute fellow, because I could make a roaring noise, clapt me on the shoulder and said, "You are a d---d hearty cock, smite my timbers!" I told him so I was, but I thought he need not swear so, and make use of such naughty words.

JESSAMY
The savage! -- Well, and did you see the man with his tricks?

JONATHAN
Why, I vow, as I was looking out for him, they lifted up a great green cloth and let us look right into the next neighbor's house. Have you a good many houses in New-York made so in that 'ere way?

JENNY
Not many; but did you see the family?

JONATHAN
Yes, swamp it; I see'd the family.

JENNY
Well, and how did you like them?

JONATHAN
Why, I vow they were pretty much like other families; -- there was a poor, good-natured, curse of a husband, and a sad rantipole of a wife.

JENNY
But did you see no other folks?

JONATHAN
Yes. There was one youngster; they called him Mr. Joseph; he talked as sober and as pious as a minister; but, like some ministers that I know, he was a sly tike in his heart for all that. He was going to ask a young woman to spark it with him, and -- the Lord have mercy on my soul! -- she was another man's wife.

JESSAMY
The Wabash!

JENNY
And did you see any more folks?

JONATHAN
Why, they came on as thick as mustard. For my part, I thought the house was haunted. There was a soldier fellow, who talked about his row de dow, dow, and courted a young woman; but, of all the cute folk I saw, I liked one little fellow --

JENNY
Aye! who was he?

JONATHAN
Why, he had red hair, and a little round plump face like mine, only not altogether so handsome. His name was -- Darby; -- that was his baptizing name; his other name I forgot. Oh! it was Wig--Wag--Wag-all, Darby Wag-all, -- pray, do you know him? -- I should like to take a sling with him, or a drap of cyder with a pepper-pod in it, to make it warm and comfortable.

JENNY
I can't say I have that pleasure.

JONATHAN
I wish you did; he is a cute fellow. But there was one thing I didn't like in that Mr. Darby; and that was, he was afraid of some of them 'ere shooting irons, such as your troopers wear on training days. Now, I'm a true born Yankee American son of liberty, and I never was afraid of a gun yet in all my life.

JENNY
Well, Mr. Jonathan, you were certainly at the play-house.

JONATHAN
I at the play-house! -- Why didn't I see the play then?

JENNY
Why, the people you saw were players.

JONATHAN
Mercy on my soul! did I see the wicked players? -- Mayhap that 'ere Darby that I liked so was the old serpent himself, and had his cloven foot in his pocket. Why, I vow, now I come to think on't, the candles seemed to burn blue, and I am sure where I sat it smelt tarnally of brimstone.

JESSAMY
Well, Mr. Jonathan, from your account, which I confess is very accurate, you must have been at the play-house.

JONATHAN
Why, I vow, I began to smell a rat. When I came away, I went to the man for my money again; you want your money? says he; yes, says I; for what? says he; why, says I, no man shall jocky me out of my money; I paid my money to see sights, and the dogs a bit of a sight have I seen, unless you call listening to people's private business a sight. Why, says he, it is the School for Scandalization. -- The School for Scandalization! -- Oh! ho! no wonder you New-York folks are so cute at it, when you go to school to learn it; and so I jogged off...

----

from Act III, scene 2

The Mall.

Enter MANLY.

It must be so, Montague! and it is not all the tribe of Mandevilles that shall convince me that a nation, to become great, must first become dissipated. Luxury is surely the bane of a nation: Luxury! which enervates both soul and body, by opening a thousand new sources of enjoyment, opens, also, a thousand new sources of contention and want: Luxury! which renders a people weak at home, and accessible to bribery, corruption, and force from abroad. When the Grecian states knew no other tools than the axe and the saw, the Grecians were a great, a free, and a happy people. The kings of Greece devoted their lives to the service of their country, and her senators knew no other superiority over their fellow-citizens than a glorious pre-eminence in danger and virtue. They exhibited to the world a noble spectacle, -- a number of independent states united by a similarity of language, sentiment, manners, common interest, and common consent, in one grand mutual league of protection. And, thus united, long might they have continued the cherishers of arts and sciences, the protectors of the oppressed, the scourge of tyrants, and the safe asylum of liberty. But when foreign gold, and still more pernicious foreign luxury, had crept among them, they sapped the vitals of their virtue. The virtues of their ancestors were only found in their writings. Envy and suspicion, the vices of little minds, possessed them. The various states engendered jealousies of each other; and, more unfortunately, growing jealous of their great federal council, the Amphictyons, they forgot that their common safety had existed, and would exist, in giving them an honourable extensive prerogative. The common good was lost in the pursuit of private interest; and that people who, by uniting, might have stood against the world in arms, by dividing, crumbled into ruin; -- their name is now only known in the page of the historian, and what they once were is all we have left to admire. Oh! that America! Oh! that my country, would, in this her day, learn the things which belong to her peace!

----

from Act IV, scene 2

MANLY leading in MARIA.

MANLY
I hope you will excuse my speaking upon so important a subject so abruptly; but, the moment I entered your room, you struck me as the lady whom I had long loved in imagination, and never hoped to see.

MARIA
Indeed, Sir, I have been led to hear more upon this subject than I ought.

MANLY
Do you, then, disapprove my suit, Madam, or the abruptness of my introducing it? If the latter, my peculiar situation, being obliged to leave the city in a few days, will, I hope, be my excuse; if the former, I will retire, for I am sure I would not give a moment's inquietude to her whom I could devote my life to please. I am not so indelicate as to seek your immediate approbation; permit me only to be near you, and by a thousand tender assiduities to endeavour to excite a grateful return.

MARIA
I have a father, whom I would die to make happy; he will disapprove --

MANLY
Do you think me so ungenerous as to seek a place in your esteem without his consent? You must -- you ever ought to consider that man as unworthy of you who seeks an interest in your heart contrary to a father's approbation. A young lady should reflect that the loss of a lover may be supplied, but nothing can compensate for the loss of a parent's affection. Yet, why do you suppose your father would disapprove? In our country, the affections are not sacrificed to riches or family aggrandizement: should you approve, my family is decent, and my rank honourable.

MARIA
You distress me, Sir.

MANLY
Then I will sincerely beg your excuse for obtruding so disagreeable a subject, and retire. [Going.

MARIA
Stay, Sir! your generosity and good opinion of me deserve a return; but why must I declare what, for these few hours, I have scarce suffered myself to think? -- I am --

MANLY
What?

MARIA
Engaged, Sir; and, in a few days, to be married to the gentleman you saw at your sister's.

MANLY
Engaged to be married! And have I been basely invading the rights of another? Why have you permitted this? Is this the return for the partiality I declared for you?

MARIA
You distress me, Sir. What would you have me say? You are too generous to wish the truth. Ought I to say that I dared not suffer myself to think of my engagement, and that I am going to give my hand without my heart? Would you have me confess a partiality for you? If so, your triumph is compleat, and can be only more so when days of misery with the man I cannot love will make me think of him whom I could prefer.

MANLY [after a pause].
We are both unhappy; but it is your duty to obey your parent -- mine to obey my honour. Let us, therefore, both follow the path of rectitude; and of this we may be assured, that if we are not happy, we shall, at least, deserve to be so. Adieu! I dare not trust myself longer with you. [Exeunt severally.

----

from Act V, scene 1

JESSAMY
"There was a certain man, who had a sad scolding wife,"--now you must laugh.

JONATHAN
Tarnation! That's no laughing matter though.

JESSAMY
"And she lay sick a-dying"; -- now you must titter.

JONATHAN
What, snigger when the good woman's a-dying! Gor, I --

JESSAMY
Yes, the notes say you must -- "and she asked her husband leave to make a will,"-- now you must begin to look grave; -- "and her husband said" --

JONATHAN
Ay, what did her husband say? Something dang'd cute, I reckon.

JESSAMY
"And her husband said, you have had your will all your life-time, and would you have it after you are dead, too?"

JONATHAN
Ho, ho, ho! There the old man was even with her; he was up to the notch -- ha, ha, ha!

JESSAMY
But, Mr. Jonathan, you must not laugh so. Why you ought to have tittered piano, and you have laughed fortissimo. Look here; you see these marks, A, B, C, and so on; these are the references to the other part of the book. Let us turn to it, and you will see the directions how to manage the muscles. This [turns over] was note D you blundered at. -- You must purse the mouth into a smile, then titter, discovering the lower part of the three front upper teeth…

----

from Act V, scene 2

CHARLOTTE'S Apartment.

Enter DIMPLE leading LETITIA.

LETITIA
And will you pretend to say now, Mr. Dimple, that you propose to break with Maria? Are not the banns published? Are not the clothes purchased? Are not the friends invited? In short, is it not a done affair?

DIMPLE
Believe me, my dear Letitia, I would not marry her.

LETITIA
Why have you not broke with her before this, as you all along deluded me by saying you would?

DIMPLE
Because I was in hopes she would, ere this, have broke with me.

LETITIA
You could not expect it.

DIMPLE
Nay, but be calm a moment; 'twas from my regard to you that I did not discard her.

LETITIA
Regard to me!

DIMPLE
Yes; I have done everything in my power to break with her, but the foolish girl is so fond of me that nothing can accomplish it. Besides, how can I offer her my hand when my heart is indissolubly engaged to you?

LETITIA
There may be reason in this; but why so attentive to Miss[225] [Charlotte] Manly?

DIMPLE
Attentive to Miss Manly! For heaven's sake, if you have no better opinion of my constancy, pay not so ill a compliment to my taste.

LETITIA
Did I not see you whisper her to-day?

DIMPLE
Possibly I might--but something of so very trifling a nature that I have already forgot what it was.

LETITIA
I believe she has not forgot it.

---

[225] [*Edit. Note.* i.e., Charlotte.]

DIMPLE
My dear creature, how can you for a moment suppose I should have any serious thoughts of that trifling, gay, flighty coquette, that disagreeable--

Enter CHARLOTTE.

DIMPLE
My dear Miss Manly, I rejoice to see you; there is a charm in your conversation that always marks your entrance into company as fortunate…

….VAN ROUGH[226]
Pray, some of you explain this; what has been the occasion of all this racket?

MANLY
That gentleman[227] can explain it to you; it will be a very diverting story for an intended father-in-law to hear.

VAN ROUGH
How was this matter, Mr. Van Dumpling?

DIMPLE
Sir, -- upon my honour, -- all I know is, that I was talking to this young lady, and this gentleman broke in on us in a very extraordinary manner.

VAN ROUGH
Why, all this is nothing to the purpose; can you explain it, Miss? [To Charlotte.]

Enter LETITIA through the back scene.

LETITIA
I can explain it to that gentleman's confusion. Though long betrothed to your daughter [to Van Rough], yet, allured by my fortune, it seems (with shame do I speak it) he has privately paid his addresses to me. I was drawn in to listen to him by his assuring me that the match was made by his father without his consent, and that he proposed to break with Maria, whether he married me or not. But, whatever were his intentions respecting your daughter, Sir, even to me he was false; for he has repeated the same story, with some cruel reflections upon my person, to Miss Manly.

JONATHAN
What a tarnal curse!

LETITIA
Nor is this all, Miss Manly. When he was with me this very morning, he made the same ungenerous reflections upon the weakness of your mind as he has so recently done upon the defects of my person.

JONATHAN
What a tarnal curse and damn, too!

---

[226] [*Edit. Note.* Maria's father.]
[227] [*Edit. Note.* Dimple.]

DIMPLE
Ha! since I have lost Letitia, I believe I had as good make it up with Maria. Mr. Van Rough, at present I cannot enter into particulars; but, I believe, I can explain everything to your satisfaction in private.

VAN ROUGH
There is another matter, Mr. Van Dumpling, which I would have you explain. Pray, Sir, have Messrs. Van Cash & Co. presented you those bills for acceptance?

DIMPLE
The deuce! Has he heard of those bills! Nay, then, all's up with Maria, too; but an affair of this sort can never prejudice me among the ladies; they will rather long to know what the dear creature possesses to make him so agreeable. [Aside.] Sir, you'll hear from me. [To Manly.]

MANLY
And you from me, Sir--

DIMPLE
Sir, you wear a sword--

MANLY
Yes, Sir. This sword was presented to me by that brave Gallic hero, the Marquis De la Fayette. I have drawn it in the service of my country, and in private life, on the only occasion where a man is justified in drawing his sword, in defence of a lady's honour. I have fought too many battles in the service of my country to dread the imputation of cowardice. Death from a man of honour would be a glory you do not merit; you shall live to bear the insult of man and the contempt of that sex whose general smiles afforded you all your happiness.

DIMPLE
You won't meet me, Sir? Then I'll post you for a coward.

MANLY
I'll venture that, Sir. The reputation of my life does not depend upon the breath of a Mr. Dimple. I would have you to know, however, Sir, that I have a cane to chastise the insolence of a scoundrel, and a sword and the good laws of my country to protect me from the attempts of an assassin --

DIMPLE
Mighty well! Very fine, indeed! Ladies and gentlemen, I take my leave; and you will please to observe in the case of my deportment the contrast between a gentleman who has read Chesterfield and received the polish of Europe and an unpolished, untravelled American.
[Exit.

Enter MARIA.

MARIA
Is he indeed gone? --

LETITIA
I hope, never to return.

VAN ROUGH
I am glad I heard of those bills; though it's plaguy unlucky; I hoped to see Mary married before I died.

MANLY
Will you permit a gentleman, Sir, to offer himself as a suitor to your daughter? Though a stranger to you, he is not altogether so to her, or unknown in this city. You may find a son-in-law of more fortune, but you can never meet with one who is richer in love for her, or respect for you.

VAN ROUGH
Why, Mary, you have not let this gentleman make love to you without my leave?

MANLY
I did not say, Sir--

MARIA
Say, Sir! -- I -- the gentleman, to be sure, met me accidentally.

VAN ROUGH
Ha, ha, ha! Mark me, Mary; young folks think old folks to be fools; but old folks know young folks to be fools. Why, I knew all about this affair. This was only a cunning way I had to bring it about. Hark ye! I was in the closet when you and he were at our hours. [Turns to the company.] I heard that little baggage say she loved her old father, and would die to make him happy! Oh! how I loved the little baggage! And you talked very prudently, young man. I have inquired into your character, and find you to be a man of punctuality and mind the main chance. And so, as you love Mary and Mary loves you, you shall have my consent immediately to be married. I'll settle my fortune on you, and go and live with you the remainder of my life.

MANLY
Sir, I hope --

VAN ROUGH
Come, come, no fine speeches; mind the main chance, young man, and you and I shall always agree.

LETITIA I sincerely wish you joy [advancing to Maria]; and hope your pardon for my conduct.

MARIA
I thank you for your congratulations, and hope we shall at once forget the wretch who has given us so much disquiet, and the trouble that he has occasioned.

CHARLOTTE
And I, my dear Maria, -- how shall I look up to you for forgiveness? I, who, in the practice of the meanest arts, have violated the most sacred rights of friendship? I can never forgive myself, or hope charity from the world; but, I confess, I have much to hope from such a brother; and I am happy that I may soon say, such a sister.

MARIA
My dear, you distress me; you have all my love.

MANLY
And mine.

CHARLOTTE
If repentance can entitle me to forgiveness, I have already much merit; for I despise the littleness of my past conduct. I now find that the heart of any worthy man cannot be gained by invidious attacks upon the rights and characters of others; -- by countenancing the addresses of a thousand; -- or that the finest assemblage of features, the greatest taste in dress, the genteelest address, or the most brilliant wit, cannot eventually secure a coquette from contempt and ridicule.

MANLY
And I have learned that probity, virtue, honour, though they should not have received the polish of Europe, will secure to an honest American the good graces of his fair countrywomen, and, I hope, the applause of THE PUBLIC.

THE END.

~~~***~~~

Some other works by Tyler

Plays:
"May-day in Town, or New-York in an Uproar" (1787) -- a comic opera; now lost
"The Farm House, or The Female Duellists" (1796), lost
"The Georgia Spec, or Land in the Moon" (1797), lost
"The Doctor in Spite of Himself" (1797)
"The Island of Barrataria" (1797)

Sacred dramas (the dates for these I was unable to ascertain):
"The Origin of the Feast of Purim, or The Destinies of Haman"
"Mordecai"
"Joseph and His Brothers"
"The Judgement of Solomon"

Miscellaneous:

The late 1790's found Tyler a regular contributor to the very Federalist *Farmer's Museum*, published in Walpole New Hampshire; and where he teamed with Joseph Dennie in composing poems and short essays, usually of light hearted and tongue-in-cheek nature, under the pen names Colon and Spondee.

The Algerine captive, or, The life and adventures of Doctor Updike Underhill (1797) -- a novel
"Convivial song, sung at Windsor, on the evening of the Fourth of July" (1799)
"An oration, pronounced at Bennington, Vermont, on the 22d February, 1800. In commemoration of the death of General George Washington"(1800)
"A Christmas Hymn" (1807)
The Yankey in London (1809)[228]

Modern anthologies:
The Verse of Royall Tyler. Collected and edited by Marius B. Peladeau
The Prose of Royall Tyler. Collected and edited by Marius B. Peladeau

[228] This book would seem to have possibly influenced James Kirke Paulding's anglophobic *The Diverting History of John Bull and Brother Jonathan* (1812) and *A Sketch of Old England by a New England Man* (1822).
~~~

"A POLITICAL REVERIE" (Jan. 1774)

by Mercy Otis Warren

Mercy Otis Warren (1728-1814), from Plymouth, Mass., is usually not among the Revolutionary War intellectual figures we initially become acquainted with. And yet, aside *perhaps* for a few exceptional geniuses that might be named, the America of the time produced no more learned, capacious, and penetrating a mind. The sister of the celebrated firebrand James Otis and wife of the relatively inconspicuous James Warren, Mercy was also fairly influential in and around Boston in the years leading up to Lexington and Concord. Overshadowed by Hancock, Joseph Warren, and the Adamses, however, and no doubt also because she was a woman, her part in helping to the form the radical consciousness of the Bostonians has tended to be neglected. Part of the reason for this in retrospect, I think, is that not a few men found her intimidating; and although somewhat staid and old fashioned in her outlook and sensibility, it is no little remarkable how correct and prophetic she proved on so many points of fact and controversy. Much like her British contemporary, Catharine Macauley, with whom she corresponded, her grasp of the state of affairs between Britain and America, and her foresight respecting the future of the latter, reveals her to have possessed a level of understanding that one would think only a historian with the benefit of decades or more of hindsight could ever have attained.

In company with Rev. William Gordon, Dr. David Ramsay, and John Marshall, she was one of the first to write an at length and comprehensive history of the American Revolution, and of these only Ramsay can vie with her for depth of insight and wisdom of retrospective reflection. At the same time, and allowing for occasional and pardonable lapses in her information or interpretation of specific isolated events, her version exceeds the rest in balance, clarity and orderliness of composition.[229]

In addition to her very thoughtful history, Warren wrote poetry and several plays. The plays, emanating as they did from the pen of a conservative female whose day to day focus was ordinarily on family and domestic affairs, and though subsequently well spoken of by critics and literary historians, were never staged. [230] Respecting her poetry, her visionary verses on the future of America imparted a greater impact; preceding as they did the "Rising Glory of America" poems (Emory Elliott's phrase; taken from a title of one ambitious such piece co-authored by Freneau and Hugh Henry Brackenridge) of, for instance, Phillis Wheatley Peters, David Humphreys, Timothy Dwight, Philip Freneau, and Joel Barlow.[231] Certainly none bettered Warren in such mantic mini-epic. As demonstration of which, the following is "A Political Reverie," written in January 1774; that appeared in her 1790 volume (dedicated to Washington) *POEMS, Dramatic and Miscellaneous*,[232] that reveals her at her most sagacious and uncanny. We see in such a work, that for some the events of Lexington came as no surprise whatsoever, and before shots were ever fired, there was already in place a reconciliation and peace movement that wished for and sought to avert what promised to be inevitable and impending bloodshed.

~~~***~~~

As fairy forms, the elfin airy train,
And sylphs, sometimes molest the learned brain,
Delusive dreams the matron's bosom swell,
And, ancient maids, the fancied vision, tell;
So beaux and belles see routs and balls in dreams,

---

[229] All four historians, as is well known, were influenced by and relied heavily on the *Annual Register*, edited by Edmund Burke. Nonetheless, it is false, as some have done, to infer or ignorantly assume that these writers included no new or original material of their own. And in Warren's case, we might add, she sought to bring to her task the universal perspective and classical erudition of Gibbon.

[230] For more on Otis' stage compositions, see Cheryl Z. Oreovicz's "Heroic Drama for an Uncertain Age: The Plays of Mercy Otis Warren," included in *Early American Literature and Culture: Essays Honoring Harrison T. Meserole* (1992), edited by Kathryn Zabelle Derounian-Stodola, p. 192.

[231] Though be it noted, John Trumbull's "Prospect of the Future Glory of America" (1770) antedates all of them (including Warrens' "Reverie.")

[232] pp. 188-194.
~~~

And drowsy preachers chop polemic themes;
The statesman's dream, in theory creates,
New perfect forms, to govern broken states.

Logistic scribblers dream of sleeping souls,
And dreaming bucks drown reason o'er their bowls;
The doubting deist dreams of Styx and fate,
Yet laughs at fables of a future state,
'Till Charon's boat shall land him on a shore
Of which the dreamer never dreamt before:
As sportive dreams infest all ranks of men,
A dream, the visionary world, may read again.

[*This Reverie was first published January, 1774, previous to the breaking out of the Civil War, while America was oscillating between a Resistance by Arms and her ancient Love and Loyalty to Britain.*][233]

Let Grecian bards and Roman poets tell,
How Hector fought, and how old Priam fell;
Paint armies ravaging the 'Ilian coast,
Shew fields of blood and mighty battles lost;
Let mad Cassandra, with dishevell'd hair,
With streaming eye, and frantic bosom bare,
Tell dark presages, and ill boding dreams,
Of murder, rapine, and the solemn themes,
Of slaughter'd cities, and their sinking spires,
By Grecian rage wrap'd in evening fires;
To bolder pens I leave the tragic tale,
While some kind muse from Tempe's gentle vale,
With softer symphony shall touch the string,
And happier tidings from Parnassus bring.

Not Caesar's name, nor Philip's bolder son,
Who sigh'd and wept, when he'd one world undone;
Who drop'd a tear, though not from pity's source,
But grief, to find some bound to brutal force,
Shall tune my harp, or touch the warbling string;
No bold destroyers of mankind I sing;
These plunderers of men I'll greatly scorn,
And dream of nations, empires yet unborn.

I look with rapture at the distant dawn,
And view the glories of the opening morn,
When justice holds his sceptre o'er the land,
And rescues freedom from a tyrant's hand;
When patriot states in laurel crowns may rise,
And ancient kingdoms court them as allies;
Glory and valour shall be here display'd,
And virtue rear her long dejected head;
Her standard plant beneath these gladden'd skies,
Her fame extend, and arts and science rise;
While empire's lofty spreading sails unfurl'd,
Roll swiftly on towards the western world.

Long she's forsook her Asiatic throne,

[233] [*Edit. Note.* Warren's brackets.]

And leaving Afric's barb'rous burning zone,
On the broad ruins of Rome's haughty power
Erected ramparts round fair Europe's shore;
But in those blasted climes no more presides,
She, o'er the vast Atlantic surges rides,
Visits Columbia's distant fertile plains,
Where liberty, a happy goddess, reigns.

No despot here shall rule with awful sway,
Nor orphan's spoils become the minion's prey;
No more the widow'd bleeding bosom mourns,
Nor injur'd cities weep their slaughtered sons;
For then each tyrant, by the hand of fate,
And standing troops, the bane of every state,
Forever spurn'd, shall be remov'd as far
As bright Hesperus from the polar star;
Freedom and virtue mall united reign,
And stretch their empire o'er the wide domain.
On a broad base the commonwealth shall stand,
When lawless power withdraws its impious hand;
When crowns and sceptres are grown useless things,
Nor petty pr[a]etors[234] plunder here for kings.

Then bless'd religion, in her purest forms,
Beyond the reach of persecuting storms,
In purest azure, gracefully array'd,
In native majesty shall stand display'd,
'Till courts revere her ever sacred shrine;
And nobles feel her influence divine;
Princes and peasants catch the glorious flame,
And lisping infants praise Jehovah's name.

But while methought this commonwealth would rise,
And bright Millenian prospects struck my eyes,
I wept Britannia, once Europa's pride,
To fame and virtue long she stood ally'd;
This glorious queen, the mistress of the isles,
Torn up by faction, and intestine broils,
Became the prey of each rapacious arm,
Strip'd and disrob'd of every native charm.

Strong and erect, like some fair polish'd tower,
She long defy'd each neighb'ring hostile power,
And sent her brave and valiant sons in quest
Of foreign realms, who by no fear repress'd,
The sinking cliffs of Europe's happy shore,
They left behind, new climates to explore.

They quitted plenty, luxury and ease,
Tempted the dangers of the frozen seas --
While hope's lost breezes fann'd the swelling sails,
And fame and glory spurn'd the ruder gales,
And smooth'd the surge that roll'd from shore to shore,
A race of heroes safely wafted o'er.

---

[234] [*Edit. Note.* Evidently referring to Royal Governors, such as Thomas Hutchinson.]

Who pitch'd their tents beneath the dismal shade,
Where wild woods roar'd, and savages betray'd;
Cities they rear'd around barbarian coasts,
And planted vineyards o'er the barren wastes.
In Britain's lap the rich produce was pour'd,
(Which heaven, benignant, plentifully shower'd,)
'Till she, ungrateful, join'd an impious band,
And forging shackles with a guilty hand,
Broke the firm union whence her vigour grew,
Dissolv'd the bands, and cut the sinews through.

Here a bright form, with soft majestic grace,
Beckon'd me on through vast unmeasur'd space;
Beside the margin of the vast profound,
Wild echos play'd and cataracts rebound;
Beyond the heights of nature's wide expanse,
Where mov'd superb the planetary dance,
Light burst on light, and suns o'er suns display,
The system perfect, nature's God had laid.

This scale of altitude presented whole,
The various movements of the human soul;
Starting, I cry'd -- "Oh! sacred form forgive,
Or me from yonder nether world remove; --
Has freedom's genius left Britannia's shore?
And must her sleeping patriots live no more?
Arise, ye venerable shades! inspire,
Each languid soul with patriotic fire;
'Till every bosom feels a noble flame,
And emulates a Locke, or Sydney's name."

The seraph smil'd ineffably serene,
And shew'd me truth, inscrib'd on her bright mien:
She said -- "The glow from breast to breast is spread,
From sire to son the latent spark's convey'd;
Let those bless'd shades rest in their sacred urns,
Lie undisturb'd -- the glorious ardour burns,
Though far transferr'd from their lov'd native soil.
Virtue turn'd pale, and freedom left the isle,
When she stretch'd out her avaricious hand,
And shew'd her sons her hostile bloody wand;
United millions parried back the blow,
Britain recoil'd, and sadly learnt to know,
Cities with cities leagu'd, and town with town,
She trembled at her fate when half undone."

Think not this all a visionary scene,
For he who wields the grand, the vast machine;
Who bids the morn from eastern ocean rise,
And paler Cynthia cheer the midnight skies;
Who holds the balance -- who stretch'd out the line --
O'er all creation form'd the grand design,
Ten thousand worlds to scatter o'er the plain,
And spread new glories through his wide domain;
Who rules the stars, and taught the rolling spheres
To measure round the quick revolving years;

At awful distance from his radiant throne,
Suspended, this terrestial ball hangs down;
Yet still presides and watches o'er the fates,
Of all the kingdoms that his power creates.

Ere he winds up the closing act of time,
And draws the veil from systems more sublime,
In swift progression, westward throws the bowl,
'Till mighty empire crowns the spacious whole.

Then this far distant corner of the earth,
Shall boast her Decii's and her Fabii's birth;
When the young heroes, wondering, shall be told,
That Britain barter'd worth for lust of gold;
How, lost in luxury, her silken sons,
Forgot her Edwards claim'd the Bourbon crowns;
That tyrants trembled on their tott'ring throne,
And haughty monarchs fear'd Britannia's frown.

But ah! how tarnish'd her illustrious name,
Despoil'd of wealth, of grandeur, and of fame!
Buried beneath her complicated crimes,
A sad memento to succeeding times:
Dismay'd, she yet may lift her suppliant hand,
And ask protection from this injur'd land;
Whose peaceful sons will draw oblivion o'er
Unnumber'd wrongs, and [e]rase the blacken'd score:
Yet heave a sigh, and drop tire tender tear,
And weep Britannia's punishment severe;
When they researching o'er some future chart,
Scarce find the seat of mighty Brunswick's court;
For neighbouring states may seize the venal isle,
And Gallic princes distribute the spoil.
The lion, prostrate on the naked strand,
May see the lilies waving o'er the land;
May see Columbia's embrio pendants play,
And infant navies cut the wat[e]ry way;
Fame's outstretch'd wing may on the eastern gales
Leave the proud Thames, and spread her whiten'd sails.

While rising empire rears her purple crest,
Triumphant commerce hails the gladden'd west,
And steers her course to Zembla's frozen pole,
Or lands in India, free from the control
Of base, monopolizing men, combin'd
To plunder millions, and enslave mankind.
From Florida to Nova Scotian shores
She pours her treasures and unlades her stores;
Round all the globe she fails from sea to sea,
And smiles and prospers, only when she's free.

But here the sweet enchanting vision fled,
And darken'd clouds flash'd lightnings o'er my head;
The seraph solemn stretch'd abroad her hand,
The stars grew pale beneath her burnish'd wand;
On her pale front disgust and sorrow hung,

And awful accents trembled on her tongue.

Behold! she said, before these great events,
Absorb'd in tears, America laments;
Laments the ravage of her fruitful plains,
While crimson streams the peaceful villa stains.

The weeping matron sighs in poignant pain
O'er her last hope, in the rude battle slain:
The bleeding bosom of the aged sire,
Pierc'd by his son, will in his arms expire;
For death promiscuous flies from ev'ry hand,
When faction's sword is brandish'd o'er the land;
When civil discord cuts the friendly ties,
And social joy from every bosom flies;
But let the muse forbear the solemn tale,
And lend once more, the "*Grecian painter's veil.*"

AN

ACCOUNT

OF THE

GRAND FEDERAL PROCESSION.

PERFORMED AT PHILADELPHIA ON FRIDAY
THE 4TH OF JULY 1788.[235]

by Francis Hopkinson

As I not only drew up for publication the following account of the grand procession, performed at Philadelphia on the 4th of July 1788; but had no small share in planning and directing the arrangement of it, and as it was spectacle as singular in itself as the occasion was extraordinary, I have thought proper to give it a place here, that the remembrance of it may have one more chance of preservation in addition to those of the Newspapers of the time.

~~~***~~~

ON Friday the 4th of July 1788, the citizens of Philadelphia celebrated the declaration of *Independence*, made by the Thirteen United States of America on the 4th of July 1776, and the establishment of the *constitution*, or frame of government proposed by the late general convention of the states, and now solemnly adopted and ratified by ten of those states.

The rising fun was saluted with a full peal from Christ Church steeple, and a discharge of cannon from the ship, *Rising Sun*, commanded by Captain Philip Brown, anchored off Market street, and superbly decorated with the flags of nations in alliance with America.

Ten vessels, in honour of the ten dates of the present union, were dressed and arranged the whole length of the harbour; each bearing a broad white flag at the mast-head, inscribed with the names of the dates respectively in broad gold letters, in the following order; *New Hampshire*, opposite to the Northern Liberties; *Massachusetts*, opposite to Vine street; *Connecticut*, to Race street; *New Jersey*, to Arch street; *Pennsylvania*, to Market street; *Delaware* to Chesnut street; *Maryland*, to Walnut street; *Virginia* to Spruce street; *South Carolina*, to Pine street; and *Georgia*, to South street. The ships along the wharfs were also dressed on the occasion; and as a brisk south wind prevailed through the whole day, the flags and pennants were kept in full display; and exhibited a moll pleasing and animating prospect.

According to orders issued the day before, the several parts which were to compose this grand procession, began to assemble at eight o'clock in the morning, at and near the intersection of South and Third-streets.

Nine gentlemen, distinguished by white plumes in their hats, and furnished with speaking trumpets, were superintendants of the procession; viz. general *Mifflin*, general *Stewart*, colonel *Proctor*, colonel *Gurney*, colonel *Will*, colonel *Marsh*, major Moore, major Lenox, and *Mr. Peter Brown*.

The different companies of military, trades and professions, had previously met in various parts of the city, of their own appointment; where they were separately formed by their officers and conductors, and marched in order with their respective flags, devices, and machines, to the place of general rendezvous. As these companies arrived in succession, the superintendants disposed of them in the neighbouring streets in

[235] As found in *The Miscellaneous Essays and Occasional Writings of Francis Hopkinson, Esq.* (1792), Vol. 2, pp. 349-422.
~~~

such manner as that they might easily fall into the stations they were to occupy in forming the general procession, as they should be successively called upon. By this means the most perfect order and regularity was effectually preserved.

After a strict review of the streets of the city, it had been determined, that the line of march should be as follows. To commence at the intersection of South and Third-streets; thence along Third-street to Callowhill-street; thence up Callowhill-street to Fourth-street; thence along Fourth-street to Market-street; and thence to Union Green, in front of Bush-Hill -- William Hamilton, esq. having kindly offered the spacious lawn before his house at Bush-Hill for the purposes of the day.

The street commissioners had, the evening before, gone through the line of march, and directed the pavements to be swept, the trees to be lopped, and all obstacles removed.

About half after nine o'clock the GRAND PROCESSION began to move; of which the following is as correct: a detail as could be procured.

I.

Twelve axe-men, dressed in white frocks, with black girdles round their waists, and wearing ornamented caps; and headed by major *Philip Pancake*.

II.

The first city troop of [Philadelphia] light dragoons, commanded by captain *Miles*.

III.

INDEPENDENCE.

John Nixon, esq. on horseback, bearing the staff and cap of liberty; under the cap a white silk flag, with these words, "FOURTH OF JULY, 1776," in large gold letters.

IV.

Four pieces of artillery, with a detachment from the train, commanded by captains *Morel* and *Fisher*.

V.

FRENCH ALLIANCE.

Thomas Fitzsimons, esq. on horseback, carrying a flag of white silk, bearing three fleurs de lys, and thirteen stars in union over the words "SIXTH OF FEBRUARY, 1778," in gold characters. The horse on which he rode was the same on which count Rochambeau rode at the siege of Yorktown.

VI.

CORPS of light infantry commanded by captain *A. G. Claypoole*, with the standard of the first regiment.

VII.

DEFINITIVE TREATY OF PEACE.

George Clymer, esq. on horseback, carrying a staff adorned with olive and laurel: the words -- "Third of September, 1783," in gold letters pendant from the staff.

VIII.

Colonel John Shee, on horseback, carrying a flag, blue field, bearing an olive and laurel wreath over the words, "WASHINGTON, *the friend of his country*" in silver letters: the staff adorned with olive and laurel.

IX.

The city troop of light dragoons, captain *W. Bingham*, commanded by major *W. Jackson*.

X.

Richard Bache, esq. on horseback, as a herald, attended by a trumpet, proclaiming "a new era!" the words, "NEW ERA," in gold letters, pendant from the herald's staff -- and also the following lines:

"Peace o'er our land her olive wand extends,
"And white rob'd innocence from heav'n descends;
"The crimes and frauds of anarchy shall fail,
"Returning justice lifts again her scale."

XI.

CONVENTION OF THE STATES.

The honourable *Peter Muhlenburg, esq.* on horseback, carrying a blue flag, with the words -- "SEVENTEENTH OF SEPTEMBER, 1787," in silver letters.

XII.

A band of music performing a grand march, composed by Mr. *Alexander Reinagle* for the occasion.

XIII.

THE CONSTITUTION.

The hon. chief juftice [Thomas] *M'Kean*; the hon. judge *Atlee*; the hon. judge *Rush* -- in their robes of office; seated in a lofty ornamented car, in form of a large Eagle, drawn by six white horses; the chief justice supported a tall staff, on the top of which was the cap of liberty; under the cap, the *New Constitution* framed and ornamented; and immediately under the Constitution, the words -- "THE PEOPLE" -- in large gold letters affixed to the staff. The car was made by Messrs. *George* and *William Hunter*. The carriage was painted light blue, 20 feet long: the hind wheels 8 feet, and the fore wheels 6½ feet in diameter. The body, mounted on springs, was 13 feet high, in the shape of a bald eagle -- from the head to the tail 13 feet -- the bread emblazoned with 13 silver stars in a sky-blue field; and underneath, a shield bearing 13 stripes, alternate red and white. The dexter talons of the eagle embraced an olive branch: the sinister [i.e., the left talons] grasped thirteen arrows.

XIV.

CORPS of light infantry, commanded by captain *Heysham*, with the standard of the third regiment.

XV.

Ten gentlemen, representing the states that had ratified the federal constitution; each carrying a small flag, bearing the name of the state he represented, in gold letters, and walking arm in arm, emblematical of the union, viz.

Duncan Ingraham esq.	New-Hampshire.
Jona. Williams, jun. esq.	Massachusetts.
Jared Ingersol, esq.	Connecticut.
Samuel Stockton, esq.	New-Jersey
James Wilson, esq.	Pennsylvania
Col. Thomas Robinson,	Delaware
Hon. J. E. Howard, esq.[236]	Maryland
Colonel [Christian] Febiger,	Virginia
W. Ward Burrows, esq.	S. Carolina
George Meade, esq.	Georgia

XVI.

Col. *William Williams*, on horseback, in complete armour, bearing on his arm a shield emblazoned with the arms of the United States.

XVII.

The Montgomery troop of light horse, commanded by captain *James Morris*.

XVIII.

The consuls and representatives of foreign states in alliance with America, in an ornamented car drawn by four horses: viz.

Capt. *Thomas Bell*, with the flag of the United States of America.

Barbe de Marbois, *esq*, vice consul of France.

J. H. C. Heinneken, *esq*. consul of the United Netherlands, with the flag of Holland.

Charles Helstedt, *esq*. consul general of Sweden, with the Swedish flag.

Charles W. Lecke, *esq*. with the flag of Prussia.

Thomas Barclay, *esq*. with the flag of Morocco.

XIX.

The hon. *Francis Hopkinson, esq*. judge of the admiralty, wearing in his hat a gold anchor, pendant on a green ribband, preceded by the register's clerk, carrying a green bag filled with rolls of parchment, the word ADMIRALTY in large letters on the front of the bag.

James Read, esq. register of the admiralty court, wearing a silver pen in his hat.

Clement Biddle, esq. marshal of the admiralty, carrying a silver oar, decorated with green ribbands.

---

236 [*Edit. Note.* Of Cowpens fame.]

XX.

The wardens of the port, and the tonnage officer.

XXI.

COLLECTOR of the customs and naval officer.

XXII.

Peter Baynton, esq. as a citizen, and col. *Isaac Melchor*, as an Indian chief, in a carriage, smoaking the calumet of peace together. The sachem magnificently dressed according to the Indian custom: his head adorned with scarlet and white plumes; jewels of silver hanging from his nose and ears: ten firings of wampum round his neck; the broad belt of peace and brotherly love in his hand: cloathed with a richly ornamented vest and other decorations suitable to the character.

XXIII.

The Berks county troop, consisting of 30 dragoons, commanded by capt. *Ph. Strubing.*

XXIV.

The NEW ROOF,[237] or GRAND FEDERAL EDIFICE; on a carriage drawn by ten white horses. This building was in the form of a dome, supported by 13 Corinthian columns, raised on pedestals proper to that order: the fri[e]ze decorated with 13 stars. Ten of the columns were complete, but three left unfinished. On the pedestals of the columns were inscribed, in ornamented cyphers, the initials of the 13 American States. On the top of the dome was a handsome cupola, surmounted by a figure of plenty, bearing a cornucopia, and other emblems of her character. The dimensions of this building were as follows -- 10 feet diameter -- 11 feet to the top of the cornice -- the dome 4 feet high -- the cupola 5 feet high -- the figure of plenty 3½ feet high -- the carriage on which the building was mounted 3 feet high -- the whole 36 feet in height. Round the pedestal of the edifice, these words, "IN UNION THE FABRIC STANDS FIRM."

This elegant edifice was begun and finished in the short space of four days by Messrs. *William Williams & Co.*

The grand edifice was followed by architects and house-carpenters, in number 450, carrying insignia of the trade, preceded by Messrs. *Benjamin Loxley, Gunning Bedford, Thomas Nevil, Levi Budd, Joseph Ogilby*, and *William Roberts*, displaying designs in architecture, &c. -- Mr. *George Ingels* bore the house carpenter's standard. -- Motto -- " JUSTICE AND BENEVOLENCE."

To this corps, the saw makers and file cutters attached themselves; headed by Messrs. *John Harper* and *William Cook*, with a flag -- a hand and a saw-mill-saw, gilt, on a pink field.

On the floor of the grand edifice were ten chairs for the accommodation of ten gentlemen, viz. Messrs. *Hilary Baker, George Latimer, John Wharton, John Nesbitt, Samuel Morris, John Brown, Tench Francis, Joseph Anthony, John Chaloner*, and *Benjamin Fuller.* These gentlemen sat as representatives of the citizens at large, to whom the federal constitution was committed previous to its ratification.

When the grand edifice arrived at *Union Green*, these gentlemen gave up their seats to the representatives of the states, mentioned in article XV, who entered the temple, and fixed their flags to the corinthian columns, to which they respectively belonged. In the evening, the edifice, with the ten gentlemen

---

[237] [*Edit. Note.* i.e., the Federal Constitution and Union. Hopkinson used the same metaphor of a roof in a poem he penned celebrating the national charter. Ostensibly then this float was prompted by his own conceptualization.]

representing the states *now in union*, was brought back in great triumph, and with loud huzzas, and left in the area before the state-house.

XXV.

The Pennsylvania society of *Cincinnati*, and militia officers.

XXVI.

CORPS of light infantry, commanded by captain *Rose*, with the standard of the fifth regiment.

XXVII.

The agricultural society, headed by their president *Samuel Powel, esq.* A flag borne by major *Samuel Hodgdon*, on a buff coloured ground in an oval compartment; *industry* represented by a ploughman, driving a plough, drawn by oxen, followed by the goddess of plenty, bearing a cornucopia in her left, and a fickle in her right, hand. A view of an American farm in the back ground -- Motto -- "*Venerate the plough.*"

XXVIII.

FARMERS, headed by Messrs. Richard Peters, Richard Willing, Samuel Meredith, Isaac Warner, George Gray, William Peltz, -- Burkhart, and Charles Willing. Two ploughs, one drawn by four oxen, directed by Richard Willing, esq. in the dress and character of a farmer, the other drawn by two horses, and directed by Mr. -- Burkhart, followed by a sower sowing feed, with a number of farmers, millers, &c. N. B. This conspicuous and interesting part of the procession cannot be minutely described, as the gentlemen who conducted it live in the country; and there was not time for procuring from them a particular account of the arrangement.

XXIX.

The *manufacturing society*, with their spinning and carding machines, looms, &c. Mr. *Gallaudet* carried the flag; the device, on which was a beehive standing in the beams of the sun -- bees issuing from the hive. The flag a blue silk: motto -- "*In its rays we shall feel new vigour*" in gold letters: followed by *Robert Hare*, esq. the managers of the society, subscribers to the institution, committee for managing the manufacturing fund, and subscribers to the fund.

The carriage 30 feet in length, 18 feet wide, and 13 feet high, neatly covered with white cotton, of the society's manufacture, drawn by ten large bay horses. On this carriage was placed the carding machine, worked by two men, carding cotton at the rate of 50 lb weight per day. Also a spinning machine of 80 spindles, worked by a woman (a native of, and instructed in the city) drawing cotton suitable for fine jeans or federal rib. On the right hand of the stage was placed a lace loom, and a workman weaving a rich scarlet and white livery lace. On the left, a man weaving jean on a large loom, with a fly shuttle. -- Behind the looms was fixed the apparatus of Mr. *Hewson*, printing muslins of an elegant chintz pattern; Mr. *Lang*, designing and cutting prints for shawls; on the right sat Mrs. *Hewson* and her four daughters penciling a piece of sprigged chintz of Mr. Hewson's printing, all dressed in cottons of their own manufacture. On the back part of the carriage, on a lofty staff, was displayed the callicoe printer's flag; in the centre 13 stars on a blue field, and 13 red stripes on a white field; round the borders of the flag were printed 37 different patterns of various colours; one of them a very elegant bed furniture chintz of fix colours, as specimens of printing done at Philadelphia. Motto -- "*May the union government protect the manufactures of America.*" The several machines, and the different branches of the manufactory, were all in action during the whole time of the procession. This carriage was followed by the weavers of the factory, and others of the same trade, about 100 in number, having the weaver's flag carried in front -- a rampant lion on a green field, holding a shuttle in his dexter paw -- Motto -- "*May government protect us.*" The cotton card makers annexed themselves to this society.

XXX.

CORPS of light infantry, commanded by captain *Robinson*, with the standard of the sixth regiment.

XXXI.

THE MARINE SOCIETY.

Captain *William Greenway*, carrying a globe, attended by captains *Heysham* and *Albertson*, with spy glasses in their hands. Ten captains, five a-breast, each carrying a quadrant, viz. *J. Woods, J. Ashmead, William Miller, Samuel Howell, John Souder, Robert Bethell, W. Allen, W. Tanner, Leeson Simmons*, and *George Atkinson*, followed by the members of the society, six a-breast, carrying trumpets, spy glasses, charts, &c. and wearing each a badge in his hat, representing a ship under sail. -- 89 in number,

XXXII.

THE FEDERAL SHIP *UNION*,

MOUNTING 20 guns, commanded by *John Green, esq.* captain *S. Smith*, *W. Belcher*, and Mr. *Mercer*, lieutenants; four young boys in uniform, as midshipmen; the crew, including officers, consisted of 25 men. The ship Union was 33 feet in length; her width and rigging in proportion to that length. Her bottom was the barge of the ship *Alliance*, and the same which formerly belonged to the *Serapis*, and was taken in the memorable engagement of captain *Paul Jones*, in the *Bon Homme Richard*, with the *Serapis*, The *Union* was a matter-piece of elegant workmanship, decorated with emblematical carvings, and finished throughout, even to a stroke of the painter's brush. And, what is truly surprising, she was begun and finished in less than four days: viz. she was begun at eleven o'clock on Monday morning the 30th of June, and was brought complete to the place of rendezvous, on the Thursday evening following, fully prepared to join in the general procession. The workmanship and appearance of this beautiful object commanded universal attention and applause, and did great and merited honour to the artists of Philadelphia, who were concerned in her construction. She was mounted on a carriage drawn by ten horses. A large meet of canvas was tacked all around along her water line, and, extending over a light frame, hung down to the ground, fo as to conceal the wheels and machinery; and the canvas painted to represent the sea, so that nothing incongruous appeared to offend the eye. The ceremonies of setting sail, receiving a pilot on board, trimming her fails to the wind, according to the several courses of the line of march, throwing the lead when she approached near to Union Green, her arrival there, casting anchor, being hailed and welcomed with three cheers, and the captain forwarding his dispatches to the president of the United States, &c. &c. &c. were all performed with the strictest maritime propriety. But neither time, nor the space allotted for this account, will permit such a detail as would do justice to captain *Green* and his crew, and to the builders and workmen concerned in the constructing and finishing this beautiful and conspicuous feature in the grand procession.

The ship was followed by the pilots of the port, with their boat, named "*the Federal Pilots*," under the command of Mr. *Isaac Roach*, who sheared along side the ship *Union* at the appointed place, and put Mr. *Michael Dawson* on board as pilot; then took his station in the procession, attended and took the pilot off again on her arrival.

BOAT BUILDERS.

A frame representing a boat builder's shop, 18 feet long, 8 wide, and 13 high, mounted on a carriage drawn by horses. On the top of the frame was placed the ship Union's Barge, elegantly finished. On the ensign staff, a flag, blue field, quartered with 13 stripes, in the field an Ax and an adze crossing each other -- Motto "*By these we live*" The barge 10 feet long, manned with a cockswain and six little boys as bargemen, dressed in white linen uniform, decorated with blue ribbands. On the platform underneath the barge, were seven hands at work, building a boat 13 feet long, which was actually set up and nearly completed during the procession. The whole machine was constructed with great skill, and drawn by four bright bay horses belonging to, and under the conduct: of, Mr *Jacob Toy*, followed by 40 Boat Builders, headed by Messrs *Bowyer Brooks* and *Warwick Hale*.

SAIL MAKERS.

A flag, carried by Capt. Joseph Rice, representing an inside view of a sail loft, with matters and men at work -- On the top Thirteen Stars -- in the fly 5 vessels -- Motto -- "May commerce flourish, and industry be rewarded:" followed by a number of masters, journeymen and apprentices.

SHIP CARPENTERS.

HEADED by Messrs. Francis Grice and John Norris, with the draft of a ship on the flocks, and cases of instruments in their hands. A flag, on which was represented a ship on the stocks carried by *Manuel Eyres, Esq*. supported by Messrs. Harrison, Rice, Brewster, and Humphreys; followed by mast-makers, caulkers and workmen, to the amount of 330, all wearing badges in their hats representing a ship on the stocks, and sprigs of white oak.

SHIP JOINERS.

NICHOLAS YOUNG, conductor, his son carrying a cedar staff before him; Robert M'Mullan master workman -- William M'Mullan and S. Ormes, with a flag, bearing the company's arms. viz. a. binnacle and hen-coop, crooked plains, and other tools of the profession, thirteen stripes and Thirteen Stars -- 10 of them in full splendour -- Motto -- "By these we support our families," followed by 25 of the trade, wearing sprigs of cedar in their hats.

ROPE-MAKERS and SHIP-CHANDLERS.

The flag, carried in front by Richard Tittermary, representing a Rope Yard, with 10 men spinning and 3 standing idle, with their hemp about their waists -- Motto -- "May commerce flourish." Next in front, as leaders, were J. Tittemary, sen. and G. Goodwin, being the oldest of the trade; followed by masters, journeymen and apprentices, with hemp round their waists, &c. about 60 in number.

MERCHANTS and TRADERS.

Their standard, the flag of a Merchant Ship of the United States -- in the union 10 illuminated flars, 3 only traced out. On one side of the flag a ship, *the Pennsylvania*, with an inscription, 4th *July* 1788. On the reverse of the flag, a globe and a scroll, with these words -- "par tout le mond." The flag staff terminated with a silver cone, to which a mariner's compass was suspended by a ring. The standard borne by Mr Nesbit. Thomas Willing, Esq. attended by Messrs. Charles Pettit, John Wilcocks, John Ross, and Tench Coxe, the merchants committee; then the body of merchants and traders, and after them a train of clerks and apprentices, preceded by Mr *Saintonge*, carrying a large ledger.

CORPS of light infantry, commanded by capt. Sproat, with the standard of the 4th regiment.

TRADES and PROFESSIONS.

N. B. The order of the several trades, except those concerned in the construction and fitting out a ship and house carpenters, was determined by lot.

XXXIII.

CORDWAINERS.

A carriage drawn by four horses, representing a cordwainer's shop, in which were six men actually at work: the shop hung round with shoes, boots, &c. Mr Alexander Rutherford conductor, Messrs. Elisha Gordon and Martin Bish, Assistants, followed by a committee of nine, three a-breast. Mr James.

Roney, junior, standard bearer. The standard -- The cordwainers arms on a crimson field: above the arms, *Crispin* holding a laurel branch in his right hand, and a scroll of parchment in his left; three hundred cordwainers following, six a-breast, each wearing a white leathern apron, embellished with the company's arms, richly painted.

XXXIV.

COACH PAINTERS.

With a flag, ornamented with the insignia of the art, followed by ten of the profession, carrying pallets and pencils.

XXXV.

CABINET and CHAIR MAKERS.

Mr. Jonathan Goslelow carrying the scale and dividers; Mr. Jedediah Snowden with the rules of architecture; four of the oldest masters; Mr. James Lee, attended by three masters bearing the standard, or cabinet maker's arms, elegantly painted and gilt, on a blue field, ornamented with thirteen stars; ten radiant and three unfinished; below the arms, two hands united -- Motto -- "*By unity we support society*" The makers six a-breast, wearing linen aprons and buck's tails in their hats, preceding *the work-shop*, seventeen feet long, nine feet eight inches wide, and fourteen feet high, on a carriage drawn by four horses; two signs projecting from the shop, and inscribed "Federal cabinet and chair shop;" one on each side; Mr. John Brown, with journeymen and apprentices at work in the shop. The shop followed by journeymen and apprentices, six a-breast, wearing lined aprons and buck's tails in their hats; the aprons were all of American manufacture -- one hundred in train.

XXXVI.

BRICK MAKERS.

A large flag of green silk, on which was represented a brick-yard; hands at work; a kiln burning; at little distance a federal city building -- Motto "*It was hard in Egypt, but this prospect makes it easy*." Ten master brick makers, headed by Mr. David Rose, senior, and followed by one hundred workmen in frocks and trowsers, with tools, &c.

XXXVII.

HOUSE, SHIP, and SIGN PAINTERS.

Arms, three shields argent, on a field azure; crest, a hand holding a brush, proper -- Motto -- "*Virtue alone is true nobility*." The stage fourteen feet by seven; on it a mill for manufacturing colours; a glazing table, with a stone for grinding paint; the stage furnished with pots, sashes, tools, &c. The business on the stage conducted by Messrs. Stride, Wells, Cowen, Deveter, and M'Elwee. The flag borne by Mr. Fausburg, as oldest painter, supported by Messrs Flinn and Fullerton, followed by the artists, six a-breast, carrying gilded brushes, diamonds, gold hammers, glazing knives, &c. sixty eight in procession.

XXXVIII.

PORTERS,

Led by John Lawrence and George Green, on each side a porter dressed, leading a horse and dray; the horse richly decorated with blue, white, and red ribbands -- on the dray, five barrels of superfine flower; on the head of each barrel, the words "Federal flour;" the dray followed by John Jacobs and 40 porters. The standard borne by David Sparks, of light blue silk; the device thirteen stripes, thirteen stars, three of them clowded; a horse and dray, four barrels on the dray, and a porter loading a fifth -- Motto -- "*May industry ever be encouraged*;" the standard, followed by a number of porters; Andrew Dyer and Joseph Greenwold brought up the rear, all wearing white aprons, tied with ribbands of blue silk, and carrying whips, ornamented with blue, white, and red ribbands; the officers wore sashes of blue silk. After the procession, the five barrels of federal flour were delivered to the overseers for the use of the poor.

XXXIX.

CLOCK and WATCH-MAKERS.

The company's arms, neatly painted on a silk flag -- Motto -- "*Time rules all things*;" headed by Mr. J. Wood, and followed by twenty three members.

XL.

FRINGE and RIBBAND WEAVERS.

Mr J. Williams, carrying a blue staff, capped with a gilt ball; across the staff 10 wires, to which were suspended implements and specimens of the art. The fringe, lace, and line shuttles were each charged with a quill of shute to shew that they were all in employ -- The ribband shuttle empty. In the gilt ball was fixed a wire, 18 inches long, from which flowed a ribband of ten stripes -- Immediately below the cross-wires, a paper, inscribed with verses, composed by Mr Williams on the occasion.

XLI.

BRICK-LAYERS.

Headed by Messrs. *Nicholas Hicks, William Johnson*, and *Jacob Grass*, with their aprons and trowels; a flag with the following device; the federal city rising in a forest, workmen building it, and the sun illuminating it -- Motto -- "*Both buildings and rulers are the works of our hands*." The flag attended by Messrs. C. Souder, W. Marsh, and Jos. Wildy, supported by Messrs. J. Robbins, P. Waglom, T. Mitchell J. Boyd, Burton Wallace, M. Groves, J. Souder, Edward M'Kaighen, Alexander M'Kinley, ten master bricklayers, wearing aprons, and carrying trowels, plum-rules, &c. followed by 55 of the trade.

XLII.

TAYLORS.

Headed by Messrs. Barker, Stille, Martin, and Tatem, carrying a white flag, bearing the company's arms -- Motto -- "By union our strength encreases;" followed by 250 of the trade.

XLIII.

INSTUMENT MAKERS, TURNERS, WINDSOR-CHAIR-MAKERS, and SPINNING-WHEEL MAKERS.

CONDUCTED by captain J. Cornish. Mr. John Stow, bearing the standard, viz. the turner's arms, with the addition of a spinning-wheel on one side, and a windsor chair on the other -- Motto -- "*By faith we obtain*." Messrs. G. Stow, and M. Fox, carrying small columns, representing the several branches of turner's work. Followed by Messrs. Anthony and Mason, with a group of musical instruments, and sixty workmen in green aprons.

XLIV.

CARVERS and GILDERS.

The carvers and gilders exhibited an ornamented car, on a federal plan; viz. it was 13 feet by 10 on the floor, whereon was erected 13 pilasters richly ornamented with carved work. The capitals of 10 of them were gilt, and labelled with the names of the dates in the order in which they acceded to the new constitution: the remaining three left somewhat unfinished. About 3 feet above the floor, a level railing united to the pilasters, denoting the equality of the subjects. In the centre a column 10 feet high, with laurel twining round it; and on the top a bud of general *Washington*, crowned with laurel, dressed in the American uniform, with thirteen stars on a collar. The column was supported by 10 tight stays from the 10 finished pilasters: three slack stays hanging from the unfinished pilaslers. Over the general's bust, the American standard was displayed.

In the centre of the front of the carriage was the head of Phidias, he most eminent of ancient carvers, with emblematical figures supporting him. On the inside of the front railing, a large figure for the head of a ship, richly carved and painted: and the whole outside of the car decorated all round with figures of the seasons, the cardinal virtues, and various devices.

Before the car, walked the artists of the several branches, headed by Mr. Cutbush, ship carver, and Messrs. Reynolds and Jugiez, house furniture and coach carvers, together with a number of young artists, wearing blue ribbands round their necks, to which were suspended medallions of ten burnished gold stars on a blue ground. Amongst these, one carried a figure of *Ceres*, another, *Fame*, with her trumpet, announcing the federal union, and another a corinthian column, complete. In the car a number of artists at work, superintended by Mr. Rush, ship carver.

XLV.

COOPERS.

Conducted by Mr. D. Dolbey. An elegant flag of the cooper's arms, embellished with thirteen stars -- Motto -- "*May commerce flourish -- Love as brethren*." After the flag, Mssrs. W. King, R. Babe, and J. Lunch, followed by 150 coopers, in white leathern aprons, and wearing badges in their hats.

XLVI.

PLANE MAKERS.

Mr. W. Martin in front, with the standard, viz. a white field; a smoothing plane on the top; in the middle a pair of spring dividers, three planes, a brace, a square, and a gauge -- Motto -- "*Truth*:' followed by 8 workmen.

XLVII.

WHIP and CANE MAKERS.

A machine on a carriage, a boy in it at work, platting a whip; followed by Mr M'Callister and 3 journeymen, carrying articles of the trade on the top of a flag -- Motto -- "*Let us encourage our own manufactures*."

XLVIII.

BLACKSMITHS, WHITE SMITHS,
and NAILORS.

A machine drawn by nine horses, representing a Smiths manufactory, being a frame 10 by 15 feet, and 9 feet high, with a real brick chimney extending 3 feet above the roof and completely furnished for use. In front of the building, three master Blacksmiths, viz. N. Brown, N. Hess, and W. Perkins supporting the standard -- The Smiths arms highly ornamented -- Motto -- "By hammer in hand, all arts do stand." The Manufactory was in full employ during the procession -- Mr I. Mingler, and his assistant C. Keyser, completed a set of plough irons out of old swords; worked a sword into a sickle, turned several horse-shoes, and performed several jobs on demand.

Mr. J. Goodman, jun. white smith, finished a complete pair of pliars, a knife, and some machinery, and other work, on demand.

Messrs. A. Fessinger and B. Brummel forged, finished, and sold a number of spikes, nails, and broad tacks; all which was performed in the street during the procession. The whole was under the conduct of Messrs. Godfrey Gebler, David Henderson, G. Goddard, Ja. Esler, Lewis Prahl, and J. Eckfelt; followed by two hundred brother black-fmiths, white-smiths, and nailers.

XLIX.

COACH MAKERS.

Preceded by Mr. John Bringhurst, in a phaeton drawn by 2 horses, carrying a draft of a coach on a white silk flag. A stage nine feet high, sixteen feet long, and eight feet wide, on a carriage drawn by four horses, representing a shop, Mr. G. Way, master workman, a body and carriage-maker, a wheelwright, a trimmer, and a harness-maker, all at work, and a painter ornamenting a body. On each side of the stage, the words, "*No tax on American carriages*," In the center was erected the standard, of yellow silk, emblazoned with the arms of the profession, viz. three coaches on a blue field; the chariot of the sun appearing through the clouds -- Motto -- "*The clouds dispelled, we shine forth*;" the staff decorated with the implements of the trade. Ten masters, each bearing a yellow silk flag, with the names of the dates in union, in letters of gold, on a blue field; five before and five behind the stage; the whole followed by one hundred and fifty workmen.

L.

POTTERS.

A flag, on which was neatly painted a kiln burning, and several men at work in the different branches of the business -- Motto -- "*The potter hath power over his clay.*" -- A machine, drawn by horses, on which was a potter's wheel and men at work. A number of cups, bowls, mugs, &c. were made during the procession, followed by twenty potters, headed by Messrs. C. Percy and M. Gilbert, wearing linen aprons of American manufacture.

LI.

HATTERS.

Led by Mr. A. Tybout; the standard borne by Mr. J. Gordon, viz. on a white field, a hat in hand 5 on each side a tassel band; the crest, a beaver; motto, on a crimson garter in gold letters; "*With the Industry of the beaver we support our rights*;" followed by one hundred and twenty four hatters.

LII.

WHEEL WRIGHTS.

A stage drawn by two horses, five men working upon it, making a plough, and a speed for a waggon wheel. The standard, a blue flag -- Motto -- "*The united wheel-wrights*;" followed by twenty two of the trade, headed by Messrs. Conrad, Robinson, and Nicholas Reep.

LIII.

TIN-PLATE WORKERS.

PRECEDED by J. Finnaur and Martin Riser, carrying the standard with the company's arms, followed by workmen in green aprons.

LIV.

SKINNERS, BREECHES MAKERS, and GLOVERS.

Headed by Messrs. J. Lisle, and G. Cooper, the one carrying a breaking knife, the other a paring knife. The standard, borne by Mr. Shreiner, viz. on one side, a deer and a glove, on the other, the golden fleece, and below it a pair of breeches; -- Motto -- "*May our manufacture be equal in its consumption to its usefulness*;" followed by fifty eight of the trade, in buckskin breeches and gloves, and wearing buck's tails in their hats. To these Mr. J. Rogers, parchment and glue manufacturer, attached himself,

LV.

TALLOW CHANDLERS.

Mr. R. Porter, matter. Two standards. First, the company's arms on a blue field, trimmed with white, three doves with olive branches. Over the arms an angel bearing St. John Baptist's head; on each side, two blazing lamps -- Motto -- "*Let your light so shine*." Second standard, a chandelier of thirteen branches, a lighted candle in each, and thirteen stars in a silver semicircle. Inscription, "*The stars of America a light to the world*." Motto, at the bottom of the chandelier, "*United in one*." The uniform, blue and white cockades, blue aprons, bound with white, with a dove neatly painted on each, a white rod, surmounted by an olive branch, in each person's hand; twenty in number.

LVI.

VICTUALLERS.

A flag with this inscription -- "The death of anarchy and confusion, shall feed the poor." Two ax men preceding two stately oxen 30001b weight -- a label across the horns of each, the one inscribed *Anarchy* the other *Confusion* -- Ten boys dressed in white, 5 on the right and 5 on the left of the oxen, carrying small flags, with the names of the states of the union inscribed -- A band of music-conductors, Messrs P. Hall, G. Welper, P. Odenheimer and Conrad Hoff; followed by 86 master victuallers, all drest in white. The oxen were afterwards killed, the hides and tallow sold for bread, and given, with the meat, to the poor.

LVII.

PRINTERS, BOOK-BINDERS, and STATIONERS.

A stage 9 feet square, drawn by four horses-up-on the stage the federal printing press complete, with cases, and other implements of the business, furnished by ten printing offices. Men at work upon the stage in the different branches of the profession. Mr Durant, in the character of *Mercury*, in a white dress, ornamented with red ribbands, and having real wings affixed to his head and feet, and a garland of flowers round his temples -- During the procession, the press-men were at work, and struck off, and distributed amongst the people, many copies of the following ode, composed for the occasion by Francis Hopkinson, Esquire.

THE ODE.

Oh! for a muse of fire! To mount the skies,
And to a listening world proclaim;
Behold! Behold! an Empire rise!
An AEra new, time as he flies,
Hath entered in the book of fame.
On Alleghany's towering head
Echo shall stand; the tidings spread,
And o'er the lakes, and misty floods around,
An *AEra new* resound.

See where Columbia sits alone,
And from her star bespangled throne,
Beholds the gay procession move along,
And hears the trumpet and the choral song.
She hears her sons rejoice;
Looks into future times, and sees
The numerous blessings heav'n decrees;
And with her *plaudit*, joins the general voice.

"'Tis done! 'tis done! my sons, she cries,
"In war are valiant and in council wise.
"*Wisdom* and *valour* shall my rights defend,
"And o'er my vast domain those rights extend.
" Science shall flourish, genius stretch her wing,
" In native strains Columbian muses sing:
"*Wealth* crown the arts, and *Justice* cleanse her scales,
"Commerce her pon'drous anchor weigh
— — "Widespread her sails.
"And in far distant seas her flag display.

"My sons for freedom fought, nor fought in vain,
"But found a naked goddess was their gain;
"Good government alone can shew the maid
"In robes of social happiness array'd."

Hail to this festival! All hail the day!
Columbia's standard on *her roof* display;
And let the people's motto ever be,
"*United thus*, and *thus united free*."

This ode, and also one in the German language, fitted to the purpose, and printed by *Mr Steiner*, were thrown amongst the people as the procession moved along. Ten small packages, containing the above ode, and the toasts for the day, were made up and addressed to the ten states in union respectively, and these were tied to pidgeons, which, at intervals, rose from Mercury's cap and flew off, amidst the acclamations of an admiring multitude.

Mr. W. Sellers, sen. bearing the standard of the united professions; viz. azure, on a cheveron argent, an American bald eagle, volant, between two reams of paper, proper, between three Bibles closed, proper. In chief, perched on the point of the cheveron, a dove with an olive branch, of the second. Supporters, two Fames, clothed in iky-blue, flowing robes, spangled with stars argent. Crest, a Bible displayed, proper, on a wreath azure and argent. Under the escutcheon, two pens placed saltiere ways, proper -- Motto -- "*We protect, and are supported by liberty*," After the standard walked the masters of the combined professions, followed by journeymen and apprentices, each carrying a scroll, tied with blue silk binding, exhibiting the word "*Typographer*" illuminated by ten stars in union. Fifty in train.

LVIII.

SADLERS.

A sad[d]ler's shop, dressed with sadlery, and a variety of ready made work; elegant American plated furniture, &c. drawn by two fine horses. In the shop, Mr. S. Burrows, and a number of hands at work: one of whom (having the different parts in readiness) completed a neat saddle during the procession. The standard, carried by Mr. Jehosophat Polk, and J. Young, was of green silk, with the company's arms thereon, elegantly painted and gilt -- Motto -- "*Our trust is in God.*" The company was headed by Messrs. J. Stephens and J. Marr. Mr. William Haley, silver platter, joined himself to this corps, carrying a federal bit of his own workmanship.

LIX.

STONE-CUTTERS.

Three apprentices with tools, and two with the orders of the operative lodge: one with the standard in mason's order; the rest following with pieces of polished marble. Twenty in number.

IX.

BREAD and BISCUIT-BAKERS.

A standard of the bread baker's arms, properly emblazoned -- Motto -- "*May our country never want bread.*" Uniform; white shirts, and full plaited aprons, quite round the waist, with light blue sashes. A stage, with a baker's oven, complete, 6 feet in diameter. Three hands at work as the procession went on, directed by a master baker, who distributed bread to the people as it was drawn out of the oven. Headed by Mr. G. Mayer.

The biscuit baker's standard. A white flag; a bake house, and several hands at work -- Motto -- "*May the federal government revive our trade.*" Messrs. T. Hopkins and Matthias Landenberger in front of twelve matters. Messrs. I. Peters, sen. and W. Echart brought up the rear, each carrying a small peel: 150 bakers in procession.

LXI.

GUN-SMITHS.

A stage on a four wheel carriage drawn by four horses, 14 feet long and 8 feet wide, with a motto on each side in large letters: "*Federal armoury.*" A number of hands on the stage at work, under the direction of two senior matters, J. Nicholson, and J. Perkins, Abm. Morrow bearing the standard in the rear of the carriage, viz. a large white silk flag, cross guns in the middle: over the guns the cap of liberty; under the guns, the letters C P (city proof) cross pistols, with the letter V (viewed). At the end nearest the staff, a powder calk: on the opposite end three balls. The uniform, green baize aprons, with green strings.

LXII.

COPPER-SMITHS.

A car, 14 feet by 7, drawn by 4 horses, three hands working at stills and tea-kettles, under the direction of Mr. Benjamin Harbeson.

A standard, bearing the arms of the trade, decorated with emblems, and surrounded with 13 stars, carried by two, and followed by seventeen master workmen.

LXIII.

GOLD-SMITHS, SILVER-SMITHS, and JEWELLERS.

WILLIAM BALL, esq. senior member, carrying an urn. Messrs. Jo. Gee and John Germain, with the standard of white silk: on one side, the silver-smith's arms -- Motto -- "*Justitia virtutum regina.*" On the reverse, the genius of America, holding in her hand a silver urn -- Motto -- "*The purity, brightness, and solidity of this metal is emblematical of that liberty which we expect from the New Constitution.*" Her head surrounded by 13 stars; 10 very brilliant, two less bright, and one with 3 dark points, and two light ones; the last emblematical of Rhode-Island; also one other star emerging bright from the horizon, for the rising state of Kentucke. After the standard, the masters, journeymen, and apprentices. Thirty-five.

LXIV.

DISTILLERS.

On a standard of blue silk, a still, worm-tub, and implements of the business, neatly painted. The standard borne by Mr. M. Shubart; and followed by 12 distillers.

LXV.

TOBACCONISTS.

Headed by Mr John. Riley. The standard of white silk; a tobacco plant of 13 leaves, 10 in perfection, 3 not finished; a hogshead of tobacco on one side of the plant, a roll of plug tobacco, a bottle and bladder of snuff: over the plant, on the other side, 13 stars; 10 silvered, 3 unfinished. The standard carried by Mr Thomas Leiper -- Motto -- "Success to the tobacco plant;" each member wearing a green apron with blue firings, and a plume, composed of different kinds of tobacco leaves in his hat, and carrying tools of the profession in his hand. Conductors, Messrs Hamilton, Few, Stimble, and Murphey; 70 in train.

LXVI.

BRASS FOUNDERS.

Mr Daniel King in a car drawn by four grey horses, with an emblimatical standard; a furnace in blast during the procession. He finished a 3 inch howitzer, which was mounted and fired off with the artillery on Union Green. His journey-men and apprentices also neatly executed several pieces of work -- Motto on the standard -- "In vain the earth her treasure hides." The whole exhibition was at the sole expence of Mr King.

LXVII.

STOCKING MANUFACTURERS.

HEADED by Mr George Freytag -- a white standard; a pair of blue stockings across -- a cap above; finger mitts below, incircled with a gilded heart -- a gold crown with 10 points, on each point a blue star -- Motto -- "The Union of the American stocking manufacturers." Thirty in train.

LXVIII.

TANNERS and CURRIERS.

Led by Mr Geo. Leib, carrying the flag of the companys arms -- Motto -- "God be with us" -- 25 in number.

Curriers, led by Mr Geo. Oakly carrying the company's flag -- Motto -- "spes nostra Deus"-- followed by 34 of the trade, each carrying a currying knife, and wearing a blue apron and a jean coatee of our new manufactory

LXIX.

UPHOLSTERERS.

Headed by Messrs J. Mason and J. Davis. In front was carried a cushion with its drapery, on which fluttered a dove with an olive branch in its mouth, and upon its head a double scroll -- Motto -- "Be liberty thine;" followed by a cabriole sopha decorated.

LXX.

SUGAR REFINERS.

CONDUCTED by Chr. Kucher Esq. Capt Ja. Lawersyler, Messrs B. Pennington. J. Morgan, D. Mierken, Adam Coruman and H. Clause, wearing black cockades, blue sashes, and white aprons. A blue standard arms: on a gold field, the cap of liberty on a staff, between two loaves of sugar -- Motto -- "*Double refined.*" Thirteen stars in a blue field: crest, a lighted candle in a candlestick; on the foot, the word "*Proof*;" beneath, "*American manufactures*" ornamented with sugar canes; followed by thirty-six, wearing white aprons, on which were painted sugar loaves, marked 10; each carrying some implement of the trade.

LXXI.

BREWERS.

Ten in number, headed by Reuben Haines, each wearing 10 ears of barley in his hat, and a sash of hop-vines; and carrying malt-shovels and mashing oars. One dray loaded with malt and hops, and one loaded with two hogsheads and a butt, marked, *Beer, Ale, Porter*; with this inscription, "*Proper drink for Americans.*" A standard, carried by Luke Morris: the brewer's arms -- Motto -- "*Home brewed is best.*"

LXXII.

PERUKE MAKERS and BARBER SURGEONS.

Preceded by Messrs. Perrie and Tautwine, full dressed. The standard -- the company's arms, on a white field, richly decorated; viz. a pillar, the emblem of strength, surmounted with the cap of liberty, and supported by twelve hands, in gules, representing the twelve concurring states that called the grand convention. A pelican and her young, in a field, azure. The arms of the barber surgeons: a goat rampant, in full coat, argent, in a field, sable: the arms of the peruke makers, with two arms extended at top, hand in hand, the emblem of union and friendship. Supporters: a land and river horse -- Motto -- "*United we stand.*" The treasurer of the company, the trustees, the company, according to seniority, hand in hand, 6 a-breast, consisting of 72, each wearing a white sash, with a black relief down the middle, and cockades of the same, in honour of the first and great ally of the United States.

LXXIII.

ENGRAVERS.

Their armorial insignia (occasionally deviced) were, or, on a cheveron, engrailed gules (between a parallel ruler, sable, barred and studded of the first, and two gravers, saltiere ways, azure, handled of the third) three plates. Crest, a copper-plate on a sand-bag, proper; inscribed underneath, in large capitals -- ENGRAVERS.

LXXIV.

PLAISTERERS.

(No return.)

LXXV.

BRUSH-MAKERS.

A white flag, with a white boar, and a bundle of bridles over him -- Motto -- "*Federal brush manufactory*." The flag carried by Mr. Roger Flahavan, jun.

LXXVI.

STAY-MAKERS.

Represented by Mr. Francis Serre, with his first journeymen, carrying an elegant pair of ladies stays.*[238]

LXXVII.

CORPS of light infantry, commanded by captain Rees, with the standard of the second regiment.

LXXVIII.

The civil and military officers of Congress in the city.

LXXIX

The supreme executive council of Pennsylvania. His excellency the president*[239] was too much indisposed to attend.

LXXX,

The justices of the court of common pleas, and the magistrates.

LXXXI.

Sheriff and coroner, on horseback.

LXXXII.

The board of city wardens, city treasurer, and secretary of the board, clerks of the market, with standard weights and measures, constables of the watch, with his two assistants.

A BAND OF MUSIC.

TWENTY watchmen, with their flams decorated, and in their proper dress: twenty silent watchmen, with these staves: other watchmen calling the hour -- "Past ten o'clock, and a glorious STAR-LIGHT morning!" alluding to the 10 united states, and the stars of the union.

---

[238] [*Hopkinson's note*] * The several companies formed their own devices, mottos, and emblems; and the above account is taken from their returns.
[239] [*Hopkinson's note*] * Dr. Franklin.

LXXXIII.

The street commissioners.

LXXXIV.

The gentlemen of the bar, headed by the hon. Edward Shippen, esq. president of the common pleas, and William Bradford, esq. attorney general, followed by the young students in law.

LXXXV.

The clergy of the different Christian denominations, with the rabbi of the Jews, walking arm in arm.

LXXXVI.

The college of physicians, headed by their president, Dr. John Redman, and followed by the students in physic.

LXXXVII.

Students of the university, headed by the vice-provost: students of the episcopal academy, and of most of the principal schools in the city, conducted by their respective principals, professors, masters, and tutors. A small flag borne before, them, inscribed, "The rising generation."

LXXXVIIL

The county troop of horse commanded by major W. M'Pherson, brought up the rear of the whole.

Major Fullerton attended the right wing, and colonel Mentges the left wing of the line. Messrs. Stoneburner, Heiltzheimer, and Jonathan Penrose, furnished and superintended the horses for the public carriages.

This grand procession began to move from the place of rendezvous about half past nine (as was before mentioned) and the front arrived at Union Green, in front of Bush Hill, about half past twelve. The length of the line was about one mile and an half, the distance marched, about three miles. As the procession passed along Fourth Street it was saluted, in military form, by captain David Zeigler and lieutenant John Armstrong, and their company of continental troops, which happened to be in the city at the time.

A very large circular range of tables, covered with awnings, and plentifully spread with a cold collation, had been prepared the day before, by the committee of provisions. In the center of this spacious circle (about 500 feet in diameter) the *grand edifice* was placed, and the *ship Union* moored. The flags of the consuls, and other standards, were planted round the edifice.

As soon as the rear of the line arrived at *Union Green*, *James Wilson, Esq*. addressed the people, from the federal edifice, in the following

ORATION.

MY FRIENDS AND FELLOW-CITIZENS,

YOUR candid and generous indulgence I may well bespeak, for *many* reasons. I shall mention but *one*. While I *express* it, I *feel* it in all its force. My abilities are unequal -- abilities far superior to mine would be unequal to the occasion, on which I have the honour of being called to address you.

A people, free and enlightened, establishing and ratifying a system of government which they have previously considered, examined, and approved! This is the spectacle which we are assembled to celebrate; and it is the most dignified one, that has yet appeared on our globe. Numerous and splendid have been the triumphs of conquerors. From what causes have they originated? Of what consequences have they been productive? They have generally begun in ambition; they have generally ended in tyranny. But nothing tyrannical can participate of dignity; and to Freedom's eye, *Sesostris* himself appears contemptible, even when he treads on the *necks of kings*.

The senators of Rome, seated on their curule chairs, and surrounded with all their official lustre, were an object much more respectable; and we view, without displeasure, the admiration of those untutored savages, who considered them as so many gods upon earth. But who were those senators? They were only a *part* of a society; they were inverted only with *inferior* powers.

What is the object exhibited to our contemplation? A *whole people* exercising its *first and greatest power*, performing an act of *sovereignty, original and unlimited!*

The scene before us is *unexampled* as well as *magnificent*. The greatest part of governments have been the deformed offspring of force and fear. With these we deign not comparison. But there have been others who have formed bold pretensions to higher regard. You have heard of *Sparta*, of *Athens*, and of *Rome*. You have heard of their admired constitutions, and of their high prized freedom. In fancied right of these, they conceived themselves to be elevated above the rest of the human race, whom they marked with the degrading title of *barbarians*. But did they, in all their pomp and pride of liberty, ever furnish to the astonished world an exhibition similar to that which we now contemplate? Were their constitutions framed by those who were appointed for that purpose by the people? Were they submitted to the consideration of the people? Had the people an opportunity of expressing their sentiments concerning them? Were they to *stand* or *fall* by the people's approving or rejecting vote? To all thefe questions attentive and impartial history obliges us to answer in the negative. The people were either unfit to be trusted, or their law-givers were too ambitious to trust them.

The far famed establishment of *Lycurgus* was introduced by deception and fraud. Under the specious pretence of consulting the oracle concerning his laws, he prevailed on the Spartans to make a temporary experiment of them during his absence, and to *swear* that they would suffer no alteration of them till his return. Taking a disingenuous advantage of their scrupulous regard for their oaths, he prevented his return, by a voluntary death; and in this manner endeavoured to secure a proud immortality to his system.

Even *Solon*, the mild and moderating *Solon*, far from considering himself as employed only to *propose* such regulations as he should think best calculated for promoting the happiness of the commonwealth, *made* and *promulgated* his laws with all the haughty airs of absolute power. On more occasions than one, we find him boasting with much self-complacency, of his extreme forbearance and condescension, because he did not establish a disposition, in his own favour, and because he did not reduce his equals to the humiliating condition of his slaves.

Did *Numa* submit his *Institutions* to the good sense and free investigation of *Rome*? They were received in precious communications from the goddess *Egeria*, with whose presence and regard he was supremely favoured; and they were imposed on the easy faith of the citizens, as the dictates of an inspiration that was divine.

Such, my fellow-citizens, was the origin of the most splendid establishments that have been hitherto known; and such were the arts to which they owed their introduction and success.

What a flattering contrast arises from a retrospect of the scenes which we now commemorate? Delegates were *appointed* to deliberate and *propose*. They met, and performed their delegated trust. The result of their deliberations *was laid before the people*. It was discussed and scrutinized in the *fullest, freest*, and *severest* manner; by *speaking*, by *writing*, and by *printing*; by individuals, and by public bodies; by its friends, and by its *enemies*. What was the issue? Most *favourable* and most *glorious* to the system. By state after state after state, at time after time, it was ratified; in some states unanimously; on the whole, by a large and very respectable majority.

It would be improper now to examine its qualities. A decent respect for those who have accepted of it will lead us to presume that it is worthy of their acceptance. The deliberate ratifications which have taken place, at once, recommend the *system*, and the *people* by whom it has been ratified.

But why? Methinks I hear one say, Why is so much exultation displayed in celebrating this event? We are prepared to give the reasons of our joy. We rejoice, because, under this constitution, we hope to see *just government*, and to enjoy the blessings that walk in her train.

Let us begin with *peace*; the mild and modest harbinger of felicity. How seldom does the amiable wanderer choose for her permanent residence the habitations of men! In their systems, she sees too many arrangements, civil and ecclessiastical, inconsistent with the calmness and benignity of her temper. In the old world, how many millions of men do we behold unprofitable to society, burdensome to industry, the props of establishments that deserve not to be supported, the causes of distrust in times of peace, and the instruments of destruction in the times of war! Why are they not employed in cultivating useful arts, and in forwarding public improvements? Let us indulge the pleasing expectation, that such will be the *operation of government* in the United States. Why may we not hope, that, disentangled from the intrigues and jealousies of European politics, and unmolested with the alarm and solicitude to which those intrigues and jealousies give birth, our councils will be directed to the encouragement, and our strength be exerted in the cultivation, of *all the arts of peace?*

Of those, the first is AGRICULTURE -- this is true in all countries. In the United States, its truth is of peculiar importance. The subsistence of man, the materials of manufactures, the articles of of commerce; all spring originally from the soil. On agriculture, therefore, the wealth of nations is founded. Whether we consult the observations that reason will suggest, or attend to the information that history will give, we shall in each case be satisfied of the influence of government, good or bad, upon the state of *agriculture*. In a government, whose maxims are those of oppression, property is insecure: it is given, it is taken away by caprice. Where there is no security for property, there is no encouragement for industry. Without industry, the richer the soil, the more it abounds with weeds. The evidence of industry warrants the truth of these general remarks: attend to *Greece*; and compare her agriculture in *ancient* and *modern* times. *Then*, smiling harvest bore testimony to the bountiful boons of liberty: now, the very earth languishes under oppression. View the *Campania* of *Rome*: how melancholy the prospect! Which ever way you turn your afflicted eyes, scenes of desolation crowd before them. Waste and barrenness appear around you in all their hideous forms. What is the reason? With *double tyranny* the land is cursed. Open the classic page -- you trace, in chaste description, the beautiful reverse of every thing you have seen. Whence proceeds the difference? When the description was made, the force of liberty pervaded the soil.

But is *agriculture* the only art which feels the influence of government? Over *manufactures* and *commerce* its power is equally prevalent: there the same causes operate; and there they produce the same effects. The industrious village, the busy city, the crowded port -- all these are the gifts of *liberty* -- and without a good government, liberty cannot exist.

These are advantages; but these are not all the advantages that result from a system of good government. Agriculture, manufactures, and commerce will ensure to us plenty, convenience, and elegance. But is there not something still wanting to finish the man? Are *internal* virtues and accomplishments less estimable or less attractive than *external* arts and ornaments? Is the operation of government less powerful upon the *former* than upon the *latter*? By no means: upon this, as upon a preceding topic, reason and history will concur in their information and advice. In a serene mind the *sciences* and the *virtues* love to dwell. But can the mind of a man be serene, when the property, liberty, subsistence of himself, and of those for whom he feels more than for himself, depend on a tyrant's nod? If the dispirited subject of oppression can with difficulty exert his enfeebled faculties so far as to provide, on the incessant demands of nature, food, just enough to lengthen out his wretched existence, can it be expected that, in such a date, he will experience those fine and vigorous movements of the soul, without the full and free exercise of which *science* and *virtue* will never flourish? Look around to the nations that now exist. View in historic retrospect nations that have hitherto existed; the collected result will be an entire conviction of these all interesting truths: -- Where tyranny reigns, there is the country of ignorance and vice. *Where GOOD GOVERNMENT prevails, there is the country of SCIENCE and VIRTUE.* Under a *good government*, therefore, we must look for *the accomplished man*.

But shall we confine our views even here? While we wish to be accomplished *men* and *citizens*, shall we wish to be *nothing more?* While we perform our duty, and promote our happiness in *this* world, shall we bestow no regard upon *the next?* Does no connection subsist between the *two?* From this connection flows the most important of all the blessings of good government. But here let us pause: *unassisted reason* can guide us no farther: she directs us to that *heaven descended science*, by which LIFE and IMMORTALITY *have been brought to light.*

May we not now say that we have reason for our joy? But while we cherish the delightful emotion, let us remember those things which are requisite to give it *permanence* and stability. Shall we lie supine, and look in listless langour for those blessings and enjoyments to which *exertion* is inseparably attached? If we would be *happy*, we must be *active*. The *constitution*, and our *manners*, must mutually support and be supported. Even on *this* festivity, it will not be disagreeable or incongruous to review the virtues and manners that both *justify* and *adorn* it.

FRUGALITY and *temperance* first attract our attention. These simple, but powerful virtues, are the sole foundation on which a good government can rest with security: they were the virtues which nursed and educated *infant Rome*, and prepared her for all her greatness. But in the giddy hour of her prosperity, she spurned from her the obscure instruments by which it was acquired; and in their place substituted *luxury* and *dissipation*. The consequence was such as might have been expected: she preserved, for some time, a gay and flourishing appearance; but the internal health and soundness of her constitution was gone. At last she fell a victim to the poisonous draughts which were administered by her perfidious favourites. The fate of Rome, both in her *rising* and in her *falling* state, will be the fate of every other nation that shall follow *both* parts of her example.

INDUSTRY appears next among the virtues of a good citizen. Idleness is the nurse of villains. The industrious alone constitute a nation's strength. I will not expatiate on this fruitful subject: let one animating reflection suffice. In a *well constituted commonwealth*, the industry of every citizen extends beyond himself. A common interest pervades the society. *Each* gains from ALL, and *all* gain from EACH. It has often been observed, that the *sciences* flourish *all together*; the remark applies equally to *the arts*.

Your patriotic feelings attest the truth of what I say, when, among the virtues necessary to merit and preserve the advantages of a good government, I number a *warm* and *uniform* attachment to LIBERTY, and TO THE CONSTITUTION. The enemies of liberty are artful and insideous. A *counterfeit* steals her *dress*, imitates her *manners*, forges her *signature*, assumes her *name*: but the real name of the deceiver is LICENTIOUSNESS. Such is her effrontery, that she will charge liberty to her face with imposture; and she will, with shameless front, insist that herself alone is the *genuine character*, and that herself alone is entitled to the respect which the *genuine character* deserves. With the giddy and undiscerning, on whom a deeper impression is made by dauntless impudence, than by modest merit, her pretensions are often successful. She receives the honours of liberty; and liberty herself is treated as a *traitor* and an *usurper*. Generally, however, this bold impostor acts only a *secondary part*. Though she alone appear upon the stage, her motions are regulated by *dark ambition*, who stands concealed behind the curtain, and who knows that despotism, his other favourite, can always follow the success of *licentiousness*. Against these enemies of *liberty*, who act in concert, though they appear on opposite sides, the patriot citizen will keep a watchful guard.

A good constitution is the greatest blessing which a society can enjoy. Need I infer, that it is the duty of every citizen to use his best and most unremitting endeavours for preserving it pure, healthful, and vigorous? For the accomplishment of this great purpose, the exertions of no one citizen are unimportant. Let no one, therefore, harbour for a moment the mean idea that he is, and can be of no value to his country. Let the contrary manly impression animate his soul. Every one can, at *many* times, perform to the state *useful services*; and he who steadily pursues the road of patriotism has the most inviting prospect, of being able, at *some* times, to perform *eminent* ones.

ALLOW me to direct your attention, in a very particular manner, to a momentous part, which, by this constitution, every citizen will frequently be called to act. All those, in places of power and trust, will be elected, either immediately by the people, or in such a manner that their appointment will depend ultimately on such immediate election. All the *derivative* movements of government must spring from the original movement of the *people at large*. If, to *this*, they give a sufficient force, and a just direction, all the others will be governed by its controlling power. To speak without a metaphor; if the people, at their elections, take care to choose none but representatives that are *wise* and *good*, their representatives will take care, in their turn, to choose or appoint none but such as are *wise* and *good* also. The remark applies to every succeeding election and appointment. Thus the characters proper for public officers will be diffused from the *immediate elections* of the people over the remotest parts of administration. Of what immense consequence is it, then, that this primary duty should be faithfully and skillfully discharged? On the faithful discharge of it, the public happiness or infelicity under this, and every other constitution, must, in a very great measure, depend, For, believe me, no government, even the bed, can be happily administered by ignorant or vicious men. You will forgive me, I am sure, for endeavouring to impress upon your minds, in the strongest manner, the importance of this great duty. It is the first *concoction* in politics; and if an error is committed here, it can never be corrected in any subsequent *process*, the certain consequence must be *disease*. Let no one say, that he is but a *single* citizen, and that his ticket will be but one in the box; that one ticket may *turn* the election. In battle, every soldier should consider the public safety as depending on his *single* arm; at an election, every citizen should consider the public happiness as depending on his *single* vote.

A progressive state is necessary to the happiness and perfection of man. Whatever attainments are already reached, attainments still higher should be pursued. Let us therefore drive with noble emulation. Let us suppose we have done nothing while any thing yet remains to be done. Let us, with fervent zeal, press forward, and make unceasing advances in every thing that can *support, improve, refine*, or *embellish* society.

To enter into particulars under each of these heads, and to dilate them according to their importance, would be improper at this time. A few remarks on the *last* of them will be congenial with the entertainments of this auspicious day.

If we give the slightest attention to *nature*, we shall discover, that with *utility* she is curious to blend *ornament*. Can we imitate a better pattern? Public exhibitions have been the favourite amusements of some of the wisest and most accomplished nations. *Greece*, in her most shining era, considered *games* as far from being the least respectable amongst her public establishments. The shews of the *circus* evince that, on this subject, the sentiments of *Greece* were fortified by those of *Rome*.

PUBLIC processions may be so planned and executed, as to join *both* the properties of nature's rule. They may *instruct* and *improve*, while they *entertain* and *please*. They may point out the elegance or usefulness of the sciences and the arts. They may preserve the memory, and engrave the importance of great *political events*. They may represent, with peculiar felicity and force, the operation and effects of great *political truths*. The picturesque and splendid decorations around me, furnish the most beautiful and most brilliant proofs, that these remarks are far from being *imaginary*.

The commencement of our government has been eminently glorious; let our progress in every excellence be proportionably great -- it will -- it must be so. What an enrapturing prospect opens on the United States! Placid *husbandry* walks in front, attended by the *venerable* PLOUGH -- lowing herds adorn our vallies -- bleating flocks spread over our hills -- verdant meadows, enamelled pastures, yellow harvests, bending orchards, rise in rapid succession from east to west: *Plenty*, with her copious horn, sits easy, smiling, and in conscious complacency, enjoys and presides over the scenes: *Commerce* next advances in all her splendid and embellished forms. The rivers and lakes, and seas, are crowded with ships: their shores are covered with cities: the cities are filled with inhabitants: the *arts* decked with elegance, yet with simplicity, appear in beautiful variety, and well adjusted arrangement. Around them are diffused, in rich abundance, the *necessaries*, the *decencies*, and the *ornaments* of life. With heartfelt contentment, Industry beholds his honest labours flourishing and secure. Peace walks serene and unalarmed over all the unmolested regions; while liberty, virtue, and religion go hand in hand, *harmoniously protecting, enlivening,* and *exalting* all -- Happy country! MAY THY HAPPINESS BE PERPETUAL!"

After the oration, the several light companies were drawn off by captain Heysham, to an eminence, and fired a feu-de-joie of three rounds, and then the company went to dinner. No spirit or wine of any kind were introduced: American porter, beer, and cyder, were the only liquors; and of these the supplies were very abundant. The whole inner circumference of the circle of tables was lined with hogsheads, butts, and barrels of these liquors on tap. The following toasts were drank, announced by trumpets, and answered by the artillery -- a round of ten to each toast -- and these were again answered by cannon from the ship *Rising Sun*, at her moorings in the river.

TOASTS.

1. The people of the United States. 2. Honour and immortality to the members of the late federal convention.

3. GENERAL WASHINGTON.

4. The king of France. 5. The United Netherlands. 6. The foreign powers in alliance with the United States. 7. The agriculture, manufactures, and commerce of the United States. 8. The heroes who have fallen in defence of our liberties. 9. May reason, and not the sword, hereafter decide all national disputes. 10. The whole family of mankind.

It should not be omitted in this account, that the several trades furnished the devices, mottos, machines, and decorations themselves, and at the expence of their respective companies. And that nearly the whole of the work exhibited on that day, was completed between Monday morning and the Thursday evening following.

The military in general, horse, artillery, and infantry were completely dressed, and accoutred, according to the uniform of their respective corps, and made a most martial appearance; being distributed in various parts of the line, they gave a beautiful variety to the whole, and evinced that both soldiers and citizens united in favour of the new government.

The whole of this vast body was formed, and the entertainment of the day conducted, with a regularity and decorum far beyond all reasonable expectation. The foot-ways, the windows, and the roofs of the houses were crowded with spectators, exhibiting a spectacle truly magnificent and irresistibly animating. But what was most pleasing to to the contemplative mind, *universal love* and *harmony* prevailed, and every countenance appeared to be the index of a heart glowing with urbanity and rational joy. This social idea was much enforced by a circumstance, which, probably, never before occurred in such extent, viz. The clergy of almost every denomination united in charity and brotherly love. May they and their flocks so walk through life!

It is impossible to be precise in numbers on such an occasion; but averaging several opinions, there were about 5,000 in the line of procession, and about 17,000 on *union* Green. The green was entirely cleared by six o'clock in the evening; and the edifice, ship, and several machines, being withdrawn, the citizens soberly retired to their respective homes. The weather was remarkably favourable for the season; cloudy without rain, and a brisk wind from the south during the whole day. At night, the ship *Rising Sun* was handsomely illuminated in honour of this great festival.

SUCH is the account we have been enabled to give of this memorable exhibition. It is very probable there may be some omissions; if so, the committee can only assure their fellow citizens, that no neglect or offence was intended to any individual or company whatever. The shortness of the time, and the complicated nature of the task, must be their apology.

As the system of government now fully ratified, has been the occasion of much *present joy*; so, may it prove a source of much future blessing to our country and the glory of our rising empire!!!

Published by order,

FRANCIS HOPKINSON,

chairman of the committee
of arrangement,

July 8th. 1788.

N. B. This extraordinary exhibition was not undertaken in consequence of any order or recommendation of government, nor was any part of the expence borne by the public treasury. The voluntary exertions and contributions of the citizens furnished the whole.

"THE FINEST SOIL IN THE WORLD FOR THE CULTURE OF LAURELS..."

One of Gen. Greene's aides, Capt. William Pierce, Relays News from the Southern Department.

Originally a captain in the 1st Continental artillery (beginning on 30 Nov. 1776), William Leigh Pierce (1740-1789), from Virginia, was in mid-November 1780, along with Captain Nathaniel Pendleton, enlisted by Maj. Gen. Nathanael Greene in Richmond; when in Nov. 1780 the latter was making his way south to assume command of the southern army. On 30 September 1783, he was brevetted (i.e., raised in rank but without additional pay) to Major, and after the war entered politics; serving as a delegate from Georgia for the Federal Convention in 1787. While he did not remain in Philadelphia long enough to sign the Constitution (indeed, he died in only 1789), Pierce did participate and have a tangible impact on some of the debate that went on beforehand; including with respect to guidelines for how members of Congress and Senators are to be elected. Yet of particular consequence, he wrote brief sketches of the Convention delegates which are viewed as being of singular value to historians of the Constitution; though it must in fairness to the delegates be said that these sketches, while useful, are too terse to be taken as entirely just or accurate portraits.[240]

Collected for this entry in our series are a series of letters Pierce wrote in 1781-1782, and which were sent to Virginia militia cavalry officer[241] and subsequently eminent and much respected jurist and Federal judge, Saint George Tucker (1752-1827). These first appeared publically in the *Magazine of American History*, Dec. 1881, vol. VII, no. 6, pp. 431-445; as presented by editor and historian Charles Washington Coleman, Jr.; and are reproduced here -- possible errors (mostly) included -- as printed there. I did, however, insert addtional footnotes of my own, and which appear at the bottoms of the page.

Apart from providing some scarce historical gossip, Pierce's correspondence is of especial fascination; yet less so for their military reporting, than for the references and vignettes they provide of the attitudes, outlook, and social life within Greene's most intimate military circle. Taken in all, the picture Pierce draws reveals the general's "family" and higher ranking Continental commanders to have, at least in some worthy and laudable measure, been a sometimes merry and occasionally joking ensemble of gentlemen -- including at one point staging among themselves a production of Shakespeare's "Much Ado About Nothing": an unusually genial view of general staff officers in the Revolutionary War rather seldom -- less so certainly than one might wish -- brought to light.

~~~***~~~

I.

Head Quarters on the High Hills of
Santee, July 20th, 1781

My dear Sir

So very uncertain is the passage of letters through North Carolina that I am fearful my last has met with the fate of the first entrusted to the care of the *planet-struck hero*. It was a plain narrative of facts without the tinsel of language or the puff of observation, and circulated entirely for your perusal and the

---

[240] Pierce evidently dabbled (at least slightly) in verse, including *The Year: a poem, in three cantos*, David Longworth (pub.), N.Y. 1813; and "An epitaph -- intended for the monument of major general Greene" ("by William Pierce, esq., of Savannah") found in *The American Museum*, for 1789 vol. 6, p. 86; that reads:

"Like other things, this marble must decay.
The cipher'd characters shall fade away,
And naught but ruin mark this sacred spot,
Where Greene's interr'd -- perhaps the place forgot;
But time, unmeasured, shall preserve his name,
Through distant ages shall roll on his fame,
And in the heart of every good man, raise
A lasting monument of matchless praise."

[241] Tucker was wounded in Lafayette's Virginia campaign.
~~~

information of a few friends. Both your letters I have been honored with, and feel an obligation for your attention. The last particularly gave me sensible pleasure, not only because it furnished me with a succinct account of matters in Virginia, but because it demonstrates a remembrance of one who feels himself singularly happy in your friendship. If a great sincerity of affection in return can make compensation for your extreme goodness we shall have our accounts settled without the trouble of a law-suit. I thank you for your satire on Lovelace,[242] and when the amorous move shall seize me I will pluck a laurel from the branch of Daphne to ornament the temples of your muse for the performance. But pray tell me, do you bathe in Hippocrene or Helicon?

I must now invite you to our climate, and conduct you through all the hardships, dangers and mutable fortunes of the campaign, from your leaving us at Ramsay's[243] Mill to the settlement of our army on the High Hills of Santee. To begin with our peregrination, -- give a free exercise to your imagination, and keep close to our heels. A few days after the discharge of the Virginia militia, the whole army was put in motion for Camden, with views either to draw Lord Cornwallis after us, or dispossess the British of all their interior posts in South Carolina. The principle which governed this manoeuvre was the same that actuated Scipio when he led the Carthagenian hero out of Rome to the plains of Zama. The manoeuvre was not so successful, as you will presently find; but the advantages were very great and very important. On the 20th of April we arrived before the town of Camden, and on the 25th had an action, which was lost by an unfortunate order from a gentleman in the Maryland line,[244] but the consequences being trifling, we soon collected and again moved towards them. On the 28th we crossed the Wateree, and soon after Lord Rawdon evacuated Camden and retired towards Charles Town. Previous to this move General Marion and Lieut. Colo. Lee had reduced Fort Watson with 70 or 80 prisoners and a quantity of military stores. The enemy at this time held a number of little posts which it was necessary for us to strike at. Sumpter was employed before Orangeburg; Marion and Lee against fort Motte; and the main army directed its course so as to cover our detachments, and to strike as circumstances might make necessary at fort Granby -- the two last standing on the beautiful river called the Congaree. Orangeburg and Motte soon fell and gave us possession of 300 or 400 prisoners. Colo. Lee was then sent on as the advance of the army to demand a surrender of fort Granby. His gallantry and elegant military address frightened the garrison into an immediate surrender. During these operations Lord Rawdon blew up the fortress at Nelson's ferry, and destroyed a great number of military stores. Two posts only were now left to strike at -- one in the district of 96,[245] the other at Augusta in the state of Georgia. The former was made the object of the main army, the latter was committed to the management of General Pickens and Colo. Lee, who obliged the garrison to surrender after a siege of twelve or fourteen days. On the 22d of May we paraded before the walls of 96, and on the 23d opened our trenches, continuing with little intermission to carry on our approaches until the 18th of June, when, receiving certain intelligence of Lord Rawdon's approach -- who had been reenforced with a large detachment of 2000 men from Ireland[246] -- we were induced to make a push, and by a coup de main to carry one redoubt on the west side of the town, and endeavor by a partial effort on the east to fix a lodgement on their principal work as a prelude to a general storm. Lee, who had joined us about 6 or 8 days before, commanded the attack on the right and succeeded. The British fled at his approach, and gave him possession of the work. Campbell[247] commanded the covering parties on the left, and was to strike the decisive blow in case the lodgement should be made. Two forlorn hopes were chosen to effect it -- one headed by Lieut. Duval of Maryland, the other by Lieut. Seldon of Virginia,[248] two elegant and gallant young gentlemen, who waded through a shower of musket balls and took possession of the enemy's ditch, but before they could pull down any of the parapet to make a secure lodgement they both got wounded and were forced to abandon the attempt. The wound of the former was slight, but that of the latter occasioned the amputation of his right arm. He bore the operation with great firmness, and though mutilated feels himself happy that he did his duty. There is a secret and sensible pleasure communicated to the feelings of

---

[242] [*Edit. Note.* Cavalier poet, Richard Lovelace (1618–1657); perhaps most remembered for his "To Althea from Prison," and, particularly appropriate for romantic-minded soldiers, his "To Lucasta, going to the Wars."]

[243] [*Edit. Note.* More correctly spelled "Ramsey's Mill."]

[244] [*Edit. Note.* Col. John Gunby of the Maryland; though it is a mater of controversy, then and now, whether he deserved any of the blame Pierce ascribes to him.]

[245] [*Edit. Note.* That is, fort Niney-Six, S.C.]

[246] [*Edit. Note.* Made up of the 3rd, 19th, and 30th regiments of foot.]

[247] [*Edit. Note.* Lieut. Col. Richard Campbell of Virginia.]

[248] [*Edit. Note.* Isaac Duval and Samuel Selden.]

a soldier when rewarded with the approbation of his general, that lifts him above his misfortunes and never fails to make him happy even in moments of the greatest difficulty. In this unsuccessful attempt we lost 40 men killed and wounded; no more, upon my honor, notwithstanding the pompous and ridiculous puff the enemy made in the Charles Town paper. There is a certain triflingness in the composition of a British officer that only can be accounted for by their extreme ignorance and uncommon share of foppery, and which discovers itself through the medium of all their publications and through the channel of every private letter to their friends. I must beg pardon for this digression, for I was insensibly led into it from reading some of their late publications, and which, by the bye, are as eminently false as any paragraph ever read in the Brussels Gazette or London Evening Post. The General finding that if he attempted to push his operations farther against 96, that altho' success would be certain, yet the expence of blood would have been so great as to have prevented his operating to more advantage in the field during the course of the campaign, he, therefore, declined the attempt for the solid purposes of rescuing the states of South Carolina and Georgia from the fetters of tyranny, and retired with the army over the Saluda River and took up his camp about 10 miles from 96. But we never raised siege until his lordship got within fifteen miles of us. We were pursued to the Enoree River. The British never could get the better of us in a single instance. Finding they were baffled, and that all hopes of bringing us to action were over, they returned to 96, divided their force, and moved to different points at the same time. Lord Rawdon marched for the Congaree and Colo. Cruger for Long Cane settlement. The object of the former was to establish a post on the Congaree, and that of the latter to destroy by plunder and fire all the means of subsistence left for the virtuous inhabitants of that settlement. In consequence of this manoeuvre General Greene moved with the army towards the Congaree and obliged his lordship to retire to Orangeburg without effecting his purpose. At the same time our light dragoons and a party of mounted infantry moved down the country to intercept Colo. Stewart, who was on his march with 400 British troops from Dorchester to join the army at Orangeburg, but in this we failed and a junction was formed without the loss of a man. The next step necessary to be taken was to form a junction of all our forces and attack his Lordship at Orangeburg. General Sumpter and Marion were ordered with the two regiments of cavalry to join us without loss of time; which being effected, we moved down and took a position within three miles of the town. Every preparation was made for the attack, but on reconnoitering the place we found the British so advantageously posted that it was impossible to get at them with any hopes of success. The town stands on the north branch of the Edisto upon a lofty eminence, with a bridge across the river, over which they could pass and possess a narrow neck of country in safety in case of a disaster, and at any time defend the bridge from any attack from us by a large brick prison strongly fortified within the town of Orangeburg, and placed within four hundred yards of the head of the bridge. His lordship had taken a position here to wait the arrival of Colo. Cruger, who had by this time returned from his plundering expedition, evacuated 96, and was on his march to join him. From the peculiar situation of the country through which Cruger passed, it was impossible to get at him, so that we were obliged to challenge Mr. Rawdon and endeavor to make him move out and fight us. But he refused it, and we were under the necessity of changing our plan of operation, and prepared to strike at the posts the enemy occupied below. Sumpter was ordered down to Monk's [Monck's] Corner, and Marion sent to Dorchester -- one within 30 miles of Charles Town and the other little upwards of twenty -- whilst Lieut. Colo. Lee, with his Legion, was to parade at the very gates of Charles Town, and cut off their supplies and convoys. The main army at the same time filed off, crossed the two rivers, Congaree and Wateree, and encamped on the High Hills of Santee on the 16th instant to refresh and get ready for future operations. The great object of the move into the lower country is to draw the enemy down to the seaboard and prevent their establishing posts in the upper country. The manoeuvre will most undoubtedly produce this consequence, or else they will lose all their troops at Monk's [Monck's] Corner and Dorchester, and hazard even the loss of Charles Town itself.

If we take a retrospective view of things, look at the variety of circumstances and consult the consequences of our operations during the campaign, it must be acknowledged that this army has done as much as ever was done by any body of men in any country or in any age. We began in January with the destruction of Tarleton, and continued fighting them in general action and skirmishes until the present moment, harrassing the enemy upon every occasion, and never letting an opportunity slip where we could possibly strike them to advantage. Their loss is generally acknowledged to be (including Tarleton's defeat, the battle of Guilford, and the battle before Camden) at least 4000 men. Ours has been considerable, but it fell chiefly on the militia. The difficulties we have gone through are almost incredible, for -- except the time we lay before 96 -- we have been constantly marching; and, upon the most moderate calculation, have travelled over 1500 or 2000 miles of this southern country.

Such scenes of desolation, bloodshed and deliberate murder I never was a witness to before! Wherever you turn the weeping widow and fatherless child pour out their melancholy tales to wound the feelings of humanity. The two opposite principles of whiggism and toryism have set the people of this country to cutting each other's throats, and scarce a day passes but some poor deluded tory is put to death at his door. For the want of civil government the bands of society are totally disunited, and the people, by copying the manners of the British, have become perfectly savage. This I hope will prove a lesson to Virginia, and teach her to guard against the consequences of British influence.

I should be ungenerous to pass over in silence the obligations we are under to the ladies of South Carolina, and particularly those of Charles Town, who have upon so many occasions given such distinguishing marks of patriotism and firmness. They take every occasion to testify their attachment to our cause, and express their good wishes for our success. When the union rose was established in honor of our al.iance with France, the ladies' shoes were ornamented with them as a compliment to the American officers; and they wore them publicly through the streets of Charlestown, until an impertinent puppy of a British officer ordered a negro fellow to kiss one of them as she was innocently walking out one morning. When General Greene arrived, they substituted green ribbons, which still continues to be the fashion. They have uniformly discovered their disgust to the British, and would never visit an assembly or concert given by them during the course of the last winter. When Mr. Balfour -- the commandant of Charles Town -- sent upwards of one hundred of the virtuous inhabitants on board the prison ship as victims of retaliation for the enormities (as he is pleased to express it) committed on the tories by our militia, the ladies accompanied them in a grand procession down to the wharf, took an affectionate leave of them, and bid them make the generous sacrifice with all that becoming dignity which is peculiar to the sentiments of the Whigs.

Having now written you a longer letter by a sheet and a half than ever I did to any body before, I think I may venture to conclude without incurring your displeasure. I must beg you to make my compliments acceptable to your lady, and assure General Lawson and Colo. Randolph[249] of my esteem. The General [Greene] often mentions you in terms of warm friendship, and desires you to accept his compliments in a very particular manner. All the [military] family with Carrington and Williams[250] join and send you a present of their good wishes. Fight on, my dear Colonel; keep up the *gaieté de coeur*, pluck laurels, and deserve the favors of your wife.

I am, my dear sir,
your most obt and very
humble servant,

Wm. Pierce, Jr.

P. S. -- Captain Eggleston[251] of the Legion a few days ago charged a body of British cavalry and took 1 Captain, 1 Lieut., 1 Cornet, and 45 privates with their horses and accoutrements complete.

Colonel Dart[252] begs you to accept his respects and pay his compliments to your lady and Mrs. Harleston. As the widow is a South Carolinian, I love her altho' I never saw her.

It is reported here that Colonel Innis[253] was seized with an *appoplectic fit* just as he was answering one of my letters, and that he died a few days after the stroke in a state of *repentance*. Let his departed soul be kept in *spirits* by the sound of his monumental inscription -- "Alas, poor *Bacchus*!"

---

249 [*Edit. Note.* Robert Lawson and Beverley Randolph, two commanders in he Virginia militia.]
250 [*Edit. Note.* Cols. Edward Carrington and Otho Holland Williams.]
251 [*Edit. Note.* Joseph Eggleston; and speaking in reference to an ambush actually carried out, not by Eggleston, but by Capt. James Armstrong of the Legion; on 3 July 1781 near Congaree Creek, S.C.]
252 [*Edit. Note.* John Sanford Dart, Greene's deputy clothier general.]

~~~***~~~

II.

Headquarters High Hills of Santee
July 23d, 1781

My dear Sir

I wrote you a long letter a few days ago, and -- unless it has met with some misfortune -- must be in your possession before you can possibly get this. Since the date of that letter, fresh matter has turned up to make this necessary. I mentioned to you that Sumpter, Marion, and Lee had gone below to strike at Dorchester, Monk's [Monck's] Corner, &c. &c. &c. The garrison at Monk's Corner fled but were pursued and left a number of men with all their baggage, about 200 horses, and four or five wagons. Several prisoners were taken at the Quarter House, near Charles Town; and a stroke would have been made at Dorchester, but Lord Rawdon moved down from Orangeburg with 1,000 men, and prevented the blow. The number of prisoners taken in the expedition amounts to about 150, including seven commissioned officers. The Legion upon this occasion, as upon every other, behaved with great gallantry. The militia also did their duty with honor.

We are gathering a respectable force together, and perhaps before many weeks shall pass away, we shall again be struggling in some bloody conflict. Mischief is a-brewing by the General, who keeps us in constant hot water, and never fails to make us fight.

[*note*. -- The remainder of this letter has been lost]

~~~***~~~

III.

Camden, South Carolina,
August 26th, 1781

Dear Sir

On the receipt of this letter you must do me the justice to say that I am a faithful correspondent. Ere this, all my letters must have reached you; and if so you stand indebted to me for two very long ones.

Our army -- after having taken a resting spell on the High Hills of Santee and in some measure recruited of its fatigues -- marched up to this place yesterday, and is now crossing the ferry here in order to approach the enemy on the Congaree River. Mischief is again on foot. Something must happen ere long, but I dare not hope for complete success yet awhile. If we recover South Carolina and Georgia, we shall be satisfied. Everything goes on well, and I hope will not be interrupted by any ill timed accident.

Skirmishes happen frequently, but no stroke of any consequence has been made since Sumpter's affair at Shoebricks [Shubrick's].

The enemy have, in open violation of all the laws of humanity and justice, hanged a Colonel Haynes[254] of our militia at Charles Town, a gentleman of a polite and finished character, with a large and extensive fortune. For this very extraordinary piece of conduct General Greene is determined to enforce the lex talionis upon some British officer.

I beg you make my respects to your lady, to Colo. Randolph, and to all the gentlemen who may do me the honor to enquire after me.

---

[253] [*Edit. Note*. Ostensibly Lieut. Col.Alexander Innes of the South Carolina Royalists Regt., seriously wounded at Musgrove's Mill and later convalescing in Charleston, is meant; however, Innes survived the war and exactly what "letters" to him Pierce speaks of here is uncertain.]

[254] [*Edit. Note*. Col. Isaac Hayne.]

I am, Sir, &c, &c.

~~~***~~~

IV.

Philadelphia, Oct. 20, 1781[255]

Sir

Permit me to introduce to your acquaintance and civilities, Mr. Crouch, a gentleman who is on his way to South Carolina. He merits all that can be said of a good character.

I have delivered my dispatches to Congress, and am happy to find that our bloody efforts meet with their approbation. The British fleet has sailed from New York, and ere this letter can reach you will, no doubt, be on the borders of Virginia.

My respects attend your lady, and believe me to be most sincerely your friend, &c, &c.

~~~***~~~

V.

December 28th, 1781

Hon'ble Sir

I consider it as a capital misfortune that I could not have had the honor of seeing you before I left Virginia; but as disappointments are incident to man, I must bear it as one.

I congratulate you on your late advancement, and should be happy to know by the first opportunity how many grades there are between a Lieutenant Colonel and a Privy Councellor.

I have the honor to be with the most h'ble submission, and with all due deference and respect.

Your most obedient and most humble servant, &c, &c.

(*Superscription*)
The Hon'ble St. George Tucker, Esqr.
Lieut. Colonel, and Member
of the Privy Council,
&c. &c. &c.
Virginia

~~~***~~~

VI.

[*Colonel Tucker's Reply*].

Respected friend

Thy letter entrusted to the care of thine and my friend Beverley Randolph was delivered unto me this day. The vain superscription thereon did but too well correspond with the writing which became visible when the folds of the paper were opened. Verily, my friend, I fear that thou hast conceived that I have

[255] [*Edit. Note.* Pierce was in Philadelphia delivering news of Eutaw Springs to Congress, As was customary in such instances of reported victory, the messenger was himself given an award of such kind. In Pierce's case, Congress on 29 October, 1781 "Resolved, that MajorGeneral Greene be desired to present the thanks of Congress to Captain Pierce, his Aide-de-Camp, in testimony of his particular activity and good conduct during the whole action at Eutaw Springs, (S. C), and that a sword be presented to Captain Pierce, who bore the General's dispatches, giving an account of the victory, and that the Board of War take order herein."]
~~~

drank of the fountain of vanity, and that my inward man is puffed up with the waters thereof, as the inconsiderate children of the world are puffed up with drinking of the juice of the grape or of that reed which produces the sugar.

Frances, the wife of my bosom, had told me that thou hadst visited our dwelling whilst I was journeying towards the east. Verily I was sore troubled that I was not at home when thou didst call; for I desired exceedingly to have communed with thee concerning many things. Much did I wish to see how that sword became thy thigh wherewith thou wert succinct by the rulers of the people. If thy future deeds shall merit equally of thy country thou mayst hope in due time to arrive at a seat in her private councils, seeing that thou art at this time in a probationary state by being admitted to participate of the private consultations of the rulers, of the armies.

That thou mayst fulfill this partial hope untainted with the vanities which contaminate the minds of youth is the sincere wish of thy friend in all good works.

(*Superscription*)
to
william pierce, the younger,
in the family of the ruler of
the southern army of america.

~~~***~~~

VII.

Head Quarters, Ponpon, South
Carolina, Feby. 6th, 1782

Dear Sir

Your Quaker[256] epistle of the 30th of December was delivered to me a few days ago by your brother, Dr. [Thomas Tudor] Tucker. It groaned exceedingly under the weight of the spirit, and had you not dated it at your ordinary dwelling place I should have sworn that you had written it in a religious fit at some Quaker meeting house, or at the council board upon Shockho Hill, at Richmond. But, be that as it may, I sincerely congratulate you on the discovery of your admirable talents for the character of Simon Pure. God grant that you may be happy under the influence of the spirit, and that all your days may roll away in pleasantness and peace.

Yes, sir, I was at Bizarre, and had the happiness to see Mrs. Tucker. It would have been an additional pleasure to me to have seen her much respected lord at home, and to have chatted with him about the roaring of cannon and bursting of shells at York. What a scene for a poet! I can easily conceive the delight of your spirits upon that occasion, and the infinite deal of pleasure which your poetic genius must have enjoyed. Every cannon ball no doubt was accompanied with a flight of figurative ideas, and the bursting of every shell served but to expand and scatter the sparks of an elevated fancy. I could wish to see some of your pieces since the siege. I am told that you have undertaken to equip and ornament the Goddess of Liberty in an American dress, disdaining with a becoming pride the fashions of Versailles, Madrid, and London. I doubt not your success, for it is universally acknowledged that you are a man of taste. But, by the way of digression, for I hate to dwell long on trifles, have you finished your chapter on noses, and calculated with a mathematical exactness the weight and velocity of that piece of shell which so wounded and hurt the extremity of yours on the 15th of October, 1781? Will you have occasion to repair to the promontory shortly? As these two interrogatories are interesting to me, I beg you will answer them catagorically. Think not that it is idle curiosity in me; be assured I esteem my friend too much not to wish his welfare.

And now, sir, to be serious, I will talk to you about the state of things in this country. I arrived at Headquarters on the 17th ultimo, and found our army situated in a fine, rich country, on the banks of

---

256 [*Edit. Note.* Greene himself, it will be recalled, was a Quaker.]
~~~

Ponpon. Our advanced posts and patroling parties covered the whole country between this and the Quarter House. The enemy were locked up in Charles Town. Except the capture of some few dragoons on both sides, nothing of any consequence has turned up since the opening of the New Year. Wayne has gone into Georgia, and by late information from that quarter he has confined the enemy to Savannah; so that unless they get strongly reinforced (which, by the bye, I expect will happen in a very little time), they will only have an opportunity of peeping at us through the key holes. The people of both these Southern States have passed through a variety of changes and a choice of difficulties and misfortunes. The human mind, perhaps, owing to the fluctuating state of politics for the last two years, has undergone the most strange and surprising revolutions that ever were known in any age or country. Interest, which is the prevailing passion with all mankind, has, by the nature of the war, appeared in so many different shapes, and such has been the various modes of pursuit, that the principles of men get warped in searching after a circumspect mode of conduct to avoid the censure of the contending parties. Some characters, indeed, withstood the storms unshaken, and sacrificed to the shrines of liberty and public honor their domestic ease and fortunes in the most magnanimous manner. Others, on the other hand, have been uniform in their opposition, and have favored the British measures through all the mutations of fortune. Such men appear to have a fixed principle for the governing rule of their conduct, and, although they stand confessed my enemies, yet I cannot help admiring and esteeming them. But I have the pleasure now to inform you that the people throughout the whole country appear to be our friends. They seem disposed to adopt any measures that may be thought well calculated for the public good. The Assembly of the State is now sitting at Jacksonborough, a little town within 30 miles of Charles Town. They are determined to exert every nerve to bring a regular force into the field, and search out all the means in their power to put their Continental line once more upon a respectable footing. An attempt was made by Colo. Laurens to pass a law for the raising of a negro corps, but it would not go down. The fears of the people started an alarm, and the force of interest annihilated the scheme.

But during the exertions of all the States both to the southward and the northward of you, pray what is Virginia about? My dear friend, she is so reproached by everybody that it is almost dishonorable to be a Virginian. Scarce a day passes but I have my feelings hurt, yet dare not say a word because I can find no excuse for her neglect. And yet she will tell you that she has done more than any other State; that she has exhausted her treasury, and spilt more lavishly the blood of her countrymen. Yes, Virginia has bled, it is true; her troops have fought with honor, and she had once a reputation that was envied and admired by all the continent, but time or something else has extinguished the fire of her military ardor, and all her former greatness has sunk into disgrace. Nothing can recover her from contempt but some bold and determined plan to establish her Continental line once more, for since the fall of Charles Town she has never had anything but detachments of eighteen months men in the field to keep the name of Virginia alive. Her officers have been loitering at home distressed in their circumstances, and quite ashamed of their situation for want of command. At this moment the Virginia troops in camp do not amount to more than sixty; and what has become of the party that was to march from Cumberland Court House heaven knows, for we do not. This is, in fact, the true picture of her situation without the aid of coloring or the force of exaggeration. Weep over it if you love your country, and use all your influence to mend and reform her manners.

Never was I more agreeably disappointed in any country as I have been in South Carolina. Indeed, I never saw anything to equal the fertility of it. Everything grows in the most luxuriant manner, and the rice swamps afford the finest soil in the world for the culture of *laurels*. And what adds to the beauty of the country, everybody lives well, the ladies are gay, and the gentlemen merry. Hospitality stands porter at every door and conducts you with an officious welcome to the board of plenty. I love the people most heartily. They possess a liberality of thinking that pleases me much; no religious prejudices, nor ill grounded pride, disturb the repose of society. They possess a dignity in their manner that is striking; but it is so softened with affability and freedom that you feel no restraint from their consequence or great riches. To their other good qualities they add the great virtue of gratitude. The Legislature of South Carolina have with an unanimous voice voted General Greene 10,000 guineas to be laid out as he may please in land and negroes. Is not that a very dignified present? A people so disposed will always meet with faithful services. Here will I hold.

For this long letter you must repay me with the news of Virginia and furnish me with Hayes' newspaper. I must entreat you, too, to send me a copy of your poem on liberty; and when you have time, that you will wait on Mrs. Tucker with my most respectful compliments, and tell Miss Hall and Miss Rind that I am their most obedient servant. The General, who really loves you, wishes you health and happiness.

I am, dear sir, &c.

~~~***~~~

VIII.

Head Quarters, So. Carolina, near
Dorchester, April 6th, 1782

My dear sir

I mean this as an apology for the absurd, disconnected scrawl by Col. Williams. It was written after dinner when the Madeira began to operate, and when I was scarcely able to think methodically. Added to this, Williams and others were dealing out such a torrent of wit that I was nearly overwhelmed. This is my excuse, and if you will forgive me I will promise never to write to you such another letter.

I am indebted to you many thanks for your last letter by Major Burnet;[257] but I wish you had given me more news and less of politics. I will not join you in the abuse of our public measures. I find the more the military complain, the more opposed are the civil to their interest. I will suppose that they will do the best they can for the general good. The Assembly are to meet immediately, and I dare say they will be impressed with the necessity of doing something for the recovery of their reputation. I wish they would take it into their heads to give each of General Greene's aids a good riding horse, at the same time that they present the General with a couple.

Virginia, I hear, is full of reports. One day we are beaten, the next, we are conquerors, and sometimes Charles Town is in our possession. Believe none of them, my dear sir, for they are all false. We have just taken a position at Bacon's Bridge, upon Ashley River, within two miles of Dorchester and a little upwards of twenty from Charles Town. This is meant as a challenge, and if I am not mistaken will shortly produce a fight. We have it reported with marks of authenticity that the enemy are making preparations for the field. But I think their efforts will be too feeble to ensure them any advantage from a general action; therefore, such an event is much to be wished for on our part. We have the best troops in the world to fight them with, and the whole army put such implicit confidence in General Greene that we shall struggle with great obstinacy to obtain a victory should they see fit to hazard a battle.

In the time between the date and the reception of this letter the die will probably be cast, and the fate of many a poor soldier be determined. Pray for us.

The loyalists in Charles Town and upon the islands within its vicinity are very much dissatisfied with their situation. They complain bitterly of their ill-usage, and desert every day to the American standard. The confiscation law and the act of amercement passed by the Assembly of this State have put the tories into a state of insanity, and all they want is the gibbet and halter to put an end to their existence. General Leslie has turned advocate for them, and reasons, in a letter to General Greene, on the injustice and impolicy of the law, with all the pomp and *ingenuity of a county court lawyer*. Indeed, the composition savors a good deal of the style of an academical exercise. The answer which the General returned to it was, in my opinion, proper. He informed His Excellency that he had no control over the civil power, and, therefore, could give no serious answer to it, but referred him to the executive of the State to have the matter properly inquired into and adjusted.

On Sunday last a large fleet with some broken corps, a number of women, and about 150 officers, sailed for New York. At the same time a fleet of empty transports sailed for Europe.

---

[257] [*Edit. Note*. Another of Greene's aides, Ichabod Burnet.]
~~~

In a little excursion which the enemy made a few days ago over Cooper River, they captured Judge Pendleton and Mayor Hym.[258] The former was going the circuit and the latter to George Town on public business.

Every part of Georgia is still in our possession except Savannah. The Indians who favored the British interest are very much dissatisfied with their friends, the Tories. Some have been put to death by them. Upwards of 300 of the Creeks who were on their way to Savannah -- finding themselves deceived have returned home disgusted and exasperated to the last degree.

Mrs. Greene arrived at camp about a week ago, after having experienced nearly as many difficulties as the famous Lady Ackland,[259] who accompanied her husband in Burgoyne's northern expedition in the campaign of '77. She is, however, recovered of her fatigue, and assumes an uncommon air of cheerfulness. Your civilities and Mrs. Tucker's extreme politeness are spoken of with great gratitude.

Morris and Pendleton[260] join me in their most respectful compliments to your lady, Miss Hall, and Miss Rind. Tell Colo. Randolph that I have the greatest friendship for him and shall write to him in two or three days.

I am, dear sir, &c.

~~~***~~~

IX.

Head Quarters, South Carolina
May 19th, 1782

My dear Friend
I wrote to you not long since, and as I do not mean to be ceremonious, I shall embrace this opportunity of writing to you again.

We have lately offered the enemy action, but they would not fight us. General Greene, at the head of the light infantry and all the cavalry of the army, went down to their lines, paraded in front of their works, and dined at Accabu without an insult.

The 19th and 30th regiments, consisting of about 1,000 men, were lately detached for Jamaica under the command of Brigadier General O'Hara.

By a handbill just sent out of Charles Town, we are informed of the defeat of Count de Grasse in the West Indies.[261] The action happened on the 12th ultimo, between the islands of Dominica and Guadaloupe. It was a bloody and obstinate conflict, and terminated with the loss of the Ville de Paris -- in which Count de Grasse -- and five other ships of the line, one of which was sunk. Admiral Rodney had 39 sail and Count de Grasse only 33. He had not formed a junction with the Spanish fleet. Both fleets are much damaged, and from the nature of the battle, it is one of the greatest that perhaps ever was fought. The celebrated action between Hawke and Conflans off Ushant in '59,[262] seems to be nothing to it. By Rodney's letter we learn that it lasted from seven o'clock in the morning to half-past six in the afternoon without a moment's intermission. I hope the victory will rather prove splendid than advantageous.

Adieu! make my respects to your lady and family, and believe me to be sincerely

Your friend, &c. &c.

---

[258] [*Edit. Note. Major* Edmund Hyrne?]
[259] [*Edit. Note.* Lady Harriet Acland , also spelled Ackland.]
[260] [*Edit. Note.* Capts. Lewis Morris, Jr. and Nathaniel Pendleton; two other of Greene's aides.]
[261] [*Edit. Note.* The Battle of the Saintes, 9-12 April 1782.]
[262] [*Edit. Note.* The Battle of Quiberon Bay, 20 Nov. 1759.]
~~~

P. S. Will you send me the paper with my letter respecting Colos. L. & W. [Lee & Washington].

~~~***~~~

X.

Headquarters, Ashley Hill
So. Carolina, July 10th, 1782

My dear sir

Every proof that I have of your friendship is like so many draughts of pleasure to my feelings. I thank you for your letter by General Moultrie. It gives me not a little satisfaction to find that your volatile powers are still awake. It is well for you that the scorching days of Phoebus are not as severe in Virginia as they are in South Carolina, or you would, as I do, feel too languid and indifferent to be gay. For my part I am burning at this moment. The mercury is up at 102, and I am sure more Promethean heat can be extracted from my body than would warm the constitution of an hundred Laplanders.

I join you most heartily in your address to heaven, and as I cannot help figuring to myself the appearance of your *sacerdotal fiz*, I feel even at this moment the enthusiasm of religion. The office of chaplain is at your service; the General desires me to inform you so. The birth of the Dauphin is to be celebrated, and you are to have the management of the *Te Deum*. By way of farce to the entertainment Shakespear's celebrated comedy of "*Much ado about Nothing*" is to be performed by the officers of the army.

We have been amused with a variety of reports lately respecting the evacuation of Savannah; but, depend upon it, as yet no such event has happened. Preparations are now making which indicate something of the sort; but there is so much finesse and cunning practiced in a military life that it is difficult to determine conclusively upon any circumstance.

General Wayne has lately had a successful skirmish with a party of Creek Indians near Savannah. Some few were killed and wounded on both sides. General Wayne has conducted himself since he has had the command in Georgia with great propriety; the people of that country seem very much pleased with him.

The sanguine part of our army think Charles Town will be evacuated very shortly; but I confess I can see no reason to indulge the opinion. The British seem well satisfied with their situation, but they do not appear as if they wished to risque anything. Our army has taken a position within 15 miles of the town and as yet continue very healthy.

For a detail of *minutia*, I take leave to refer you to Captain Carnes,[263] who will do me the honor of delivering this letter. He is a gentleman well informed, an agreeable companion and an elegant soldier. Take him by the hand, embrace him as a friend, and cherish him as a valuable acquaintance.

The General, Mrs. Greene, and the family join me in compliments to Mrs. Tucker, yourself and family. I am, sir, with great esteem, &c.

~~~***~~~

XI.

Head Quarters, South Carolina

July 14th, 1782

My dear sir

---

[263] [*Edit. Note.* Patrick Carnes of the infantry of Lee's Legion.]

An official dispatch has just arrived, announcing General Wayne to be in the town of Savannah. The enemy evacuated it on the nth, and are now on their way to Charles Town.

This is a fortunate event for the distressed State of Georgia, and of great political consequence to the United States.

Colo. Balfour, commandant of Charles Town, has been tried by a Court Martial for supplying the American army with clothing and military accoutrements;[264] but he was acquitted with honor. Poor fellow; I expect fate has fixed him the object of retaliation for the unfortunate Colo. Haynes.

Yours in haste, in business and confusion.

~~~***~~~

XII.

July 16th, 1782

Dear sir
I have enclosed for your amusement a poem written by Captain Barry[265] of the British army. I have not a comment to make. Read it and present it to Mrs. Tucker. Yours sincerely, &c.

~~~***~~~

XIII.

Head Quarters, South Carolina
Nov. 14th, 1782

My dear sir
Between two inclinations I am most delicately embarrassed. On one hand a very sincere friendship urges me to write; on the other, a pride -- which, I believe, belongs to me as a Virginian -- persuades me to be silent. Like Garrick between Thalia and Melpomene, I am at a loss to which I should yield. Nothing could place me in this situation, sir, but the neglect which you have shown to my three last letters. They must either have miscarried, or you are so immersed in business that you cannot take time to answer them. I will suppose the former, and once more endeavor to draw your attention to the burning regions of So. Carolina.

Our camp is still on Ashley Hill, on the south side of the river, and within fifteen miles of Charles Town. The enemy still keeps possession of the town, but are now making every preparation to abandon this country altogether, and I believe will evacuate the town by the first of next month. Our hopes and expectations are raised to the highest pitch. Bacchus will be highly honored, and every man seems already as nimblefooted as if he intended to dance off the campaign at his heels. The *sirve* [sic] has no longer any influence over his animal powers, but all is life, gaity and spirits. Suicide is advocated with great warmth; but every man seems too happy with his existence to sanctify the principle with the sacrifice of his life.

Just this moment I am honored with your letter by Mr. Osborne. I thank you very sincerely, as I feel a new flow of spirits in consequence of it. Your criticism on Barry's poem, I dare say, is just; but as I know very little of metrical composition, I shall not tell you what my private observations were. Barry is one of those kind of characters who acts contrary in every instance to common sense, and would fain make the world believe by attempting *great things* he is a *great man*. But nature, who denies him the bounty of genius, is seen slumbering through all his performances; and the goddess, as if she were ashamed of herself, often seeks retirement behind the curtain of obscurity.

---

[264] [*Edit. Note*. This remark, of course, is apparently made in jest; with Balfour having been made infamous among the Americans for his harsh severity toward the "rebels."]
[265] [*Edit. Note*. Henry Barry (1749-1822) Deputy Adjutant General of the British Army, and Secretary to Balfour.]

The General and Mrs. Greene desire their respects to Mrs. Tucker and yourself. Pendleton, Carrington, and Burnet join me in compliments to yourself and family.

I am, dear sir, &c.

P. S. I will write to you more fully when we get to Charles Town.

~~~***~~~

XIV.

Head Quarters, South Carolina
December 15th, 1782

My dear sir

The enemy have at length evacuated Charles Town, and our army is now in possession of it. The event, so long expected has completed the honors of the southern army.

If we look back to that period when General Greene first took the command in this department, and compare the low condition of the American army with the powerful superiority of the British, we shall be surprised at the rapidity of our success.

In December, '80, when the General joined the army at Pedee, he had only 12,000 men,[266] including hospital patients, convalescents, and detachments. The enemy, according to the Parliamentary Register, had (including their several garrisons) upwards of 15,000 disciplined troops, with an able and active general at their head.

The operations commenced in January with great and unexpected success on our side. Morgan, with an handful of men, defeated Tarleton near the Pacolet. This gave spirits to our army and a spring to the hopes of the people in North Carolina, which Lord Cornwallis observing, wisely pushed forward with great fury, obliged us to retire, and by throwing the whole country into one general alarm totally effaced the consequences of the victory. General Greene collected a body of militia on his retreat, and with a force that was constantly fluctuating between the numbers of two and four thousand gave his lordship battle at Guilford Court house. We lost the field, but we gained the advantages of a victory. In a few days the enemy retreated and we pursued them to Deep river, from whence they filed off towards Wilmington, and we pushed forward into South Carolina. On the 12th of April, we arrived before Camden; on the 15th the enemy sallied and gave us battle at Hobkirk Hill, defeated us, and obliged us to retreat. But we soon recovered, pressed down again, and compelled them to evacuate their works. Fort Watson, Fort Motte, Fort Granby, Orangeburg and Augusta, with all their garrisons, fell one after the other. They blew up their works at Nelson's Ferry, abandoned Dorchester, left Ninety-six after a severe siege of twenty-one days, in which a most enormous quantity of blood was spilt; and on the 8th of September we fought them at the Eutaw Springs in a general action, and gained a glorious victory. We next compelled them to quit Stono, to evacuate Savannah, and yesterday to give up Charles Town, by which General Greene has ended a glorious and honorable command in the southern world.

The Carolinians, so long oppressed, are now likely to enjoy the blessings of peace and tranquility. One universal joy seems to reign through the whole country. The fetters of tyranny are taken off, and the goddess of liberty seems to be the companion of every one. I feel myself exceedingly interested in the happiness of these people. They are hospitable, generous and polite.

---

266 [*Edit. Note.* This 12,000 and the subsequent 15,000 are a bit mystifying; as neither Greene nor Cornwallis ever had any such numbers under their command in the south. Possibly they are a transcription error, and what instead was originally meant was 1,200 and 1,500 -- roughly the numbers of the opposing sides in Continentals and Regulars respectively (and not counting militia) prior to the arrival of Maj. Gen Alexander Leslie's reinforcement that joined Cornwallis in Jan 1781.]
~~~

I beg you, sir, to make my respects to your lady and family, and believe me to be with sincere esteem, your most obt. sert.

Wm. Pierce, Jr.

"THE PROUDEST DAY"

Historical novelist Charles G. Muller's
Dramatization of the Battle of Lake Champlain, Sept. 11, 1814.

The life of American author Charles G. Muller's (1897-1978) spanned an active and varied career, and that was not infrequently tied in with some form of public service, whether with respect to the military, politics, or charity. Starting out as a naval aviator in World War 1, he subsequently served in the American Red Cross ambulance unit in France; later traveled around the globe; wrote for several newspapers and other publications as well as published a number of books; worked on navy training films in World War II; served as a consultant and in public relations, and became noticeably involved in several charitable organizations, including becoming a vociferous advocate for Alcoholics Anonymous and acting as chairman for the Greater New York Fund, one of the predecessors of the United Way. Today, Cornell University, his alumni, houses an extensive collection of his works and papers.

Muller might, as Alexandre Dumas thought himself, be deemed more a novelizing historian than a historical novelist. And among his writings of historical fiction, he penned two novels about the War of 1812, namely: *The Proudest Day: Macdonough on Lake Champlain* (1960), and *The Darkest Day: 1814, The Washington-Baltimore Campaign* (1963). Though the latter is still in print, somewhat strangely the former, a masterwork of its kind, is not so; nor has been for a very long time. Personally, I find this puzzling as I frankly treasured *The Proudest Day*[267] since I first read it decades ago (by way of a paperback), and I never knew a novel that could better compete so well with a *first rate* movie when it came to excitement and drama; though it must be understood most of the thrills in *Proudest Day* occur in the climactic battle scenes. The rest of the novel focuses chiefly on Macdonough's trying and patient efforts to build up and keep together his squadron. And yet these earlier chapters are engrossing and historically informative in their own right in preparing the moral groundwork and necessary preliminaries to the grand finale.

This said, in the way of an excerpt, I reproduce here the battle itself as an encouragement and to readers to seek out the rest of the book, and which in addition to the aforesaid "lead-up" includes map, chart, diagram, footnotes, other unusual and particular historical research material, bibliography, and finally a not little touching, and what will for some be surprising, epilogue.[268]

~~~***~~~

Ch. 8

Sunday, September 11h, 1814, dawned clear and cloudless over Lake Champlain. Along her quiet shores gulls soared screaming harsh and loud at the wooded mountains taking on their red and gold autumnal foliage. On just such a day, almost exactly two years ago the Commodore recalled, Lieutenant Thomas Macdonough had first come to the lake.

Outside Cumberland Head British flagship *Confiance* hove to, he used the night's favoring wind to lead the enemy squadron up from Isle la Motte, her topsails rising new and white over the Head.

To *Saratoga*, a messenger brought news of a gig rowed close to Plattsburg Bay with a British officer who examined the American fleet's disposition and put back to the frigate. That would be Captain Downie.

At 7 A.M. Downie's fleet stood for Plattsburg Bay. Bending to their oars, the Cumberland Head guard boat crew drove toward their own fleet with signals flying.

---

[267] First published by John Day Co. in 1960.

[268] For such as are novices on the subject of sailor's jargon, and which no doubt is most people, the six key terms to learn to save you much confusion in reading nautical accounts, whether fictional or historical, are:

* Bow vs. Stern: Front end vs. rear end.

* Larboard (or Port) vs. Starboard: "Port," like "left," as in *to one's left*, has four letters; and therefore you also know that "Starboard" means "right" or *to the right*.

* Leeward vs. Windward. The direction the wind *is going* (Lee) versus the direction it is *coming from* (Wind), but usually expressed of course in terms of *blowing*.

For a more complete glossary, see: *The Seaman's Friend: A Treatise on Practical Seamanship* (1841) by Richard Henry Dana, Jr., author of that timeless nautical classic *Two Years Before the Mast* (1840).
~~~

The American vessels beat to quarters and prepared for action.

On *Saratoga's* quarterdeck at 8 A.M., with his officers in their best uniforms, the Commodore watched the British sail into sight at a distance of six miles. His heart pounded. Around his spyglass, his hand felt moist, clammy. He had waited a long time for this moment.

He controlled his voice. "Midshipman Bellamy," he requested softly, "will you have the kindness to make the agreed signal?"

Original signal officer of the Lake Champlain quadroon, Aze proudly sent the Commodore's message flags up to Saratoga's masthead for all the fleet to see:

IMPRESSED SEAMAN CALL ON EVERY MAN TO DO HIS DUTY.

Solemnly then, while the crew looked on from their stations, the Commodore read to his officers the ancient church prayer for those about to engage in battle on the sea. "...stir up Thy strength, O Lord, and come and help us, for Thou givest not always battle to the strong, but canst save by many or by few...through Jesus Christ, our Lord."

Lieutenant Gamble reported final preparations completed. The flagship stood ready; splinter screens rigged, pumps in order, and the chief caulker provided with hemp plugs, sheet lead, nails, and slings for lowering men overside to close shot holes and pound fresh caulking into *Saratoga's* hull.

Forty yards inshore from the line of ships stood the squadron's ten gunboats, two off *Eagle's* larboard bow, two between the brig and *Saratoga*, three between the flagship and *Ticonderoga*, three between the schooner and *Preble*. Kept in position by their sweeps, their guns could fire a continuous barrage of twelve-, eighteen-, and twenty-four pound balls between the vessels when the enemy came up.

It took the British another hour to round Cumberland Head and move in for battle.

A sloop came first, filled with civilians and, as the Commodore's glass revealed, many women. Spectators, so sure of British victory that they dared enter the bay! The shores too, as far as he could see were lined with spectators, but Americans all. Keeping well to leeward, the sloop stood down toward Crab Island.

First of the fighting ships around the Head came *Finch* (once American sloop *Growler*), followed by *Confiance*, *Linnet*, and *Chubb* (Lieutenant Sydney Smith's former *Eagle*.)

Hauling up to the wind in a line abreast, formidable, they lay to for their lateen-rigged galleys to sail up and join them. The Commodore got his first look at *Confiance*.

Eleazer Williams' rangers had described her accurately -- enormous, in a class with ocean-going *Constellation*. She carried the gundeck of a heavy frigate, a spacious topgallant forecastle on which she mounted four heavy carronades and a long twenty-four pounder on a circle, and a poop deck mounting two heavy carronades. *Confiance* could fire a seventeen-gun broadside of 432 pounds; *Saratoga's* broadside metal weighed 414.

Passing to leeward of their ships, the British gunboats formed a line abreast. At 9 A.M. the quick beat of their drums calling to quarters wafted across the bay, and ships and galleys, close-hauled on the starboard tack, moved en masse against the American squadron.

The Commodore watched warily.

Leading, *Chubb* stood well to windward of *Eagle*, at the head of the American line. *Linnet's* course would bring her too, on *Eagle's* bow.

Confiance advanced like a great dog intent on making short work of a small opponent, laying her course to fetch a position ahead of *Saratoga*; far enough ahead to concentrate her fire power on the American, with the American unable perhaps to bring her full broadside to bear.

Finch and the British gunboats stood for *Ticonderoga* and *Preble*.

The enemy strategy came clear. In the van, *Chubb* and *Linnet* aimed to take on *Eagle* while the British flagship set about subduing the American flagship; in the rear, *Finch* and the gunboats sought to reduce *Ticonderoga* and *Preble*.

His heart pounding again, the Commodore patiently waited. The enemy had no sea room to turn his line; nor could they double it, because of the shoal off Crab Island. If they continued to stand in, bows on, he could spring his ship to meet them. If they anchored, they must anchor within reach of his carronades, since he had not left them enough water between his line and Cumberland Head to stay out of range. Come on, and be damned!

The American sailing masters already had set about springing their vessels to bear broadside on the oncoming squadron, and the Commodore knew that the quiet, before-battle expectations that filled *Saratoga* also filled the other ships as they awaited the flagship's signal to open fire.

While the enemy inched closer, the Commodore continued to contain his impatience. A few minutes more -- to bring them within effective range. A few yards more…

Four guns blasted in rapid succession. Fire flashed and black smoke almost enveloped *Eagle*. Bob Henley! Ignoring orders to wait, he had opened fire -- short! The Commodore's fingers clenched tight around his glass. He --

Of a sudden *Saratoga's* forecastle resounded with raucous crowing as Cookie's chickens, startled by *Eagle's* booming broadside, flew hysterically out of the galley. Explosive shouts of laughter immediately followed as a single cockerel, perched on the foremast bell and flapping its wings, cried angrily. While the Commodore, officers, and seamen stood entranced in spite of themselves, the furious bird flew into the starboard rigging and continued to flap and crow lustily.

"It's Oscar!" Lieutenant Gamble shouted above the uproar. "That's giving 'em what for Champ!"[269]

Like fog before a gale, tension departed *Saratoga* in laughter and the crew spontaneously cheered the bird's favorable augury.

Eagle's continuing fire now reached *Chubb*; the moment had come.

Bending over his favorite gun, the Commodore turned its breech-sight thumbscrew for the elevation needed to reach *Confiance*, lined it up with the fixed reinforce sight, and touched a match to the vent. As the twenty-four pounder trumpeted the Commodore's deadly welcome to the enemy, Aze Bellamy had the "close action" flag run up, signaling the American fleet to open fire.

Even before *Saratoga's* guns blasted their first broadside, a terrific roar swept the flagship's deck. For Captain White Young's soldiers, acing as marines in her tops, shouted down that the Commodore's greeting shot, landing near *Confiance's* outer hawshole, had torn the length of her deck and carried away her wheel.

At the same moment -- 9:30 A.M. -- rockets, balls, and shells rose over the Saranac River, and Prevost began his attack on Macomb.

Ch. 9

The Commodore kept in close touch with all parts of his ship, using Aze Bellamy and *Saratoga's* many midshipmen for messengers. As action developed, he would dispatch them with instructions to other vessels. Glass to eye, he swept the bay.

The British advanced steadily and, he forced himself to admit, gallantly, in their attempt to achieve a commanding positions. He also appreciated, however, how greatly they underestimated his gunners' ability to annoy and how grievously they'd overestimated their own power to endure. *Confiance* could take little more punishment from *Saratoga's* guns; their fire had already cut away the enemy flagship's larboard anchor and spare anchor in the larboard forechains, hanging by the stoppers ready to let go.

The wind lightened as the Commodore held his glass on the frigate to check the havoc of his guns, and he saw *Confiance* turn into the wind a quarter of a mile and let go a kedge. But in bringing up with her starboard bower, the frigate fouled the kedge, which became useless.

While Downie strained to secure *Confiance*, letting her halyards run and hauling up her courses, *Chubb* and *Linnet* still stood in, farther to windward; until *Linnet* fired a broadside at *Saratoga* from a favorable position forward of *Eagle's* beam and dropping anchor. *Chubb*, kept under way, and *Finch*, with gunboat support, fetched up abreast of *Ticonderoga*.

The handsome manner in which Downie secured *Confiance*, withholding his fire until he had performed his duty, prepared the Commodore in part for the sheet of fire that flashed him warning of the frigate's first broadside.

Directly *Saratoga* at principally from twenty-four pound, double-shotted British guns leveled to pointblank range and coolly sighed, almost eight hundred pounds of iron smashed into the American flagship with a blow that seemed to lift her out of the water. *Saratoga* writhed like a stricken whale. Splinters flew over her deck like matchwood. Shrieks and cries arose into the rigging as torn bodies fell beside her guns in pools of blood.

---

[269] [*Editor's Note.* As well as being here both historical and humorous, the event of a bird seemingly auguring the outcome of a fight is ironically reminiscent of something from a battle scene in Homer or Vergil.]

From the quarterdeck, the Commodore made out nearly half his ship's complement lying dead, wounded, stunned. He watched dazed men slowly pick themselves up. Then he counted forty wounded and dead by the *Confiance's* single broadside.

While midshipmen directed the lowering of the wounded to the cockpit, the disposal of dead away from the guns, and the remounting where possible of dismounted cannons, the Commodore saw blood pour from the gundeck's scuppers like rain off a roof. And from the bow Midshipman Montgomery brought him word of Peter Gamble, killed without a scratch while sighting a gun, dead from the force of a split quoin driven against his chest.

The Commodore sent George Beale, the purser, to help Lieutenant Vallette with his own and Gamble's gun divisions. And until Downie might try to board *Saratoga*, he sent the acing marines down from the tops -- where their muskets could not reach the enemy -- to join Captain Youngs and his other soldiers wherever the guns could use them.

The flagship resumed her fire. The battle became a steady carronading.

Twenty minutes from the opening of the blast, *Eagle* threw a crippling broadside into *Chubb* at the head of the line. The British sloop drifted down on *Saratoga*, in the line of fire between American ship and British frigate. From *Saratoga's* bow, George Beale put a shot into hapless *Chubb* and she immediately struck her colors.

"Take possession," the Commodore ordered Midshipman Platt.

From *Saratoga's* launch, Plattsburg's native son threw the prize line. When he crossed the flagship's stern, towing the captured sloop to the mouth of the Savanac, he shouted: "Nearly half her crew killed and wounded, sir." Then: "Captain Downie reported dead on *Confiance*."

In the ensuing hour, the battle raged up and down the line.

Eagle and *Saratoga* bore the full brunt of every gun *Confiance* and *Linnet* could bring to bear. Encouragingly, *Eagle* sent word that Joseph Smith, wounded early in the action, had returned to duty, as had Lieutenant Spencer.

On *Ticonderoga*, Lieutenant Cassin walked the taffrail in a hail of canister and grapeshot to direct a fire that time and time again beat back the British galleys, some of which reached within a boat's length of the schooner. Finding the schooner's matches useless for firing the division's guns, Midshipman Paulding fired them by flashing his pistol at their vents. Superintending duty with the springs, Lieutenant Stansbury disappeared from the bulwarks forward, cut in two by round shot.

Making no effort to hide his excitement, Midshipman Monteath returned from the end of the line with news that Lieutenant Budd and his veterans, using springs and two sweeps out of *Preble's* stern port, had kept the sloop broadside to bear on *Finch* and four British galleys -- each with more men than *Preble's* entire crew! Boatswain Rose was dead. Aware that he could expect no assistance from the fleet, Budd intended to keep pouring grape into the enemy, get his mainsail on, and go close aboard *Finch*.

Meanwhile the American gunboats had accounted for two enemy galleys sunk. Maintaining their order of battle, these aggressive bantams kept pitching into the frigate.

Black smoke, pouring up from both fleets, clouded the azure sky. Cannon balls -- many in deliberate ricochet fire -- skipped over the millpond-smooth water between the ships, to enter their target near the waterline. Hurtling chain shot tore through the rigging, to make decks shambles. Hot shot from *Confiance's* furnace set fires on board *Saratoga* and burned her spanker boom over the quarterdeck.

To the Commodore it became increasingly apparent, however, that *Confiance's* blasts lost power with each roar of the frigates great guns. Whereas her firs and second broadsides had cut to pieces nearly all the hammocks on the American flagship rail, succeeding fire came higher and higher, cutting the standing rigging farther from the deck. Elevation of *Confiance's* guns got higher with each broadside -- and less effective! Having once leveled them to pointblank range, her gunners no doubt failed properly to replace their loosened quoins at each discharge.

But *Saratoga's* death toll rose with every broadside. Midships, Cookie sprawled -- long, lean, awkward as in life -- beside a silenced carronade. His wife, stepping over his body, carried powder to the next active gun. And before the Commodore looked away, a ball entered the gun port where she reached the powder to the loader, drove her across the deck, and left her crumpled form dangling on the larboard rail -- head down, dead. His cheek gashed, the boy John Kortz had barely enough clothes left intact to cover his nakedness.

Returning from captured *Chubb*, anchored under the shore forts, Midshipman Platt's launch took an eighteen-pound shot in her middle that sank her and left the officer and his crew struggling in the water among the doughty galleys. But when, waterlogged, he finally made *Saratoga*, Platt brought the good news that General Macomb had repulsed Prevost's every effort to cross the Saranac fords and bridges.

Macomb still stood firm. So he intended to stand -- with his regulars, with Mooers' New York militia, with Strong's Vermont volunteers.

As guns on both sides went out of action, dismounted and disabled by direct hits or flying splinters, the cannonading gradually decreased. Disposing available midshipmen in a desperate effort to remount some of the ship silenced starboard guns, the Commodore found *Eagle* bearing down on his larboard under topsails, to anchor by the stern between the flagship and the schooner.

Henley again! Leaving *Saratoga* at the head of the line to bear the brunt of *Confiance's* and *Linnet's* combined fire!

In the new position, Henley could bring his fresh larboard guns to bear on either *Confiance* or *Linnet*. But by winding the brig he could have done that without leaving his assigned station. Was he trying to fight this battle all by himself, with his own strategy? What a time to throw away the squadron's agreed-on plans and play lone wolf! [270]

Aze Bellamy shouted in the Commodore's ear: "Lieutenant Vallette reports all starboard batteries are out of action, sir, with the exception of a single carronade amidships and your long gun."

The Commodore listened as if in shock. Two pieces left on the flagship to fire. One lieutenant left alive to help fight *Saratoga*. Her crew decimated; her decks covered with their blood and mangled bodies.

He saw Aze looking at him strangely. What did the boy perceive in his face? The end? But Aze could not discern that! No thought of defeat had ever held him...no before this moment. Why now? Curious, he should finally think of losing. Curious, too, he should remember at this particular time that old saw about men not winning wars -- only one man! What do you say now, Grandfather Denning?

He shook himself, blinked his eyes. Had he been hit? His head cleared. He pointed amidships to *Saratoga's* venerable old sailing master with Joe Barron splicing a torn rope tackle on the last remaining carronade.

"Tell Mr. Brum to wind the ship a once," he barked at Aze. "Have Mister Vallette prepare the larboard batteries while we get the ship around."

The Commodore bent over the long gun again. As he sighted, the carronade amidships also fired; but its navel bolt broke and the cannon hurtled off its carriage to plunge down the main hatch. In almost the same instant, a round shot from the enemy's frigate struck the spanker boom over the Commodore's head, cut the boom -- already weakened by *Confiance's* hot-shot fire -- and hurled the savage spar down on the long twenty-four pounder. Gun and Commander smashed to *Saratoga's* deck together.

Ch. 10

Holding his breath, Commodore Macdonough struggled in a swirling, submerging vortex. His arms lashed out, to push him up for air. He heard voices. If only he could hold out a few seconds more, two or three seconds, just one, just..."

Opening his eyes he looked up. Torn rigging and shattered yardarms cut a ragged pattern across the smoke-fogged sky. Aze Bellamy's agonized face hung over him. A subbed of the spanker boom pinned his legs to the deck. The long gun canted at a preposterous angle.

"He's coming to!"

Aze's shout filled the quarterdeck, and many hands finished clawing away the debris and helped the Commodore groggily to his feet.

---

[270] [*Edit.* MacDonough, in his all too brief autobiography, states: "The Saratoga lost many of her men. The Ticonderoga behaved with much gallantry. The Eagle, Capt. Henley, quitted the station assigned her and took another where she kept up her fire upon the enemy. As regards this act of this vessel I am decidedly of opinion her duty was to remain in the station assigned her as long as it was possible for her to maintain it. Her list of killed and wounded would show what necessity she was under to change her station, and even that evidence of her disability was made up of the names of wounded men, in part, who had only been so scratched or slightly hurt as not to merit the name of wounded, among whom was Lt. Spencer, who had a bit of skin by some means torn off his face. Mr. Loomis (I believe acting master) earnestly requested that his name should not appear among the wounded. Had the Saratoga been beaten, as, during the latter part of the action she had the fire of the brig which had been opposed to the Eagle upon her, as well as that of the Confiance, the day in all human probability would have fallen to the enemy. The smaller vessels did their duty." See *Life of Commodore Thomas MacDonough, U.S. Navy* (1909) by Rodney MacDonough, p. 30.]

Brum and the seamen, having clapped on the hawser that led to starboard quarter, had brought the flagship's stern up over the kedge. But there she hung, with not enough wind to force her bows around.

Taking advantage of *Saratoga's* silent guns, *Confiance* had attempted also to wind so that her unused starboard guns could come into action. Her fire had temporarily ceased.

But as *Saratoga* rode by her kedge and a line bent to a bight in the stream cable, her stern under *Linnet's* raking broadside, the British brig kept up a steady and well-directed fire on the American flagship's afterdeck.

Still groggy, swaying unsteadily on his feet, the Commodore surveyed the crisis. In an instant he saw that *Saratoga* lay helpless until Sailing Master Brown could wind her; under *Linnet's* broadside now; under *Confiance's* also, as soon as the frigate got around.

"Send the men forward until our guns bear," he ordered. Then he, too, took shelter.

As Sailing Master Brum roused with his men on the line to the stream cable, the minutes mounted. Linnet's devastating round shot poured into the defenseless flagship. And before the Commodore's eyes, a crashing ball catapulted a mast splinter across the deck to rip every stretch of clothing off the laboring Philip Brum -- everything but the large blue-and-white kerchief around his neck.

Without a word the stark-naked sailing master yanked a frayed lanyard off the nearest disabled gun and with it tied his handkerchief at his waist, like an apron. Without a word he went back to rousing with his men on the line to the stream cable, and slowly the ship wound until her aftermost gun bore on *Confiance*.

Ordering Vallette to man the single gun, and prepare to man the next as it came to bear, and the next until *Saratoga's* full broadside roared in unison, the Commodore of a sudden saw that *Confiance* failed longer to wind. Hauling on her springs merely forced her ahead. The British frigate could not bring her starboard broadside to bear!

So Commodore Macdonough came to the moment he'd waited so patiently for! The moment to make up for all the humiliations of two frustrating years! Where was Joe Barron? He would relish this.

"Mr. Barron's in the cockpit," said Aze, "critically injured sir, sir."

Joe, too!

Then, like a genie's gift, the Commodore's victory vanished. For his flagship would go no farther around; but stood nearly end on to the wind, with only two fresh guns in play. Linnet raked her with a deadly fire. He'd fought -- and lost!

With his fine plans destroyed, with his dead lying mutilated on the deck, with all but two of his guns out of action, Commodore Macdonough stood alone. No matter how much his men loved him, no matter how loyal, how patriotic, brave, self-sacrificing, in this crisis they could do nothing to help. When he fell, they fell with him.

His mind filled with tumbling pictures, words, remembered faces...Ann in her wedding gown, Hank de Koven dropping the ring, little Augusta and Charlotte Shaler pertly carrying their flower-girl violets...Grandfather Denning's "In you hands, son, our whole national future may rest."

He looked down at his hands, almost black with powder and smoke. In these hands, his hands...Well, Grandfather Denning, at least we all tried. We did our best. We...

What tricks did his mind play? And why at a time like this? Beat? Why, they'd just got the enemy where they wanted him! He seized a trumpet from the hands of a midshipman

"Mr. Brum!" he ordered. "The hawser from the kedge to the larboard quarter...get it forward under the bows. Then pass it aft to the starboard quarter."

With an exultant shout as he comprehended, the naked sailing master put his men on the hawser. Slowly, powerfully, they brought it under the bows and walked it aft.

Under Brum's skillful guidance the seamen sprang the ship's stern to the westward...until all her guns lined up to present a fresh and complete broadside to *Confiance* and *Linnet*!

The Commodore's heart bounded. With every blast of *Saratoga's* guns and carronades, with every belch of flame and smoke that hurled 414 pounds of deadly Vergennes and Charlestown iron at the British frigate, his heart bounded higher. From his head caulker came reports that the flagship, hulled more than fifty times, remained tight. Bless Noah Brown!

For two hours the battle had waxed and waned. For two hours the advantage had gone from one side to the other. Now the fighting had reached its peak.

Saratoga's guns continued to pour metal into the frigate.

Eagle and most of the galleys, still in battleline, kept up their galling fire on *Confiance* and *Linnet*.

But five British gunboats opened an attack on *Ticonderoga*, seeking desperately to close and board. As earlier in the fight, however, the Commodore saw Steve Cassin leap on the schooner's rail to direct her fire against the enemy galleys. Thank you God for men like Steve!

At the end of the line, *Preble*, having made a stretch inshore to avoid pursuing British galleys which had poured immense quantities of grape into her, now stood down for *Finch* which, aground off Crab Island, still flew her British colors.

From *Saratoga's* midships the crash of a ball and a shout brought the Commodore's gaze to a still tumbling officer and the shot box on which he had stood. The Commodore's heart sank. But Elie Vallette slowly, deliberately picked himself off the deck, examined his shredded uniform, shrugged his Gargantuan shoulders, and resumed charge of his guns.

John Vance, the Narragansett Indian whose torn canvas shirt and trousers bared much of his coppery skin, showed his beautifully white and even teeth as he called out to Aze Bellamy, near the Commodore: "Lookee," Vance shouted, pointing to a gaping cannon-ball cut in the glazed that he wore above the single gold ring in his right ear, "how the damned John Bulls have spoiled my hat!"

Then the Indian bent to the deck, picked up John Roberts, the gentle carpenter who took such pride in lifting pork brine with his fingers grasping only the top of the rim of the barrel, and tenderly carried the limp giant below to have his shattered leg cut off. In the blood-splashed cockpit, the Commodore knew, Surgeon Briggs already had amputated Midshipman Graham's.

Through the battle smoke, the Commodore saw not a mast in either squadron that could stand to make sail on. Lower rigging, nearly all shot away, hung down as if just placed over the mastheads.

With Aze Bellamy beside him, the Commodore watched his flagship's destructive fire reduce the enemy's frigate to utter helplessness. Her masts and yards looked like bunches of broken matches; her sails -- so freshly white and new two hours ago -- like bundles of old rags What kept her riddled hull afloat?

Still girdled in part by his neckerchief and ready at a command to spring *Saratoga* to any position, Sailing Master Brum could not contain himself. "I've been on Lake Erie, Commodore," he shouted admiringly, "and as a tactician and a fighter, Perry can't be mentioned in the same breath with you, sir!"[271]

At that moment *Confiance* struck.

The instant her colors came down, Brum went to work -- springing the flagship to bear on *Linnet*. And the Commodore, looking quickly around for an officer to go on board surrendered *Confiance*, fastened on Captain Youngs in the ships waist. Smiling as he recalled Alex Macomb's perennial protests over supplying the navy with solders, he turned to Aze.

"Ask Captain Youngs," he said, "to do me the honor of taking possession of the frigate."

With *Saratoga's* fire concentrated on the British brig, Aze resumed his place at the Commodore's side. Their powder-blackened faces complemented their begrimed hands and torn uniforms. Aze beamed, unable to conceal the swelling of his heart.

"Sir," he said, "this is a proud day for the United States."

He looked at the Commodore with the concentrated devotion of their two years together on the Lake. "I think this is the proudest day our country ever saw."

Aze's own proud smile remained as a last sixteen-pound ball from the enemy's *Linnet* flew over the flagship's rail. Decapitating the midshipman, the ball drove Aze's severed head into the Commodore's chest, and as the Commodore hurtled across the quarterdeck he heard an anguished cry fill the ship before he crashed, unconscious and covered with blood, into a starboard scupper.

With seaman shouting that their Commander had been killed, George Beale raced to the quarterdeck. Lifting Aze's head from the shaken Commodore's hands, the purser turned away from the tears he saw.

On his feet, Commodore Macdonough grimly watched *Linnet* wilt under *Saratoga's* withering fire. Fifteen minutes later, he saw her strike. *Finch* -- and all the British galleys still afloat -- immediately struck too.

Of sixteen British ensigns that had flown over Plattsburg Bay two hours and a half ago, not one remained aloft. Not a single enemy vessel remained to contest the ascendancy of Lake Champlain.

---

[271] [*Edit. Note.* This comment vindicating the conclusions of subsequently digested history is altogether out of place, as well as being in conflict with the already well-built up mood and vantage point of the contemporary participants. For this reason it should be marked as the only portion of this battle chapter that shows an overt lapse of aesthetic judgement on author Muller's part. Such retrospective assement of what is *then* supposed to be transpiring is best left to a more formal historical presentation, and here, as historical fiction, too much acts as a rhythm distracting and believability impeding anachronism.]

In his mind the Commodore framed a message to William Jones [Madison's Secretary of the Navy]: "The Almighty has been pleased to grant us a signal victory…"

When Midshipman Monteath brought news from General Macomb that Prevost's army had started a precipitous retreat toward Canada, the Commodore still paced back and forth on the flagship's quarterdeck, still gazing at his powder-blackened hands, tinged with red.

"Thank you," he said to the young midshipman as he would have spoken to Aze. He continued to look at his hands as he added: "Our country's thanks to all you boys…you men…for evicting our enemy…" His voice trailed…"forever, I hope."

A Stroll Through
THE AMERICAN MUSEUM *(1787-1792)*

Magazines, that is monthly or quarterly publications, first made their appearance in North America in about the middle of the eighteenth century, and were usually modeled on, if not outright copies of, the British *Gentleman's Magazine* (est. 1731) and *London Magazine* (1732). And if patriotism was not a sufficient incentive for American magazine publishers and editors to attempt something original, charges of imitation, cultural subservience, and absence of literary creativity in the America were. At best, and this was rare, American magazines of this period rarely stayed afloat for more than a few years; with a little over a year, if that long, being the more common length of a run. If literary historians of later generations are to be believed, these efforts were largely failures; and there is no lack of sneering.[272] Although the overall picture these pundits present is a bit distorting and rather unfair, their harshness is not without grounds. For wading through such volumes of periodicals today is no easy task and requires immense patience of a casual reader. Eighteenth century magazines have been characterized as a collection, storehouse, assemblage of widely diverse topics and literary forms, and there is so much there -- with topics ranging from botany, biology, agriculture, history, poetry and literature, politics, government, foreign affairs, cooking, psychology, trade, numismatics, medicine, zoology, entomology, manufacturing, meteorology, oceanography, etc. -- that perusing them is not unlike trying to digest elegant chaos.

This said, if one *is* willing to spend the time digging -- *mining* being an very apt metaphor for this kind of endeavor -- odds are good that efforts of finding something interesting and unique will not go unrewarded. Furthermore, too often overlooked is that the magazines were an effective way of edifying the public and bringing them in on subjects otherwise left to specialists, and to that extent they were an incalculably important educational and democratizing influence. By means of them, everyone came together to learn and discuss, and in this way they aided in informing and, in turn, empowering people to become better citizens at a peculiarly pivotal juncture in Western history. At the same time, in doing so they provided the necessary trial and error needed for publishers to learn how to improve them, and thus laid the foundation for later higher quality journals, such as *The Port Folio*, *The Analectic Magazine* and *The North American Review*. On the other hand, it might be argued that aiming towards higher standards may have resulted in leaving much of the previous and more democratic readership behind.

American magazines published in the eighteenth century, predominantly (but not exclusively) issued out of Boston, Philadelphia, and New York, and came under titles such as: *The Massachusetts Magazine*; *The American Apollo*; *The United States Magazine*; *The Universal Asylum and Columbian Magazine*; The *Worcester Magazine*; *The Monthly Magazine and American Review*; *The American Moral and Sentimental Magazine*; *The National Magazine*, and *The Omnium Gatherum*. But possibly the most prominent is Irish-Catholic immigrant and Philadelphia publisher Mathew Carey's (1760-1839) *The American Museum, or Repository of Ancient and Modern Fugitive Pieces, &c. Prose and Poetical*. Along with *Columbian Magazine*, the *Museum* was the most popular American periodical of its brief day; though with most of its contents being simply re-published pieces and articles distilled from and that first appeared separately in newspapers.

Making the acquaintance of Benjamin Franklin in Paris, Carey also met there Lafayette who recommended him to George Washington; while providing him with funds to buy him a printing press in America. After landing here and setting himself up in Philadelphia in 1784, Carey commenced a fairly successful and lasting career as a publisher; while, as *both* idealist and savvy propagandist, playing an important role in helping to shape the consciousness and values of the fledgling nation; overtime putting forth from his printing house numerous books (including a dictionary), pamphlets, maps; as well as several periodicals.

---

[272] e.g., "No literary periodical before 1800 deserves individual consideration." William B. Cairns, *The Cambridge History of American Literature*, vol. II (1918), edited by Trent, et al., ch. XX "Magazines, Annuals, and Gift-books, 1783-1850," p. 162.
"Because material was not copyrighted, editors saw no reason not to fill their pages with *pirated* selections." (my italics) Michael T. Gilmore, *The Cambridge History of American Literature,* vol. 1: 1590-1820 (1994), Bercovitch editor, p. 559.

The following are some gleanings of his *American Museum,* and which, it is hoped, will serve to prove, or at least aid in proving, my aforesaid thesis for those willing to demand of themselves requisite patience with such magazines: *"Seek and ye shall find."*

~~~***~~~

Account of the life and death of Edward Drinker, who died on the 17th of November, 1782. In a letter to a friend: said to have been written by Benjamin Rush, M. D. &c.

EDWARD DRINKER was born on the 24th of December 1680, in a small cabin, near the present corner of Walnut and Second-streets, in the city of Philadelphia. His parents came from a place called Beverly, in Massachusetts-bay. The banks of the Delaware, on which the city of Philadelphia now stands, were inhabited, at the time of his birth, by Indians, and few Swedes and Hollanders. He has often talked to his companions of picking whortle berries, and catching rabbits, on spots now the most improved and populous of the city. He recollected the second time William Penn came to Pennsylvania, and used to point to the place where the cabin stood, in which he and his [Quaker] friends, that accompanied him, were accommodated, upon their arrival. At twelve years of age he went to Boston, where he served his apprenticeship to a cabinet-maker. In the year 1745, he returned to Philadelphia, with his family, where he lived until the time of his death. He was four times married, and had eighteen children, all of whom were by his first wife. At one time of his life, he sat down, at his own table, with fourteen of his children. Not long before his death, he heard of the birth of a grandchild, the fifth in succession to himself.

He retained all his faculties till the last year of his life. Even his memory, so early and generally diminished by age, was but little impaired. He not only remembered the incidents of his childhood or youth*[273], but the events of the latter years; and so faithful was his memory to him, that his son has informed me he never heard him tell the same story twice, but to different persons, and in different companies. His eyesight failed him, many years before his death, but his hearing was uniformly perfect and unimpaired. His appetite was good till within a few days before his death. He generally eat [sic] a hearty breakfast of a pint of tea or coffee, as soon as he got out of his bed, with bread and butter in proportion. He eat likewise at eleven o'clock, and never failed to eat plentifully at dinner of the grossest solid food. He drank tea in the evening, but never eat any supper; he had lost all his teeth thirty years before his death, which was occasioned, his son says, by drawing excessive hot smoke of tobacco into his mouth; but the want of suitable mastication of his food, did not prevent its speedy digestion, nor impair his health. Whether the gums, hardened by age, supplied the place of his teeth in a certain degree, or whether the juices of the mouth and stomach became so much more acrid by time, as to perform the office of dissolving the food more speedily and more perfectly, I know not, but I have often observed, that old people are most disposed to excessive eating, and that they suffer fewest inconveniencies from it. He was inquisitive after news in the last years of his life. His education did not lead him to increase the stock of his ideas any other way. But it is a fact well worth attending to, that old age, instead of diminishing, always increases the desire of knowledge. It must afford some consolation to those who expect to be old, to discover, that the infirmities to which the decays of nature expose the human body, are rendered more tolerable by the enjoyments that are to be derived from the appetite for sensual and intellectual food.

He was remarkably sober and temperate. Neither hard labour, nor company, nor the usual afflictions of human life, nor the wastes of nature, ever led him to an improper or excessive use of strong drink. For the last twenty-five years of his life, he drank twice every day of toddy, made with two table spoons full of spirit, in half a pint of water. His son, a man of fifty nine years of age, told me that he had

[273] * [*Footnote in the original by, presumably, Benjamin Rush*] It is remarkable that the incidents of childhood and youth are seldom remembered or called forth until old age. I have sometimes been led, from this and other circumstances, to suspect, that nothing is ever lost that is lodged in the memory, however it may be buried for a time by a variety of causes. How often do we find the transactions of early life, which we had reason to suppose were lost from the mind forever, revived in our memories by certain accidental fights or sounds, particularly by certain notes or airs in music? I have known a young man speak French fluently, when drunk, that could not put two sentences of that languge together, when sober. He had been taught perfectly, when a boy, but had forgotten it from disuse. The countess of L—v—l was nursed by a Welsh woman, from whom she learned to speak her language, which she soon forgot, after she had acquired the French, which was her mother tongue. In the delirium of a fever many years afterwards, she was heard to mutter words which none of her family or attendants understood. An old Welsh woman came to see her, who soon perceived that the sounds which were so unintelligible to the family, were the Welsh language. When she recovered, she could not recollect a single word of the language she had spoken in her sickness. I can conceive great advantages may be derived from this retentive power in our memories, in the advancement of the mind towards perfection in knowledge (so essential to its happiness) in a future world.
~~~

never seen him intoxicated. The time and manner in which he used spiritous liquors, I believe, contributed to lighten the weight of his years, and probably to prolong his life. "Give wine to him that is of a heavy heart, and strong drink to him that is ready to perish with age, as well as with sickness. Let him drink and forget his sorrow, and remember his misery no more."

He enjoyed an uncommon share of health, insomuch that in the course of his long life, he never was confined more than three days to his bed. He often declared, that he had no idea of that most distressing pain, called the head ach[e]. His steep was interrupted a little in the last years of his life with a deduction on his breast, which produced what is commonly called the old man's cough.

The character of this aged citizen was not summed up in his negative quality of temperance; he was a man of the most amiable temper; old age had not curdled his blood; he was uniformly chearful and kind to every body; his religious principles were as steady, as his morals were pure. He attended public worship about thirty years in the rev. dr. Sproat's church, and died in a full assurance of a happy immortality. The life of this man is marked with several circumstances which perhaps have seldom occurred in the life of an individual; he saw and heard more of those events which are measured by time, than have ever been seen or heard by any man since the age of the patriarchs; he saw the same spot of earth, which at one period of his life was covered with wood and bushes, and the receptacle of beasts and birds of prey, afterwards become the seat of a city not only the first in wealth and arts in the new, but rivalling in both, many of the first cities in the old world. He saw regular streets, where he once pursued a hare; he saw churches rising upon morasses, where he had often heard the croaking of frogs; he saw wharfs and warehouses, where he had often seen Indian savages draw fish from the river for their daily subsistence, and he saw ships of every size and use, in those streams, where he had often seen nothing but Indian canoes; he saw a stately edifice, filled with legislators, astonishing the world with their wisdom and virtue, on the same spot, probably, where he had seen an Indian council fire; he saw the first treaty ratified between the newly confederated powers of America and the ancient monarchy of France, with all the formalities of parchment and seals, the same spot, probably, he once saw William Penn ratify his first and last treaty with the Indians, without the formality of pen, ink, or paper; he saw all the intermediate stages through which a people pass, from the most simple to the highest degree of civilization. He saw the beginning and end of the empire of Great-Britain in Pennsylvania. He had been the subject of successive crowned heads, and afterwards became a willing citizen of a republic; for he embraced the liberties and independence of America in his withered arms, and triumphed in the last year of his life, in the salvation of his country.[274]

~~~***~~~

The origin of tobacco: by dr. Franklin.

A Swedish minister took occasion to inform the chiefs of the Susquehannah Indians, in a kind of sermon, of the principal historical facts on which the christian religion is founded; and particularly the fall of our first parents, by eating an apple. When the sermon was over, an old Indian orator replied, "what you have told us is very good; we thank you for coming so far to tell us those things you have heard from your mothers; in return, we will tell you what we heard from ours.

"In the beginning, we had only flesh of animals to eat; and if they failed, we starved; two of our hunters, having killed a deer, and broiled a part of it, saw a young woman descend from the clouds, and seat herself on a hill hard by. Said one to the other, 'It is a spirit, perhaps, that has smelt our venison; let us offer some of it to her.' They accordingly gave her the tongue; she was pleased with its flavour, and said, 'your kindness shall be rewarded; come here thirteen moons hence, and you will find it.' They did so, and found, where her right hand had touched the ground, maize growing: where her left hand had been, kidney-beans; and where her back-side had been, they found tobacco." The Swedish minister was disgusted. "What I told you, said he, is sacred truth: yours is fable, fiction, and falsehood." The Indian, offended in his turn, replied, "My friend, your education has not been a good one; your mothers have not done you justice; they have not well instructed you in the rules of common civility. You saw that we, who understand and practice these rules, believed all your stories; why then do you refuse to believe ours? We believe, indeed, as you have told us, that it is bad to eat apples; it had been better that they had all been made into cyder; but

[274] Vol. II, no. 1, for July 1787, pp. 73-75.
~~~

we would not have told you so, had you not disbelieved the method by which we first obtained maize, kidney-beans and tobacco."[275]

~~~***~~~

An oration, delivered at the north church in Hartford, at the meeting of the society of the Cincinnati, July the fourth, 1787, in commemoration of the independence of the united states. By Joel Barlow, esq. Published by desire of said society.

Mr. President, gentlemen of the society, and fellow citizens,

ON the anniversary of so great an event, as the birth of the empire in which we live, none will question the propriety of pasting a few moments in contemplating the various objects suggested to the mind by the important occasion. But at the present period, while the blessings, claimed by the sword of victory, and promised in the voice of peace, remain to be confirmed by our future exertions -- while the nourishment, the growth, and even the existence of our empire depend upon the united efforts of an extensive and divided people -- the duties of this day ascend from amusement and congratulations to a serious patriotic employment.

We are assembled, my friends, not a boast, but to realize -- not to initiate our national vanity by a pompous relation of past achievements in the council, or in the field; but, from a modest retrospect of the truly dignified part already acted by our countrymen -- from an accurate view of our present situation -- and from an anticipation of the scenes that remain to be unfolded -- to discern and satirize the duties that still await us, as citizens, as soldiers, and as men.

Revolutions in other countries have been effected by accident. The faculties of human reason and the rights of human nature have been the sport of chance and the prey of ambition. And when indignation has burst the bonds of slavery, to the destruction of one tyrant, it was only to impose the manacles of another. This arose from the imperfection of that early stage of society, which necessarily occasioned the foundation of empires on the eastern continent to be laid in ignorance, and which induced a total inability of foreseeing the improvements of civilization, or of adapting the government to a state of social refinement.

I shall but repeat a common observation, when I remark, that on the western continent the scene was entirely different, and a new task, totally unknown to the legislators of other nations, was imposed upon the fathers of the American empire.

Here was a people thinly scattered over an extensive territory, lords of the soil on which they trod, commanding a prodigious length of coast and an equal breadth of frontier -- a people habituated to liberty, professing a mild and benevolent religion, and highly advanced in science and civilization. To conduct such a people in a revolution, the address must be made to reason, as well as to the passions. And to reason, to the clear understanding of these variously affected colonies, the solemn address was made.

A people thus enlightened, and capable of discerning the connexion of causes with their remotest effects, waited not the experience of oppression in their own persons; which they well knew would render them less able to conduct a regular opposition. But in the moment of their greatest prosperity, when every heart expanded with the increasing opulence of the British American dominions, and every tongue united in the praises of the parent state and her patriot king, when many circumstances concurred, which would have rendered an ignorant people secure and inattentive to their future interests -- at this moment the eyes of the American Argus were opened to the first and most plausible invasion of the colonial rights.

In vain were we told, and perhaps with the greatest truth and sincerity, that the monies levied in America were all to be expended within the country, and for our benefit; equally idle was the policy of Great Britain, in commencing her new system by a small and almost imperceptible duty, and that upon very few articles. It was not the quantity of the tax, it was not the mode of appropriation, but it was the right of the demand, which was called in question. Upon this the people deliberated: this they discussed in a cool and dispassionate manner: and this they opposed, in every shape that an artful and systematic ministry could devise, for more than ten years, before they assumed the sword.

This single circumstance, aside from the magnitude of the object, or the event of the contest, will stamp a peculiar glory on the American revolution, and mark it as a distinguished era in the history of

[275] Vol. II, no. 1, for July 1787, p. 86.
~~~

mankind; that sober reason and reflexion have done the work of enthusiasm, and performed the miracles of gods. In what other age or nation has a laborious and agricultural people, at ease upon their own farms, secure and distant from the approach of fleets and armies, tide-waiters, and stamp-masters, reasoned before they had felt, and, from the dictates of duty and conscience, encountered dangers, distress, and poverty, for the sake of securing to posterity a government of independence and peace? The toils of ages and the fate of millions were to be sustained by a few hands. The voice of unborn nations called upon them for safety; but it was a still small voice, the voice of rational reflexion. Here was no Cromwell to inflame the people with bigotry and seal, no Caesar to reward his followers with the spoils of vanquished foes, and no territory to acquire by conquest. Ambition, superstition, and avarice, those universal torches of war, never illumined an American field of battle. But the permanent principles of sober policy spread through the colonies, reused the people to assert their rights, and conducted the revolution.

It would be wandering from the objects which ought to occupy our present attention, again*[276] to recount the numerous acts of the British parliament which compose that system of tyranny designed for the subjugation of America: neither can we indulge in the detail of those memorable events, which marked our various stages of resistance, from the glooms of unsuccessful supplication, to the splendor of victory and acknowledged sovereignty. The former were the theme of senatorial eloquence, producing miracles of union and exertion in every part of the continent, till we find them preserved far everlasting remembrance in that declaratory act of independence, which gave being to an empire, and dignified the day we now commemorate; the latter are fresh in the memory of every person of the least information. It would be impertinence, if not a breach of delicacy, to attempt a recital of those glorious achievements, especially before an audience, part of whom have been distinguished actors in the scene, others the anxious and applauding spectators. To the faithful historian we resign the task -- the historian, whom it is hoped the present age will deem it their duty, as well as their interest, to furnish, encourage, and support.

Whatever praise is due for the task already performed, it is certain that much remains to be done. The revolution is but half completed. Independence and government were the two objects contended for: and but one is yet obtained. To the glory of the present age, and the admiration of the future, our severance from the British empire was conducted upon principles as noble, as they were new end unprecedented in the history of human actions. Could the same generous principles, the same wisdom and unanimity be exerted in effecting the establishment of a permanent federal system, what an additional lustre would it pour upon the present age! a lustre hitherto unequalled; a display of magnanimity, for which mankind may never behold another opportunity.

Without an efficient government, our independence will cease to be a blessing. Shall that glow of patriotism and unshaken perseverance, which have been so long conspicuous in the American character, desert us at our utmost need? Shall we lose sight of our own happiness, because it has grown familiar by a near approach? Shall thy labours, O Washington, have been bestowed in vain? Hast thou conducted us to independence and peace, and shall we not receive the blessings at thy hands? Where are the shades of our fallen friends? and what is their language on this occasion? [Joseph] Warren, [Richard] Montgomery, [Hugh] Mercer, [David] Wooster, [Alexander] Scammel, and [John] Laurens, all ye hosts of departed heroes! rich is the treasure you have lavished in the cause, and prevalent the price you have paid for our freedom. Shall the purchase be neglected? the fair inheritance lie without improvement, exposed to every daring invader? Forbid it, honour; forbid it, gratitude; and oh, may heaven avert the impending evil.

In contemplating the price of our independence, it will never be forgotten, that it was not entirely the work of our own hands; nor could it probably have been established, in the same term of time, by all the blood and treasure that America, unassisted, was able to furnish for the contest. Much of the merit is due, and our warmest acknowledgments shall ever flow to that illustrious monarch, the father of nations and friend of the distrest -- that monarch who by his early assistance taught us not to despair; and who, when we had given a sufficient proof of our military virtue and perseverance, joined us in alliance, upon terms of equality; gave us a rank and credit among the maritime nations of Europe; and furnished fleets and armies, money and military stores, to put a splendid period to the important conflict.

Where shall we find language to express a nation's gratitude for such unexampled goodness and magnanimity? my friends, it is not to be done with language. Our sense of obligation for favours received from heaven, is best expressed by a wise improvement. Does Louis ask for more? and can duty be satisfied

[276] [*Footnote in the original*] * This oration was preceded by the lecture of the act of independence; which, by an order of this state society, is in future to make part of their public exercises at every annual meeting.

with less? Unite in a permanent federal government; put your commerce upon a respectable footing; your arts, and manufactures, your population, your wealth and glory will increase; and when a hundred millions of people are comprised within your territory, and made happy by your sway, then shall it be known, that the hand of that monarch assisted in planting the vine, from which so great a harvest is produced. His generous heart shall exult in the prospect: his royal descendants, fired by the great example, shall imitate his virtues: and the world shall unite in his praise.

Here shall that pride of the military character, the gallant FAYETTE, find his compensation for a life of disinterested service; whose toils have not ceased with the termination of the war; and whose successful endeavours to promote our interest, in commercial and political arrangements, can only be equalled by his achievements in the field. How will the posterity of that nobleman, and that of the other brave officers of his nation, who have fought by your sides, on reviewing the American history, rejoice in the fame of their fathers; nor even regret the fate of those who bled in so glorious a field! An acknowledgement of the merits of Rochambeau and Chastellux, D'Estaing, De Grasse, De Barras, and the other heroes of the French army and navy -- affection to the memory of our brethren and companions who have bled in our battles -- reverence to the advice of our illustrious commander in chief, and of all those sages and patriots who have composed our councils, from the time of the first congress to the present moment -- honour to our worthy creditors in Europe -- a regard to the conduct of the imperial sovereigns of Russia and Germany, who evince to the world that they revere the cause of liberality and human happiness, in which we drew the sword -- a respect to the memory of the venerable Frederic of Prussia, whose dying hand put the signature to a treaty of commerce with the united states, upon the most liberal principles that ever originated in a diplomatic council -- a sacred regard to ourselves and to all posterity -- and, above all, a religious gratitude to our heavenly Benefactor, who hath hitherto smiled upon our endeavours -- call upon us, in the language of a thousand tongues, for firmness, unanimity, and perseverance, in completing the revolution, and establishing the empire.

The present is justly considered an alarming crisis: perhaps the most alarming that America ever saw. We have contended with the most powerful nation, and subdued the bravest and best appointed armies: but now we have to contend with ourselves, and encounter passions and prejudices, more powerful than armies, and more dangerous to our peace. It is not for glory, it is for existence that we contend.

Much is expected from the federal convention now sitting at Philadelphia: and it is a happy circumstance that so general a confidence from all parts of the country is centred in that respectable body. Their former services, as individuals, command it, and our situation require, it. But although much is expected from them, yet more is demanded from ourselves.

The first great object is to convince the people of the importance of their present situation: for the majority of a great people, on a subject which they understand, will never act wrong. If ever there was a time, in any age or nation, when the fate of millions depended on the voice of one, it is the present period in these states. Every free citizen of the American empire ought now to consider himself as the legislator of half mankind. When he views the amazing extent of territory, settled, and to be settled under the operation of his laws -- when, like a wise politician, he contemplates the population of future ages -- the changes to be wrought by the possible progress of arts, in agriculture, commerce, and manufactures -- the increasing connexion and intercourse of nations, and the effect of one rational political system upon the general happiness of mankind -- his mind, dilated with the great idea, will realize a liberality of feeling which leads to a rectitude of conduct. He will see that the system to be established by his suffrage, is calculated for the great benevolent purposes of extending peace, happiness, and progressive improvement to a large proportion of his fellow creatures. As there is a probability that the system to be proposed by the convention may answer this description, there is some reason to hope it will be viewed by the people with that candour and dispassionate respect which is due to the importance of the subject.

While the anxiety of the feeling art is breathing the perpetual sigh or the attainment of so great an object, it becomes the strongest duty of the social connexion, to enlighten and harmonize the minds of our fellow citizens, and point them to a knowledge of their interests, as an extensive federal people, and fathers of increasing nations. The price put into their hands is great, beyond all comparison; and, as they improve it, they will entail happiness or misery upon a larger proportion of human beings, than could be affected by the conduct of all the nations of Europe united.

Those who are possessed of abilities or information in any degree bore the common rank of their fellow citizens, are called upon by every principle of humanity, to diffuse a spirit of candour and rational enquiry upon these important subjects.

[John] Adams, to his immortal honour, and the timely assistance of his country, has set the great example. His treatise[277] in defence of the constitutions, though confined to the state republics, is calculated to do infinite service, by correcting thousands of erroneous sentiments arising from our inexperience; sentiments which, if uncorrected in this early stage of our existence, will be the source of calamities without measure and without end. Should that venerable philosopher and statesman be induced to continue his enquiries, by tracing the history of confederacies, and with his usual energy and perspicuity, delineate and defend a system adapted to the circumstances of the united states -- I will not say he could deserve more from his distrest country, but he would crown a life of patriotic labours, and render an essential service to the world.

While America enjoys the peculiar felicity of seeing those, who have conducted her councils and her battles, retire, like Cincinnatus, to the humble labours of the plough, it must be remembered, that she there expects a continuance of their patriotic exertions. The society of the Cincinnati, established upon the most benevolent principles, will never lose sight of their duty, in rendering every possible aid, as citizens, to that community which they have defended, as soldiers. They will rejoice, that, although independence was the result of force, yet government is the child of reason. As they are themselves an example of the noblest effort of human nature, the conquest of self, in obeying the voice of their country, and exchanging the habits, the splendor, and importance of military life, for domestic labour and poverty -- they will readily inculcate on others, the propriety of sacrificing private and territorial advantages, to the good of the great majority, the salvation of the united states.

Slaves to no party, but servants of the whole, they have wielded the sword of every state in the union, and bled by the side of her sons. Their attachments are as extensive as their labours. Friendship and charity, the great pillars of their institution, will find their proper objects, through the extended territory; and seek the happiness of all.

While we contemplate the endearing objects of our association -- and indulge in the gloomy pleasure of recollecting that variety of suffering which prompted the sympathetic soldier to institute this memorial of his friendship -- fraternal affection recalls the scene of parting; and enquires with solicitude the fate of our beloved companions.

Since the last anniversary, the death of general [Robert] Howe has diminished the number of our brethren, and called for the tribute of a tear. With some of the foibles, incident to human nature, he possessed many valuable accomplishments. His natural good understanding he had embellished with considerable attention to polite literature. As a soldier, he was brave -- as an officer, attentive to discipline; he commanded with dignity and obeyed with alacrity; and whatever talents he possessed, were uniformly and cheerfully devoted to the service of his country.

But a few weeks previous to that period, the much lamented deaths of [Tench] Tilghman and [Alexander] M'Dougall were successively announced, and the tidings received, with a peculiar poignancy of grief. What citizen of the American empire does not join the general voice of gratitude, when contemplating the merits of those distinguishing officers; and swell the tide of sympathy with his bereaved country, when deprived of their future assistance? They were ornaments to the states in which they lived, as well as to the profession in which they acquired their glory.

Amiable and heroic Tilghman! short was the career of thy fame: but much hast thou performed for thy country. Of thee shall it ever be remembered, that no social virtue was a stranger to thy breast, and no military achievement too daring for thy sword. While we condole with thy afflicted father for the loss of so dear a son, permit the tear of friendship to flow for its own bereavement: and as oft as the anniversary of this day shall assemble the companions of thy life, to rejoice in the freedom of their country, they shall mingle a sigh to thy lasting memory, and bewail thy untimely fate,

Untimely also was the death of the brave and patriotic M'Dougall. Though many years were worn away in his unremitted labours for the public safety -- though his early and decided exertions against the claims of Great Britain had an essential influence in determining the conduct of the province in which he resided -- though he was the nerve of war, the wisdom of council and one of our principal supporters in the acquest [sic] of independence -- yet these but shew us the necessity of such characters in establishing the blessings of the acquisition. While it shall require the same wisdom and unshaken fortitude, the same patience and perseverance, to rear the fabric of our empire, as it did to lay the foundation -- patriotism and valour in sympathetic affection will bemoan the loss of M'Dougall.

---

[277] [*Edit. Note. A Defence of the Constitutions of Government of the United States of America* (1787).]

Happy would it be for America, thrice happy for the feelings of sorrowing friendship, could the list of our deceased companions be closed even with the names of those worthy heroes. But heaven had bestowed too much glory upon the life of the favourite Greene, to allow it a long duration.

My affectionate auditory will anticipate more than can be uttered, in the melancholy duty of contemplating his distinguished excellence. To any assembly that could be collected in America, vain would be the attempt to illustrate his character, or embellish the scene of his exploits. It is a subject to be felt, but not to be described. To posterity, indeed, it may be told, as an incentive to the most exalted virtue and astonishing enterprise, that the man, who carried in his native genius all the resources of war, and the balance of every extreme of fortune -- who knew the advantages to be derived from defeat, the vigilance of military arrangement, the rapidity and happy moment of assault, the deliberate activity of battle, and the various important uses of victory -- that the man who possessed every conceivable quality of a warrior, was, in his public and private character, without a foible or a fault; that all the amiable as well as heroic virtues were assembled in his soul: and that it was the love, of a rational and enlightened age, and not the stupid stare of barbarity, that expressed his praise.

The map of America may designate the vast extent of conquered country recovered by his sword: the future traveller, in the southern stares, may be pointed, by the peasant, to the various regions containing monuments of his valour and his skill; where, amid his marches and countermarches, his studied retreats and his rapid approaches, every advantage, given to the enemy, was resumed with ten-fold utility and certain conquest. The historic muse, as a legacy to future ages, may transmit with heroic dignity the feats of her favourite chief: but who shall transmit the feelings of the heart -- or give the more interesting representation of his worth? the hero will remain; but the man must be lost.

The grief of his bereaved consort, aggravated by the universal testimony of his merit, we hope will receive some alleviation from the ardent sympathy of thousands, whose hearts were penetrated with his virtues, and whose tears would have flowed upon his hearse.

But we will not open afresh the wounds, which we cannot close. The best eulogium of the good and great is expressed by an emulation of their virtues. As those of the illustrious Greene were equally useful in every department, in which human society can call a man to act, every friend to America must feel the want of his assistance, in the duties that remain to be performed. Yet, as these duties are of the rational and pacific kind, the performance is more attainable, and emulation the better encouraged. In military operations, none but the soldier can be distinguish; nor any but the fortunate are sure of rendering service: but here is a theatre of action for every citizen of a great country: in which the smallest circumstance will have its weight, and on which infinite consequences will depend.

The present is an age of philosophy, and America, the empire of reason. Here, neither the pageantry of courts, nor the glooms of superstition, have dazzled or beclouded the mind. Our duty calls us to act worthy of the age and the country that gave us birth. Though inexperience may have betrayed us into errors -- yet they have not been fatal: and our own discernment will point us to their proper remedy.

However defective the present confederated system may appear -- yet a due consideration of the circumstances, under which it was framed, will teach us rather to admire its wisdom, than to murmur at its faults. The same political abilities, which were displayed in that institution, united with the experience we have had of its operation, will doubtless produce a system, which will stand the test of ages, in forming a powerful and happy people.

Elevated with the extensive prospect, we may consider present inconveniencies as unworthy of regret. At the close of the war, an uncommon plenty of circulating specie, and a universal passion for trade, tempted many individuals to involve themselves in ruin, and injure the credit of their country. But these are evils which work their own remedy. The paroxysm is already over. Industry is increasing faster than ever it declined; and, with some exceptions, where legislative authority has sanctioned fraud, the people are honestly discharging their private debts, and increasing the resources of their wealth.

Every possible encouragement for great and generous exertions is now presented before us. Under the idea of a permanent and happy government, every point of view, in which the future situation of America can be placed, fills the mind with peculiar dignity; and opens an unbounded field of thought. The natural resources of the country are inconceivably various and great. The enterprising genius of the people promises a most rapid improvement in all the arts that embellish human nature. The blessings of a rational government will invite emigrations from the rest of the world; and fill the empire with the worthiest and happiest of mankind; while the example of political wisdom and felicity, here to be displayed, will excite emulation through the kingdoms of the earth; and meliorate the condition of the human race.

In the pleasing contemplation of such glorious events, and comparing the scenes of action that adorn the western hemisphere, with what has taken place in the east, may we not apply to our country the language of the prophet of Israel, though spoken on a different occasion -- "The glory of this latter house shall be greater than the former, saith the Lord of hosts:" -- peace to any disorders that may at present subsist among us -- peace to the contending passions of nations -- peace to this empire, to future ages, and through the extended world?[278]

~~~***~~~

Complaining regulated.

---------*Nunc fera querelis*
Haud justis assurgis, et irrita jurgia
jactas.[279]

COMPLAINTS of bad times have been common in all ages. No period was ever so good, but many would think, former days were not so bad, and present days might be better. This is a period remarkable for complaints. Whether there be sufficient cause for them, I will not say. Every man, in this matter, will judge for himself. "Scarcity of cash, heavy taxes, frequent suits, severity of creditors, bad debts, ill management of public affairs," &c. &c. are common topics of conversation in most companies But I cannot find that complaining has mended the times: for they still continue the same. Since complaining is so considerable a part of the business of the day, it is necessary some rules should be prescribed, to guide us in so important an affair. Until better are provided, I would recommend the following:

Never complain of any thing before you have examined it, and are sure that it is an evil. Judge not of a matter merely from its present appearance, or from your present feelings: but consider its natural tendency, and probable consequences; for, however disagreeable it may be at present -- yet, if it be naturally productive of superior good, it is not, on the whole, an evil, or proper matter of complaint,

If you are not capable, at present, of making a proper judgment of its probable tendency, suspend your complaints, till you are wiser, or can see the issue. Never complain of that as a grievance, which is necessary to prevent or remove something worse.

Complain not of that which could not have been prevented, or cannot be remedied: this would be impiety, as well as folly: for it would be murmuring at providence.

Complain not of that which proceeds from your own choice, or your own conduct: but silently censure your error; and, from your experience, learn wisdom and virtue.

Never complain of that which it is in your power to mend. Remove the evil: and there will be nothing to complain of. Complain not of that which becomes painful merely' from the irregularity of your own temper: but correct your temper: and then all will be well.

Never complain of the conduct of others, when you act in the same manner, or in a manner that shews you have the fame disposition, and would act like them, in the same circumstances: but first reform yourself: and then, perhaps, your example will do something to reform them.

Complain not of that in the great which is faulty only in part: but wish to destroy what only wants mending. Would you throw away your only coat, because the tailor erred in the cut of the cuff?

Complain not, when complaints do no good. This is spending your breath, and disturbing your mind in vain.

Never complain of mere trifling inconveniencies. This shews a trifling mind. Complain not of that which you do not, and cannot, understand. This indicates rashness.

Complain not of disappointments, which originate from unreasonable and extravagant expectations. Bring your views down to the standard of nature: and your disappointments will be few and small. Never serve, like a piece of inanimate nature, to echo other people's complaints: perhaps, they are designing men, and want you to be their tool.

Never complain of a matter after it has been fully explained, and unanswerably justified. This would be obstinacy and perverseness.

---

[278] Vol. II, no. 2, for August 1787, pp. 135-142.
[279] [*Edit. Note. Aeneid*, Book X, line 95: "-- now you raise complaints without justice, and incite distracting quarrels."]
~~~

Never complain to shew your own importance, or to make a noise, perhaps you will raise a noise that you did not expect; and sink, from opposed importance, into real insignificance.

Never complain of that which in no respect concerns you: nor search their faults, for the sake of talking about them. This is to be a busy only in other men's matters.

Complain not of grievances, but with a view to remove them; nor in misconduct in others, but for the end of reforming it. If no good end can be answered, you may as well be silent.

But, you will say, "these are riling[?][280] rules: may we not complain at them?" What matter is it whether you do or not? Let every man study his own duty, and comply with his own obligations; know himself, and assess his faults; be as good as he might, and by his example make others as good as he can; conduct as generously as he thinks others ought to conduct; and fill his sphere as well as he thinks others ought to fill theirs: and he will see less evil to complain of, and be less disposed to complain of what he sees.[281]

~~~***~~~

Efficacy of black-berry jelly -- Recipe for making it.

AS the season for making a jelly of black-berries has arrived, it may be proper to communicate the following account of its very remarkable efficacy, in that dreadful disorder, the gravel and stone.

A gentleman, who for many years had been afflicted with this dreadful complaint, was persuaded to take every night going to bed the quantity of a large nutmeg of this jelly. The effect of which was, that the stone was broken to pieces, and voided in grannels, some of them nearly the size of pepper-corns, manifestly appearing so be portions of a much larger substance. The gentleman, though more than four score, is now enabled to discharge these stony particles without much difficulty, and finds no other inconvenience than a frequent irritation to urinate.

To make the jelly: take black berries before they are quite ripe when turned red; pick them and put them into a pot, tie them up close and put them in a kettle of water. Let them stand over the fire, until they are reduced to a pulp. Then strain them: and to a pint of juice put pound of powdered sugar. Boil it to a jelly: and put it up for use.[282]

~~~***~~~

Verses written at sea, in a heavy gale.
By Philip Freneau

HAPPY the man, who safe on shore
Now trims at home his evening fire;
Unmov'd, he hears the tempests roar,
That on the tufted groves expire.
   Alas! on us they doubly fall:
   Our feeble barque must bear them all.

Now to their haunts the birds retreat:
The squirrel seeks his hollow tree:
Wolves in their shaded caverns meet:
All, all are blest but wretched we.
   Foredoom'd a stranger to repose,
   No rest th' unsettled ocean knows.

While o'er the dark abyss we roam,
Perhaps (whate'er the pilots say)
We saw the Sun descend in gloom,

---

280 [*Edit. Note*. Text here is illegible.]
281 Vol. II, no. 2, for August 1787, p. 174.
282 Vol. II, no. 2, for August 1787, p. 178.

No more to see his rising ray.
    But buried low, by far too deep,
    On coral beds, unpitied, sleep.

But what a strange, uncoasted strand
Is that, where Death permits no day?
No charts have we, to mark that land,
No compass to direct that way.
    What pilot shall explore that realm?
    What new Columbus take the helm?

While death and darkness both sit round,
And tempests rage with lawless pow'r,
Of friendship's voice I hear no sound,
No comfort in this dreadful hour,
    What friendship can in tempests be?
    What comforts on this angry sea?

The barque accumstom'd to obey,
No more the trembling pilots guide:
Alone she gropes her trackless way,
While mountains burst on either side:
    Thus skill and science both must fall,
    And ruin is the lot of all.[283]

~~~***~~~

To the memory of the brave, accomplished, and patriotic col. John Laurens, who in the 27th year of his age, was killed in an engagement with a detachment of the British from Charleston, near the river Cambaheee [Combahee], *South-Carolina, August, 1782. By Philip Freneau.*

SINCE on her plains this gen'rous chief expir'd,
Whom sages honour'd, and whom France admir'd;
Does fame no statues to his mem'ry raise,
Nor swells one column to record his praise?
Where her palmetto shades th' adjacent deeps,
Affection sighs, and Carolina weeps!

Thou, who shalt stray where death this chief confines,
Approach, and read the patriot in these lines:
Not from the dust the muse transcribes his name,
And more than marble shall declare his fame;
Where scenes more glorious his great soul engage,
Contest thrice worthy in that closing page;
When conqu'ring time to dark oblivion calls,
The marble totters, and the column falls.

Laurens! thy tomb while kindred hands adorn,
Let northern muses, too, inscribe your urn --
Of all, whose names on death's black list appear,
No chief, that perish'd, claim'd more grief sincere;
Not one, Columbia, that thy bosom bore,
More tears commanded, or deserv'd them more! --
Grief at his tomb shall heave th' unweary'd sigh,
And honour lift the mantle to her eye:

---

[283] Vol. II, no. 2, for August 1787, p. 202.
~~~

Fame thro' the world his patriot name shall spread,
By heroes envy'd and by monarchs read:
Just, generous, brave -- to each true heart ally'd:
The Briton's terror, and his country s pride;
For him the tears of war-worn soldiers ran,
The friend of freedom, and the friend of man.

Then what is death, compar'd with such a tomb,
Where honour fades not, and fair virtues bloom?
Ah! what is death, when fame like *this* endears
The brave man's favourite, and his country's tears! [284]

~~~***~~~

Letter on Slavery. By a negro.

I AM one of that unfortunate race of men, who are distinguished from the rest of the human species, by a black skin and woolly hair -- disadvantages of very little moment in themselves, but which prove to us a source of the greatest misery, because there are men, who will not be persuaded, that it is possible for a human soul to be lodged within a sable body. The West Indian planters could not, if they thought us men, so wantonly spill our blood; nor could the natives of this land of liberty, deeming us of the same species with themselves, submit to be instrumental in enslaving us, or think us proper subjects of a sordid commerce. Yet, strong as the prejudices against us are, it will not, I hope, on this side of the Atlantic, be considered as a crime, for a poor african not to confess himself a being of an inferior order to those, who happen to be of a different colour from himself; or be thought very presumptuous, in one who is but a negro, to offer to the happy subjects of this free government, some reflexions upon the wretched condition of his countrymen. They will not, I trust, think worse of my brethren, for being discontented with so hard a lot as that of slavery; nor disown me for their fellow creature, merely because I deeply feel the unmerited sufferings, which my countrymen endure.

It is neither the vanity of being an author, nor a sudden and capricious gall of humanity, which has prompted the present design. It has been long conceived, and long been the principal subject of my thoughts. Ever since an indulgent master rewarded my youthful services with freedom, and supplied me at a very early age with the means of acquiring knowledge, I have laboured to understand the true principles, on which the liberties of mankind are founded, and to possess myself of the language of this country, in order to plead the cause of those who were once my fellow slaves, and if possible to make my freedom, in some degree, the instrument of their deliverance.

The first thing then, which seems necessary, in order to remove those prejudices, which are so unjustly entertained against us, is to prove that we are men -- a truth which is difficult of proof, only because it is difficult to imagine, by what arguments it can be combated. Can it be contended, that a difference of colour alone can constitute a difference of species? -- if not, in what single circumstance are we different from the rest of mankind? what variety is there in our organization ? what inferiority of art in the fashioning of our bodies? what imperfection in the faculties of our minds ? -- Has not a negro eyes? has not a negro hands, organs, dimensions, senses, affections, passions ? -- fed with the fame food; hurt with the fame weapons, subject to the same diseases; healed by the same means; warmed and cooled by the same summer and winter, as a white man is? if you prick us, do we not bleed ? if you poison us, do we not die ? are we not exposed to all the same wants? do we not feel all the same sentiments -- are we not capable of all the same exertions -- and are we not entitled to all the same rights, as other men?[285]

---

[284] Vol. II, no. 5, for November 1787, pp. 514-515. [*Edit. Note.* In another published version of this poem, found in *The Army Correspondence of Col. John Laurens 1777-1778* (1857), edited by William Gilmore Simms, p. 56., the last stanza reads:

Then what is death, compar'd with such a tomb,
Where honour fades not, and fair virtues bloom?
When silent grief on every face appears,
The tender tribute of a nation's tears;
Ah! what is death, when deeds like his thus claim
The brave man's homage, and immortal fame!]

[285] [*Edit. Note.* These last sentences are ostensibly and intended echoes of Shylock's speech in *The Merchant of Venice*, Act III, sc. 1.]
~~~

Yes -- and it is said we are men, it is true; but that we are men, addicted to more and worse vices, than those of any other complexion; and such is the innate perverseness of our minds, that nature seems to have marked us out for slavery. -- Such is the apology-perpetually made for our masters, and the justification offered for that universal proscription, under which we labour.

But I supplicate our enemies, to be, though for the first time, just in their proceedings towards us; and to establish the fact, before they attempt to draw any conclusion from it. Nor let them imagine, that this can be done, by merely asserting, that such is our universal character. It is the character, I grant, that our inhuman masters have agreed to give us, and which they have too industriously and too successfully propagated, in order to palliate their own guilt, by blackening the helpless victims of it, and to disguise their own cruelty under the semblance of justice. Let the natural depravity of our character be proved -- not by appealing to declamatory invectives, and interested representations, but by shewing, that a greater proportion of crimes have been committed by the wronged slaves of the plantations, than by the luxurious inhabitants of Europe, who are happily strangers to those aggravated provocations, by which our passions are every day irritated and incensed. Shew us, that, of the multitude of negroes, who have, within a few years, transported themselves to this country*[286], and who are abandoned to themselves; who are corrupted by example, prompted by penury, and instigated, by the memory of their wrongs, to the commission of every crime -- shew us, I say, (and the demonstration, if it be possible, cannot be difficult) that a greater proportion of these, than of white men, have fallen under the animadversion of justice, and have been sacrificed to your laws. Though avarice may slander and insult our misery, and though poets heighten the horror of their fables, by representing us as monsters of vice -- the fact is, that, if treated like other men, and admitted to a participation of their rights, we should differ from them in nothing, perhaps, but in our possessing stronger passions, nicer sensibility, and more enthusiastic virtue.

Before so harsh a decision was pronounced upon our nature, we might have expected -- if sad experience had not taught us, to expect nothing but injustice from our adversaries -- that some pains would have been taken, to ascertain, what our nature is; and that we should have been considered, as we are found in our native woods, and not as we now are -- altered and perverted by an inhuman political institution. But, instead of this, we are examined, not by philosophers, but by interested traders; not as nature formed us, but as man has depraved us -- and from such an enquiry, prosecuted under such circumstances, the perverseness our dispositions is said to be established. Cruel that you are! you make us slave; you implant in our minds all the vices, which are, in some degree, inseparable from that condition ; and you then impiously impute to nature, and to God, the origin of those vices, to which you alone have given birth; and punish in us the crimes, of which you are yourselves the authors.

The condition of slavery is in nothing more deplorable, than in its being so unfavourable to the practice of every virtue. The surest foundation of virtue, is the love of our fellow-creatures; and that affection takes its birth, in the social relations of men to one another. But to a slave these are all denied. He never pays or receives the grateful duties of a son -- he never knows or experiences the fond solicitude of a father -- the tender names of husband, of brother, and of friend, are to him unknown. He has no country to defend and bleed for -- he can relieve no sufferings -- for he looks around in vain, to find a being more wretched than himself. He can indulge no generous sentiment -- for, he sees himself every hour treated with contempt and ridicule, and distinguished from irrational brutes, by nothing, but the severity of punishment. Would it be surprising, if a slave, labouring under all these disadvantages -- oppressed, insulted, scorned, and trampled on -- should come at last to despise himself -- to believe the calumnies of his oppressors -- and to persuade himself, that it would be against his nature, to cherish any honourable sentiment, or to attempt any virtuous action? Before you boast of your superiority over us, place some of your own colour (if you have the heart to do it) in the same situation with us; and see, whether they have such innate virtue, and such unconquerable vigour of mind, as to be capable of surmounting such multiplied difficulties, and of keeping their minds free from the infection of every vice, even under the oppressive yoke of such a servitude.

But, not satisfied with denying us that indulgence, to which the misery of our condition gives us so just a claim, our enemies have laid down other and stricter rules of morality, to judge our actions by, than those by which the conduct of all other men is tried. Habits, which in all human beings, except ourselves, are thought innocent, are, in us, deemed criminal -- and actions, which are even laudable in white men,

---

[286] [*Footnote in the original*] * This letter was originally published in England, where the number of negroes is considerably encreased, since the late war in America.

become enormous crimes in negroes. In proportion to our weakness, the strictness of censure is increased upon us; and as resources are withheld from us, our duties are multiplied. The terror of punishment is perpetually before our eyes: but we know not, how to avert it, what rules to act by, or what guides to follow. We have written laws, indeed, composed in a language we do not understand, and never promulgated: but what avail written laws, when the supreme law, with us, is the capricious will of our overseers? To obey the dictates of our own hearts, and to yield to the strong propensities of nature, is often to incur severe punishment; and by emulating examples, which we find applauded and revered among Europeans, we risk inflaming the wildest wrath of our inhuman tyrants.

To judge of the truth of these assertions, consult even those milder and subordinate rules for our conduct, the various codes of your West India laws -- those laws, which allow us to be men, whenever they consider us as victims of their vengeance, but treat us only like a species of living property, as often as we are to be the objects of their protection -- those laws, by which (it may be truly said) that we are bound to suffer, and be miserable, under pain of death. To resent an injury, received from a white man, though of the lower rank, and to dare to strike him, though upon the strongest and grossest provocation, is an enormous crime. To attempt an escape from the cruelties exercised over us, by flight, is punished with mutilation, and sometimes with death. To take arms against masters, whose cruelty no submission can mitigate, no patience exhaust, and from whom no other means of deliverance are left, is the most atrocious of all crimes; and is punished by a gradual death, lengthened out by torments, so exquisite, that none, but those who have been long familiarized, with West Indian barbarity, can hear the bare recital of them without horror. And yet I learn from writers, whom the Europeans hold in the highest esteem, that treason is a crime, which cannot be committed by a slave against his master; that a slave stands in no civil relation towards his master, and owes him no allegiance; that master and slave are in a state of war; and if the slave take up arms for his deliverance, he acts not only justifiably, but in obedience to a natural duty, the duty of self-preservation. I read in author, whom I find venerated by our oppressors, that to deliver one's self and one's countrymen from tyranny, is an act of the sublimest heroism. I hear Europeans exalted, as the martyrs of public liberty, the saviours of their country, and the deliverers of mankind -- I see their memories honoured with statues, and their names immortalized in poetry -- and yet when a generous negro is animated by the same passion, which ennobl'd them -- when he feels the wrongs of his countrymen as deeply, and attempts to revenge them as boldly -- I see him treated by those same Europeans, as the most execrable of mankind, and led out, amidst curses and insults, to undergo a painful, gradual, and ignominious death*[287]: and thus the same Briton, who applauds his own ancestors, for attempting to throw off the easy yoke, imposed on them by the Romans, punishes us, as detested parricides, for seeking to get free from the cruelest of all tyrannies, and yielding to the irresistible eloquence of an African Galgacus or Boadicea.

Are then the reason and the morality, for which Europeans so highly value themselves, of a nature so variable and fluctuating, as to change with the complexion of those, to whom they are applied? -- Do the rights of nature cease to be such, when a negro is to enjoy them? -- Or does patriotism, in the heart of an African, rankle into treason?

A free negro. [288]

~~~***~~~

Letter from an Indian chief to his friends in the state of New York.

Dear sir,

YOUR letter came safe to hand. To give you entire satisfaction, I must, I perceive, enter into the discussion of a subject, on which I have often thought. My thoughts were my own, and being so different from the ideas entertained among your people, I should have certainly carried them with me to the grave, had I not received your obliging favour. You ask then, whether, in my opinion, civilization is favourable to human happiness? In answer to the question, it may be observed, that there are degrees of civilization from Can[n]ibals to the most polite European nations; the question is not, whether a degree of refinement is not conducive to happiness, but, whether you, or the natives of this land, have obtained the happy medium? On this subject, we are at present, I presume, of very different opinions; you will, however, allow me in some respects to have had the advantage of you in forming my judgment. I was, sir, born of Indian parents, and

[287] [*Footnote in the original*] * For a remarkable instance of this species of barbarous cruelty – see vol.1 [?-illegible] of this work, page 210.

[288] Vol. VI, no. 1, for July 1789, pp. 77-80.
~~~

lived, while a child, among those you are pleased to call savages; I was afterwards sent to live among the white people, and educated at one of your schools; since which period, I have been honoured, much beyond my deserts, by an acquaintance with a number of principal characters both in Europe and America. After all this experience, and after every exertion to divest myself of prejudice, I am obliged to give my opinion in favor of my own people. I will now, as well as I am able, collect together and set before you, some of the reasons that have influenced my sentiments on the subject before us.

In the governments you call civilized, the happiness of the people is constantly sacrificed to the splendor of empire; hence your code of civil and criminal laws have had their origin; and hence your dungeons and prisons, I will not enlarge on an idea so singular in civilized life, and perhaps disgraceful to you; and will only observe, that among us, we have no law but that written on the heart of every rational creature by the immediate finger of the great Spirit of the universe himself. We have no prisons -- we have no pompous parade of courts; and yet judges are as highly esteemed among us, as they are among you, and their decisions as highly revered; property, to say the least, is as well guarded, and crimes are as impartially punished. We have among us no splendid villains, above the controul of that law, which influences our decisions; in a word, we have no robbery under the colour of law -- daring wickedness here is never suffered to triumph over helpless innocence -- the estates of widows and orphans are never devoured by enterprising sharpers. Our sachems, and our warriors, eat their own bread, and not the bread of wretchedness. No person, among us, desires any other reward for performing a brave and worthy action, than the consciousness of serving his nation. Our wise men are called fathers -- they are truly deserving the character; they are always accessible -- I will not say to the meanest of our people -- for we have none mean, but such as render themselves so by their vices.

Civilization creates a thousand imaginary wants, that continually distress the human mind. I remember to have read, while at one of your schools, the saying of a philosopher to this purport, "The real wants of human nature are very few;" on this maxim our people practice, without ever having learned to read. We do not hunger and thirst after those superfluities of life, that are the ruin of thousands of families among you. Our ornaments, in general, are simple and easily obtained. Envy and covetousness, those worms that destroy the fair flower of human happiness, are unknown in this climate.

The palaces and prisons among you, form a most dreadful contrast. Go to the former places, and you will see, perhaps, a deformed piece of earth swelled with pride, and assuming airs, that become none but the Spirit above. Go to one of your prisons -- here description utterly fails! -- certainly the sight of an Indian torture, is not half so painful to a well informed mind. Kill them, if you please -- kill them, too, by torture; but let the torture last no longer than a day. Let it be, too, of such a nature, as has no tendency to unman the human mind. Give them an opportunity, by their fortitude in death, of entitling themselves to the sympathy of the human race, instead of exciting in them the mortifying reflexion of being enveloped in the gulph of eternal infamy. Those you call savages, relent -- the most furious of our tormentors exhausts his rage in a few hours, and dispatches the unhappy victim with a sudden stroke.

But for what are many of your prisoners confined? For debt! Astonishing! and will you ever again call the Indian nations cruel? -- Liberty, to a rational creature, as much exceeds property, as the light of the sun does that of the most twinkling star: but you put them on a level, to the everlasting disgrace of civilization. Let me ask, is there any crime in being in debt? While I lived among the white people, I knew many of the most amiable characters contract debts, and I dare say with the best intentions. Both parties at the time of the contract, expected to find their advantage. The debtor, I suppose, by a train of unavoidable misfortunes, fails. Here is no crime, nor even a fault; and yet your laws put it in the power of that creditor, to throw the debtor into jail, and confine him there for life: a punishment infinitely worse than death to a brave man. And I seriously declare, that I had rather die by the most severe tortures ever inflicted by any savage nation on the continent, than languish in one of your prisons for a single year. Great Maker of the world! and do you call yourselves christians? I have read your bible formerly, and should have thought it divine, if the practice of the most zealous professor had corresponded with his professions. Does then the religion of him whom you call your Saviour, inspire this conduct, and lead to this practice? Surely no. It was a sentence that once struck my mind with some force, that "a bruised reed he never broke." Cease then, while these practices continue among you, to call yourselves christians, lest you publish to the world your hypocrisy. Cease to call other nations savage, while you are tenfold more the children of cruelty, than they.[289]

~~~***~~~

---

[289] Vol. VI, no. 3, for September 1789, pp. 226-227.
~~~

An HYMN *to* RESIGNATION

Written by a clergyman of Philadelphia.

Oh! from that high and holy sphere,
Where, thron'd in light, you dwell,
Sweet maid, in all thy charms descend
To gild my humble cell.

Thy presence heightens ev'ry bliss,
Draws out the sting of woe,
Allures to brighter worlds above.
And makes an heav'n below.

The pilgrim, roving all night long,
Through trackless wilds forlorn,
Oft sighs oppres'd, and sighs, again,
The wish'd return of morn.

So I, in sorrow's gloomy night,
Condemn'd a while to stray.
Look up, with ardent eye, to heav'n,
And ask the devious way.

Inconstant as the idle wind,
That sports with ev'ry flow'r,
When earthly friends by turns drop off,
Friends of our brighter hour;

Do thou, mild cherub, fill my breast
With all that's good and wise.
Snatch me from earth's tumultuous scenes,
And lead me to the skies.

There kindred spirits ne'er deceive,
Soul mingles there with soul;
Sweet sympathy and truth are there.
And love cements the whole.

More welcome to this sorrowing heart,
O pensive queen, thy strain,
Than all the joys mad Riot gives
To soothe his clam'rous train.

You shade the poor man's evening walk
With wreaths of endless green,
And when the lamp of life declines,
You tend the last dread scene.

Oh! then from heav'n, thy holy sphere.
Where, thron'd in light, you dwell;
Come, Resignation, sainted maid.
And gild my humble cell. [290]

---

[290] Vol. VI, no. 2, for August 1789, pp. 173-174.

EARLY DAYS IN THE NAVY

During these at present, as I write this, excoriating months of summer, I am taking a break from my more usual studies to brush up on my immediate familiarity with the history of the post-Revolutionary War United States Navy. Among the volumes I've thus far, or else mostly, finished are Stephen W.H. Duffy's *Captain Blakeley and the Wasp: The Cruise of 1814,* and *A Gentlemanly and Honorable Profession: The Creation of the U.S. Naval Officer Corps, 1794-1815* by Christopher McKee -- both veritable classics of their kind.

Duffy's biography of Master Commandant Johnston Blakeley is singularly splendid. Here's some first-rate research and accompanied by descriptions of naval actions that could hold their own in drama and excitement with some of the masters of nautical fiction; by an author who knows the technical niceties of sea faring and ocean survival in an early 19th century sailing ship breasting the waves in time of war. As well, the book ends up being surprisingly moving: Blakeley, having lost his entire (immediate) family at a young age, makes his way up the ladder in the emergent U.S. navy; encountering daunting and trying challenges along the way; finds time to get married; finally sets sail after a protracted and tedious fitting out of his new vessel; wins two incredible and stunning battles; only to shortly after be *mysteriously* lost at sea with his victorious men and ship.[291] While Duffy's facts and data could be shored up at points and be profitably served by further analysis, exploration and development of what he presents (including perhaps philosophical-artistic development), this shortcoming can be pardoned given what a magnificent job he's done gathering up the requisite materials.

The book concludes with an anonymous tribute poem to Blakeley and the officers and crew of the *Wasp* (p. 329) as it first (?) appeared in the *Newburyport* [Mass.] *Herald*, 23 July 1816. I found out later, however, that Duffy's, though perhaps given its brevity is better as poetry, is not the complete version; having discovered in an 1838 edition of the *Army and Navy Chronicle* (vol. VI, no. 21, Washington, Thurs, May 24, 1838, p. 329) this:

The following beautiful lines on the melancholy fate of a noble ship and her daring crew, have never before appeared in print. They were written in 1815 or 1816 by a highly gifted and accomplished young lady, for several years a resident of the District of Columbia, but now no more.

To the Memory of the Officers
of the U.S. Sloop of War Wasp
Lost at sea in 1814.

by MISS C. W. B., OF NEWBURYPORT, MASS.

No more shall Blakeley's thunder roar,
Along the stormy deep.
Far distant from Columbia's shore,
His tombless ruins sleep.
Yet long Columbia's sons shall tell.
How Blakeley fought -- bow Blakeley fell.

Though long on foamy billows cast,
The battle's fury braved,
And still unsullied on thy mast,
The starry banner waved,
Unconquered shall Columbia be,
While she can boast of sons like thee.

Oh! Sleep -- the battle's rage no more

---

[291] There is even an "Ishmael" in the way of Midshipman David Geisinger who was sent home on a prize ship shortly before the *Wasp* disappeared in ostensibly the eastern or south Atlantic.

Shall animate thy breast,
No sound on Lethe's silent shore,
Disturbs the warrior's rest;
No wave molests its peaceful tide,
No navies on its waters ride.

Nor will the muse refuse a tear,
O'er Reilly's[292] corse to flow;
Or one less generous and sincere,
On Tillinghast[293] bestow.
Farewell! no warlike sound again
Shall rouse you from the watery main.[294]

And shall the oblivious waves that roll
O'er Baury's[295] lifeless breast,
Drown the remembrance of that soul,
That asked no other rest?
No! ocean shrouds thy earthly part --
Thy deepest grave is in the heart.

Still in our hearts, by love illumed,
The gentle Clarke[296] is urned,
Whose hand was prompt to heal the wound.
His pitying spirit mourned.
Farewell! thou hast nor night nor morn,
Nor requiem, save the howling storm.

Quite different from the Blakeley biography is Christopher McKee's *A Gentlemanly and Honorable Profession: The Creation of the U.S. Naval Officer Corps, 1794-1815.* While mostly an academic and scholarly work, it has its fair share of ordinary human interest elements. Though I take exception to his psycho-analyzing contemporary portrait paintings of individual officers, he gives us rarely seen information and insights into the United States navy in its formative years that makes for a most unique and indispensable history.[297] Among the many and varied treasures contained in his book is Midshipman William Taylor Skiddy's report of the battle between the *Hornet* and the *Penquin* (pp. 147-149), and that originated with Skiddy's autobiography "The Ups and Downs of Life at Sea." I subsequently uncovered two other versions of his story in *History of Stamford, Connecticut: from its settlement in 1641, to the Present Time* (1868) by Elijah Baldwin Huntington (pp. 356-358), and "The Hornet's Sting and Wing" by P. S. P. Conner found in *New England Magazine*, Nov. 1900, Vol. XXIII, no. 3 (pp. 268-275.) All three renderings somewhat diverge with each other as to what is included and the way some sentences are phrased and worded; though this last anomaly is a fairly minor difficulty. Not having Skiddy's original at hand myself, and to attempt to rectify this (for some) conflicting state of texts, I edited and spliced together the following version that combines as much of Skiddy's account as all three make available -- though without in any way claiming that mine be necessarily preferred to the others.

~~~***~~~

March 15th, 1815.[298] We arrived off the island of Tristian d'Aurca [Tristan da Cunha], in latitude 37 degrees south and 11 degrees longitude west. Our [*acting*, he was formally only a midshipman at the

[292] First Lieutenant James Reilly. Duffy's text here reads "course," rather than "corse;" the latter apparently being the correct word.
[293] Second Lieutenant Thomas G. Tillinghast.
[294] Duffy and the *Newburyport Herald's* text of the poem ends here.
[295] Midshipman, but acting Third Lieutenant Frederick Baury.
[296] Midshipman William Montague Clarke.
[297] One striking and little known point brought out by McKee is that a little over half of the U.S. Navy's enlisted personnel between 1794 and 1815 was comprised of foreign born (predominantly British) sailors, p. 219n.
[298] [*Edit. Note.* This is an error as the correct date of the meeting between the opposing ships is March 23rd.]
~~~

time] first lieutenant David Conner had just landed when the signal was made for him to return, in consequence of a strange sail heaving in sight and standing down before the wind for us. We hove to and took our dinner (it was duff-day)[299] while she was running down. The duff was hardly swallowed when the drum beat to quarters. In a few minutes all was ready for action, every eye watching the stranger. He soon luffed to on our weather-quarter (starboard) about pistol shot off, hoisted the British flag, and gave us a gun. This we did not notice -- waiting for him to shoot ahead more. He then gave us the first broadside.

The moment his guns flashed, ours were in operation; and, strange to say, in five minutes I perceived the blood running from his scuppers, when they almost stopped firing. Our little captain [James Biddle[300]] ordered us to cease firing; when the enemy, thinking we were disabled, renewed his fire, -- and of course we soon convinced him of his mistake. He then, as a last alternative, ran his bowsprit between our main and mizzen mast, with the intention of carrying us by boarding.

I was standing with the first lieutenant, in the third division, on the quarter deck (three after guns on each side) and was soon in command of this division -- first lieutenant, Mr. Conner, having been severely wounded at the commencement of the action. This brave officer was standing near my right arm. I was then assisting the working the second gun from aft, and after taking aim he inquired of me how the enemy looked, and I just answered that from appearances his time had nearly expired, when a shot struck him (Mr. Conner) in the groin. I watched the effect of the wound, and soon observed him whiten from loss of blood. I attempted to assist him out of the way of the guns and, stopping abreast of the mizzen mast, asked him if I should send him below. Putting his hand over the wound, he said, 'No, I'll see it out.' He then sank down on the deck beside the mast. The captain observing this despatched [sic] his aid, Midshipman Samuel Phelps, to help him below, and I continued in charge of the third division.

The jib-halyards being shot away, the fore tack was hauled down to veer the ship. The enemy was now foul of us, and all hands were called to repel boarders; we immediately mounted the hammock cloths and the enemy's booms; the shout of 'Board' and cheers from our boys soon thinned off the crowd on their forecastle deck, and it required all the exertions of our captain and officers to prevent our men from boarding; had they done so the enemy would have suffered much; many of them were now dodging below and some left their first lieutenant (MacDonald) standing alone on the forecastle. Many muskets were levelled at him, but were prevented, by our officers, from firing on so brave a man. He then enquired of our leader, Second Lieutenant Newton, the name of the ship, and was answered, "the United States sloop Hornet;" he then waved his sword and walked aft.

Our ship in shooting ahead carried away his bowsprit, tore away all our mizzen rigging, and the enemy swung across our stem. Our captain was standing aft on the arm chest speaking to them, when their foremast fell along the lee waist. The marines in the foretop clung with their muskets to the rigging as the mast fell on deck, and then jumped forward, fired and wounded our captain. They made an attempt also at this time to rake us with their bow-guns, then pointed on our stern; I was standing in the larboard stern port in front of their two bow-guns, only about twelve feet from us. The greater part of our crew then being aft to prevent their boarding, I certainly expected to see many of our party fall at that fire. Had these guns been well directed, many of us must have been killed; but fortunately at that very moment the sea lifted our ship's stern and the shot went under the counter into the sea. Our ship now came round on the other tack (larboard), and I played my division into them, raking them fore and aft. They again cried quarters, and our wounded captain came and ordered me to cease firing.

Our antagonist proved to be H. B. M. sloop-of-war Penguin, Captain [James] Dickinson [also seen spelled, for example, in Fenimore Cooper and Theodore Roosevelt's naval histories as "Dickensen"] (one of Lord Nelson's favorites), who was killed during the action by a ball through the heart. This was a new vessel, mounting sixteen thirty-two pound carronades, two long nines, and one twelve-pounder on the forecastle. They reported fifteen men killed and twenty-eight wounded; but they had a number of men from

---

299 [McKee: "One day a week, in both the U.S. and British navies, the ship's company received -- in place of beef -- flour, suet [the residue of fat left over from cooked beef], and currants or raisins with which to make a duff, a stiff pudding boiled in a bag or steamed." *A Gentlemanly and Honorable Profession*, p. 147n.]

300 [*Edit. Note.* Nephew of Captain Nicholas Biddle of the *Randoph* vs. *Yarmouth* engagement.]

the Medway seventy-four, and were sent expressly from the Cape of Good Hope to cruise for the Young Wasp privateer, of twenty-two long guns. We made out, by the rolls on board of her, twenty-five killed. Several of the wounded died. The Hornet was of the same length, one foot less beam, guns of the same calibre, one more in number than the Penguin. The Hornet had. before the action, 130 men; the Penguin had 158 men, including volunteers from the Medway -- 28 difference. The Hornet had one man killed and eleven wounded, and this all in the after third division. The poor fellow that was killed was a six-foot marine, named Town, from Vermont; he was firing over my head, and I suddenly perceived his brains on my shoes -- and, on turning, I observed the top of his skull had been taken off by a ball. As he was now much in the way, I shoved him through one of the ports overboard. After the fight came the most painful and heart-sickening sight of poor fellows, who only a few minutes since were well and joyful, now all mangled by balls and splinters. Groans were heard from all quarters. We were now employed getting the prisoners on board, unbending and bending sails, repairing rigging, and replacing as soon as possible all damages. This called us from the dying groans of the wounded. The surgeons were all employed amputating limbs and dressing wounds. The prize was taken in tow, and night veiled the dismal scene. The next morning the Penguin was scuttled and sunk; Captain Dickinson was buried with the honors of war, his own officers and marines being allowed to perform the ceremony.

When our little captain was wounded a man from one of my guns pulled off his old checked shirt, tore it in strips, took hold of Captain Biddle, and wound this round his neck. He [Biddle], then holding his bandage himself, was asked by one of our officers if he thought himself much hurt, when he replied "No, no, give it to the damned rascals!"[301] This shot was fired, recollect, after they had once given up. After the action was over, the doctor ([Surgeon Benjamin P.] Kissam) came to the captain (who was still at his post, holding onto his neck) and asked him if he would go down and have his wound dressed? The captain answered that, if he had got through with the rest, he believed he would go, and then we heard that the ball had passed through his neck and out through his collar behind.

One of our men on board the Penguin picked up a hat on the quarter deck in which he found a man's head that had been shot off. He very deliberately pull[ed] the head out, looked at it saying, "Matey, you don't now require a hat," put it on his own head and dispatched the other overboard. I have seen him with this hat on often in New York. The sailors were also looking out for the legs amputated, that they might get some shoes and stockings, as the doctor did not take the trouble to pull them off. One very remarkable occurrence, and that that was one of the English midshipmen, a young man who sat on the wardroom table, smiling and talking and joking with one of his wounded shipmates near him who had lost a leg, while the doctor amputated one of his [own] legs, without the least emotion. When it was off, "Never mind," said he, "Bond (his messmate wounded), we will soon get on sticks and have fun with the girls yet." The poor fellow was on crutches when removed on board the Tom Bowline [the U.S. squadron's storeship] with the other prisoners, took cold, and had his leg amputated a second time by their own surgeon. Poor fellow, he died. Bond I often met at St. Salvador, Brazil.

---

[301] [*Edit. Note.* J. F. Cooper, *History of the Navy of the United States of America* (1839), p. 342: "The vessels lay in this position but a minute or two, the American raking, when the sea lifted the Hornet ahead, carrying away her mizzen-rigging, davits and spanker boom, the enemy swinging round and hanging on the larboard quarter. At this moment Captain Biddle sent the master forward to set the foresail, with a view to part the vessels, when an officer on board the English ship called out that she surrendered. The positions prevented any other firing than that of small arms; this was ordered to cease, and Captain Biddle sprang upon the taffrail to inquire if the enemy submitted. He was within thirty feet of the forecastle of the English vessel, when two marines on board her discharged their muskets at him. The ball of one just missed the chin, and, passing through the skin of the neck, inflicted a severe, but fortunately not a dangerous wound. This incident drew a discharge of muskets from the Hornet, which killed the two marines; the American ship drew ahead at that instant, and the enemy lost his bowsprit and foremast as the vessels separated.

"The Hornet now wore round, with a fresh broadside to bear, and was about to throw in a raking fire, when twenty men appeared at the side and on the forecastle of the enemy, raising their hands for quarter, and eagerly calling out that they had struck. The excitement on board the American ship, however, was so great, in consequence of the manner in which their gallant captain had received his wound, that it was with the utmost difficulty Captain Biddle and his officers could prevent the people from pouring in another broadside."]

As a last minute afterthought, below are some additional personal musings on a separate but related 1812 naval topic.

While I am neither disposed nor situated at the moment to write a formal piece or article on the subject, I could not help wanting to add a little something about my reaction to the O.H. Perry vs. Jesse Duncan Elliott controversy regarding the latter's dilatoriness in supporting Perry at the Battle of Lake Erie. The mystery is simply this -- how could Elliott have avoided being engaged for two hours? The response of Elliott's detractors was either that he was cowardly or else designing to gain glory for himself (i.e., once Perry and the *Lawrence* "went under.") In examining diverse perspectives on this question, and which have over many, many years been taken on to amazingly prolix and vituperative length, it seems one explanation has been overlooked -- namely that Elliott's fault was one of indecision (i.e., "What am I to do?...*I don't know.*") -- rather than fear of battle or envy of his commander. Two things happened to cause this 1) Perry's orders that the fleet maintain its line of battle combined with 2) Perry's violating his own instructions to remain in line and going dashing after the British himself. This then put Elliott in a position of a) having to disobey his commander's earlier instructions, and b) to act on his own initiative. Not sure that he could or should do either, this caused him to be indecisive. He arguably could not disobey his prior orders; while at the same time Perry was rash to assume Elliott necessarily would take the initiative. Per chance too, though we have no way ourselves of knowing this, *pride* was a factor in making Elliott reluctant to have Perry *force him*, without advanced notice or warning, to act on his own; and which could further remind him that technically the rules were on his side. So yes, we can say then Elliott may be considered at fault for his indecisiveness, but this is *far less* impugning of his *character* than the charges of timidity and or conspiracy.

AMERICAN MUSIC:
Remembering Samuel Woodworth

In a review of the 1818 edition of Samuel Woodworth's[302] *Poems, Odes, Songs, and other Metrical Effusions*, an unnamed author for *The Analectic Magazine* (the same Philadelphia periodical that in 1813 and 1814 had been edited by Washington Irving) wrote:

"The literary productions of our country, seem at last to have taken a start; and we may now venture to hope, that the charge of barrenness which has been brought against the American mind, will be disproved. Poetry, in particular, which has heretofore been treated as an exotic, and bore evident marks of its foreign extraction, has of late been discovered in various quarters of the union, and cultivated with considerable success. It is true, that of the many poetical works which now issue from the press, there are few which will bear a comparison with the effusions of our trans-atlantic brethren: Yet an impetus being once given, we have no doubt, that in a comparatively short time, poets equal to those of other nations will spring up. In the mean time, however, there will be numerous failures; and hundreds on whom the true inspiration hath not descended, will light their farthing candles at the eternal lamp of some great master, and successively disappear. Of the works before us, we think that of Mr. Woodworth entitled to the preference: both from the marks of genius visible in it, and the situation and life of the author...

"The poetry of Mr. Woodworth although containing nothing very striking, is still we think entitled to no small share of praise. The language is almost uniformly harmonious, and we often see traits of nature and simplicity; and what we cannot help liking, Americanisms and American allusions. At all events, he is no copier of foreign poets and foreign ideas. We see no reason why, with so much to delight and interest around us, we should resort to the 'crambe bis cocta'[303] of the British poets. We love to find our own scenery and manners in verse, and not those of any other country; and have no doubt that the Delaware, the Missouri, or the Ohio would flow as harmoniously through American lyrics, as .the Tweed, the Thames, or the Avon. The longest poem in the book, is a kind of half satire, half eulogy on New Haven and the manners and customs of our New England brethren. It is written in many parts with considerable force and spirit, although on the whole not entitled to great praise...

"The smaller pieces in this volume are chiefly patriotic songs on the naval victories, written in a popular style, but rather overdoing the matter. We have no objection to seeing them, however, as they contribute to the support of a national feeling, that great desideratum of the republic..."[304]

By about the late 19th century, the verdict on Woodworth was that he was best and, in effect, only to be remembered for his song "The Old Oaken Bucket" (originally titled "The Bucket.") Even sympathetic Samuel Adams Drake, in his delightful *A Book of New England Legends and Folklore in Prose and Poetry* (1901), states: "His (Woodworth's) reputation rests upon this one stroke of genius. He never wrote anything better than this beautiful lyric, which is capable of hushing the most boisterous assemblies into silence..."[305]

Yet in his prime, Woodworth was viewed with distinguished favor by some of early America's most noted authors and critics, including, among others, Washington Irving, Fitz-Greene Halleck, James Kirke Paulding, and William Cullen Bryant -- not to mention as well Sir Walter Scott. When Edgar Allan Poe reviewed Rufus Wilmot Griswold's *The Poets and Poetry of America* (1842), he bemoaningly took Griswold to task for only including Woodworth's name among a number who had been dumped into the "Various" poets category; i.e., instead of devoting an special section to him (Woodworth, by the way, had died in the same year Griswold's anthology was published.)

---

[302] Born in Scituate, Massachusetts, Woodworth (1784-1842) was the youngest child of Revolutionary War veteran Benjamin Woodworth. At various times he lived in Baltimore, New Haven, and New York City, but ended up spending most of his life and career in the latter metropolis.

[303] "Cabbage boiled twice."

[304] *The Analectic Magazine*, Volume 12, July 1818, pp. 66-72.

[305] pp. 373-374

Where then does Woodworth's merit lie? Perhaps someplace in between his admirers and dismissers. For one thing, "The Old Oaken Bucket" was far from being his only catchy tune. His "Patriotic Diggers" and "The Hunters of Kentucky" (wonderfully recorded in modern times by folk singer Wallace House) are now equally as memorable. His prose fiction and plays, such as the novel *The Champions of Freedom* (1816), though deserving much less attention than his verse, are at least valuable in furnishing colorful glimpses and vivid vignettes of life, including public gatherings and theater, in the very young United States. Yet all seem to agree that if Woodworth *is* to be famous, it must be for his poetry.

But there's the rub also. As a poet, Woodworth was usually and merely passing competent. While warm and amiable for his unbounded optimism and buoyant cheerfulness, there is rarely depth of thought or profundity of imagination in him. In retrospect and like Irish bard Thomas Moore (by whom he was much inspired), what made him *truly* great was his natural talent as a lyricist.[306] It is the *musicality* of his verse, marked by clean rhythms, purity of phrase, and a mellifluous choice of words, that sets him alongside if not above other American writers in this category of composition. So much so, that perhaps Woodworth might have achieved more deserved renown if he had been as well a musical composer -- say, something along the lines of Stephen Foster. To help verify the point then, we've collected here selections of Woodworth at some of his best in this department.

~~~***~~~

FREEDOM'S STAR.

Hail, Star of Freedom, hail!
Whose splendor ne'er shall fail,
In peace or war;
Long shall thy golden ray
O'er these blessed regions play,
While millions own the sway
Of Freedom's Star.

Our sires, a pilgrim band,
Who sought this promised land,
From realms afar,
Spurned fell oppression's sway,
And dared the pathless way,
Led by the golden ray
Of Freedom's Star.

Their sons, with kindred flame,
Have earned an equal fame,
In peace and war!
Determined to be free,
Have fought by land and sea,
Led on to victory,
By Freedom's Star!

Beneath her temple's dome,
Here wanderers find a home
From realms afar!
Blest in their happy choice,
Here will they long rejoice,

[306] Moore, in later years, humbly down-played his own talent as a poet. In a letter dated "Sloperton [Cottage, Bromham, Wiltshire, England]," 3 Dec. 1843, and written to an unknown recipient, he stated: "...the Publick has been so long and abundantly dosed with my versicles that they must, by this time, I think, be as tired of them as I am myself. I must likewise add that if I ever do commit verse again I am bound by promise to let an old & dear friend of mine have the refusal of it. Wishing you every success both in verse and song, I am, dear Madam..." *private collection.*]
~~~

And with united voice,
Hail Freedom's Star![307]

~~~***~~~

FREEDOM'S CONSTELLATION.

Glory gilds the western skies
With bright irradiation,
Where brilliant stars so oft arise
In Freedom's constellation.
See the glittering orbs revolve
Around the sun of Union!
And never shall the tie dissolve
Which holds them in communion.
This exalts Columbia's cause,
And gilds her reputation;
This secures her earth's applause,
And Heaven's approbation.

Long shall live Columbia's name,
In patriotic story,
And long around her brow shall flame
A bright, unsullied glory.
Virtue's panoply she wears,
Her weapons truth and justice;
The olive-branch her standard bears,
In Heaven alone her trust is.
This exalts Columbia's cause, &c.

Mild religion's lucid ray
Her glowing prospect brightens,
And superstition shuns the day
Which literature enlightens.
Charity's celestial flame
Here sheds its mild effulgence,
For every party, sect, and name,
Enjoys the same indulgence.
This exalts Columbia's cause, &c.

Freemen reap the fertile soil
Their valor has defended,
And smiling plenty crowns the toil
Which health and hope attended.
Exiles here a refuge find,
Secure from persecution,
And bless the wisdom that designed
Our glorious constitution.
This exalts Columbia's cause, &c.

See our mighty realm increase,
Since independence crowned it,
And its growth shall never cease,
Till oceans only bound it.

---

[307] *The Poetical Works of Samuel Woodworth* (1861), Vol. II, pp. 87-88.
~~~

Still Columbia never fights
For conquest or for plunder;
Nothing but insulted right
Can wake her martial thunder.
This exalts Columbia's cause, &c.

See Neptune with the lakes allied --
No legendary story --
The god of ocean gains a bride
Where Perry wedded glory.
See potent steam's resistless charm
Uniting distant places,
Till Mississippi's giant arm
The Hudson's form embraces.
This exalts Columbia's cause &c.

Hail, thou mistress of the West!
Where freemen hold dominion,
Where the dove may safely rest
Beneath the eagle's pinion.
Long as Cynthia wheels her car,
Or Phœbus holds his station,
Be virtue still the brightest star
In Freedom's Constellation.
This exalts Columbia's cause,
And gilds her reputation;
This secures her earth's applause,
And Heaven's approbation.[308]

~~~***~~~

THE VICTOR COMES, HUZZA!

Flee, busy care! the god of war
Will guard him in the fray,
And where the rudest dangers are,
His plume is seen to play.
Where martial banners proudly wave,
And flashing blades appear,
There moves the leader of the brave,
His heart unknown to fear
The routed foe, retreating,
To freemen yield the day;

The roll of joy is beating,
The field is ours, huzza!

My hero claims the brightest wreath,
The loudest note of fame,
Let Music's voice his praises breath,
And bards repeat his name.
He comes to bless my longing arms,
And cheer his lonely bride;
Safe from the battle's rude alarms,

[308] Vol. II, pp. 88-91.
~~~

He comes in martial pride.
He comes with smiles returning,
In triumph's glittering car;
The torch of joy is burning,
The victor comes, huzza![309]

~~~***~~~

INDEPENDENCE.

Come, crowd around the festive board,
And join the song with one accord,
Be every breast with pleasure stored,
And care and envy send hence.
Our dear-bought freedom we will praise,
Dear-bought freedom -- dear-bought freedom --
Our dear-bought freedom we will praise,
The right of our descendants;
Our dear-bought freedom we will praise,
And every glowing heart shall raise
The chorus of our joyful lays,
Columbia's Independence.

Be party rancor banished hence,
For peace is virtue's recompense;
Friendship and love on no pretence
Should ever meet with hinderance.
Let sons of freedom e'er agree --
Sons of freedom -- sons of freedom --
Let sons of freedom e'er agree,
In amity's attendance;
Let sons of freedom e'er agree,
For why should men, existing free,
Deform with discord's stormy sea --
Columbia's Independence!

We here assemble to rejoice
That patriots, with united voice,
Once rose and made this manly choice,
For them and their descendants.
They freedom's eagle raised on high --
Freedom's eagle -- freedom's eagle --
They freedom's eagle raised on high,
Amid the stars' resplendence;
They freedom's eagle raised on high,
And swore to fight or bravely die,
If foreign despots dare deny
Columbia's Independence.

Bellona goads her foaming steeds,
Beneath her car Oppression bleeds,
And Tyranny with haste recedes,
With all his cursed attendants;
Our patriot fathers gained the day --
Patriot fathers -- patriot fathers --

---

[309] Vol. II, pp. 92-93.
~~~

Our patriot fathers gained the day,
For them and their descendants;
Our patriot fathers gained the day,
For which we raise the joyful lay,
And on our banners still display
Columbia's Independence.

Then Freedom bade her temple rise,
Whose fabric every foe defies,
While joyous seraphs from the skies
Bestow their glad attendance;
And shades of martyrs smiling see --
Shades of martyrs -- shades of martyrs --
And shades of martyrs smiling see
The joy of their descendants;
And shades of martyrs smiling see
Their sons united, brave, and free,
And yearly hail, with mirth and glee,
Columbia's Independence.[310]

~~~***~~~

THE PATRIOTIC DIGGERS.

Johnny Bull beware,
Keep at proper distance,
Else we'll make you stare
At our firm resistance;
Let alone the lads
Who are freedom tasting,
Recollect our dads
Gave you once a basting.
Pickaxe, shovel, spade,
Crowbar, hoe, and barrow,
Better not invade,
Yankees have the marrow.
To protect our rights
'Gainst your flints and triggers,
See on Brooklyn Heights
Our patriotic diggers;
Men of every age,
Color, rank, profession,
Ardently engage,
Labor in succession.

Pickaxe, shovel, spade,
Crowbar, hoe, and barrow,
Better not invade,
Yankees have the marrow.

Grandeur leaves her towers,
Poverty her hovel,
Here to join their powers
With the hoe and shovel.

---

[310] Vol. II, pp. 100-102.
~~~

Here the merchant toils
With the patriot sawyer,
There the laborer smiles,
Near him sweats the lawyer.
Pickaxe, shovel, spade,
Crowbar, hoe, and barrow,
Better not invade,
Yankees have the marrow.

Here the mason builds
Freedom's shrine of glory,
While the painter gilds
The immortal story.
Blacksmiths catch the flame,
Grocers feel the spirit,
Printers share the fame,
And record their merit.
Pickaxe, shovel, spade,
Crowbar, hoe, and barrow,
Better not invade,
Yankees have the marrow,

Scholars leave their schools
With their patriot teachers;
Farmers seize their tools,
Headed by their preachers.
How they break the soil!
Brewers, butchers, bakers,
Here the doctors toil,
There the undertakers.
Pickaxe, shovel, spade,
Crowbar, hoe, and barrow,
Better not invade,
Yankees have the marrow.

Bright Apollo's sons
Leave their pipe and tabor,
'Mid the roar of guns
Join the martial labor;
Round the embattled plain
In sweet concord rally,
And in freedom's strain
Sing the foe's finale!
Pickaxe, shovel, spade,
Crowbar, hoe, and barrow,
Better not invade,
Yankees have the marrow.

Plumbers, founders, dyers,
Tinmen, turners, shavers,
Sweepers, clerks, and criers,
Jewellers, engravers,
Clothiers, drapers, players,
Cartmen, hatters, tailors,
Gaugers, sealers, weighers,
Carpenters, and sailors.

Pickaxe, shovel, spade,
Crowbar, hoe, and barrow,
Better not invade,
Yankees have the marrow.

Better not invade;
Recollect the spirit
Which our dads displayed,
And their sons inherit;
If you still advance,
Friendly caution slighting,
You may get, by chance,
A bellyful of fighting.
Pickaxe, shovel, spade,
Crowbar, hoe, and barrow,
Better not invade,
Yankees have the marrow.[311]

~~~***~~~

COLUMBIA, THE PRIDE OF THE WORLD.

Oh, there is a region, a realm in the West,
To Tyranny's shackles unknown,
A country with union and liberty blest,
That fairest of lands is our own.
Where commerce has opened her richest of marts,
Where freedom's bright flag is unfurled,
The garden of science, the seat of the arts,
Columbia, the pride of the world.

The rays of her glory have lighted the earth,
While Tyranny's minions, dismayed,
Acknowledged her prowess, admitted her worth,
And shrunk at the flash of her blade.
For conquest or plunder she never contends,
For freedom, her flag is unfurled;
And foemen in battle, in peace are thy friends,
Columbia, the pride of the world.

Her clime is a refuge for all the oppressed,
Whom tyranny urges to roam;
And every exile we greet as a guest,
Soon feels like a brother at home.
Then hail to our country, the land of our birth,
Where freedom's bright flag is unfurled;
The rays of whose glory have lighted the earth,
Columbia, the pride of the world.[312]

~~~***~~~

[311] Vol. II, pp. 105-107.
[312] Vol. II, pp. 112-113.

ODE, SUNG AT THE CELEBRATION OF INDEPENDENCE BY THE SOCIETY OF JUVENILE PATRIOTS.

[AN EARLY JUVENILE PRODUCTION.]

When from our shores Bellona's car
Recoiled amid dread scenes of war;
The guardian genius of our land
Gave listening freemen this command --
"Revere fair Freedom's chosen son,
Protect with life the prize he won."

High on her right the hero stood,
Victorious from the fields of blood,
And poised to heaven his reeking blade,
As witness to the vow he made: --
"This arm, with Heaven for its shield,
Shall e'er protect the dear-bought field."

The goddess heard the solemn vow,
And twined the laurel round his brow;
While swelled the anthem to his praise,
And spheres responsive caught the lays --
"Revere the hero, Washington,
For he your independence won."

Then, while we consecrate the day
Which gave our land its lawful sway,
Let all our bosoms glow with fires
Becoming sons of hero sires;
Swear ne'er to forfeit what they won,
While earth revolves around the sun.

And while our goblets flow with wine,
While rich libations grace the shrine,
In clouds of incense to the skies
Let this inspiring theme arise: --
"The youth of freedom e'er will be
Champions of sacred Liberty."

While Mars' red banner floats unfurled,
O'er the blood-deluged eastern world,
Here, Peace shall bless us with her reign,
While Virtue, Right, and Faith remain;
And let mad Europe blush to see
That Peace can dwell with Liberty.

But if our foes should e'er conspire
To kindle Freedom's funeral pyre,
And slaves of tyrants join the band
To subjugate their native land,
Our youth, indignant, then shall rise,
And save the dearly-purchased prize.

Our fathers fought, and scorned to yield,
But drove Oppression from the field;

Then gave this mandate with the prize,
To unborn patriots yet to rise: --
"Protect the blessing we bestow,
And guard your rights from every foe."

Then, youthful patriots, rise, and swear
To hold the glorious name you bear;
Your dear-bought freedom to maintain,
While ocean, earth, or sky remain;
And, like your fathers, still to be
Independent, great, and free.[313]

~~~***~~~

WASHINGTON'S BIRTHDAY.

While festive joys our hearts inspire,
Awake the patriotic lyre
With chords of light and tones of fire,
To sing a hero's worth;
And let our voices swell the lay,
Again to celebrate the day,
Illumed with Glory's brightest ray,
The day that give him birth.

Ennobled by himself alone,
His glory so resplendent shone,
That regal sceptre, crown, and throne,
Would but have dimmed its rays;
Devoted to his country's cause,
The champion of her rights and laws,
His children are heaven's applause
And earth's united praise.

In halls of state, and fields of blood,
He like a firm Colossus stood,
His object still Columbia's good,
His trust in Heaven alone;
But when the avenging deed was done,
And Freedom's host the field had won,
Then was immortal Washington
Throned in a nation's love.

When War's dread fiend had stayed his hand,
And dove-eyed Peace had blessed the land,
The hero sheathed the conquering wand,
Which independence won;
His valor made our country free,
Secured our rights and liberty,
Then let us celebrate with glee
The birth of Washington.[314]

---

313 Vol. II, pp. 113-115.
314 Vol. II, pp. 129-130.
~~~

~~~***~~~

A TRIBUTE TO LAFAYETTE.

What is true greatness? In the Eternal Mind
'T is wisdom, love, and potency combined;
In man, his image, it is truth in thought,
Embraced, beloved, and into action brought;
In one bright spirit all these virtues met,
And blessed the world with glorious Lafayette,
Whose feelings, thoughts, and acts united, ran
To one grand point -- the happiness of man.
No blemish stained the escutcheon which he bore;
If he loved glory -- he loved virtue more:
Heir to a splendid name, rank, title, power,
And princely fortune -- from the elysian bower
Of youthful wedlock, which an Eden bloomed
By breath of angel tenderness perfumed,
He tore himself away -- at Freedom's call,
In Freedom's cause resolved at stand or fall.
From a voluptuous court, where all caressed,
He flew to join her votaries in the West;
Here, with a stripling's arm, he bared the blade,
The drooping cause of Liberty to aid;
Resolved for glory's dazzling goal to run,
And share the prize with none but Washington.

Was this not greatness? -- Triumph or defeat --
The furious onset -- masterly retreat --
Skill, courage, patience, conduct, and address --
Yet great in all -- till crowned with bright success
He saw our country free; with laurelled brow
Beheld her God-like chief resume the plough;
Then sought his much-loved, native land again,
To beard the fiend Oppression in his den,
Bearing a torch from Freedom's blazing shrine,
Which lights the world, and will for ever shine.

Whether beheld in Victory's brightest hour,
Or as a fugitive from lawless power;
In the dark cells of Olmutz, crushed with chains,
Still not a spot his laurel chaplet stains.
Freed by Napoleon's arms -- e'en gratitude
His love of truth and virtue ne'er subdued.
With manly pride he princely honors spurned,
And to his fireside -- loved La Grange -- returned.
Was greatness his, whom cursed ambition fired
To mount a throne -- or Lafayette's, retired?

But time rolled on -- the hero came once more,
And millions hailed him "Welcome to our shore!"
That was a triumph "meet for gods to view,
And men, like gods"-- what monarchs never knew.
But oh! the moral grandeur of that hour,
When introduced beneath our senate's dome,
That solemn conclave hailed him "Welcome home!"
~~~

Leaves human language destitute of power
To do it justice. It was more sublime
Than any scene upon the page of time.

And when he saw the sages of the land,
Convened to place in one deserving hand
The reins of power, the car of state to guide,
In peace or war, whatever fate betide;
A chief installed without the vain parade
Which dazzles vassals, when their king are made:
Fired with the moral grandeur of the scene,
With tear-drops gushing from an eye serene,
He saw -- he heard -- and, with high-throbbing breast,
Pronounced Columbia's sons supremely blest.

But lo! in France oppression reigns again,
And Lafayette, at three-score years and ten,
Plucks from the Bourbon brow the jewelled crown,
While the weak despot, shrinking from his frown,
Yields him the sceptre, flying in disgrace --
The last, the worst of that degenerate race!
Millions of hearts, and hands, and voices, now
Had placed upon the patriot's silvery brow
That dazzling diadem -- but he was yet
Greater than monarchs -- he was Lafayette!
On younger brows he placed the glittering thing,
And swore allegiance to the new-made king:
This was true greatness -- for this act surpassed
The loftiest stretch of thought -- it was the last --
And it approached so near the heavenly goal,
Earth could no longer hold so pure a soul;
But, filled with virtue, wisdom, truth, and love,
'T was called to wear a diadem above.
We mourn him not on this august occasion --
We celebrate his heavenly coronation![315]

This tribute to the memory and virtues of Lafayette, was recited by William Wiley, Esq., at the Chatham-street chapel, in the city of New York, on the evening of the eighteenth of December, 1834, preparatory to a eulogy on the life and character of the distinguished patriot.

~~~***~~~

THE IRISH ORPHAN.

CITIZEN.
Irish maiden, whither fly you?
Whence the moisture on your cheek?
Danger here shall not come nigh you --
Tell me what, and whom, you seek.

IRISH GIRL.
Pity, sir, a hapless stranger,
Friendless on a foreign shore!
Much, alas! I fear of danger --
I'm from Erin, just come o'er.

---

[315] Vol. II, pp. 133-136.
~~~

CITIZEN.
Where 's your kindred, friend, protector?
Sure you ventured not alone?
Had you not some kind director?
Father, brother -- have you none?

IRISH GIRL.
Yes I have -- I had a brother,
Once a widowed parent's stay;
Yes, alas! I had a mother
Both by fate were snatched away!

CITIZEN.
Then, an orphan, unprotected,
You have left your native isle,
To Columbia's shore directed,
Where you meet no kindred smile?

IRISH GIRL.
No -- a parent, and a brother,
With me from oppression run;
Death deprived me of my mother --
Cruel Britons *pressed* her son.

Under Freedom's banner sailing,
Just in view of Freedom's shore,
Brightening prospects Hope was hailing,
Whispering future bliss in store:

When we spied the flag of Britain,
Where foreboding fancy read
Some impending evil written --
How my bosom beat with dread!

First a shot our course arrested,
Then their slaves disgraced our deck,
Fathers from their children wrested!
Son from parent's -- sister's neck!

"Spare!" I cried, "oh, spare my brother!
Spare him for a parent's sake!"
"Save! oh, save him!"' cried my mother,
"Or his sister's heart will break!"

Smiling pirates! they but mocked us!
Laughed at fond affection's grief!
And with brutal language shocked us,
While we wept without relief!

But when from us they departed,
Shrieks of anguish pierced the air!
Then my mother, broken-hearted
Fell, the victim of despair!

Pity, then, a hapless stranger,

Friendless on a foreign shore!
Oh, protect a maid from danger,
Who for comfort looks no more.

CITIZEN.
Yes, fair daughter of oppression!
Exile from Hibernia's plains,
Victim of that cursed aggression
Which the flag of freedom stains:

Here I swear to be thy brother;
See a sister in my wife;
Find a parent in my mother,
I'll protect thee with my life.[316]

~~~***~~~

BOLIVAR'S LAST WORDS.

"I pity and forgive."

Ye powers, from each oppressor,
Preserve my country's wreath,
And if my death can bless her,
Oh, then I welcome death.
Though malice wield her scourge,
E'en when I cease to live,
Here on the grave's terrific verge,
"'I pity and forgive."'

I planted freedom's banner
Where tyranny had reigned,
And heard the glad hosanna
For rights our arms regained;
But now they trample on my heart,
Yet ere I cease to live,
Though in my soul I feel the smart,
"I pity and forgive."[317]

~~~***~~~

CONSTITUTION AND JAVA.

Yankee tars! come, join the chorus,
Shout aloud the patriot strain;
Freedom's flag, again victorious,
Floats triumphant o'er the main.
Hail the gallant Constitution!
Hull immortalized her name;
Bainbridge, round it in profusion
Pours the golden blaze of fame.

Scarce had Fame her Hull rewarded,

---

[316] Vol. II, pp. 148-151.
[317] Vol. II, pp. 151-152.

Ere intrepid Bainbridge rose,
Eager while the world applauded,
To subdue his country's foes.
Hail the gallant Constitution, &c.

Hull, on board the Constitution,
Sank his foe beneath the flood;
Fired with equal resolution,
Bainbridge sought the scene of blood.
Hail the gallant Constitution, &c.

Lambert met him on the Java,
Fierce the hot contention rose --
Like the streams of Etna's lava,
Fell our vengeance on the foes
Hail the gallant Constitution, &c.

Neptune shunned the fierce commotion,
Saw his realm with carnage spread,
Saw our fire illume the ocean,
Covered with the floating dead.
Hail the gallant Constitution, &c.

Twice had Time his glass inverted,
While the strife deformed the flood,
Ere the fiend of death, diverted,
Ceased to glut on human blood.
Hail the gallant Constitution, &c.

See, our foe, upon the billow,
Floats a wreck without a spar --
Lowly lies on ocean's pillow,
Many a brave and gallant tar.
Hail the gallant Constitution, &c.

Hark! his lee gun speaks submission,
Bid our vengeful tars forbear --
Mercy views the foe's condition,
Sees a bleeding brother there.
Hail the gallant Constitution, &c.

Man the boats! the foe, confounded,
Yields to our superior fire;
Board the prize! relieve the wounded!
Ere in anguish they expire.
Hail the gallant Constitution, &c.

Ah! the fight was hard contested,
Groaning there an hundred bleed,
Sixty-nine has death arrested,
From their floating prisons freed.
Hail the gallant Constitution, &c.

Clear the wreck! she can not swim, boys;
See! she follows the Guerriere!
Now your cans fill to the brim, boys,

Sing our navy's bright career.
Hail the gallant Constitution, &c.

Toast the heroes famed in story,
Hull, Decatur, Rodgers, Jones;
Bainbridge, chief in naval glory,
Smiling Freedom joyfully owns.
Hail the gallant Constitution!
Hull immortalized her name;
Bainbridge, round it in profusion
Pours the golden blaze of fame.[318]

~~~***~~~

UNITED STATES AND MACEDONIAN.

The banner of Freedom high floated unfurled,
While the silver tipped surges in low homage curled,
Flashing bright round the bow of a ship under sail,
In fight, like the tempest -- in speed, like the gale.
She bears our country's name,
She builds our country's fame,
The bold United States disdains to yield or fly;
Her motto is "Glory -- we conquer or die."

All canvass expanded the gale to embrace,
The ship cleared for action, still nearing the chase;
The foeman in view -- every bosom beats high,
All eager for conquest, or ready to die.
Columbia's gallant tars,
Who sail beneath her stars,
Shall ne'er be known to yield -- shall ne'er ignobly fly;
Their motto is "Glory -- we conquer or die."

Still rapidly lessens the distance between,
Till the gay-floating streamers of Britain are seen;
Till our quick-sighted chief could with rapture espy,
The cross, like a meteor, gleaming on high.
To gild our country's name,
To rival Hull in fame,
The brave Decatur now resolves the fight to try --
His motto is "Glory -- we conquer or die."

Now Havoc stands ready with optics of flame,
And battle-hounds strain on the start for the game;
The blood-demons rise on the surge for their prey,
While Pity, dejected, awaits the dread fray.
But Freedom's gallant sons,
Now stationed at their guns,
Remember Freedom's wrongs, and smother Pity's sigh;
Their motto is "Glory -- we conquer or die."

Now the lightning of battle gleams horribly red
While a tempest of iron, and a hailstorm of lead,

---

[318] Vol. II, pp. 159-161.
~~~

Like a flood on the foe was so copiously poured,
That his mizzen and topmasts soon went by the board.
Still fight Columbia's tars
Beneath the stripes and stars,
For still their country's flag is proudly floating high,
Their motto is "Glory -- we conquer or die."

The contest continued with horrible roar,
The demons of vengeance still feasting on gore;
'Till more than a hundred of Britain's brave sons,
Lay bleeding on deck by the side of their guns:
When low the cross descends,
And quick the battle ends,
The Macedonian yields, her streamers kiss the wave;
Our motto is "Glory -- we conquer to save."

Let Britain no longer lay claim to the seas,
For the trident of Neptune is ours if we please;
While Hull, and Decatur, and Jones[319] are our boast,
In vain their huge navy may threaten our coast.
They gild Columbia's name,
They build Columbia's fame;
And to revenge our wrongs, to battle eager fly;
Their motto is "Glory -- we conquer or die."[320]

~~~***~~~

PERRY AND M'DONOUGH:
OR, ERIE AND CHAMPLAIN.

Hail to the day which arises in splendor,
Shedding the lustre of victory far!
Long shall its glory illume September,
Which twice beheld freemen the victors in war.
Roused by the spirit of heaven-born Freedom,
Perry her lightning pours over the lake;
His falchion a meteor glitters to lead them,
And swift on the foemen in thunders they break.
Loud swells the cannon's roar,
Round Erie's sounding shore,
Answered in volleys by musketry's voice;
Till Britain's cross descends,
And the haughty foe bends --
Victory! glory! Columbians, rejoice!

Hail to the day which in splendor returning,
Lights us to conquest and glory again;
Time told a year -- still the war-torch was burning,
And threw its red ray on the waves of Champlain;

Roused by the spirit that conquered for Perry,
Dauntless M'Donough advanced to the fray;

---

[319] [*Edit. Note*. Capt. Jacob Jones of the *Wasp* versus *Frolic* encounter.]
[320] Vol. II, pp. 156-158.
~~~

Instant the glory that brightened Lake Erie,
Burst on Champlain with the splendor of day
Loud swells the cannon's roar
On Plattsburgh's bloody shore,
Britons retreat from the tempest of war;
Prevost deserts the field,
While the gallant ships yield --
Victory! glory! Columbians, huzza!

Hail to the day which, recorded in story,
Lives the bright record of unfading fame!
Long shall Columbians, inspired by its glory,
Hail its returning with joyous acclaim.
Victory scattered profusely the laurel,
Over our heroes, on land and on flood;
Britain, astonished, relinquished the quarrel,
Peace saw her olive arise from the blood.
Now cannons cease to roar,
Round Freedom's peaceful shore,
Silent and hushed is the war-bugle's voice;
Let festive joys increase
In the sunshine of peace,
Peace gained by victory! Freemen, rejoice![321]

The engagement on Lake Erie, between Commodores Perry and Barclay, occurred September 10, 1813, and that of Lake Champlain, between M'Donough and Downie, Sept. 11, 1814. Sir George Prevost, commander of the British land-forces, made a hasty retreat after the capture of Commodore Downie's fleet.

~~~***~~~

THE HUNTERS OF KENTUCKY.

Ye gentlemen and ladies fair,
Who grace this famous city,
Just listen, if ye've time to spare,
While I rehearse a ditty;
And for the opportunity,
Conceive yourselves quite lucky,
For 't is not often that you see,
A hunter from Kentucky.
Oh! Kentucky, the hunters of Kentucky,
The hunters of Kentucky .

We are a hardy free-born race,
Each man to fear a stranger,
Whate'er the game, we join in chase,
Despising toil and danger;
And if a daring foe annoys,
Whate'er his strength and forces,
We'll show him that Kentucky boys
Are "alligator horses."
Oh! Kentucky, &c.

I s'pose you've read it in the prints,
How Packenham attempted

[321] Vol. II, pp. 167-168.
~~~

To make Old Hickory Jackson wince,
But soon his scheme repented;
For we with rifles ready cocked,
Thought such occasion lucky,
And soon around the general flocked
The hunters of Kentucky .
Oh! Kentucky, &c.

You've heard, I s'pose, how New Orleans
Is famed for wealth and beauty --
There's girls of every hue, it seems,
From snowy white to sooty:
So Packenham he made his brags,
If he in fight was lucky,
He'd have their girls and cotton bags,
In spite of Old Kentucky.
Oh! Kentucky, &c.

But Jackson, he was wide awake,
And wasn't scared at trifles;
For well he knew what aim we take,
With our Kentucky rifles;
So he led us down to Cypress swamp,
The ground was low and mucky;
There stood John Bull, in martial pomp,
And here was Old Kentucky.
Oh! Kentucky, &c.

A bank was raised to hide our breast,
Not that we thought of dying,
But then we always like to rest,
Unless the game is flying;
Behind it stood our little force --
None wished it to be greater,
For every man was half a horse,
And half an alligator.
Oh! Kentucky, &c.

They did not let our patience tire,
Before they showed their faces --
We did not choose to waste our fire,
So snugly kept our places;
But when so near we saw them wink,
We thought it time to stop them;
And 't would have done you good, I think.
To see Kentucky pop them.
Oh! Kentucky, &c.

They found at last, 't was vain to fight
Where lead was all their booty,
And so they wisely took to flight,
And left us all the beauty.
And now, if danger e'er annoys,
Remember what our trade is,
Just send for us Kentucky boys,
And we'll protect you, ladies.

Oh! Kentucky, the hunters of Kentucky,
The hunters of Kentucky.[322]

~~~***~~~

A FOURTH OF JULY CELEBRATION.

Where's Roberts, that red-headed fellow?
I wanted to give him a call, sir;
They told me down there in the cellar,
I'd find him up here in the hall, sir.
I've come from the country, you know,
For farming is my occupation;
To see what you city folks show
On a fourth of July celebration.
Umpti-uddity, &c.

To Hobok I rode in a wagon,
And sailed over the river in style, sir;
For the boat had a pole with a flag on,
And a big pot of water to boil, sir.
The stovepipe was smoking like fury,
An iron thing bobbed up and down, sir,
And all, just to make, I assure you,
A wheel in the water go round, sir.

We landed, at length, in your city,
Without the least morsel of dread, sir,
For I thought it a wonderful pity,
If I couldn't find the Bull's Head, sir.
So I travelled right up to Broadway,
Where gridirons are laid out in the street, sir,
For wood is so scarce here, they say,
The sun has to boil all the meat, sir.

The people were thicker than mustard,
Each girl with her beautiful lips, sir,
Looked sweeter than honey or custard,
And smiled like a basket of chips, sir;
The windows were chuck full of gay things,
And boys in every shop, sir,
Were buying those little red playthings,
That cracked away pop-ity pop! sir.

The crowd it grew thicker and thicker,
Along by the Park iron fence, sir,
Where gingerbread, cherries, and liquor,
Were spread upon tables in tents, sir.
There was lobsters, and oysters, and clams,
Green pease, new potatoes, and gravy,
With pigs ready roasted, and hams,
Enough to provision the navy.

The Park was all crowded with people,

[322] Vol. II, pp. 7-10.
~~~

And so was the big City-Hall, sir,
Chuck full, from the steps to the steeple,
The gallery, windows, and all, sir.
They were waiting to see the procession,
And sure enough, after a while, sir
Mechanics of every profession,
Formed a line that extended a mile, sir.
And there was the veteran corps,
Each member an old seventy-sixer,
In the very same dress that he wore,
When he peppered John Bull for his tricks, sir.
Each man who had courage and pluck,
And boasted political stamina,
In his hat had the tail of a buck,
In honor of Mister St. Tammany.

And then came a beautiful ship,
I'm sorry I couldn't get near her;
All handsomely rigged and equipped,
With a neat little fellow to steer her.
And there was a seven-foot Venus,
As big as the wife of a giant,
They said it was one Mrs. Genius,
I mean to ask Halleck or Bryant.

But don't let's forget the brave fellows,
Whose things at a fire never fail, sir,
They work 'em all one like a bellows,
And every one spouts like a whale, sir.
All these, with a thousand more people,
Marched off, for their edification,
To a building without any steeple,
To hear Hooper Cumming's oration.

Then I heard such a fifing and drumming,
I axed the folks what was to pay, sir,
They told me the soldiers were coming,
All marching along in Broadway, sir.
And soon in the Park was paraded,
The strength of our city, I'll bet, sir,
With no other view, I'm persuaded,
But to honor the brave Lafayette, sir.

Then there was the famous balloon,
That travels ten miles in a minute,
Set out on a voyage to the moon,
With a *parley vous Francais* man in it;
Besides a boat-race on the water,
Where one of them travelled so fast, sir,
I wonder how 't other one caught her,
Without e'er a sail or a mast, sir.

So, having seen everything new,
I thought I would finish the day, sir,
By coming with Sally and Sue,
And Ichabod, here to the play, sir.

But if you should relish my song,
I'll make you another and bring it;
Much better, because not so long,
And red-headed Roberts shall sing it.

Sung by Mr. Roberts at the Chatham Theatre, in 1825, in the character of a country boy.[323]

A Partial Listing of Literary Works by Samuel Woodworth

Note. Woodworth also wrote a good deal of shorts stories, poems, essays, and miscellaneous and occasional pieces printed in magazines and periodicals or performed in the theater not included here.

* "New-Haven: a poem, satirical and sentimental, with critical, humorous, descriptive, historical, biographical, and explanatory notes" (1809) by Selim[324] Woodworth
* *An oration delivered before the New-York Typographical Society at their second anniversary, on the fourth of July, 1811* (1811) by George Ashbridge; which included an ode by Woodworth.
* "Beasts at Law, or, Zoologian Jurisprudence: a poem, satirical, allegorical, and moral : in three cantos, translated from the Arabic of Sampfilius Philocrin, Z.Y.X.W. &c., &c., whose fables have made so much noise in the East, and whose fame has eclipsed that of Aesop; with notes and annotations" (1811)
* *The First Attempt, or, Something new: Being a picture of truth, drawn from the nature of things as they really exist* (1811)
* "Quarter-day, or, The horrors of the first of May: a poem" (1812)
* "The Heroes of the Lake: a poem, in two parts" (1814) by Amulans Sequor [pseudonym]
* *Bubble & Squeak, or, A Dish of all Sorts: Being a collection of American poems* (1814)
* *The Champions of Freedom, or, The mysterious chief: a romance of the nineteenth century, founded on the events of the War, between the United States and Great Britain, which terminated in March, 1815* (1816)
* "The Complete Coiffeur, or, An essay on the art of adorning natural, and of creating artificial, beauty" (1817) by J.B.M.D. Lafoy [pseudonym]
* *The poems, odes, songs, and other metrical effusions, of Samuel Woodworth* (1818)
* "The Deed of Gift: a comic opera in three acts" (1822)
* "An Excursion of the Dog-Cart: a poem, by an imprisoned debtor." (1822)
* "La Fayette, or, The Castle of Olmutz: a drama in three acts" (1824)
* "The Widow's Son, or, Which is the Traitor: a melo-drama in three acts" (1825) by Samuel Woodworth; music by J.H. Swindells.
* "The Forest Rose, or, American Farmers: a drama in two acts" (1825)
* "The life and confession of James Hudson, who was executed on Wednesday the 12th January, 1825, at the falls of Fall Creek, for the murder of Logan, an Indian Chief of the Wyandott nation, to which is added an account of his execution. The whole written and published at the request of the deceased." (1825)
* "King's Bridge cottage: a revolutionary tale founded on an incident which occurred a few days previous to the evacuation of N. York by the British: a drama in two acts" (1826)
* *Melodies, duets, trios, songs, and ballads, pastoral, amatory, sentimental, patriotic, religious, and miscellaneous. Together with metrical epistles, tales and recitations. By Samuel Woodworth. Second edition, comprising many late productions never before published.* (1830)
* *Festivals, Games, and amusements: ancient and modern* (1831) by Horatio Smith; with contributions by Woodworth
* *Dixon's*[325] *Oddities. A glorious collection of ... songs; as song by Mr. G. Dixon, at New-York, Philadelphia, Boston, Baltimore and New Orleans theatres -- Including the new national song, composed and sung on the day of the celebration of the French revolution; to which is added, the ode, written by Mr. S. Woodworth for the same occasion* (1842)
The Poetical Works of Samuel Woodworth (1861), edited by his son, Frederick A. Woodworth.

---

[323] Vol. II, pp. 29-33.
[324] A pen-name.
[325] A popular comic stage singer.

PRESERVING THE NATION'S HONOR:
Capt. Joshua Barney and the Patuxent River Flotilla of 1814.

Not long after the cannon of the naval War of 1812 fell silent, the fight resumed, and to this day even continues, on paper and in print between British and American partisans. This battle of the scholars could be said to have originated with popular American histories, such as Thomas Clark's well-meaning but rather fast and loose *Naval History of the United States* (1813 and 1814), and, in addition, more credible personal accounts and memoirs, such as Captain David Porter's thrilling *Journal of a Cruise Made to the Pacific Ocean* (1822)[326] that incited the exasperated ire of former British attorney William James (1780-1827); who responded with his multi-volume *Naval History of Great Britain from the declaration of war by France in February 1793 to the accession of George IV in January 1820* (1822-24, & 1837). This monumental and impressive, if as many will feel imperfect and sometimes flawed work (volume 6 in particular), was gallantly and coolly answered by James Fenimore Cooper's *The History of the Navy of the United States* (1839);[327] followed by the even more meticulous *The Navy of the United States from the commencement 1775 to 1853* (1853) by Lieut. George Foster Emmons, USN. Later and even more indignantly, James' work received an unapologetically thunderous broadside from Theodore Roosevelt's *The Naval War of 1812* (1882) -- with and in our own time some and more of the same from both sides of the Atlantic (and Canada) -- though in hopefully a better humored and more good humored and friendly manner than the earlier historians felt necessary. While most everyone is quick to see errors and misjudgments in these or the writings of their respective opponents, what is unfortunately and too often overlooked is that *all* these aforenamed writers, whatever their shortcomings in a given instance as historians, have *something* worth saying and being heard, and a student is much misguided who turns a deaf ear in *wholesale* prejudice to any one of them.[328]

It was only very recently that I myself had and took the time to go through Cooper's tome; which as survey and overview has much to recommend it. Although far from seamless as a narrative; while occasionally suffering from the author's sometimes strained and confusing prose, his history is a *must read* for purposes of furnishing the broad picture, and I am sorry I had not already read it many years ago. Moreover, in many portions it makes for some genuinely exciting, touching, and or droll history-telling; such as (though not exclusively) in these sections:

* The Barbary States, the Birth of the Federal navy, and the Quasi-War with France (vol. I, chs. 14-16)
* The War with Tripoli (vol. 1, ch. 18; vol. II, chs. 1-6)
* Chase of the *Constitution* under Capt. Isaac Hull by a British squadron (vol. ii, ch. 10)
* Capt. Porter and the *Essex* (vol. II, chs. 13-15)
* Battle of Lake Borgne 1814 (vol. II, ch. 22)
* Joshua Barney and the defense of Washington, D.C. in 1814

Joshua Barney (1759-1818) is an exceptionally memorable figure because he was one of the few who signally distinguished himself and covered himself with glory in *both* the Revolution *and* the War of 1812.[329] If, as is averred, only a minority of valiant and undaunted individuals saved the country from foreign invasion in those two struggles, he would most certainly can be deemed one of those most noble

---

[326] Perhaps also (and along with *Narrative of the Most Extraordinary and Distressing Shipwreck of the Whale-Ship Essex, of Nantucket; Which was Attacked and Finally Destroyed by a Large Spermaceti-Whale* [1821] by Chase Owen) an inspiration for Melville's *Moby Dick*?

[327] Cooper put out an abridged version in 1841 which, though some will find more convenient, is inferior as both a chronicle and keepsake compared to the complete edition.

[328] As we've noted elsewhere previously, for a nautical primer, including a handy glossary of terms incomprehensible to most laymen and otherwise indispensable for reading such books, see *The Seaman's Friend: A Treatise on Practical Seamanship* (1841) by Richard Henry Dana, Jr. at: http://www.archive.org/details/seamansfriendcon00danarich

[329] He was also unique as a American naval officer for being, like Capt. John Barry and Lieut. Stephen Cassin (which latter fought with distinction in command of the *Ticonderoga* at the battle of Lake Champlain), a Roman Catholic; see Norton pp. 147-148, 156. A most welcome and extremely useful, if perhaps too hastily penned and edited, modern biography is *Joshua Barney: Hero of the Revolution and 1812* (2000) by Louis Arthur Norton; also of interest are *A Biographical Memoir of the Late Commodore Joshua Barney* (1832) by Mary Barney (Barney's daughter-in-law), and *Sailor of Fortune: The Life and Adventures of Commodore Barney, U.S.N.* (1940) by Hulbert Footner.

and illustrious few; warring with a youthful zeal and determination rarely matched even in those heroic times. That he else and afterward appears to have also subsequently lived a relatively pacific, prosperous, and happy domestic and family life for a military officer adds further to his appeal.

The following then is Cooper's coverage of Barney involvement in the War of 1812. Most notably, Barney's naval service in that conflict saw him leading President Jefferson's ignominious gunboats. As bad a reputation as they have received, it must be observed that those gunboats saw much action in the War of 1812; and a number of them were commanded with encouraging success; so that their fault lay not some much in their use but rather in the government's over reliance on them.

~~~***~~~

~ from Chapter XXI of Cooper's *History of the Navy of the United States* (1839) Vol. 2, pp. 215-221.

The general peace that, owing to the downfall of Napoleon, so suddenly took place in Europe, afforded England an opportunity of sending large reinforcements in ships and troops to America. Regiments that had entered France from Spain, were embarked in the Loire, with that object; and a land force of more than thirty thousand men was soon collected in the interior, or on the American coast. The ships, also, were much increased in number; and it would seem that there was a moment when some in England were flattered with the belief of being able to dictate such terms to the republic, as would even reduce its territory, if they did not affect its independence. In carrying on the war, two separate plans appear to have been adopted. One aimed at conquest -- the other at harassing the coast, and at inflicting the injuries that characterise [sic] a partisan warfare.

In furtherance of the latter intention, a considerable force in ships and troops assembled in the waters of the Chesapeake early in the summer, when the enemy attempted expeditions of greater importance, and which were more creditable to his arms than many in which he had been previously engaged, against small, exposed, and defenceless [sic] villages. The warfare of 1813 had induced the government to equip a stronger force in the Chesapeake than it had originally possessed, and Captain Joshua Barney, the officer whose name has already been mentioned [See *History of the Navy*, vol. I, ch. 11, pp. 149-153], with distinction, as the captor of the General Monk, was placed at its head.[330] The vessels of the flotilla under the orders of Captain Barney were principally barges, carrying heavy guns, though there were a few galleys, and a schooner or two.

It would exceed the limits of a work of this nature, to enter into a minute relation of all the skirmishes to which the predatory warfare of the English, in the Chesapeake, gave rise; but it is due to the officers and men employed against them to furnish an outline of their services. On various occasions parties from the ships had conflicts with the detached militia, or armed citizens, who were frequently successful. Although it is a little anticipating events, it may be mentioned here, that, in one of these skirmishes, Captain Sir Peter Parker, of the Menelaus, was killed, and his party driven off to its ship. In several other instances captures were made of boats and their crews, the people of the country frequently displaying a coolness and gallantry that were worthy of trained soldiers. On the whole, however, the vast superiority of the enemy in numbers, and his ability to choose his time and place of attack, gave the English the advantage, and their success was usually in proportion.

The presence of Captain Barney's flotilla compelled the enemy to be more guarded, and his small vessels became cautious about approaching the shallow waters in calms, or in light winds. On the 1st of June this active and bold officer left the Patuxent [River], with the Scorpion, two gun-boats, and several large barges, in chase of two schooners. He was closing fast, by means of sweeps, when a large ship was discovered to the southward. Just at this moment the wind shifted, bringing the enemy to windward, blowing fresh, and becoming squally. Signal was made for the flotilla to return to the Patuxent, as the weather was particularly unfavourable for that description of force, and the ship proved to be a two-decker. On re-entering the river, the wind came ahead, when the gun-boats began to sweep up under the weather

[330] [*Edit. Note.* As a result of the naval battle that took place in Delaware/New Jersey Bay, 8 April 1782, with Barney flying the flag of the Pennsylvania Navy while escorting a small convoy of American merchantmen out of Philadelphia.]
~~~

shore. One of the latter being in some danger, Captain Barney anchored with the Scorpion and the other boats, and opened a fire, which immediately drove the enemy schooners out of the river. On this occasion, the English pushed a barge in front, which began to throw Congreve rockets. By this essay it was found that the rockets could be thrown farther than shot, but that they could not be directed with any certainty. The ship of the line anchored at the mouth of the Patuxent; the enemy's barges kept hovering about it, and the American flotilla was anchored about three miles within the river.

Between the 4th and 8th of June, the enemy was joined by a rasée [razee] and a sloop-of-war, when Captain Barney removed his flotilla up the river, to the mouth of St. Leonard's creek. On the morning of the 8th, the British were seen coming up the river, the wind being fair, with a ship, a brig, two schooners, and fifteen barges, which induced Capt. Barney to remove up St. Leonard's about two miles, when he anchored in a line abreast, and prepared to receive an attack. At 8 A. M., the ship, brig, and schooners anchored at the mouth of the creek, and the barges entered it, with the rocket boat in advance.

Captain Barney now left the Scorpion and the two gun-boats at anchor, and got his barges, thirteen in number, under way, when the enemy retreated towards their vessels outside. In the afternoon, the same manoeuvre was repeated, the enemy's barge throwing a few rockets without effect.

On the afternoon of the 9th, the ship of the line having sent up a party of men, the enemy entered the creek again, having twenty barges, but, after a smart skirmish, retired. The object of these demonstrations was probably to induce the Americans to burn their vessels, or to venture out within reach of the guns of the ships, but the latter were commanded by an officer much too experienced and steady to be forced into either measure without sufficient reason. On the 11th, a still more serious attempt was made with twenty-one barges, having the two schooners in tow. Capt. Barney met them again, and, after a sharper encounter than before, drove them down upon their large vessels. On this occasion the pursuit was continued until the rasée, which, by this time, had ascended the Patuxent, and the brig opened a fire on the Americans. In this affair the English are supposed to have suffered materially, especially one of the schooners. A shot also struck the rocket-boat.

Some small works were now thrown up on the shore, to protect the American flotilla, and the blockade continued. In the mean time, Captain [Samuel] Miller of the marine corps joined the flotilla, and a considerable force of militia was collected under Colonel [Decius] Wadsworth, of the ordnance service. The enemy had also brought a frigate, in addition to the rasée, off the mouth of the creek. The largest of these vessels was believed to be the Severn, and the smallest the Narcissus, thirty-two. On the 26th, an attempt was made by the united force of the Americans to raise the blockade. The cannonade was close, for the species of force employed; and it lasted two hours, when the Severn cut, and was run on a sand-bank to prevent her sinking.*[331] It is said that a raking shot ripped a plank from her bow, and placed her in imminent danger. Shortly after, in company with the Narcissus, she dropped down the river and went into the bay. In this handsome affair the flotilla lost thirteen men in killed and wounded; but it effectually raised the blockade, and induced the enemy to be more cautious.

The portion of the flotilla that was in the Patuxent, remained in that river until the middle of August, when the enemy commenced that series of movements which terminated in his advance upon Washington. On the 16th, Captain Barney received intelligence that the British were coming up the Patuxent in force, when he sent an express to the navy department for instructions. The answer was, to land the men, and join the army that was hurriedly assembling for the defence of the coast, under General [William H.] Winder, and, if pressed, to burn the flotilla.

On the 21st, the news was received that the enemy had landed a force of four or five thousand men at Benedict [Maryland; some 35 miles southeast of Washington, D.C.], and that he was marching in the direction of the capital. Captain Barney immediately landed four hundred of his party, leaving the vessels in charge of Mr. Frazier, with orders to set fire to them if attacked, and to join the main body with as little delay as possible. The next day this order was executed, a strong detachment of seamen and marines approaching the flotilla to attack it.

---

[331] [*Cooper's Footnote*] By some accounts this ship was the Loire.

On the 22nd, Captain Barney joined the assemblage of armed citizens, that was called an army, at the wood-yard. The next day he marched into Washington, and took up his quarters in the marine barracks. After a good deal of uncertainty concerning the movements of the enemy, it was understood he was marching directly on Washington, and that it was intended to fight him at Bladensburgh. The flotilla-men and marines left the yard on the morning of the 24th, and they arrived at the battle-ground on a trot, and were immediately drawn up about a mile to the west of Bladensburgh, holding the centre of General Winder's position. After a sharp skirmish in front, where the enemy suffered severely in crossing a bridge, the militia fell back, and the British columns appeared, following the line of the public road. The entire force of the flotilla-men and marines was about five hundred men; and they had two eighteens, and three twelve pounders, ship's guns, mounted on travelling carriages. Captain Barney took command of the artillery in person, while Captain Miller had the disposition of the remainder of the two parties, who were armed as infantry. The marines, seventy-eight men in all, formed a line immediately on the right of the guns, while the seamen, three hundred and seventy men, were drawn up a little in their rear, and on the right flank of the marines, on ground that permitted them to fire over the heads of the latter. Although the troops that were falling back did not halt, Captain Barney held his position, and as soon as the enemy began to throw rockets, he opened on him, with a sharp discharge of round and grape. The column was staggered, and it immediately gave ground. A second attempt to advance was repulsed in the same manner, when the enemy, who, as yet, had been able to look down resistance by his discipline, advancing steadily in column, was obliged to make an oblique movement to his left, into some open fields, and to display. Here he threw out a brigade of light troops in open order, and advanced in beautiful style, upon the command of Captain Barney, while the head of a strong column was kept in reserve in a copse in its rear. Captain Miller, with the marines, and that portion of the seamen who acted as infantry, met the charge in the most steady and gallant manner, and, after a sharp conflict, drove the British light troops back upon their supporting column.[332] In this conflict, the English commanding officer, in advance, Colonel [William] Thornton, with his second and third in rank, Lieutenant-Colonel Wood and Major Brown, were all wounded, and left on the field. The marines and seamen manifested the utmost steadiness, though it was afterwards ascertained that the light troops brought up in their front amounted to about six hundred men.

There can be no question that a couple of regular regiments would now have given the Americans the day, but no troops remained in line, except the party under Captain Barney, and two detachments on his right, that were well posted. Having been so roughly handled, the enemy made no attempt to advance directly in front of the seamen and marines, but, after forcing the troops on their right from the field, by a demonstration in that direction, they prepared to turn the rear of Captain Barney, in order to surround him. While these movements were going on in front, a party of light troops had been thrown out on the enemy's right, and the militia having abandoned the ground, they were also beginning to close upon the Americans that stood. By this time Captain Barney, Captain Miller, and several other officers were wounded; and victory being impossible, against odds so great, an order was given to commence a retreat. The defence had been too obstinate to admit of carrying off the guns, which were necessarily abandoned. All the men retired, with the exception of the badly wounded; among the latter, however, were Captain Barney and Captain Miller, who both fell into the enemy's hands. The loss of the latter, in front of the seamen and marines, on this occasion, was near three hundred men, in killed and wounded. Of the marines nearly one-third were among the casualties; and the flotilla-men suffered considerably, though in a smaller proportion.

The people of the flotilla, under the orders of Captain Barney, and the marines, were justly applauded for their excellent conduct on this occasion. No troops could have stood better, and the fire of both artillery and musketry has been described as to the last degree severe. Captain Barney, himself, and Captain Miller, of the marine corps, in particular, gained much additional reputation, and their conspicuous gallantry caused a deep and general regret, that their efforts could not have been sustained by the rest of the army.

As the enemy took possession of Washington, a perfectly defenceless straggling town of some eight or nine thousand inhabitants, that evening, and a considerable force in ships was ascending the

---

[332] [*Edit. Note.* The sailors and marines when attacking, it is said (though unconfirmed by me), called on their comrades to "board 'em" or words to similar effect. And see Norton, p. 180.]

Potomac, it was thought necessary to destroy the public property at the navy yard. At that time a frigate, of the first class, called the Columbia, was on the stocks, and the Argus, 18, and Lynx, 12, had not long been launched. A small quantity of stores and ammunition had been removed, but on the night of the 24th, fire was communicated to the remainder. It is difficult to say why the vessels 'afloat were not scuttled, a measure that would have allowed of their being raised again, as it would have been impossible for the enemy to injure ships in that state, and much less to remove them. Indeed the expediency of setting fire to anything has been questioned, since the enemy could not have done more. It is, however, just to remember that the sudden retreat of the English could not have been foreseen, and that they had a commanding naval force in the Potomac. The loss in vessels was not great; the Columbia, 44, on the stocks, and the Argus, 18, being the only two destroyed that were of any value. The Lynx escaped, and it would seem that the enemy was in too great a hurry to do her any injury. On this occasion the Boston, 28, was burned, though the ship was condemned. The hulk of the New York, 36, escaped, but all the naval stores were consumed.

It is worthy of remark, that this, and the instance in which the Adams was burned in the Penobscot, were the only cases in the war in which the enemy, notwithstanding his numerous descents, was ever able to destroy any public cruiser by means of his troops. In this respect the difference between the war of 1812 and that of 1775 is strikingly apparent. During the former contest, indeed, the enemy: succeeded in no assault on any place of size, although, encouraged by his success at Washington, an attempt was shortly after made on Baltimore....

[In a subsequent footnote, pp. 223n-225n, Cooper states:]

Joshua Barney was born in Baltimore, July 6th, 1759. He went to sea young, and by some accidental circumstances was early thrown into the command of a valuable ship. At the commencement of the war of the Revolution, or in October, 1775, he entered on board the Hornet, 10, which was fitted at Baltimore, as a master's mate, and sailed in the expedition under Com. [Esek] Hopkins, against the Bahamas. The Hornet was separated from the squadron by bad weather, and returned to port alone. He next joined the Sachem, 10, Captain Alexander, as a lieutenant, though his name is not found on the regular list of the service, until July 20th, 1781, when it appears by the side of those of Dale and Murray. From this fact it is to be inferred that the first commissions regularly received from Congress, by either of those distinguished young sailors, were given at that time. But Mr. Barney served even as a first lieutenant of a frigate at a much earlier day. He was in that station on board the Virginia, 28, when taken by the enemy; and he also served in the same rank, on board the Saratoga, 16. Mr. Barney escaped the fate of the Saratoga, in consequence of having been in a prize.

After serving in a very gallant manner on board of different vessels of former command, less than half of his flotilla having been destroyed in the Patuxent, Mr. Barney was appointed to the Hyder Ally.[333] For the manner in which he received this command, and the brilliant action he fought in that ship, the reader is referred to the text. From the year 1782 to that of 1784, Captain Barney served in the General Washington, (late General Monk,) being most of the time employed as a despatch vessel, or on civil duty of moment. It is not easy to say what was the regular rank of Captain Barney at this period. That he was a lieutenant in the public marine is certain, but it does not so clearly appear that he was appointed to be a captain. Of his claim to this distinction there is no question, though it would seem that the peculiar state of the country prevented this act of justice from being performed. When the General Washington was sold, Captain Barney retired to private life, and, like all his brother officers of the marine of the Revolution, was disbanded.

In 1794, Captain Barney was one of the six captains appointed in the new navy, but he declined taking the commission on account of the name of Captain Talbot preceding his own. In 1796 Captain Barney went to France, and not long after he was induced to enter the French navy, with the rank of *chef de division*. On the 28th of May he sailed from Rochfort for St. Domingo, in L'Harmouie, 44, having La Railleuse, 36, in company, and under his orders. After cruising some time with these ships, to which a third was subsequently added, he got the command of La Meduse and L'Insurgente, the latter being the frigate

[333] [*Edit. Note.* Named after the Mysore sultan in India, Hyder Ali (1720-1782); who successfully defied British rule there. His son, Tipu Sultan (1750-1799), also became an intrepid fighter for Indian liberty and widely hailed national folk-hero.]

that was eventually lost in the American navy. With these two ships he came to America, and was watched for several months by a superior English squadron. The manner in which Com. Barney got to sea, when he was ready to sail, has always been greatly admired. The French frigates dropped down gradually towards the sea, the enemy moving out before them, until the former had anchored just within the capes, and the latter were watching them in the offing. As soon as it became dark, Com. Barney lifted his anchors and stood up the bay, until far enough to be out of sight, when he again brought up. The next morning, missing him, the English supposed he had got to sea in the night, and made sail in chase. Com. Barney, in the mean while, followed his enemies off the coast, altering his course in time to avoid them.

In 1800, Com. Barney quitted the French service, and returned home, He was engaged in commerce until the war of 1812. The navy by that time had become too regular to allow of his being received into it, and he accepted the command of a privateer. He made only one cruise in this vessel, and in 1813 was put at the head of the flotilla in the Chesapeake, with the rank of a captain in the navy, though not properly in the service. His gallant conduct in that station has been shown. After the war of 1812, he held a civil station under the government, and died in Kentucky, to which stale he had removed, December 1st, 1818, in the 59th year of his age. The wound received at Bladensburg is supposed to have caused his death.

Captain Barney, or Com. Barney, as it was usual to call him, in consequence of his rank in the French service, was a bold, enterprising, and highly gallant officer. His combat with the Monk was one of the neatest naval exploits on record; and in all situations he manifested great spirit, and the resources of a man fitted to command. There is little question that he would have been one of the most distinguished officers in the service, had he remained in it; and, as it is, few Americans enjoy a more enviable professional reputation. Captain Barney is said to have been engaged in twenty-six combats, all of which were against the English, and in nearly all of which he was successful.

An Ode
"TO THE LIBERTY AND INDEPENDENCE OF THE UNITED STATES"

By Francisco Manuel de Nascimento.

Historians Clinton Rossitor in *The First American Revolution: The American Colonies on the Eve of Independence* (1933, 1956), and Max Savelle in *Seeds of Liberty: The Genesis of the American Mind* (1948) cogently, and with extensive evidence and documentation to back their claims, demonstrate how a dramatic political, cultural and religious break of America from Britain and Europe was taking place several decades before the fighting at Lexington and Concord. To supplement this both important and correct interpretation, it is yet warranted as well to observe that chronologically the American Revolutionaries were preceded in their bid for liberty by General Pasquale Paoli's (1725-1807) Corsican Republic (versus the French),[334] Poland's Bar Confederation of 1768-1772 (versus Russia), and, as we have noted elsewhere, the rebellion of Chief Pontiac of the Ottawas in 1763.

Of course, the influence of John Locke and other English Puritan writers[335] -- with the Puritans, after all being, the forerunners of the Whigs -- on such as Benjamin Franklin, John Adams and Thomas Jefferson is well known; as is the impact of Montesquieu and the political theorists of the French Enlightenment: American notions of political equality being, to a large degree, a joint by product of Dutch/English Protestant revolt and 17th-18th century scientific rationalism. Frankin's deft witticisms, when he was acting the part of ambassador to France, smacked no little of Voltaire's outlook and style of repartee; while his fur cap and assumed persona of the American rustic with down-to-earth good sense made him a popular, real life representative of Rousseau's natural ideal.

But, as we know, whatever colonial America picked up from Europe it returned in reciprocal and ample proportion; with the success of the American Revolution serving as a material impetus in encouraging and giving hope to subsequent radical and liberation movements in France, the Netherlands, Ireland, and, as well, South America; while providing a boost to nationalism and a searching for (and defining of) a modern national identity in almost every country in Europe.

The decisive role of Beaumarchais in helping America to win its independence needs little reminder. But less familiar to us is the impact of largely lesser known poets, artists, and thinkers in urging direct French support and involvement in the American war; such as L. Chavannes de la Giraudiere, Antoine Serieys, and Abbe Raynal who wrote ambitious epics, fervid poetical essays, stage plays, odes, and *cantates* on the American cause for Liberty. Indeed it comes somewhat as a surprise to learn there were some Frenchmen who chided and faulted Louis XVI and his ministers for delaying armed intervention too long. Finally, how ironic it is, now in retrospect, to realize that it was Rochambeau's *Royal* expeditionary force that was the very first army of "liberation" of modern times.

But such warm advocates for America, ardent as they were, did not always or necessarily represent the greater majority in France. Some, including Lafayette at one despondent point in late 1779, viewed many Americans cynically; blaming them for, among other charges, their economic poverty, lack of culture, and absence of a potent central government. Yet such harsh misgivings as time went on appear to have become more the exception. And a comparatively larger number of Frenchmen, albeit with predictable reservations characteristic of that skeptical and wary people, were impressed by and felt affinity for American notions of: reward based merit (rather than on birth);[336] casual candor and freedom of expression; the intellectual boldness and modest sobriety of American women (who visited France); and the concern for social, including racial, equality articulated by some Americans. Sometimes such perceived

---

[334] Paoli, Pennsylvania, site of Anthony Wayne's defeat, received it name from "General Paoli's Tavern;" which earlier had served as a gathering place for local Pennsylvania revolutionaries. Ironically, Paoli ultimately received most support for his movement from the British.

[335] The works of John Milton, for one, are replete with references to a love of liberty and rustic virtue, and a disdain of greed and royal corruption; sentiments that were habitually echoed in the political and literary writings of American Revolutionary authors.

[336] Among these was Greco-French Revolutionary verse writer André Chénier, guillotined by Robespierre, and who before he died left fragments of an unfinished poetical epic entitled *L'Amerique*.

virtues and examples of virtue were occasionally more the result of imagination than fact; yet imagined or no, they did act as a palpable stimulus to the subsequent aspirations of Revolutionary France.[337]

Aside perhaps from the states that sent mercenaries to fight alongside the British, for most Germans America was something remote,[338] and for which information on was relatively sparse. In Book XVII of his autobiography *Dichtung und Wahrheit*, Goethe wrote:

"[W]e wished the Americans all success, and the names of Franklin and Washington began to shine and sparkle in the political and warlike firmament. Much had been accomplished to improve the condition of humanity, and now when a new and well-meaning king of France evinced the best intentions of doing away a multitude of abuses and of limiting himself to the noblest ends, of introducing a regular and efficient system of political economy, of dispensing with all arbitrary power and of ruling by order as by right alone; the brightest hope spread over the world, and youth most confidently promised itself and the race a fair and a majestic future..."

Although Walter Wadepuhl in his most informative *Goethe's Interest in the New World* (1934) dismisses this passage as more a product of Goethe's mature elderly reflections than the poet's accurately reporting history; Goethe in his later years assuredly did manifest a forthright appreciation for what America represented, and made up for lost time by more closely educating himself on both the people and their culture. Oddly, however, the only famous American he himself ever appears to have met was Aaron Burr in 1810; when the latter appeared at the Weimar court; on a prospective mineral and business venture that ultimately fell though.[339] Yet however belated Goethe's enthusiasm, it *can* be noted that Schiller in his drama "Kabale und Liebe" ("Intrigue and Love," 1784) parodies a firing squad that shoots poor, young Germans refusing to sign on with the Hessians being sent to America (Act II, scn. 2.) As well, and perhaps more astonishing, the famous *Sturm und Drang* literary movement received its designation from a stage drama by Friedrich Maximilian Klinger, and which employed the phrase "Sturm und Drang" as its title (though the play was first named "Der Wirrwarr" [1776] and shortly after changed.) It presents the story of a young Englishman going to America at the commencement of the Revolution to fight against it, but who, due in part to a romance with an American girl, ends up espousing the rebels' cause and ideals.

But lesser known of the European enthusiasts for American Liberty was Portuguese poet Francisco Manuel de Nascimento, also known as "Filinto Elysio" (1734-1819); and who counted Chateaubriand -- himself an author famous for passionate novellas centered on highly imaginative and evocative American locales and themes -- among his chief admirers. It is well to remember that in several countries on the continent, such as Spain and Portugal, the Enlightenment entered by way of royal courts and even some church clerics; of which in the latter case Nascimento was one; rather than by way of ground-level populist movements as some might suppose. Moreover, some peoples, whether in America or Europe, did not seek freedom for themselves until aroused and goaded into doing so by wealthy societal elites. Sometime in probably the mid-1780's, Nascimento, living in exile in Paris wrote *To the Liberty and Independence of the United States*, but which upon looking I was at a loss to find an English translation for. Securing then the help of a friend of mine, Louis Chirillo, who knows Portuguese reasonably well as a second language, we attempted a translation of that ode; with what follows being the result of our joint efforts. First, let me be plain in saying that neither of us considers ourselves properly qualified for such an undertaking; and if anything has been misworded we don't flinch at assuming full reproach. But as we have, as best as we can tell, got most it right, we hope that under the circumstances this is at least sufficient to help make the poem more available to English speaking readers.

~~~***~~~

---

[337] For a most splendid and edifying, if perhaps too brief, exposition of French reaction to the American Revolutionary War, see: "Revolution and the Muse: The American War of Independence in Contemporary French Poetry" by John L. Brown, *The William and Mary Quarterly*, Third Series, Vol. 41, No. 4 (Oct., 1984), pp. 592-614; and available at: http://www.jstor.org/pss/1919155

[338] Not so unlike how later South America's revolutions -- as often as not inevitably used as accessories to U.S. diplomacy directed against Spain; for purposes of acquiring Florida or Texas -- were often oddly remote to many freedom loving Americans.

[339] Wadepuhl, pp. 21-22.
~~~

To the Liberty and Independence of the United States.

What is it that I hear, ye Gods?
My ivory lyre
That reposes, after illustrious glory
I sang superbly of resolute Albuquerque,[340]
Untouched it resonates
Inviting the hand of the indolent bard!

Respectable prodigy!
I accept the blissful welcome:
Offered to the high Muse, who excites you,
Appointing me to sonorous meters.
I have already taken notice of the chords
And, subject to my ear, the song fits.

That of the Sisyonian[341] beach
Part of the uncertain Agenorian,[342]
Searching for the timid and beautiful Irma
In the deceptive Touro[343] of each brow;
And bending forward the craggy
Elongated tips of the rocky cliffs:

By strange seas
Trampling insane fears,
By way of Columbus, and by also the illustrious [Vasco de] Gama
Western flags here will be fluttering
Among people who kneel
Before divine-men, of the lords of thunder.

The Tritons, impatient
Of unbroken seas,
With boldness are unleashed, so intoxicated
By the bolder dweller of the far West,
They depose the young ingrate
Before the throne of the azure Tyrant.

Neptune enraged
From the throne he hurls wrath,
And with powerful arm, shakes the bottom
Of the sea, that surges and breaks off;
The rough shoots,
From mountain to mountain,
Of the bleached wood.

Already here, Cabral,[344] discovers

---

[340] [*Edit. Note.* Afonso de Albuquerque (1453-1515), Portuguese Admiral and colonial Governor in India.]
[341] [*Edit. Note.* Sicyonian?]
[342] [*Edit. Note.* Agenor was the father of Europa.]
[343] [*Edit. Note.* The reference here is unclear; this particular stanza being more elusive than any other in its meaning to we the translators. However, we could note as a possibly *related* explanation Isaac Touro (1738–1783), American Rabbi and later British Loyalist, originally from Amsterdam; who'd led a Portuguese Sephardic congregation in Newport, Rhode Island. His son, Judah Touro (1775-1854) served with General Jackson in the defense of New Orleans in 1815, and was wounded there. Of note, Haym Solomon (1740-1785), whose immense financial contribution to the Revolutionary cause is generally well known, himself, though born in Poland, was also of Sephardic-Portuguese extraction.]
[344] [*Edit. Note.* Pedro Alvares Cabral (c.1467-c.1520), Portuguese explorer and reputed discoverer of Brazil.]

The undiscovered Brasils:
With the heavily dripping briny frocks
Kissing the golden beaches;
And to the people who greet you,
Ignorant of the coming spears and chains.

Goodness, Innocence,
Which immemorial reigns
In the benevolent realms of the golden candle,
Yet from the customs of frightened Europe,
People forsake the pitiful *People*!
…Therefore to Liberty.

The unstained wings
Throw down tyranny,
With free air he acquitted himself,
That saw evil slavery from afar,
Clothes costuming saints,
Comes now this climate requiring bliss.

The wind unfurls itself
And the candles already white
That the dark bloody laws bring,
They bring ropes, chains, binds
(Liberty in exchange)
To Nations little familiar with crime.

America groans under the weight
That insolence aggravates
Vices of the cohort spotted:
The poison is poured out of Europe,
And the silent valleys tremble
With the throaty roar of brass.

Themis, with hands to her face
Suddenly her eyes shut
When facing the blazing fires,
The King handcuffed, the hangman thirsty
By the evil gold devotee
Cutting off innocent heads.

But...What sweet violence
Removes from me such
Scenes of horror? That which spills my nectar
Muse, by the heavy dead limbs,
Harm that touches, as light,
The blue translucent waves?

This liquor bathed,
The sweet Orpheus
Thus following the provident Calliope,
From the seas of Greece to the unknown Nile,
When the Egyptian mystery
Wanted to register, all-Knowing miser.

Hail, leafy woods!

Hail, placid asylum
From the outlaw breed liberty!
There I see the temple its portico, immense,
That does not leave closed
Its bronze doors, its artful ceilings...

There I see, still carved
In this robust tree,
The grateful name of the most human Penn:
Even yet the customs are, what he plants,
Breathing in these fertile fields,
Made fresh by the dew of kind tolerance.

Here, in rough terrain
The indigenous savage
Seated and accepted
The price for land already given:
An outstanding example
Compared to infamy's record
Of capture by plagues!

No more, no more, oh Muse!
No more anger to ignite me...
I feel the running blood beaten,
The brain assailing me with acute flames
Of fatal fire:
Already Jupiter from the future plucks the notes.

As, smiling and with right hand,
Thirteen regions discourse!
As the Lily[345] hands break the yoke
And take them -- Liberty -- in a firm ring!
As their right-hands grasp it,
Upsurge their breasts with pride and hope!

Loosen free the banners
To your earnest nod,
Philosopher Franklin, you who snatched
From the heavens the bolt, the scepter to tyranny!
And to your alarm, Boston,
The helper Lily flies [to you] triumphant.

By honor and armed valor,
Washington, there hast risen,
And to the undecided Congress instilled faith:
You are its wall and its shield,
As formerly, in Lazio,
The wary Fabius [Maximus] was to oppressed Rome.

The allies safeguarded,
The tyrants exhausted,
Eternal are the crests of thy glory,
That grows triumphant, in the vicinity,
Like circles grow

---

[345] [*Edit. Note*. France.]

In the center of a lake that is disturbed.

In this untainted land,
Sane Philosophy, poorly accepted
Will come to sit on its throne;
And more lenient laws govern the world
With men more human,
With the radius of Truth, the light spreads.

Already rich in wisdom,
The Philadelphians gather as a host.[346]
They will conquer Europe with good teaching;
Without bayonets, without enslaving cannon,
They will plant generously
The branches of restored Liberty:

Those of flowering Hymettos
Honey bees,
Between the supported wings of Zephyrus,
Will demand with wishful flight
The remote pastures,
In which to fashion sweetening combs.

~~~***~~~

[The original text]

À Independência dos Estados-Unidos

Que é que ouço, oh Deuses?
A minha ebúrnea lira
Que repousa, depois que a clara glória
Cantei soberbo do Albuquerque duro,
Não tocada ressoa
E do vate incurioso a mão convida!

Respeitável prodígio!
Aceito o auspício fausto:
Feitos altos a Musa, que te excita,
Em grandíloquo metro me aparelha.
Já me assinala as cordas
E, ao meu sujeito ouvido, o canto ajusta.

Qual da Siciónia praia
Parte o Agenório incerto,
Buscando a linda Irmã mal-confiada
No falaz Touro de necada fronte;
E dobra ansioso as crespas
Pontas dos alongados promontórios:

---

346 [*Edit. Note.* While there were some Quakers and former Quakers among the revolutionaries, such as Nathanael Greene and Thomas Paine, by and large Quakers tended to be neutrals or loyalists in the Revolutionary War; indeed, some Brethren were disowned by the sect for joining the American rebels. Despite this, and like Nascimento, several notable French intellectuals took it for granted that the Quakers, due to their egalitarian outlook (i.e., "brethren" without priests or clerics), represented a major power and ideological block underpinning American Independence efforts. To their credit, the Quakers were the only sect that formally advocated the abolition of slavery. Some Quakers, however, were accused of taking on the exclusivity and tightly clanish character of Jews in order to get in on and reap the traditional financial advantages of that ancient people, *The History of the Jews of Philadelphia* (1956) by Edwin Wolf and Maxwell Whiteman, pp. 44, 112.]
~~~

Por insólitos mares
Calcando insanos medos,
De alem Colombo, de aquí o ínclito Gama
Vão tremular ocidentais bandeiras
Entre povos que ajoelham
Ante homens-numes, dos trovões senhores.

Os Tritões, insofridos
Que os não-rompidos mares,
Com desatado arrojo, assim devasse
Do extremo Ocaso o morador afouto,
Depõem a ingrata nova
Ante o trono do cérulo Tirano.

Neptuno enfurecido
Do sólio se arremessa
E, c'o braço potente, abala o fundo
Do mar, que se amontoa e se espedaça;
Que encapelado atira,
De serra em serra, os descorados lenhos.

Eis já, Cabral, descobres
Os Brasis não buscados:
C'os salgados vestidos gotejando,
Pesado, beijas as douradas praias;
E aos povos que te hospedam,
Ignaro de vindouro, os grilhoes lanças.

A Bondade, a Inocência,
Que imemoriais imperam
Nos reinos não-avaros da áurea vela,
Dos costumes da Europa espavoridas,
As gentes desamparam,
Miserandas!... Entao a Liberdade

As asas, não-manchadas
De baixa tirania,
Soltou isenta, pelos ares livres,
Mal que avistou a Escravidão, ao longe,
Roupas trajando santas,
Vir esses climas demandar ditosos.

Ao vento se desfraldam
E as velas já branquejam
Que as leis escuras trazem, sanguinosas,
Trazem cordas, grilhoes, trazem seguros
(Da Liberdade em troco)
Para as Nações que o crime mal-conhecem.

Geme a América ao peso
Que insolente lhe agrava
Dos vícios a coorte maculosa:
O veneno da Europa se derrama,
E os mudos vales troam
C'o trémulo fragor do bronze rouco.

Témis, c'as mãos ao rosto,
Súbito os olhos cerra
Quando encara as fogueiras flamejando,
O rei manietado, o algoz sedento,
Pelo ouro mal-devoto,
Decepando as cabeças inocentes.

Mas… Que doce volência
Me retira de tanta
Cena de horrores? Qual me esparges néctar,
Musa, pelos mortais pesados membros,
Que mal toco, ligeiro,
As azuladas transparentes ondas?

Deste licor banhado,
O dulcíssono Orfeu
Assim seguia a próvida Calíope,
Desde os mares da Grécia ao Nilo ignoto,
Quando o mistério egípcio
Quis registar, de alto Saber avaro.

Salve, copado bosque!
Salve, plácido asilo
Da casta foragida liberdade!
Lá vejo o templo seu aprico, imenso,
Que encerrar-se não deixa
De brônzeas portas, de artezoados tectos…

Lá vejo, inda entalhado
Nessa árvore robusta,
Do humaníssimo Penn o nome grato:
Inda os costumes sãos, que ele plantar,
Recendem nestas veigas,
Orvalhados de amiga tolerância.

Aquí, nos terões toscos
Sentados, aceitavam
Os selvagens indígenas o preço
Da terra já além dada: exemplo insigne
Que insculpirá infâmia
Nos que as plagas não-suas cativaram!

Não mais, não mais, oh Musa!
Não mais furor me acendas…
Sinto o sangue correr atropelado,
O cérebro assaltar-me aguda chama
De fatídico incêndio:
Já do futuro a Jove arranco as chaves.

Como, risonha e destra,
Treze regiões discorre!
Como c'as alvas mãos mlhes quebra o jugo
E as toma –a Liberdade- em anel firme!
Como as dextras lhe enlaça,
Sopra, em seus peitos, brios, esperanças!

Soltam-se os pendões livres
Ao teu sisudo aceno,
Filósofo Flanklin, que arrebataste
Aos céus o raio, o ceptro à tirania!
E ao teu aviso, em Bóston,
O Lírio ajudador tremula, ovante.

De honra e valor armado,
Washington, alí te ergues,
E ao Congresso indeciso a fé abonas:
Tu és sua muralha e seu escudo,
Qual noutrora, no Lácio,
O Fábio tardador à aflita Roma!

Os sócios protegidos,
Os tiranos exaustos
São eternos brazões da tua glória,
Que cresce triunfal, na redondeza,
Comos os círculos crescem
Em lago que no centro foi ferido.

Neste limpo terreno,
Virá assentar seu trono
A sã Filosofia, mal-aceita;
E leis mais brandas regerão o mundo
Quando homens mais humanos,
C'o raio da Verdade, a luz espalhem.

Já de sapiência ricos,
Enxames filadélfios
Vão conquistar com almo ensino a Europa;
Sem baionetas, sem canhões escravos,
Vão planta generoso
Ramos da restaurada Liberdade:

Quais do florido Himeto
Melíficas abelhas,
Entre as asas do Zéfiro amparadas,
Vão demandar con voo desejoso
As remotas devesas,
Que hão-de adoçar c'os fabricandos favos.

IN THE SHADOWS OF LIBERTY:
Charles Brockden Brown and Nascent American Gothic

"The flattering reception that has been given, by the public, to Arthur Mervyn, has prompted the writer to solicit a continuance of the same favour, and to offer to the world a new performance. America has opened new views to the naturalist and politician, but has seldom furnished themes to the moral painter. That new springs of action, and new motives to curiosity should operate; that the field of investigation, opened to us by our own country, should differ essentially from those which exist in Europe, may be readily conceived. The sources of amusement to the fancy and instruction to the heart, that are peculiar to ourselves, are equally numerous and inexhaustible. It is the purpose of this work to profit by some of these sources; to exhibit a series of adventures, growing out of the condition of our country, and connected with one of the most common and most wonderful diseases or affections of the human frame.

"One merit the writer may at least claim; that of calling forth the passions and engaging the sympathy of the reader, by means hitherto unemployed by preceding authors. Puerile superstition and exploded manners; Gothic castles and chimeras, are the materials usually employed for this end. The incidents of Indian hostility, and the perils of the western wilderness, are far more suitable; and, for a native of America to overlook these, would admit of no apology. These, therefore, are, in part, the ingredients of this tale, and these he has been ambitious of depicting in vivid and faithful colours. The success of his efforts must be estimated by the liberal and candid reader."

~ Preface to *Edgar Huntly* (1801)

"I saw him [in Philadelphia], a little time before his death. I had never known him -- never heard of him -- never read any of his works. He was in a deep decline. It was the month of November -- our Indian summer -- when the air is full of smoke. Passing a window one day I was caught by the sight of a man -- with a remarkable physiognomy -- writing, at a table, in a dark room. The sun shown directly upon his head. I shall never forget it. The dead leaves were falling then -- It was Charles Brockden Brown."

~ painter Thomas Sully, 1809.[347]

Following a glorious founding and elated beginning, it wasn't long before the fledgling United States began feeling the affects of new, strange and disturbing problems that had their origins both domestically and abroad. America's economy had generally been on the rise before and during the revolution, and with increased wealth came rising populations and, in turn, concomitant problems of crime and sickness; with war itself soon resuming on both the frontier and, not long after, in and from Europe as well.

It was during this both confident yet sometimes troubling transition period that there entered on the cultural scene one of the most precocious (for his time) and enigmatic authors the United States ever produced, Charles Brockden Brown (1771-1810), from Philadelphia, and whose person and life seems almost as fraught with mystery and puzzles as any of his novels.[348] Doubtless he stands out as a peculiar anomaly in the America of his generation. While it is commonly stated that he influenced the work of Hawthorne, Poe, and Melville (not to mention several others), outside of suggestions or echoes of Brown's style in their writings, I myself have yet to come across a specific or explicit reference by any of these three to him.[349] This is by no means to say that none exist, but it will be a somewhat remarkable find for someone to inform me specifically of such. On the other hand, early American playwright, painter, and theater historian William Dunlap, and noted historian William Prescott, it is known, *did* write short biographies of him.[350] Dunlap is interesting because as well as being a personal associate of Brown's, both he and the latter evinced a pronounced interest in drama and which greatly impacted their subsequent work. In addition, both were members of the "Friendly Club"[351] of New York; which 1796 belles-lettres confraternity; also included the highly respected minister, "Connecticut Wit," and later Yale College

---

[347] Duyckinck *Cyclopaedia of American Literature* (1854-1875.), vol. 1, pp. 611-612.

[348] Though typically situated in Pennsylvania, they were written in New York (city) 1798-1801. Brown composed four; of which these are extant: *Wieland* (1798), *Ormond* (1799), *Arthur Mervyn* (in two parts, 1799 and 1800), *Memoirs of Stephen Calvert* (1799-1800), *Edgar Huntly* (1801); and also later two sentimental romances *Clara Howard* (1800) and *Jane Talbot* (1801). While it might be pointed out that Philip Frenau's lengthy poem "The House of Night" (1779) should be awarded honors as the first and most decidedly impressive work of American Gothic literature, we *can* make the distinction of saying that Freneau's is a work of verse; and Brown's *Wieland* the first in prose form. Ironically, Brown, in later years, effectively disavowed and lamented his gothic novels; even though they are now the sole basis of his famous reputation.

[349] Among Brown's European admirers were Shelley and Sir Walter Scott; the latter evincing this by his naming some of his characters in *Guy Mannering, or The Astrologer* (1815) after Brown himself and after Brown's own creation Arthur Mervyn. Cooper, on the other hand, makes not so flattering reference to *Edgar Huntley* in the preface to the very first edition (1821) of *The Spy*.

[350] Worth mentioning also is Brown's interesting obituary found in the 1810 installment of *The American Register* (1811), vol. VII, pp, 169-170, and for which publication Brown had been an editor.

[351] Friendly Clubs were a *type* of gathering for their time, rather than a specific or proper name; formed as a venue in which to discuss matters legal, political, philosophical, and literary; with Brown's group then being one such.

president Timothy Dwight, and Elihu Hubbard Smith, a physician (who specialized in psychology) and colleague of Benjamin Rush, devotee of literature,[352] close friend, and significant influence on Brown. While Brown's father had been a pro-American pacifist Quaker during the Revolution, Dunlap's father had been a loyalist surgeon who served in the British Army -- so that the Friendly Club was distinctive as a gathering of thinkers who originally hailed from diverse ends of the revolutionary political spectrum with a joint concern in literature and social (including moral) reform. About four years later Brown was part of avid Federalist Joseph Dennie's anglophile Philadelphia literary circle, and in this we encounter something of a paradox. For although Brown had ardently welcomed Enlightenment reformation of mankind, like the Federalists he shrank in frank disgust at French Revolutionary *egalité*.[353]

Possibly the oddest and most overlooked thing about Brown, who first trained to be a lawyer, is that he was, by temperament, an entertainer.[354] Yes, a sociologist, crusader for progress, an astute and eager psychologist, visionary aesthete, and literary artiste of (later) high repute -- but also, as author, a flamboyant showman -- who but for his pathologically introspective nature might have proved a wonder as a stage dramatist. In fact, his mystery and detective novels (and I think it is fair to categorize them as that; though they are scarcely denoted such) have in them scenes to rival German Expressionist cinema of the early 20th century in originality, and surreal matter and events visually dramatic in their elements and composition.

Yet in Brown, sensationalism, insane behavior, and eccentric characters are not mere entertainment but devices inextricably connected to his purpose of drawing attention to a variety of moral and psychological conflicts and dilemmas taking place behind the backdrop of public society; crying out to be addressed. Moreover, Brown probably took up literature due in some degree to his initial disillusionment with the power of churches to reform people; so that, as with Freneau and Barlow, writing for the public became a substitute religious calling.[355] And yet what in truth was sour about religion was not religion itself, but its occasional seizure by forces both earthly and unearthly of both insincere, crooked, and, in some instances, even sinister and malevolent -- a phenomena glaringly exhibited to view in Brown's horrific *Wieland*.[356] So that as time went on Brown himself would seemed to have come to realize that the fault lay not with religion but rather with others who corrupted it. He came to lay the Gothic novel aside, wrote instead two of a sentimental type, married, and returned to a more orthodox religious outlook while continuing to write and speak out on public affairs in magazines he edited and published pieces he composed.

The reportorial or journalistic manner of Daniel Defoe, and that punctiliously leaves (almost) no detail unturned or unanalyzed, is quite evident in Brown's work, as is Joseph Addison's narrative style.[357] He was further strongly influenced by the sociological and psychological novels of English author William Godwin; yet with Brown's allowing himself free rein to innovate and expand on the former. His style also draws heavily on the conventional 18th century novel: such as the reliance on the picaresque and episodic; on the use of letters, like in Samuel Richardson and Brown's American predecessor William Hill Brown (1765-1793) in the latter's *The Power of Sympathy* (1789),[358] to tell much of the tale; except that in

---

352 Smith is also sometimes included as one of the Connecticut, or Hartford, Wits, i.e., along with Dwight, Joel Barlow, John Trumbull, David Humphreys, Lemuel Hopkins, and Richard Alsop. In 1793 he published *American Poems, Original and Selected*; the first such anthology of its kind.

353 It is not inconceivable that Brown's sending President Jefferson a complimentary copy of *Wieland* may have been prompted by an unstated or implied desire to ridicule Jefferson's faith in the common people.

354 In the positive and best sense of the title.

355 Brown, it should be added, came to see himself as an *outcast* Quaker. "Arch-heretic" and human rights zealot Thomas Paine of course, was also brought up in a Quaker family.

356 *Very curiously*, the novel's title character (and who murders his children after hearing what he thinks is the voice of "God" commanding such), and according to the fictional narrator's own explanation, is described as a distant relative of the *real life*, and then still living, Wiemar poet Christoph Martin Wieland (1733-1813). Wieland, as well as exerting a profound influence on Goethe's poetry (compare for example aspects of the former's fantastic *Oberon* to *Faust* part II); was an eloquent, Voltaire-like critic against religious fraud and fanaticism, particularly in his novel *The History of Agathon* (1766-67), and which Brown was well acquainted with.

357 Compare, for instance, Addison's short story "Theodosius and Constantia," Spec. 164, Sept. 7, 1711, with the sort of multi-layered plot formula and character presentation Brown uses in his own fiction.

358 Said by some to be the first American novel, but technically that honor goes to *The Adventures of Alonso* (1775) by Thomas Atwood Gibbes of Warburton, Maryland; though the setting and character of that work is entirely European.

Brown's case the epistles, of say such as would be used by Richardson's characters, are turned into very lengthy *spoken* narratives. Often in his given novel, Brown (or else his character that speaks) belabors a point, sometimes obsessively; but always in a steady and singularly lucid manner; with the sentences of even Brown's distraught or bewildered prisoners, wanderers, and fugitives being models of crisp succinctness and clarity. He strings together the weirdest and baffling of occurrences while not infrequently, and in effect, then asking the thinking reader to explain how his character(s) got or ended up there where they were; and. Moreover, as a means of raising serious questions as to what *actually* motivates human actions. Nor would it be stretching things to liken his narratives to dreams, filled with constantly shifting and changing events; where seldom, if ever, is anything adequately resolved. That he was at times dismaying readers with recountings of inexplicably lurid events and bizarre crimes does not, at least in his earlier years, seemed to have bothered him; so that one sometimes is perplexed or at least left wondering as to the design behind his brand of shock story-telling. True, had he written at a later period in American history than he did, we would not be nearly so surprised by such an approach. But writing for the era in which he lived, such introduction or bringing in of the graphic, grotesque, and diabolical in real life situations, for fiction purposes, is no little peculiar.[359] Some have suspected Brown may have had more humor to him than on the surface appears. Be that as it may, certainly his characters themselves are conspicuously humorless. Rather ludicrously, *Arthur Mervyn*, after all sorts of bitterly drawn out, tragic and medically agonizing ordeals, ends on a note of romance. Was there in this, as averred by some, intended sarcasm aimed at his novel's main character, or rather was he making an appeal to hope amid the ruins?

In that same novel the preponderance of the events that occur in relation to the devastating Yellow Fever plague that struck Philadelphia -- then the nation's capitol[360] -- in 1793, and which took the lives of some 5,000 people, including that of Brown's intellectual mentor Elihu Hubbard Smith. Rather ingeniously, Brown uses the epidemic as a motif that thematically reflects and complements the *moral* maladies pervading the beleaguered city: greed, murder, forgery, acrimonious jealousies and rivalries, intrigues, robbery, prostitution, infant mortality, unpaid debts that imply crime and or bring about imprisonment of someone,[361] and an often cold indifference to other's suffering generally.

As way of introduction for some, what ensues are portions of *Mervyn* directly describing the pestilence. Mervyn has come to the city in order to find Wallace, the fiancée of an acquaintance of his (Susan Hadwin); whom it is feared has succumbed to the plague. If you are unfamiliar with the novel it is not required to know and understand quite all what is going on or alluded to here. All that *is* necessary is to permit yourself to accompany Mervyn on what is a typically strange odyssey of one of Brown's typically strange characters in order to experience the startling power of Brown's innovative brand of eerie drama.

~~~***~~~

Chapter XV.

These meditations did not enfeeble my resolution, or slacken my pace. In proportion as I drew near the city, the tokens of its calamitous condition became more apparent. Every farm-house was filled with supernumerary tenants, fugitives from home, and haunting the skirts of the road, eager to detain every passenger with inquiries after news. The passengers were numerous; for the tide of emigration was by no means exhausted. Some were on foot, bearing in their countenances the tokens of their recent terror, and filled with mournful reflections on the forlornness of their state. Few had secured to themselves an asylum; some were without the means of paying for victuals or lodging for the coming night; others, who were not thus destitute, yet knew not whither to apply for entertainment, every house being already overstocked with inhabitants, or barring its inhospitable doors at their approach.

---

[359] In chapter 30 of *Arthur Mervyn* for example there is a scene where the protagonist matter-of-factly buries a plague victim, sans coffin or shroud, in someone's backyard.
[360] i.e., from 1790 to 1800.
[361] Samuel Woodworth, John Pendleton Kennedy, and other contemporaries of Brown were outspoken against imprisonment for debt; viewing it as an unnecessarily cruel and counterproductive measure. It wasn't till 1833 that the US ended Federal imprisonment for insolvent debtors; with other states following up till about 1850 when the practice was finally ended. So oppressive was the law until its revocation that even some of the country's most famous citizens and leaders, such as James Wilson, Robert Morris, and Henry Lee, it will be recalled, served time in jail for falling into arrears.
~~~

Families of weeping mothers and dismayed children, attended with a few pieces of indispensable furniture, were carried in vehicles of every form. The parent or husband had perished; and the price of some movable, or the pittance handed forth by public charity, had been expended to purchase the means of retiring from this theatre of disasters, though uncertain and hopeless of accommodation in the neighbouring districts.

Between these and the fugitives whom curiosity had led to the road, dialogues frequently took place, to which I was suffered to listen. From every mouth the tale of sorrow was repeated with new aggravations. Pictures of their own distress, or of that of their neighbours, were exhibited in all the hues which imagination can annex to pestilence and poverty.

My preconceptions of the evil now appeared to have fallen short of the truth. The dangers into which I was rushing seemed more numerous and imminent than I had previously imagined. I wavered not in my purpose. A panic crept to my heart, which more vehement exertions were necessary to subdue or control; but I harboured not a momentary doubt that the course which I had taken was prescribed by duty. There was no difficulty or reluctance in proceeding. All for which my efforts were demanded was to walk in this path without tumult or alarm.

Various circumstances had hindered me from setting out upon this journey as early as was proper. My frequent pauses to listen to the narratives of travellers contributed likewise to procrastination. The sun had nearly set before I reached the precincts of the city. I pursued the track which I had formerly taken, and entered High Street after nightfall. Instead of equipages and a throng of passengers, the voice of levity and glee, which I had formerly observed, and which the mildness of the season would, at other times, have produced, I found nothing but a dreary solitude.

The market-place, and each side of this magnificent avenue, were illuminated, as before, by lamps; but between the verge of Schuylkill [River] and the heart of the city I met not more than a dozen figures; and these were ghost-like, wrapped in cloaks, from behind which they cast upon me glances of wonder and suspicion, and, as I approached, changed their course, to avoid touching me. Their clothes were sprinkled with vinegar, and their nostrils defended from contagion by some powerful perfume.

I cast a look upon the houses, which I recollected to have formerly been, at this hour, brilliant with lights, resounding with lively voices, and thronged with busy faces. Now they were closed, above and below; dark, and without tokens of being inhabited. From the upper windows of some, a gleam sometimes fell upon the pavement I was traversing, and showed that their tenants had not fled, but were secluded or disabled.

These tokens were new, and awakened all my panics. Death seemed to hover over this scene, and I dreaded that the floating pestilence had already lighted on my frame. I had scarcely overcome these tremors, when I approached a house the door of which was opened, and before which stood a vehicle, which I presently recognised to be *a hearse*.

The driver was seated on it. I stood still to mark his visage, and to observe the course which he proposed to take. Presently a coffin, borne by two men, issued from the house. The driver was a negro; but his companions were white. Their features were marked by ferocious indifference to danger or pity. One of them, as he assisted in thrusting the coffin into the cavity provided for it, said, "I'll be damned if I think the poor dog was quite dead. It wasn't the *fever* that ailed him, but the sight of the girl and her mother on the floor. I wonder how they all got into that room. What carried them there?"

The other surlily muttered, "Their legs, to-be-sure."

"But what should they hug together in one room for?"

"To save us trouble, to-be-sure."

"And I thank them with all my heart; but, damn it, it wasn't right to put him in his coffin before the breath was fairly gone. I thought the last look he gave me told me to stay a few minutes."

"Pshaw! He could not live. The sooner dead the better for him; as well as for us. Did you mark how he eyed us when we carried away his wife and daughter? I never cried in my life, since I was knee-high, but curse me if I ever felt in better tune for the business than just then. Hey!" continued he, looking up, and observing me standing a few paces distant, and listening to their discourse; "what's wanted? Anybody dead?"

I stayed not to answer or parley, but hurried forward. My joints trembled, and cold drops stood on my forehead. I was ashamed of my own infirmity; and, by vigorous efforts of my reason, regained some degree of composure. The evening had now advanced, and it behooved me to procure accommodation at some of the inns.

These were easily distinguished by their *signs*, but many were without inhabitants. At length I lighted upon one, the hall of which was open and the windows lifted. After knocking for some time, a young girl appeared, with many marks of distress. In answer to my question, she answered that both her parents were sick, and that they could receive no one. I inquired, in vain, for any other tavern at which strangers might be accommodated. She knew of none such, and left me, on someone's calling to her from above, in the midst of my embarrassment. After a moment's pause, I returned, discomfited and perplexed, to the street.

I proceeded, in a considerable degree, at random. At length I reached a spacious building in Fourth Street, which the signpost showed me to be an inn. I knocked loudly and often at the door. At length a female opened the window of the second story, and, in a tone of peevishness, demanded what I wanted. I told her that I wanted lodging.

"Go hunt for it somewhere else," said she; "you'll find none here." I began to expostulate; but she shut the window with quickness, and left me to my own reflections.

I began now to feel some regret at the journey I had taken. Never, in the depth of caverns or forests, was I equally conscious of loneliness. I was surrounded by the habitations of men; but I was destitute of associate or friend. I had money, but a horse-shelter, or a morsel of food, could not be purchased. I came for the purpose of relieving others, but stood in the utmost need myself. Even in health my condition was helpless and forlorn; but what would become of me should this fatal malady be contracted? To hope that an asylum would be afforded to a sick man, which was denied to one in health, was unreasonable…

I immediately directed my steps towards the habitation of Thetford. Carriages bearing the dead were frequently discovered. A few passengers likewise occurred, whose hasty and perturbed steps denoted their participation in the common distress. The house of which I was in quest quickly appeared. Light from an upper window indicated that it was still inhabited.

I paused a moment to reflect in what manner it became me to proceed. To ascertain the existence and condition of Wallace was the purpose of my journey. He had inhabited this house; and whether he remained in it was now to be known. I felt repugnance to enter, since my safety might, by entering, be unawares and uselessly endangered. Most of the neighbouring houses were apparently deserted. In some there were various tokens of people being within. Might I not inquire, at one of these, respecting the condition of Thetford's family? Yet why should I disturb them by inquiries so impertinent at this unseasonable hour? To knock at Thetford's door, and put my questions to him who should obey the signal, was the obvious method.

I knocked dubiously and lightly. No one came. I knocked again, and more loudly; I likewise drew the bell. I distinctly heard its distant peals. If any were within, my signal could not fail to be noticed. I paused, and listened, but neither voice nor footsteps could be heard. The light, though obscured by window-curtains, which seemed to be drawn close, was still perceptible.

I ruminated on the causes that might hinder my summons from being obeyed. I figured to myself nothing but the helplessness of disease, or the insensibility of death. These images only urged me to persist in endeavouring to obtain admission. Without weighing the consequences of my act, I involuntarily lifted the latch. The door yielded to my hand, and I put my feet within the passage.

Once more I paused. The passage was of considerable extent, and at the end of it I perceived light as from a lamp or candle. This impelled me to go forward, till I reached the foot of a staircase. A candle stood upon the lowest step.

This was a new proof that the house was not deserted. I struck my heel against the floor with some violence; but this, like my former signals, was unnoticed. Having proceeded thus far, it would have been absurd to retire with my purpose uneffected. Taking the candle in my hand, I opened a door that was near. It led into a spacious parlour, furnished with profusion and splendour. I walked to and fro, gazing at the objects which presented themselves; and, involved in perplexity, I knocked with my heel louder than ever; but no less ineffectually.

Notwithstanding the lights which I had seen, it was possible that the house was uninhabited. This I was resolved to ascertain, by proceeding to the chamber which I had observed, from without, to be illuminated. This chamber, as far as the comparison of circumstances would permit me to decide, I believed to be the same in which I had passed the first night of my late abode in the city. Now was I, a second time, in almost equal ignorance of my situation, and of the consequences which impended, exploring my way to the same recess.

I mounted the stair. As I approached the door of which I was in search, a vapour, infectious and deadly, assailed my senses. It resembled nothing of which I had ever before been sensible. Many odours had been met with, even since my arrival in the city, less supportable than this. I seemed not so much to smell as to taste the element that now encompassed me. I felt as if I had inhaled a poisonous and subtle fluid, whose power instantly bereft my stomach of all vigour. Some fatal influence appeared to seize upon my vitals, and the work of corrosion and decomposition to be busily begun.

For a moment, I doubted whether imagination had not some share in producing my sensation; but I had not been previously panic-struck; and even now I attended to my own sensations without mental discomposure. That I had imbibed this disease was not to be questioned. So far the chances in my favour were annihilated. The lot of sickness was drawn.

Whether my case would be lenient or malignant, whether I should recover or perish, was to be left to the decision of the future. This incident, instead of appalling me, tended rather to invigorate my courage. The danger which I feared had come. I might enter with indifference on this theatre of pestilence. I might execute, without faltering, the duties that my circumstances might create. My state was no longer hazardous; and my destiny would be totally uninfluenced by my future conduct.

The pang with which I was first seized, and the momentary inclination to vomit, which it produced, presently subsided. My wholesome feelings, indeed, did not revisit me, but strength to proceed was restored to me. The effluvia became more sensible as I approached the door of the chamber. The door was ajar; and the light within was perceived. My belief that those within were dead was presently confuted by sound, which I first supposed to be that of steps moving quickly and timorously across the floor. This ceased, and was succeeded by sounds of different but inexplicable import.

Having entered the apartment, I saw a candle on the hearth. A table was covered with vials and other apparatus of a sick-chamber. A bed stood on one side, the curtain of which was dropped at the foot, so as to conceal any one within. I fixed my eyes upon this object. There were sufficient tokens that some one lay upon the bed. Breath, drawn at long intervals; mutterings scarcely audible; and a tremulous motion in the bedstead, were fearful and intelligible indications.

If my heart faltered, it must not be supposed that my trepidations arose from any selfish considerations. Wallace only, the object of my search, was present to my fancy. Pervaded with remembrance of the Hadwins; of the agonies which they had already endured; of the despair which would overwhelm the unhappy Susan when the death of her lover should be ascertained; observant of the lonely condition of this house, whence I could only infer that the sick had been denied suitable attendance; and reminded, by the symptoms that appeared, that this being was struggling with the agonies of death; a sickness of the heart, more insupportable than that which I had just experienced, stole upon me.

My fancy readily depicted the progress and completion of this tragedy. Wallace was the first of the family on whom the pestilence had seized. Thetford had fled from his habitation. Perhaps as a father and husband, to shun the danger attending his stay was the injunction of his duty. It was questionless the conduct which selfish regards would dictate. Wallace was left to perish alone; or, perhaps, (which, indeed, was a supposition somewhat justified by appearances,) he had been left to the tendance of mercenary wretches; by whom, at this desperate moment, he had been abandoned.

I was not mindless of the possibility that these forebodings, specious as they were, might be false. The dying person might be some other than Wallace. The whispers of my hope were, indeed, faint; but they, at least, prompted me to snatch a look at the expiring man. For this purpose I advanced and thrust my head within the curtain.

Chapter XVI.

The features of one whom I had seen so transiently as Wallace may be imagined to be not easily recognised, especially when those features were tremulous and deathful. Here, however, the differences were too conspicuous to mislead me. I beheld one in whom I could recollect none that bore resemblance. Though ghastly and livid, the traces of intelligence and beauty were undefaced. The life of Wallace was of more value to a feeble individual; but surely the being that was stretched before me, and who was hastening to his last breath, was precious to thousands.

Was he not one in whose place I would willingly have died? The offering was too late. His extremities were already cold. A vapour, noisome and contagious, hovered over him. The flutterings of his pulse had ceased. His existence was about to close amidst convulsion and pangs.

I withdrew my gaze from this object, and walked to a table. I was nearly unconscious of my movements. My thoughts were occupied with contemplations of the train of horrors and disasters that pursue the race of man. My musings were quickly interrupted by the sight of a small cabinet, the hinges of which were broken and the lid half raised. In the present state of my thoughts, I was prone to suspect the worst. Here were traces of pillage. Some casual or mercenary attendant had not only contributed to hasten the death of the patient, but had rifled his property and fled.

This suspicion would, perhaps, have yielded to mature reflections, if I had been suffered to reflect. A moment scarcely elapsed, when some appearance in the mirror, which hung over the table, called my attention. It was a human figure. Nothing could be briefer than the glance that I fixed upon this apparition; yet there was room enough for the vague conception to suggest itself, that the dying man had started from his bed and was approaching me. This belief was, at the same instant, confuted, by the survey of his form and garb. One eye, a scar upon his cheek, a tawny skin, a form grotesquely misproportioned, brawny as Hercules, and habited in livery, composed, as it were, the parts of one view.

To perceive, to fear, and to confront this apparition were blended into one sentiment. I turned towards him with the swiftness of lightning; but my speed was useless to my safety. A blow upon my temple was succeeded by an utter oblivion of thought and of feeling. I sunk upon the floor prostrate and senseless.

My insensibility might be mistaken by observers for death, yet some part of this interval was haunted by a fearful dream. I conceived myself lying on the brink of a pit, whose bottom the eye could not reach. My hands and legs were fettered, so as to disable me from resisting two grim and gigantic figures who stooped to lift me from the earth. Their purpose, me thought, was to cast me into this abyss. My terrors were unspeakable, and I struggled with such force, that my bonds snapped and I found myself at liberty. At this moment my senses returned, and I opened my eyes.

The memory of recent events was, for a time, effaced by my visionary horrors. I was conscious of transition from one state of being to another; but my imagination was still filled with images of danger. The bottomless gulf and my gigantic persecutors were still dreaded. I looked up with eagerness. Beside me I discovered three figures, whose character or office was explained by a coffin of pine boards which lay upon the floor. One stood with hammer and nails in his hand, as ready to replace and fasten the lid of the coffin as soon as its burden should be received.

I attempted to rise from the floor, but my head was dizzy and my sight confused. Perceiving me revive, one of the men assisted me to regain my feet. The mist and confusion presently vanished, so as to allow me to stand unsupported and to move. I once more gazed at my attendants, and recognised the three men whom I had met in High Street, and whose conversation I have mentioned that I overheard. I looked again upon the coffin. A wavering recollection of the incidents that led me hither, and of the stunning blow which I had received, occurred to me. I saw into what error appearances had misled these men, and shuddered to reflect by what hairbreadth means I had escaped being buried alive.

Before the men had time to interrogate me, or to comment upon my situation, one entered the apartment, whose habit and mien tended to encourage me. The stranger was characterized by an aspect full of composure and benignity, a face in which the serious lines of age were blended with the ruddiness and smoothness of youth, and a garb that bespoke that religious profession with whose benevolent doctrines the example of Hadwin had rendered me familiar.

On observing me on my feet, he betrayed marks of surprise and satisfaction. He addressed me in a tone of mildness:--

"Young man," said he, "what is thy condition? Art thou sick? If thou art, thou must consent to receive the best treatment which the times will afford. These men will convey thee to the hospital at Bush Hill."

The mention of that contagious and abhorred receptacle inspired me with some degree of energy. "No," said I, "I am not sick; a violent blow reduced me to this situation. I shall presently recover strength enough to leave this spot without assistance."

He looked at me with an incredulous but compassionate air:-- "I fear thou dost deceive thyself or me. The necessity of going to the hospital is much to be regretted, but, on the whole, it is best. Perhaps, indeed, thou hast kindred or friends who will take care of thee?"

"No," said I; "neither kindred nor friends. I am a stranger in the city. I do not even know a single being."

"Alas!" returned the stranger, with a sigh, "thy state is sorrowful. But how camest thou hither?" continued he, looking around him; "and whence comest thou?"

"I came from the country. I reached the city a few hours ago. I was in search of a friend who lived in this house."

"Thy undertaking was strangely hazardous and rash; but who is the friend thou seekest? Was it he who died in that bed, and whose corpse has just been removed?"

The men now betrayed some impatience; and inquired of the last comer, whom they called Mr. Estwick, what they were to do. He turned to me, and asked if I were willing to be conducted to the hospital.

I assured him that I was free from disease, and stood in no need of assistance; adding, that my feebleness was owing to a stunning blow received from a ruffian on my temple. The marks of this blow were conspicuous, and after some hesitation he dismissed the men; who, lifting the empty coffin on their shoulders, disappeared.

He now invited me to descend into the parlour; "for," said he, "the air of this room is deadly. I feel already as if I should have reason to repent of having entered it."

He now inquired into the cause of those appearances which he had witnessed. I explained my situation as clearly and succinctly as I was able.

After pondering, in silence, on my story, -- "I see how it is," said he; "the person whom thou sawest in the agonies of death was a stranger. He was attended by his servant and a hired nurse. His master's death being certain, the nurse was despatched by the servant to procure a coffin. He probably chose that opportunity to rifle his master's trunk, that stood upon the table. Thy unseasonable entrance interrupted him; and he designed, by the blow which he gave thee, to secure his retreat before the arrival of a hearse. I know the man, and the apparition thou hast so well described was his. Thou sayest that a friend of thine lived in this house: thou hast come too late to be of service. The whole family have perished. Not one was suffered to escape."

This intelligence was fatal to my hopes. It required some efforts to subdue my rising emotions. Compassion not only for Wallace, but for Thetford, his father, his wife and his child, caused a passionate effusion of tears. I was ashamed of this useless and childlike sensibility; and attempted to apologize to my companion. The sympathy, however, had proved contagious, and the stranger turned away his face to hide his own tears.

"Nay," said he, in answer to my excuses, "there is no need to be ashamed of thy emotion. Merely to have known this family, and to have witnessed their deplorable fate, is sufficient to melt the most obdurate heart. I suspect that thou wast united to some one of this family by ties of tenderness like those which led the unfortunate *Maravegli* hither."

This suggestion was attended, in relation to myself, with some degree of obscurity; but my curiosity was somewhat excited by the name that he had mentioned, I inquired into the character and situation of this person, and particularly respecting his connection with this family.

"Maravegli," answered he, "was the lover of the eldest daughter, and already betrothed to her. The whole family, consisting of helpless females, had placed themselves under his peculiar guardianship. Mary Walpole and her children enjoyed in him a husband and a father."

The name of Walpole, to which I was a stranger, suggested doubts which I hastened to communicate. "I am in search," said I, "not of a female friend, though not devoid of interest in the welfare of Thetford and his family. My principal concern is for a youth, by name Wallace."

He looked at me with surprise. "Thetford! this is not his abode. He changed his habitation some weeks previous to the *fever*. Those who last dwelt under this roof were an Englishwoman and seven daughters."

This detection of my error somewhat consoled me. It was still possible that Wallace was alive and in safety. I eagerly inquired whither Thetford had removed, and whether he had any knowledge of his present condition.

They had removed to No.--, in Market Street. Concerning their state he knew nothing. His acquaintance with Thetford was imperfect. Whether he had left the city or had remained, he was wholly uninformed.

It became me to ascertain the truth in these respects. I was preparing to offer my parting thanks to the person by whom I had been so highly benefited; since, as he now informed me, it was by his interposition that I was hindered from being enclosed alive in a coffin. He was dubious of my true condition, and peremptorily commanded the followers of the hearse to desist. A delay of twenty minutes, and some medical application, would, he believed, determine whether my life was extinguished or suspended. At the end of this time, happily, my senses were recovered.

Seeing my intention to depart, he inquired why, and whither I was going. Having heard my answer,-- "Thy design," resumed he, "is highly indiscreet and rash. Nothing will sooner generate this fever than fatigue and anxiety. Thou hast scarcely recovered from the blow so lately received. Instead of being useful to others, this precipitation will only disable thyself. Instead of roaming the streets and inhaling this unwholesome air, thou hadst better betake thyself to bed and try to obtain some sleep. In the morning, thou wilt be better qualified to ascertain the fate of thy friend, and afford him the relief which he shall want."

I could not but admit the reasonableness of these remonstrances; but where should a chamber and bed be sought? It was not likely that a new attempt to procure accommodation at the inns would succeed better than the former.

"Thy state," replied he, "is sorrowful. I have no house to which I can lead thee. I divide my chamber, and even my bed, with another, and my landlady could not be prevailed upon to admit a stranger. What thou wilt do, I know not. This house has no one to defend it. It was purchased and furnished by the last possessor; but the whole family, including mistress, children, and servants, were cut off in a single week. Perhaps no one in America can claim the property. Meanwhile, plunderers are numerous and active. A house thus totally deserted, and replenished with valuable furniture, will, I fear, become their prey. To-night nothing can be done towards rendering it secure, but staying in it. Art thou willing to remain here till the morrow?

"Every bed in the house has probably sustained a dead person. It would not be proper, therefore, to lie in any one of them. Perhaps thou mayest find some repose upon this carpet. It is, at least, better than the harder pavement and the open air."

This proposal, after some hesitation, I embraced. He was preparing to leave me, promising, if life were spared to him, to return early in the morning. My curiosity respecting the person whose dying agonies I had witnessed prompted me to detain him a few minutes.

"Ah!" said he, "this, perhaps, is the only one of many victims to this pestilence whose loss the remotest generations may have reason to deplore. He was the only descendant of an illustrious house of Venice. He has been devoted from his childhood to the acquisition of knowledge and the practice of virtue. He came hither as an enlightened observer; and, after traversing the country, conversing with all the men in it eminent for their talents or their office, and collecting a fund of observations whose solidity and justice have seldom been paralleled, he embarked, three months ago, for Europe.

"Previously to his departure, he formed a tender connection with the eldest daughter of this family. The mother and her children had recently arrived from England. So many faultless women, both mentally and personally considered, it was not my fortune to meet with before. This youth well deserved to be adopted into this family. He proposed to return with the utmost expedition to his native country, and, after the settlement of his affairs, to hasten back to America and ratify his contract with Fanny Walpole.

"The ship in which he embarked had scarcely gone twenty leagues to sea, before she was disabled by a storm, and obliged to return to port. He posted to New York, to gain a passage in a packet shortly to sail. Meanwhile this malady prevailed among us. Mary Walpole pole was hindered by her ignorance of the nature of that evil which assailed us, and the counsel of injudicious friends, from taking the due precautions for her safety. She hesitated to fly till flight was rendered impracticable. Her death added to the helplessness and distraction of the family. They were successively seized and destroyed by the same pest.

"Maravegli was apprized of their danger. He allowed the packet to depart without him, and hastened to rescue the Walpoles from the perils which encompassed them. He arrived in this city time enough to witness the interment of the last survivor. In the same hour he was seized himself by this disease: the catastrophe is known to thee.

"I will now leave thee to thy repose. Sleep is no less needful to myself than to thee; for this is the second night which has passed without it." Saying this, my companion took his leave.

I now enjoyed leisure to review my situation. I experienced no inclination to sleep. I lay down for a moment, but my comfortless sensations and restless contemplations would not permit me to rest. Before I entered this house, I was tormented with hunger; but my craving had given place to inquietude and loathing. I paced, in thoughtful and anxious mood, across the floor of the apartment.

I mused upon the incidents related by Estwick, upon the exterminating nature of this pestilence, and on the horrors of which it was productive. I compared the experience of the last hours with those pictures which my imagination had drawn in the retirements of *Malverton*. I wondered at the contrariety that exists between the scenes of the city and the country; and fostered, with more zeal than ever, the resolution to avoid those seats of depravity and danger.

Concerning my own destiny, however, I entertained no doubt. My new sensations assured me that my stomach had received this corrosive poison. Whether I should die or live was easily decided. The sickness which assiduous attendance and powerful prescriptions might remove would, by negligence and solitude, be rendered fatal; but from whom could I expect medical or friendly treatment?

I had indeed a roof over my head. I should not perish in the public way; but what was my ground for hoping to continue under this roof? My sickness being suspected, I should be dragged in a cart to the hospital; where I should, indeed, die, but not with the consolation of loneliness and silence. Dying groans were the only music, and livid corpses were the only spectacle, to which I should there be introduced.

Immured in these dreary meditations, the night passed away. The light glancing through the window awakened in my bosom a gleam of cheerfulness. Contrary to my expectations, my feelings were not more distempered, notwithstanding my want of sleep, than on the last evening. This was a token that my state was far from being so desperate as I suspected. It was possible, I thought, that this was the worst indisposition to which I was liable.

Meanwhile, the coming of Estwick was impatiently expected. The sun arose, and the morning advanced, but he came not. I remembered that he talked of having reason to repent his visit to this house. Perhaps he, likewise, was sick, and this was the cause of his delay. This man's kindness had even my love. If I had known the way to his dwelling, I should have hastened thither, to inquire into his condition, and to perform for him every office that humanity might enjoin; but he had not afforded me any information on that head.

Chapter XVII.

It was now incumbent on me to seek the habitation of Thetford. To leave this house accessible to every passenger appeared to be imprudent. I had no key by which I might lock the principal door. I therefore bolted it on the inside, and passed through a window, the shutters of which I closed, though I could not fasten after me. This led me into a spacious court, at the end of which was a brick wall, over which I leaped into the street. This was the means by which I had formerly escaped from the same precincts.

The streets, as I passed, were desolate and silent. The largest computation made the number of fugitives two-thirds of the whole people; yet, judging by the universal desolation, it seemed as if the solitude were nearly absolute. That so many of the houses were closed, I was obliged to ascribe to the cessation of traffic, which made the opening of their windows useless, and the terror of infection, which made the inhabitants seclude themselves from the observation of each other.

I proceeded to search out the house to which Estwick had directed me as the abode of Thetford. What was my consternation when I found it to be the same at the door of which the conversation took place of which I had been an auditor on the last evening!

I recalled the scene of which a rude sketch had been given by the *hearse-men*. If such were the fate of the master of the family, abounding with money and friends, what could be hoped for the moneyless and friendless Wallace? The house appeared to be vacant and silent; but these tokens might deceive. There was little room for hope; but certainty was wanting, and might, perhaps, be obtained by entering the house. In some of the upper rooms a wretched being might be immured; by whom the information, so earnestly desired, might be imparted, and to whom my presence might bring relief, not only from pestilence, but famine. For a moment, I forgot my own necessitous condition, and reflected not that abstinence had already undermined my strength.

I proceeded to knock at the door. That my signal was unnoticed produced no surprise. The door was unlocked, and I opened. At this moment my attention was attracted by the opening of another door near me. I looked, and perceived a man issuing forth from a house at a small distance.

It now occurred to me, that the information which I sought might possibly be gained from one of Thetford's neighbours. This person was aged, but seemed to have lost neither cheerfulness nor vigour. He had an air of intrepidity and calmness. It soon appeared that I was the object of his curiosity. He had, probably, marked my deportment through some window of his dwelling, and had come forth to make inquiries into the motives of my conduct.

He courteously saluted me. "You seem," said he, "to be in search of some one. If I can afford you the information you want, you will be welcome to it."

Encouraged by this address, I mentioned the name of Thetford; and added my fears that he had not escaped the general calamity.

"It is true," said he. "Yesterday himself, his wife, and his child, were in a hopeless condition. I saw them in the evening, and expected not to find them alive this morning. As soon as it was light, however, I visited the house again; but found it empty. I suppose they must have died, and been removed in the night."

Though anxious to ascertain the destiny of Wallace, I was unwilling to put direct questions. I shuddered, while I longed to know the truth.

"Why," said I, falteringly, "did he not seasonably withdraw from the city? Surely he had the means of purchasing an asylum in the country."

"I can scarcely tell you," he answered. "Some infatuation appeared to have seized him. No one was more timorous; but he seemed to think himself safe as long as he avoided contact with infected persons. He was likewise, I believe, detained by a regard to his interest. His flight would not have been more injurious to his affairs than it was to those of others; but gain was, in his eyes, the supreme good. He intended ultimately to withdraw; but his escape to-day, gave him new courage to encounter the perils of to-morrow. He deferred his departure from day to day, till it ceased to be practicable."

"His family," said I, "was numerous. It consisted of more than his wife and children. Perhaps these retired in sufficient season."

"Yes," said he; "his father left the house at an early period. One or two of the servants likewise forsook him. One girl, more faithful and heroic than the rest, resisted the remonstrances of her parents and friends, and resolved to adhere to him in every fortune. She was anxious that the family should fly from danger, and would willingly have fled in their company; but while they stayed, it was her immovable resolution not to abandon them.

"Alas, poor girl! She knew not of what stuff the heart of Thetford was made. Unhappily, she was the first to become sick. I question much whether her disease was pestilential. It was, probably, a slight indisposition, which, in a few days, would have vanished of itself, or have readily yielded to suitable treatment.

"Thetford was transfixed with terror. Instead of summoning a physician, to ascertain the nature of her symptoms, he called a negro and his cart from Bush Hill. In vain the neighbours interceded for this unhappy victim. In vain she implored his clemency, and asserted the lightness of her indisposition. She besought him to allow her to send to her mother, who resided a few miles in the country, who would hasten to her succour, and relieve him and his family from the danger and trouble of nursing her.

"The man was lunatic with apprehension. He rejected her entreaties, though urged in a manner that would have subdued a heart of flint. The girl was innocent, and amiable, and courageous, but entertained an unconquerable dread of the hospital. Finding entreaties ineffectual, she exerted all her strength in opposition to the man who lifted her into the cart.

"Finding that her struggles availed nothing, she resigned herself to despair. In going to the hospital, she believed herself led to certain death, and to the sufferance of every evil which the known inhumanity of its attendants could inflict. This state of mind, added to exposure to a noonday sun, in an open vehicle, moving, for a mile, over a rugged pavement, was sufficient to destroy her. I was not surprised to hear that she died the next day.

"This proceeding was sufficiently iniquitous; yet it was not the worst act of this man. The rank and education of the young woman might be some apology for negligence; but his clerk, a youth who seemed to enjoy his confidence, and to be treated by his family on the footing of a brother or son, fell sick on the next night, and was treated in the same manner."

These tidings struck me to the heart. A burst of indignation and sorrow filled my eyes. I could scarcely stifle my emotions sufficiently to ask, "Of whom, sir, do you speak? Was the name of the youth -- his name -- was --"

"His name was Wallace. I see that you have some interest in his fate. He was one whom I loved. I would have given half my fortune to procure him accommodation under some hospitable roof. His attack was violent; but, still, his recovery, if he had been suitably attended, was possible. That he should survive removal to the hospital, and the treatment he must receive when there, was not to be hoped.

The conduct of Thetford was as absurd as it was wicked. To imagine the disease to be contagious was the height of folly; to suppose himself secure, merely by not permitting a sick man to remain under his roof, was no less stupid; but Thetford's fears had subverted his understanding. He did not listen to arguments or supplications. His attention was incapable of straying from one object. To influence him by words was equivalent to reasoning with the deaf.

"Perhaps the wretch was more to be pitied than hated. The victims of his implacable caution could scarcely have endured agonies greater than those which his pusillanimity inflicted on himself. Whatever be the amount of his guilt, the retribution has been adequate. He witnessed the death of his wife and child, and last night was the close of his own existence. Their sole attendant was a black woman; whom, by frequent visits, I endeavoured, with little success, to make diligent in the performance of her duty."

Such, then, was the catastrophe of Wallace. The end for which I journeyed hither was accomplished. His destiny was ascertained; and all that remained was to fulfill the gloomy predictions of the lovely but unhappy Susan. To tell them all the truth would be needlessly to exasperate her sorrow. Time, aided by the tenderness and sympathy of friendship, may banish her despair, and relieve her from all but the witcheries of melancholy.

Having disengaged my mind from these reflections, I explained to my companion, in general terms, my reasons for visiting the city, and my curiosity respecting. Thetford. He inquired into the particulars of my journey, and the time of my arrival. When informed that I had come in the preceding evening, and had passed the subsequent hours without sleep or food, he expressed astonishment and compassion.

"Your undertaking," said he, "has certainly been hazardous. There is poison in every breath which you draw, but this hazard has been greatly increased by abstaining from food and sleep. My advice is to hasten back into the country; but you must first take some repose and some victuals. If you pass Schuylkill before nightfall, it will be sufficient."

I mentioned the difficulty of procuring accommodation on the road. It would be most prudent to set out upon my journey so as to reach *Malverton* at night. As to food and sleep, they were not to be purchased in this city.

"True," answered my companion, with quickness, "they are not to be bought; but I will furnish you with as much as you desire of both, for nothing. That is my abode," continued he, pointing to the house which he had lately left. "I reside with a widow lady and her daughter, who took my counsel, and fled in due season. I remain to moralize upon the scene, with only a faithful black, who makes my bed, prepares my coffee, and bakes my loaf. If I am sick, all that a physician can do, I will do for myself, and all that a nurse can perform, I expect to be performed by *Austin*.

"Come with me, drink some coffee, rest a while on my mattress, and then fly, with my benedictions on your head."

These words were accompanied by features disembarrassed and benevolent. My temper is alive to social impulses, and I accepted his invitation, not so much because I wished to eat or to sleep, but because I felt reluctance to part so soon with a being who possessed so much fortitude and virtue.

He was surrounded by neatness and plenty. Austin added dexterity to submissiveness. My companion, whose name I now found to be Medlicote, was prone to converse, and commented on the state of the city like one whose reading had been extensive and experience large. He combated an opinion which I had casually formed respecting the origin of this epidemic, and imputed it, not to infected substances imported from the East or West, but to a morbid constitution of the atmosphere, owing wholly or in part to filthy streets, airless habitations, and squalid persons.

As I talked with this man, the sense of danger was obliterated, I felt confidence revive in my heart, and energy revisit my stomach. Though far from my wonted health, my sensation grew less comfortless, and I found myself to stand in no need of repose.

Breakfast being finished, my friend pleaded his daily engagements as reasons for leaving me. He counselled me to strive for some repose, but I was conscious of incapacity to sleep. I was desirous of escaping, as soon as possible, from this tainted atmosphere, and reflected whether any thing remained to be done respecting Wallace.

It now occurred to me that this youth must have left some clothes and papers, and, perhaps, books. The property of these was now vested in the Hadwins. I might deem myself, without presumption, their representative or agent. Might I not take some measures for obtaining possession, or at least for the security, of these articles?

The house and its furniture were tenantless and unprotected. It was liable to be ransacked and pillaged by those desperate ruffians of whom many were said to be hunting for spoil even at a time like this. If these should overlook this dwelling, Thetford's unknown successor or heir might appropriate the whole. Numberless accidents might happen to occasion the destruction or embezzlement of what belonged to Wallace, which might be prevented by the conduct which I should now pursue…

Chapter XVIII.

I wandered over this deserted mansion, in a considerable degree, at random. Effluvia of a pestilential nature assailed me from every corner. In the front room of the second story, I imagined that I discovered vestiges of that catastrophe which the past night had produced. The bed appeared as if some one had recently been dragged from it. The sheets were tinged with yellow, and with that substance which is said to be characteristic of this disease, the gangrenous or black vomit. The floor exhibited similar stains.

There are many who will regard my conduct as the last refinement of temerity, or of heroism. Nothing, indeed, more perplexes me than a review of my own conduct. Not, indeed, that death is an object always to be dreaded, or that my motive did not justify my actions; but of all dangers, those allied to pestilence, by being mysterious and unseen, are the most formidable. To disarm them of their terrors requires the longest familiarity. Nurses and physicians soonest become intrepid or indifferent; but the rest of mankind recoil from the scene with unconquerable loathing.

I was sustained, not by confidence of safety, and a belief of exemption from this malady, or by the influence of habit, which inures us to all that is detestable or perilous, but by a belief that this was as eligible an avenue to death as any other; and that life is a trivial sacrifice in the cause of duty.

I passed from one room to the other. A portmanteau, marked with the initials of Wallace's name, at length attracted my notice. From this circumstance I inferred that this apartment had been occupied by him. The room was neatly arranged, and appeared as if no one had lately used it. There were trunks and drawers. That which I have mentioned was the only one that bore marks of Wallace's ownership. This I lifted in my arms with a view to remove it to Medlicote's house.

At that moment, methought I heard a footstep slowly and lingeringly ascending the stair. I was disconcerted at this incident. The footstep had in it a ghost-like solemnity and tardiness. This phantom vanished in a moment, and yielded place to more humble conjectures. A human being approached, whose office and commission were inscrutable. That we were strangers to each other was easily imagined; but how would my appearance, in this remote chamber, and loaded with another's property, be interpreted? Did he enter the house after me, or was he the tenant of some chamber hitherto unvisited; whom my entrance had awakened from his trance and called from his couch?

In the confusion of my mind, I still held my burden uplifted. To have placed it on the floor, and encountered this visitant, without this equivocal token about me, was the obvious proceeding. Indeed, time only could decide whether these footsteps tended to this, or to some other, apartment.

My doubts were quickly dispelled. The door opened, and a figure glided in. The portmanteau dropped from my arms, and my heart's blood was chilled. If an apparition of the dead were possible, (and that possibility I could not deny,) this was such an apparition. A hue, yellowish and livid; bones, uncovered with flesh; eyes, ghastly, hollow, woe-begone, and fixed in an agony of wonder upon me; and locks, matted and negligent, constituted the image which I now beheld. My belief of somewhat preternatural in this appearance was confirmed by recollection of resemblances between these features and those of one who was dead. In this shape and visage, shadowy and death-like as they were, the lineaments of Wallace, of him who had misled my rustic simplicity on my first visit to this city, and whose death I had conceived to be incontestably ascertained, were forcibly recognised.

This recognition, which at first alarmed my superstition, speedily led to more rational inferences. Wallace had been dragged to the hospital. Nothing was less to be suspected than that he would return alive from that hideous receptacle, but this was by no means impossible. The figure that stood before me had just risen from the bed of sickness, and from the brink of the grave. The crisis of his malady had passed, and he was once more entitled to be ranked among the living.

This event, and the consequences which my imagination connected with it, filled me with the liveliest joy. I thought not of his ignorance of the causes of my satisfaction, of the doubts to which the circumstances of our interview would give birth, respecting the integrity of my purpose. I forgot the artifices by which I had formerly been betrayed, and the embarrassments which a meeting with the victim of his artifices would excite in him; I thought only of the happiness which his recovery would confer upon his uncle and his cousins.

I advanced towards him with an air of congratulation, and offered him my hand. He shrunk back, and exclaimed, in a feeble voice, "Who are you? What business have you here?"

"I am the friend of Wallace, if he will allow me to be so. I am a messenger from your uncle and cousins at *Malverton*. I came to know the cause of your silence, and to afford you any assistance in my power."

He continued to regard me with an air of suspicion and doubt. These I endeavoured to remove by explaining the motives that led me hither. It was with difficulty that he seemed to credit my representations. When thoroughly convinced of the truth of my assertions, he inquired with great anxiety and tenderness concerning his relations; and expressed his hope that they were ignorant of what had befallen him.

I could not encourage his hopes. I regretted my own precipitation in adopting the belief of his death. This belief had been uttered with confidence, and without stating my reasons for embracing it, to Mr. Hadwin. These tidings would be borne to his daughters, and their grief would be exasperated to a deplorable and perhaps to a fatal degree.

There was but one method of repairing or eluding this mischief. Intelligence ought to be conveyed to them of his recovery. But where was the messenger to be found? No one's attention could be found disengaged from his own concerns. Those who were able or willing to leave the city had sufficient motives for departure, in relation to themselves. If vehicle or horse were procurable for money, ought it not to be secured for the use of Wallace himself, whose health required the easiest and speediest conveyance from this theatre of death?

My companion was powerless in mind as in limbs. He seemed unable to consult upon the means of escaping from the inconveniences by which he was surrounded. As soon as sufficient strength was regained, he had left the hospital. To repair to *Malverton* was the measure which prudence obviously dictated; but he was hopeless of effecting it. The city was close at hand; this was his usual home; and hither his tottering and almost involuntary steps conducted him.

He listened to my representations and counsels, and acknowledged their propriety. He put himself under my protection and guidance, and promised to conform implicitly to my directions. His strength had sufficed to bring him thus far, but was now utterly exhausted. The task of searching for a carriage and horse devolved upon me.

In effecting this purpose, I was obliged to rely upon my own ingenuity and diligence. Wallace, though so long a resident in the city, knew not to whom I could apply, or by whom carriages were let to hire. My own reflections taught me, that this accommodation was most likely to be furnished by innkeepers, or that some of those might at least inform me of the best measures to be taken. I resolved to set out immediately on this search. Meanwhile, Wallace was persuaded to take refuge in Medlicote's apartments; and to make, by the assistance of Austin, the necessary preparation for his journey.

The morning had now advanced. The rays of a sultry sun had a sickening and enfeebling influence beyond any which I had ever experienced. The drought of unusual duration had bereft the air and the earth of every particle of moisture. The element which I breathed appeared to have stagnated into noxiousness and putrefaction. I was astonished at observing the enormous diminution of my strength. My brows were heavy, my intellects benumbed, my sinews enfeebled, and my sensations universally unquiet…

I went from one tavern to another. One was deserted; in another the people were sick, and their attendants refused to hearken to my inquiries or offers; at a third, their horses were engaged. I was determined to prosecute my search as long as an inn or a livery-stable remained unexamined, and my strength would permit.

To detail the events of this expedition, the arguments and supplications which I used to overcome the dictates of avarice and fear, the fluctuation of my hopes and my incessant disappointments, would be useless. Having exhausted all my expedients ineffectually, I was compelled to turn my weary steps once more to Medlicote's lodgings…

On entering Medlicote's house, my looks, which, in spite of my languors, were sprightly and confident, flattered Wallace with the belief that my exertions had succeeded. When acquainted with their failure, he sunk as quickly into hopelessness. My new expedient was heard by him with no marks of satisfaction. It was impossible, he said, to move from this spot by his own strength. All his powers were exhausted by his walk from Bush Hill…

This interval allowed him to reflect upon the past, and to inquire into the fate of Thetford and his family. The intelligence which Medlicote had enabled me to afford him was heard with more satisfaction than regret. The ingratitude and cruelty with which he had been treated seemed to have extinguished every sentiment but hatred and vengeance. I was willing to profit by this interval to know more of Thetford than I already possessed. I inquired why Wallace had so perversely neglected the advice of his uncle and cousin, and persisted to brave so many dangers when flight was so easy.

"I cannot justify my conduct," answered he. "It was in the highest degree thoughtless and perverse. I was confident and unconcerned as long as our neighbourhood was free from disease, and as long as I forbore any communication with the sick; yet I should have withdrawn to Malverton, merely to gratify my friends, if Thetford had not used the most powerful arguments to detain me. He laboured to extenuate the danger.

"Why not stay," said he, "as long as I and my family stay? Do you think that we would linger here, if the danger were imminent? As soon as it becomes so, we will fly. You know that we have a country-house prepared for our reception. When we go, you shall accompany us. Your services at this time are indispensable to my affairs. If you will not desert me, your salary next year shall be double; and that will enable you to marry your cousin immediately. Nothing is more improbable than that any of us should be sick; but, if this should happen to you, I plight my honour that you shall be carefully and faithfully attended.

"These assurances were solemn and generous. To make Susan Hadwin my wife was the scope of all my wishes and labours. By staying, I should hasten this desirable event, and incur little hazard. By going, I should alienate the affections of Thetford; by whom, it is but justice to acknowledge, that I had hitherto been treated with unexampled generosity and kindness; and blast all the schemes I had formed for rising into wealth.

"My resolution was by no means steadfast. As often as a letter from *Malverton* arrived, I felt myself disposed to hasten away; but this inclination was combated by new arguments and new entreaties of Thetford.

"In this state of suspense, the girl by whom Mrs. Thetford's infant was nursed fell sick. She was an excellent creature, and merited better treatment than she received. Like me, she resisted the persuasions of her friends, but her motives for remaining were disinterested and heroic.

"No sooner did her indisposition appear, than she was hurried to the hospital. I saw that no reliance could be placed upon the assurances of Thetford. Every consideration gave way to his fear of death. After the girl's departure, though he knew that she was led by his means to execution, yet he consoled himself by repeating and believing her assertions, that her disease was not *the fever*.

"I was now greatly alarmed for my own safety. I was determined to encounter his anger and repel his persuasions; and to depart with the market-man next morning. That night, however, I was seized with a violent fever. I knew in what manner patients were treated at the hospital, and removal thither was to the last degree abhorred.

"The morning arrived, and my situation was discovered. At the first intimation, Thetford rushed out of the house, and refused to re-enter it till I was removed. I knew not my fate, till three ruffians made their appearance at my bedside, and communicated their commission.

"I called on the name of Thetford and his wife. I entreated a moment's delay, till I had seen these persons, and endeavoured to procure a respite from my sentence. They were deaf to my entreaties, and prepared to execute their office by force. I was delirious with rage and terror. I heaped the bitterest execrations on my murderer; and by turns, invoked the compassion of, and poured a torrent of reproaches on, the wretches whom he had selected for his ministers. My struggles and outcries were vain.

"I have no perfect recollection of what passed till my arrival at the hospital. My passions combined with my disease to make me frantic and wild. In a state like mine, the slightest motion could not be endured without agony. What then must I have felt, scorched and dazzled by the sun, sustained by hard boards, and borne for miles over a rugged pavement?

"I cannot make you comprehend the anguish of my feelings. To be disjointed and torn piecemeal by the rack was a torment inexpressibly inferior to this. Nothing excites my wonder but that I did not expire before the cart had moved three paces.

"I knew not how, or by whom, I was moved from this vehicle. Insensibility came at length to my relief. After a time I opened my eyes, and slowly gained some knowledge of my situation. I lay upon a mattress, whose condition proved that a half-decayed corpse had recently been dragged from it. The room was large, but it was covered with beds like my own. Between each, there was scarcely the interval of three feet. Each sustained a wretch, whose groans and distortions bespoke the desperateness of his condition.

"The atmosphere was loaded by mortal stenches. A vapour, suffocating and malignant, scarcely allowed me to breathe. No suitable receptacle was provided for the evacuations produced by medicine or disease. My nearest neighbour was struggling with death, and my bed, casually extended, was moist with the detestable matter which had flowed from his stomach.

"You will scarcely believe that, in this scene of horrors, the sound of laughter should be overheard. While the upper rooms of this building are filled with the sick and the dying, the lower apartments are the scene of carousals and mirth. The wretches who are hired, at enormous wages, to tend the sick and convey away the dead, neglect their duty, and consume the cordials which are provided for the patients, in debauchery and riot.

"A female visage, bloated with malignity and drunkenness, occasionally looked in. Dying eyes were cast upon her, invoking the boon, perhaps, of a drop of cold water, or her assistance to change a posture which compelled him to behold the ghastly writhings or deathful *smile* of his neighbour.

"The visitant had left the banquet for a moment, only to see who was dead. If she entered the room, blinking eyes and reeling steps showed her to be totally unqualified for ministering the aid that was needed. Presently she disappeared, and others ascended the staircase, a coffin was deposited at the door, the wretch, whose heart still quivered, was seized by rude hands, and dragged along the floor into the passage.

"Oh! how poor are the conceptions which are formed, by the fortunate few, of the sufferings to which millions of their fellow-beings are condemned. This misery was more frightful, because it was seen to flow from the depravity of the attendants. My own eyes only would make me credit the existence of wickedness so enormous. No wonder that to die in garrets, and cellars, and stables, unvisited and unknown, had, by so many, been preferred to being brought hither.

"A physician cast an eye upon my state. He gave some directions to the person who attended him. I did not comprehend them, they were never executed by the nurses, and, if the attempt had been made, I should probably have refused to receive what was offered. Recovery was equally beyond my expectations and my wishes. The scene which was hourly displayed before me, the entrance of the sick, most of whom perished in a few hours, and their departure to the graves prepared for them, reminded me of the fate to which I, also, was reserved.

"Three days passed away, in which every hour was expected to be the last. That, amidst an atmosphere so contagious and deadly, amidst causes of destruction hourly accumulating, I should yet survive, appears to me nothing less than miraculous. That of so many conducted to this house the only one who passed out of it alive should be myself almost surpasses my belief.

"Some inexplicable principle rendered harmless those potent enemies of human life. My fever subsided and vanished. My strength was revived, and the first use that I made of my limbs was to bear me far from the contemplation and sufferance of those evils."

A VOICE CRYING OUT IN THE WILDERNESS:
The Speeches of Chief Tecumseh

"The native American has been generally despised by his white conquerors for his poverty and simplicity. They forget, perhaps, that his religion forbade the accumulation of wealth and the enjoyment of luxury. To him, as to other single-minded men in every age and race, from Diogenes to the brothers of Saint Francis, from the Montanists to the Shakers, the love of possessions has appeared a snare, and the burdens of a complex society a source of needless peril and temptation. Furthermore, it was the rule of his life to share the fruits of his skill and success with his less fortunate brothers. Thus he kept his spirit free from the clog of pride, cupidity, or envy, and carried out, as he believed, the divine decree -- a matter profoundly important to him...

"There was undoubtedly much in primitive Christianity to appeal to this man, and Jesus' hard sayings to the rich and about the rich would have been entirely comprehensible to him. Yet the religion that is preached in our churches and practiced by our congregations, with its clement of display and self-aggrandizement, its active proselytism, and its open contempt of all religions but its own, was for a long time extremely repellent. To his simple mind, the professionalism of the pulpit, the paid exhorter, the moneyed church, was an unspiritual and unedifying thing, and it was not until his spirit was broken and his moral and physical constitution undermined by trade, conquest, and strong drink, that Christian missionaries obtained any real hold upon him. Strange as it may seem, it is true that the proud pagan in his secret soul despised the good men who came to convert and to enlighten him!...

"...When distinguished emissaries from the Father at Washington, some of them ministers of the gospel and even bishops, came to the Indian nations, and pledged to them in solemn treaty the national honor, with prayer and mention of their God; and when such treaties, so made, were promptly and shamelessly broken, is it strange that the action should arouse not only anger, but contempt? The historians of the white race admit that the Indian was never the first to repudiate his oath.

"It is my personal belief, after thirty-five years' experience of it, that there is no such thing as 'Christian civilization.' I believe that Christianity and modern civilization are opposed and irreconcilable, and that the spirit of Christianity and of our ancient religion is essentially the same...

"Such are the beliefs in which I was reared -- the secret ideals which have nourished in the American Indian a unique character among the peoples of the earth. Its simplicity, its reverence, its bravery and uprightness must be left to make their own appeal to the American of to-day, who is the inheritor of our homes, our names, and our traditions. Since there is nothing left us but remembrance, at least let that remembrance be just!"

~ Dr. Charles Alexander Eastman, aka Ohiyesa, *The Soul of the Indian* (1900), pp. 9-24, 171.[362]

The migration westward of masses of Americans and transplanted Europeans following the Revolutionary War was from the beginning beset with elements out of which bitter strife and tragic loss of life were the ineluctable result, viz.: the ousting of long settled Indians, greed on the part of settlers and real estate magnates, government officials promoting a wide and vigorous expansion policy;[363] left over scores to settle from the Revolutionary War; with no doubt a not inconsiderable amount of the diabolical thrown to keep the flames of hatred, prejudice, and revenge recurrently fanned. And even if the vast majority of both Indians and whites were opposed to flagrant theft, cruelty, and related outrages, there were always enough bad whites and bad Indians to exacerbate matters and ruin things for the rest. Even Shawnee Chief Tecumseh (1768-1813),[364] one of the most warm proponents of war against United States encroachment, realized it was incumbent on the Indians themselves to maintain a higher moral dignity if they were to defeat the whites. And yet as much as he tried, even his efforts could not succeed in curbing the rank savagery and brutality of some of his own adherents and allies -- a failing which, sure enough as he could have predicted, did, by giving his opponents a real or seeming pretext, have a devastating effect on undermining Indian military efforts and claims for justice.

---

[362] See: http://www.archive.org/details/soulindian01unkngoog

[363] Including linking the Eastern states with the Mississippi for economic purposes; and the Southern states with the Gulf of Mexico.

[364] Which properly pronounced, by the way, sounds more like "Te-coom-suh" than "Te-cuhm-suh." It is said to mean "Panther Across The Sky;" that is "Shooting Star."

It is little appreciated that *legal technicalities* won the west as much as much as money, (albeit perhaps "well-meaning") con-artists, guns, liquor, and disease. In spirit the United States was hypocrite in its dealings with the Natives insofar that it was careful to deny the latter the opportunity of self-determination, democratically combine, and choose their own representatives; just as the British had denied the same of the colonists. And since the Indians were not allowed the choice of uniting, it then became a relatively easy matter of assailing them piecemeal -- which is in fact and of course how they were in the end conquered.

To add to their difficulties, the Indians generally did not have resources, patience, and discipline to fight a standing army, and organizationally and logistically speaking were little better than militia. Yet when the United States threw their own militia at the Indians the Natives on a number of occasions managed to triumph against them -- as at Harmar's Defeat (Oct. 19-22, 1790) and The Battle of the Wabash (Nov. 4, 1791). At the Wabash (aka "St. Clair's Defeat"), the worst military catastrophe the United States *ever* suffered at the hands of the Indians, indigenous leaders Miami Chief Michikinikwa (Little Turtle) and Shawnee Chief Weyapiersenwah (Blue Jacket) against St. Clair played roles not unlike that of Shelby and Campbell against Ferguson; and rank these chiefs with King Philip, Pontiac, Black Hawk, Sitting Bull, Red Cloud, Geronimo, Modoc Captain Jack, Chief Joseph, for highest military honors in AmerIndian history. Looking at the map, it comes as a bit of surprise how deeply into the interior these earliest battles were fought; that is on the border of present day states Ohio and Indiana, and which serves to show how aggravated and provoked the Natives were by United States demands and aggression.

When Tecumseh tried to unite the tribes against the invaders he was pursuing a cause that was late in coming and had little real hope of succeeding. If we remember him today with admiration it was for the valiant and honor-saving gesture of what he attempted; for few then or later expected it was feasible for him to accomplish what he set out on to do. For one thing (among the many we might mention), the Indians were not all communalists; some themselves owned slaves. Further, like the U.S. in the Revolutionary War, they were not without some in their midst who were ready to sell their own people for a price; others who (like the Loyalists of the Revolutionary War; per the British) understandably felt it more safe and practical to side with the United States, and as earlier mention it was necessary to maintain a certain moral integrity for purposes of providing the Indian movement with political (or what we might now call public relations) credibility. In order then to prevail, Tecumseh in other words had to be both Congress and George Washington -- a most ambitious of tasks to state it mildly.

Yet if Tecumseh did have one quality that *might* have made it all possible it was his famous skill as an orator. Both friend and foe alike expressed great respect for his force and ability in this regard. Perhaps then the best way to remember and commemorate him is by his speeches. For this purpose therefore I have assembled a number that have come down to us. How accurate they are in reporting what was originally spoken is open to question. But they would nonetheless seem to be authentic in their parts and in substance if not always in word for word detail.

~~~***~~~

Speech given in response to the establishment by the U.S. of Fort Dearborn (present day Chicago) as recalled by Chief Simon Pokagon of the Potawatomi Nation. This appeared as part of a larger article by Pokagon, "The Massacre[365] *of Fort Dearborn at Chicago;" found in* Harper's New Monthly Magazine, *vol. XCVIII, No. 586, March 1899, pp. 649-656. States Pokagon: "My father and many others who listened to the speeches of Tecumseh many times repeated to me his words when I was a boy, but it was impossible to give an idea of their spirit and power."*

Before me stand the rightful owners of kwaw-notchi-we au-kee [this beautiful land].

[365] Also known as the battle of Fort Dearborn, 15 August 1812. Pokagan's article in *Harper's* also furnishes a moving, very informative (on a number of levels), and by all appearances, accurate and trustworthy account of the same. I would reproduce it here in its entirety but for the need to stay within the bounds of our allotted topic.
~~~

The Great Spirit in His wisdom gave it to you and your children to defend, and placed you here.

But ä-te-wä [alas!] the incoming race, like a huge serpent, is coiling closer and closer about you.

And not content with hemming you in on every side, they have built at She-gog-ong [Chicago], in the very center of our country, a military fort, garrisoned with soldiers, ready and equipped for battle.

As sure as waw-kwen-og [the heavens] are above you they are determined to destroy you and your children and occupy this goodly land themselves.

Then they will destroy these forests, whose branches wave in the winds above the graves your fathers, chanting their praises.

If you doubt it, come, go with me eastward or southward a few days' journey along your ancient mi-kan-og [trails], and I will show you a land you once occupied made desolate.

There the forests of untold years have been hewn down and cast into the fire!

There be-sheck-kee and waw-mawsh-ka-she [the buffalo and deer] pe-nay-shen and ke-gon [the fowl and fish], are all gone.

There the woodland birds, whose sweet songs once pleased your ears, have forsaken the land, never to return.

And waw-bi-gon-ag [the wild flowers], which your maidens once loved to wear, have all withered and died.

You must bear in mind these strangers are not as you -- they are devoid of natural affection, loving gold or gain better than one another, or ki-tchi-tchag [their own souls].

Some of them follow on your track as quietly as maw-in-gawn [the wolf] pursues the deer, to shoot you down, as you hunt and kill mé-she-bé-zhe (the panther).

But a few years since I saw with my own eyes a young white man near the O-hi-o River who was held by our people as a prisoner of war. He won the hearts of his captors with his apparent friendship and good-will, while murder was in his heart.

They trusted him as they trusted one another. But he most treacherously betrayed their confidence, and secretly killed not less than nech-to-naw [twenty] before his crimes were detected, and then he had fled.

After this, when Chief [Josiah] Harmar [a United States general] invited some of our head men to meet him at Fort Harmar to try and settle our war spirits, that same young man lay in wait, and secretly shot down me-no au-nish-naw-by [a good Indian man] just as he reached the treaty grounds; and yet for that outrageous crime he went unpunished, and today is being petted by wau-be au-nene-eg [white men] as you pet him who kills mé-she-bé-zhe [the panther].

I speak of this case -- and there are many of them within my own personal knowledge -- that you may know our enemies are cunning, crafty, and cruel, without honor, without natural affection.

When we were many and strong, and they were few and weak, they reached out their hands for wido-kaw-ké-win [help], and we filled them with wie-aus and maw-daw-min [meat and corn]; we lived wa-naw-kiwen [in peace] together; but now they are many and strong, and we are getting few and weak, they waw nen-dam [have forgotten] the deep debt of mawmo-i-wendam [gratitude] they owe us, and are now scheming to drive us towards ke-so [the setting sun], into desert places far from ke-win [home] and da-na ki aukee [our native land].

Eh [yes], they come to us with lips smoother than bi-me-da [oil], and words sweeter than amose-póma [honey], but beware of them! The venomous amo [wasp] is in their odaw [heart], and their dealing with us when we have not tamely submitted, has ever been maw-kaw-te and ashki-koman [powder and lead]; against such mau-tchi au-nene [wicked men] our only pagos-seni-ma [hope], our only inin-ijim [safety] is in joining all our tribes, and then, and not until then, will we be able to drive the soulless invaders back! Fail in this, and awak-ani-win [slavery] and ne-baw [death] are ours!

And lastly, do not forget that what peace you have enjoyed the past 50 years in your homes and on your hunting grounds you entirely owe to the brave Pontiac, who, at the risk of his own life, destroyed the forts of your enemies around the Great Lakes, driving the white invaders back.

~~~***~~~

Speech given at Vincennes to General and Governor William Henry Harrison, 12 (or as given elsewhere, 11) August 1810; as presented in American Eloquence: A Collection of Speeches and Address *(1857) by Frank Moore, pp. 354-356. Moore in turn quotes from* Biography and History of the Indians of North America *(1818), by Samuel G. Drake, and notes "Mr. Drake, the author from whom this speech is taken, expresses some doubts of the correctness of this version of it; but adds: 'nevertheless it may give the true meaning. One important paragraph ought to be added, which was, that the Americans had driven them from the sea-coast, and that they would shortly push them into the lakes, and that they were determined to make a stand where they were.'"*
As preface, Moore explains "Tecumseh received the stamp of greatness from the hand of nature, and had his lot been cast in a different state of society, he would have shone as one of the most distinguished of men. He was endowed with a powerful mind, with the soul of a hero. There was an uncommon dignity in his countenance and manners; by the former he was easily discovered after death, among the rest of the slain, for he wore no insignia of distinction. When girded with a silk sash, and told by General [Henry] Proctor that he was made a brigadier in the British service, for his conduct at Brownstown and Magagua, he returned the present with respectful contempt. Born with no title to command but his native greatness, every tribe yielded submission to him at once, and no one ever disputed his precedence. Subtle and firm in war, he was possessed of uncommon eloquence; his speeches might bear a comparison with those of the most celebrated orators of Greece or Rome. His invective was terrible, as may be seen in the reproaches which he applied to General Proctor, a few days previous to his death. His form was uncommonly elegant; his stature about six feet, and his limbs were perfectly proportioned. He was honorably interred by the Americans, who respected him, as an inveterate, but a magnanimous enemy.[366] He left a son, who, when his father fell, was about seventeen years of age, and who fought by his side. To this son, the King of England, in 1814, sent a present of a handsome sword, as a mark of respect for the memory of his father.
"In 1809 Governor Harrison purchased of the Delawares and other tribes of Indians, a large tract of country on both sides of the Wabash, and extending up the river sixty miles above Vincennes. Tecumseh was absent during the time of the negotiation, and at his return expressed great dissatisfaction with the sale. On the twelfth of August of the next year (1810) he met the governor in council at Vincennes, when he addressed him as follows:"

It is true I am a Shawanee. My forefathers were warriors. Their son is a warrior. From them I only take my existence; from my tribe I take nothing. I am the maker of my own fortune; and oh! that I could make that of my red people, and of my country, as great as the conceptions of my mind, when I think of the Spirit that rules the universe. I would not then come to Governor Harrison, to ask him to tear the treaty and to obliterate the landmark; but I would say to him, sir, you have liberty to return to your own country. The being within, communing with past ages, tells me that once, nor until lately, there was no white man on this continent. That it then all belonged to red men, children of the same parents, placed on it by the Great Spirit that made them, to keep it, to traverse it, to enjoy its productions, and to fill it with the same race. Once a happy race. Since made miserable by the white people, who are never contented, but always encroaching. The way, and the only way to check and to stop this evil, is for all the red men to unite in claiming a common and equal right in the land, as it was at first, and should be yet; for it never was divided, but

[366] [*Edit. Note.* Accounts vary as to what happened to Tecumseh himself and his remains; with the truth of which yet to be formally settled.]
~~~

belongs to all for the use of each. That no part has a right to sell, even to each other, much less to strangers; those who want all, and will not do with less.

The white people have no right to take the land from the Indians, because they had it first; it is theirs. They may sell, but all must join. Any sale not made by all is not valid. The late sale is bad. It was made by a part only. Part do not know how to sell. It requires all to make a bargain for all. All red men have equal rights to the unoccupied land. The right of occupancy is as good in one place as in another. There cannot be two occupations in the same place. The first excludes all others. It is not so in hunting or travelling; for there the same ground will serve many, as they may follow each other all day; but the camp is stationary, and that is occupancy. It belongs to the first who sits down on his blanket or skins which he has thrown upon the ground; and till he leaves it no other has a right.[367]

~~~***~~~

Speech to the Creeks at Tuckabatchee (in modern day Alabama) in October 1811; as recorded by Sam Dale; see The Life and times of General Sam Dale, the Mississippi Partisan *(1860) by John Francis Hamtramck (1809-1884), pp. 59-61. Dale was an Indian fighter; so it is not unreasonable to surmise that the version he gives is or may be biased in order to depict Tecumseh in a more that usual hostile light.*

In defiance of the white warriors of Ohio and Kentucky, I have traveled through their settlements, once our favorite hunting grounds. No war-whoop was sounded, but there is blood on our knives. The Pale-faces felt the blow, but knew not whence it came.

Accursed be the race that has seized on our country and made women of our warriors. Our fathers, from their tombs, reproach us as slaves and cowards. I hear them now in the wailing winds.

The Muscogee was once a mighty people. The Georgians trembled at your war-whoop, and the maidens of my tribe, on the distant lakes, sung the prowess of your warriors and sighed for their embraces.

Now your very blood is white; your tomahawks have no edge; your bows and arrows were buried with your fathers. Oh!

Muscogees, brethren of my mother, brush from your eyelids the sleep of slavery; once more strike for vengeance; once more for your country. The spirits of the mighty dead complain. Their tears drop from the weeping skies. Let the white race perish.

They seize your land; they corrupt your women; they trample on the ashes of your dead!

Back, whence they came, upon a trail of blood, they must be driven.

Back! back, ay, into the great water whose accursed waves brought them to our shores!

Burn their dwellings! Destroy their stock! Slay their wives and children! The Red Man owns the country, and the Pale-faces must never enjoy it.

War now! War forever! War upon the living! War upon the dead! Dig their very corpses from the grave. Our country must give no rest to a white man's bones.

This is the will of the Great Spirit, revealed to my brother, his familiar, the Prophet of the Lakes. He sends me to you.

All the tribes of the north are dancing the war-dance. Two mighty warriors across the seas will send us arms.

---

[367] [*Edit. Note.* For a significantly extended and more complete version of this same speech, see: http://www.snowwowl.com/hhtecumsehsspeech.html Though what their source is they don't state.]
~~~

Tecumseh will soon return to his country. My prophets shall tarry with you. They will stand between you and the bullets of your enemies. When the white men approach you the yawning earth shall swallow them up.

Soon shall you see my arm of fire stretched athwart the sky. I will stamp my foot at Tippecanoe, and the very earth shall shake.[368]

~~~***~~~

Address to the Osages 1811; as per Memoirs of a Captivity Among the Indians of North America, from childhood to the age of nineteen: with Anecdotes Descriptive of Their Manners and Customs *(1823), by John Dunn Hunter (1798?–1827), pp. 45–48.*

Brothers, we all belong to one family; we are all children of the Great Spirit; we walk in the same path; slake our thirst at the same spring; and now affairs of the greatest concern lead us to smoke the pipe around the same council fire!

Brothers, we are friends; we must assist each other to bear our burdens. The blood of many of our fathers and brothers has run like water on the ground, to satisfy the avarice of the white men. We, ourselves, are threatened with a great evil; nothing will pacify them but the destruction of all the red men.

Brothers, when the white men first set foot on our grounds, they were hungry; they had no place on which to spread their blankets, or to kindle their fires. They were feeble; they could do nothing for themselves. Our fathers commiserated their distress, and shared freely with them whatever the Great Spirit had given his red children. They gave them food when hungry, medicine when sick, spread skins for them to sleep on, and gave them grounds, that they might hunt and raise corn. Brothers, the white people are like poisonous serpents: when chilled, they are feeble and harmless; but invigorate them with warmth, and they sting their benefactors to death.

The white people came among us feeble; and now that we have made them strong, they wish to kill us, or drive us back, as they would wolves and panthers.

Brothers, the white men are not friends to the Indians: at first, they only asked for land sufficient for a wigwam; now, nothing will satisfy them but the whole of our hunting grounds, from the rising to the setting sun.

Brothers, the white men want more than our hunting grounds; they wish to kill our old men, women, and little ones.

Brothers, many winters ago there was no land; the sun did not rise and set; all was darkness. The Great Spirit made all things. He gave the white people a home beyond the great waters. He supplied these grounds with game, and gave them to his red children; and he gave them strength and courage to defend them.

Brothers, my people wish for peace; the red men all wish for peace; but where the white people are, there is no peace for them, except it be on the bosom of our mother.

Brothers, the white men despise and cheat the Indians; they abuse and insult them; they do not think the red men sufficiently good to live. The red men have borne many and great injuries; they ought to suffer them no longer. My people will not; they are determined on vengeance; they have taken up the tomahawk; they will make it fat with blood; they will drink the blood of the white people.

---

[368] [*Edit. Note.* As happened, prophecies made by Tecumseh and his brother Tenskwatawa, the prophet, regarding earthquakes and a comet as well proved true; in the case of the comet thanks to astronomical forecasts provided by the British. Similar and strange predictions made by Indians also took place in the related United States War with the Creeks (1813-1814).]
~~~

Brothers, my people are brave and numerous; but the white people are too strong for them alone. I wish you to take up the tomahawk with them. If we all unite, we will cause the rivers to stain the great waters with their blood.

Brothers, if you do not unite with us, they will first destroy us, and then you will fall an easy prey to them. They have destroyed many nations of red men, because they were not united, because they were not friends to each other.

Brothers, The white people send runners amongst us; they wish to make us enemies, that they may sweep over and desolate our hunting grounds, like devastating winds, or rushing waters.

Brothers, our Great Father [the King of England] over the great waters is angry with the white people, our enemies. He will send his brave warriors against them; he will send us rifles, and whatever else we want -- he is our friend, and we are his children.

Brothers, who are the white people that we should fear them? They cannot run fast, and are good marks to shoot at: they are only men; our fathers have killed many of them: we are not squaws, and we will stain the earth red with their blood.

Brothers, the Great Spirit is angry with our enemies; he speaks in thunder, and the earth swallows up villages, and drinks up the Mississippi. The great waters will cover their lowlands; their corn cannot grow; and the Great Spirit will sweep those who escape to the hills from the earth with his terrible breath.

Brothers, we must be united; we must smoke the same pipe; we must fight each other's battles; and, more than all, we must love the Great Spirit: he is for us; he will destroy our enemies, and make all his red children happy.

~~~***~~~

Speech to and at a conference with William Henry Harrison at Vincennes in 1811; reported in Tecumseh and the Shawnee Prophet *(1878), by Edward Eggleston and L. E. Seelye, pp. 182-86.*

Brother: I wish you to listen to me well. As I think you do not clearly understand what I before said to you, I will explain it again. Brother, since the peace war made, you have killed some of the Shawnees, Winnebagoes, Delawares, and Miamis, and you have taken our land from us, and I do not see how we can remain at peace if you continue to do so. You try to force the red people to do some injury. It is you that are pushing them on to do mischief. You endeavor to make distinctions. You wish to prevent the Indians doing as we wish them -- to unite, and let them consider their lands as the common property of the whole; you take tribes aside and advise them not to come into this measure; and until our design is accomplished we do not wish to accept of your invitation to go and see the President. The reason I tell you this, you want, by your distinctions of Indian tribes in allotting to each a particular tract of land, to make them to war with each other. You never see an Indian come and endeavor to make the white people do so. You are continually driving the red people; when, at last, you will drive them into the Great Lake, where they can't either stand or walk.

Brother, you ought to know what you are doing with the Indians. Perhaps it is by direction of the President to make those distinctions. It is a very bad thing, and we do not like it. Since my residence at Tippecanoe we have endeavored to level all distinctions -- to destroy village chiefs, by whom all mischief is done. It is they who sell our lands to the Americans. Our object is to let our affairs be transacted by warriors.

Brother, this land that was sold and the goods that were given for it were only done by a few. The treaty was afterwards brought here, and the Weas were induced to give their consent because of their small numbers. The treaty at Fort Wayne was made through the threats of Winnemac; but in future we are prepared to punish those chiefs who may come forward to propose to sell the land. If you continue to
~~~

purchase of them it will produce war among the different tribes, and at last, I do not know what will be the consequence to the white people.

Brother, I was glad to hear your speech. You said that if we could show that the land was sold by people that had no right to sell, you would restore it. Those that did sell did not own it. It was me. These tribes set up a claim, but the tribes with me will not agree with their claim. If the land is not restored to us you will see, when we return to our homes, how it will be settled. We shall have a great council, at which all the tribes will be present, when we shall show to those who sold that they had no right to the claim that they set up; and we will see what will be done to those chiefs that did sell the land to you. I am not alone in this determination; it is the determination of all the warriors and red people that listen to me. I now wish you to listen to me. If you do not, it will appear as if you wished me to kill all the chiefs that sold you the land. I tell you so because I am authorized by all the tribes to do so. I am the head of them all; I am a warrior, and all the warriors will meet together in two or three moons from this; then I will call for those chiefs that sold you the land and shall know what to do with them. If you do not restore the land, you will have a hand in killing them.

Brother, do not believe that I came here to get presents from you. If you offer us any, we will not take. By taking goods from you, you will hereafter say that with them you purchased another piece of land from us…It has been the object of both myself and brother to prevent the lands being sold. Should you not return the land, it will occasion us to call a great council that will meet at the Huron village, where the council-fire has already been lighted, at which those who sold the lands shall be called, and shall suffer for their conduct.

Brother, I wish you would take pity on the red people and do what I have requested. If you will not give up the land and do cross the boundary of your present settlement, it will be very hard, and produce great troubles among us. How can we have confidence in the white people? When Jesus Christ came on earth, you killed him and nailed him on a cross. You thought he was dead, but you were mistaken. You have Shakers among you, and you laugh and make light of their worship. Everything I have said to you is the truth. The Great Spirit has inspired me, and I speak nothing but the truth to you…Brother, I hope you will confess that you ought not to have listened to those bad birds who bring you bad news. I have declared myself freely to you, and if any explanation should be required from our town, send a man who can speak to us. If you think proper to give us any presents, and we can be convinced that they are given through friendship alone, we will accept them. As we intend to hold our council at the Huron village, that is near the British, we may probably make them a visit. Should they offer us any presents of goods, we will not take them; but should they offer us powder and the tomahawk, we will take the powder and refuse the tomahawk. I wish you, brother, to Consider everything I have said as true, and that it is the sentiment of all the red people that listen to me.

~~~***~~~

Speech to British Maj. Gen. Henry Proctor given shortly before the battle of the Thames, Oct. 5, 1805; said to have been found among Proctor's captured papers following that conclusive engagement. American Eloquence: A Collection of Speeches and Address *(1857) by Frank Moore, pp. 354-356.*

Father, listen to your children! you have them now all before you. The war before this our British father gave the hatchet to his red children, when old chiefs were alive. They are now dead. In that war our father was thrown on his back by the Americans, and our father took them by the hand without our knowledge; and we are afraid that our father will do so again at this time.

Summer before last, when I came forward with my red brethren, and was ready to take up the hatchet, in favor of our British father, we were told not to be in a hurry, that he had not yet determined to fight the Americans.
~~~

Listen! When war was declared, our father stood up and gave us the tomahawk, and told us that he was ready to strike the Americans; that he wanted our assistance, and that ho would certainly get us our lands back, which the Americans had taken from us.

Listen! You told us, at that time, to bring forward our families to this place, and we did so: -- and you promised to take care of them, and that they should want for nothing, while the men would go and fight the enemy. That we need not trouble ourselves about the enemy's garrisons; that we knew nothing about them, and that our father would attend to that part of the business. You also told your red children, that you would take good care of your garrison here, which made our hearts glad.

Listen! When we were last at the Rapids, it is true we gave you little assistance. It is hard to fight people who live like ground-hogs.

Father, listen! Our fleet has gone out; we know they have fought:[369] we have heard the great guns: but know nothing of what has happened to our father with one arm.[370] Our ships have gone one way, and we are much astonished to see our father tying up every thing and preparing to run away the other, without letting his red children know what his intentions are. You always told us to remain here and take care of our lands. It made our hearts glad to hear that was your wish. Our great father, the King, is the head, and you represent him. You always told us that you would never draw your foot off British ground; but now, father, we see you are drawing back, and we are sorry to see our father doing so without seeing the enemy. We must compare our father's conduct to a fat animal that carries its tail upon its back, but when affrighted, it drops it between its legs and runs off.

Listen, Father! The Americans have not yet defeated us by land; neither are we sure that they have done so by water -- we therefore wish to remain here and tight our enemy, should they make their appearance. If they defeat us, we will then retreat with our father.

At the battle of the Rapids,[371] last war, the Americans certainly defeated us; and when we retreated to our father's fort in that place, the gates were shut against us -- We were afraid that it would now be the case, but instead of that, we now see our British father preparing to march out of his garrison.

Father! You have got the arms and ammunition which our great father sent for his red children. If you have an idea of going away, give them to us, and you may go and welcome, for us. Our lives are in the hands of the Great Spirit. We are determined to defend our lands, and if it is his will, we wish to leave our bones upon them.

---

[369] [*Edit. Note.* That is at the Battle of Lake Erie, 10 Sept. 1813.]
[370] [*Edit. Note.* Commander Robert Heriot Barclay, and who had lost his left arm in naval fighting in 1809.]
[371] [*Edit. Note.* Fallen Timbers, 20 August 1794.]

NATURE, WILLIAM CULLEN BRYANT,
AND THE POETRY OF HOPE

"It must however be allowed, that the poetry of the United States, though it has not reached that perfection to which some other countries have carried theirs, is yet even better than we could have been expected to produce, considering that our nation has scarcely seen two centuries since the first of its founders erected their cabins on its soil, that our literary institutions are yet in their infancy, and that our citizens are just beginning to find leisure to attend to intellectual refinement and indulge in intellectual luxury, and the means of rewarding intellectual excellence. For the first century after the settlement of this country, the few quaint and unskilful specimens of poetry which yet remain to us, are looked upon merely as objects of curiosity, are preserved only in the cabinet of the antiquary, and give little pleasure, if read without reference to the age and people which produced them. A purer taste began after this period to prevail -- the poems of the Rev. John Adams, written in the early part of the eighteenth century, which have been considered as no bad specimen of the poetry of his time, are tolerably free from the faults of the generation that preceded him, and show the dawnings of an ambition of correctness and elegance. The poetical writings of Joseph Green, Esq. who wrote about the middle of the same century, have been admired for their humour and the playful ease of their composition.

"But, previous to the contest which terminated in the independence of the United States, we can hardly be said to have had any national poetry. Literary ambition was not then frequent amongst us -- there was little motive for it, and few rewards. We were contented with considering ourselves as participating in the literary fame of that nation, of which we were a part, and of which many of us were natives, and aspired to no separate distinction..."

~ William Cullen Bryant, in a review of Solyman Brown's *Essay on American Poetry* (1818); for *The North American Review*, no. 22, July 1818.[372]

If, poetically speaking, Walt Whitman is our hearty *comrade* and fellow amidst the vast teeming throng of life, William Cullen Bryant (1794-1878), who distinctly impacted Whitman's nature-based cosmic outlook, is by comparison a solemn, yet credible, *father* figure. Those who are more than casually acquainted with the writings of both authors will know immediately what I am talking about. Added to this, how odd it is that Bryant (who spanned from 1794 to 1817), like Father Time, *both* preceded *and* survived some of his famous contemporaries in American Literature; as for instance: John Pendleton Kennedy (1795-1870), Nathaniel Hawthorne (1804-1864), William Gilmore Simms (1806-1870), Edgar Allan Poe (1809-1849), Henry David Thoreau (1817-1862); while a second group outlived him by no more than a decade or less: Ralph Waldo Emerson (1803-1882), Henry Wadsworth Longfellow (1807-1882), Emily Dickinson (1830-1886), Sidney Lanier (1842-1881), and John Greenleaf Whittier (1807-1892).

With then such and what developed into a sage and elderly persona, somewhat humorous it is to learn that in his youth Bryant was a fairly brash political agitator armed with a vitriolic pen. His background was respectable and staid enough: he traced ancestors back to Mayflower settlers John Alden and Priscilla Mullins; of Longfellow's celebrated *Courtship of Miles Standish*; having been otherwise born of devout Calvinist-Puritan stock[373] on the family farm in bucolic Cummington, (western) Massachusetts. Yet his first efforts at writings were heated, even embarrassingly so, invectives against the administrations of Jefferson and Madison. Likewise, he was keenly supportive of the British against Napoleon, and during the War of 1812 sided rather with secessionist New Englanders than the United States in that conflict.

With time, however, he became more subdued and carefully avoiding, as best he could, heated quarrels in the political arena. He intended first to be an attorney, and briefly set up a law practice. But drawn to literary pursuits, he put that aside and took up writing poetry, articles, and reviews for then recently founded journals; finally settling down as an editor of the New York City *Evening Post*; from which position he ended up deriving most of his income in the course of his life. As well as gaining honored renown as a bard, he was not infrequently called upon as an orator for public occasions and events, including giving memorial addresses on the passings of James Fenimore Cooper, Washington Irving and Fitz-Greene Halleck; all of whom personally knew and held Bryant in high regard.

Although he has been rightly characterized at the American Wordsworth, Bryant's substrata roots, as literary historian William Ellery Leonard points out,[374] were in 18th century poets like James Thomson, Mark Akenside, Thomas Young, William Cowper, and, in addition Isaac Watt.[375] Penning as many poems

---

[372] Solyman Brown's work is so generally affected and feeble in spirit and imagination that one can't but wonder whether it were a hoax designed to lampoon American literature. Bryant, in any case, in summation makes quite clear he does not like the book.

[373] The hymns of Isaac Watts had made a strong and lasting impression on him as a boy.

[374] See Leonard's essay on the poet found in *The Cambridge History of American Literature* (1917), vol. 1, edited by Trent, Erskine, Sherman, Van Doren, ch. 5, pp. 260-278; and which is one of most erudite, and just appraisals of Bryant in print.

[375] Bryant later wrote "I may be said to have been nurtured on Watt's devout poems composed for children."

with Indian themes as he did, one would surmise Philip Freneau was an influence also. If so, this could only have come after Bryant put aside his strong anti-Jefferson feelings; as his initial respect for Freneau was grudging.[376] Wordsworth, Robert Burns, and Henry Kirke White were others who subsequently left their mark on his work; not least of which White whose gravity of manner often surfaces in Bryant's usual verse technique.

In his lifetime he was nigh universally admired generally, and it would be something to find anything bad spoke or writ of him by his contemporaries; Edgar Allan Poe, for one and for example, being no little lavish in his praise.[377] Yet with the change of generations Bryant has tended to have fallen out of favor with much of conventional literary criticism. While this is to be regretted, it is to a degree understandable. Too frequently Bryant succumbs to contrived and artificial 19th century figures of speech and modes of expression; which if we browse through him superficially make him seem trivial. Two things, however, need to be said in response to this. First, Bryant like any poet had his better and less than better poems, and his superior efforts are more than adequate to sustain his stature as one of this country's first rank poets. Secondly, resonating throughout the general corpus of his work is a mature and profound vision of life that still inspires and will move sensitive readers deeply. And, to be candid and speaking from personal experience, what therapy and a comfort it is sometimes to curl up in a snug spot imbibing his warm, albeit sometimes somber yet nevertheless hopeful and positive view of things that draws on both Nature and religion for its strength. Together with Audubon, Thoreau, and Whitman, no one else in white American culture ever served as a better mouthpiece for Nature's voice plaintively calling to us amid the ravages and disturbing throes of the modern living.

Bryant's most familiar poems are his "Thanatopsis" (1811, pub. 1817) "The Ages" (1821), and "To a Waterfowl" (1816, pub. 1818). Yet in the interest of bringing attention to some of his lesser known pieces, assembled here is a sampling of other pieces that also display him at some of his most moving and, for that reason, excellent.[378]

~~~***~~~

A WINTER PIECE.

The time has been that these wild solitudes,
Yet beautiful as wild, were trod by me
Oftener than now; and when the ills of life
Had chafed my spirit--when the unsteady pulse
Beat with strange flutterings--I would wander forth
And seek the woods. The sunshine on my path
Was to me as a friend. The swelling hills,
The quiet dells retiring far between,
With gentle invitation to explore
Their windings, were a calm society
That talked with me and soothed me. Then the chant
Of birds, and chime of brooks, and soft caress
Of the fresh sylvan air, made me forget
The thoughts that broke my peace, and I began
To gather simples by the fountain's brink,
And lose myself in day-dreams. While I stood
In nature's loneliness, I was with one
With whom I early grew familiar, one

---

[376] See the earlier quoted review of Solyman Brown's *Essay on American Poetry* (1818); *The North American Review*, no, 22, July 1818.
[377] See Poe's "The Poetic Principle," *Home Journal*, series for 1850, no. 36 (whole number 238), August 31, 1850, p. 1, cols. 1-6; available at http://www.eapoe.org/works/essays/poetprnb.htm
[378] Bryant also wrote a number of short stories. One of which, "The Skeleton's Cave" and that appeared in the multi-authored collection *Tales of the Glauber Spa* (1832), can be found in .pdf at:
http://archive.org/details/TheSkeletonsCaveByWilliamCullenBryant
~~~

Who never had a frown for me, whose voice
Never rebuked me for the hours I stole
From cares I loved not, but of which the world
Deems highest, to converse with her. When shrieked
The bleak November winds, and smote the woods,
And the brown fields were herbless, and the shades,
That met above the merry rivulet,
Were spoiled, I sought, I loved them still, -- they seemed
Like old companions in adversity.
Still there was beauty in my walks; the brook,
Bordered with sparkling frost-work, was as gay
As with its fringe of summer flowers. Afar,
The village with its spires, the path of streams,
And dim receding valleys, hid before
By interposing trees, lay visible
Through the bare grove, and my familiar haunts
Seemed new to me. Nor was I slow to come
Among them, when the clouds, from their still skirts,
Had shaken down on earth the feathery snow,
And all was white. The pure keen air abroad,
Albeit it breathed no scent of herb, nor heard
Love-call of bird, nor merry hum of bee,
Was not the air of death. Bright mosses crept
Over the spotted trunks, and the close buds,
That lay along the boughs, instinct with life,
Patient, and waiting the soft breath of Spring,
Feared not the piercing spirit of the North.
The snow-bird twittered on the beechen bough,
And 'neath the hemlock, whose thick branches bent
Beneath its bright cold burden, and kept dry
A circle, on the earth, of withered leaves,
The partridge found a shelter. Through the snow
The rabbit sprang away. The lighter track
Of fox, and the racoon's broad path, were there,
Crossing each other. From his hollow tree,
The squirrel was abroad, gathering the nuts
Just fallen, that asked the winter cold and sway
Of winter blast, to shake them from their hold.

But Winter has yet brighter scenes,--he boasts
Splendours beyond what gorgeous Summer knows;
Or Autumn with his many fruits, and woods
All flushed with many hues. Come when the rains
Have glazed the snow, and clothed the trees with ice;
While the slant sun of February pours
Into the bowers a flood of light. Approach!
The incrusted surface shall upbear thy steps,
And the broad arching portals of the grove
Welcome thy entering. Look! the massy trunks
Are cased in the pure crystal; each light spray,
Nodding and tinkling in the breath of heaven,
Is studded with its trembling water-drops,
That stream with rainbow radiance as they move.
But round the parent stem the long low boughs
Bend, in a glittering ring, and arbours hide
The glassy floor. Oh! you might deem the spot

The spacious cavern of some virgin mine,
Deep in the womb of earth--where the gems grow,
And diamonds put forth radiant rods and bud
With amethyst and topaz--and the place
Lit up, most royally, with the pure beam
That dwells in them. Or haply the vast hall
Of fairy palace, that outlasts the night,
And fades not in the glory of the sun;--
Where crystal columns send forth slender shafts
And crossing arches; and fantastic aisles
Wind from the sight in brightness, and are lost
Among the crowded pillars. Raise thine eye,--
Thou seest no cavern roof, no palace vault;
There the blue sky and the white drifting cloud
Look in. Again the wildered fancy dreams
Of spouting fountains, frozen as they rose,
And fixed, with all their branching jets, in air,
And all their sluices sealed. All, all is light;
Light without shade. But all shall pass away
With the next sun. From numberless vast trunks,
Loosened, the crashing ice shall make a sound
Like the far roar of rivers, and the eve
Shall close o'er the brown woods as it was wont.

And it is pleasant, when the noisy streams
Are just set free, and milder suns melt off
The plashy snow, save only the firm drift
In the deep glen or the close shade of pines,--
'Tis pleasant to behold the wreaths of smoke
Roll up among the maples of the hill,
Where the shrill sound of youthful voices wakes
The shriller echo, as the clear pure lymph,
That from the wounded trees, in twinkling drops,
Falls, mid the golden brightness of the morn,
Is gathered in with brimming pails, and oft,
Wielded by sturdy hands, the stroke of axe
Makes the woods ring. Along the quiet air,
Come and float calmly off the soft light clouds,
Such as you see in summer, and the winds
Scarce stir the branches. Lodged in sunny cleft,
Where the cold breezes come not, blooms alone
The little wind-flower, whose just opened eye
Is blue as the spring heaven it gazes at--
Startling the loiterer in the naked groves
With unexpected beauty, for the time
Of blossoms and green leaves is yet afar.
And ere it comes, the encountering winds shall oft
Muster their wrath again, and rapid clouds
Shade heaven, and bounding on the frozen earth
Shall fall their volleyed stores rounded like hail,
And white like snow, and the loud North again
Shall buffet the vexed forest in his rage.

~~~***~~~
~~~

THE WEST WIND.

Beneath the forest's skirts I rest,
  Whose branching pines rise dark and high,
And hear the breezes of the West
  Among the threaded foliage sigh.

Sweet Zephyr! why that sound of woe?
  Is not thy home among the flowers?
Do not the bright June roses blow,
  To meet thy kiss at morning hours?

And lo! thy glorious realm outspread--
  Yon stretching valleys, green and gay,
And yon free hill-tops, o'er whose head
  The loose white clouds are borne away.

And there the full broad river runs,
  And many a fount wells fresh and sweet,
To cool thee when the mid-day suns
  Have made thee faint beneath their heat.

Thou wind of joy, and youth, and love;
  Spirit of the new-wakened year!
The sun in his blue realm above
  Smooths a bright path when thou art here.

In lawns the murmuring bee is heard,
  The wooing ring-dove in the shade;
On thy soft breath, the new-fledged bird
  Takes wing, half happy, half afraid.

Ah! thou art like our wayward race;--
  When not a shade of pain or ill
Dims the bright smile of Nature's face,
  Thou lovest to sigh and murmur still.

~~~***~~~

THE INDIAN GIRL'S LAMENT.

An Indian girl was sitting where
  Her lover, slain in battle, slept;
Her maiden veil, her own black hair,
  Came down o'er eyes that wept;
And wildly, in her woodland tongue,
This sad and simple lay she sung:

"I've pulled away the shrubs that grew
  Too close above thy sleeping head,
And broke the forest boughs that threw
  Their shadows o'er thy bed,
That, shining from the sweet south-west,
The sunbeams might rejoice thy rest.
~~~

"It was a weary, weary road
  That led thee to the pleasant coast,
Where thou, in his serene abode,
  Hast met thy father's ghost:
Where everlasting autumn lies
On yellow woods and sunny skies.

"Twas I the broidered mocsen made,
  That shod thee for that distant land;
'Twas I thy bow and arrows laid
  Beside thy still cold hand;
Thy bow in many a battle bent,
Thy arrows never vainly sent.

"With wampum belts I crossed thy breast,
  And wrapped thee in the bison's hide,
And laid the food that pleased thee best,
  In plenty, by thy side,
And decked thee bravely, as became
A warrior of illustrious name.

"Thou'rt happy now, for thou hast passed
  The long dark journey of the grave,
And in the land of light, at last,
  Hast joined the good and brave;
Amid the flushed and balmy air,
The bravest and the loveliest there.

"Yet, oft to thine own Indian maid
  Even there thy thoughts will earthward stray,--
To her who sits where thou wert laid,
  And weeps the hours away,
Yet almost can her grief forget,
To think that thou dost love her yet.

"And thou, by one of those still lakes
  That in a shining cluster lie,
On which the south wind scarcely breaks
  The image of the sky,
A bower for thee and me hast made
Beneath the many-coloured shade.

"And thou dost wait and watch to meet
  My spirit sent to join the blessed,
And, wondering what detains my feet
  From the bright land of rest,
Dost seem, in every sound, to hear
The rustling of my footsteps near."

~~~***~~~

RIZPAH.

And he delivered them into the hands of the Gibeonites, and they hanged them in the hill before the Lord; and they fell all seven together, and were put to death in the days of the harvest, in the first days, in the beginning of barley-harvest.
And Rizpah, the daughter of Aiah, took sackcloth, and spread it for her upon the rock, from the beginning of harvest until the water dropped upon them out of heaven, and suffered neither the birds of the air to rest upon them by day, nor the beasts of the field by night. 2 SAMUEL, xxi. 10.
~~~

Hear what the desolate Rizpah said,
As on Gibeah's rocks she watched the dead.
The sons of Michal before her lay,
And her own fair children, dearer than they:
By a death of shame they all had died,
And were stretched on the bare rock, side by side.
And Rizpah, once the loveliest of all
That bloomed and smiled in the court of Saul,
All wasted with watching and famine now,
And scorched by the sun her haggard brow,
Sat mournfully guarding their corpses there,
And murmured a strange and solemn air;
The low, heart-broken, and wailing strain
Of a mother that mourns her children slain:

"I have made the crags my home, and spread
On their desert backs my sackcloth bed;
I have eaten the bitter herb of the rocks,
And drunk the midnight dew in my locks;
I have wept till I could not weep, and the pain
Of my burning eyeballs went to my brain.
Seven blackened corpses before me lie,
In the blaze of the sun and the winds of the sky.
I have watched them through the burning day,
And driven the vulture and raven away;
And the cormorant wheeled in circles round,
Yet feared to alight on the guarded ground.
And when the shadows of twilight came,
I have seen the hyena's eyes of flame,
And heard at my side his stealthy tread,
But aye at my shout the savage fled:
And I threw the lighted brand to fright
The jackal and wolf that yelled in the night.

"Ye were foully murdered, my hapless sons,
By the hands of wicked and cruel ones;
Ye fell, in your fresh and blooming prime,
All innocent, for your father's crime.
He sinned--but he paid the price of his guilt
When his blood by a nameless hand was spilt;
When he strove with the heathen host in vain,
And fell with the flower of his people slain,
And the sceptre his children's hands should sway
From his injured lineage passed away.

"But I hoped that the cottage roof would be
A safe retreat for my sons and me;
And that while they ripened to manhood fast,
They should wean my thoughts from the woes of the past.
And my bosom swelled with a mother's pride,
As they stood in their beauty and strength by my side,
Tall like their sire, with the princely grace
Of his stately form, and the bloom of his face.

"Oh, what an hour for a mother's heart,

When the pitiless ruffians tore us apart!
When I clasped their knees and wept and prayed,
And struggled and shrieked to Heaven for aid,
And clung to my sons with desperate strength,
Till the murderers loosed my hold at length,
And bore me breathless and faint aside,
In their iron arms, while my children died.
They died--and the mother that gave them birth
Is forbid to cover their bones with earth.

"The barley-harvest was nodding white,
When my children died on the rocky height,
And the reapers were singing on hill and plain,
When I came to my task of sorrow and pain.
But now the season of rain is nigh,
The sun is dim in the thickening sky,
And the clouds in sullen darkness rest
Where he hides his light at the doors of the west.
I hear the howl of the wind that brings
The long drear storm on its heavy wings;
But the howling wind and the driving rain
Will beat on my houseless head in vain:
I shall stay, from my murdered sons to scare
The beasts of the desert, and fowls of air."

~~~***~~~

THE AFRICAN CHIEF.

Chained in the market-place he stood,
A man of giant frame,
Amid the gathering multitude
That shrunk to hear his name--
All stern of look and strong of limb,
His dark eye on the ground:--
And silently they gazed on him,
As on a lion bound.

Vainly, but well, that chief had fought,
He was a captive now,
Yet pride, that fortune humbles not,
Was written on his brow.
The scars his dark broad bosom wore,
Showed warrior true and brave;
A prince among his tribe before,
He could not be a slave.

Then to his conqueror he spake--
"My brother is a king;
Undo this necklace from my neck,
And take this bracelet ring,
And send me where my brother reigns,
And I will fill thy hands
With store of ivory from the plains,
And gold-dust from the sands."
~~~

"Not for thy ivory nor thy gold
  Will I unbind thy chain;
That bloody hand shall never hold
  The battle-spear again.
A price thy nation never gave
  Shall yet be paid for thee;
For thou shalt be the Christian's slave,
  In lands beyond the sea."

Then wept the warrior chief, and bade
  To shred his locks away;
And one by one, each heavy braid
  Before the victor lay.
Thick were the platted locks, and long,
  And closely hidden there
Shone many a wedge of gold among
  The dark and crisped hair.

"Look, feast thy greedy eye with gold
  Long kept for sorest need:
Take it--thou askest sums untold,
  And say that I am freed.
Take it--my wife, the long, long day,
  Weeps by the cocoa-tree,
And my young children leave their play,
  And ask in vain for me."

"I take thy gold--but I have made
  Thy fetters fast and strong,
And ween that by the cocoa shade
  Thy wife will wait thee long."
Strong was the agony that shook
  The captive's frame to hear,
And the proud meaning of his look
  Was changed to mortal fear.

His heart was broken--crazed his brain:
  At once his eye grew wild;
He struggled fiercely with his chain,
  Whispered, and wept, and smiled;
Yet wore not long those fatal bands,
  And once, at shut of day,
They drew him forth upon the sands,
  The foul hyena's prey.

~~~***~~~

AN INDIAN AT THE BURIAL-PLACE OF HIS FATHERS.

It is the spot I came to seek,--
  My fathers' ancient burial-place
Ere from these vales, ashamed and weak,
  Withdrew our wasted race.
It is the spot--I know it well--
Of which our old traditions tell.
~~~

For here the upland bank sends out
  A ridge toward the river-side;
I know the shaggy hills about,
  The meadows smooth and wide,--
The plains, that, toward the southern sky,
Fenced east and west by mountains lie.

A white man, gazing on the scene,
  Would say a lovely spot was here,
And praise the lawns, so fresh and green,
  Between the hills so sheer.
I like it not--I would the plain
Lay in its tall old groves again.

The sheep are on the slopes around,
  The cattle in the meadows feed,
And labourers turn the crumbling ground,
  Or drop the yellow seed,
And prancing steeds, in trappings gay,
Whirl the bright chariot o'er the way.

Methinks it were a nobler sight
  To see these vales in woods arrayed,
Their summits in the golden light,
  Their trunks in grateful shade,
And herds of deer, that bounding go
O'er hills and prostrate trees below.

And then to mark the lord of all,
  The forest hero, trained to wars,
Quivered and plumed, and lithe and tall,
  And seamed with glorious scars,
Walk forth, amid his reign, to dare
The wolf, and grapple with the bear.

This bank, in which the dead were laid,
  Was sacred when its soil was ours;
Hither the artless Indian maid
  Brought wreaths of beads and flowers,
And the gray chief and gifted seer
Worshipped the god of thunders here.

But now the wheat is green and high
  On clods that hid the warrior's breast,
And scattered in the furrows lie
  The weapons of his rest;
And there, in the loose sand, is thrown
Of his large arm the mouldering bone.

Ah, little thought the strong and brave
  Who bore their lifeless chieftain forth--
Or the young wife, that weeping gave
  Her first-born to the earth,
That the pale race, who waste us now,
Among their bones should guide the plough.

They waste us--ay--like April snow
  In the warm noon, we shrink away;
And fast they follow, as we go
  Towards the setting day,--
Till they shall fill the land, and we
Are driven into the western sea.

But I behold a fearful sign,
  To which the white men's eyes are blind;
Their race may vanish hence, like mine,
  And leave no trace behind,
Save ruins o'er the region spread,
And the white stones above the dead.

Before these fields were shorn and tilled,
  Full to the brim our rivers flowed;
The melody of waters filled
  The fresh and boundless wood;
And torrents dashed and rivulets played,
And fountains spouted in the shade.

Those grateful sounds are heard no more,
  The springs are silent in the sun;
The rivers, by the blackened shore,
  With lessening current run;
The realm our tribes are crushed to get
May be a barren desert yet.

~~~***~~~

SEVENTY-SIX.

What heroes from the woodland sprung,
  When, through the fresh awakened land,
The thrilling cry of freedom rung,
And to the work of warfare strung
  The yeoman's iron hand!

Hills flung the cry to hills around,
  And ocean-mart replied to mart,
And streams whose springs were yet unfound,
Pealed far away the startling sound
  Into the forest's heart.

Then marched the brave from rocky steep,
  From mountain river swift and cold;
The borders of the stormy deep,
The vales where gathered waters sleep,
Sent up the strong and bold,--

As if the very earth again
  Grew quick with God's creating breath,
And, from the sods of grove and glen,
Rose ranks of lion-hearted men
  To battle to the death.
~~~

The wife, whose babe first smiled that day,
  The fair fond bride of yestereve,
And aged sire and matron gray,
Saw the loved warriors haste away,
  And deemed it sin to grieve.

Already had the strife begun;
  Already blood on Concord's plain
Along the springing grass had run,
And blood had flowed at Lexington,
  Like brooks of April rain.

That death-stain on the vernal sward
  Hallowed to freedom all the shore;
In fragments fell the yoke abhorred--
The footstep of a foreign lord
  Profaned the soil no more.

~~~***~~~

CATTERSKILL FALLS.

Midst greens and shades the Catterskill leaps,
  From cliffs where the wood-flower clings;
All summer he moistens his verdant steeps
  With the sweet light spray of the mountain springs;
And he shakes the woods on the mountain side,
When they drip with the rains of autumn-tide.

But when, in the forest bare and old,
  The blast of December calls,
He builds, in the starlight clear and cold,
  A palace of ice where his torrent falls,
With turret, and arch, and fretwork fair,
And pillars blue as the summer air.

For whom are those glorious chambers wrought,
  In the cold and cloudless night?
Is there neither spirit nor motion of thought
  In forms so lovely, and hues so bright?
Hear what the gray-haired woodmen tell
Of this wild stream and its rocky dell.

'Twas hither a youth of dreamy mood,
  A hundred winters ago,
Had wandered over the mighty wood,
  When the panther's track was fresh on the snow,
And keen were the winds that came to stir
The long dark boughs of the hemlock fir.

Too gentle of mien he seemed and fair,
  For a child of those rugged steeps;
His home lay low in the valley where
  The kingly Hudson rolls to the deeps;
But he wore the hunter's frock that day,
And a slender gun on his shoulder lay.
~~~

And here he paused, and against the trunk
  Of a tall gray linden leant,
When the broad clear orb of the sun had sunk
  From his path in the frosty firmament,
And over the round dark edge of the hill
A cold green light was quivering still.

And the crescent moon, high over the green,
  From a sky of crimson shone,
On that icy palace, whose towers were seen
  To sparkle as if with stars of their own;
While the water fell with a hollow sound,
'Twixt the glistening pillars ranged around.

Is that a being of life, that moves
  Where the crystal battlements rise?
A maiden watching the moon she loves,
  At the twilight hour, with pensive eyes?
Was that a garment which seemed to gleam
Betwixt the eye and the falling stream?

'Tis only the torrent tumbling o'er,
  In the midst of those glassy walls,
Gushing, and plunging, and beating the floor
  Of the rocky basin in which it falls.
'Tis only the torrent--but why that start?
Why gazes the youth with a throbbing heart?

He thinks no more of his home afar,
  Where his sire and sister wait.
He heeds no longer how star after star
  Looks forth on the night as the hour grows late.
He heeds not the snow-wreaths, lifted and cast
From a thousand boughs, by the rising blast.

His thoughts are alone of those who dwell
  In the halls of frost and snow,
Who pass where the crystal domes upswell
  From the alabaster floors below,
Where the frost-trees shoot with leaf and spray,
And frost-gems scatter a silvery day.

"And oh that those glorious haunts were mine!"
  He speaks, and throughout the glen
Thin shadows swim in the faint moonshine,
  And take a ghastly likeness of men,
As if the slain by the wintry storms
Came forth to the air in their earthly forms.

There pass the chasers of seal and whale,
  With their weapons quaint and grim,
And bands of warriors in glittering mail,
  And herdsmen and hunters huge of limb.
There are naked arms, with bow and spear,
And furry gauntlets the carbine rear.

There are mothers--and oh how sadly their eyes
  On their children's white brows rest!
There are youthful lovers--the maiden lies,
  In a seeming sleep, on the chosen breast;
There are fair wan women with moonstruck air,
The snow stars flecking their long loose hair.

They eye him not as they pass along,
  But his hair stands up with dread,
When he feels that he moves with that phantom throng,
  Till those icy turrets are over his head,
And the torrent's roar as they enter seems
Like a drowsy murmur heard in dreams.

The glittering threshold is scarcely passed,
  When there gathers and wraps him round
A thick white twilight, sullen and vast,
  In which there is neither form nor sound;
The phantoms, the glory, vanish all,
With the dying voice of the waterfall.

Slow passes the darkness of that trance,
  And the youth now faintly sees
Huge shadows and gushes of light that dance
  On a rugged ceiling of unhewn trees,
And walls where the skins of beasts are hung,
And rifles glitter on antlers strung.

On a couch of shaggy skins he lies;
  As he strives to raise his head,
Hard-featured woodmen, with kindly eyes,
  Come round him and smooth his furry bed
And bid him rest, for the evening star
Is scarcely set and the day is far.

They had found at eve the dreaming one
  By the base of that icy steep,
When over his stiffening limbs begun
  The deadly slumber of frost to creep,
And they cherished the pale and breathless form,
Till the stagnant blood ran free and warm.

~~~***~~~

THE ANTIQUITY OF FREEDOM.

  Here are old trees, tall oaks and gnarled pines,
That stream with gray-green mosses; here the ground
Was never trenched by spade, and flowers spring up
Unsown, and die ungathered. It is sweet
To linger here, among the flitting birds
And leaping squirrels, wandering brooks, and winds
That shake the leaves, and scatter, as they pass,
A fragrance from the cedars, thickly set
With pale blue berries. In these peaceful shades--
~~~

Peaceful, unpruned, immeasurably old--
My thoughts go up the long dim path of years,
Back to the earliest days of liberty.

Oh FREEDOM! thou art not, as poets dream,
A fair young girl, with light and delicate limbs,
And wavy tresses gushing from the cap
With which the Roman master crowned his slave
When he took off the gyves. A bearded man,
Armed to the teeth, art thou; one mailed hand
Grasps the broad shield, and one the sword; thy brow,
Glorious in beauty though it be, is scarred
With tokens of old wars; thy massive limbs
Are strong with struggling. Power at thee has launched
His bolts, and with his lightnings smitten thee;
They could not quench the life thou hast from heaven.
Merciless power has dug thy dungeon deep,
And his swart armorers, by a thousand fires,
Have forged thy chain; yet, while he deems thee bound,
The links are shivered, and the prison walls
Fall outward; terribly thou springest forth,
As springs the flame above a burning pile,
And shoutest to the nations, who return
Thy shoutings, while the pale oppressor flies.

Thy birthright was not given by human hands:
Thou wert twin-born with man. In pleasant fields,
While yet our race was few, thou sat'st with him,
To tend the quiet flock and watch the stars,
And teach the reed to utter simple airs.
Thou by his side, amid the tangled wood,
Didst war upon the panther and the wolf,
His only foes; and thou with him didst draw
The earliest furrows on the mountain side,
Soft with the deluge. Tyranny himself,
Thy enemy, although of reverend look,
Hoary with many years, and far obeyed,
Is later born than thou; and as he meets
The grave defiance of thine elder eye,
The usurper trembles in his fastnesses.

Thou shalt wax stronger with the lapse of years,
But he shall fade into a feebler age;
Feebler, yet subtler. He shall weave his snares,
And spring them on thy careless steps, and clap
His withered hands, and from their ambush call
His hordes to fall upon thee. He shall send
Quaint maskers, wearing fair and gallant forms,
To catch thy gaze, and uttering graceful words
To charm thy ear; while his sly imps, by stealth,
Twine round thee threads of steel, light thread on thread
That grow to fetters; or bind down thy arms
With chains concealed in chaplets. Oh! not yet
Mayst thou unbrace thy corslet, nor lay by
Thy sword; nor yet, O Freedom! close thy lids
In slumber; for thine enemy never sleeps,

And thou must watch and combat till the day
Of the new earth and heaven. But wouldst thou rest
Awhile from tumult and the frauds of men,
These old and friendly solitudes invite
Thy visit. They, while yet the forest trees
Were young upon the unviolated earth,
And yet the moss-stains on the rock were new,
Beheld thy glorious childhood, and rejoiced.

~~~***~~~

"THE MAY SUN SHEDS AN AMBER LIGHT."

The May sun sheds an amber light
On new-leaved woods and lawns between;
But she who, with a smile more bright,
Welcomed and watched the springing green,
Is in her grave,
Low in her grave.

The fair white blossoms of the wood
In groups beside the pathway stand;
But one, the gentle and the good,
Who cropped them with a fairer hand,
Is in her grave,
Low in her grave.

Upon the woodland's morning airs
The small birds' mingled notes are flung;
But she, whose voice, more sweet than theirs,
Once bade me listen while they sung,
Is in her grave,
Low in her grave.

That music of the early year
Brings tears of anguish to my eyes;
My heart aches when the flowers appear;
For then I think of her who lies
Within her grave,
Low in her grave.

~~~***~~~

WAITING BY THE GATE

Beside a massive gateway built up in years gone by,
Upon whose top the clouds in eternal shadow lie,
While streams the evening sunshine on quiet wood and lea,
I stand and calmly wait till the hinges turn for me.

The tree-tops faintly rustle beneath the breeze's flight,
A soft and soothing sound, yet it whispers of the night;
I hear the wood-thrush piping one mellow descant more,
And scent the flowers that blow when the heat of day is o'er.

Behold, the portals open, and o'er the threshold, now,

There steps a weary one with a pale and furrowed brow;
His count of years is full, his allotted task is wrought;
He passes to his rest from a place that needs him not.

In sadness then I ponder how quickly fleets the hour
Of human strength and action, man's courage and his power.
I muse while still the wood-thrush sings down the golden day,
And as I look and listen the sadness wears away.

Again the hinges turn, and a youth, departing, throws
A look of longing backward, and sorrowfully goes;
A blooming maid, unbinding the roses from her hair,
Moves mournfully away from amid the young and fair.

O glory of our race that so suddenly decays!
O crimson flush of morning that darkens as we gaze!
O breath of summer blossoms that on the restless air
Scatters a moment's sweetness, and flies we know not where!

I grieve for life's bright promise, just shown and then withdrawn;
But still the sun shines round me: the evening bird sings on,
And I again am soothed, and, beside the ancient gate,
In this soft evening sunlight, I calmly stand and wait.

Once more the gates are opened; an infant group go out,
The sweet smile quenched forever, and stilled the sprightly shout.
O frail, frail tree of Life, that upon the greensward strows
Its fair young buds unopened, with every wind that blows!

So come from every region, so enter, side by side,
The strong and faint of spirit, the meek and men of pride.
Steps of earth's great and mighty, between those pillars gray,
And prints of little feet, mark the dust along the way.

And some approach the threshold whose looks are blank with fear,
And some whose temples brighten with joy in drawing near,
As if they saw dear faces, and caught the gracious eye
Of Him, the Sinless Teacher, who came for us to die.

I mark the joy, the terror; yet these, within my heart,
Can neither wake the dread nor the longing to depart;
And, in the sunshine streaming on quiet wood and lea,
I stand and calmly wait till the hinges turn for me.

THE DAVIDSON SISTERS IN RETROSPECT

When Edgar Allan Poe came to review[379] the poetical "remains" Lucretia (1808-1825) and Margaret Davdison (1823-1838), victims of tuberculosis at a very young age, he rightly refused to let the tragic circumstances of their brief lives and untimely deaths hold undue sway over his literary judgment; and as he was inclined to think had, albeit perhaps understandably, been the case with Robert Southey, Catherine Sedgwick, and Washington Irving. Although ostensibly moved like everyone else over the two sisters sad end,[380] he was not *so* especially impressed by their poems; noting that he had seen verse of better quality written by other youngsters and yet who (presumably) garnered nothing like the sympathetic notoriety the Davdison's received. Yes, the girls distinctly showed encouraging promise. Yet the fact remained they had not, in their writings, attained quite to the level of excellence others attributed to them, but which perhaps they *might* have achieved had they lived long enough. Moreover, Poe must have felt, as perhaps did Washington Irving (Margaret's biographer) also, that readers were being manipulated into unduly favoring the girls' writings simply out of pity for them; possibly suspecting that the mother, in her pride, grief, and ambition, was forcing the matter. That so many of the girls poems morbidly deal with mortality and the fleetingness of life only contributes to this impression.[381]

Yet even if the poetry of the Davidson girls taken by itself was usually and not, all in all, exactly stupendous, their tale is nonetheless remains an engrossing one. As well as being a priceless and unusual record of what it was like being a young American girl in the early part of the nineteenth century, there is something not a little stirring and heroic in Margaret's effort to please her mother, memorialize her elder sister and mourn other lost siblings, while facing death herself so prematurely. To compound matters, it seems further not altogether implausible that the Davidsons found themselves, unwittingly or no, possibly contending with other-worldly personages intruding upon their lives. In reading Lucretia's biography, she strikes one as having been a haunted child of sorts; in one instance, secretly drawing pictures with cryptic letters written on the reverse side of them and which she didn't want her mother to see (and then later burning after the mother did discover them), and at other times reportedly falling into strange trances. As for Margaret, the mother states:

"Her visions were usually of an unearthly cast, -- about heaven and angels. She was wandering among the stars; her sainted sisters were her pioneers; her cherub brother walked hand-in-hand with her through the gardens of Paradise! I was always an early riser; but after Margaret began to decline I never disturbed her until time to rise for breakfast, a season of social intercourse in which she delighted to unite, and from which she was never willing to be absent. Often when I have spoken to her she would exclaim, 'Mother, you have disturbed the brightest visions that ever mortal was blessed with! I was in the midst of such scenes of delight! Cannot I have time to finish my dream?' And when I told her how long it was until breakfast, 'It will do, she would say, and again lose herself in her bright imaginings; for I considered these as moments of inspiration rather than sleep. She told me it was not sleep. I never knew but one, except Margaret, who enjoyed this delightful and mysterious source of happiness; that one was her departed sister Lucretia. When awaking from these reveries, an almost ethereal light played about her eye, which seemed to irradiate her whole face. A holy calm pervaded her manner, and in truth she looked more like an angel who had been communing with kindred spirits in the world of light, than anything of a grosser nature."[382]

---

[379] *See The Works of the Late Edgar Allan Poe*, edited by Rufus Wilmot Griswold (1850-1856); Volume III: *The Literati, &c.*, pp. 219-228; available at: http://www.eapoe.org/works/criticsm/dvdson.htm

[380] For the text of Washington Irving's biographical sketch of Margaret Davidson (found in *Biographies and Miscellanies* (1866) published by his brother Pierre), and written with no inconsiderable assistance from Margaret's mother, see: http://archive.org/details/MargaretMillerDavidsonByWashingtonIrving

[381] Is it only a coincidence that Margaret's would-be magnum opus was named "Leonore," and that Poe much later used the name "Lenore" for his dearly departed (poetical) love who'd found a home with "the angels?" On the other hand, German poet Gottfried August Bürger's (1747–1794) famous ballad "Lenore" (1773) could very likely have been the original source for both Davidson and Poe's use of that title name.

[382] And Margaret herself in a letter to a friend wrote: "You ask what I think of animal magnetism? My dear Hetty, I have not troubled my head about it. I hear of it from every quarter, and mentioned so often with contempt, that I have thought of it only as an absurdity. If I understand it rightly, the leading principle is the influence of one mind upon another; there is undoubtedly such an influence, to a reasonable degree, but as to throwing one into a magnetic sleep -- presenting visions before their eyes of scenes passing afar off, it seems almost too ridiculous! Still it may all be *true!*"

And what role the mother, not to mention the father, physician Oliver Davidson, acted in all that transpired is potentially a telling question. Was the mother, despite her own protestations and denials, exerting undue pressure on Margaret to emulate her sister while at the same time trying unwisely, albeit actuated by benevolent intention, to promote and campaign for the latter's status as a literary celebrity; thus adding to the already strenuous and unnatural stresses placed on Margaret? It is wrenchingly touching as we follow the mother and Irving's account of Margaret to see the latter attempting to brave the cruel and merciless storms of a very brief life through poetry and being a good and dutiful girl. Herself trapped, faced with death, what was she to do? And yet in hindsight she did marvelously,[383] and it is this it turns out that makes some of the Davidson's sisters better poems worth remembering. Not, as Poe feared, out of pity, but because the poems are an integral part of a real life drama that is a supreme and humbling inspiration of its kind.

The poems are largely imitative in voice, and the girls not infrequently resort to mechanically formulated apostrophes, stale 19th century wordings, and stiff, antiquated phrasing ("Brother!" used in a vocative sense, for example.) Lucretia seems to have been markedly influenced by Byron; often has a certain brooding quality, and an inventive turn such that she might, for purposes of conveniently differentiating the two, be considered moody and imaginative Coleridge in contrast to Margaret's optimistic and affectionate Wordsworth. While it is only well and prudent, as Poe did, to downplay the superiority of the girls' poems, and taking the *poems of themselves*, still a number are notwithstanding passing good, or better than, and do show admirable talents, intelligence, and imaginations; which, had the girls survived, might have justly earned them a place among or near the world's great poets: this in combination with the part (as mentioned) the poems play in helping to tell the astonishing, curious and poignant story of their lives. A story that as a life lesson, as Samuel F. B. Morse (one of Lucretia's biographers), Southey, Segwick and Irving realized, that is assuredly worth the hearing. To illustrate, I've collected here a number of pieces of both Lucretia and Margaret that reflect and help to convey these merits.

Selected poems of LUCRETIA DAVIDSON

ON AN AEOLIAN HARP.

What heavenly music strikes my ravished ear,
So soft, so melancholy, and so clear?
And do the tuneful Nine then touch the lyre,
To fill each bosom with poetic fire?

Or does some angel strike the sounding strings,
Catching from echo the wild note he sings?
But hark! another strain, how sweet, how wild!
Now rising high, now sinking low and mild.

And tell me now, ye spirits of the wind,
O, tell me where those artless notes to find!
So lofty now, so loud, so sweet, so clear,
That even angels might delighted hear!

But hark! those notes again majestic rise,
As though some spirit, banished from the
Had hither fled to charm Aeolus wild,
And teach him other music sweet and mild.

Then hither fly, sweet mourner of the air,

[383] If occasionally stumbling (or impelled to stumble at someone else's prompting) when it came to public relations; where, for instance, in a letter to a friend of her own age, Margaret clumsily affects laughter in praising *Legend of Sleepy Hollow* -- reading of which missive probably made Irving wince a little in embarrassment.

Then hither fly, and to my harp repair;
At twilight chant the melancholy lay,
And charm the sorrows of thy soul away.

~~~***~~~

PETITION OF OLD COMB[384]

Dear mistress, I am old and poor,
My teeth decayed and gone;
Oh! give me but one moment's rest,
For mark, I'm tott'ring down.

Thy raven locks for many a day,
I've bound around thy brow;
And now that I am old and lame,
I prithee let me go.

Have I not, many a weary hour,
Peep'd o'er thy book or pen;
And seen what this poor mangled form
Will ne'er behold again?

A faithful servant I have been,
But ah! my day is past;
And all my hope, and all my wish,
Is liberty at last.

Mark but the glittering well fill'd shelf,
Where my companions lie;
Are they not fairer than myself,
And younger far than I?

Oh! then in pity hie thee there,
Where thousands wait thy call,
And twine one in thy raven hair,
To shroud my shameful fall.

My days are hast'ning to their close,
Crack! crack! goes every tooth;
A thousand pains, a thousand woes,
Remind me of my youth.

Adieu then -- in distress I die --
My last hold fails me now;
Adieu, and may thy elf locks fly,
For ever 'round thy brow.

~~~***~~~

THE LAST FLOWER OF THE GARDEN.

(Written in her thirteenth year.)

[384] [*Edit. Note.* This was written as an allegorical message of sorts to her mother; though quite what Lucretia meant to impart or communicate we leave to others to speculate.]

The last flower of the garden was blooming alone,
The last rays of the sun on its blushing leaves shone;
Still a glittering drop on its bosom reclined,
And a few half-blown buds 'midst its leaves were entwined.

Say, lonely one, say, why ling'rest thou here?
And why on thy bosom reclines the bright tear?
'T is the tear of a zephyr -- for summer 'twas shed,
And for all thy companions now withered and dead.

Why ling'rest thou here, when around thee are strown
The flowers once so lovely, by Autumn blasts blown?
Say, why, sweetest flowret, the last of thy race,
Why ling'rest thou here the lone garden to grace?

As I spoke, a rough blast, sent by Winter's own hand,
Whistled by me, and bent its sweet head to the sand;
I hastened to raise it -- the dew-drop had fled,
And the once lovely flower was withered and dead.

~~~***~~~

ON THE BIRTH OF A SISTER.[385]

(Written in her fifteenth year.)

Sweet babe, I cannot hope that thou'lt be freed
From woes, to all, since earliest time, decreed;
But mayst thou be with resignation blessed,
To bear each evil, howsoe'er distressed.

May Hope her anchor lead amid the storm,
And o'er the tempest rear her angel form!
May sweet Benevolence, whose words are peace,
To the rude whirlwinds softly whisper "cease!"

And may Religion, Heaven's own darling child,
Teach thee at human cares and griefs to smile;
Teach thee to look beyond this world of wo,
To Heaven's high fount, whence mercies ever flow.

And when this vale of tears is safely passed,
When Death's dark curtain shuts the scene at last,
May thy freed spirit leave this earthly sod,
And fly to seek the bosom of thy God.

~~~***~~~

PROPHECY II.

TO ANOTHER LADY.

(Written in her sixteenth year.)

---

385 [*Edit. Note.* i.e., Margaret.]

I have told a maiden of hours of grief,
Of a bleeding heart, of a joyless life;
I have read her a tale of future wo;
I have marked her a pathway of sorrow below;
I have read on the page of her blooming cheek,
A darker doom than my tongue dare speak.
Now, maiden, for thee, I will turn mine eye
To a brighter path through futurity.
The clouds shall pass from thy brow away,
And bright be the closing of life's long day;
The storms shall murmur in silence to sleep,
And angels around thee their watches shall keep;
Thou shalt live in the sunbeams of love and delight,
And thy life shall flow on 'till it fades into night;
And the twilight of age shall come quietly on;
Thou wilt feel, yet regret not, that daylight hath flown;
For the shadows of evening shall melt o'er thy soul,
And the soft dreams of Heaven around thee shall roll,
'Till sinking in sweet, dreamless slumber to rest,
In the arms of thy loved one, still blessing and blest,
Thy soul shall glide on to its harbour in Heaven,
Every tear wiped away -- every error forgiven.

~~~***~~~

TO A STAR.

(Written in her fifteenth year.)

Thou brightly-glittering star of even,
Thou gem upon the brow of Heaven,
Oh! were this fluttering spirit free,
How quick 't would spread its wings to thee.

How calmly, brightly dost thou shine,
Like the pure lamp in Virtue's shrine!
Sure the fair world which thou mayst boast
Was never ransomed, never lost.

There, beings pure as Heaven's own air,
Their hopes, their joys together share;
While hovering angels touch the string,
And seraphs spread the sheltering wing.

There cloudless days and brilliant nights,
Illumed by Heaven's refulgent lights;
There seasons, years, unnoticed roll,
And unregretted by the soul.

Thou little sparkling star of even,
Thou gem upon an azure Heaven,
How swiftly will I soar to thee,
When this imprisoned soul is free.

~~~***~~~

TO A FRIEND,
WHOM I HAD NOT SEEN SINCE MY CHILDHOOD.

(Written in her sixteenth year.)

And thou hast marked, in childhood's hour,
The fearless boundings of my breast,
When fresh as Summer's opening flower,
I freely frolicked, and was blessed.

Oh! say, was not this eye more bright?
Were not these lips more wont to smile?
Methinks that then my heart was light,
And I a fearless, joyous child.

And thou didst mark me gay and wild,
My careless, reckless laugh of mirth;
The simple pleasures of a child,
The holiday of man on earth.

Then thou hast seen me in that hour,
When every nerve of life was new,
When pleasures fanned youth's infant flower,
And Hope her witcheries round it threw.

That hour is fading, it has fled,
And I am left in darkness now;
A wand'rer towards a lowly bed,
The grave, that home of all below.

~~~***~~~

AMERICA.

(Written in her seventeenth year.)

And this was once the realm of nature, where
Wild as the wind, tho' exquisitely fair,
She breath'd the mountain breeze, or bow'd to kiss
The dimpling waters with unbounded bliss.
Here in this Paradise of earth, where first
Wild mountain liberty began to burst,
Once Nature's temple rose in simple grace,
The hill her throne, the world her dwelling place.
And where are now her lakes so still and lone,
Her thousand streams with bending shrubs o'ergrown?
Where her dark cat'racts tumbling from on high,
With rainbow arch aspiring to the sky?
Her tow'ring pines with fadeless wreaths entwin'd,
Her waving alders streaming to the wind?
Nor these alone, -- her own, -- her fav'rite child,
All fire; all feeling; man untaught and wild;
Where can the lost, lone son of nature stray?
For art's high car is rolling on its way;
A wand'rer of the world, he flies to drown
The thoughts of days gone by and pleasures flown,
~~~

In the deep draught, whose dregs are death and woe,
With slavery's iron chain conceal'd below.
Once thro' the tangled wood, with noiseless tread
And throbbing heart, the lurking warrior sped,
Aim'd his sure weapon, won the prize, and turn'd
While his high heart with wild ambition burn'd,
With song and war-whoop to his native tree,
There on its bark to carve the victory.
His all of learning did that act comprise,
But still in *nature's* volume doubly wise.

The wayward stream which once with idle bound,
Whirl'd on resistless in its foaming round,
Now curb'd by art flows on, a wat'ry chain
Linking the snow-capp'd mountains to the main.
Where once the alder in luxuriance grew,
Or the tall pine its tow'ring branches threw
Abroad to Heav'n, with dark and haughty brow,
There mark the realms of plenty smiling now;
There the full sheaf of Ceres richly glows,
And Plenty's fountain blesses as it flows;
And man, a brute when left to wander wild,
A reckless creature, nature's lawless child,
What boundless streams of knowledge rolling now,
From the full hand of art around him flow!
Improvement strides the surge, while from afar,
Learning rolls onward in her silver car;
Freedom unfurls her banner o'er his head,
While peace sleeps sweetly on her native bed.
The muse arises from the wildwood glen,
And chants her sweet and hallow'd song again,
As in those Halcyon days, which bards have sung,
When hope was blushing, and when life was young.
Thus shall she rise, and thus her sons shall rear
Her sacred temple *here*, and only *here*,
While Percival, her lov'd and chosen priest,
For ever blessing, tho' himself unblest,
Shall fan the fire that blazes at her shrine,
And charm the ear with numbers half divine.

~~~***~~~

A SONG.

(Written in her fifteenth year.)

Life is but a troubled ocean,
Hope a meteor, love a flower
Which blossoms in the morning beam,
And withers with the evening hour.

Ambition is a dizzy height,
And glory, but a lightning gleam;
Fame is a bubble, dazzling bright,
Which fairest shines in fortune's beam.
~~~

When clouds and darkness veil the skies,
And sorrow's blast blows loud and chill,
Friendship shall like a rainbow rise,
And softly whisper -- peace, be still.

~~~***~~~

A VIEW OF DEATH.

When bending o'er the brink of life,
My trembling soul shall stand,
Waiting to pass death's awful flood,
Great God! at thy command;

When weeping friends surround my bed,
To close my sightless eyes,
When shattered by the weight of years
This broken body lies;

When every long lov'd scene of life
Stands ready to depart,
When the last sigh which shakes this frame
Shall rend this bursting heart;

Oh thou great source of joy supreme,
Whose arm alone can save,
Dispel the darkness that surrounds
The entrance to the grave.

Lay thy supporting gentle hand
Beneath my sinking head,
And with a ray of love divine,
Illume my dying bed.

Leaning on thy dear faithful breast,
I would resign my breath,
And in thy loved embraces lose
The bitterness of death.

~~~***~~~

KINDAR BURIAL SERVICE.

VERSIFIED.

We commend our brother to thee, O earth!
To thee he returns, from thee was his birth!
Of thee was he formed, he was nourished by thee;
Take the body, O earth! the spirit is free.

O air! he once breathed thee, through thee he survived,
And in thee and with thee his pure spirit lived;
That spirit hath fled, and we yield him to thee;
His ashes be spread, like his soul, far and free.

O fire! we commit his dear relics to thee,
Thou emblem of purity, spotless and free;
May his soul, like thy flames, bright and burning arise
To its mansion of bliss, in the star-spangled skies.

O water! receive him; without thy kind aid
He had parched 'neath the sunbeams or mourned in the shade;
Then take of his body the share which is thine,
For the spirit hath fled from its mouldering shrine.

~~~***~~~

THE WIDE WORLD IS DREAR.

(Written in her sixteenth year.)

O Say not the wide world is lonely and dreary!
O say not that life is a wilderness waste!
There's ever some comfort in store for the weary,
And there's ever some hope for the sorrowful breast.

There are often sweet dreams which will steal o'er the soul,
Beguiling the mourner to smile through a tear,
That, when waking, the dew-drops of mem'ry may fall,
And blot out, forever, "the wide world is drear."

There is hope for the lost, for the lone one's relief,
Which will beam o'er his pathway of danger and fear;
There is pleasure's wild throb, and the calm "joy of grief,"
O then say not the wide world is lonely and drear!

There are fears that are anxious, yet sweet to the breast,
Some feelings, which language ne'er told to the ear,
Which return to the heart, and there lingering rest,
Soft whispering, this world is not lonely and drear.

'Tis true that the dreams of the evening will fade,
When reason's broad sunbeam shines calmly and clear;
Still fancy, sweet fancy, will smile o'er the shade,
And say that the world is not lonely and drear.

O then mourn not that life is a wilderness waste!
That each hope is illusive, each prospect is drear,
But remember that man, undeserving, is blest,
And rewarded with smiles for the fall of a tear.

~~~***~~~

THE FEAR OF MADNESS.

WRITTEN WHILE CONFINED TO HER BED, DURING HER LAST ILLNESS.

There is a something which I dread,
It is a dark, a fearful thing;
It steals along with withering tread,
Or sweeps on wild destruction's wing.

That thought comes o'er me in the hour
Of grief, of sickness, or of sadness;
'Tis not the dread of death -- 'tis more,
It is the dread of madness.

Oh! may these throbbing pulses pause,
Forgetful of their feverish course;
May this hot brain, which burning, glows
With all a fiery whirlpool's force,

Be cold, and motionless, and still,
A tenant of its lowly bed,
But let not dark delirium steal --

****

[Unfinished.]

(This was the last piece she ever wrote.)

~~~~~~******~~~~~~

Selected Poems of MARGARET DAVIDSON

TO A FLOWER.

The blighting hand of winter
Has laid thy glories low;
Oh, where is all thy beauty?
Where is thy freshness now!

Summer has pass'd away,
With every smiling scene,
And nature in decay
Assumes a mournful mien.

How like adversity's rude blast
Upon the helpless one,
When hope's gay visions all have pass'd,
And to oblivion gone.

Yet winter has some beauties left,
Which cheer my heart forlorn;
Nature is not of charms bereft,
Though shrouded by the storm.
~~~~~~

I see the sparkling snow;
I view the mountain tops;
I mark the frozen lake below,
Or the dark rugged rocks.

How truly grand the scene!
The giant trees are bare,
No fertile meadows intervene,
No hillocks fresh and fair;

But the cloud-capp'd mountains rise,
Crown'd with purest whiteness,
And mingle with the skies,
That shine with azure brightness.

And solitude, that friend so dear
To each reflecting mind,
Her residence has chosen here
To soothe the heart refined.

1831.

~~~***~~~

HOME.

(Verses written when nine years of age.)

Yonder orb of dazzling light
Sinks beneath the robe bf night,
And the moon, so sweetly pale,
Waits to lift her silver veil.
One by one the stars appear,
Glittering in the heavenly sphere,
And sparkling in their bright array,
Welcome in the close of day.
But home, that sacred, pure retreat,
Where dwells my heart in all that's sweet,
And my own stream, where oft I've stray'd,
And mark'd the beams that o'er it play'd,
Is far away, o'er the waters blue,
Far from my fondly straining view.

1832.

~~~***~~~

STANZAS.

The power of mind, the force of genius,
Oh, what human heart can tell,
Or the deep and stirring thoughts,
Which in the poet's bosom dwell!

The high and holy dreams of heaven,
Which raise the soul above
This world of care, this sphere of sin,

To realms of light and love.

Oh, who can tell its energy?
The spirit's power and might,
When genius, with sublimest force,
Appoints its upward flight,--

And lifts the struggling soul above
This prison-house of clay,
To roam amid the fancied realms
Of glory and of day!

And breathes immortal vigour
To sustain it through this life,
The index of a higher world,
With power and beauty rife.
Oh, how sublime the very thought,
That this frail form of mine
Contains a spirit destined soon
In purer worlds to shine.

T' unfold its infant energies,
In an immortal clime,
And far more glorious become
Each passing hour of time.

That it contains the heavenly germ
Of future being now,
Created there to beautify,
Where clearer waters flow.

And there expand the glowing bud,
'Mid worlds of light and love,
Through the bright realms of ether,
In glory still to rove.

~~~***~~~

FRAGMENT.

Oh, for a something more than this,
To fill the void within my breast,
A sweet reality of bliss,
A something bright but unexpress'd.

My spirit longs for something higher
Than life's dull stream can e'er supply,
Something to feed this inward fire,
This spark, which never more can die.

I'd dwell with all that nature forms
Of wild or beautiful or gay,
Bow, when she clothes the heaven with storms,
And join her in her frolic play.

I'd hold companionship with all
~~~

Of pure, or noble, or divine,
With glowing heart adoring fall,
And kneel at nature's sylvan shrine.

My soul is like a broken lyre,
Whose loudest, sweetest chord is gone,
A note half trembling on the wire,
A heart that wants an echoing tone.

Where shall I find this shadowy bliss,
This shapeless phantom of my mind,
This something words can ne'er express,
So vague, so faint, so undefined?

Language! thou never canst portray
The fancies floating o'er my soul,
Thou ne'er canst chase the clouds away,
Which o'er my changing visions roll.

1837.

~~~***~~~

FRAGMENT.

Oh, I have gazed on forms of light,
Till life seem'd ebbing in a tear,
Till in that fleeting space of sight,
Were merged the feelings of a year.

And I have heard the voice of song,
Till my full heart gush'd wild and free,
And my rapt soul would float along
As if on waves of melody.

But while I glow'd at beauty's glance,
I long'd to feel a deeper thrill,
And while I heard that dying strain,
I sigh'd for something sweeter still.

I have been happy, and my soul
Free from each sorrow, care, regret,
Yet ever in those hours of bliss,
I long'd to find them happier yet

Oft o'er the darkness of my mind,
Some meteor thought has glanced at will,
'Twas bright -- but ever have I sigh'd
To find a fancy brighter still.

Why are these restless, vain desires,
Which always grasp at something more
To feed the spirit's hidden fires,
Which burn unseen, unnoticed soar!

Well might the heathen sage have known
~~~

That earth must fail the soul to bind,
That life, and life's tame joys alone,
Could never chain the ethereal mind.[386]

1837.

~~~***~~~

STANZAS.

Oh, who may tell the joy, the bliss,
Which o'er the realm of fancy streams,
The varied scenes of light and life,
Which deck the poet's world of dreams?

The ransom'd soul may speed its flight,
To live and glow in realms above;
May bathe in floods of endless light,
And live eternal years of love.

But oh, what voice hath e'er reveal'd
The glories of that blest abode,
Save the faint whisperings of the soul,
The mystic monitors of God!

Thus may the poet's spirit dance
And revel in his world of joy,
May form creations at a glance,
And myriads at a word destroy.

But mortal ear can never hear
The music of that seraph band;
Nought save the faint, unearthly tones
Just wafted from that spirit-land.

None but the poet's soul can know
The wild and wondrous beauty there;
The streams of light, which ever flow,
The ever music-breathing air.

His spirit seeks this heaven awhile,
Entranced in glowing dreams of bliss;
Lives in the muses' hallow'd smile,
And bathes in founts of happiness.

Then, when he sinks to earth again,
His hand awakes the trembling lyre,
He strives to breathe a burning strain,
Kindled at fancy's altar-fire.
But oh, how frail the trembling notes,
Compared * * *
* * * *

[386] [*Edit. Note.* Compare to the closing lines of David Humphreys' "Addressed to My Friends at Yale College on My Leaving Them to Join the Army" (1776).]
~~~

1837.

~~~***~~~

LINES

WRITTEN AFTER SHE HERSELF BEGAN TO FEAR THAT HER DISEASE WAS PAST REMEDY.

I once thought life was beautiful,
I once thought life was fair,
Nor deem'd that all its light could fade
And leave but darkness there.

But now I know it could not last --
The fairy dream has fled!
Though thirteen summers scarce have past
Above this youthful head.

Yes, life -- 'twas all a dream -- but now
I see thee as thou art;
I see how slight a thing can shade
The sunshine of the heart.

I see that all thy brightest hours,
Unmark'd, have pass'd away;
And now I feel how sweet they were,
I cannot bid them stay.

In childish love or childish play
My happiest hours were spent,
While scarce my infant tongue could say
What joy or pleasure meant.

And now, when my young heart looks up,
Life's gayest smiles to meet;
Now, when in youth her brightest charms
Would seem so doubly sweet;

Now fade the dreams which bound my soul
As with the chains of truth!
Oh that those dreams had stay'd awhile,
To vanish with my youth!

Oh! once did hope look sweetly down,
To check each rising sigh;
But disappointment's iron frown
Has dimm'd her sparkling eye.

And once I loved a brother too,
Our youngest and our best,
But death's unerring arrow sped,
And laid him down to rest.

*****
* * * * *****
~~~

But now I know those hours of peace
Were never form'd to last;
That those fair days of guileless joy
Are past -- for ever past!

January, 1837.

WHIG AND TORY IN *HORSE-SHOE ROBINSON*

"We have seen war in its horrors," exclaimed Mildred, with an involuntary vivacity; "and here it is in all its romance!"
~ *Horse-Shoe Robinson*, ch. 41.

For his time, Baltimore born Joseph Pendleton Kennedy would seemed to have *just about* done and had it all; which for our purposes we can summarize by listing some highlights. He began his career as an attorney; fought at the battle of Bladensburg while serving in the Maryland militia; disenchanted with practicing law, he took up writing; and wrote three novels -- two of which became popular and successful. His main focus, however, was not literature but politics and he became a busy statesman; acting for many years as an assembly member, including Speaker, of the Maryland legislature. Later he was elected U.S. Congressman (on the Whig platform) from the same state, and subsequently went on, like fellow literary lights James Kirke Paulding and U.S. historian George Bancroft, to be appointed Secretary of the Navy. He knew or was the personal acquaintance of most, if not quite all, of many of the eminent American authors of his era; as well as being a correspondent with some well-known British ones, including Charles Dickens and William Makepeace Thackeray. Although a devoted lover of the South, he was pro-Union during the Civil War; arguing that it was the collective, not individual, states that found our country and won its independence.[387] At the same time, he was one of those who thought slavery a bad idea, and encouraged its overtime and gradual eradication. To cap it all off, he was a devout Presbyterian and a reputed credit to his congregation.[388]

His two (aforesaid) *successful* novels were *Swallow Barn, or A Sojourn in the Old Dominion* (1832), and *Horse-Shoe Robinson: A Tale of the Tory Ascendancy* (1835). The first was a sentimental and semi-comical tale of nostalgia, written in the affectionate and warm hearted manner of Washington Irving; that told the story of neighboring plantations in (what was then becoming) Old Virginia. While the first is critically considered his best work overall, it was *Horse-Shoe Robinson*, a humorous historical romance set during the Revolutionary War in (mostly) South Carolina in 1780, that earned Kennedy most acclaim.

Although *Horse-Shoe Robinson* is in part yet another attempt at an American based *Waverly* spin-off, Kennedy's work has the advantage over such as Cooper in that there is a greater emphasis on realism; while simultaneously humor is far more prominent and lively an ingredient to the story. With respect to realism, Kennedy was ahead of his time in presenting Black slaves as more human and intelligent than, say, they appear in William Gilmore Simms. True, he occasionally has one of his characters, such as Horse-Shoe Robinson himself, ridicule or speak condescendingly of them, but not so Kennedy himself; who draws them in a believable and reasonably (and for his time) respectful manner. He is matter-of-fact candid in displaying the foibles and faults as well as strengths of his heroes; including, for instance, detailing their punctual concern for eating; or the rank villainy of other characters, such Horse-Shoe's guide who insists on (literally) skinning a captured wolf alive.[389]

As history, *Horse-Shoe Robinson* is fairly fast and loose at times but mostly faithful to the record. As well as brief recreations of the battles of Musgrove Mill and King's Mountain, it includes what we today might refer to as cameo appearances by loyalist Alexander Innes,[390] Francis Marion, James Williams, William Campbell, Tarleton, Cornwallis, Archibald McArthur, Patrick Ferguson, Isaac Shelby; with repeated references to Sumter, Elijah Clark, and Pickens. And it is interesting to note that Kennedy's work antedated Simms' southern Revolutionary War novels, and even in some-wise would seem to have prompted them. On the whole, *Horse-shoe Robinson* is overly lengthy; while suffering from excessive digressions and unnecessarily protracted conversations (the latter device regrettably typical of American

---

[387] Maj. Arthur Butler, a *Continental* (S.C.) officer and who plays a pivotal role, is in the end rescued from his British captivity by the Southern *militia*.
[388] A good introduction to Kennedy and his work, and from which much of the above is taken, is Ernest E. Leisy's lead-in to the 1937 edition of *Horse-Shoe Robinson* (American Book Company.)
[389] In Simms' *Mellichampe: A Legend of the Santee* (1836) a character not dissimilarly cruelly stabs a dog to keep him quiet.
[390] Kennedy mistakenly spells his last name as "Innis."

novels of the time.) Where the book succeeds rather and chiefly is in its individual scenes and characters; administered in extracted doses.

The star of the tale is said by Kennedy in his introduction to have been based on a real Galbraith Robinson (who'd fought and related anecdotes of his experiences in the Revolution), and there's no reason to think that this wasn't technically and in part the case. Notwithstanding, Horse-Shoe as much as anything is more of a general type: a male southerner: hardy, fearless, given to both joking and philosophizing. He's Natty Bumppo, but Natty Bumppo given more to wit making and wise-cracking than Cooper's creation -- such that Kennedy here is something of an ancestor of Mark Twain and Will Rogers. Here, to illustrate, are some notable Horse Shoe-isms:

* *Horse Shoe came to the fire-side, and took a chair, saying, "I larnt that, Colonel, in the campaigns. A man picks up some good everywhere, if he's a mind to; that's my observation."* [Introduction]

* *"When danger stares you in the face," replied Horse Shoe, "the best way is not to see it. It is only in not seeing of it, that a brave man differs from a coward: that's my opinion."* [ch. 2]

* *"A good stomach enough, but not much in it. I'll tell you another observation I made: when a man travels all night long on an empty stomach, he ought either to fill it next morning or make it smaller."*
"And how is that to be managed, friend Horse Shoe?"
"Indian fashion," replied the sergeant. "Buckle your belt a little tighter every two or three hours. A man may shrivel his guts up to the size of a pipe stem. But I found a better way to get along than by taking in my belt --" [ch. 2]

* *"It is my opinion, ma'am, the best thing the women can do, in these here wars, is to knit; and leave the fighting of it out, to us who hav'n't faces to be spoiled by bad weather and tough times."* [ch. 5]

* *"It's the custom of our country," rejoined Horse Shoe, "I don't know what it may be in yourn, to larn a little about the business of every man we meet; but we do it by fair, out-and-out question and answer -- all above board, and we hold in despise all sorts of contwistifications, either by laying of tongue-traps, or listening under eaves of houses."* [ch. 6]

* *"In our country," replied Horse Shoe, "we generally like to get a share of whatever new is stirring, and, though we don't practise much with cudgels, yet, to sarve a turn, we do, now and then, break a head or so; and, consarning that fist work you happened to touch upon, we have no condesentious scruples against a fair rap or two over the knowledge-box, and the tripping-up of a fractious chap's heels, in the way of a sort of a rough-and-tumble, which, may be, you understand. You have been long enough here, mayhap, to find that out."* [ch. 6]

* *"They didn't want to have no uproar with me, Major [Arthur] Butler. They knowed me, that although I wa'n't a quarrelsome man, they would'a got some of their necks twisted if I had seen occasion: in particular, I would have taken some of mad Archy's crazy fits out of him--by my hand I would, major! But I'll tell you,--I made one observation, that this here sort of carrying false colors goes against a man's conscience: it doesn't seem natural for a man, that's accustomed and willing to stand by his words, to be heaping one lie upon top of another as fast as he can speak them. It really, Major Butler, does go against my grain."* [ch. 12]

* *"If the worst comes to the worst, major, the rule is run or fight. We can manage that, at any rate, for we have had a good deal of both in the last three or four years."* [ch. 12]

* *"There is some good things," said the sergeant, "in this world that's good, and some that's bad. But I have always found that good and bad is so mixed up and jumbled together, that you don't often get much of one without a little of the other. A sodger's a sodger, no matter what side he is on; and they are the naturalest people in the world for fellow-feeling. One day a man is up, and then the laugh's on his side; next day he is down, and then the laugh's against him. So, as a sodger has more of these ups and downs*

than other folks, there's the reason his heart is tenderer towards a comrade than other people's. Here's your health, sir. This is a wicked world, and twisted, in a measure, upside down; and it is well known that evil communications corrupts good manners; but sodgers were made to set the world right again, on its legs, and to presarve good breeding and Christian charity. So there's a sarmon for you, you tinkers!" [ch. 18]

* *"As heavy a lump, certainly," replied the officer [one of Tarleton's]. "This, you say, is the first time you have been in Carolina?"*

"To my knowledge," replied the [masquerading] sergeant. [ch. 47]

Of particular relevance to historians of the American Revolution is Kennedy's faithful portrayal of southern whigs and tories. Here is a view of Revolutionary War combatants on both sides interacting in a manner which -- outside of, say, fellow southern novelist William Gilmore Simms -- we scarce ever get a chance to see and hear. To spare such as who haven't read the book the digging, here is an excellent sample of this very case in point, taken from chapter 18. Robinson and the S.C. Continental officer Maj. Arthur Butler, taken prisoner, are being escorted by their captors, a gang of roguish, yet conscience weighingly human, tories.

~~~*~~~

It was with the most earnest solicitude that Butler and his companion watched the course of events, and became acquainted with the character of the ruffians into whose hands they had fallen. The presence of James Curry in this gang excited a painful consciousness in the mind of the soldier, that he had powerful and secret enemies at work against him, but who they were was an impenetrable mystery. Then the lawless habits of the people who had possession of him, gave rise to the most anxious distrust as to his future fate: he might be murdered in a fit of passion, or tortured with harsh treatment to gratify some concealed malice. His position in the army was, it seemed, known too; and, for aught that he could tell, his mission might be no secret to his captors. Robinson's sagacity entered fully into these misgivings. He had narrowly observed the conduct of the party who had made them prisoners, and with that acute insight which was concealed under a rude and uneducated exterior, but which was strongly marked in his actions, he had already determined upon the course which the safety of Butler required him to pursue. According to his view of their present difficulties it was absolutely necessary that he should effect his escape, at whatever personal hazard. Butler, he rightly conjectured, was the principal object of the late ambuscade; that, for some unknown purpose, the possession of this officer became important to those who had procured the attack upon him, and that James Curry had merely hired this gang of desperadoes to secure the prize. Under these circumstances, he concluded that the Major would be so strictly guarded as to forbid all hope of escape, and that any attempt by him to effect it would only be punished by certain death. But, in regard to himself, his calculation was different. "First," said he, "I can master any three of this beggarly crew in an open field and fair fight; and, secondly, when it comes to the chances of a pell-mell, they will not think me of so much account as to risk their necks by a long chase; their whole eyes would undoubtedly be directed to the Major." The sergeant, therefore, determined to make the attempt, and, in the event of his success, to repair to Sumpter, who he knew frequented some of the fastnesses in this region; or, in the alternative, to rally such friends from the neighboring country as were not yet overawed by the Tory dominion, and bring them speedily to the rescue of Butler. Full of these thoughts, he took occasion during the night, whilst the guard were busy in cooking their venison, and whilst they thought him and his comrade wrapt in sleep, to whisper to Butler the resolution he had adopted.

"I will take the first chance to-morrow to make a dash upon these ragamuffins," he said; "and I shall count it hard if I don't get out of their claws. Then, rely upon me, I shall keep near you in spite of these devils. So be prepared, if I once get away, to see me like a witch that travels on a broomstick or creeps through a keyhole. But whisht! The drunken vagabonds mustn't hear us talking."

Butler, after due consideration of the sergeant's scheme, thought it, however perilous, the only chance they had of extricating themselves from the dangers with which they were beset, and promised the most ready co-operation; determining also, to let no opportunity slip which might be improved to his own
~~~

deliverance. "Your good arm and brave heart, Galbraith, never stood you in more urgent stead than they may do to-morrow," was his concluding remark.

When morning broke the light of day fell upon a strange and disordered scene. The drunken and coarse wretches of the night before, now lessened in number and strength by common broil and private quarrel, lay stretched on their beds of leaves. Their motley and ill-assorted weapons lay around in disarray; drinking cups and empty flasks were scattered over the trodden grass, the skin and horns of the buck, and disjointed fragments of raw flesh were seen confusedly cast about beneath the tree, and a conspicuous object in the scene were the clots of blood and gore, both of men and beast, that disfigured the soil. Two new-made graves, or rather mounds, hastily scratched together and imperfectly concealing the limbs of the dead, prominently placed but a few feet from the ring of last night's revelry, told of the disasters of the fight at the ford. The brushwood fire had burned down into a heap of smouldering ashes, and the pale and sickly features of the wounded trooper were to be discerned upon a pallet of leaves, hard by the heap of embers, surrounded by the remnants of bones and roasted meat that had been flung carelessly aside. In a spot of more apparent comfort, sheltered by an overhanging canopy of vines and alder, lay Butler stretched upon his cloak, and, close beside him, the stout frame of Horse Shoe Robinson. In the midst of all these marks of recent riot and carousal, sat two swarthy figures, haggard and wan from night-watching, armed at every point, and keeping strict guard over the prisoners.

The occasional snort and pawing of horses in the neighboring wood showed that these animals were alert at the earliest dawn; whilst among the first who seemed aware of the approach of day, was seen rising from the earth, where it had been flung in stupid torpor for some hours, the bloated and unsightly person of Hugh Habershaw, now much the worse for the fatigue and revelry of the preceding night. A savage and surly expression was seated on his brow, and his voice broke forth more than ordinarily harsh and dissonant, as he ordered the troop to rouse and prepare for their march.

The summons was tardily obeyed; and while the yawning members of the squad were lazily moving to their several duties and shaking off the fumes of their late debauch, the captain was observed bending over the prostrate form of Gideon Blake, and directing a few anxious inquiries into his condition. The wounded man was free from pain, but his limbs were stiff, and the region of the stab sore and sensitive to the least touch. The indications, however, were such as to show that his wound was not likely to prove mortal. By the order of Habershaw, a better litter was constructed, and the troopers were directed to bear him, by turns, as far as Christie's, where he was to be left to the nursing of the family. It was a full hour before the horses were saddled, the scattered furniture collected, and the preparations for the march completed. When these were accomplished the prisoners were provided with the two sorriest horses of the troop, and they now set forward at a slow pace, under the escort of four men commanded by James Curry. The two troopers who bore the sick man followed on foot; Habershaw with the remainder, one of whom had appropriated Captain Peter, whilst he led the horses of the dismounted men, brought up the rear.

On the journey there was but little spoken by any member of the party; the boisterous and rude nature of the men who composed the troop seemed to have been subdued by sleep into a temper of churlish indifference or stolid apathy. Peppercorn, or James Curry, as the reader now recognizes him, strictly preserved his guard over the prisoners, manifesting a severity of manner altogether different from the tone of careless revelry which characterized his demeanor on the preceding night. It never relaxed from an official and sullen reserve. A moody frown sat upon his brow, and his communication with the prisoners was confined to short and peremptory commands; whilst, at the same time, he forbade the slightest intercourse with them on the part of any of the guard. During the short progress to Christie's he frequently rode apart with Habershaw; and the conversation which then occupied these two was maintained in a low tone, and with a serious air that denoted some grave matter of deliberation.

It was more than an hour after sunrise when the cavalcade reached the point of their present destination. There were signs of an anxious purpose in the silence of the journey, broken as it was only by low mutterings amongst the men, above which sometimes arose an expression of impatience and discontent, as the subject of their whispered discussions appeared to excite some angry objection from several of the party; and this mystery was not less conspicuous in the formal order of the halt, and in the pause that followed upon their arrival at the habitation.

The house, in front of which they were drawn up, was, according to the prevailing fashion of the time, a one-storied dwelling covering an ample space of ground, built partly of boards and partly of logs, with a long piazza before it, terminating in small rooms, made by inclosing the sides for a few feet at either extremity. Being situated some twenty paces aside from the road, the intervening area was bounded by a fence through which a gate afforded admission. A horse-rack, with a few feeding troughs, was erected near this gate; and a draw-well, in the same vicinity, furnished a ready supply of water. With the exception of a cleared field around the dwelling, the landscape was shaded by the natural forest.

A consultation of some minutes' duration was held between Habershaw and Curry, when the order to dismount was given, accompanied with an intimation of a design to tarry at this place for an hour or two; but the men, at the same time, were directed to leave their saddles upon their horses. One or two were detailed to look after the refreshment of the cattle, whilst the remainder took possession of the principal room. The first demands of the troop were for drink, and this being indulged, the brute feeling of conviviality which in gross natures depends altogether upon sensual excitement, began once more to break down the barriers of discipline, and to mount into clamor.

The scenes of the morning had made a disagreeable impression upon the feelings of Butler and his comrade. The changed tone and the ruffian manners of the band, the pause, and the doubts which seemed to agitate them, boded mischief. The two prisoners, however, almost instinctively adopted the course of conduct which their circumstances required. They concealed all apprehension of harm, and patiently awaited the end. Horse Shoe even took advantage of the rising mirth of the company when drink began to exhilarate them, and affected an easy tone of companionship which was calculated to throw them off their guard. He circulated freely amongst the men, and by private conference with some of the individuals around him, who, attracted by his air of confiding gaiety, seemed inclined to favor his approaches of familiarity, he soon discovered that the gang were divided in sentiment in regard to some important subject touching the proposed treatment of himself and his friend. A party, at least, he was thus made aware, were disposed to take his side in the secret disputes which had been in agitation. He was determined to profit by this dissension, and accordingly applied himself still more assiduously to cultivate the favorable sentiment he found in existence.

Whilst breakfast was in preparation, and Habershaw and Curry were occupied with the wounded man in an adjoining apartment, the sergeant, playing the part of a boon companion, laughed with the rioters, and, uninvited, made himself free of their cups.

"I should like to know," he said to one of the troopers, "why you are giving yourselves all this trouble about a couple of simple travelers that happened to be jogging along the road? If you wanted to make a pitched battle you ought to have sent us word; but if it was only upon a drinking bout you had set your hearts, there was no occasion to be breaking heads for the honor of getting a good fellow in your company, when he would have come of his own accord at the first axing. There was no use in making such a mighty secret about it; for, as we were travelling the same road with you, you had only to show a man the civility of saying you wanted our escort, and you should have had it at a word. Here's to our better acquaintance, friend!"

"You mightn't be so jolly, Horse Shoe Robinson," said Shad Green--or, according to his nickname, Red Mug, in a whisper; "if some of them that took the trouble to find you, should have their own way. It's a d----d tight pull whether you are to be kept as a prisoner of war, or shoved under ground this morning without tuck of drum. That for your private ear."

"I was born in old Carolina myself," replied Horse Shoe, aside to the speaker; "and I don't believe there is many men to be found in it who would stand by and see the rules and regulations of honorable war blackened and trod down into the dust by any cowardly trick of murder. If it comes to that, many as there are against two, our lives will not go at a cheap price."

"Whisht!" returned the other, "with my allowance, for one, it shan't be. A prisoner's a prisoner, I say; and damnation to the man that would make him out worse."

"They say you are a merry devil, old Horse Shoe," exclaimed he who was called Bow Legs, who now stepped up and slapped the sergeant on the back. "So take a swig, man; fair play is a jewel!--that's my doctrine. Fight when you fight, and drink when you drink--and that's the sign to know a man by."

"There is some good things," said the sergeant, "in this world that's good, and some that's bad. But I have always found that good and bad is so mixed up and jumbled together, that you don't often get much of one without a little of the other. A sodger's a sodger, no matter what side he is on; and they are the naturalest people in the world for fellow-feeling. One day a man is up, and then the laugh's on his side; next day he is down, and then the laugh's against him. So, as a sodger has more of these ups and downs than other folks, there's the reason his heart is tenderer towards a comrade than other people's. Here's your health, sir. This is a wicked world, and twisted, in a measure, upside down; and it is well known that evil communications corrupts good manners; but sodgers were made to set the world right again, on its legs, and to presarve good breeding and Christian charity. So there's a sarmon for you, you tinkers!"

"Well done, mister preacher!" vociferated a prominent reveller. "If you will desert and enlist with us you shall be the chaplain of the troop. We want a good swearing, drinking, and tearing blade who can hold a discourse over his liquor, and fence with the devil at long words. You're the very man for it! Huzza for the blacksmith!"

"Huzza for the blacksmith!" shouted several others in the apartment.

Butler, during this scene, had stretched himself out at full length upon a bench, to gain some rest in his present exhausted and uncomfortable condition, and was now partaking of the refreshment of a bowl of milk and some coarse bread, which one of the troopers had brought him.

"What's all this laughing and uproar about?" said Habershaw, entering the room with Curry, just at the moment of the acclamation in favor of the sergeant "Is this a time for your cursed wide throats to be braying like asses! We have business to do. And you, sir," said he, turning to Butler, "you must be taking up the room of a half dozen men on a bench with your lazy carcase! Up, sir; I allow no lolling and lying about to rascally whigs and rebels. You have cost me the death of a dog that is worth all your filthy whig kindred; and you have made away with two of the best men that ever stept in shoe leather. Sit up, sir, and thank your luck that you haven't your arms pinioned behind you, like a horse thief."

"Insolent coward," said Butler, springing upon his feet; "hired ruffian! you shall in due time be made to pay for the outrage you have inflicted upon me."

"Tie him up!" cried Habershaw; "tie him up! And now I call you all to bear witness that he has brought the sentence upon himself; it shall be done without waiting another moment. Harry Gage, I give the matter over to you. Draw out four men, take them into the yard, and dispatch the prisoners off-hand! shoot the traitors on the spot, before we eat our breakfasts! I was a fool that I didn't settle this at daylight this morning--the rascally filth of the earth! Have no heart about it, men; but make sure work by a short distance. This is no time for whining. When have the Whigs shown mercy to us!"

"It shall be four against four, then!" cried out Shadrach Green, seconded by Andrew Clopper; "and the first shot that is fired shall be into the bowels of Hugh Habershaw! Stand by me, boys!"

In a moment the parties were divided, and had snatched up their weapons, and then stood looking angrily at each other as if daring each to commence the threatened affray.

"Why, how now, devil's imps!" shouted Habershaw. "Have you come to a mutiny? Have you joined the rebels? James Curry, look at this! By the bloody laws of war, I will report every rascal who dares to lift his hand against me!"

"The thing is past talking about," said the first speaker, coolly. "Hugh Habershaw, neither you nor James Curry shall command the peace if you dare to offer harm to the prisoners. Now, bully, report that as my saying. They are men fairly taken in war, and shall suffer no evil past what the law justifies. Give them up to the officer of the nearest post--that's what we ask--carry them to Innis's camp if you choose; but whilst they are in our keeping there shall be no blood spilled without mixing some of your own with it, Hugh Habershaw."

"Arrest the mutineers!" cried Habershaw, trembling with rage. "Who are my friends in this room? Let them stand by me, and then--blast me if I don't force obedience to my orders!"

"You got off by the skin of your teeth last night," said Green, "when you tried to take the life of Gideon Blake. For that you deserved a bullet through your skull. Take care that you don't get your reckoning this morning, captain and all as you are."

"What in the devil would you have?" inquired Habershaw, stricken into a more cautious tone of speech by the decided bearing of the man opposed to him.

"The safety of the prisoners until they are delivered to the commander of a regular post; we have resolved upon that!" was the reply.

"Curry!" said Habershaw, turning in some perplexity to the dragoon as if for advice.

"Softly, Captain; we had better have a parley here," said Curry, who then added in a whisper: "There's been some damned bobbery kicked up here by the blacksmith. This comes of giving that fellow the privilege of talking."

"A word, men," interposed Horse Shoe, who during this interval had planted himself near Butler, and with him stood ready to act as the emergency might require. "Let me say a word. This James Curry is my man. Give me a broadsword and a pair of pistols, and I will pledge the hand and word of a sodger, upon condition that I am allowed five minutes' parole, to have a pass, here in the yard, with him--it shall be in sight of the whole squad--I pledge the word of a sodger to deliver myself back again to the guard, dead or alive, without offering to take any chance to make off in the meantime. Come, James Curry, your word to the back of that, and then buckle on your sword, man. I heard your whisper."

"Soldiers," said Curry, stepping into the circle which the party had now formed round the room, "let me put in a word as a peace-maker. Captain Habershaw won't be unreasonable. I will vouch for him that he will fulfil your wish regarding the conveying of the prisoners to a regular post. Come, come, let us have no brawling! For shame! put down your guns. There may be reason in what you ask, although it isn't so much against the fashion of the times to shoot a Whig either. But anything for the sake of quiet amongst good fellows. Be considerate, noble captain, and do as the babies wish. As for Horse Shoe's brag--he is an old soldier, and so am I; that's enough. We are not so green as to put a broadsword and a brace of pistols into the hands of a bullying prisoner. No, no, Horse Shoe! try another trick, old boy! Ha, ha, lads! you are a set of fine dashing chaps, and this is only one of your mad-cap bits of spunk that boils up with your liquor. Take another cup on it, my merry fellows, and all will be as pleasant as the music of a fife. Come, valiant Captain of the Tiger, join us. And as for the prisoners--why let them come in for snacks with us. So there's an end of the business. All is as mild as new milk again."

"Well, well, get your breakfasts," said Habershaw gruffly. "Blast you! I have spoiled you by good treatment, you ungrateful, carnivorous dogs! But, as Peppercorn says, there's an end of it! So go to your feeding, and when that's done we will push for Blackstock's."

The morning meal was soon despatched, and the party reassembled in the room where the late disturbance had taken place. The good-nature of Robinson continued to gain upon those who had first taken up his cause, and even brought him into a more lenient consideration with the others. Amongst the former I have already noted Andrew Clopper, a rough and insubordinate member of the gang, who, vexed by some old grudge against the fat captain, had efficiently sustained Green in the late act of mutiny, and who now, struck with Horse Shoe's bold demeanor towards Curry, began to evince manifest signs of a growing regard for the worthy sergeant. With this man Horse Shoe contrived to hold a short and secret interview that resulted in the quiet transfer of a piece of gold into the freebooter's hand, which was received with a significant nod of assent to whatever proposition accompanied it. When the order of "boot and saddle" was given by Habershaw, the several members of the troop repaired to their horses, where a short time was spent in making ready for the march; after which the whole squad returned to the porch and occupied the few moments of delay in that loud and boisterous carousal which is apt to mark the conduct of such an ill-organized body in the interval immediately preceding the commencement of a day's ride. This was a moment of intense interest to the sergeant, who kept his eyes steadily fixed upon the movements of Clopper, as that individual lingered behind his comrades in the equipment of his horse. This solicitude did not, however, arrest his seeming mirth, as he joined in the rude jests of the company and added some sallies of his own.

"Give me that cup," he said at length, to one of the men, as he pointed to a gourd on a table; "before we start I have a notion to try the strength of a little cold water, just by way of physic, after all the liquor we have been drinking," and, having got the implement in his hand, he walked deliberately to the draw-well, where he dipped up a draught from the bucket that stood on its brink. As he put the water to his lips and turned his back upon the company, he was enabled to take a survey of the horses that were attached to the rack near him: then, suddenly throwing the gourd from him, he sprang towards his own trusty steed, leaped into his saddle at one bound, and sped, like an arrow from a bow, upon the highway. This exploit was so promptly achieved that no one was aware of the sergeant's purpose until he was some twenty paces upon his journey. As soon as the alarm of his flight was spread, some three or four rifles were fired after him in rapid succession, during which he was seen ducking his head and moving it from side to side with a view to baffle the aim of the marksmen. The confusion of the moment in which the volley was given rendered it ineffectual, and the sergeant was already past the first danger of his escape.

"To horse and follow!" resounded from all sides.

"Look to the other prisoner!" roared out Habershaw; "if he raises his head blow out his brains! Follow, boys, follow!"

"Two or three of you come with me," cried Curry, and a couple of files hastened with the dragoon to their horses. Upon arriving at the rack it was discovered that the bridles of the greater part of the troop were tied in hard knots in such a manner as to connect each two or three horses together.

A short delay took place whilst the horsemen were disentangling their reins, and Curry, being the first to extricate his steed, mounted and set off in rapid pursuit. He was immediately followed by two others.

At the end of half an hour the two privates returned and reported that they had been unable to obtain a view of the sergeant or even of Curry. Shortly afterwards the dragoon himself was descried retracing his steps at a moderate trot towards the house. His plight told a tale upon him of discomfiture. One side of his face was bleeding with a recent bruise, his dress disarranged and his back covered with dust. The side of his horse also bore the same taint of the soil.

He rode up to Habershaw--who was already upon the road at the head of the remaining members of the squad, having Butler in charge -- and informed him that he had pursued the sergeant at full speed until he came in sight of him, when the fugitive had slackened his gait as if on purpose to allow himself to be overtaken.

"But, the devil grip the fellow!" he added, "he has a broad-side like a man-of-war! In my hurry I left my sword behind me, and, when I came up with him, I laid my hand upon his bridle; but, by some sudden sleight which he has taught his horse, he contrived, somehow or other, to upset me--horse and all--down a bank on the road-side. And, when I lay on the ground sprawling, do you think the jolly runagate didn't rein up and give me a broad laugh, and ask me if he could be of any *sarvice* to me? He then bade me good bye, saying he had an engagement that prevented him from favoring me any longer with his company. Gad! it was so civilly done that all I could say was, luck go with you, Mr. Horse Shoe; and, since we are to part company so soon, may the devil pad your saddle for you! I'll do him the justice to say that he's a better horseman than I took him for. I can hardly begrudge a man his liberty who can win it as cleverly as he has done."

"Well, there's no more to be said about it," remarked Habershaw. "He is only game for another day. He is like a bear's cub; which is as much as to signify that he has a hard time before him. He would have only given us trouble; so let him go. Now, boys, away for Blackstock's; I will engage I keep the fox that's left safely enough."

With these words the troop proceeded upon their march.

THE FOE OF TYRANTS:

Italian poet Vittorio Alfieri's "L'America Libera" (1781; 1783)

It is perhaps relatively few who *readily* associate Italy with the American Revolution, and yet a number of Italians, particularly men of arts and letters, became some of its ardent and prominent supporters. Four of the latter that conspicuously stand out in this regard are Filippo Mazzei (1730-1816),[391] from Tuscany, physician, political historian, and agricultural innovator and colleague of Thomas Jefferson; Lorenzo Da Ponte (1749-1838), of Venice, Mozart's librettist for "Marriage of Figaro," "Don Giovanni," and "Cosi Fan Tutte;" who emigrated to America and found a welcome home there; Carlo Botta (1766-1837), from the Piedmont-Turin region, and who penned *Storia della guerra dell'Independenza d'America* ("History of the War of Independence of America," 1809) -- one of the Revolutionary War's most respected and frequently cited early histories; and poet and dramatist Vittorio Alfieri (1749-1803).

Alfieri, also from the Piedmont, was one of the most widely honored of Italian playwrights of his era, being much to the tragic stage what Carlo Goldoni (1707-1793), of Venice, was to comedy. Like Lord Byron, he was both a noble (in his case a Count) and a revolutionary. A friend of Beaumarchais, who of course acted a pivotal role in having military French aid sent to the rebelling American colonies, Alfieri was in many ways typical of the 18th century enlightened cosmopolitan and philosophically nation-less European, traveling as far as Sweden and Russia, as well as other parts of the continent, to share and sample other countries' ways of life and government -- and usually displeased with what he found when it came to the latter. And like a number of giants of the Age or Reason, he was emotionally quite temperamental. His was a soul literally aflame for freedom while simultaneously seething with incandescent hatred of despotism; whether legal or cultural. This was no little reflected in his tragedies in which, following philosopher Giambattista Vico, he presented tyranny as a result of the conflict between man's *selfish* nature and his inherent need to be a member of collective society; the most famous of these plays being his "Saul" (1782). Later in life, he became an animated advocate of the French Revolution only to become bitterly disillusioned by its missteps and excesses. As well, he no doubt viewed such as Napoleon as proof of his adopted thesis that the insatiable ambition of some is what ultimately leads men into chains. He warmly embraced the American cause for Liberty, yet perhaps little realized that it too was not without its men, although also well-meaning, who used the event as vehicle for career advancement.[392]

In 1781 he wrote a series of four, and in 1783 a fifth, odes entitled *L'America Libera*; in which he serves up a doughty and ecstatic reverie of his thoughts and feelings on America's plight and struggle. The result is, in some respects and in hindsight, an occasionally puerile work, full of bombastic declamations and some exaggerated praising. Yet on the positive side, the fervor that animates Alfieri is indubitably soulful and sincere; and it is still possible to read these American Odes with some patriotic pleasure.[393]

As a poet is his own master -- as he must be if he is any serious composer of verse -- hope for freedom comes most fittingly from the words and voice of such as he. And if Alfieri's choices of arguments and allusions are not now always so compelling as originally intended, his lively and inextinguishable fire glows throughout and provides those already disposed to love liberty and to wish for the improved dignity of the human race continued hope.

Here then are some excerpts; as translated by Adolph Caso.[394]

---

[391] Mazzei's enthusiasm and dedication on behalf of the American cause is no where better expressed than in his dispatches to Gov. Jefferson, written from Paris, March to May 1780; in which he (acting as a purchaser of munitions in France on behalf of the state of Virginia) at length and most meticulously describes the state of European political affairs in relation to Britain's then current war with her former colonies. See *Calendar of Virginia State Papers* (1875), vol. 1, edited by Wm. P. Palmer, pp. 339-352. Jefferson, who spoke and wrote the language fluently, probably felt a greater affinity for Italian culture and manners than that of any other European nation; and which admiration and sympathy we are regularly reminded of by the name and character of his famous hilltop home. France, however we should add, was also very close to Jefferson's heart and thoughts, and English traveler John Davis remarked that Jefferson's prose more resembled French than English.

[392] It is interesting to note that Henry Lee IV wrote a studious biography of Napoleon; clearly assigning an association, at least in his own mind, with his much loved, and lauded by himself, father.

[393] Alfieri, we might further note, also dedicated his "Bruto Primo" ("Brutus the First," 1788), a drama about Lucius Junius Brutus, to Washington, "The Liberator of America."

[394] As drawn from Caso's *Alfieri's Ode to American Independence*, Branden Press Publishers, Boston, 1976.

~~~***~~~

First Ode --
Reasons for War

I.

Is this a warlike trumpet I hear,
Coming from the immense ocean
Whose waters have not yet been sailed?
What streaking arrows are filling the sky?
What thunderous steel breaks the air?
There is no reason why so much blood
Should be spilling over those innocent shores
Whose people, not yet tarnished by wealth,
Had grown safe and free under their laws,
And unaware of the evil
That is clogging all of Europe.
Who is unburdening their peace?
What wicked fury, what crude
Impious thought disturbs their union?
T'is the wrath of a King blind to beauty,
And to vile ministers, and ugly cupidity.

V.

What? Not even you [people of Britain] are staying?
How can you! You've sold
Your own free votes to those
Chosen for the ability
To satiate in debauchery and rioting
And as much in drinking and in eating.
Oh plunder of despots!
Aren't there enough slave sin England
To satisfy your greed?
Must you also go to the American shores
To play your treacherous game?
Children of your blood,
They're made to spend their days in plight.
Once you were their mother;
Now you're the witch threatening them with death
For the past six years, and more.

Second Ode --
The Warring People

II.

Caught between bondage and death
Those generous sons of Liberty await,
Afflicted, tired and grieved.
Fate has all but taken their hearts,
Not because they are lacking in gold –
Virtue is never in need of it,
But because they lack arms and bread.
They stare at each other mercifully,
~~~

Knowing they have to die for their country,
While their women and children
Practically starve
Within their beloved homes.
Hearing the little ones ask for bread
And there being none
Is the lowest level of human misery.
Worse, they must bid them goodbye forever.

IV.

Yet some say: Who are
These new liberators
Stepping down magnanimously
To bring together glory and results?
Are these the new men of Europe,
Forged on the spirit of humanity
The likes of which is not known today,
That have come to deal a blow to tyranny
And to build dykes against the tides?
Those, whom Philip derided
For being armed with the slingshot,
Fate would have it
They should receive the highest virtues?
They gained liberty with their blood;
Now they've come to give life
To a Liberty about to languish.

VIII.

Already the night has lifted its veil;
From the reign of Neptune
The sweet sails rise with the sun.
The ship appears with the early light,
Flying its linen against the sky,
Its beautiful and shimmering lily [France]
Masted and unfolded to the gilded Mars.
Fitted with provisions and their arms,
They're already covering the fields
In pursuit of the haughty Briton.
What invincible sword will strike?
Who will be the worth my subject
To be immortalized in verses?
Who will bring honor to his birthplace
And make the countrymen proud?
To him, of Muses, a trophy for all time!

Third Ode --
Lafayette

IV.

Let the Goddess of Sparta
Be the only [one] to inspire disdain
Into this youthful heart:

He understands and speaks no more.
Already, he's hurled himself
Of the stormy and evil royal court.
Oh happy desire for fame and glory!
He's bidding his wife goodbye.
She, whom nature has more than made
Beautiful and chaste,
Now stands alone as well.
Fearlessly, he bids here farewell
Amidst the kisses and the tears.
She'd rather die than let him go,
But all's in vain, for he has gone.

V.

Why do you weep? Can't you see,
Glory is taking him to radiant paths
Whose imprints fill his heart alone?
Once the novice warrior,
Now he trains without respite
And guards our liberty day and night.
He's learned to use his weapons
To kill as must be done.
He is a marvel to the Americans,
Who are impressed with this one man;
Every part of his body,
His each and every vibrant cell
Long for that freedom,
Of which no other is convinced as he.
So, let your weeping turn to song,
For tears are not becoming to your eyes.

VI.

See for yourself: he's a born leader;
Prudence and valour abound.
He's like those great ones
Whom men willingly obey and love
Though they may be much the elders.
His enemies are awed
By the respect he commands;
Even the most envious of men
Respects the nobility of his ways.
Look what the gilded lily
Has brought together: men ready to battle
There, where the action is fierce,
Where in the midst he will shine.
Mars and Liberty are his friends:
He will be known forever
So long he leaves the corrupted court behind.

Fourth Ode --
Praises for General Washington

II.

But where so suddenly
Has this burning fantasy taken me?
Doors are opening wide,
And the caves of Tenaurus within sight:
Let him enter into eternal darkness
He who has glazed his heart with steel.
The Sun pushes me ahead,
And the laws of the Abyss broken.
I enter. Behind me already,
The there headed dog,
The frightful steerman of the black river,
And the horrendous shrieks of the damned.
Lethe is nearby,
The sweet river of life
Where immortal flowers of many colors
Embank the slow running water.

IV.

I see the once proud woman, now in tears,
Speak to the council,
Telling of the vicissitudes on earth.
Her tears and stories inflame the hearts
Of those magnanimous souls…
"Worry not, oh Goddess," one replied;
"The man to stimulate the heroes
Is coming with all his sacred fury.
Do your part to help regain
The liberty they have lost,
And fight against the enemy;
Destroy them if you must.
We're going to give you back
That which you have us once:
Gather the gifts you can find,
And let your champion honor them."

VI.

With her noble booty secure,
The Goddess spread her wings
And flew joyfully forth
To bring the news to the camp,
And to join the league of her brothers –
All sworn to preserve their traditions
Or die a thousand deaths
As old man Cato [the younger] did in Utica.[395]
In complete admiration,

---

[395] [*Edit. Note.* To the majority of 18th century writers, thinkers, and statesmen, virtuous (ancient) Rome was *Republican* Rome; with concomitant reference often made to Hannibal. Rarely, by comparison, is praise ever bestowed on any emperors; except possibly with respect to the military prowess of Caesar. Simon Bolivar was one figure who drew inspiration from ancient Rome's Republican foundations, and it was no coincidence that it was in Rome itself, on the summit of Monte Sacro in 1805, that he made his solemn and historic vow to uplift his country from control by Spain's monarchy.]

They gather around the captain
To listen to his words.
In full view of his fearless eyes,
She displayed the many gifts,
Enough to make the enemy fall.
Come, Englishmen, see for yourselves
How vain your efforts will be now.

VII.

I've seen your arrogant faces before:
Large numbers alone raise your chins.
The good they will do you now
Against a leader with solid men behind
And each respecting the other's life,
Fighting as they must
To inflict their wounds
When you least expect them to.
For all these years, and risking life,
The mighty stood the camp
In behalf of the mother country
Even to the last man and sword
That She may never perish.
The trap has finally worked:
The Briton is buying his soul away.
This is the meaning of liberty to him.

VIII.

Go, Washington, seek
The treacherous enemies of liberty
And deal with them you must.
No other battle
Shall be memorable and great
As this one you must fight.
Already you're pursuing the enemy,
Inflicting upon them your last woes.
Oh worthy victory of your great heart!
Few are the dead
And the rest are surrounded,
Ready to lay down the arms,
The mismatched boldness,
And their honor, if ever they had any.
Mankind will be forever grateful
For what you've done, of Washington.

Fifth Ode --
The Peace of 1783

I.

The sweet chorus of celestial voices
Sings over the gentle breezes
That fill the hearts of men with joy,
And almost restores those late martyrs:

The cries of war have ceased,
And blood no longer colors the rivers.
Men seem more forgiving of each other
While the harvests sway to the wind.
The shepherds take heart again,
Now that the fields are free,
And return to their songs of old,
While on the other side
The kings wipe the abundant sweat
Of their brows, pondering,
As they sit on their gilded thrones,
The recent undertakings and defeats.

II.

The man of the Leopard emblem,
Who wanted a tighter yoke around his English
And conquer a new land in the Americas,
Has only caused the breakdown
Of his British throne.
The French King, with the jocund air,
And the blonde Dutchman,
Have achieved a peace without war;
And the disillusioned besieger [Spain]
Of the unconquerable Gibraltar
Is left to brood in his own dead silence:
This victorious league has given
Little more than tears.
Well can America go proudly forth
With her first arms – an America
That boats the image of perfect liberty.

III.

Now, dense ignorance breaks out
Which old age itself involves,
Showing me a whirling fire
That shatters, burns, and turns to dust
Any intense and impious crowd
To make an infamous game of our service.
It is a power that gives birth
To a howling and impetuous wind
That blows from the west with such force
That in its vortex it pulls
That most audacious and superb of plants
And carries them forth
Where the bad seeds take root
In Asia as on the original soil.
The dark clouds have disappeared;
Faith and virtue are back again.

VII.

[Yet] How can I sing of peace
When half the world is in arms,

And not know why, while the other
Live sin fear, and without bread,
Choosing to remain stupid and immobile?
Call this liberty, which is protected
By he who rules with absolute power?
A war was fought,
And the enemy never [really] slaughtered --
Wasn't this the greatest of evils?
And men died in its behalf.
Can a sweet smelling potion,
Drawn from bad weeds and given to drink,
Enervate the bodies and minds of men?
T'is an evil from far off India [i.e., the riches of]
Come to enslave and make America poor.

VIII.

Marathon, Termopoli [Thermopylae],
The ominous day of Cannae itself!
Those were the days when soldiers fought
To protect their homes,
Going from Tile to Bactria,
Never once fighting for money
Or being the pawns of evil leaders.
Those were the times
When Peace and Liberty in Athens' apron lay,
Her men free to speak their thoughts,
And the arts flourishing everywhere;
But in our age,
They're sidelined or lost.
What am I to sing about? And to whom?
I look around and weep:
Force alone rules this world!

"THE FLOURISHING VILLAGE"
from Timothy Dwight's *Greenfield Hill* (1794)

The Connecticut (or, as they are also denoted, "Hartford") Wits,[396] were simply a "Friendly Club," or philosophical (what we would call "scientific") and cultural association, of academic and professional people, i.e., a lawyer, clergymen, former Continental army men (one turned author; another legislator), a doctor, and a merchant; who in the early to late 1780s for various reasons just happen to find themselves following their respective vocations in or near to Hartford; with most of them having direct ties to Yale College either as faculty and or as former students there. The foremost among these Hartford Wits were John Trumbull (second cousin of the Revolutionary War painter of the same name), a practicing attorney; Timothy Dwight, instructor at Yale (and later President of the same) and vicar of (not too distant) Greenfield, Connecticut; Joel Barlow, former army chaplain, Hartford newspaper publisher (of *The American Mercury*), and sometime public orator (among his several occupations); David Humphreys, one of Washington's aide de camps then serving as a representative in the Connecticut assembly; Lemuel Hopkins, a physician; Richard Alsop, a businessman; and Theodore Dwight, Timothy's staunchly Federalist brother, barrister and journalist. Others who are also every now and then listed as members are Elihu Hubbard Smith, (also) a medical doctor, intellectual tutor to Brockden Brown, and the first publisher of an anthology of American poetry (1793); and Yale tutor and also attorney, Josiah Meigs.

Despite their different vocations and employments, all were avid patriots and Federalists[397] who shared a deep and abiding interest in poetry and literature; and who used that medium to help lay and form the foundations of what they hoped to be the national character and culture. Indignant and disgusted at rising protest movements that threatened to undermine national unity, such as Shays' Rebellion and disgruntled agitators who grudged Continental army offers being granted (by Congress) five years pay in lieu of the original promised half-pay for life,[398] they responded to such as these with a joint mock epic entitled *The Anarchiad* (1786-87), ridiculing the radicals. Barlow acted as editor and writer in chief of the group, but with each "wit" contributing some great or small portion to the larger work. In addition, they put out a series of satirical prose essays and short pieces called *American Antiquities* written on similar topics and in a similar humorous vein. These various writings first appeared before the public in newspapers, in particular *The New Haven Gazette and Connecticut Magazine,* and it was through such mediums that they gained national attention. Although the overall impact and later influence of the Connecticut wits was relatively slight, possibly because, as well as being mostly Federalists, they were seen as too removed from and too intellectually elite for most ordinary people, they were nevertheless constituted an impressive assemblage of learning, talent, and wisdom; each of whom produced some literary work or other of lasting historical, if not always (as some may argue) lasting artistic, merit.[399]

Two of the Wits we would take *this* occasion to specifically focus on are Trumbull and Dwight.

Trumbull is most famous as an author for his comic epic *M'Fingal* (1775-1782), written in the manner of Samuel Butler's *Hudibras* and Alexander Pope's satires; which lampoons a fictional Tory M'Fingal and his Don Quixote-like encounters and struggles with the often tumultuous and rowdy American Whigs. Like Francis Hopkinson, Trumbull later put poetry aside and devoted himself mostly to the legal profession. Yet *M'Fingal* in several respects is a finely penned pasquinade, worthy of Pope. But also like Pope, Trumbull's sparkling wit and gift for drawing analogy from animals, insects, and

---

[396] And whom we previously made mention of in our monograph on Joel Barlow and David Humphreys.

[397] Upon a trip to France in 1788, Barlow much to the dismay of his colleagues turned Jacobin, and subsequently became a warm supporter of Jefferson and Madison. It is interesting to parallel him in this regard with John Quincy Adams, also a one time Federalist; who although not a Connecticut Wit in many ways emulated them in his own love of poetry and admirable literary achievements; not least of which his astounding diary of 51 volumes which he diligently kept from 1779 to 1848, and which is housed with the Adams Family Papers at the Massachusetts Historical Society. Noah Webster (1758-1843), author of the famous dictionary, be it noted, is also sometimes mentioned at as one of the Connecticut Wits, but even if allowed that honor was not one of its original members.

[398] "[Following a decisive victory] the first moment of the public safety is devoted to gratitude and joy; but the second is diligently occupied by envy and calumny." Edward Gibbon, *The Decline and Fall of the Roman Empire*, vol. IV, ch. 30.

[399] A series of biographies of Connecticut Wits John Trumbull, David Humphreys, Lemuel Hopkins, Timothy Dwight, and Joel Barlow -- not least informative and illuminating for their being written in 1798 -- appears in Joseph Dennie, et al.'s, *The Spirit of the Farmer's Museum and Lay Preacher's Gazette* (1801) published at Walpole, N.H., pp. 123-149.

commonplace articles, and occurrences does not so much evoke laughter as much as mirth; while the sing-song quality of the heroic couplets tends overtime to become somewhat tiresome and monotonous. Moreover, his choice of targets periodically rings false: e.g., repeated slights at British valor (*that* was never a problem of long or deserving note) or fairly absurd insinuations of inquisitorial popery in the Royal government. Still and otherwise, as a conveyor of good spirit and gay fellowship, as well as richly and intricately wrought jewel of a composition, there is ample in *M'Fingal* to be praised and admired by connoisseurs of verse. Trumbull also produced some fervently patriotic as well as *very* routine 18th century sentimental poetry[400] which speak well of his ability as a meticulous and erudite, if not altogether stirring, craftsman. Of note, he ended up an esteemed and respected judge and jurist, and outlasted the other Hartford Wits by passing away in 1831.

Perhaps the most imposing and impressive, if not necessarily the most popular,[401] of all the Wits was erudite scholar and thinker with a broad range of interests the Reverend Timothy Dwight. Both a formal educator and Calvinist-Congregationalist minister, Dwight was another of Jonathan Edwards' illustrious progeny (in this case his grandson). He displayed an extraordinary acumen on various topics; showing himself to be both able, learned, and profound in matters scientific, religious, and literary. His main body of writings of particular interest to us today are his *Travels in New England and New York* (1821-1822) -- invaluable, not to mention absorbing, as a historical record of his times -- and his poetry.

Respecting this last, Dwight's two most ambitious poetical works are his *The Conquest of Canaan: A Poem in Eleven Books* (1785), a massive Biblical epic written as an allegory on the Revolutionary War and the struggle to establish American society, and his *Greenfield Hill* (1794). While it's been something fashionable among literary historians to brush *Conquest* aside as an unreadable, elephantine tome like Barlow's *Columbiad*, it even so deserves credit as a spiritually endowed and imaginative effort. Perhaps also it ought in fairness to be viewed as one of those works deserving of more attention, for historical reasons if less so for poetical ones, *if and whenever* we finally have the leisure to examine and savor the thing with more patience. The problem here seems to be one of available time as much as anything, and one suspects there is or may be more genius to it than is conventionally allowed. But a *final* conclusion on its place and due in our canon of domestic scripture at least perhaps needs to be postponed.

Greenfield Hill, on the other hand, is easily the more attractive, winsome and winning of the pair of Dwight's epic poems. The greater part of it was penned in 1787, but published with finishing touches in 1794. Notwithstanding the reputation it has acquired among some as a stiff and contrived academic exercise -- Dwight deliberately set out to reproduce, in addition to that of Vergil's *Georgics*, the styles and address of various English poets, including Thomson, Young, Cowper, and Prior[402] -- *Greenfield Hill* is in many portions a lush and genuinely beautiful work that, with it concomitant appeal to both Nature and high ideals presages the writings of Bryant and Whitman -- each of which poets, rightly or no and like almighty Greek deities, seems to have, in chronological sequence, toppled his immediate predecessor in literary significance. Written in regular iambic pentameter occasionally interspersed with (for a New England clergyman) a flamboyant hendecasyllabic line, it is composed as visionary essay, with occasional digression on historical events, including a lament for the vanished Pequod tribe (while yet rationalizing the fate of such and similar Indians as to a large degree unavoidable); the bane of Black slavery; and a tragical recounting of the British burning of Fairfield, Connecticut; yet whose main theme is the extolling of Nature, high morals -- such as hard work and plain, unencumbered living, and the burgeoning of American liberty.

As a selection from this sometimes underrated and neglected treasure of from our nation's past and heritage, we've chosen for our purpose Part II, "The Flourishing Village" -- titled purposely in contrast to and comparison with Goldsmith's "The Deserted Village."

---

[400] And which can be well likened to the affected and formulaic romantic poems of Revolutionary War North Carolina governor Thomas Burke.

[401] Among others, Dwight locked theological and political horns with Ethan Allen over the Vermont (would-be) "Every Man"'s controversial *Reason the Only Oracle of Man: Or, A Compendious System of Natural Religion* (1784).

[402] It is no small irony that although the Wits espoused the idea of creating and fashioning American forms of writing and expression they without exception were unabashed British imitators.

~~~***~~~

FAIR Verna! loveliest village of the west;
Of every joy, and every charm, possess'd;
How pleas'd amid thy varied walks I rove,
Sweet, cheerful walks of innocence, and love,
And o'er thy smiling prospects cast my eyes,
And see the seats of peace, and pleasure, rise,
And hear the voice of Industry resound,
And mark the smile of Competence, around!
Hail, happy village! O'er thy cheerful lawns,
With earliest beauty, spring delighted dawns;
The northward sun begins his vernal smile;
The spring-bird carols o'er the cressy rill:
The shower, that patters in the ruffled stream,
The ploughboy's voice, that chides the lingering team,
The bee, industrious, with his busy song,
The woodman's axe, the distant groves among,
The waggon, rattling down the rugged steep,
The light wind, lulling every care to sleep,
All these, with mingled music, from below,
Deceive intruding sorrow, as I go.

How pleas'd, fond Recollection, with a smile,
Surveys the varied round of wintery toil!
How pleas'd, amid the flowers, that scent the plain,
Recalls the vanish'd frost, and sleeted rain;
The chilling damp, the ice-endangering street,
And treacherous earth that slump'd beneath the feet.

Yet even stern winter's glooms could joy inspire:
Then social circles grac'd the nutwood fire;
The axe resounded, at the sunny door;
The swain, industrious, trimm'd his flaxen store;
Or thresh'd, with vigorous flail, the bounding wheat,
His poultry round him pilfering for their meat;
Or slid his firewood on the creaking snow;
Or bore his produce to the main below;
Or o'er his rich returns exulting laugh'd;
Or pledg'd the healthful orchard's sparkling draught:
While, on his board, for friends and neighbours spread,
The turkey smoak'd, his busy housewife fed;
And Hospitality look'd smiling round,
And Leisure told his tale, with gleeful sound.

Then too, the rough road hid beneath the sleigh,
The distant friend despis'd a length of way,
And join'd the warm embrace, and mingling smile,
And told of all his bliss, and all his toil;
And, many a month elaps'd, was pleas'd to view
How well the houshold far'd, the children grew;
While tales of sympathy deceiv'd the hour,
And Sleep, amus'd, resign'd his wonted power.

Yes! let the proud despise, the rich deride,
~~~

These humble joys, to Competence allied:
To me, they bloom, all fragrant to my heart,
Nor ask the pomp of wealth, nor gloss of art.
And as a bird, in prison long confin'd,
Springs from his open'd cage, and mounts the wind,
Thro' fields of flowers, and fragrance, gaily flies,
Or re-assumes his birth-right, in the skies:
Unprison'd thus from artificial joys,
Where pomp fatigues, and fussful fashion cloys,
The soul, reviving, loves to wander free
Thro' native scenes of sweet simplicity;
Thro' Peace' low vale, where Pleasure lingers long,
And every songster tunes his sweetest song,
And Zephyr hastes, to breathe his first perfume,
And Autumn stays, to drop his latest bloom:
'Till grown mature, and gathering strength to roam,
She lifts her lengthen'd wings, and seeks her home.

But now the wintery glooms are vanish'd all;
The lingering drift behind the shady wall;
The dark-brown spots, that patch'd the snowy field;
The surly frost, that every bud conceal'd;
The russet veil, the way with slime o'erspread,
And all the saddening scenes of March are fled.

Sweet-smiling village! loveliest of the hills!
How green thy groves! How pure thy glassy rills!
With what new joy, I walk thy verdant streets!
How often pause, to breathe thy gale of sweets;
To mark thy well-built walls! thy budding fields!
And every charm, that rural nature yields;
And every joy, to Competence allied,
And every good, that Virtue gains from Pride!

No griping landlord here alarms the door,
To halve, for rent, the poor man's little store.
No haughty owner drives the humble swain
To some far refuge from his dread domain;
Nor wastes, upon his robe of useless pride,
The wealth, which shivering thousands want beside;
Nor in one palace sinks a hundred cots;
Nor in one manor drowns a thousand lots;
Nor, on one table, spread for death and pain,
Devours what would a village well sustain.

O Competence, thou bless'd by HEAVEN's decree,
How well exchang'd is empty pride for thee!
Oft to thy cot my feet delighted turn,
To meet thy chearful smile, at peep of morn;
To join thy toils, that bid the earth look gay;
To mark thy sports, that hail the eve of May;
To see thy ruddy children, at thy board,
And share thy temperate meal, and frugal hoard;
And every joy, by winning prattlers giv'n,
And every earnest of a future HEAVEN.

There the poor wanderer finds a table spread,
The fireside welcome, and the peaceful bed.
The needy neighbour, oft by wealth denied,
There finds the little aids of life supplied;
The horse, that bears to mill the hard-earn'd grain;
The day's work given, to reap the ripen'd plain;
The useful team, to house the precious food,
And all the offices of real good.

There too, divine Religion is a guest,
And all the Virtues join the daily feast.
Kind Hospitality attends the door,
To welcome in the stranger and the poor;
Sweet Chastity, still blushing as she goes;
And Patience smiling at her train of woes;
And meek-eyed Innocence, and Truth refin'd,
And Fortitude, of bold, but gentle mind.

Thou pay'st the tax, the rich man will not pay;
Thou feed'st the poor, the rich man drives away.
Thy sons, for freedom, hazard limbs, and life,
While pride applauds, but shuns the manly strife:
Thou prop'st religion's cause, the world around,
And shew'st thy faith in works, and not in sound.

Say, child of passion! while, with idiot stare,
Thou seest proud grandeur wheel her sunny car;
While kings, and nobles, roll bespangled by,
And the tall palace lessens in the sky;
Say, while with pomp thy giddy brain runs round,
What joys, like these, in splendour can be found?
Ah, yonder turn thy wealth-inchanted eyes,
Where that poor, friendless wretch expiring lies!
Hear his sad partner shriek, beside his bed,
And call down curses on her landlord's head,
Who drove, from yon small cot, her houshold sweet,
To pine with want, and perish in the street.
See the pale tradesman toil, the livelong day,
To deck imperious lords, who never pay!
Who waste, at dice, their boundless breadth of soil,
But grudge the scanty meed of honest toil.
See hounds and horses riot on the store,
By HEAVEN created for the hapless poor!
See half a realm one tyrant scarce sustain,
While meagre thousands round him glean the plain!
See, for his mistress' robe, a village sold,
Whose matrons shrink from nakedness and cold!
See too the Farmer prowl around the shed,
To rob the starving houshold of their bread;
And seize, with cruel fangs, the helpless swain,
While wives, and daughters, plead, and weep, in vain;
Or yield to infamy themselves, to save
Their sire from prison, famine, and the grave.

There too foul luxury taints the putrid mind,
And slavery there imbrutes the reasoning kind:

There humble worth, in damps of deep despair,
Is bound by poverty's eternal bar:
No motives bright the etherial aim impart,
Nor one fair ray of hope allures the heart.

But, O sweet Competence! how chang'd the scene,
Where thy soft footsteps lightly print the green!
Where Freedom walks erect, with manly port,
And all the blessings to his side resort,
In every hamlet, Learning builds her schools,
And beggars' children gain her arts, and rules;
And mild Simplicity o'er manners reigns,
And blameless morals Purity sustains.

From thee the rich enjoyments round me spring,
Where every farmer reigns a little king;
Where all to comfort, none to danger, rise;
Where pride finds few, but nature all supplies;
Where peace and sweet civility are seen,
And meek good-neighbourhood endears the green.
Here every class (if classes those we call,
Where one extended class embraces all,
All mingling, as the rainbow's beauty blends,
Unknown where every hue begins or ends)
Each following, each, with uninvidious strife,
Wears every feature of improving life.
Each gains from other comeliness of dress,
And learns, with gentle mein to win and bless,
With welcome mild the stranger to receive,
And with plain, pleasing decency to live.
Refinement hence even humblest life improves;
Not the loose fair, that form and frippery loves;
But she, whose mansion is the gentle mind,
In thought, and action, virtuously refin'd.
Hence, wives and husbands act a lovelier part,
More just the conduct, and more kind the heart;
Hence brother, sister, parent, child, and friend,
The harmony of life more sweetly blend;
Hence labour brightens every rural scene;
Hence cheerful plenty lives along the green;
Still Prudence eyes her hoard, with watchful care,
And robes of thrift and neatness, all things wear.

But hark! what voice so gaily fills the wind?
Of care oblivious, whose that laughing mind?
'Tis yon poor black, who ceases now his song,
And whistling, drives the cumbrous wain along.
He never, dragg'd, with groans, the galling chain;
Nor hung, suspended, on th' infernal crane;
No dim, white spots deform his face, or hand,
Memorials hellish of the marking brand!
No seams of pincers, scars of scalding oil;
No waste of famine, and no wear of toil.
But kindly fed, and clad, and treated, he
Slides on, thro' life, with more than common glee.
For here mild manners good to all impart,

And stamp with infamy th' unfeeling heart;
Here law, from vengeful rage, the slave defends,
And here the gospel peace on earth extends.

He toils, 'tis true; but shares his master's toil;
With him, he feeds the herd, and trims the soil;
Helps to sustain the house, with clothes, and food,
And takes his portion of the common good:
Lost liberty his sole, peculiar ill,
And fix'd submission to another's will.
Ill, ah, how great! without that cheering sun,
The world is chang'd to one wide, frigid zone;
The mind, a chill'd exotic, cannot grow,
Nor leaf with vigour, nor with promise blow;
Pale, sickly, shrunk, it strives in vain to rise,
Scarce lives, while living, and untimely dies.

See fresh to life the Afric infant spring,
And plume its powers, and spread its little wing!
Firm is it's frame, and vigorous is its mind,
Too young to think, and yet to misery blind.
But soon he sees himself to slavery born;
Soon meets the voice of power, the eye of scorn;
Sighs for the blessings of his peers, in vain;
Condition'd as a brute, tho' form'd a man.
Around he casts his fond, instinctive eyes,
And sees no good, to fill his wishes, rise:
(No motive warms, with animating beam,
Nor praise, nor property, nor kind esteem,
Bless'd independence, on his native ground,
Nor sweet equality with those around;)
Himself, and his, another's shrinks to find,
Levell'd below the lot of human kind.
Thus, shut from honour's paths, he turns to shame,
And filches the small good, he cannot claim.
To sour, and stupid, sinks his active mind;
Finds joys in drink, he cannot elsewhere find;
Rule disobeys; of half his labour cheats;
In some safe cot, the pilfer'd turkey eats;
Rides hard, by night, the steed, his art purloins;
Serene from conscience' bar himself essoins;
Sees from himself his sole redress must flow,
And makes revenge the balsam of his woe.

Thus slavery's blast bids sense and virtue die;
Thus lower'd to dust the sons of Afric lie.
Hence sages grave, to lunar systems given,
Shall ask, why two-legg'd brutes were made by HEAVEN;
Home seek, what pair first peopled Afric's vales,
And nice Monboddo calculate their tails.

O thou chief curse, since curses here began;
First guilt, first woe, first infamy of man;
Thou spot of hell, deep smirch'd on human kind,
The uncur'd gangrene of the reasoning mind;
Alike in church, in state, and houshold all,

Supreme memorial of the world's dread fall;
O slavery! laurel of the Infernal mind,
Proud Satan's triumph over lost mankind!

See the fell Spirit mount his sooty car!
While Hell's black trump proclaims the finish'd war;
Her choicest fiends his wheels exulting draw,
And scream the fall of God's most holy law.
In dread procession see the pomp begin,
Sad pomp of woe, of madness, and of sin!
Grav'd on the chariot, all earth's ages roll,
And all her climes, and realms, to either pole.
Fierce in the flash of arms, see Europe spread!
Her jails, and gibbets, fleets, and hosts, display'd!
Awe-struck, see silken Asia silent bow!
And feeble Afric writhe in blood below!
Before, peace, freedom, virtue, bliss, move on,
The spoils, the treasures, of a world undone;
Behind, earth's bedlam millions clank the chain,
Hymn their disgrace, and celebrate their pain;
Kings, nobles, priests, dread senate! lead the van,
And shout "Te-Deum!" o'er defeated man.

Oft, wing'd by thought, I seek those Indian isles,
Where endless spring, with endless summer smiles,
Where fruits of gold untir'd Vertumnus pours,
And Flora dances o'er undying flowers.
There, as I walk thro' fields as Eden gay,
And breathe the incense of immortal May,
Ceaseless I hear the smacking whip resound;
Hark! that shrill scream! that groan of death-bed sound!
See those throng'd wretches pant along the plain,
Tug the hard hoe, and sigh in hopeless pain!
Yon mother, loaded with her sucking child,
Her rags with frequent spots of blood defil'd,
Drags slowly fainting on; the fiend is nigh;
Rings the shrill cowskin; roars the tyger-cry;
In pangs, th' unfriended suppliant crawls along,
And shrieks the prayer of agonizing wrong.

Why glows yon oven with a sevenfold fire?
Crisp'd in the flames, behold a man expire!
Lo! by that vampyre's hand, yon infant dies,
It's brains dash'd out, beneath it's father's eyes.
Why shrinks yon slave, with horror, from his meat?
HEAVENs! 'tis his flesh, the wretch is whipp'd to eat.
Why streams the life-blood from that female's throat?
She sprinkled gravy on a guest's new coat!

* * * * * *
* * * * * *

Why croud [crowd] those quivering blacks yon dock around?
Those screams announce; that cowskin's shrilling sound.
See, that poor victim hanging from the crane,
While loaded weights his limbs to torture strain;

At each keen stroke, far spouts the bursting gore,
And shrieks, and dying groans, fill all the shore.
Around, in throngs, his brother-victims wait,
And feel, in every stroke, their coming fate;
While each, with palsied hands, and shuddering fears,
The cause, the rule, and price, of torment bears.

Hark, hark, from morn to night, the realm around,
The cracking whip, keen taunt, and shriek, resound!
O'ercast are all the splendors of the spring;
Sweets court in vain; in vain the warblers sing;
Illusions all! 'tis Tartarus round me spreads
His dismal screams, and melancholy shades.
The damned, sure, here clank th' eternal chain,
And waste with grief, or agonize with pain.
A Tartarus new! inversion strange strange of hell!
Guilt wreaks the vengeance, and the guiltless feel.
The heart, not form'd of flint, here all things rend;
Each fair a fury, and each man a fiend;
From childhood, train'd to every baleful ill,
And their first sport, to torture, and to kill.

Ask not, why earthquakes rock that fateful land;
Fires waste the city; ocean whelms the strand;
Why the fierce whirlwind, with electric sway,
Springs from the storm, and fastens on his prey,
Shakes HEAVEN, rends earth, upheaves the cumbrous wave,
And with destruction's besom fills the grave:
Why dark disease roams swift her nightly round,
Knocks at each door, and wakes the gasping sound.

Ask, shuddering ask, why, earth-embosom'd sleep
The unbroken fountains of the angry deep:
Why, bound, and furnac'd, by the globe's strong frame,
In sullen quiet, waits the final flame:
Why surge not, o'er yon isles it's spouting fires,
'Till all their living world in dust expires.
Crimes sound their ruin's moral cause aloud,
And all HEAVEN, sighing, rings with cries of brother's blood.

Beside yon church, that beams a modest ray,
With tidy neatness reputably gay,
When, mild and fair, as Eden's seventh-day light,
In silver silence, shines the Sabbath bright,
In neat attire, the village housholds come,
And learn the path-way to the eternal home.
Hail solemn ordinance! worthy of the Skies;
Whence thousand richest blessings daily rise;
Peace, order, cleanliness, and manners sweet,
A sober mind, to rule submission meet,
Enlarging knowledge, life from guilt refin'd,
And love to God, and friendship to mankind.
In the clear splendour of thy vernal morn,
New-quicken'd man to light, and life, is born;
The desert of the mind with virtue blooms;
It's flowers unfold, it's fruits exhale perfumes;

Proud guilt dissolves, beneath the searching ray,
And low debasement, trembling, creeps away;
Vice bites the dust; foul Error seeks her den;
And God, descending, dwells anew with men.
Where yonder humbler spire salutes the eye,
It's vane slow turning in the liquid sky,
Where, in light gambols, healthy striplings sport,
Ambitious learning builds her outer court;
A grave preceptor, there, her usher stands,
And rules, without a rod, her little bands.
Some half-grown sprigs of learning grac'd his brow:
Little he knew, though much he wish'd to know,
Inchanted hung o'er Virgil's honey'd lay,
And smil'd, to see desipient Horace play;
Glean'd scraps of Greek; and, curious, trac'd afar,
Through Pope's clear glass, the bright Mæsonian star.
Yet oft his students at his wisdom star'd,
For many a student to his side repair'd,
Surpriz'd, they heard him Dilworth's knots untie,
And tell, what lands beyond the Atlantic lie.

Many his faults; his virtues small, and few;
Some little good he did, or strove to do;
Laborious still, he taught the early mind,
And urg'd to manners meek, and thoughts refin'd;
Truth he impress'd, and every virtue prais'd;
While infant eyes, in wondering silence, gaz'd;
The worth of time would, day by day, unfold,
And tell them, every hour was made of gold.
Brown Industry he lov'd; and oft declar'd
How hardly Sloth, in life's sad evening, far'd;
Through grave examples, with sage meaning, ran,
Whist was each form, and thus the tale began.

"Beside yon lonely tree, whose branches bare
Rise white, and murmur to the passing air,
There, where the twining briars the yard enclose,
The house of Sloth stands hush'd in long repose."

"In a late round of solitary care,
My feet instinct to rove, they knew not where,
I thither came. With yellow blossoms gay,
The tall rank weed begirt the tangled way:
Curious to view, I forc'd a path between,
And climb'd the broken stile, and gaz'd the scene."

"O'er an old well, the curb half-fallen spread,
Whose boards, end-loose, a mournful creaking made;
Poiz'd on a leaning post, and ill-sustain'd,
In ruin sad, a mouldering swepe remain'd;
Useless, the crooked pole still dangling hung,
And, tied with thrumbs, a broken bucket swung."

"A half-made wall around the garden lay,
Mended, in gaps, with brushwood in decay.
No culture through the woven briars was seen,

Save a few sickly plants of faded green:
The starv'd potatoe hung it's blasted seeds,
And fennel struggled to o'ertop the weeds,
There gaz'd a ragged sheep, with wild surprise,
And too lean geese upturn'd their slanting eyes."

"The cottage gap'd, with many a dismal yawn,
Where, rent to burn, the covering boards were gone;
Or, by one nail, where others endwise hung,
The sky look'd thro', and winds portentous rung.
In waves, the yielding roof appear'd to run,
And half the chimney-top was fallen down."

"The ancient cellar-door, of structure rude,
With tatter'd garments calk'd, half open stood.
There, as I peep'd, I saw the ruin'd bin;
The sills were broke; the wall had crumbled in;
A few, long-emptied casks lay mouldering round,
And wasted ashes sprinkled o'er the ground;
While, a sad sharer in the houshold ill,
A half-starv'd rat crawl'd out, and bade farewell."

"One window dim, a loop-hole to the sight,
Shed round the room a pale, penurious light;
Here rags gay-colour'd eked the broken glass;
There panes of wood supplied the vacant space."

"As, pondering deep, I gaz'd, with gritty roar,
The hinges creak'd, and open stood the door.
Two little boys, half-naked from the waist,
With staring wonder, ey'd me, as I pass'd.
The smile of Pity blended with her tear --
Ah me! how rarely Comfort visits here!"

"On a lean hammoc, once with feathers fill'd,
His limbs by dirty tatters ill conceal'd,
Tho' now the sun had rounded half the day,
Stretch'd at full length, the lounger snoring lay:
While his sad wife, beside her dresser stood,
And wash'd her hungry houshold's meagre food,
His aged sire, whose beard, and flowing hair,
Wav'd silvery, o'er his antiquated chair,
Rose from his seat; and, as he watch'd my eye,
Deep from his bosom heav'd a mournful sigh --
"Stranger, he cried, once better days I knew;"
And, trembling, shed the venerable dew.
I wish'd a kind reply; but wish'd in vain;
No words came timely to relieve my pain:
To the poor parent, and her infants dear,
Two mites I gave, besprinkled with a tear;
And, fix'd again to see the wretched shed,
Withdrew in silence, clos'd the door, and fled."

"Yet this so lazy man I've often seen
Hurrying, and bustling, round the busy green;
The loudest prater, in a blacksmith's shop;

The wisest statesman, o'er a drunken cup;
(His sharp-bon'd horse, the street that nightly fed,
Tied, many an hour, in yonder tavern-shed)
In every gambling, racing match, abroad:
But a rare hearer, in the house of God."

"Such, such, my children, is the dismal cot,
Where drowsy Sloth receives her wretched lot:
But O how different is the charming cell,
Where Industry and Virtue love to dwell!"

"Beyond that hillock, topp'd with scatter'd trees,
That meet, with freshest green, the hastening breeze,
There, where the glassy brook reflects the day,
Nor weeds, nor sedges, choke its crystal way,
Where budding willows feel the earliest spring,
And wonted red-breasts safely nest, and sing,
A female Worthy lives; and all the poor
Can point the way to her sequester'd door."

"She, unseduc'd by dress and idle shew,
The forms, and rules, of fashion never knew;
Nor glittering in the ball, her form display'd;
Nor yet can tell a diamond, from a spade.
Far other objects claim'd her steady care;
The morning chapter, and the nightly prayer;
The frequent visit to the poor man's shed;
The wakeful nursing, at the sick man's bed;
Each day, to rise, before the early sun;
Each day, to see her daily duty done;
To cheer the partner of her houshold cares,
And mould her children, from their earliest years.

"Small is her house; but fill'd with stores of good;
Good, earn'd with toil, and with delight bestow'd.
In the clean cellar, rang'd in order neat,
Gay-smiling Plenty boasts her casks of meat,
Points, to small eyes, the bins where apples glow,
And marks her cyder-butts, in stately row.
Her granary, fill'd with harvest's various pride,
Still sees the poor man's bushel laid aside;
Here swells the flaxen, there the fleecy store,
And the long wood-pile mocks the winter's power:
White are the swine; the poultry plump and large;
For every creature thrives, beneath her charge."

"Plenteous, and plain, the furniture is seen;
All form'd for use, and all as silver clean.
On the clean dresser, pewter shines arow [a-row];
The clean-scower'd bowls are trimly set below;
While the wash'd coverlet, and linen white,
Assure the traveller a refreshing night."

"Oft have I seen, and oft still hope to see,
This friend, this parent to the poor and me,
Tho' bent with years, and toil, and care, and woe,

Age lightly silver'd on her surrow'd brow,
Her frame still useful, and her mind still young,
Her judgment vigorous, and her memory strong,
Serene her spirits, and her temper sweet,
And pleas'd the youthful circle still to meet,
Cheerful, the long-accustom'd task pursue,
Prevent the rust of age, and life renew;
To church, still pleas'd, and able still, to come,
And shame the lounging youth, who sleep at home."

"Such as her toils, has been the bright reward;
For HEAVEN will always toils like these regard.
Safe, on her love, her truth and wisdom tried,
Her husband's heart, thro' lengthened life, relied;
From little, daily saw his wealth increase,
His neighbours love him, and his houshold bless;
In peace and plenty liv'd, and died resign'd,
And, dying, left six thousand pounds behind.
Her children, train'd to usefulness alone,
Still love the hand, which led them kindly on,
With pious duty, own her wise behest,
And, every day, rise up, and call her bless'd."

"More would ye know, of each poor hind enquire, 1.
Who sees no sun go down upon his hire;
A cheerful witness, bid each neighbour come;
Ask each sad wanderer, where he finds a home;
His tribute even the vilest wretch will give,
And praise the useful life, he will not live."

"Oft have the prattlers, God to me has giv'n,
The flock, I hope, and strive, to train for HEAVEN,
With little footsteps, sought her mansion dear,
To meet the welcome, given with heart sincere;
And cheer'd with all, that early minds can move,
The smiles of gentleness, and acts of love,
At home, in lisping tales, her worth display'd,
And pour'd their infant blessings on her head."

"Ye kings, of pomp, ye nobles proud of blood,
Heroes of arms, of science sages proud!
Read, blush, and weep, to see, with all your store,
Fame, genius, knowledge, bravery, wealth, and power,
Crown'd, laurell'd, worshipp'd, GODs beneath the sun,
Far less of real good enjoy'd, or done."

Such lessons, pleas'd, he taught. The precepts new 1.
Oft the young train to early wisdom drew;
And, when his influence willing minds confess'd,
The children lov'd him, and the parents bless'd;
But, when by soft indulgence led astray,
His pupil's hearts had learn'd the idle way,
Tho' constant, kind, and hard, his toils had been,
For all those toils, small thanks had he, I ween.

Behold yon humbler mansion lift its head! 1.

Where infant minds to science door are led.
As now, by kind indulgence loos'd to play,
From place to place, from sport to sport, they stray,
How light their gambols frolic o'er the green!
How their shrill voices cheer the rural scene!
Sweet harmless elves! in Freedom's houshold born,
Enjoy the raptures of your transient morn;
And let no hour of anxious manhood see
Your minds less innocent, or bless'd, or free!

See too, in every hamlet, round me rise
A central school-house, dress'd in modest guise!
Where every child for useful life prepares,
To business moulded, ere he knows its cares;
In worth matures, to independence grows,
And twines the civic garland o'er his brows.

Mark, how invited by the vernal sky,
Yon cheerful group of females passes by!
Whose hearts, attun'd to social joy, prepare
A friendly visit to some neighbouring fair.
How neatness glistens from the lovely train!
Bright charm! which pomp to rival tries in vain.

Ye Muses! dames of dignified renown,
Rever'd alike in country, and in town,
Your bard the mysteries of a visit show;
For sure your Ladyships those mysteries know:
What is it then, obliging Sisters! say,
The debt of social visiting to pay?

'Tis not to toil before the idol pier;
To shine the first in fashion's lunar sphere;
By sad engagements forc'd, abroad to roam,
And dread to find the expecting fair, at home!
To stop at thirty doors, in half a day,
Drop the gilt card, and proudly roll away;
To alight, and yield the hand, with nice parade;
Up stairs to rustle in the stiff brocade;
Swim thro' the drawing room, with studied air;
Catch the pink'd beau, and shade the rival fair;
To sit, to curb, to toss, with bridled mien,
Mince the scant speech, and lose a glance between;
Unfurl the fan, display the snowy arm,
And ope, with each new motion, some new charm:
Or sit, in silent solitude, to spy
Each little failing, with malignant eye;
Or chatter, with incessancy of tongue,
Careless, if kind, or cruel, right, or wrong;
To trill of us, and ours, of mine, and me,
Our house, our coach, our friends, our family,
While all th' excluded circle sit in pain,
And glance their cool contempt, or keen disdain:
T' inhale, from proud Nanking, a sip of tea,
And wave a curtsey trim, and flirt away:
Or waste, at cards, peace, temper, health and life,

Begin with sullenness, and end in strife,
Lose the rich feast, by friendly converse given,
And backward turn from happiness, and HEAVEN.

It is, in decent habit, plain and neat,
To spend a few choice hours, in converse sweet;
Careless of forms, to act th' unstudied part,
To mix in friendship, and to blend the heart;
To choose those happy themes, which all must feel,
The moral duties, and the houshold weal,
The tale of sympathy, the kind design,
Where rich affections soften, and refine;
T' amuse, to be amus'd, to bless, be bless'd,
And tune to harmony the common breast;
To cheer, with mild good-humour's sprightly ray,
And smooth life's passage, o'er its thorny way;
To circle round the hospitable board,
And taste each good, our generous climes afford;
To court a quick return, with accents kind,
And leave, at parting, some regret behind.

Such, here, the social intercourse is found; 1.
So slides the year, in smooth enjoyment, round.

Thrice bless'd the life, in this glad region spent,
In peace, in competence, and still content;
Where bright, and brighter, all things daily smile,
And rare and scanty, flow the streams of ill;
Where undecaying youth sits blooming round,
And Spring looks lovely on the happy ground;
Improvement glows, along life's cheerful way,
And with soft lustre makes the passage gay.
Thus oft, on yonder Sound, when evening gales
Breath'd o'er th' expanse, and gently fill'd the sails,
The world was still, the HEAVENs were dress'd in smiles,
And the clear moon-beam tipp'd the distant isles,
On the blue plain a lucid image gave,
And capp'd, with silver light, each little wave;
The silent splendour, floating at our side,
Mov'd as we mov'd, and wanton'd on the tide;
While shadowy points, and havens, met the eye,
And the faint-glimmering landmark told us home was nigh.

Ah, dire reverse! in yonder eastern clime,
Where heavy drags the sluggish car of time;
The world unalter'd by the change of years,
Age after age, the same dull aspect wears;
On the bold mind the weight of system spread,
Resistless lies, a cumbrous load of lead;
One beaten course, the wheels politic keep,
And slaves of custom, lose their woes in sleep;
Stagnant is social life; no bright design,
Quickens the sloth, or checks the sad decline.
The friend of man casts round a wishful eye,
And hopes, in vain, improving scenes to spy;
Slow o'er his head, the dragging moments roll,

And damp each cheerful purpose of the soul.

Thus the bewilder'd traveller, forc'd to roam
Through a lone forest, leaves his friends, and home;
Dun evening hangs the sky; the woods around
Join their sad umbrage o'er the russet ground;
At every step, new gloom inshrouds the skies;
His path grows doubtful, and his fears arise:
No woodland songstress soothes his mournful way;
No taper gilds the gloom with cheering ray;
On the cold earth he laps his head forlorn,
And watching, looks, and looks, to spy the lingering morn.

And when new regions prompt their feet to roam, .
And fix, in untrod fields, another home,
No dreary realms our happy race explore,
Nor mourn their exile from their native shore.
For there no endless frosts the glebe deform,
Nor blows, with icy breath, perpetual storm:
No wrathful suns, with sickly splendour glare,
Nor moors, impoison'd, taint the balmy air,
But medial climates change the healthful year;
Pure streamlets wind, and gales of Eden cheer;
In misty pomp the sky-topp'd mountains stand,
And with green bosom humbler hills expand:
With flowery brilliance smiles the woodland glade;
Full teems the soil, and fragrant twines the shade.
There cheaper fields the numerous houshold charm,
And the glad sire gives every son a farm;
In falling forests, Labour's axe resounds;
Opes the new field; and wind the fence's bounds;
The green wheat sparkles; nods the towering corn;
And meads, and pastures, lessening wastes adorn.
Where howl'd the forest, herds unnumber'd low;
The fleecy wanderers fear no prowling foe;
The village springs; the humble school aspires;
And the church brightens in the morning fires!
Young Freedom wantons; Art exalts her head;
And infant Science prattles through the shade.
There changing neighbours learn their manners mild;
And toil and prudence dress th' improving wild:
The savage shrinks, nor dares the bliss annoy;
And the glad traveller wonders at the joy.

All hail, thou western world! by HEAVEN design'd
Th' example bright, to renovate mankind.
Soon shall thy sons across the mainland roam;
And claim, on far Pacific shores, their home;
Their rule, religion, manners, arts, convey,
And spread their freedom to the Asian sea.
Where erst six thousand suns have roll'd the year
O'er plains of slaughter, and o'er wilds of fear,
Towns, cities, fanes, shall lift their towery pride;
The village bloom, on every streamlets side;
Proud Commerce' mole the western surges lave;
The long, white spire lie imag'd on the wave;

O'er morn's pellucid main expand their sails,
And the starr'd ensign court Korean gales.
Then nobler thoughts shall savage trains inform;
Then barbarous passions cease the heart to storm:
No more the captive circling flames devour;
Through the war path the Indian creep no more;
No midnight scout the slumbering village fire;
Nor the scalp'd infant stain his gasping sire:
But peace, and truth, illume the twilight mind,
The gospel's sunshine, and the purpose kind.
Where marshes teem'd with death, shall meads unfold;
Untrodden cliffs resign their stores of gold;
The dance refin'd on Albion's margin move,
And her lone bowers rehearse the tale of love.
Where slept perennial night, shall science rise,
And new-born Oxfords cheer the evening skies;
Miltonic strains the Mexic hills prolong,
And Louis murmur to Sicilian song.

Then to new climes the bliss shall trace its way, 1.
And Tartar desarts hail the rising day;
From the long torpor startled China wake;
Her chains of misery rous'd Peruvia break;
Man link to man; with bosom bosom twine;
And one great bond the house of Adam join:
The sacred promise full completion know,
And peace, and piety, the world o'erflow.

LAFAYETTE TRIUMPHANT:
His 1824-1825 Tour and Reception in the United States

Even for the momentous and historic times, in both America and Europe, in which he lived, the Marquis de Lafayette (more properly "La Fayette") led one of the most singularly adventurous and astounding of lives. His biography reads as much like a story-book or legend as any real person's life possibly could. Born to nobility, he became one of leading champions for liberty of his era, and managed to be both a companion of enlightened old order aristocrats and new world radicals. His instrumental and distinctly vital role in the American Revolution lies in this simple fact: neither Washington or Rochambeau, for all their honorable amicability, could have jointly coordinated and inspired Franco-American war effort as smoothly and harmoniously as they did without his assistance.[403] Among other startling occurrences encountered or that befell him that might be enumerated: when as political *moderate* in 1792 he fled Jacobin France for the Netherlands, en route to secure a passage to America, he was taken and made prisoner by the Austrians on grounds that *he was a Revolutionary*.[404] He subsequently spent six years in a Bastille-like dungeon in Olmutz; where due to the unhealthy and peculiarly harsh circumstances of his confinement he lost much of his hair. It was only when in 1797 that the victorious Bonaparte came to power that the latter demanded and obtained his release. In spite of this, Lafayette was no fan of Napoleon, and would not serve under him. Napoleon, for his part, tended to treat the Marquis as an impractical idealist, and did not take him all that seriously. Following the Restoration in 1814-1815, the Marquis then incurred the restrictive, and in some respects deserved (given his involvement in several independence movements at home and elsewhere) ban on his public activities by the Ultra-Royalists.

And yet though largely viewed with suspicion or dissatisfaction by both reactionaries and extreme liberals in his own country, in America his worship as a hero did not fall that very short of Washington himself. In 1824, President James Monroe extended him an invitation to visit the United States, and which he accepted. The ensuing welcome was possibly the greatest celebration -- and that heart felt and sincere -- shown toward a then living person the world has ever seen. And few, if any, in all of history could have experienced such widespread adulation and affection as did Lafayette when, at age 67, he toured all 24 states of the Union. As well as the unprecedented marvel of the event in and of itself and what it says about Lafayette (who for all the excitement in his own life found time to read the romances of Sir Walter Scott), the accounts of the innumerable receptions and festivities arranged for him serves as an often amusing and touching commentary on the then character of the youthful nation. In them we catch glimpses of groups and individuals on practically all levels of society, and the result is a rare and remarkable portrait of how people were and lived in during the "Era of Good Feeling."

Two works that are especially helpful as sources on the subject are Frederick Butler's *Memoirs of the Marquis De La Fayette, Major-General in the Revolutionary Army of the United States of America, Together with His Tour Through the United States* (1825) and Amos Andrew Parker's *Recollections of General Lafayette on His Visit to the United States in 1824 and 1825* (1879).[405] In the case of Amos Andrew Parker, not only was he present at a number of stops on Lafayette's visits, but he also had the opportunity to converse with him personally, and a portion of his *Recollections* consists of an interview he had with "The General" (as Lafayette was titled in America) that is startlingly modern in its presentation, and such as we might find on, say, a news show like "60 Minutes." Here, for instance, is an extract from the same.

"His friendship for Washington, he said, could not be expressed by words. It was the friendship of David and Jonathan repeated. Although double his own age, and more sedate and less impulsive, yet their cordial intimacy, in the long and vexing scenes of the revolution, had never been disturbed. Although unlike, they were in agreement with each other. If he had at any time been a spur to Washington, more

[403] Though Chastellux, and who did a superb job, was the formal liaison between Rochambeau and Washington, Lafayette acted as a morale enhancer and, as it were, psychological unifier of the alliance.
[404] Although a supporter of the French king, Lafayette refused, upon asked by the Austrians and Prussians, to join émigré officers fighting France; and it was on this grounds that it was decided to keep him a prisoner.
[405] As some supplements to these, see also "Lafayette's Last Visit to America" by Ella Rodman Church, *The Magazine of American History*, May 1881, vol. 6, no. 5, p. 321-339, and Alexander Garden's *Anecdotes of the American Revolution* (Second series, 1828).

often he had been a curb to himself. Washington had been censured for his want of energy in the prosecution of the war, but he thought, wrongfully. He could not do as he would for the lack of means, and could not disclose to the public his destitution without informing the enemy also; and at times, had the enemy known his condition, it would have been fatal.

"Washington did not lack energy, but it was regulated by prudence. He never made long speeches to his army, or boasted of what he had done, or was about to do; and yet, when thoroughly aroused, the stoutest heart would quail before him. He had been his aid, when he mounted his charger on the eve of a battle, rode round the army, took his position in front, while his soldiers passed in review before him, and then wave an adieu with his hat, and not a word spoken; yet his face would glow with emotion, and his appearance and bearing were more powerful than words. His soldiers understood him, and were ready to fight to the utmost; and woe to the foe they encountered." [406]

Butler's chronicle on the other hand, evidently taken chiefly from contemporaneous newspaper reports, has its own advantage of being more detailed and thorough with regard to Lafayette's tour itself; so that it is with this in mind we proffer the following extended excerpts. There is *much* we didn't which we might well have included from Butler's text, and it was by no means an easy task choosing what and what not to include. This allowed for, the proceeding will at least serve to give you a general idea of this scarcely paralleled moment in the annals of *humanity*.

~~~***~~~

General La Fayette, accompanied by his son, George Washington La Fayette. Mr. Auguste Le Vasseur a companion, and one servant, arrived in the harbour of New York on the morning of the 15th of August, in the ship Cadmus, captain Allyn, after a pleasant passage of 31 days from Havre. The fact of his arrival was made known by the Telegraph at an early hour, and it spread through the city with electrical rapidity. Broadway was soon thronged, and the Battery crowded with people, who sallied forth with the expectation that the hero and veteran of two revolutions, might come directly to the city. The arrangements of the city authorities, however, for his reception, having been seasonably communicated to him, he landed at Staten Island, and was conducted to the seat of the Vice President, where he remained through the day, and passed the night. Fort La Fayette fired a salute as the ship passed, and a handsome salute was fired as the General landed.

In the city the national flag was immediately hoisted and displayed at all the public places during the day…

~~~***~~~

The Committee of Arrangements of the Corporation having accepted the proffered services of the steam-ship Robert Fulton, and the steam-boats Chancellor Livingston, Oliver Ellsworth, Henry Eckford, Connecticut, Bellona, Olive Branch, Nautilus, &c.; they were all superbly dressed with flags and streamers of every nation, and directed to meet and form an aquatic escort between the south part of the Battery and Governor's Island, and thence proceed in order to Staten Island. The spectacle, as the boats were assembling, was truly interesting and beautiful. The Battery was crowded with respectable people of both sexes; Castle Garden was filled, and every boat that arrived to take its station was completely crowded with elegant dressed ladies and gentlemen. The appearance of the Robert Fulton, as she came down East River, from the Navy Yard, escorted by the Connecticut and Oliver Ellsworth, all superbly decorated, was rich beyond description. Her yards were manned to the round-tops, with about 200 seamen from the Constitution, who made an elegant appearance, and a battalion of marines, under the command of Major Smith, was on board, with a band of music, and many of the Naval Officers upon this station, together with several ladies and private gentlemen.

Arrived at the place of rendezvous, the several vessels comprising the fleet took their station, and proceeded in regular order to the quarantine, as follows: -- First, the Chancellor Livingston, on board of

---

[406] *Recollections of General Lafayette*, pp. 63-64.

which were the committee of the Corporation, Major General Morton and suite, a number of the members of the Cincinnati, including Colonels Willette, Varick, Trumbull, Platt, and others, together with a few ladies, several officers and professors from West Point, accompanied by the excellent military band attached to that institution. On the right of the Chancellor, and about a length in rear, was the Connecticut, and on the left, to correspond, was the Oliver Ellsworth. Directly in the rear of the Chancellor, was the Robert Fulton, whose lofty masts and wide-spread arms, which literally swarmed with men, towered proudly above her less pretending, but not less gay and beautiful consorts. On the right of the Robert Fulton, about a length in the rear, was the Bellona, and on the left, the Henry Eckford, in a station to correspond; and the squadron was closed by the Olive Branch and Nautilus. The signals exchanged, and the steam-boats having attained their stations, as above stated, the squadron got under weigh, amidst the cheers of thousands of delighted spectators. The view of this fleet will perhaps never be forgotten. It was not only unique, but beyond a doubt, one of the most splendid spectacles ever witnessed on this part of the globe. The squadron, bearing six thousand of our fellow citizens, majestically took her course towards Staten Island, there to take on board our long expected and honoured guest. At 1 o'clock the fleet arrived at Staten Island, and in a few minutes, a Landau was seen approaching the Hotel, near the ferry. The Marquis, the Vice-President, and the Ex-Governor Ogden, of New-Jersey, having alighted, a procession was formed, and the venerable stranger, supported by these gentlemen, followed by all the officers of the Island, and a crowd of citizens, passing through a triumphal arch, round which was tastefully entwined the French and American colours. As soon as the Marquis and suite entered on the broad stairs, connected with, and leading to the steam-boat which was to convey him to the city, he was received by the committee of the Common Council, who conducted him on board the Chancellor Livingston. On entering this splendid vessel, the marines paid him military honours. He was now introduced to the committees from most of our honoured Associations, and the General Officers, representing the Infantry. The West Point band all this time was playing "See the Conquering Hero Comes," "*On pent on etre mieux*," "Hail Columbia," and the "Marseilles Hymn." The steam ship now fired a salute, and the whole squadron got under weigh for the city, in the same order as before, except that the Bellona and Olive Branch, fastened each side of the Cadmus, (the ship which brought the General from France,) decorated with colours, and filled with passengers, majestically moved up the Bay. The sea was smooth and placid, and the breeze cool and agreeable. Decidedly the most interesting sight, was the reception of the General by his old companions in arms: Colonel Marinus Willette, now in his eighty-fifth year, General Van Courtland, General Clarkson. and the other worthies, whom we have mentioned. Colonel Fish, General Lewis, and several of his comrades were absent. He embraced them all affectionately, and Colonel Willette again and again. He knew and remembered them all. It was a re-union of a long separated family.

After the ceremony of embracing and congratulations were over, he sat down along-side of Colonel Willet, who grew young again, and fought all his battles o'er. "Do you remember," said he, "at the battle of Monmouth, I was volunteer aid to General Scott? I saw you in the heat of battle. You were but a boy, but you were a serious and sedate lad. Aye, aye; I remember well. And on the Mohawk, I sent you fifty Indians, and you wrote me, that they set up such a yell, that they frightened the British horse, and they ran one way and the Indians another."

No person who witnessed this interview, will ever forget it; many an honest tear was shed on the occasion. The young men retired at a little distance, while the venerable soldiers were indulging recollections, and were embracing each other again and again; and the surrounding youth silently dropt the tear they could no longer restrain. Such sincere, such honest feelings, were never more plainly or truely [sic] expressed. The sudden changes of the countenance of the Marquis, plainly evinced the emotions he endeavored to suppress. He manfully supported this truly trying situation for some time, when a revolutionary story from the venerable Willette, recalled circumstances long passed: the incident, the friend alluded to, made the Marquis sigh; and his swelling heart was relieved, when he burst into tears. The sympathetic feelings extended to all present; and even the hardy tar rubbed away the tear he could no longer restrain. The scene was too affecting to be continued, and one of the Cincinnati, anxious to divert the attention of the Marquis, his eyes floating with tears, announced the near approach of the steam-ship. The Marquis advanced to the quarter railing, where he was no sooner perceived by the multitude, than an instantaneous cheer most loudly expressed the delight they experienced. The other steam-boats in succession, presented themselves, and passed, each giving three enthusiastic cheers. The Marquis was delighted, and especially with the activity and quickness, with which 200 of our gallant seamen manned the yards of the steam frigate, previous to the salute. About 2 o'clock P. M. the fleet arrived off the Battery. What an impressive scene -- 3000 men, making a splendid appearance, formed in line with a battering train. The ramparts and parapets of the Castle, were lined with ladies and gentlemen. The flag-staff, the windows, and even the roofs of the houses facing the Bay, were literally crowded with spectators. Hundreds of boats and wherrys surrounded the Battery. The Marquis left the Chancellor Livingston in a barge, commanded by Lieutenant Mix, of the Navy, accompanied by the committee of the Corporation, and the Cincinnati, the Generals of Infantry, &c.; and landed amidst the cheers and acclamations of 30,000 people, who filled the Castle, Battery, and surrounding grounds within sight. The Marquis now entered the Castle, which was tastefully carpeted from the landing place to the receiving rooms. He then partook of some refreshment, and was introduced to some distinguished citizens. Perceiving the restless anxiety of nearly 3000 persons in the Castle, to see the General, the Marquis advanced to the centre of the erea [sic] of the Castle, and was greeted with loud cheers, expressive of as honest and generous feelings, as were ever spontaneously manifested by any people on the face of the earth. From Castle Garden he proceeded with the appointed committee, and the military and naval officers, to review the line of troops from the division of state artillery, under the command of Brigadier General Benedict. The muster was, on this occasion, unusually numerous and splendid, each corps vying with the others in paying a tribute of respect to the soldier of the revolution, the friend and companion of Washington. After the review, the General entered a barouche, drawn by four horses, accompanied at the request of the committee, by General Morton.

The committee of the Corporation, accompanied by the General's son. George Washington La Fayette, and his secretary, Mr. La Vasseur, followed the carriages. The General was escorted by a corps of cavalry, and at the head of the column of the troops, proceeded up Broadway to the City Hall. The crowds which had assembled to pay honour to the respected visitor, and to be gratified with a view of his person, were such as almost to prevent the passage of the carriages and the troops, The scene could not but have afforded to the General the most delightful gratifications. -- The houses to the very roofs were filled with spectators, and to the incessant cheers of the multitude, graceful female signified their welcome by the silent, but not less graceful and affecting testimony of the waving of handkerchiefs...

~~~***~~~

To the affectionate address of the French gentlemen [i.e., French residents of New York City], the Marquis La Fayette replied as follows:

"It is a great happiness for me, on my arrival in this land of liberty, to receive the address of my countrymen.

"At the moment of my departure, the testimonials of affectionate attachment of many of my fellow citizens, the parting accents from the shores of France, left in my heart the most grateful emotions. I delight to participate with you, the feelings which I experienced in this happy American land, to which I am bound by so many ties. We also, patriots of 1789, sought to establish the national dignity, the security of property, and the happiness of our beautiful France, upon the sacred foundations of liberty and equality. Notwithstanding our misfortunes, the cotemporaries of that epoch will inform you, that the revolution of '89, has greatly ameliorated the condition of an immense majority of the people. Do not let us despair of the cause of liberty: it is still dear to the hearts of Frenchmen; and we shall one day have the felicity of seeing it established in our beloved country."

At 12 o'clock, the Nautical Society, chiefly composed of our most respectable masters of vessels, assembled on board the ship Cadmus, Captain Allyn, where they were formed in regular order, and proceeded through some of our principal streets, to the City Hall. Here they were severally introduced to the General, who received them in his usual frank and cordial manner. -- Many of the members he recognized as old acquaintances, and expressed his gratification at meeting them, in the warmest terms...

~~~***~~~

The interesting and impressive visit at New York, thus being closed -- at an early hour on Friday morning, a scene of general bustle and activity commenced, preparatory to the departure of the General for Boston. His suite consisted of his son, and M. La Vasseur, who accompanied him on his voyage from

France, and four of the Alderman of N. York. The city corporation had provided an elegant carriage; to accommodate him on his journey to Boston, and deputed four of their number to attend him on his route. At 7 o'clock, the Horse Artillery, commanded by Colonel Arcularius, paraded in Broadway, in front of Washington Hall; and at 8 o'clock, they took up their line of march to Harlaem [sic], where they superceded the escort which accompanied him to that place. This escort consisted of a squadron of cavalry, the Corporation in carriages, the Fayette Guards, the General, Field, and Staff officers of the Artillery and Infantry of the city, and a number of citizens mounted. The General breakfasted with Philip Hone, Esq. at half past 7, and repaired immediately afterwards to his lodgings at the City Hotel, whence the whole cavalcade moved up Broadway, to Bond-street; and thence up the Third Avenue. The streets were thronged with people, and the General, who rode uncovered, repeatedly returned their expressions of kindness and attachment, by bowing…

~~~***~~~

The following extract of a letter from a young Lady at Greenwich, bearing date Friday evening, August 20th, will further illustrate the reception of the Marquis on his route:

"The news that the Marquis de La Fayette was to pass through this town to-day, was received yesterday afternoon. Nothing however was done, and I began to fear that old Connecticut would disgrace itself; but this morning, the spirit of '76 appeared to animate all ranks and descriptions. Orders were given for the troops to proceed to Byram, and escort the General to Norwalk, where, it was understood, the New-Haven troop would be in waiting. Fortunately, it entered into the heads of a few, that an arch, erected over Putnam's Hill, would have a fine effect. A number of ladies volunteered their services in erecting and adorning it; and the Reverend Doctor Lewis, who was himself a chaplain in the revolutionary army, was requested to write a short inscription. The inscription which was hung in the centre, surrounded by a wreath of sweet briar and roses, was as follows: -- "This arch, on the hill rendered memorable by the brave General Putnam, is erected in honor of the illustrious, the Marquis De La Fayette -- the early and distinguished champion of American liberty, and the tried friend of Washington." The arch was very tastefully enwreathed, and from its top waved the flag which the regiment of this place carried in the battle of Whiteplains [White Plains].

"After waiting till nearly 5 o'clock, our ears were glad[d]ened with the sound of their approach. The cannon which had been previously sent on, fired, the church bell rang a merry peal, and hundreds of spectators, of both sexes, stationed on and about the hill, welcomed the General with loud huzzas, and waving of hats and handkerchiefs. When the Marquis arrived at Tracy's Hotel, (within 40 rods of the arch,) he dismounted, and was there introduced to the venerable Doctor Lewis, who took him by the hand, and (as near as I can recollect,) addressed him as follows:

"'Sir, -- With the millions of America, I welcome you to this land of freedom, and rejoice that God has spared my life to see that veteran General, who so eminently distinguished himself in procuring her liberties.'

"The Marquis then advanced to the arch, supported by the Reverend Doctor Lewis, and his son, the present minister of the parish. The inscription was read to him by the latter. He appeared much pleased and affected, advanced a few steps, bowed to the gentlemen who were stationed on one side of the hill, turned to the ladies on the other side, and said, -- 'My friends, I am very much obliged to you for the attention you have paid to me, and feel happy to find myself among you.'

"He then walked down the hill, took his carriage, and proceeded on his journey, expecting to lodge at Norwalk, or Bridgeport to night. On parting with him, Doctor Lewis said, 'Sir, America loves you' -- 'And, Sir,' said the Marquis, 'I truly love America'"…

~~~***~~~

At Saugatuck the militia were prepared throughout the day, to fire a salute; but owing to the lateness of the hour when the cavalcade approached, it being 10 at night, the villagers could do no more than give their loud huzzas, as the General passed. Mill River Bridge was handsomely decorated with colours, by the captains of the coasting vessels at anchor in the harbour…[407]

~~~***~~~

It would have been impossible to have travelled through the towns of Connecticut without feeling a part of the enthusiasm which pervaded all classes. Even the poor lads who drove the carriages entered fully into the common feeling, and seemed proud of their honours. They wore silk ribbons fastened to the button holes of their waistcoats, by way of distinction; and while waiting to receive their illustrious passenger, usually became persons of no inconsiderable interest and attention with the hundreds who stood around. "Behave pretty now, Charley," said the driver of La Fayette's coach, to one of his horses, "behave pretty, Charley -- you are going to carry the greatest man in the world"…

~~~***~~~

The Marine Artillery, stationed on the Dexter Training Ground, pealed their welcome as he passed, and the General soon entered the populous part of the town. In passing through High and Westminster-streets, and until he arrived at the court-house, he was welcomed by that most expressive token of affectionate interest, the waving of white handkerchiefs by the fair hands of the ladies, who crowded every building from which they could obtain a view of this distinguished personage.

Many females, we observed, in the excess of their feelings, suspended this token of welcome, to gaze more intently at the object whom they appeared alone to see in the whole procession, and many a fine eye was wet with the gush of a tear, which the rush of so many sublime and sympathetic emotions sent warm from the heart.

On arriving in front of the State-House, the General alighted, and was received in a peculiarly interesting manner. The poplar avenue, leading to the building, was lined on each side with nearly two hundred misses, arrayed in white, protected by a file of soldiers on each side, and holding in their hands bunches of flowers, which (as the General proceeded up the avenue, supported by the Governor's Aids) they strewed in his path, at the same time waving their white handkerchiefs. The General was afterwards pleased to express the peculiar and high satisfaction he took in this simple and touching arrangement.

On reaching the landing of the stairs, the General turned towards the multitude, and at the same moment, the veteran Captain Stephen Olney, (who served under the General repeatedly, and was the first to force the enemy's works at Yorktown, in which he was seconded, at another point, almost simultaneously, by La Fayette) approached the General, who instantly recognized his old companion in arms, and embraced and kissed him in the most earnest and affectionate manner. A thrill went through the whole assembly, and scarcely a dry eye was to be found among the spectators, while the shouts of the multitude, at first suppressed, and then uttered in a manner tempered by the scene, evinced tie deep feeling and proud associations it had excited…

~~~***~~~

The dwelling houses and stores on the streets [of Boston] through which the procession was conducted, were crowded with inhabitants in every part. The ladies thus situated, caught the enthusiasm of the occasion, waved their white handkerchiefs, and, with smiles and gladness, greeted the veteran hero, who appeared affected and delighted by these demonstrations of a joyful welcome. The moment La Fayette arrived at the line of the city, the bells struck and rang merry peals, while the procession was passing through the streets.

---

407 [*Edit. Note.* Nathaniel Hawthorne in his short story "The Bald Eagle" (1832) gives a sarcastic account of one Connecticut town that went to elaborate lengths to celebrate Lafayette's visit; only to learn too late, and to their inebriated disappointment, that the Marquis would not be able to attend their patriotic festivities.]
~~~

Excepting the cavalcade, the procession passed through the Common from Boylston to Park-street, on the eastern margin, and between two lines of children, of both sexes, belonging to the several schools in the city. Their ages were from about eight to twelve, and nearly three thousand in number. Their dress was neat and uniform; the misses in white, and the masters in white pantaloons and blue spencers. They also wore ribbands on their breasts, stamped with a miniature likeness of La Fayette. As the carriage in which the General rode was passing, one of the misses darted from the line where she was standing, and begged to speak with him. She was handed into the carriage, and by the Mayor presented to La Fayette, who pressed an affectionate kiss on her blooming, yet blushing cheek. She had confidence, however, to address him, and place a wreath of flowers which she held, on his head. He made her a short but affectionate reply, and placed the wreath on the seat of the carriage. Attached to the wreath of flowers was a small piece of paper, carefully folded, which contained these lines; said to be composed by the mother of the child.

"An infant hand presents these blushing flowers,
Glowing and pure as childhood's artless hours,
Where roses bloom, and buds of *promise* smile,
Repaying with their charms the culturer's toil.

Oh! *take them* Father, they were culled *for you!*
(Still bright with warm *affection's* sacred dew --)
O let them live in thy benignant smile,
And o'er thy *brow of glory* bloom awhile!

'Twined with the *laurel* Fame on thee bestowed,
When thy *young heart* with patriot ardour glow'd;
Self *exiled* from the charms of *wealth* and *love*,
And *home*, and *friends*, thou didst our *champion prove*.
And, by the side of Glorious Washington,
Didst make our grateful country *all thine own!*

Go, fragile offering, speak the ardent joy
Our bosoms feel, which *Time* can ne'er destroy!"

Arches were thrown across several of the principal streets, through which La Fayette was conducted, covered with evergreens and flowers, and containing appropriate mottos. There were two in Washington-street, the largest and part of the distance, the widest street in the City. -- On one of these was very legibly written -- "1776--Washington and La Fayette. *Welcome La Fayette -- A Republic not ungrateful*." On the other

"WELCOME LA FAYETTE."
"The Fathers in glory shall sleep,
Who gather'd with thee to the fight!;
But the sons will eternally keep
The tablet of gratitude bright.
We bow not the, neck
And we bend not the knee,
But our hearts, La Fayette.
We surrender to thee."

The lines were from the pen of a citizen of Boston, whose poetic talents had often delighted the public, and who had received the highest praise from those capable of appreciating the productions of genius.

~~~***~~~

[Lafayette to the Pres. of the Mass. Society of Cincinnati, in Roxbury]:
~~~

"Amidst the inexpressible enjoyments which press upon my heart, I could not but feel particularly eager and happy to meet my beloved brothers in arms. Many, many, I call in vain; and at the head of them, our matchless paternal Chief, whose love to an adopted son, I am proud to say, you have long witnessed -- But while we mourn together, for those we have lost, while I find a consolation in the sight of their relations and friends, it is to me a delightful gratification to recognize my surviving companions of our revolutionary army -- that army so brave, so virtuous, so united by mutual confidence and affection. That we have been the faithful soldiers of independence, freedom, and equality, those three essential requisites of national and personal dignity and happiness; that we have lived to see those sacred principles secured to this vast Republic, and cherished elsewhere by all generous minds, shall be the pride of our life, the boast of our children, the comfort of our last moments. -- Receive, my dear brother soldiers, the grateful thanks, and constant love of your old companion and friend."

~~~***~~~

At about half past 8 o'clock, he arrived at the bridge, (over the draw of which was thrown a handsome arch,) under the escort of the Boston company of cavalry, which immediately joined the other battalion; when the whole moved towards the Hotel.

On the arrival of the procession at the Hotel, which was very handsomely decorated with flags and ever-greens, the following address was delivered to the General by John White, Esq. the Chairman of the Committee of Arrangements:

"General -- The inhabitants of this town have chosen me their organ, to greet you with a sincere and hearty welcome, on this joyful occasion. A duty on which I enter with mingled emotions of profound veneration, gratitude and affection towards you, Sir, our nation's early, disinterested and unvarying friend and benefactor.

"The deep, intense, and indelible feelings of this free and happy republic towards you, General, whoso eminently and successfully contributed to raise her to her present proud and powerful attitude among the nations of the earth, can be no more forcibly illustrated, than in that spontaneous homage of the heart, which you see displayed around you, on your arrival upon our favoured shores; and which, like a halo of glory, encircles you in your progress through our country. This, General, is a language not to be misunderstood, compared with which the most laboured declamation must be faint and powerless.

"Although your present appearance among us, like the transit of a brilliant and beneficent planet, commissioned to proclaim good will to man, in its rapid career among innumerable worlds, is short and fleeting, the emanations of the bright and joyous light which it sheds around you, will continue with us to guide our steps, and cheer our hearts to the latest moment of our existence.

"Permit me now, General, to express my individual joy at the happy consummation of those ardent wishes, which I had the honour to express to you twelve years since, in your native country -- for you have re-visited us, and you see that 'all hearts and arms are open to receive you."

To this the General made a very affectionate reply.

The General was then conducted to the Hall, where he was introduced by the chairman to the ladies, committee of arrangements, municipal officers, revolutionary soldiers, clergy, and many citizens, but being engaged to breakfast at Marblehead, his stay was restricted to thirty minutes. On leaving the Hotel, the General ascended the barouche, with the chairman of the committee, and the procession proceeded through the town. At the western end of the common was erected a beautiful civic arch, most elegantly decorated with ever-greens, surmounted by a wreath enclosing the following inscription:

"Welcome La Fayette! Conqueror of hearts;"

on the top of which was perched a beautiful gilt Eagle. Suspended under the arch by festoons of evergreens was a wreath, surrounding this inscription.
~~~

"Washington and La Fayette."

After passing this arch, the procession entered between two lines of children of the town, neatly and prettily dressed, who threw bouquets of flowers before the General, and into his carriage. Next in order were two long lines of the citizens, reaching to another very handsome arch of evergreen, under which was suspended a wreath surrounding these words: "October 19th, 1781." The procession continued over the common towards Market-street, through which he passed, and at its entrance passed under a beautiful canopy, formed on one side by a majestic elm, and on the, other by large trees planted for the occasion, united at the top, and tastefully hung with wreaths and garlands of flowers. At this place was the following inscription:

"Welcome La Fayette, to thee we owe the sweets of Liberty."

On the entrance of the procession to Front-street, another beautiful arch was presented, to which was suspended, under thirteen sun flowers, representing stars, this inscription: "Thou gavest to us thirteen talents. Lo! we have gained eleven more. -- Receive our gratitude." Under this inscription were eleven other sun flowers. In Broad-street was another handsome arch, made entirely of trees, wreaths and garlands, on which was the following inscription:

"The voice of ten millions welcome."

The procession then passed into Chesnut-street, and through part of Fayette-street, into Essex-street, where another magnificent arch was erected, most beautifully decorated, on the centre of which was inscribed "1776," and below this, was inscribed these words:

"The man whom the people delight to honour. -- Welcome La Fayette. -- Yorktown. -- Monmouth."

On the reverse, being the last arch, was this inscription: "Tho' lost to sight, to memory dear."

The procession moved in fine style through this arch, and proceeded to the eastern boundary line of the town, where the Lynn escort delivered their illustrious guest to the authorities of Marblehead. A salute of 13 guns was fired by the Lynn and Danvers Artillery, on the entrance of the General upon the lines of the town, and another of 24 guns when he passed over the Common. All the bells of the town were rung while he was in it...

~~~***~~~

The General and his suite arrived at Middletown, Upper Houses, about 6 o'clock. -- When the Boat first appeared, a salute of 13 guns was fired. -- At the landing place, he was received by a deputation, composed of thirteen distinguished citizens of Middletown, with the first Marshal; and escorted by a squadron of cavalry, commanded by Colonel R. Wilcox. proceeded to the bridge which crosses the northern line of the city. -- He was here received by the corps of Artillery, Riflemen and Light Infantry, under the command of Colonel Walter Boothe, of the 10th Regiment of Infantry, who joined in escorting him to the large and elegant building occupied by Mr. Charles Francis, where preparations had been made for giving him an elegant dinner. The windows and tops of houses were thronged with females, who were constantly waving their handkerchiefs, as expressive of their feelings at seeing him. On his arrival at the house, he was addressed by the Mayor, to which he made an appropriate reply. After which the Mayor presented him to the several members of the Common Council, gentlemen of the Clergy, and the veterans of the Revolution. He was then persuaded to take a seat in the Barouche, and was escorted through the principal streets in the city; the houses were brilliantly illuminated, and added much to the magnificence of the scene. On his arrival at the Boat, he was cheered by the multitude who had followed him. At 7 o'clock he again embarked on the beautiful Connecticut, and though the evening was lowering, all the villages on the river were illuminated, bands of music were playing, and cannon firing. Mr. Ellsworth, one of the liberal proprietors of the Boat, had also provided a band which answered the salutes from the shore. Before
~~~

reaching Saybrook, the weather cleared, the moon burst forth in its calm and serene splendour, to witness the enthusiasm of the ladies of that and the neighboring towns, who, though it was late at night, were drawn up dressed in white, on a platform, and music, cannon and brilliant illuminations were prepared to honor the Guest of the Nation. He then tranquilly and safely descended the Sound…

~~~***~~~

General La Fayette returned from his Eastern tour, and landed in New-York, from on board of the Steam-Boat Oliver Ellsworth, September 5, about 1 o'clock, P. M. A national salute was fired from the Franklin 74, at the Navy Yard, as he passed. The citizens along the shores and wharves of East River, for two miles, kept up a continued acclamation for the whole distance. The Oliver Ellsworth was decorated with flags, and had on board a fine band of music. He was received at the Fulton-street wharf by the Committee of the Corporation, and conducted to his lodgings at the City Hotel. The streets were filled with people, whose anxiety to see him was unabated.

The anniversary of the birth day of La Fayette, the 6th September, when he attained his 67th year, having been selected by the Cincinnati veterans, to give him a dinner, he was escorted at the appointed hour to Washington Hall, by the La Fayette Guards. The room was splendidly and tastefully decorated: over the head of the General was sprung a triumphal arch of laurels and evergreens, in the centre of which appeared a large American eagle, with a scroll in its beak bearing the words "September 6th, 1757," (the day and year in which he was born.) On its right, a scroll bearing, "Brandywine, 11th September 1777"; on its left. "Yorktown, 19th October, 1781." In the rear of the General's chair was planted the grand standard of the Society, entwined with the national color of thirteen stripes. On the right was a shield, bearing a rising sun ; on the left, a shield with the State Arms. In the centre of the room, there was a splendid star, studded with others of less magnitude. From this star two broad pendants from the Franklin 74, were crossed and carried to the four corners of the room. At the lower end of the room was a most exquisite transparency, executed by Childs, representing the Goddess of Liberty, with an eagle holding a wreath of laurels. In her left hand was a scroll with the word "Welcome." On its right was a column, on which was placed forty muskets, forty pistols, and forty swords ; on its left a similar one; beneath it a shield with thirteen American stripes, and thirteen stars supported by two six-pounders, as likewise a coat of mail of steel, such as were worn by Napoleon's cuirassiers; and on the right and left ten field drums. Around the room were tastefully displayed 60 banners, bearing the names of distinguished officers of the revolution, who had fallen in battle. together with the regimental standards of the corps of artillery, and a number of trophies of our navy, which were handsomely tendered by Captain Rogers, and Lieutenant Goldsborough...

~~~***~~~

On Thursday the Fire Department mustered to the utmost of their strength, and paraded in the park, where the General, (after returning from the Oratorio given by the Choral Society in St. Paul's Church,) viewed their engines, and the other apparatus belonging to the dauntless guardians of the city.

All the Fire Engines in the city, amounting to 44, with hook and ladder companies, and two engines from Brooklyn, were arranged in a line around the park, and all the Firemen stood a little in advance, holding their drag ropes. After passing round the line, the General returned to the hall, and made his appearance on the piazza, where he remained in company with Thomas Franklin, Chief Engineer, and many ladies and gentlemen, to witness the exhibition.

In the centre of the Park, the ladders of the company were erected in the form of a Pyramid, on the top of which was placed a miniature house, filled with combustibles. The Engines having all approximated the centre, to within a suitable distance, and having been charged with water, at a signal the house was fired, and forty-six powerful water spouts were all directed at the object in an instant. The spectacle for the moment was beautiful beyond description. Such was the skill of the engineers that every spout seemed to strike the common centre, and a mighty fountain in the form of a colossal column, or cone, was thus, as if by enchantment, in the twinkling of an eye, beheld rushing up and descending like a shower of liquid silver. When the sun shone out the fountain sparkled all over like a palace of ice, or a magnificent dome of crystal; and the wind now and then blew upon the spray and carried off a cloud of vapour: the arch of a rainbow appeared above, with all its brilliant colours. The engines appeared to great advantage; they were all in the finest order.

On Friday, in pursuance of an invitation from the Trustees of the Free Schools of New-York, the General visited some of the Schools, and afterwards reviewed the whole collected for that purpose in the Park.

A large class of the scholars in the female school recited the following lines:

Welcome Hero, to the West,
To the land thy sword hath blest!
To the country of the *Free*,
Welcome, *Friend of Liberty!*

Grateful millions guard thy fame,
Age and youth revere thy name,
Beauty twines the wreath for thee,
Glorious *Son of Liberty!*

Years shall speak a nation's love,
Wheresoe'er thy footsteps move,
By the choral paean met --
Welcome, welcome, *La Fayette!*

At 1 o'clock, the General, by particular invitation, visited the African Free School, which embraces 7 or 800 scholars; about 450 were present on the occasion. Here it was announced to him that under the Presidency of the Honorable John Jay in 1788, he was elected an Honorary member of this Society, which the Marquis well recollected.

The General then retired to his lodgings for a few moments, until the children of all the schools could be assembled in the Park; he then returned and reviewed the whole, to the number of about 5000, arranged by their teachers ill regular order, and surrounded by at least 5000 spectators. The scene was truly interesting, and afforded a peculiar gratification to the General, who well knew that the schools of America were the nurseries of freedom, and the basis of American liberty...

~~~***~~~

Immediately in front of the gate which forms the first entrance to the Garden, was erected a pyramid of the height of seventy-five feet, brilliantly illuminated, and surmounted by a double triangle, likewise illuminated, presenting the appearance of a star encircling the letter F. The Bridge leading to the Castle [in New York City], which stands off from the Battery, into the bay 250 feet, was this evening an immense covered way, carpeted the entire distance, hung with numerous lamps, and decorated with ever-greens. Through this magnificent entrance, the company found their way into the interior of the Garden.

The Castle, which is a circle, and covers a surface of about 600 feet, was enclosed with an awning at an altitude of seventy-five feet, the dome of which was supported in the centre by a column dressed with pale blue and white, and inscribed with the names of men immortalized with that of La Fayette, in the cause of freedom. This column was encircled with an immense cut glass chandalier [sic], composed of thirteen separate ones, representing the thirteen original states; while it formed at its summit, the centre, whence hung the flags, signals and standards of various nations, looped and festooned with much good taste, making a covering for the company, and a splendid military and naval dress for the coarser canopy above.

This object, which was the first that met the eye, and formed at the base but a slight obstruction, had a very imposing appearance, and produced a fine effect. The whole seemed to operate like a charm upon the visitor, as he entered, who, with elevated and sparkling eyes, and with looks of enraptured admiration, came forward from the massy and low-browed entrance, with increased grace in his step, and airy lightness in his feelings. Every one seemed to feel at home, and to appropriate the scene and its pleasures to his individual enjoyment and use.
~~~

The roof was supported by thirteen transparent columns, capped with a circle of light, and based with the armorial insignia of the several states, under a shield of the Union, to denote their dependence on the same, and richly flanked with a falling drapery. Between the columns were to be seen the names of the original states, in gilded letters, encircled by laurel wreaths, and suspended between American ensigns, and a profusion of "striped bunting."

The General made his appearance about 10 o'clock. Immediately the dance and the song was at an end. The military band struck up a military air, and La Fayette was conducted through a column of ladies and gentlemen, to a splendid pavilion, immediately opposite to the great entrance. Not a word was spoken of gratulation -- so profound and respectful, and intellectual, was the interest which his presence excited; nothing but a subdued and universal clap broke the general silence, and that but for a moment.

The interior of the pavilion, which was composed of white cambric, festooned, arid otherwise varied with sky blue, and surmounted with an American Eagle, over the letter F, was richly furnished. Among other interesting objects, we noticed a bust of Hamilton, placed under a Corinthian pillar, and illuminated with a beautiful lamp.

But the most interesting of all the exhibitions were those presented in front of the pavilion, and seen from it, immediately over the entrance to the Garden. A triumphal arch of about ninety feet space, adorned with laurel, oak, and festoons of flags, &c. was seen, based upon pillars of cannon fifteen feet high. A bust of Washington, supported by a golden eagle, was placed over the arch, as the presiding deity. Within the arch was a painting, nearly 25 feet square, of a fine colossal figure, representing the Genius of our country, rising in her native majesty and strength, supported by the American Eagle, and exhibiting a scroll inscribed to Fayette, with the words -- "Honoured be the faithful patriot."

Soon after the General entered, the painting just alluded to, was slowly raised, which exhibited to the audience a beautiful transparency, representing La Grange, the mansion of La Fayette. The effect was as complete as the view was unexpected and imposing. Another subdued clap of admiration followed this tasteful, and appropriate, and highly interesting display…

~~~***~~~

After a brief and pertinent reply, the General accepted of an invitation to visit the seat of Edward P. Livingston, Esq. which is situated but a short distance to the north, upon the same elevated and beautiful plain. His reception was equally cordial and flattering as before. An excellent cold collation, together with refreshments of every suitable kind, were served up. And while the company were partaking of these, the steam-boat Richmond, Captain William Wiswall, came gaily down, and anchored alongside of the James Kent, having on board Major-General Jacob Rutsen Van Rensselaer, and suite, Brigadier-General Fleming, and suite, the Mayor of Hudson, (Rufus Reed, Esq.) Dr. Tallman, late Mayor, and Colonel Strong, as delegates from the city of Hudson, together with the Hudson Band, and two elegant uniform companies, under the command of Colonel Edwards. This formidable addition to the company already on the ground, repaired immediately to the seat of Mr. E. P. Livingston, from whence, after refreshments were served out to them by Mr. L. and Commodore Wiswall in person, General La Fayette was escorted back to the seat of his liberal entertainer. As night came on, the troops and crowd from the country dispersed, and the Hudson troops were taken on board of the steam-boat James Kent, where refreshments were ordered, and the forward deck and cabin assigned to them for the night. In the evening the whole of Mr. L's. splendid suite of apartments were brilliantly lighted up, and an elegant ball was given in honor of the General's company. The assemblage was very numerous, and a brilliant circle of ladies, arrayed in all the charm of health, beauty, and rich and elegant dresses, were contributing to the festivity and joy of the occasion, by "tripping the light fantastic toe," or by conversation sparkled with wit, or adorned by the graces of polished manners and education. Among the guests this evening, in addition to those already named, were the Honorable Edward Livingston, of New Orleans, the Honorable Walter Patterson, Captain Ridgeley, of the Navy, the Honorable Peter R. Livingston, A. Vanderpool, Esq. of Kinderhook, Mrs. Montgomery, (widow of the gallant General who fell at Quebec,) and many others whose names are not recollected. During the evening a sumptuous supper was served up in a style of magnificence rarely, if ever equalled in this country. The
~~~

room selected for this part of the fete, was an extensive Greenhouse, or Orangery, and the effect was indescribably fine. The tables had been made and fitted for this occasion, and were spread beneath a large grove of Orange and Lemon trees, with bending branches of fruit, and many other species of exotic shrubs and plants. Flora also, had profusely scattered her blossoms; and the whole scene seemed to partake of enchantment. The beholder stood Sizing, as if bound by the wizzard spell of the Magician. The night was dark and rainy; but this contributed to the general effect of the fete, inasmuch as the darkness heightened the effect of the thousand lamps by which the surrounding groves were illuminated. There was also a fine exhibition of fireworks, which had been prepared and brought from New-York for the occasion. It having been found inconvenient to provide suppers for so many on board of the boat, the whole detachment of troops were invited by Mr. L. to supper in the Green house, which invitation was accepted. At 10 o'clock, General La Fayette retired from this scene of gaiety and beauty, and at two the hall was closed, and the company separated, not only highly gratified with the entertainment, but with the manner in which it was got up and imparted to his guests, by Mr. L. whose style of living closely approximates that of the real English gentleman, and whose wealth is equalled by his kindness and liberality...

~~~***~~~

General La Fayette briefly replied to the address, after which the members of the Common Council were severally presented to him. A most interesting and affecting spectacle was then presented; sixty-eight veterans of the revolution, who had collected from the different parts of the county, formed a part of the procession, and were next presented; and it so happened that several of them were officers, and many of them soldiers who had served with La Fayette. Notwithstanding that they were admonished that the greatest haste was necessary, yet every one had something to say; and when they grasped his friendly hand, each seemed reluctant to release it. One of them came up with a sword in his hand, which, as he passed, he remarked was "given to him by the Marquis," at such a place, "in Rhode Island." Another, with a tear glistening in his eye, as he shook the hand of the General, observed -- "You, Sir, gave me the first guinea I ever had in my life -- I shall never forget that"...

~~~***~~~

On Sunday morning, the General stopped at Red-Hook and visited Mrs. Montgomery, widow of General Montgomery, who fell in storming the city of Quebec, December 1775, where he met a numerous collection of friends, and partook of a sumptuous dinner. About 2 o'clock, the General took an affectionate leave of Mrs. Montgomery and guests, and retired on board of the steam-boat, on his way to New-York. At 7 o'clock the boat came to at Fishkill landing, and the General called on Mrs. Dewitt, grand-daughter of the former President Adams, where he was courteously as well as splendidly received, amidst a numerous collection of friends assembled to greet their country's guest. To add to the enjoyments of this interview, the General had the pleasure of shaking cordially by the hand another of his brave Light Infantry, adding, "the Light Infantry were a brave corps, and under my immediate command." "Yes," returned the old soldier, "and you gave us our swords and plumes." The General made but a short stay, took leave of his friends, and returned to the boat under a salute of three hearty cheers...

~~~***~~~

On the arrival of General La Fayette upon the shore of New-Jersey, he was waited upon by General Dayton, Colonel Kinney, and Major Kean, of the suite of Governor Williamson, and conducted to Lyon's Hotel, where he was received by the Governor himself, and introduced to a number of distinguished citizens of New-Jersey. While here, a foil basket of large and delicious peaches were presented to the General, from the extensive fruitery of Mr. Taphagan. The General was accompanied to Jersey by the Mayor, Recorder, Members of the Common Council, the Society of Cincinnati, and several other gentlemen, all of whom were politely invited to visit and join in the festivities at Newark, and dine with the company at Elizabethtown. After remaining a five minutes, the General, with his Excellency Governor Williamson entered a superb carriage, drawn by four beautiful bay horses, and a cavalcade was formed, which proceeded leisurely towards Newark, escorted by a squadron of New Jersey cavalry, and two companies which had been invited from N. York. Arrived at Bergen, it was found that the inhabitants of that little town had assembled at the Inn, and were so anxious to pay their respects to the General that he
~~~

was constrained to alight for a moment. Here, unexpectedly, he was formally addressed by a delegation from the town, and presented with a superb cane made from an apple-tree under which Washington and La Fayette dined, when passing through that town, during the revolution, and which was blown down by the violent gale of the 3d of September, in 1821, The cane is richly mounted with gold, and bears the following inscription: -- "La Fayette," on the top, and round the head the words -- "Shaded the hero and his friend Washington, in 1779 -- Presented by the Corporation of Bergen, in 1824"...

~~~***~~~

To which [i.e., the address of Pennsylvania Gov. Schultze at Morrisville, outside Philadelphia] General La Fayette made the following reply:

"Sir -- On the happy moment, long and eagerly wished for, when I once more tread the soil of Pennsylvania, I find in her affectionate welcome, so kindly expressed by her first magistrate, a dear recollection of past favours, and a new source of delightful gratifications. The very names of this State and her Capitol, recall to the mind those philanthropic and liberal sentiments, which have marked every step of their progress.

"Pennsylvania has been the theatre of most important events; a partaker in the arduous toils and meritorious sacrifices, which insured the success of our glorious and fruitful revolution. I particularly thank you, Sir, for your gratifying mention of my personal obligation to the Pennsylvania line, nor will I ever forget, that on Pennsylvania ground, not far from this spot, I enjoyed, for the first time, the delight to find myself under American tents, and in the family of our beloved Commander in Chief. Now, Sir, Pennsylvania is in full possession, and reaps all the prosperities, and happy consequences of that great national union, of those special institutions, which, by offering in a self-governed people the most perfect example of .social order that ever existed, have reduced to absurdity and ridicule the anti-popular arguments of pretended statesmen in other countries. In whatever manner I may be disposed of, by the duties and feelings in which you have been pleased to sympathize, I shall ever rank this day among the most fortunate in my life; and while I beg your excellency personally to accept my cordial acknowledgements, I have the honour to offer to him, as Governor of the State, a tribute of profound gratitude, and respected devotion, to the citizens of Pennsylvania."

Having ascended his barouche and six, the General proceeded on his way; and did not reach Frankford until seven o'clock in the evening -- such being the throngs which lined the roads, and the number of the welcomes offered, and which he could not refuse. He passed the night at Frankford...

~~~***~~~

The whole appearance of this truly Grand Procession [in Philadelphia] was, august and imposing. As it passed, La Fayette! La Fayette! sprang from the voices of a multitude that rolled on, and on, and on, like wave after wave of the ocean, in numbers we shall not presume to name, [but which were estimated at 200,000,][408] -- La Fayette beat in every heart -- La Fayette hung on every tongue -- La Fayette glowed in every cheek -- La Fayette glistened in every swimming eye -- La Fayette swelled on every gale. The whole city and country appeared to have arrayed themselves in all their glory, and beauties and strength, at once to witness and adorn the majesty of the spectacle; and the fashionable part of the community seemed determined to exhibit the perfection of taste in the beauty of the decoration of their persons, and the richness of their attire. In Chesnut street, wreaths were cast into the barouche, as it passed, and many of them were from the fair hands of the Quakeresses.

After the procession had passed through the principal streets, the front halted at the old State House, which contains the Hlil in which the Declaration of Independence was signed in 1776.

Here the General alighted, passed under a most magnificent triumphal arch, and was conducted to the Hall, which is forty feet square, and was decorated in a most splendid manner. Among the decorations

[408] [*Edit. Note.* Comment in square brackets is contained in the original text.]

was a Statue of Washington, and Portraits of William Penn, Franklin, Robert Morris, Francis Hopkinson, Greene, Wayne, Montgomery, Hamilton, Gates, Rochambeau, Charles Carrol, M'Kean, Jefferson;[409] Hancock, Adams, Madison, Monroe, and Charles Thompson. The portrait of Washington, by Peale, occupied the first place, and was most splendidly decorated. Here were assembled the City authorities, the Society of Cincinnati, the Judges, Officers of the Army and Navy, and the Committee of Arrangements, all seated on superb sofas. The Governor of the State having been presented, General La Fayette, Judge Peters, and George Washington La Fayette were introduced, the company all standing. The Mayor of the city then welcomed the Guest...

~~~***~~~

[In Baltimore]

"Welcome, thrice welcome, General, to the soil of Maryland. Nothing that we can do, can too strongly express to you the affection and respect which we entertain for your person and your principles, or the joy with which we receive you among us, as a long absent Father upon a visit to his children."

The Governor then conducted him to the Tent, where he found the Society of the Cincinnati, the patriarchs of the revolution -- here he was received and embraced by all of them -- the scene was one of the most impressive and heart-touching, that was ever witnessed -- all were convulsed into tears, but they were tears of the most heart-felt joy and gratulation.

Colonel John E. Howard, the hero of Cowpens, and President of the Cincinnati Society, when the first emotion had subsided, addressed the General in the name of the Society, who in his reply, declared that "language could not express his feelings with meeting with his brothers in arms, in the Tent of their common friend, the beloved Washington." He then most affectionately embraced his old friends, Charles Carroll, of Carrollton, one of the signers of the Declaration of Independence, General Beeson, General Strieker, Colonel Howard, and all the aged members of the association, while tears rolled down their venerable cheeks. He shook hands with the younger members in the most cordial manner, looked frequently with an enquiring eye round the Tent, and seemed deeply affected. On discovering part of Washington's camp equipage, he said in an under voice, "I remember!" There was not a dry eye in the Tent.

The General and invited guests then retired to an adjoining Marquee, to an excellent breakfast prepared for the occasion, when many recollections of former days were brought forcibly to mind; and when this repast closed, the General was conducted to his barouche, accompanied as before by all the civil and military authorities present. When, he had taken his seat, Charles Carroll, General Smith, and Colonel Howard, were handed into the same barouche, which was followed by another containing George Washington La Fayette, whose warm reception we should have noticed before, Colonel Bentalou and two other gentlemen, and other carriages followed...

~~~***~~~

His reception by Mr. Monroe President of the United States, was most cordial and honorable. He called on the President, the day of his arrival in Washington, as before mentioned. The next day he was with Mr. Monroe both at breakfast and dinner, and on Thursday, the President gave a public dinner in honor of La Fayette, at which were present, the Heads of Departments, many distinguished public characters from various parts of the United States, and the principal officers of the army and navy. While in Washington, he also visited the Secretaries of State, of the Treasury, and of War, and Major General Brown, of the United States army.

General La Fayette rode over to Georgetown on Thursday, having been earnestly invited by the Mayor and corporation to visit that city; and the citizens demonstrated their gratitude and joy on the occasion, by a military escort, and a respectable procession. But the most acceptable offering was such as

[409] [*Edit. Note.* Although many are no doubt aware of his sojourn of a week at Monticello, less known perhaps is that Lafayette also visited and or stayed at the homes of John Adams, James Madison, and Joseph Bonaparte.]

he had received in all other places, the spontaneous and cordial salutations of the whole people. On Friday, he visited the navy yard, by invitation of the veteran Commodore Tingey. His reception here was remarkably brilliant and impressive; he was accompanied by many distinguished citizens and public functionaries; and the attentions of the naval veteran were honorable to himself and highly gratifying to General La Fayette. He dined again on Friday with President Monroe; and on Saturday proceeded on his proposed visit to Alexandria, and Yorktown. He was accompanied as far as the Potomac by the Mayor and committee of arrangements from Washington, escorted by the Georgetown cavalry. On the south side of the river, he was received by the deputation of Alexandria, attended by many other citizens, and several officers of the army and navy of the United States...

~~~***~~~

He entered the Ancient Dominion at Alexandria, at noon on the 16th, every where accompanied, escorted, and welcomed with the offerings of all hearts, hands, and voices. The parade of military exceeded 1500. In the procession was a car with "the tent of Washington.["] The procession passed through thronged streets, by crowded houses, under splendid arches, and amidst the roar of welcome, and shouts of transport. On the apex of a magnificent arch was perched a live mountain Eagle, of extraordinary size, who spread his wings when the General passed, and seemed to unite to their welcome. On his way he was met by another of those interesting and affecting sights -- a body of two hundred young boys and misses, who, while one of the latter chanted a beautiful paean, strewed flowers in his path. He was here addressed by the Mayor, the Common Council, his brother Masons and others. Salutes of artillery were fired at intervals. At the public dinner given to him, Mr. Secretary Adams, Commodores Rodgers and Porter, General Macomb and other distinguished citizens, were guests. The toasts were good and the volunteers numerous. "Our distinguished Guest -- the People's prisoner," was one of them. The General held a levee in the evening. The public buildings and many private houses were brilliantly illuminated.

On the Sabbath General La Fayette proceeded to Mount Vernon, and visited the tomb of Washington, his revered Father and Friend. While here, he was presented, by Mr. Custis, with a ring containing a portion of the hair of the Sainted Hero, together with the masonic sash and jewel formerly belonging to the Great Mason, accompanied with the following address:

"Last of the Generals of the army of Independence! At this awful and impressive moment, when, forgetting the splendour of a triumph greater than Roman consul ever had, you bend with reverence over the remains of Washington, the child of Mount Vernon presents you with this token, containing the hair of him, whom while living you loved, and to whose honored grave you now pay the manly and affecting tribute of a patriots and a soldier's tear.

"The ring has ever been an emblem of the union of hearts from the earliest ages of the world; and this will unite the affections of all the Americans to the person and posterity of La Fayette, now and hereafter. And when your descendants of .a distant day shall behold this valued relic, it will remind them of the heroic virtues of their illustrious sire, who received it, not in the palaces of princes, or amid the pomp and vanities of life, but at the laurelled grave of Washington.

"Do you ask -- Is this the Mausoleum befitting the ashes of a Marcus Aurelius, or the good Antonius? I tell you, that the father of his country lies buried in the hearts of his countrymen; and in those of the brave, the good, the free, of all ages and nations. Do you seek for the tablets which are to convey his fame to immortality? They have long been written in the freedom and happiness of their country. These are the monumental trophies of Washington the great; and will endure when the proudest works of art have "dissolved and left not a wreck behind."

"Venerable man! Will you never tire in the cause of freedom and human happiness Is it not time that you should Test from your labours, and repose on the bosom of a Country, which delights to love and honor you, and will teach her children's children to bless your name and memory? Surely, where liberty dwells, there must be the country of La Fayette.
~~~

"Our fathers witnessed the dawn of your glory, partook of its meridian splendour; and oh, let their children enjoy the benign radiance of your setting sun. And when it shall sink in the horizon of nature, here, here with pious duty, we will form your sepulchre; and, united in death as in life, by the side of the great chief you will rest in peace, till the last trump awakes the slumbering world, and calls your virtues to their great reward.

"The joyous shouts of millions of freemen hailed your returning foot-print on our sands. The arms of millions are opened wide to take you to their grateful hearts; and the prayers of millions ascend to the throne of the Eternal, that the choicest blessings of heaven may cheer the latest days of La Fayette."

General La Fayette having received the ring, pressed it to his bosom, and replied --

"The feelings, which at this awful moment oppress my heart, do not leave the power of utterance. I can only thank you, my dear Custis, for your precious gift. I pay a silent homage to the tomb of the greatest and best of men, my paternal friend"...

~~~***~~~

On this day, Monday 18th, the reception was purely civic, not a soldier appeared under arms. But on the 19th, the military spectacle was imposing and brilliant. Soon after breakfast, La Fayette walked from his quarters, to the tent of Washington surrounded by the Committee of Arrangements and others. Numbers were then introduced to him -- many ladies, the veteran soldiers of the revolution, citizens from other states, and all quarters of Virginia. The classic ground of Yorktown was converted into a camp; and the harbor was filled with vessels, steam-boats, &c. In the midst of the camp the tent of Washington had a conspicuous situation, near the House where its illustrious owner had his Head Quarters in 1782. -- To this the General repaired, and received the visits of the Ladies, strangers, &c. -- after which he was introduced to Col. Win. I. Lewis, of Campbell, who delivered an address suitable to the occasion.

Leaving this he passed under a splendid triumphal arch, erected on the spot where once stood the redoubt, which. La Fayette stormed, and which bore the names of La Fayette, Hamilton, and Laurens. The other redoubt stormed by the French troops, bore an Obelisk, bearing the names of Viomenil, Dupont, Dumas, De Noailles, Rochambeau, and De Grasse. On every part of the battle ground were to be found balls, shells, and fragments of bombs, the interesting evidences of the ardor and peril with which the capture of York was characterized. -- The General, in his splendid barouche, accompanied by the Governor of Virginia, Chief Justice Marshal, and Mr. Secretary Calhoun, proceeded to the arch, where he was received by General Taylor, and addressed as follows:

"General -- On behalf of my comrades, I bid you welcome. They come to greet you, with no pageantry, intended to surprise by its novelty, or dazzle by its splendour. But they bring you, General, an offering which wealth could not purchase, nor power constrain. On this day, associated with so many thrilling recollections; on this spot, consecrated by successful valour, they come to offer you this willing homage of their hearts.

"Judge, General, of their feelings at this moment by your own. Every thing around them speaks alike to their senses and sensibilities. These plains, where the peaceful ploughshare has not yet effaced the traces of military operations, these half decayed ramparts, this ruined village, in which the bomb's havoc is still every where visible, tell us of past warfare: and remind us of that long, arduous and doubtful struggle, on the issue of which depended the emancipation of our country.

"On yonder hillock, the last scene of blood was closed by the surrender of an army; and the liberty of our nation permanently secured. With what resistless eloquence does it persuade our gratitude and admiration for the gallant heroes, to whose noble exertions we owe the countless blessings which our free institutions have conferred upon us?

"The spot on which we stand, was once a redoubt occupied by our enemy. With how rapid a pencil does imagination present the blooming chieftain, by whom it was wrested from his grasp. Can we be here,
~~~

and forget that superior to the prejudices which then enchained even noble minds, he perceived in the first and almost hopeless struggles of a distant and obscure colony, the movement of that moral power, which was destined to give a new direction and character to political institutions, and to improve human happiness. Can we forget, that, deaf to the solicitations of power, of rank, and of pleasure, with a noble prodigality, he gave to our country his sword, his treasure, and the influence of his example.

"And when in the aged warrior who stands before us, we recognize that youthful chieftain, with what rapidity does memory retrace the incidents of his eventful life? With what pleasure do we see his manhood realize the promise of his youth? In senates or in camps, in the palaces of kings, or in their dungeons, we behold the same erect and manly spirit. At one time, tempering the licentiousness of popular feeling; at another restraining the extravagance of power, and always regardless of every thing but the great object of his life, the moral and political improvement of mankind.

"General -- In the brightest days of antiquity, no artificial stimulus of rank, or power, or wealth, was required to excite noble minds to acts of generous daring. A wreath of laurel, or of oak, was at once the proof and the reward of illustrious merit. For this, statesmen meditated, warriors bled, and eloquence soared to its sublimest heights. The prize was invaluable; for, it was won only by merit. It detracted, however, somewhat from its worth, that it was conferred by the partiality of compatriots, and in the fervor of admiration, inspired by recent success.

"Your life, General, illustrious throughout, in this also is distinguished. -- Time, which dims the lustre of ordinary merit, has rendered yours more brilliant. After a lapse of nearly half a century, your triumph is decreed by the sons of those who witnessed your exploits.

"Deign then, General, to accept the simple but expressive token of their gratitude and admiration. Suffer their leader to place upon your veteran brow, the only crown it would not disdain to wear, the blended emblems of civic worth and martial prowess. It will not pain you. General, to perceive some scattered sprigs of melancholy cypress, intermingled with the blended leaves of laurel and oak. Your heart would turn from us with generous indignation, if on an occasion like this, amid the joyous acclamations which greet you every where, were heard no sighs of grateful recollection for those gallant men who shared your battles, but do not, cannot, share your triumph. The wreath which our gratitude has woven, to testify our love for you, will lose nothing of its fragrance, or its verdure, though time hang upon its leaves some tears of pious recollection of the friend of your early youth: in war the avenger, in peace, the father of his country.

"In behalf then, of all the chivalry of Virginia; on this redoubt, which his valour wrested from the enemy at the point of the bayonet; I place on the head of Major General La Fayette this wreath of double triumph: --won by numerous and illustrious acts of martial prowess, and by a life devoted to the happiness of the human race. In their names, I proclaim him alike victorious in arms and acts of civil polity. In bannered fields, a hero -- in civil life, the benefactor of mankind."

La Fayette was deeply affected. There was a solemn earnestness in his manners, a touching sensibility in his whole countenance, which most deeply impressed every observer. Many wept all were moved. When General Taylor had closed his address, he was about to fix the civic wreath upon the General's head. But the considerate veteran, always himself, always attentive to the slightest proprieties of word and action, caught the hovering wreath as it approached his brow with his right hand, and respectfully bowing, dropt it to his side, when he thus replied:

"I most cordially thank you, my dear general, and your companions in arms, for your affectionate welcome, your kind recollections, and the flattering expressions of jour friendship. Happy I am to receive them on these already ancient lines, where the united arms of America and France have been gloriously engaged in a holy alliance, to support the rights of American Independence, and the sacred principle of the sovereignty of the people. Happy also to be so welcomed on the particular spot where my dear Light Infantry comrades acquired one of their honourable claims to public love and esteem.

You know. Sir, that in this business of storming redoubts, with unloaded arms and fixed bayonets, the merit of the deed is in the soldiers who execute it; and to each of them, I am anxious to acknowledge their equal share of honour. Let me, however, with affection and gratitude, pay a special tribute to the gallant name of Hamilton, who commanded the attack, to the three field officers who seconded him, Gimat, Laurens and Fish, the only surviving one, my friend now near me. In their name, my dear General, in the name of the Light Infantry, those we have lost, as well as those who survive, and only in common with them, I accept the crown with which you are pleased to honour us, and I offer you the return of the most grateful acknowledgements."

The General was not apprized of the address or the offering of the wreath; but with his never-ceasing readiness he turned round, and drawing Colonel Fish to the front, said, "*Here, half of this wreath belongs to you.*" "No, Sir," replied the Colonel "it is all your own." "Then," rejoined La Fayette, putting it into the Colonel's hand, "take it, and preserve it as our common property." The whole scene was strongly marked with the moral sublime...

~~~***~~~

To which address, General La Fayette replied, in a tone in which energy of character and sensibility of feeling were most interestingly blended, to the following effect:

"Mr. Speaker, and Gentlemen of the [U.S.] House of Representatives:

"While the people of the United States, and their honorable Representatives in Congress have deigned to make choice of me, one of the American veterans, to signify in his person, their esteem for our joint services and their attachment to the principles for which we have had the honour to fight and bleed, I am proud and happy to share those extraordinary favours with my dear revolutionary companions yet, it would be, on my part, uncandid and ungrateful not to acknowledge my personal share in those testimonies of kindness, as they excite in my breast emotions which no adequate words could express.

"My obligations to the United States. Sir, far exceed any merit I might claim. They date from the time when I had the happiness to be adopted as a young soldier, a favoured son of America. -- They have been continued to me during almost half a century of constant affection and confidence, and now, sir, thanks to your most gratifying invitation, I find myself greeted by a series of welcomes, one hour of which would more than compensate for the public exertions and sufferings of a whole life.

"The approbation of the American people and their Representatives, for my conduct during the vicissitudes of the European Revolution, is the highest reward I could receive. Well may I stand, "firm and erect," when, in their names, and by you, Mr. Speaker, I am declared to have, in every instance, been faithful to those American principles of liberty, equality, and true social order, the devotion to which, as it has been from my earliest youth, so shall it continue to be to my latest breath.

"You have been pleased, Mr. Speaker, to allude to the peculiar felicity of my situation, when, after so long an absence, I am called to witness the immense improvements, the admirable communications, the prodigious creations of which we find an example in this city, whose name itself is a venerated palladium; in a word, all the grandeur and prosperity of these happy United Slates, which, at the same time they nobly secure the complete assertion of American Independence, reflect on every part of the world the light of a far superior political civilization.

"What better pledge can be given of a persevering national love of liberty, when those blessings are evidently the result of a virtuous resistance to oppression, and the institutions founded on the rights of man and the Republican principle of self-government. No, Mr. Speaker, posterity has not begun for me -- since in the sons of my companions and friends, I find the same public feelings, and permit me to add the same feelings in my behalf, which I have had the happiness to experience in their fathers.

"Sir, I have been allowed, forty years ago, before a Committee of a Congress of thirteen States, to express the fond wishes of an American heart. -- On this day I have the honor, and enjoy the delight, to
~~~

congratulate the Representatives of the Union, so vastly enlarged, on the realization of those wishes, even beyond every human expectation, and upon the almost infinite prospects we can with certainty anticipate.

"Permit me, Mr. Speaker, and gentlemen of the House of Representatives, to join, to the expression of those sentiments, a tribute of my lively gratitude, affectionate devotion, and profound respect."

After the General and the Members had resumed their seats, and a short pause ensued, Mr. Mitchell, the organ of the Committee of reception, moved an adjournment.

The motion was agreed to, and the House was adjourned to Monday.

The Speaker then descended from the Chair, and most affectionately saluted the General. His example was followed by the Members of the House, individually, and some time was spent in this agreeable manner before the General retired.

The sublime and touching realities of this whole scene surpass the powers of imagination; every eye, every ear and every heart were wholly engrossed by the magnitude of the object before them. Nothing is to be found in the whole field of Grecian or Roman story, as a parallel to this. Of all the proud triumphs through which the veteran hero has passed since he first landed upon the shores of America, this was not only the most glorious, but must have been the most interesting to his feelings.

The scene in the Senate was not less interesting and imposing than that of the House; and it is well understood, that General La Fayette is the only public character that has ever been received by the Senate of the United States. This virgin honor was reserved for the man who was truly the most deserving.

On Monday, December 20th, Mr. Hayne, from the committee to whom was referred the subject of making provision for General La Fayette, reported to the Senate a bill, providing, that the sum of 200,000 dollars be granted to Major General La Fayette; also, one complete and entire township of land, to be located upon any of the public lands that remain unsold.

On Tuesday, December 21st, this bill passed the Senate, and on Wednesday, December 22d, the bill passed the House of Representatives.

Some slight objections were made to the bill while Under discussion in Congress, which were remarks by way of inquiry for information, rather than serious opposition, which led one of the members, in a conversation with General La Fayette, to offer a delicate apology; but the General with great *naivete* interrupted him, by adding -- "*I too Sir am of the opposition*. The gift is so munificent, so far exceeding the services of the individual, that had I been a member of Congress, I must have voted against it"...

~~~***~~~

General La Fayette commenced his tour from Washington, through the southern and western states, about the first of March.

In his course he visited the principal towns in the states of North and South Carolina, Georgia, Alabama. Louisiana, Mississippi, Tennessee, Missouri, Kentucky, Illinois, Indiana and Ohio. He visited Pittsburg[h], and returned to Albany, by the way of Buffalo and the western canal. From Albany he proceeded directly to Boston, through Springfield, where he arrived on the 16th of June...

~~~***~~~

The author regrets extremely that the limits of this work will not permit him to give a particular description of the interesting scenes that awaited the General throughout this whole tour. It must however, be remembered, that descriptions of scenes the most interesting, of feelings the most sublime and touching, and of characters the most exalted, loose their intended effect, by being too minutely dwelt upon, or too often repeated, and become irksome and tedious. A general sameness necessarily prevails throughout the whole; as in the Atlantic so in the western tour of General La Fayette, all classes of citizens vied with each other in expressing the grateful emotions of their hearts to the guest of the nation, the veteran hero, and the patriot benefactor of America.

The orators of the country, the surviving heroes of the revolution, the patriots and sages, the fair daughters of Columbia, with their numerous, offspring, and the whole mass of citizens, all with one acclaim welcomed the man whom their united hearts delight to honor. The same military parades, civic feasts, cordial and affectionate addresses, triumphal arches, splendid balls, and soldiers tears, that shewed the joys of kindred souls, greeted the arrival of La Fayette in every place he visited, throughout this extensive route, from Washington to Charleston, to New Orleans, to St. Louis, to Cincinnati, to Pittsburg, to Buffalo, to Albany, and to Boston, a distance of more than 4000 miles.

These were not the momentary triumphs of a conqueror, who returns flushed with some recent victory; but the triumphs of the hearts of other generations, who rise up to bless the patriot hero of their country, who took their fathers by the hand, led them to victory and glory; and when he had given them an exalted rank among the nations of the earth, stepped aside, and left them to pursue their enjoyments of freedom, happiness and honor. Again, after a lapse of nearly fifty years, he comes, at the united voice of more than 10,000,000 of people, as free, as happy, and as independent, as the nature of man can possibly become, to receive the welcome plaudits of the nation.

More than 3000 miles of the western tour of General La Fayette were a pathless desert when he last visited America; now they can proudly boast of nine new and valuable states, covered with rich and flourishing cities, towns and villages; possessing a free, a virtuous, and an intelligent population; richly enjoying all that is essential to the happiness of man. Throughout this vast interior, the forests have bowed to the ax of the wood-man, cities, towns and villages, roads, canals, manufactures, commerce, and the arts and sciences, have risen into being, as by the wand of the magician; and the all-propelling power of steam has greatly facilitated the social and commercial intercourse throughout the vast circuit of this western route.

The changes throughout the eastern or Atlantic tour, in a period of forty or fifty years, far surpass every thing of the kind, either in ancient or modern story, and must have been almost incredible to the patriot hero; but the changes of the west are far greater, and must have appeared to bins like so much of the section of a new creation. The sublime realities of this whole scene, when taken collectively, surpass the powers of the pen or the pencil, and are vast beyond the stretch of imagination.

THE KNICKERBOCKERS RESCUE SANTA CLAUS

"...from the dawn of recollection, until within a few years since, I lived wholly in the Country, and there spent the happiest days of my life.

The Dawn of youth serenely smil'd
And jocund danced the hours along;
I roved my native woodlands wild,
And wak'd blithe Echo with my song.

To be sure my 'douce Amie,' I was no great Singer – but there were no listeners Save Miss Echo and as She repeated my Song no doubt She was pleased with it..."
~ To Sally Hanlon, New York, 3rd Sept. 1802.[410]

Now that there's a cloud pending over the authorship of "A Visit from Saint Nicholas" (1823),[411] who in heaven's name is there left that can possibly save the tarnished name of "Santa?" Never fear! The Knickerbocker authors -- Washington Irving and James Kirke Paulding -- are here to retrieve the day! For "A Visit" was not Mr. Claus' (or as he was better back then "Saint Nicholas")[412] earliest debut in popular American culture. That honor goes to Irving's *A History of New-York, from the Beginning of the World to the End of the Dutch Dynasty* (1809) written, as you know, under the pseudonymous name and fictional creation Diedrich Knickerbocker (from whence the name originated of the Irving, Paulding, et al. school of New York writers.[413]) Most notably in chapters 5 and 7 of the same work, we find some of the very same attributes of the "jolly old elf" as we find in "A Visit": that is, he rides his sleigh over the rooftops bringing presents to children; smokes a pipe with a wreath of smoke circling his face; stockings are hung by the chimney for him to fill; and he's described as "laying his finger beside his nose and winking hard with one eye" (ch.7). Whoever it was therefore who wrote "A Visit from Saint Nicholas" indubitably derived no little of his material directly from Irving.

But where then does James Kirke Paulding come in? Paulding (whom Irving addressed and personally referred to as "Jim") was, in company with Irving and Irving's brother William[414], one of the co-authors of the earlier *Salmagundi* (1807-1808) series of humor essays, poems, and sketches. And it is not in the least inconceivable that Irving picked up much of his information on and understanding of the New York Dutch, including their language, from Paulding; the latter himself of that descent[415] -- including perhaps details on their ideas regarding Saint Nicholas. Moreover, Paulding was a helpful aid to Irving's public relations. For not all Dutch New Yorkers looked very kindly on his historical parody; including Walt Whitman, for one, who took offense at Irving's "buffonery." Paulding then, being a stalwart ally and friend,

---

[410] *The Letters of James Kirke Paulding*, Edited by Ralph M. Aderman, p. 22.

[411] While there does appear to be some argument to support the claim of Henry Livingston, Jr.'s writing that famous poem, it seems highly improbable that Clement Clarke Moore engaged in premeditated and willful fraud. And the mistaken attribution, granting such to be the case, may have stemmed from a misunderstanding on the part of Moore's children, and that Moore subsequently so acted and went along with it to spare himself, and them, potential embarrassment. Of note, it is said Livingtson was a Major in the 3rd New York Regiment led by Colonel James Clinton, and served in Canada in the 1775 campaign; however, I don't find him listed in the *Heitman Register*. His cousin, however, Col. Henry Beekman Livingston (1750-1851) is. The latter's sister Janet, by the way, was the wife of Maj. Gen. Richard Montgomery.

[412] The name "Santa Claus" itself is a pardonable mispronunciation of the Dutch "Sinter Klaas." Depending on the story-teller, he makes his visits on Christmas Eve, New Years Eve, or possibly both.

[413] Including, informally (since they wrote more or less independently of each other), Joseph Rodman Drake, George P. Morris, Nathaniel Parker Willis, Robert Charles Sands, Lydia Maria Child, P. Hamilton Myers; and in the lyric and poetical branch of the same: Henry Livingtson, Jr., Fitz-Greene Halleck, Samuel Woodworth, Clement Clarke Moore, Gulian Crommelin Verplanck, Charles Fenno Hoffman, and James Gates Percival.

[414] Paulding, by the bye, was also William Irving's brother-in-law.

[415] In keeping with our Continental Army series theme, Paulding's own Revolutionary War pedigree was nothing to sneeze at. His father, William, was an active commissary who supplied both the Continental Army in New York, under Maj. Gen. James Clinton, and the state militia. His uncle, John was, along with David Williams and Isaac Van Wart, one of the three militiamen who captured André. Paulding mother was Catharine Ogden; member of the famous New Jersey clan of Ogdens who produced several Revolutionary War notables, including Samuel and Matthias Ogden. In addition to his *Life of Washington* (1835), Paulding also wrote *The Old Continental, or The Price of Liberty* (1846), a mostly delectable, if haphazardly organized and episodic, historical novel set in the Revolutionary War Westchester County, and which includes at length accounts of the Jersey prison ship and the notorious Sugar House prison (both mentioned by Ethan Allen in his *Narrative*), as well as numerous other to be expected period places, events, and persons. His *The Dutchman's Fireside* (1831), another particular favorite of ours we should mention, occurs during the French and Indian War.

joined Irving in having comic fun at the expense of the early Dutch settlers, and thus demonstrated that the Dutch New Yorkers, himself being one, need not receive the jest harshly.

It was one of Paulding's signal traits to decide and express himself as he felt -- with little or no qualm or concern as to who might disapprove. He had all manner of curious ideas on various subjects. Today his pro-slavery views and relentless and overdone tirades against British cultural despotism, and his desire for a solely *sail*-going navy in the growing industrial age (evidently for aesthetic reasons) sound like so much foolishness. Yet the important thing to keep in mind is that Paulding had the feisty courage and determination to think and speak for himself; regardless of whether or not others liked it. And it is in this regard that his remains a most refreshing perspective on life and he himself a voice regenerating the human soul; even if particular opinions of his were, in retrospect, in wild error. As for his pro-slavery stance, he seemed to have be motivated by a desire to remain friendly with southerners, and thus preserve the struggling Union; as well, based on his visits to Virginia,[416] was persuaded to think that Blacks could be well cared for and happy in their arbitrary station. And further in fairness, be it noted, he does, despite his ridicule of everyone present, including Blacks, depict the latter in his comic novels (such as *Konigsmarkke: The Long Finn*) with indubitable warmth and thinly concealed affection. Sadly however, and somewhat like the country itself, it must be admitted that in later years and as he, a democrat, became more deeply embroiled in national politics, coming to serve briefly as Martin Van Buren's Secretary of the Navy and subsequently his informal campaign advisor, he grew more intransigent and bigoted; in his letters treating the Black and Red races with unbecoming and paranoid scorn that contrasted sharply with his more open minded youth.

"Yes," you say, "but what does this all have to do with Santa Claus?" I'm getting to that. In 1836 Paulding published a collection of stories entitled *The Book of Saint Nicholas*; doubtless in part intended as a holiday gift book, in which Father Christmas appears in most of them. True, Paulding is as much indebted to Irving as the author of "A Visit." And yet *The Book of Saint Nicholas* is no little precious to us for delving into the Saint Nicholas, or Santa, legend, in greater depth; and thereby providing an added dimension to the notions and ideas surrounding the venerated joy and gift bearer. In Irving, Saint Nicholas is a kind of briefly attending guest star; while in "A Visit" he rides swiftly out of sight before you have hardly time to properly make his acquaintance. Paulding, on the other hand, takes us into his very thoughts and haunts, and provides us with diverse scenarios involving different sorts of people; all the more welcome as vehicles by which Santa's character, circa 1810-1840, can be better grasped and appreciated. The following then is a tale chosen from this story collection that we fondly hope will bring back to you, who are unfamiliar with the book, sweet and cordial memories you presumably never had.[417]

~~~***~~~

CLAAS SCHLASCHENSCHLINGER.

Thrice blessed St. Nicholas! may thy memory and thine honours endure for ever and a day! It is true that certain arch calumniators, such as Romish priests, and the like have claimed thee as a Catholic saint, affirming, with unparalleled insolence, that ever since the pestilent heresy of the illustrious John Calvin, there hath not been so much as a single saint in the Reformed Dutch Church. But beshrew these keepers of fasts, and other abominations, the truth is not, never was, nor ever will be in their mouths, or their hearts! Doth not everybody know that-.the blessed St. Nicholas was of the Reformed Dutch Church, and that the cunning Romanists did incontinently filch him from us to keep their own calendar in countenance? The splutterkins! But I will restrain the outpourings of my wrath, and contenting myself with having proved that the good saint was of the true faith, proceed with my story, which is of undoubted authority, since I had it from a descendant of Claas Schlaschenschlinger himself, who lives in great honour and glory at the Waalboght on Long Island, and is moreover a justice of the peace and deacon of the church.

---

[416] In political temperament and wittily sarcastic manner of pleading, Paulding bears reasonable comparison with John Randolph.

[417] Of perhaps further and curious note, the famous Castle of Otranto, as Walpole himself relates it, is tellingly located next store to a church of *St. Nicholas!* The latent and possibly suspicious meaning of this is made more evident when we learn that Walpole's celebrated and fantastic gothic history first saw publication in 1764 -- on *December 24th!*
~~~

Nicholas, or, according to the true orthography, Claas Schlaschenschlinger, was of a respectable parentage, being born at Saardam, in our good faderland, where his ancestors had been proprietors of the greatest windmill in all the country round, ever since the period when that bloody tyrant, Philip of Spain, was driven from the Low Countries by the invincible valour of the Dutch, under the good Prince of Orange. It is said in a certain credible tradition, that one of the family had done a good turn to the worshipful St. Nicholas, in secreting him from the persecutions of the Romanists, who now, forsooth, claim him to themselves! and that ever afterwards the saint took special interest and cognizance in their affairs.

While at Saardam, little Claas, who was the youngest of a goodly family of seventeen children, was observed to be a great favourite of St. Nicholas, whose namesake he was, who always brought him a cake or two extra at his Christmas visits, and otherwise distinguished him above his brothers and sisters; whereat they were not a little jealous, and did sometimes slyly abstract some of the little rogue's benefactions, converting them to their own comfort and recreation.

In the process of time, Claas grew to be a stout lad, and withal a little wild, as he did sometimes neglect the great windmill, the which he had charge of in turn with the rest of his brothers, whereby it more than once came to serious damage. Upon these occasions, the worthy father, who had a reverend care of the morals of his children, was accustomed to give him the bastinado; but as Claas wore a competent outfit of breeches, he did not much mind it, not he; only it made him a little angry, for he was a boy of great spirit. About the time, I say, that Claas had arrived at the years of two or three and twenty, and was considered a stout boy for his age, there was great talk of settling a colony at the Manhadoes, which the famous Heinrick Hudson had discovered long years before. Many people of good name and substance were preparing to emigrate there, seeing it was described as a land flowing with milk and honey -- that is to say, abounding in shad and herrings -- and affording mighty bargains of beaver and other skins.

Now Claas began to cherish an earnest longing to visit these parts, for he was tired of tending the windmill, and besides he had a natural love for marshes and creeks, and being a shrewd lad, concluded that there must be plenty of these where beavers and such like abounded. But his father and the Vrouw Schlaschenschlinger did eschew and anathematize this notion of Claas's, and placed him apprentice to an eminent shoemaker, to learn that useful art and mystery. Claas considered it derogatory to the son of the proprietor of the greatest windmill in all Saardam to carry the lapstone, and wanted to be a doctor, a lawyer, or some such thing. But his father told him in so many words, that there were more lawyers than clients in the town already, and that a good cobbler saved more people from being sick, than all the doctors cured. So Claas became apprentice to the shoemaking business, and served out his time, after which he got to be his own master, and determined to put in practice his design of visiting the Manhadoes, of which he had never lost sight.

After much ado, Mynheer Schlaschenschlinger, and the good vrouw, consented unwillingly to let him follow the bent of his inclinations, and accordingly all things were got ready for his departure for the New World, in company with a party which was going out Under that renowned Lord Michael Paauw, who was proceeding to settle his domain of Pavonia, which lieth directly opposite to NewAmsterdam. Mynheer Schlaschenschlinger fitted out his son nobly, and becoming the owner of the largest windmill in all Saardam, equipping him with awls, and knives, and wax, and thread, together with a bench, and a goodly lapstone, considering in his own mind that the great scarcity of stones in Holland might, peradventure, extend to the Manhadoes. Now all being prepared, it was settled that Claas should depart on the next day but one, the next being St. Nicholas his day, and a great festival among the people of Holland.

According to custom, ever since the days of the blessed saint, they had a plentiful supper of waffles and chocolate -- that pestilent beverage tea not having yet come into fashion -- and sat up talking of Claas, his adventures, and what he would see and hear in the Manhadoes, till it was almost nine o'clock. Upon this, mynheer ordered them all to bed, being scandalized at such unseasonable hours. In the morning when Claas got up, and went to put on his stocking, he felt something hard at the toe, and turning it inside out, there fell on the floor the bowl of a pipe of the genuine Meershaum, which seemed to have been used beyond memory, since its polish was a thousand times more soft and delightsome than ivory or tortoise shell, and its lustre past all price. Would that the blessed Saint would bestow such a one on me!

Claas was delighted; he kissed it as if he had been an idolatrous Romanist -- which, by the blessing of Saint Nicholas was not – and bestowing it in the bottom of his strong oaken chest, resolved, like unto a prudent Dutchman, never to use it, for fear of accidents. In a few hours afterwards, he parted from his parents, his family, and his home; his father gave him a history of the bloody wars and persecutions of Philip of Spain; a small purse of guilders, and abundance of advice for the government of his future life; but his mother gave him what was more precious than all these -- her tears, her blessing, and a little Dutch Bible with silver clasps. Bibles were not so plenty then as they are now, and were considered as the greatest treasures of the household. His brothers and sisters took an affectionate farewell of him, and asked his pardon for stealing his Newyear cookies. So Claas kissed his mother, promising, if it pleased Heaven, to send her stores of herrings and beaver. skins, whereat she was marvellously comforted; and he went on his way, as it were sorrowfully rejoicing.

I shall pass over the journey, and the voyage to the Manhadoes, saving the relation of a curious matter that occurred after the ship had been about ninety days at sea, and they were supposed to be well on their way to the port of New-Amsterdam. It came into the heads of the passengers to while away the time as they were lying to one day with the sails all furled, except one or two, which I name not, for a special reason, contrary to the practice of most writers -- namely, because I am ignorant thereof -- having the sails thus furled, I say, on account of certain suspicious-looking clouds, the which the captain, who kept a bright lookout day and night, had seen hovering overhead, with no good intentions, it came into the noodles of divers of the passengers to pass the time by opening their chests, and comparing their respective outfits, for they were an honest set of people, and not afraid of being robbed.

When Claas showed his lapstone, most of the company, on being told the reasons for bringing it such a long distance, held up their hands, and admired the foresight of his father, considering him an exceeding prudent and wise man to think of such matters. Some of them wanted to buy it on speculation, but Claas was too well acquainted with its value to set a price on it. While they were thus chaffering, an old sailor, who had accompanied the renowned Heinrick Hudson as cabin boy, in his first voyage to the Manhadoes, happening to come by and hear them, swore a great Dutch oath, and called Claas a splutterkin for bringing stones all the way from Holland, saying that there were enough at the Manhadoes to furnish lapstones for the whole universe. Whereupon Claas thought to himself, "What a fine country it must be, where stones are so plenty."

In process of time, as all things, and especially voyagings by sea, have an end, the vessel came in sight of the highlands of Neversink -- vulgarly called by would-be learned writers, Navesink -- and Claas and the rest, who had never seen such vast mountains before, did think that it was a wall, built up from the earth to the sky, and that there was no world beyond.

Favoured by a fine south wind, whose balmy freshness had awakened the young spring into early life and beauty, they shot like an arrow from a bow through the Narrows, and sailing along the heights of Staaten Island, came in sight of the illustrious city of New-Amsterdam, which, though at that period containing but a few hundred people, I shall venture to predict, in some future time, may actually number its tens of thousands.

Truly it was a beautiful city, and a beautiful sight as might be seen of a spring morning. As they came through Buttermilk Channel, they beheld with delighted astonishment the fort, the church, the governor's house, the great dock jutting out into the salt river, the Stadt Huys, the rondeel, and a goodly assemblage of houses, with the gable ends to the street, as before the villainous introduction of new fashions, and at the extremity of the city, the gate and wall, from whence Wall-street deriveth its name. But what above all gloriously delighted Claas, was a great windmill, towering in the air, and spreading its vast wings on the rising ground along the Broadway, between Liberty and Courtlandt streets, the which reminded him of home and his parents. The prospect rejoiced them all mightily, for they thought to themselves, "We have come to a little Holland far over the sea,"

So far as I know, it was somewhere about the year of our Lord one thousand six hundred and sixty, or thereabout, and in the month of May, that Claas landed in the New World; but of the precise day of the month I cannot be certain, seeing what confusion of dates hath been caused by that idolatrous device of Pope Gregory, called the New Style, whereby events that really happened in one year are falsely put down to another, by which means history becomes naught. The first thing he thought of, was to provide himself a home, for be it known it was not then the fashion to live in taverns and boarding houses, and the man who thus demeaned himself was considered no better than he should be; nobody would trust or employ him, and he might consider it a special bounty of the good St. Nicholas, if he escaped a ride on the wooden horse provided for the punishment of delinquents. So Claas looked out for a pleasant place whereon to pitch his tent. As he walked forth for this end, his bowels yearned exceedingly for a lot on the Broad-street, through which ran a delightful creek, crooked like unto a ram's horn, the sides of which were low, and, as it were, juicy with the salt water which did sometimes overflow them at spring tides, and the full of the moon. More especially the ferry house, with its never to be forgotten weathercock, did incite him sorely to come and set himself down thereabout. But he was deterred by the high price of lots in that favoured region, seeing they asked him as much as five guilders for the one at the corner of the Broad and Wall streets, a most unheard-of price, and not to be thought of by a prudent man like Claas Schlaschenschlinger.

So he sought about elsewhere, though he often looked wistfully at the fair meads of the Broadstreet, and nothing deterred him from ruining himself by gratifying his longings, but the truly excellent expedient of counting his money, which I recommend to all honest people, before they make a bargain. But though he could not settle in Broadstreet, he resolved in his mind to get as nigh as possible, and finding a lot with a little puddle of brackish water in it large enough for a goose pond, nigh unto the wall and gate of the city, and just at the head of what hath lately been called Newstreet -- then the region of unsettled lands -- he procured a grant thereof from the schout, scheepens, and burgomasters, who then ruled the city, for five stivers, being the amount of fees for writing and recording the deed by the Geheim Schryver.

Having built himself a comfortable house, with a little stoop to it, he purchased a pair of geese, or, to be correct and particular, as becometh a conscientious historian, a goose and gander, that he might recreate himself with their gambols in the salt puddle, and quietly sat himself down to the making and mending of shoes. In this he prospered at first indifferently well, and thereafter; mightily, when the people found that he made shoes, some of which were reported never to wear out; but this was, as it were, but a sort of figure of speech to express their excellent qualities.

Every Sunday, after church, in pleasant weather, Claas, instead of putting off his Sunday suit, as was the wont of the times, used to go and take a walk in the Ladies' Valley, since called Maiden Lane, for everything has changed under those arch intruders, the English, who, I believe, in their hearts, are half Papists. This valley was an exceeding cool, retired, and pleasant place, being bordered by a wood, in the which was plenty of pinkster blossoms in the season. Being a likely young fellow, and dressed in a goodly array of breeches and what not, he was much noticed, and many a little damsel cast a sheep's eye upon him as he sat smoking his pipe of a summer afternoon under the shade of the trees which grew plentifully in that quarter. I don't know how it was, but so it happened, that in process of time he made acquaintance with one of these, a buxom creature of rare and unmatchable lineaments and dimensions, insomuch that she was considered the beauty of New-Amsterdam, and had refused even the burgomaster, Barendt Roeloffsen, who was taxed three guilders, being the richest man of the city. But Aintjie was not to be bought with gold; she loved Claas because he was a solid young fellow, who plucked for her the most beautiful pinkster blossoms, and was the most pleasant companion in the world, for a ramble in the Ladies' Valley.

Report says, but I believe there was no great truth in the story, that they sometimes Queested*[418] together, but of that I profess myself doubtful. Certain it is, however, that in good time they were married, to the great content of both, and the great discontent of the burgomaster, Barendt Roeloffsen.

In those days young people did not marry to set up a coach, live in fine houses filled with rich furniture, for which they had no use, and become bankrupt in a few years. They began in a small way, and

[418] [*Footnote in the original*] * This word is untranslatable.

increased their comforts with their means. It was thus with Claas and his wife, who were always employed in some useful business, and never ran into extravagance, except it may be on holydays. In particular Claas always feasted lustily on St. Nicholas his day, because, he was his patron saint, and he remembered his kindness in faderland.

Thus they went on prospering as folks always do that are industrious and prudent, every year laying up money, and every year increasing their family; for be it known, those who are of the true Dutch blood, always apportion the number of children to the means of providing for them. They never are caught having children for other people to take care of. But be this as it may, about this time began the mischievous and oppressive practice of improving the city, draining the marshes, cutting down hills, and straightening streets, which hath since grown to great enormity in this city, insomuch that a man may be said to be actually impoverished by his property.

Barendt Roeloffsen, who was at the head of the reformers, having a great estate in vacant lands, which he wanted to make productive at the expense of his neighbours -- Barendt Roeloffsen, I say, bestirred himself lustily to bring about what he called, in outlandish English, the era of improvement, and forthwith looked around to see where he should begin. I have always believed, and so did the people at that time, that Barendt singled out Claas his goose pond for the first experiment, being thereunto impelled by an old grudge against Claas, on account of his having cut him out with the damsel he wished to marry, as before related.

But, however, Barendt Roeloffsen, who bore a great sway among the burgomasters, on account of his riches, got a law passed, by hook or by crook, for draining Claas his pond, at his own expense, making him pay at the same time for the rise in the value of his property, of which they did not permit him to be the judge, but took upon themselves to say what it was. The ancestors of Claas had fought valiantly against Philip of Spain, in defence of their religion and liberty, and he had kept up his detestation of oppression by frequently reading the account of the cruelties committed in the Low Countries by the Spaniard, in the book which his father had given him on his departure from home. Besides, he had a great admiration, I might almost say affection, for his goose pond, as is becoming in every true Dutchman. In it he was accustomed to see, with singular delight, his geese, now increased to a goodly flock, sailing about majestically, flapping their wings, dipping their necks into the water, and making a noise exceedingly tuneful and melodious. Here, too, his little children were wont to paddle in the summer days, up to their knees in the water, to their great contentment as well as recreation, thereby strengthening themselves exceedingly. Such being the case, Claas resisted the behest of the burgomasters, declaring that he would appeal to the laws for redress if they persisted in trespassing on his premises. But what can a man get by the law at any time, much less when the defendant, as in this case, was judge as well as a party in the business? After losing avast deal of time, which was as money to him, and spending a good portion of what he had saved for his children, Claas was at length cast in his suit, and the downfall of his goose pond irrevocably decreed.

It was a long time before he recovered this blow, and when he did, Fortune, as if determined to persevere in her ill offices, sent a blacksmith from Holland, who brought over with him the new and diabolical invention of hobnails, the which he so strenuously recommended to the foolish people, who are prone to run after novelties, that they, one and all, had their shoes stuck full of nails, whereby they did clatter about the streets like unto a horse newly shod. As might be expected, the business of shoemaking decreased mightily upon this, insomuch that the shoes might be said to last for ever; and I myself have seen a pair that have descended through three generations, the nails of which shone like unto silver sixpences. Some people supposed this was a plot of Barendt Roeloffsen, to complete the ruin of poor Claas; but whether it was or not, it is certain that such was the falling off in his trade, on account of the pestilent introduction of hobnails, that, at the end of the year, Claas found that he had gone down hill at a great rate. The next year it was still worse, and thus, in the course of a few more, from bad to worse, he at last found himself without the means of support for himself, his wife, and his little children. But what shows the good ness of Providence, it is worthy of record, that from this time his family, miraculously as it were, ceased to increase.

Neither begging nor running in debt without the prospect of paying was in fashion in those days, nor were there any societies to invite people to idleness and improvidence by the certainty of being relieved from their consequences without the trouble of asking. Claas tried what labouring day and night would do, but there was no use in making shoes when there was nobody to buy them. His good wife tried the magic of saving; but where there is nothing left to save, economy is to little purpose. He tried to get into some other business, but the wrath of Barendt Roeloffsen was upon him, and the whole influence of the burgomasters stood in his way on account of the opposition he had made to the march of improvement. He then offered his house and lot for sale; but here again his old enemy Barendt put a spoke in his wheel, going about among the people and insinuating that as Claas had paid nothing for his lot, the title was good for nothing. So one by one he tried all ways to keep want from his door; but it came at last, and one Newyear's eve, in the year of our Lord -- I don't know what, the family was hovering round a miserable fire, not only without the customary means of enjoying the festivity of the season, but destitute of the very necessaries of life.

The evening was cold and raw, and the heavy moanings of a keen northeast wind announced the approach of a snow storm. The little children cowered over the almost expiring embers, shivering with cold and hunger; the old cat lay half buried in the ashes to keep herself warm; and the poor father and mother now looked at the little flock of ragged -- no, not ragged -- the mother took care of that; and industry can always ward off rags and dirt. But though not ragged or dirty, they were miserably clad and worse fed; and as the parents looked first at them and then at each other, the tears gathered in their eyes until they ran over.

"We must sell the silver clasps of the Bible my mother gave me, wife," said Claas, at last.

"The Goodness forbid," said she; "we should never prosper after it."

"We can't prosper worse than we do now, Aintjie."

"You had better sell the little book about the murders of the Spaniards, that you sometimes read to me."

"It has no silver clasps, and will bring nothing," replied Claas, despondingly, covering his face with his hand, and seeming to think for a few moments. All at once he withdrew his hand, and cried,

"The pipe! the meershaum pipe! it is worth a hundred guilders!" and he ran to the place where he had kept it so carefully that he never used it once in the whole time he had it in his possession.

He looked at it wistfully, and it brought to his mind the time he found it in his stocking. He thought of his parents, his brothers, his sisters, and old faderland, and wished he had never parted from them to visit the New World. His wife saw what was passing in his heart, and said, "Never mind, dear Claas, with these hundred guilders we shall get on again by the blessing of the good St. Nicholas, whose namesake you are."

Claas shook his head, and looked at the meershaum, which he could not bear to part with, because, somehow or other, he could not help thinking it was the gift of St. Nicholas. The wind now freshened, and moaned more loudly than ever, and the snow began to come in through the crevices of the door and windows. The cold increased apace, and the last spark of fire was expiring in the chimney. There was darkness without and within, for the candle, the last they had, was just going out.

Claas, without knowing what he was doing, rubbed the pipe against his sleeve, as it were mechanically.

He had scarcely commenced rubbing, when the door suddenly opened, and without more ado, a little man, with a right ruddy good-humoured face, as round as an apple, and a cocked beaver, white with snow, walked in, without so much as saying, "By your leave," and sitting himself by the side of the yffrouw [sic], began to blow at the fire, and make as if he was warming his fingers, though there was no fire there, for that matter.

Now Claas was a good-natured fellow, and though he had nothing to give, except a welcome, which is always in the power of everybody, yet he wished to himself he had more fire to warm people's fingers. After a few moments, the little man rubbed his hands together, and looking around him, with a good-humoured smile, said, "Mynheer Schlaschenschlinger, methinks it might not be amiss to replenish this fire a little; 'tis a bitter cold night, and my fingers are almost frostbitten."

"Alack, mynheer," quoth Claas, "I would, with all my heart, but I have nothing wherewith to warm myself and my children, unless I set fire to my own house. I am sorry I cannot entertain thee better."

Upon this the little man broke the cane with which he walked into two pieces, which he threw in the chimney, and thereupon the fire began to blaze so cheerfully that they could see their shadows on the wall, and the old cat jumped out of the ashes, with her coat well singed, which made the little jolly fellow laugh heartily.

The sticks burnt and burnt, without going out, and they were soon all as warm and comfortable as could be. Then the little man said,

"Friend Claas, methinks it would not be much amiss if the good vrouw here would bestir herself to get something to eat. I have had no dinner today, and come hither on purpose to make merry with thee. Knowest thou not that this is Newyear's eve?"

"Alack!" replied Claas, "I know it full well; but we have not wherewithal to keep away hunger, much less to make merry with. Thou art welcome to all we have, and that is nothing."

"Come, come, Friend Claas, thou art a prudent man, I know, but I never thought thou wert stingy before. Bestir thyself, good Aintjie, and see what thou canst find in that cupboard. I warrant there is plenty of good fare in it."

The worthy yffrouw looked rather foolish at this proposal, for she knew she would find nothing there if she went; but the little man threatened her, in a good-humoured way, to break the long pipe he carried stuck in his cocked hat, over her nightcap, if she didn't do as he bid her. So she went to the cupboard, resolved to bring him out the empty pewter dishes, to show they had nothing to give him. But when she opened the cupboard, she started back, and cried out aloud, so that Claas ran to see what was the matter; and what was his astonishment to find the cupboard full of all sorts of good things for a notable jollification.

"Aha!" cried the merry little man, "you're caught at last. I knew thou hadst plenty to entertain a stranger withal; but I suppose thou wantedst to keep it all to thyself. Come, come! bestir thyself, Aintjie, for I am as hungry as a schoolboy."

Aintjie did as she was bid, wondering all the time who this familiar little man could be; for the city was not so big, but that she knew by sight everybody that lived in it, and she was sure she had never seen him before.

In a short time there was a glorious array of good things set out before them, and they proceeded to enjoy themselves right lustily in keeping of the merry Newyear's eve. The little man cracked his jokes, patted little Nicholas -- Claas, his youngest son, who was called after his father -- on the head; chucked Aintjie under the chin; said he was glad she did not wed the splutterkin Barendt Roeloffsen, and set them so good an example, that they all got as merry as crickets.

By-and-by the little man inquired of Claas concerning his affairs, and he gave him an account of his early prosperity, and how he had declined, in spite of all he could do, into poverty and want; so that he had nothing left but his wife, his children, his Dutch Bible, his history of the Low Country wars, and his meershaum pipe.

"Aha!" quoth the little man, "you've kept that, hey! Let me see it."

Claas gave it to him, while the tears came into his eyes, although he was so merry, to think that he must part with it on the morrow. It was the pride of his heart, and he set too great a value on it to make any use of it whatever.

The little man took the pipe, and looking at it, said, as if to himself,

"Yes; here it is! the very identical meershaum out of which the great. Calvin used to smoke. Thou hast done well, Friend Claas, to preserve it; and thou must keep it as the apple of thine eye all thy life, and give it as an inheritance to thy children."

"Alack!" cried Aintjie, "he must sell it to-morrow, or we shall want wherewithal for a dinner."

"Yea," said Claas, "of a truth it must go tomorrow!"

"Be quiet, splutterkin!" cried the little man, merrily; "give me some more of that spiced beverage, for I am as thirsty as a dry sponge. Come, let us drink to the Newyear, for it will be here in a few minutes."

So they drank a cup to the jolly Newyear, and at that moment the little boys and negroes, who didn't mind the snow any more than a miller does flour, began to fire their cannon at a great rate; whereupon the little man jumped up, and cried out,

"My time is come! I must be off, for I have a great many visits to pay before sunrise."

Then he kissed the yffrouw with a hearty smack, just as doth the illustrious Rip Van Dam, on the like occasions; patted little Nicholas on the head, and gave him his blessing; after which he did incontinently leap up the chimney and disappear. Then they knew it was the good St. Nicholas, and rejoiced mightily in the visit he had paid them, looking upon it as an earnest that their troubles were over.

The next morning the prudent housewife, according to custom, got up before the dawn of day to put her house in order, and when she came to sweep the floor, was surprised to hear something jingle just like money. Then opening the embers, the sticks which the good saint had thrown upon the fire again blazed out, and she descried a large purse, which, on examination, was found filled with golden ducats. Whereupon she called out to Claas, and they examined the purse, and found fastened to it a paper bearing this legend: --

"THE GIFT OF SAINT NICHOLAS."

While they stood in joyful wonder, they heard a great knocking and confusion of tongues outside the door, and the people calling aloud upon Claas Schlaschenschlinger to come forth; whereupon he went forth, and, to his great astonishment, found that his little wooden house had disappeared in the night, and in its place was standing a gorgeous and magnificent mansion of Dutch bricks, two stories high, with three windows in front, all of a different size; and a door cut right out of the corner, just as it is seen at this blessed day.

The neighbours wondered much, and it was whispered among them, that the fiend had helped Claas to this great domicil[e], which was one of the biggest in the city, and almost equal to that of Barendt Roeloffsen. But when Claas told them of the visit of St. Nicholas, and showed them the purse of golden ducats, with the legend upon it, they thought better of it, and contented themselves with envying him heartily" his good fortune.

I shall not relate how Claas prospered ever afterwards, in spite of his enemies the burgomasters, who, at last, were obliged to admit him as one of their number; or how little Aintjie held up her head among the highest; or how Claas ever after eschewed the lapstone, and, like a worshipful magistrate, took to bettering the condition of mankind, till at length he died, and was gathered to his forefathers, full of years and honours.

All I shall say is, that the great house in Newstreet continued in the family for several generations, until a degenerate descendant of Claas, being thereunto incited by the d--l, did sell it to another degenerate splutterkin, who essayed to pull it down. But mark what followed. No sooner had the workmen laid hands on it, than the brickbats began to fly about at such a rate, that they all came away faster than they went; some with broken heads, and others with broken bones, and not one could ever be persuaded to meddle with it afterwards.

And let this be a warning to any one who shall attempt to lay their sacrilegious hands on the Last of The Dutch Houses, the gift of St. Nicholas, for whoever does so, may calculate, to a certainty, on getting well peppered with brickbats, I can tell them.

THE NOVEL AS THEATER IN JAMES FENIMORE COOPER'S *THE PILOT* (1823)

James Fenimore Cooper's *The Pilot: A Tale of the Sea* (1823), set during the American Revolution, is arguably one of the most influential novels, and with few peers, in all of American literature. Never before had an author so infatuated himself and his readers with the sea and sea faring matters; while introducing, at least for moderns, the notion of man against the elements. And in these regards, *The Pilot* vividly foreshadowed not only the nautical fiction of Herman Melville and Joseph Conrad, as others have already observed, but also that of Jack London and Ernest Hemingway. The ocean itself, with sky, sun, clouds, and stars as companions, is carefully delineated, described, and developed as if it too were a central character in the complex of *human* events.

Cooper himself effectively characterized his work as so many "rude sketches" (ch. 35), and, like some of his other novels, is not without its shortcomings, not least of which improbability of plot. Exactly what the mission of the American ships is and why they find themselves off the northern coast of England, and, *just coincidentally*, near St. Ruth's Abbey, the then abode of the love interests of three naval officers serving the American cause, i.e., Griffith (with Katherine Plowden), Barnstable (Cecilia Howard), and the pilot "John Gray" (Alice Dunscombe) is never very plausibly explained. It's a wonder that Cooper, who is so scrupulously careful to dovetail and weave together the particulars of his story on so many points, should be guilty of such a conspicuous omission; and there are other and similar creaks in the story line. In addition, Cooper often has a convoluted, round about, and abstruse way of wording himself; that will invariably annoy readers, and who can't help at times finding themselves puzzled as to quite what he is talking about; all the more so, when the point made is one that might otherwise have been made succinctly in a single sentence or two. Yet on the positive side, Cooper on other occasions has a knack for evoking moods very well, such as the feeling of being amid the tossing waves, and it is no little uncanny after putting the book down between readings to afterward feel oneself still imbued with the same.

The character of the book's title has been likened to John Paul Jones, indeed some critics assume the latter is on whom the mysterious Englishman "John Gray" is based. But this seems to be an error, or at best an over simplification, because John Gray is a persona unique and unlike almost anyone else we've seen. At times he seems to represent the true heart and spirit of the British naval tradition that spawned both British and American navies. At other times he is nationless wanderer seeking justice and adventure wherever there's a fight. At yet others, he acts as Providence itself dispensing to men their fate -- including perhaps even the outcome of the Revolutionary War itself. Moreover, we might add, Jones was not the first independent sailor to attempt fighting the British in their home waters, and had his antecedent in François Thurot, a privateer during the Seven Years War; Lambert Wickes, a Continental Navy captain from Maryland; and Irishman Gustavus Conyngham, "The Dunkirk Pirate."

And yet there is much more to *The Pilot* than its historical naval yarn, and Cooper spends almost as much time punctually tending to the tastes of the drawing room ladies, literati, scholars and historians as he does to the conventional action and romance reader. In fact in some parts Cooper uses *The Pilot* as a venue to display his interest in theater and his evidently closet aspiration to be a playwright as well as novelist.[419] A perfect illustration of this last is chapter 28 which appears to be tailor and ready made to be adapted to the stage. There is much to love about this chapter; which viewed allegorically could be said to portray in abstract encapsulation the military struggle of the American Revolution, including references and allusions to the respective combatants most seminal motives and arguments. It was all a family quarrel pertaining in part to a dispute over women, Cooper says in effect. But perhaps even more interesting, indeed some will find a riot, are the theatrics, including suspense, he employs in presenting this denouement, and which give us an amusing glimpse of what many theater-goers of the early 19th century no doubt liked to see and hear in their stage dramas.

---

[419] Cooper's *The Spy* had been successfully produced for the stage in 1822 at the Park Theater in New York City; a performance of which has been memorialized in a painting by dramatist, painter, and stage historian William Dunlap. 1823 then saw a staging of *The Pioneers*, and sure enough in the following year it was *The Pilot*.

To set the scene, the Americans sailors under Griffith and Barnstable are preparing to liberate some prisoners by surprising British Capt. Borroughcliffe and his soldiers; unaware that the latter have themselves secretly set a trap *for them*.

~~~***~~~

CHAPTER XXVIII.

"He looks abroad, and soon appears,
O'er Horncliffe-hill, a plump of spears,
Beneath a pennon gay."
Marmion.[420]

The sharp sounds of the supper-bell were ringing along the gallery, a Miss Plowden gained the gloomy passage; and she quickened her steps to join the ladies, in order that no further suspicions might be excited by her absence. -- Alice Dunscombe was already proceeding to the dining parlor, as Katherine passed through the door of the drawing-room; but Miss Howard had loitered behind, and was met by her cousin alone.

"You have then been so daring as to venture, Katherine!" exclaimed Cecilia.

"I have," returned the other, throwing herself into a chair, to recover her agitation -- "I have, Cecilia; and I have met Barnstable, who will soon be in the abbey, and its master."

The blood which had rushed to the face of Cecilia on first seeing her cousin now retreated to her heart, leaving every part of her fine countenance of the whiteness of her polished temples, as she said:

"And we are to have a night of blood!"

"We are to have a night of freedom, Miss Howard; freedom to you, and to me: to Andrew Merry [an American midshipman and also cousin to the Cecilia Howard and Katherine Plowden], to Griffith and to his companion!"

"What freedom more than we now enjoy Katherine, is needed by two young women? Think you I can remain silent, and see my uncle betrayed before my eyes? his life perhaps endangered!"

"Your own life and person will not be held more sacred, Cecilia Howard, than that of your uncle. If you will condemn Griffith to a prison, and perhaps to a gibbet, betray Barnstable, as you have threatened -- an opportunity will not be wanting at the supper-table, whither I shall lead the way, since the mistress of the house appears to forget her duty."

Katharine arose, and with a firm step and proud eye she moved along the gallery to the room where their presence was expected by the rest of the family. Cecilia followed in silence, and the whole party immediately took their several places at the board.

The first few minutes were passed in the usual attentions of the gentlemen to the ladies, and the ordinary civilities of the table; during which Katherine had so far regained the equanimity of her feelings, as to commence a watchful scrutiny of the manners and looks of her guardian and Borroughcliffe, in which she determined to persevere until the eventful hour when she was to expect Barnstable should arrive. Colonel Howard [retired British officer and caretaker of wards Cecilia and Katherine] had, however, so far got the command of himself, as no longer to betray his former abstraction. In its place Katherine fancied, at moments, that she could discover a settled look of conscious security, mingled a little with an expression of severe determination; such as, in her earlier days, she had learned to dread as sure indications of the indignant, but upright, justice of an honorable mind. Borroughcliffe, on the other hand, was cool, polite,

[420] [*Edit. Note*. By Sir Walter Scott.]
~~~

and as attentive to the viands as usual, with the alarming exception of discovering much less devotion to the Pride of the Vineyards than he commonly manifested on such occasions. In this manner the meal passed by, and the cloth was removed, though the ladies appeared willing to retain their places longer than was customary. Colonel Howard, filling up the glasses of Alice Dunscombe and himself, passed the bottle to the recruiting officer, and, with a sort of effort that was intended to rouse the dormant cheerfulness of his guests, cried:

"Come Borroughcliffe, the ruby lips of your neighbors would be still more beautiful, were they moistened with this rich cordial, and that, too, accompanied by some loyal sentiment. Miss Alice is ever ready to express her fealty to her sovereign; in her name, I can give the health of his most sacred majesty, with defeat and death to all traitors!"

"If the prayers of an humble subject, and one of a sex that has but little need to mingle in the turmoil of the world, and that has less right to pretend to understand the subtleties of statesmen, can much avail a high and mighty prince like him who sits on the throne, then will he never know temporal evil," returned Alice, meekly; "but I cannot wish death to any one, not even to my enemies, if any I have, and much less to a people who are the children of the same family with myself."

"Children of the same family!" the colonel repeated, slowly, and with a bitterness of manner that did not fail to attract the painful interest of Katherine: "children of the same family! Ay! even as Absalom was the child of David, or as Judas was of the family of the holy Apostles! But let it pass unpledged -- let it pass. The accursed spirit of rebellion has invaded my dwelling, and I no longer know where to find one of my household that has not been assailed by its malign influence!"

"Assailed I may have been among others," returned Alice; "but not corrupted, if purity, in this instance, consists in loyalty--"

"What sound is that?" interrupted the colonel, with startling suddenness. "Was it not the crash of some violence, Captain Borroughcliffe?"

"It may have been one of my rascals who has met with a downfall in passing from the festive board -- where you know I regale them to-night, in honor of our success--to his blanket," returned the captain, with admirable indifference; "or it may be the very spirit of whom you have spoken so freely, my host, that has taken umbrage at your remarks, and is passing from the hospitable walls of St. Ruth into the open air, without submitting to the small trouble of ascertaining the position of doors. In the latter case there may be some dozen perches or so of wall to replace in the morning."

The colonel, who had risen, glanced his eyes uneasily from the speaker to the door, and was evidently but little disposed to enter into the pleasantry of his guest.

"There are unusual noises, Captain Borroughcliffe, in the grounds of the abbey, if not in the building itself," he said advancing with a fine military air from the table to the centre of the room, "and as master of the mansion I will inquire who it is that thus unseasonably disturbs these domains. If as friends, they shall have welcome, though their visit be unexpected; and if enemies, they shall also meet with such a reception as will become an old soldier!"

"No, no," cried Cecilia, entirely thrown off her guard by the manner and language of the veteran and rushing into his arms. "Go not out, my uncle; go not into the terrible fray, my kind, my good uncle! you are old, you have already done more than your duty; why should you be exposed to danger?"

"The girl is mad with terror, Borroughcliffe," cried the colonel, bending his glistening eyes fondly on his niece, "and you will have to furnish my good-for-nothing, gouty old person with a corporal's guard, to watch my nightcap, or the silly child will have an uneasy pillow, till the sun rises once more. But you do not stir, sir?"

"Why should I?" cried the captain; "Miss Plowden yet deigns to keep me company, and it is not in the nature of one of the --th to desert his bottle and his standard at the same moment. For, to a true soldier, the smiles of a lady are as imposing in the parlor as the presence of his colors in the field."

"I continue undisturbed, Captain Borroughcliffe," said Katherine, "because I have not been an inhabitant, for so many months, of St. Ruth, and not learned to know the tunes which the wind can play among its chimneys and pointed roofs. The noise which has taken Colonel Howard from his seat, and which has so unnecessarily alarmed my cousin Cicely, is nothing but the Æolian harp of the abbey sounding a double bass."

The captain fastened on her composed countenance, while she was speaking, a look of open admiration, that brought, though tardily, the color more deeply to her cheeks: and he answered with something extremely equivocal, both in his emphasis and his air:

"I have avowed my allegiance, and I will abide by it. So long as Miss Plowden will deign to bestow her company, so long will she find me among her most faithful and persevering attendants, come who may, or what will."

"You compel me to retire," returned Katherine, rising, "whatever may have been my gracious intentions in the matter; for even female vanity must crimson, at an adoration so profound as that which can chain Captain Borroughcliffe to a supper-table! As your alarm has now dissipated, my cousin, will you lead the way? Miss Alice and myself attend you."

"But not into the paddock, surely, Miss Plowden," said the captain; "the door, the key of which you have just turned, communicates with the vestibule. This is the passage to the drawing-room."

The lady faintly laughed, as if in derision of her own forgetfulness, while she bowed her acknowledgment, and moved towards the proper passage: she observed:

"The madness of fear has assailed some, I believe, who have been able to affect a better disguise than Miss Howard."

"Is it the fear of present danger, or of that which is in reserve?" asked the captain; "but, as you have stipulated so generously in behalf of my worthy host here, and of one, also, who shall be nameless, because he has not deserved such a favor at your hands, your safety shall be one of my especial duties in these times of peril."

"There is peril, then!" exclaimed Cecilia; "your looks announce it. Captain Borroughcliffe! The changing countenance of my cousin tells me that my fears are too true!"

The soldier had now risen also, and, casting aside the air of badinage, which he so much delighted in, he came forward into the centre of the apartment, with the manner of one who felt it was time to be serious.

"A soldier is ever in peril, when the enemies of his king are at hand, Miss Howard," he answered: "and that such is now the case, Miss Plowden can testify, if she will. But you are the allies of both parties -- retire, then, to your own apartments, and await the result of the struggle which is at hand."

"You speak of danger and hidden perils," said Alice Dunscombe; "know ye aught that justifies your fears?"

"I know all," Borroughcliffe coolly replied.

"All!" exclaimed Katherine.

"All!" echoed Alice, in tones of horror, "If, then, you know all, you must know his desperate courage, and powerful hand, when opposed -- yield in quiet, and he will not harm ye. Believe me, believe one who knows his very nature, that no lamb can be more gentle than he would be with unresisting women; nor any lion more fierce, with his enemies!"

"As we happen not to be of the feminine gender," returned Borroughcliffe, with an air somewhat splenetic, "we must abide the fury of the king of beasts. His paw is, even now, at the outer door; and, if my orders have been obeyed, his entrance will be yet easier than that of the wolf to the respectable female ancestor of the little Red-riding-hood."

"Stay your hand for one single moment!" said Katherine, breathless with interest; "you are the master of my secret, Captain Borroughcliffe, and bloodshed may be the consequence. I can yet go forward, and, perhaps, save many inestimable lives. Pledge to me your honor, that they who come hither as your enemies, this night, shall depart in peace, and I will pledge to you my life for the safety of the abbey,"

"Oh! hear her, and shed not human blood!" cried Cecilla.

A loud crash interrupted further speech, and the sounds of heavy footsteps were heard in the adjoining room, as if many men were alighting on its floor, in quick succession. Borroughcliffe drew back, with great coolness, to the opposite side of the large apartment, and took a sheathed sword from the table where it had been placed; at the same moment the door was burst open, and Barnstable entered alone, but heavily armed.

"You are my prisoners, gentlemen," said the sailor, as he advanced; "resistance is useless, and without it you shall receive favor. Ha, Miss Plowden! my advice was that you should not be present at this scene."

"Barnstable, we are betrayed!" cried the agitated Katherine. "But it is not yet too late. Blood has not yet been spilt, and you can retire, without that dreadful alternative, with honor. Go, then, delay not another moment; for should the soldiers of Captain Borroughcliffe come to the rescue of their commander, the abbey would be a scene of horror!"

"Go you away; go, Katherine," said her lover, with impatience; "this is no place for such as you. But, Captain Borroughcliffe, if such be your name, you must perceive that resistance is in vain. I have ten good pikes in this outer room, in twenty better hands, and it will be madness to fight against such odds."

"Show me your strength," said the captain, "that I may take counsel with mine honor."

"Your honor shall be appeased, my brave soldier, for such is your bearing, though your livery is my aversion, and your cause most unholy! Heave ahead, boys! but hold your hands for orders."

The party of fierce-looking sailors whom Barnstable led, on receiving this order, rushed into the room in a medley; but, notwithstanding the surly glances, and savage characters of their dress and equipments, they struck no blow, nor committed any act of hostility. The ladies shrank back appalled, as this terrific little band took possession of the hall; and even Borroughcliffe was seen to fall back towards a door which, in some measure, covered his retreat. The confusion of this sudden movement had not yet subsided, when sounds of strife were heard rapidly approaching from a distant part of the building, and presently one of the numerous doors of the apartment was violently opened, when two of the garrison of the abbey rushed into the hall, vigorously pressed by twice their number of seamen, seconded by Griffith, Manual [commanding the American marines], and Merry, who were armed with such weapons of offence as had presented themselves to their hands, at their unexpected liberation. There was a movement on the part of the seamen who were already in possession of the room, that threatened instant death to the fugitives; but Barnstable beat down their pikes with his sword, and sternly ordered them to fall back. Surprise produced the same pacific result among the combatants; and as the soldiers hastily sought a refuge behind their own officers, and the released captives, with their liberators, joined the body of their friends, the quiet of the hall, which had been so rudely interrupted, was soon restored.

"You see, sir," said Barnstable, after grasping the hands of Griffith and Manual in a warm and cordial pressure, "that all my plans have succeeded. Your sleeping guard are closely watched in their barracks by one party; our officers are released and your sentinels cut off by another; while, with a third, I hold the centre of the abbey, and am, substantially, in possession of your own person. In consideration, therefore, of what is due to humanity, and to the presence of these ladies, let there be no struggle! I shall impose no difficult terms, nor any long imprisonment."

The recruiting officer manifested a composure throughout the whole scene that would have excited some uneasiness in his invaders, had there been opportunity for minute observation; but his countenance now gradually assumed an appearance of anxiety, and his head was frequently turned, as if listening for further and more important interruptions. He answered, however, to this appeal with his ordinary deliberation.

"You speak of conquests, sir, before they are achieved. My venerable host and myself are not so defenceless as you may chose to imagine." While speaking he threw aside the cloth of a side table, from beneath which the colonel and himself were instantly armed with a brace of pistols each. "Here are the death-warrants of four of your party, and these brave fellows at my back can account for two more. I believe, my transatlantic warrior, that we are now something in the condition of Cortes and the Mexicans, when the former overran part of your continent -- I being Cortes, armed with artificial thunder and lightning, and you the Indians, with nothing but your pikes and sling, and such other antediluvian inventions. Shipwrecks and seawater are fatal dampers of gunpowder!"

"That we are unprovided with firearms, I will not deny," said Barnstable; "but we are men who are used, from infancy, to depend on our good right arms for life and safety, and we know how to use them, though we should even grapple with death! As for the trifles in your hands, gentlemen, you are not to suppose that men who are trained to look in at one end of a thirty-two pounder, loaded with grape, while the match is put to the other, will so much as wink at their report, though you fired them by fifties. What say you, boys, is a pistol a weapon to repel boarders?"

The discordant and disdainful laughs that burst from the restrained seamen were a sufficient pledge of their indifference to so trifling a danger. Borroughcliffe noted their hardened boldness, and taking the supper bell, which was lying near him, he rang it, for a minute, with great violence. The heavy tread of trained footsteps soon followed this extraordinary summons; and presently the several doors of the apartment were opened, and filled with armed soldiers, wearing the livery of the English crown.

"If you hold these smaller weapons in such vast contempt," said the recruiting officer, when he perceived that his men had possessed themselves of all the avenues, "it is in my power to try the virtue of some more formidable. After this exhibition of my strength, gentlemen, I presume you cannot hesitate to submit as prisoners of war."

The seamen had been formed in something like military array, by the assiduity of Manual, during the preceding dialogue; and as the different doors had discovered fresh accessions to the strength of the enemy, the marine industriously offered new fronts, until the small party was completely arranged in a hollow square, that might have proved formidable in a charge, bristled as it was with the deadly pikes of the Ariel.

"Here has been some mistake," said Griffith, after glancing his eye at the formidable array of the soldiers; "I take precedence of Mr. Barnstable, and I shall propose to you, Captain Borroughcliffe, terms that may remove this scene of strife from the dwelling of Colonel Howard."

"The dwelling of Colonel Howard," cried the veteran, "is the dwelling of his king, or of the meanest servant of the crown! so, Borroughcliffe, spare not the traitors on my behalf; accept no other terms than such unconditional submission as is meet to exact from the rebellious subjects of the anointed of the Lord."

While Griffith spoke, Barnstable folded his arms, in affected composure, and glanced his eyes expressively at the shivering Katherine, who, with her companions, still continued agitated spectators of all that passed, chained to the spot by their apprehensions; but to this formidable denunciation of the master of the abbey he deemed proper to reply:

"Now, by every hope I have of sleeping again on salt water, old gentleman if it were not for the presence of these three trembling females, I should feel tempted to dispute, at once, the title of his majesty. You may make such a covenant as you will with Mr. Griffith, but if it contain one syllable about submission to your king, or of any other allegiance than that which I owe to the Continental Congress, and the State of Massachusetts, you may as well consider the terms violated at once; for not an article of such an agreement will I consider as binding on me, or on any that shall choose to follow me as leader."

"Here are but two leaders, Mr. Barnstable," interrupted the haughty Griffith; "the one of the enemy, and the other of the arms of America. Captain Borroughclffe, to you, as the former, I address myself. The great objects of the contest which now unhappily divides England from her ancient colonies can be, in no degree, affected by the events of this night; while, on the other hand, by a rigid adherence to military notions, much private, evil and deep domestic calamity must follow any struggle in such a place. We have but to speak, sir, and these rude men, who already stand impatiently handling their instruments of death, will aim them at each other's lives; and who can say that he shall be able to stay their hands when and where he will. I know you to be a soldier, and that you are not yet to learn how much easier it is to stimulate to blood than to glut vengeance."

Borroughcliffe, unused to the admission of violent emotions, and secure in the superiority of his own party, both in numbers and equipments, heard him with the coolest composure to the end, and then answered in his customary manner:

"I honor your logic, sir. Your premises are indisputable, and the conclusion most obvious. Commit then these worthy tars to the good keeping of honest Drill [i.e., the subaltern in command of Borroughcliffe's soldiers], who will see their famished natures revived by divers eatables and a due proportion of suitable fluids; while we can discuss the manner in which you are to return to the colonies, around a bottle of liquor, which my friend Manual there assures me has come from the sunny side of the island of Madeira, to be drunk in a bleak corner of that of Britain. By my palate! but the rascals brighten at the thought. They know by instinct, sir, that a shipwrecked mariner is a fitter companion to a ration of beef and a pot of porter than to such unsightly things as bayonets and boarding-pikes!"

"Trifle, not unseasonably!" exclaimed the impatient young sailor. "You have the odds in numbers, but whether it will avail you much in a deadly struggle of hand to hand, is a question you must put to your prudence: we stand not here to ask terms, but to grant them. You must be brief, sir; for the time is wasting while we delay."

"I have offered to you the means of obtaining, in perfection, the enjoyment of the three most ancient of the numerous family of the arts -- eating, drinking, and sleeping! What more do you require?"

"That you order these men, who fill the pass to the outer door, to fall back and give us room. I would take, in peace, these armed men from before the eyes of those who are unused to such sights. Before you oppose this demand, think how easily these hardy fellows could make a way for themselves, against your divided force."

"Your companion, the experienced Captain Manual, will tell you that such a manoeuvre would be very unmilitary with a superior body in your rear!"

"I have not leisure, sir, for this folly," cried the indignant Griffith. "Do you refuse us an unmolested retreat from the abbey?"

"I do."

Griffith turned with a look of extreme emotion to the ladies, and beckoned to them to retire, unable to give utterance to his wishes in words. After a moment of deep silence, however, he once more addressed Borroughcliffe in the tones of conciliation.

"If Manual and myself will return to our prisons, and submit to the will of your government," he said, "can the rest of the party return to the frigate unmolested?"

"They cannot," replied the soldier, who, perceiving that the crisis approached, was gradually losing his artificial deportment in the interest of the moment. "You, and all others who willingly invade the peace of these realms, must abide the issue!"

"Then God protect the innocent and defend the right!"

"Amen."

"Give way, villains!" cried Griffith, facing the party that held the outer door; "give way, or you shall be riddled with our pikes!"

"Show them your muzzles, men!" shouted Borroughcliffe, "but pull no trigger till they advance."

There was an instant of bustle and preparation, in which the rattling of firearms blended with the suppressed execrations and threats of the intended combatants; and Cecilia and Katherine had both covered their faces to veil the horrid sight that was momentarily expected, when Alice Dunscombe advanced, boldly, between the points of the threatening weapons, and spoke in a voice that stayed the hands that were already uplifted.

"Hear me, men! if men ye be, and not demons, thirsting for each other's blood; though ye walk abroad in the semblance of Him who died that ye might be elevated to the rank of angels! Call ye this war? Is this the glory that is made to warm the hearts of even silly and confiding women? Is the peace of families to be destroyed to gratify your wicked lust for conquest, and is life to be taken in vain, in order that ye may boast of the foul deed in your wicked revels? Fall back, then, ye British soldiers! if ye be worthy of that name, and give passage to a woman; and remember that the first shot that is fired will be buried in her bosom!"

The men, thus enjoined, shrank before her commanding mien, and a way was made for her exit through that very door which Griffith had, in vain, solicited might be cleared for himself and party. But Alice, instead of advancing, appeared to have suddenly lost the use of those faculties which had already effected so much. Her figure seemed rooted to the spot where she had spoken, and her eyes were fixed in a settled gaze, as if dwelling on some horrid object. While she yet stood in this attitude of unconscious helplessness, the doorway became again darkened, and the figure of the Pilot was seen on its threshold, clad, as usual, in the humble vestments of his profession, but heavily armed with the weapons of naval war. For an instant, he stood a silent spectator of the scene; and then advanced calmly, but with searching eyes, into the centre of the apartment.[421]

~~~~~~******~~~~~~

[421] [*Edit. Note.* The Pilot, it turns out and symbolically not unlike the French in the American Revolution, has brought a landing party from the frigate to break the deadlock at St. Ruth's.]
~~~~~~

For *The Continental Army Series* vol. II, see:
https://archive.org/details/Vol2ContinentalArmySeries
~or~
http://www.scribd.com/doc/136892381/Vol-II-THE-CONTINENTAL-ARMY-SERIES-Reality-and-Aspiration-in-the-American-Revolutionary-Era

For *The Continental Army Series...Odds and Ends*, see:
https://archive.org/details/CASOddsAndEnds
~or~
https://www.scribd.com/document/338894482/THE-CONTINENTAL-ARMY-SERIES-Odds-and-Ends

CPSIA information can be obtained
at www.ICGtesting.com
Printed in the USA
FSHW020649030119
54804FS

9 781792 982590